STUDIES IN THE TRANSMISSION OF TEXTS & IDEAS

14

EDITOR IN CHIEF

Pieter d'Hoine

EDITORIAL BOARD

Anthony Dupont
Michèle Goyens
Marleen Reynders
Stefan Schorn

SUBMISSIONS
SHOULD BE SENT TO

Marleen Reynders
marleen.reynders@kuleuven.be

Le père du siècle:
The Early Modern Reception of Jean Gerson (1363–1429)
Theological Authority between Middle Ages and Early Modern Era

by
Yelena Mazour-Matusevich

BREPOLS

© 2023, Brepols Publishers n.v., Turnhout, Belgium.

All rights reserved.
No part of this publication may be reproduced,
stored in a retrieval system, or transmitted,
in any form or by any means, electronic, mechanical,
photocopying, recording, or otherwise
without the prior permission of the publisher.

D/2023/0095/130
10.1484/M.LECTIO-EB.5.131521
ISBN 978-2-503-60225-7
e-ISBN 978-2-503-60235-6
ISSN 2565-8506
e-ISSN 2565-9626
Printed in the EU on acid-free paper.

Roadmap of Jean Gerson's post-mortem journey in Europe, 15th-16th centuries.
Artwork by Francisca Shilova.

TABLE OF CONTENTS

ACKNOWLEDGEMENTS	13
List of Abbreviations	14
INTRODUCTION	15

CHAPTER 1
THE BACKGROUND:
GERSON AND THE LONG 15TH CENTURY

Part I. Early Reception in the Empire — 29
Introduction 29; Gerson at Melk 31; University of Vienna 34; Carthusian Tradition 40; Nicolas of Cusa and Bernhard von Waging 43; Rhine Humanists: Geiler von Kaysersberg, Jacob Wimpheling and Johannes Trithemius 47; University of Tübingen: from Gabriel Biel to Conrad Summenhart 65; *Devotio moderna*: Wessel Gansfort, Jan Standonck and Johannes Mombaer 71; *Ars moriendi* 87; Early Catechization 96

Part II. Early Reception in France — 98
First Printed Editions 99; Reform-minded Clergy and Implementation of Gerson's Pastoral Program 101

Part III. Early Reception in Spain — 109

Part IV. Early Reception in Italy — 118
Antoninus of Florence 121; Pietro Ritta da Lucca 123; Josephology and Mariology. Bernardino di Busti 125; Sylvestro Mazzolini 128; Gianfrancesco Pico della Mirandola, Girolamo Savonarola, Marsilio Ficino and Christopher Columbus 130

Part V. Early Reception in Sweden — 135

Conclusion — 137

CHAPTER 2
THE PROTESTANT RECEPTION OF GERSON
Introduction 147
Part I. Gerson's Lutheran Reception 149
    Martin Luther 149; Philipp Melanchthon 171; Andreas Bodenstein von Karlstadt 183; Martin Bucer 188; German Evangelical Harmonies, Johannes Bugenhagen and Andreas Osiander 192; Second-generation Lutherans: Martin Chemnitz 199; Lutheran Historiography 208
Part II. Reception in the Reformed Tradition 220
    Huguenot Historiography: Jean Crespin, Simon Goulart 225
Conclusion 235

CHAPTER 3
CATHOLIC RECEPTION OF GERSON
Introduction 245
Part I. Catholic Reception in the Empire 248
Part II. The Catholic Reception in the Low Countries 259
    Jacobus Latomus and Godescale Rosemondt 259
Part III. The Catholic Reception in France 262
    Pastoral renewal 262; The Circle of Meaux: Guillaume Briçonnet, Marguerite de Navarre and Lefèvre d'Etaples 268; Parisian Intellectual Milieu 273
Part IV. The Catholic Reception in Spain 284
    School of Salamanca 285; Spanish Illuminati 299; Francisco de Osuna 305; John of the Cross and Teresa of Avila 312
Part V. The Early Jesuits 316
    The Question of *De Imitatione Christi* 316; Besides and Beyond *De Imitatione Christi* 320; Confession and Communion 323
Part VI. The Council of Trent 334
Conclusion 340

CHAPTER 4
THE RECEPTION OF GERSON IN ENGLAND AND SCOTLAND
Introduction 347
Part I. Gerson's Theological Influence 350
    William Perkins, Christopher Sutton, Joseph Hall, Richard Baxter 352

Part II. *The Scottish Connection*	359
Part III. *The Very Special Case: Gerson and Thomas More*	364
Part IV. *Gerson's Influence on the Growth of Common Law in England*	390
Christopher St Germain 398; Edmund Plowden 400	
Part V. *Synderesis and the Notion of Conscience in English Literary and Philosophical Traditions*	402
Conclusion	408
GENERAL CONCLUSION	413
Gerson's Future	430
BIBLIOGRAPHY	435
NAME INDEX	507

ACKNOWLEDGEMENTS

This journey began in 2004 thanks to Brian Patrick McGuire, who had asked me to contribute a chapter to the 2006 volume *Companion to Jean Gerson*. I was chosen for this task because of a small chapter on the subject of Gerson's post-mortem reception in my 2004 book *Le siècle d'or de la mystique française*. The wealth of fascinating facts and developments I accumulated while preparing this chapter could not be accommodated in a series of articles, signaling the need for a more substantial study, which became my second dissertation at EHESS in Paris, and then this book. My most heartfelt gratitude goes to my mentor Pierre-Antoine Fabre (EHESS), colleagues Thierry Amalou (Université d'Artois) and Jean-Marie Le Gall (Sorbonne) for their generosity in welcoming a complete stranger; and to Jacob Schmutz (UC Louvain), Bénédicte Sère (Paris-Nanterre) and Dominique Iogna-Prat (EHESS) for their helpful comments. I am most grateful to Wim François at KU Leuven for his unwavering support and friendship, and to Antonio Gerace at Fondazione per le scienze religiose Giovanni XXIII (FSCIRE) in Bologna for his continuous help and his faith in me. On the 'German side' I thank my former Alaska colleague Josef Glowa for his assistance with difficult middle-German passages, my dear friend Steffen Hoffman for guiding me through archives of Sondersammlungen of Albertina Library (Leipzig University) and Rudolf Schüssler (Bayreuth University) for his interest in my work. A dedicated group made of family members (Phyllis Adams, Craig Bledsoe), friends (Vlad Demine, George Fairclough and Sylvia Kim) and especially former students (Jalil Jackallen, Debbie Tilsworth, Maureen Heftinger, Katelyn Bushnell, Heather Maas-Kisha, Kat Timm, Solomon Shindler and Lisa Gilbert) proofread the manuscript. Thank you, thank you, thank you.

List of Abbreviations

Luthers Werke Weimar Ausgabe	*WA* volume number. Part number (when applicable). Page number.
Luther's Works American Edition	*LW* volume number. Page number.
Jean Gerson. Early Works, B. P. McGuire	EW 1998
Jean Gerson, *Œuvres complètes*, P. *Glorieux*	OC: volume: part (if applicable), page number
Philipp Melanchthon, *Corpus Reformatorum*	CR: volume, page
The Complete Works of St Thomas More	*CWTM* volume number: page number

INTRODUCTION

'A special grace given to one person does not apply to everyone'.
Jean Gerson[1]

This book is the first wide-ranging investigation of the reception of Jean Gerson — the most significant intellectual figure of the late medieval period, whose larger-than-life personality and mammoth legacy we are only now beginning to assess — in early modern Europe, both in Protestant and in Catholic milieus. The story of his reception is worth sharing, as it reveals many discoveries and surprises for all those interested in the reconstruction of this revolutionary period in Western history — the end of the late Middle Ages and the beginning of modern times — when European culture began to show first signs of its dissociation from what Albert Camus called 'the world of grace'[2] and Jacques Derrida the 'universe of testimony'.[3] Indeed, although Gerson himself fully belongs to the latter, his reception, in my view, has the potential to serve as a key to both the lost universe of the medieval past and the reformed world that would replace it. Paraphrasing Daniel Hobbins, one can say that his legacy is a window not just to Gerson himself but to the social realities that met his thought after his passing.[4]

Studying towering figures like Gerson is never just a mere erudition. The success of someone's ideas is not measured by their fame, but by an actual effect upon the minds and actions of

---

[1] *La Montagne de contemplation*, OC: 7:1, p. 27: 'Comment la grace singulière d'aucuns n'est mie a ensuivre de tous'. McGuire 1998, p. 90.
[2] Camus 1992, p. 21.
[3] Derrida & Stiegler 1996, p. 94. Also see Allow 2017, pp. 289–303.
[4] Hobbins 2006, p. 76.

those who come after them. In Gerson's case this effect was disproportionally large, while our understanding of it is still in its early stages. Therefore, his significance should be fully restored to posterity not only to give him credit for his contributions, but also in order to better understand his specific role in the religious, legal and cultural evolution of Western civilization. It is a matter of awareness and healthy self-reflection on our common and now more and more shared inheritance. His legacy, part of the theological foundation, which lies, hidden, at the basis of many, if not all, contemporary issues and debates, provides a significant doctrinal context, where contemporary ideas such as the concept of individual right, international law or the necessity of palliative care, find their roots. Today, when the question of the place of religion in society has lost nothing of its urgency, coming to terms with this theological basis is no longer the fief of specialized researchers, but a social necessity. For, even though we might not know it, Gerson is part of our own universe, capable of offering us 'a surer grasp of principles amid the complexities of the modern world'.[5]

The title of the book, *Le père du siècle: The Early Modern Reception of Jean Gerson (1363-1429)*, reflects the prevalence of the theme of the father — as parent, protector, generator, counselor and authority — both in his oeuvre and in his reception, providing connection between the two. Much more than a 'good witness of his time', as Zénon Kaluza, Cédric Giraud and Jacques Verger viewed him,[6] Gerson was an active maker of a modern concept of the father, in a sense becoming 'the father of the fatherhood'. What's more, already in his lifetime he assumed, first toward his siblings, then toward his students and finally even toward his contemporaries, including the royal family, the role of the father, whose vocation consisted of leading, teaching and especially consoling his spiritual children. The latter motif is part of the ideal of *bonus paster*, who, as a prelate of the Church, should be like a father to all the orphans, the poor, the prisoners and the af-

---

[5] Figgis 2011, p. 4.
[6] Kaluza 1988, p. 65. Giraud 2016, p. 257: 'nous avons retenu Jean Gerson pour plusieurs raisons qui s'additionnent pour faire du chancelier un 'bon témoin de son temps'. Verger 1995, p. 191: 'Gerson est un bon témoin.' On Gerson's contribution to the more modern idea of fatherhood see Delumeau & Roche 1990.

flicted.[7] Indeed, it is mostly, although not only, in his quality of *doctor consolatorius*, which Herbert Kraume calls his *zweiter Beiname*,[8] that Gerson would be welcomed by the future generations of theologians and spiritual leaders for the majority of whom he had remained or had become a spiritual father.

State of the Art

> 'For the late Middle Ages, the towering figure of Jean Gerson commands attention'.[9]

While there has been something of a renaissance in Gerson-related studies, with Daniel Hobbins's 2009 book *Authorship and Publicity Before Print: Jean Gerson and the Transformation of Late Medieval Learning*, Vial 2006 *Jean Gerson: théoricien de la théologie mystique*, Nancy McLoughlin's 2015 *Jean Gerson and Gender: Rhetoric and Politics in Fifteenth-Century France* and Brian Patrick McGuire's 2005 biography, *Jean Gerson and the Last Medieval Reformation*, none of the existing research deals with the subject of Gerson's legacy and reception directly. Gerson-related literature can be divided into four groups. The first group, dominated by Protestant researchers, traditionally presents Gerson as a precursor of the Reformation, from Johann Baptist Schwab's major 1873 study to Heiko A. Oberman's classic *Forerunners of the Reformation*.[10] This view has been challenged by the second group of publications, dating from the late 1980s and 1990s, and authored by unambiguously Christian researchers such as Mark S. Burrows, Catherine Brown and Brian P. McGuire, arguing that 'Gerson is no forerunner to later Protestant exegesis, but a distinctively

---

[7] Gerson, *Nova epistola pro instructione episcoporum et prelatorum ...*, in Vansteenberghe 1939, p. 40 and p. 42: *Qui orphano et pupillo et uidue et egenti et captiuo et egroto et aflicto et agricolis senebis et languoribus consumptis et onere puerorum aggrauatis etc., quia refugium esse debent atque patres, subueniant*. 'And that these [prelates] help the orphan, the child, the widow, the destitute, the prisoner, the sick and the afflicted, the old peasants and those who are consumed by diseases, etc., because they must be for them a refuge and fathers'.

[8] Kraume 1980, p. 76.

[9] Newman 2013, p. 2.

[10] Schwab 1859; Oberman 1981a.

conservative voice',[11] or should be considered as the forerunner of the Catholic Counter-Reformation instead.[12] The third group of research publications, by Heiko A. Oberman, Veronica Gerz-Von Büren, Herbert Kraume and Daniel Hobbins, is comprised of works covering the reception of Gerson shortly after his death in 1429 up until early 1500s.[13] Based on the fact that the last edition of Gerson's works was published in 1521, these studies deem Gerson's influence to have diminished with the triumph of the Reformation. The fourth, and the largest category, is focused on his role in the conciliarist movement, and includes works by Francis Oakley, Christopher Bellitto, Bénédicte Sère, Thomas Izbicki, Philippe Denis and others. This dimension of his legacy, together with the discussion of Gerson's nominalism,[14] although very important, will mostly stay outside the scope of the current study for three main reasons. The first is that, unlike practically all other aspects of Gerson's legacy, the conciliarist dimension has already received much scholarly attention in the last fifty years. In fact, it might be the only component of his legacy that received any major traction at all. Despite Philippe Denis's affirmation to the contrary, the bibliography on this subject is extensive.[15] The second, a direct consequence of the first, is that the study of the chancellor's conciliarism has a history in and of its own, with its own methodologies and a long tradition, whose inclusion in this study would require a whole different approach and a multi-volume format. Finally, since this book aims, first and foremost, at introducing unexplored dimensions of Gerson's posthumous significance, the

[11] Burrows 1991, p. 42.
[12] Brown 1987, p. 252.
[13] Oberman 1963; Gerz-Von Büren 1973; Kraume 1980.
[14] Adams 1977, pp. 144–76; Burrows 1991; Gillespie 2009; Enenkel & Melion 2010.
[15] Denis 2019, p. 369. For Gerson and Conciliarism see Morrall 1960; Schneider 1976; Skinner 1978; Sieben 1988; Nederman 1990; Monahan 1997; Ryan 1998; Oakley 1999; Oakley 2003; Oakley & Blythe 2005; Oakley 2006; Anderson 2007; Bellitto 2008; Rollo-Koster & Izbicki 2009; Oakley 2015; Sère 2016; Sère 2018. Francis Oakley addresses the issue of 'instability' regarding the definition of conciliarism: 'What people mean, however, when they refer to 'conciliarism' is far from self-evident; over the years usage has manifested a sometimes confusing degree of instability'. (Oakley 2006, pp. 182–83) Some legal researchers credit Gerson's conciliar theory as presaging 'the eventual development of representative democracy in the Western world' (Cahill 2014, p. 168).

conciliarist component does not fit this objective, as well as the general direction of the study, which focuses on the chancellor's spiritual and theological legacy.

This project also builds on the foundation of my own earlier research, which will be referenced but not repeated in the current study. The subjects explored in my earlier publications, such as the 15th century reception of Gerson by Parisian preachers, *devotio moderna*, early German humanists in Vienna, Tübingen, Strasbourg and Heidelberg, and some other topics, will reappear only in two particular circumstances. The first is when there is a new information, which may enrich or correct previously investigated developments. The second is when there is a clear need to provide factual base and context for the readers.

Objective

Since no comprehensive study of the reception of Gerson exists,[16] the book hopes to achieve precisely this primary task: to take his name out of shadow and bring him into spotlight, by showing his importance beyond the 15th century. Already in 1964 Etienne Delaruelle articulated the historical task taken up here, when he urged the necessity of undertaking such an opening study, believing, contrary to majority of Gerson's experts, that the chancellor's influence sustained and even increased in the 16th century.[17] Yet, the majority of points concerning the state of research on Gerson's legacy that Etienne Delaruelle and his team specified in *L'Église au temps du schisme* are still valid, with none of the research ideas listed in its 'Note additionnelle' realized to this day.[18] While Delaruelle hoped that a study of Gerson's influence outside

---

[16] Bast 1997, p. 18: 'Scholars have not yet attempted to gauge precisely the impact of Gerson's program'.

[17] Delaruelle, Labande & Ourliac 1964, p. 861: 'Si la première moitié du XVe siècle peut être appelée le siècle de Gerson, il ne faudrait pas croire pour autant que cette influence ait par la suite déclinée; elle n'a fait, au contraire, que croître'.

[18] 'One should not underestimate the impact of the ideology of laïcité that spread along with the Code Napoléon and the repression of the ancien régime, not only on the actual, battered relationship between State and Church, but inevitably also on historical scholarship, where the contribution by the theologians has been eclipsed almost completely' (Decock 2012, pp. 12–13).

France would take place 'un jour',[19] a relatively recent MA thesis, concerning the state of Gerson's studies after 1945, flatly asserts the absence of further research on his legacy and reception.[20] In 1960s, as today, 'Le monde gersonien est donc actuellement un chantier où tout est matière de discussion'.[21] The present study is, among other things, an exploratory response to Delaruelle's half a century old call for action, as it attempts to demonstrate Gerson's relevance beyond the 15th century and his impact on early modern movements and thinkers of great significance that paved the way for many developments still shaping our existence today.

Besides the expected influence in theology and church history, Gerson's thought left a significant imprint in jurisprudence, human rights history, education, art, music, literature and more. There is hardly an area of humanities that did not pay at least some tribute to his authority, and there is almost no political or religious movement in the West that neglected his name. Following Gerson's legacy through time and space, one crosses paths with virtually all key personalities of early modern Europe. A cohort of celebrities — Thomas More, Martin Luther, King James I, Ignatius of Loyola, Girolamo Savonarola, Christopher Columbus, Bartolomé de Las Casas and many others, relied on his writings and ideas. The last medieval reformer (McGuire) became a privileged reference in the dialogue of practically all early-modern theologians with their immediate past, and in the heated arguments these theologians had between each other. His writings and ideas became building blocks for new religious identities ranging from Lutheran to Jesuit, and among those who relied on his insights were not only Martin Luther, his main associate Philipp Melanchthon and his spiritual descendant Martin Chemnitz, but also Luther's main opponent Johannes Eck and Melanchthon's bitter foe, Lutheran theologian Matthias Flacius Illyricus. Puritans, Jesuits and King James I, who hated both, all banked on Gerson's authority and ideas. The topography of his legacy is just as broad and varied, spanning from Portugal to Scan-

---

[19] Delaruelle, Labande & Ourliac 1964, p. 862: 'Il vaudrait la peine d'étudier un jour la question du gersonisme hors de France'.
[20] Hoffman 2003.
[21] Delaruelle, Labande & Ourliac 1964, p. 865.

dinavia, and from Japan to Mexico. It is scarcely possible to exaggerate the importance of further research regarding the reception of Gerson before and during the Reformation, this book being the first, opening step toward filling a yawning gap in our understanding of his legacy.

Methodology: Organization, Sources and Theoretical Framework

The novelty of the project consists in its aim to transcend traditional historiographical boundaries, which have continuously influenced and, in my opinion, undermined, our understanding of Gerson's legacy. These boundaries are numerous: confessional, namely between Protestant and Catholic scholarships; chronological (between the fields of medieval and early modern studies); and disciplinary (between different fields of knowledge). An example of the latter is Gerson's contribution to music, which has long been known to professional musicologists, while remaining unknown to historians. Similarly, Gerson's role in the emergence of the early modern judicial order, which has recently attracted an unprecedented attention among legal scholars and philosophers, has not reached outside the field of jurisprudence.[22] His fundamental role in the history of medicine is also acknowledged exclusively in specialized publications. Finally, the project also aspires to make an important step toward overcoming the national divide in Gerson's research, namely between contemporary French, German and English-language scholarships. Such a study is certainly an ambitious undertaking fraught with great difficulty, but it should help in both dispelling the perception of Gerson's irrelevance in the early modern Europe, and break new ground. Surely, nothing approaching complete success is possible at this stage. Yet, this endeavor gives a chance of reaching certain conclusions about the place that this extraordinary man occupied after his death. This is what I have tried to do, and I shall be happy if the pages which follow stimulate teams of others to fare better.

---

[22] Prodi 2000; Bauer 2004; Varkemaa 2005; Varkemaa 2006; Varkemaa 2012; Decock 2012; Bader 2014; Decock 2017; Astorri 2019.

Avoiding confessional bias is of a particular importance in the field of Reformation studies, where, until recently, traditional perspectives remained strong and nearly all those working in it were insiders, interpreting revolutionary changes that occurred in early modern period in light of their respective religious commitments, and thus often presenting 'une construction théorique ouvertement confessionnelle'.[23] The aim to adopt, as much as possible, an analytically detached outsider perspective requires minimal information on my own biography, as a way to identify possible involvement or partiality in the issues analyzed here. To keep it short, I have no familial, cultural, historical or educational ties with Western forms of Christianity, and no personal or religious association with either Catholic or Protestant traditions. As an imperfect outsider, I am rather interested 'in presenting the story of Christian contributions to contemporary identity', which, as Carter Lindberg put it, 'is too important to be left to the Christians'[24] only. However, it does not mean that I intend, in the tradition of social historians, 'to shelve the theological-religious interpretation of the Reformation',[25] or dismiss *homo religiosus* as a mere fiction. On the contrary, I believe that the presence of *homo religiosus* is sometimes the most determining factor in shaping human existence even now, let alone in the 16th century. After all, at the center of this study is a 'theological polymath'[26] Jean Gerson, who was *homo religiosus* par excellence. Placed outside any particular religion or even, as much as possible, current ideological movements, I consider theology to be a formative anthropological factor of major importance, which needs to take a central stage in telling history, where Jean Gerson is certainly one of the most significant and interesting actors.

Of course, no writing is value-free and 'to write history amounts, for the most part, to projecting a vocabulary of order unto the confusion of realities'.[27] Even choosing terminology is a heavily charged and problematic step, as all usual terms — Refor-

---

[23] Büttgen 2011, p. 78.
[24] Lindberg 1996, p. 4.
[25] Lindberg 1996, p. 20.
[26] McGinn 2005, p. 405.
[27] Venard 2000, p. 9.

mation, Protestant, Counter-Reformation — as well as all periodizations, have been continuously contested as inadequate. Both the words 'Reformation', which was not used until the end of the 17th century, and 'Counter-Reformation' fail to please Roman Catholic historians such as John Bossy, who would just as soon drop the term Reformation altogether, or John O'Malley, who cogently argues that the phrase 'early modern Catholicism' would better designate both change and continuity than the older terms.[28]

However, since the human mind cannot function without categories, the contents of this study are organized chronologically, denominationally and geographically. Chronologically, in order to provide the reader with historical background immediately preceding the Reformation, the study begins, largely building upon existing scholarship, in the last ten years of Gerson's life, after the conclusion of the Council of Constance (chapter one). Denominationally, the book is divided, relatively equally, between Protestant and Catholic receptions (chapters two and three). Each chapter opens with an introduction, followed by concrete case studies. The geographical dimension is particularly relevant, since ideas and social processes play out differently in different locations. The impact of Gerson's thought largely depended upon local circumstances, the broader theological and political context, and the specific and ever-contingent agency of particular religious leaders and thinkers. In the unfolding of the initial roadmap of Gerson's post-mortem journey space is every bit as important as time. Spatiality, which is interdisciplinary by nature, offers a perspective in which 'geography is not relegated to an afterthought of social relations, but is intimately involved in their construction'.[29] Indeed, geography in all its expressions, as locality, environment, vicinity or neighborhood, probably shaped early modernity more than any other factor. However, using designations such as 'Germany' or the 'Netherlands' is obviously problematic and ambiguous at best, as early modern borders did not coincide with the present-day political maps. Also, due to frequent visits among religious leaders and to migrations provoked by mutual persecutions, schools and ideas traveled amazingly fast, constantly inter-

---

[28] Lindberg 1996, pp. 10–11.
[29] Warf & Arias 2009, p. 1.

mingling and changing configurations of political units, regions and even individual cities.

The greater part of the new data in chapter one concerns the reception of Gerson in Sweden and especially in Italy, new facts and documents concerning his influence on Johannes Geiler von Kaysersberg and Johannes Nider, as well as his contribution to *Ars moriendi* tradition. 16th century sources explored in the main chapters two, three and four, with the exception of the Meaux circle of French evangelicals, Martin Luther, and, partly, the philosophical 'School of Salamanca', had not been considered in relation to Gerson before this study. Thus, the degree of Gerson's significance for early 16th century Catholic German theologians such as Johannes Staupitz did not bring any notice, the fact likely explainable by a scanty interest and 'a historical pre-judgment' of the beginning of Catholic reform in general, and in German territories in particular.[30] Among the writings of famous personalities, analyzed for their relationship with Gerson's legacy, Thomas More holds a special and massive place, which, together with the chancellor's impact on British legal history through both More and Christopher St Germain, as well as some other, specifically English aspects, warrant the necessity of a separate chapter 'Gerson in England and Scotland'.[31]

Gerson-related data is gathered, whenever possible, from primary Latin, vernacular or translated sources by key historical personalities, such as Johannes Geiler von Kaysersberg's *Die Augsburger Predigten*, Johannes Nider's *Consolatorium timorae conscientiae*, Bernard von Waging's *Consolatorium tribulatorum*, Wessel Gansfort's *Farrago rerum theologicarum*, Thomas More's *Complete Works*, Martin Luther's *Werke*, Andreas Osiander's *Gesamtausgabe, Schriften und Briefe*, Johann von Staupitz's *Sämtliche Schriften*, Philipp Melanchthon's *Loci Communes*, Martin Chemnitz's *Loci theologici*, Francisco de Osuna's *Tercer abecedario spiritual*, Juan-Alphonso Polanco's *Le Directoire des confesseurs tres*

---

[30] Volkmar 2018, p. 13.

[31] Although Anglicanism is one of the major branches of the 16th-century Protestant Reformation, it is a form of Christianity that includes features of both Protestantism and Roman Catholicism. Due to this particular situation and England's 16th-century vacillations between Puritanism and Catholicism, Anglican reception of Gerson is treated in chapter four.

brief and so forth, as well as from important historical documents, such as the text of the *Confessio Augustana (Augsburg Confession)* or *Repertorium columbianum*. The investigation also includes anonymous or collective works largely based on Gerson's writings, such as German *ars moriendi* or Middle English manuals for confessors, as well as a large quantity of secondary literature. It must also be taken into account that many of Gerson's writings were published under other people's names, while his works and ideas were used without giving him credit. In the era before copyrights and the concept of plagiarism, the significance of an author cannot be measured through direct citations only. Hence, I cannot always claim, in every case, to be invulnerable to doubt in regards to Gerson's textual presence or theological influence, nor can I claim to have called everything possible into question. Such work would exceed not only this volume but my lifetime. As a general principle, I made a decision to present only the clearest cases of what may be called history of the reference to Gerson, while only briefly indicating other occurrences, which admit more scruple.

Notwithstanding, evaluating influence is always problematic for several reasons, the first being the vagueness of the concept itself. Although 'my method has been inductive, starting with case studies rather than theories',[32] this study is partly based on the techniques borrowed from modern sociology, which uses the following principles in order to measure impacts of contemporary movements or figures. Applied in historical context and re-contextualized in light of the diffusion and transformation of Gerson's legacy, these methods include:

- the General Elimination Method, which entails systematically identifying alternative causal explanations of observed results, as, for example, when Gerson's opinions concerning certain issues have to be differentiated from those of other thinkers or from the prevalent ideas of the time commonly inhaled with them.
- Contribution Analysis Method, which builds up evidence to demonstrate the contribution made by an activity or a person

---

[32] Newman 2013, p. 7.

towards observed outcomes, as in cases of Gerson's impacts on catechization, *ars moriendi* tradition, cult of St Joseph or confessional practices.

- A Case Study Method, which is a detailed and intensive examination of a specific unit of analysis — as in cases of Thomas More's reception of Gerson, early Jesuits or Lutheran historiography — eventually building into larger 'long-term syntheses' narratives. Case studies method is privileged here because it suits situations involving a new setting, or when the environment is complex or turbulent,[33] which is definitely the case of early modern Europe. Even though case study evaluations present the difficulty of not being easily generalizable, multiple case studies, as presented here, counter the latter concern by presenting a rich and varied panorama of the reception.[34] This method can also provide a deeper understanding of circumstances, actors and their motivations, while also avoiding the problem of being locked into preconceived ideas about the person or phenomenon being evaluated.[35] Naturally, such an approach is not without dangers, since a case-based study cannot, by its nature, do full justice to each historical figure treated here, and specialists of Thomas More, Teresa of Avila or Philipp Melanchthon may complain that I have misrepresented them in this way. Also, there is a problem inherent to 'long-term syntheses', as it can only provide 'a rough outline'.[36] Nevertheless, considering that the significance of Gerson for the Western intellectual history has not yet been acknowledged, case-based long-term syntheses approach is justified. Instead of taking small, careful steps forward, the book hopes to become a starting point of the future chain of research, which will take upon itself proving in minuscule detail what appears beyond certain for me: Jean Gerson's continuous and ubiquitous presence after his passing.

---

[33] Tsui & Lucas 2013, online.
[34] Balbach 1999, online.
[35] Balbach 1999, online.
[36] Elias 1969, 2, p. 407.

The notion of reception, closely related to the concept of legacy as 'something transmitted by or received from an ancestor or predecessor or from the past' (Merriam-Webster) also asks for clarification. In this book, it combines several related and mostly chronologically subsequent concepts:

- reception in its most literal sense of a welcome, as with Gerson's initial sojourn in Austria or in Lyons;
- reception as distribution, reproduction, translation and accumulation of his works, as in cases of the Carthusian Order, *devotio moderna* or Johann Staupitz;
- reception as a response to his legacy, whether through reworking or manipulation, as in cases of Johannes Geiler von Kayserberg, Philipp Melanchthon or Thomas More;
- reception as response to the response, as with the Catholic reaction to the Lutheran attitude toward the late medieval chancellor.

Since in the 15th and 16th centuries these types of reception were not isolated from one another, the same person or institution could be simultaneously or subsequently involved in more than one of these types. Thus, those who received the exiled chancellor at Melk became active in first distribution efforts, while one of the principal recipients of his theology, Gabriel Biel, also translated and published his works. Indubitably, the distribution effort already represents, in and of itself, a type of response, a reaction and an approval, as only an author in whom the reading public is potentially interested can become an object of such efforts. On the other hand, response to an influence through citing and reworking affects distribution, in a complicated, controversial, and oftentimes unpredictable way.

Finally, a study of reception also poses the problem of continuity or discontinuity models, which both imply a teleological perspective. Although both modes will be signaled when appropriate, it is Volker Leppin's idea to view the relation between late Middle Ages and the 16th century as that of change in polarities, that appears to offer a particularly useful theoretical framework. Leppin's suggestion that tensions, which had existed in late Middle Ages as cultural tendencies were transformed in the 16th century into institutional ones [37] applies to the chancellor's reception, since Gerson, whom Leppin never mentions, was involved in all polarities listed by the German scholar. Among these tension-generating polarities are philosophical, between realists and nominalists, theological, between *via antiqua* and *via moderna*, political, between papacy and conciliarism, cognitive, between humanism and scholasticism, as well as between humanism and monasticism, social, between secular and professional religiosity, university and monastic orders, and institutional, between monastic tradition and non-monastic communities such as *devotio moderna* or even little home-based communes such as the one that Gerson helped to create for his own sisters. To this list could be added nascent national tensions in which Gerson also played a significant role both during his lifetime and post-mortem. His centrality to all major issues of his time, whose tension will increase in the 16th century to the point of becoming actual conflicts, makes the French chancellor a reference with a capital R.

---

[37] Leppin 2010.

CHAPTER 1

THE BACKGROUND: GERSON AND THE LONG 15TH CENTURY

> 'Once it was Alexander of Hales who was the reigning authority; then came Thomas and after him Duns Scotus; Albertus dominated his age, as Gerson did his'.
> Desiderius Erasmus[1]

Part I. Early Reception in the Empire

Introduction

The period of early reception corresponds to the long 15th Century (1400–1520s),[2] an age characterized by prodigious cultural, political and religious changes to which Gerson's role was central. It was also the time when the reception of Gerson throughout Europe began, and where the future developments in his legacy are rooted. His star status in the 15th century is beyond doubt. With 210 editions published between 1455 and 1500, he scores as the seventh best-selling author far above Petrarch (thirty-fourth) or Boccaccio (forty-eighth). Among those who still matter today only St Augustine (sixth), Thomas Aquinas (fourth), and Cicero (third) are ahead of him.[3] With a view to the chancellor's key importance for this time period, this chapter seeks to achieve the balancing act of presenting new or lesser-known facts concerning the early stages of the reception of Gerson, while still providing sufficient references to the already existing research without repeating previous publications. In addition to these two goals and in accordance with the study's spatial approach, this chapter

---

[1] Erasmus 1994, Letter 1581 to Noel Béda p. 153.
[2] Van Engen 2008, p. 260: 'This address focuses on the 1370s to 1520s, the long 15th century as some now say, and more particularly on religious and church history'.
[3] Milway 2000, p. 142.

offers a geographically inclusive view of Gerson's early reception in Europe.

This reception was diffused through three distinct but interconnected channels: monastic milieu, humanist circles, and universities. Contrary to Paul Payan's affirmation that the chancellor's influence was 'naturellement plus importante en France',[4] all three conduits were initially more active in propagating Gerson's works in what is now the Low Countries, Austria, Switzerland, and especially Germany than in his homeland.[5] Several factors contributed to Gerson's posthumous success in this cultural chronotope — configuration of time and space — forming what came to be known as his 'Germanic passage'.[6] One factor was numerical: the Empire was producing three times as many manuscripts as France was, a phenomenon that Daniel Hobbins called 'the textual avalanche'.[7] Another factor was quantitative. The distribution of Gerson's writings and ideas profited mightily from the location of the general ecumenical council at the imperial city of Constance (Konstanz) from 1414 to 1418. The council became a nexus circulating Gerson's books in the heart of the Empire. There, Gerson's works were introduced to the new reading public of 15th century Germany, which was then both the most pious and the most literate land that it has ever been,[8] as well as to the booming Northern and Central European book markets.[9] The desire for church reform formed another powerful ground for Gerson's highly positive reception in the Empire.[10] Then there was the Zeitgeist, which Gerson both shaped and expressed in his works: a response to the desire for reform expressed in a new form of practical devotional theology, known as *Frömmigkeitstheologie*, to which both the clergy and 'the self-confident urban laity'[11]

---

[4] Payan 2006, p. 219.
[5] Kraume 1980, p. 82: 'Gerson gegen Ende des 15. Jahrhunderts in Deutschland besser bekannt war als in Frankreich selbst'.
[6] Mazour-Matusevich 2006, pp. 963–87; Mazour-Matusevich 2006, pp. 357–400; Mazour-Matusevich 2010, pp. 632–51.
[7] Hobbins 2006, p. 194.
[8] Saak 2017, p. 16.
[9] Hobbins 2006, pp. 193–94.
[10] Hamm 1977, p. 75 & p. 77.
[11] François & Soen 2018, Introduction, p. 10.

were already particularly receptive during his lifetime.[12] The fact that by the end of the 15th century the principal oracle of the *devotio moderna* (a Germanic phenomenon as well) was none other than the chancellor of Paris University,[13] further reinforced the special connection between the French late medieval chancellor and religious circles in this part of Europe.

Gerson at Melk

The Benedictine monastery of Melk, located on a rocky base overlooking the Danube river, was the place where Gerson's Germanic passage began. It began, right after the Council of Constance, as a personal failure and loss. The epic Council turned out to be the culmination of all the paradoxes and contradictions of Gerson's complex personality and life — both the summit of his career that propelled him from a peasant's son to a preeminent status in Europe, and the point of no return in the literal and figurative sense of this expression. The Council epitomized his greatest achievement as an ecclesiastical leader and a dedicated servant of the Church: the end of the Western Schism. It also brought about his fateful involvement in the condemnation and gruesome execution of Jan Hus (1369–1415) and Jerome of Prague (1379–1416), a deeply disturbing fact in the chancellor's biography otherwise untarnished by violence and cruelty.[14] As if in retribution for his treatment of the Czechs, he, the powerful chancellor of the University of Paris, adviser of kings and princes and the star theologian of his time — himself became a victim of persecution. His persistent struggle *contra doctrinam pestiferam iubentam tyranos per insidias interfici*[15] or the tyrannicide theory, earned him condemnation in Paris, then occupied by Anglo-Burgundian

---

[12] See Hamm, 1977, pp. 464–971.

[13] Debongnie 1928, p. 255. Martinstal *devotio moderna* monastery's reading list in Leuven includes all printed editions by Gerson (Martinstal list in Staubach 1997, p. 429).

[14] For an excellent analysis of Gerson – Hus conflict see Prügl 2013.

[15] *Dialogus Apologeticus*, OC: 6, pp. 296–97: *Monicus: Petis cur terminata per generale Concilium non fuerit causa fidei contra doctrinam pestiferam iubentam tyranos per insidias interfici per quoslibet, etiam ordine iuris nec diuini nec humini seruato, et confoederatione qualibet non obstante.* 'Monicus: 'You ask why the cause of faith was not settled by the general Council against the pestiferous doctrine ordering that tyrants could be murdered by whomever with treacherous attacks

forces,[16] and transformed him into a homeless wanderer or *peregrinus* (according to his favorite expression) with powerful lords, and even his former colleagues, conspiring against his very life. His numerous epitaphs do not exaggerate when they state that he suddenly lost all that he managed to accomplish, accumulate and secure in his spectacular social ascent: status, academic position, income, home, library, and friends.[17] Unable to go back, he traveled to Tyrol, accompanied (according to a legend which will be discussed further on) by only a friend and a dog.[18]

This life-changing experience must have had a powerful effect on the formerly powerful man, and in 1418 Melk's monks probably met a different Gerson. His own accounts of his internal state of turmoil are found in *Dialogus Apologeticus* and *De consolatione theologiae*, written immediately after the Council. *Dialogus*, written first, reflects his inner transition from shock to resentment, from resentment to acceptance and from acceptance to the beginning of recovery. Anyone familiar with the grieving process can identify with these three stages. Only at the very end, the *Dialogus* reveals its author's capacity to redirect his gaze away from his pain-

(ambushes) and furthermore when the system of either divine or human laws, despite any confederation, is not upheld'.

[16] The tyrannicide controversy and the ensuing open conflict with the head of House of Burgundy John the Fearless (1371–1419) earned the chancellor the condemnation *in absentia*, making his return to Paris impossible. After the Council of Constance, he went to Tyrol and then to Lyons. For Gerson's biography see McGuire 2005. On the tyrannicide controversy see Coville 1974; Esquivel 1979; Guenée 1992; Figgis 1999; Izbicki, Bellitto 2000; Turchetti 2001; Vaughan 2002; Pascoe 2005; Schnerd 2005; Mazour-Matusevich 2013.

[17] Fredericus Hekelius (Johann Friedrich Hekel), *Donatus moralizatus uenerabilis magistri Iohannes de Gerson, Praefatio ad lectorem* (no pagination): *Caeterum hic Gerson noster, dissoluto Concilio Constantiensi, cui non fine laude intersuit, Domo patria, Cognatis, Amicis, Dignitatibus, Rebusque omnibus [...] est priuatus atque exspoliatus ut Lugdunum confugare illi necessum fuerit, ubi quod & non Parisiis, uitae huius miserae & inconstantis fatur d. XII. Jul. M. CCCC. XXIX. Aetatis suae 66, in Domino Iesu placide est mortuus.* 'Thus he [Gerson] was deprived and despoiled of his home, acquaintances, friends, dignities, and all things, including spiritual matters, and sought out by many enemies to the extent that it was necessary for him to seek refuge not in Paris but in Lyons, and, where his unhappy and erratic life ended on July 12, 1429, at the age of 66, when he peacefully passed away in our Lord Jesus Christ'. This epitaph, with slight variations, is found in the 1580 *Index Chronologicus* by Abraham Buchholzer, *Catalogue of Historical Description* by Wolfgang Krüger, and *Index Chronologicus* by Elia Reusner.

[18] L'Écuy 1832, p. 251.

ful recent past, turning 'inward to his spiritual life'.[19] Abruptly thrown out of the commotion of an active political life, disillusioned, worn out and resentful, the fifty-five-year-old chancellor was left with what no one could take away from him, and what he was soon to rediscover as truly his own: his love of writing and meditation, which for him were one and the same.

This mindset, favoring detachment and internal reflection, naturally influenced his demeanor and the impression he left on Melk's brothers, who perceived him not as a mighty church politician, but as a spiritual writer absorbed in contemplation. This does not mean, of course, that his contemplative tendencies emerged only at that stage of his life. They had always been present in his writings.

But it was only in his involuntary retirement that these tendencies had the opportunity to fully blossom and fully absorb him, unhindered by worldly concerns. In fact, shifting away from his initial distress, Gerson ended up viewing his forced withdrawal from the active life as a deliverance and an act of God's mercy, allowing him to finally focus on his main concerns — theology and pastoral care:

> *His interim contentus, habes enim De theologica consolatione grandius opusculum, tecum habita, gratus Deo qui te segregauit ab his sollicitudinibus et pro ceteris in potestate constitutes ora, compatiens, flens et lugens.*[20]

Gerson must have left a lasting impression in Melk, since the first German manuscript translations of his works originate from there, including his future best-seller *Opus tripartitum*. His contemporary at Melk and likely his personal acquaintance, Benedictine monk Johannes Wischler von Freinsheim (1383–1455), translated *Opus*' third part in Latin as *Scientia mortis*. The second translation of the same text also came from Melk, authored by an affiliate of Vienna University, Heinrich von Preussen.[21] By 1483

---

[19] McGuire 2005, p. 283.

[20] *Dialogus Apologeticus*, OC: 6, p. 304. 'Meanwhile, safe from those people, now you have the greater work *The Consolation of Theology*, carried with you, [and], thanks to God, who separated you from these cares, now you also are able to work for others, suffering, crying and grieving'.

[21] Rudolf 1957, p. 68.

catalogue at Melk already 'lists forty-three manuscripts containing one or more Gerson's texts'.[22] The consonance between Gerson's post-Constance disposition and Melk spirituality could not be greater: like-minded people met at the right place and at the right time. Melk's monks, leaders of the reform movement among monasteries in the Empire, welcomed a kindred spirit. This happenstance doubtless influenced the reception of the chancellor's writings in German lands in the years immediately following his passing, as other monasteries soon joined Melk in the production of German manuscript translations of Gerson's works. His *De remediis contra pusillanimitatem* and *Super Magnificat* were translated anonymously at the monastery in Tegernsee, which would collect thirty-nine manuscripts of his works.[23] German monks Thomas Finck and Wolfgang Walcher translated the vernacular French treatise *De mendicité spirituelle*.[24] Several translations also came from the movement of *devotio moderna*.[25]

University of Vienna

While the monastic milieu might have been the most receptive to Gerson's influence at first, his impact in academia was ultimately not less prominent. In fact, in the context of the 15th century Empire, these two spheres of intellectual and spiritual life were not juxtaposed but closely connected, with both students and faculty circulating between the two venues. Gerson's association with the University of Vienna, the Empire's most important theological school, is of particular importance. According to a later tradition promoted by early German humanists, the Vienna connection was a direct continuation of Gerson's sojourn at Melk. According to this belief, the exiled and dispossessed chancellor was contacted by Albrecht V, Duke of Austria (1397–1439), who allegedly offered him protection and professorship at the Theology Department of the young University of Vienna (founded in 1365, the first students matriculated in

---

[22] Hobbins 2006, p. 202.
[23] Kraume 1980, p. 42. Besides Kraume, for the first reception see Pascoe 1973; McGuire 2005.
[24] Kraume 1980, p. 55 & p. 64. Hohenadel 2015, p. 51.
[25] Kraume 1980, p. 50.

1385). Although Gerson allegedly declined the offer — a believable response considering his mood after the Council — he enjoyed a great reputation among the University's faculty. His writings addressing the daily needs of the clergy met with an immediate popularity among representatives of the Vienna school of *Pastoraltheologie* such as Thomas Peuntner (1360/80–1439), Peuntner's teacher, Nikolaus von Dinkelsbühl (real name Prüntzlin or Prunczlein, 1360–1433), Johannes Nider (1380–1438), and Oswald de Corda (13?–1434). The latter, a Vienna alumnus and author of a manual for Carthusian copyists and correctors of Latin manuscripts, *Opus pacis*, corresponded with Gerson, and translated several of his French works into Latin.[26] Vienna scholars chose Gerson as their model, since 'Jerome, Augustine, Gerson, and Heinrich of Langenstein [were] superior to the neoclassical poets of Italian humanism because the former employed language practically rather than artificially'.[27] 'Practically' here means theologically, that is applying linguistic prowess and classical erudition as a medium for a greater purpose, theology, rather than as a goal in and of itself. For the Vienna faculty, caught at the crossroad between classicist Renaissance Italy and traditional medieval scholasticism, Gerson embodied a new type of theologian who, while passionate for affective theology, was open 'toward the first stirrings of humanist, rhetorical renewal at Paris'.[28] The combination of humanistic concerns with an earnest spiritual quest for contemplative life was what the Vienna faculty found inspirational in Gerson.

As for the scholastic philosopher, theologian and mathematician Heinrich von Langenstein (1325–1397), his life presents some rather curious similarities to Gerson's, to the point of causing confusion. Langenstein studied at the University of Paris, favored the idea of a general council as the remedy for the suppression of the Schism in his 1381 *Epistola concilii pacis*, had mystical tendencies, and even authored an ascetic treatise with the same

---

[26] Egan 2001, p. 179.
[27] Martin 1992, p. 38.
[28] Martin 1992, p. 54. On Gerson as an early humanist see Ouy 1970; Ouy 1982; Ouy 1993; Roccati 1992; Ouy 1995; Mazour-Matusevich 2003.

title as Gerson's text:[29] *Speculum animæ*. Langenstein's *Speculum* was published in Strasbourg in 1507 by the main editor of Gerson texts Jacob Wimpheling. Furthermore, after leaving his position in Paris, Langenstein was invited in 1384 by Albrecht III, Duke of Austria (1349–1395), to come to Vienna in order to assist in the foundation of the theological faculty of the newly founded university. Unlike Gerson, Heinrich von Langenstein accepted the offer and spent the remainder of his life teaching fundamental theology, exegesis, and canon law in Vienna. The association of their names and the intriguing parallels between the two men's biographies might have been responsible for the lasting confusion between these two authors. In the middle of the 16th century, the English jurist Christopher St Germain still attributed Langenstein's writings to Gerson, further contributing to the misperception, which was to continue for at least two more centuries. It also makes one wonder whether some facts from Heinrich von Langenstein's life have actually been confused with Gerson's story.

Yet, Heinrich von Langenstein might not be the only person to act as a possible prototype for Gerson's German passage. The chancellor's story of traveling through German lands and spreading ancient knowledge also corresponds to the biography of a Benedictine monk Peter von Rosenheim (1380–1433). Fra Peter not only participated in the Council of Constance — where he must have met and heard Gerson personally — but he also stayed at the Melk monastery, apparently around the same time as Gerson.[30] This energetic monk also left a long-lasting impression at Melk and was credited with bringing humanist ideas from Italy to Vienna. Later, von Rosenheim reformed Salzburg's Benedictine monastery, which 'became a stimulating intellectual and spiritual center from the middle of the 15th century'.[31] The library of this monastery was particularly famous for offering vernacular translations of Latin works, including those by Gerson.[32] The bio-

---

[29] While Langenstein's *Speculum animae* was written between 1382–1384, the exact date of the completion of Gerson's *Miroir de l'ame* is unknown. See Willshire 1874, p. 34.
[30] Posset 2005, p. 20.
[31] Posset 2005, p. 20.
[32] Posset 2005, p. 20.

graphical similarities between Gerson, Heinrich von Langenstein, and Peter von Rosenheim, rather than being mere coincidences, might reveal a commonality of ideas and goals aimed at the reform of religious life.

The link between Gerson and Johannes Nider, Dominican theologian and dean of the Vienna faculty, is well established.[33] Nider certainly knew the chancellor personally. While at Constance, 'the assembly of the electrified intellectuals',[34] Nider attended the chancellor's speeches, which made a big impression on him. His dependence on Gerson leaves no room for doubt. His major work *Consolatorium timoratae conscientiae*, 'derives its lessons directly from Gerson',[35] drawing on several works 'zusammenkompiliert'.[36] The chancellor is mentioned directly at least twenty-two times as *Magistro Io. De Gersono, cancellarius parisieni*, *Cancellarius* or even simply *Ioannnis*. Concerning confessions, Part I of *Consolatorium* relies on what *Cancellarius Parisiensis in suo tripartite [Opus tripartitum] sic dicens*,[37] while Part III, heavy with Gerson's textual presence, is dependent on *Libro suo de consolatione theologie, tractatu de pollutione Cancellari de gersono, tractatu de contractibus* and *De uita spirituali animae* as its direct sources. In chapter VII, chapters from XV to XX, as well as in chapters XXII, XXIIII and XXVII *uerba sunt per totum Cancellarii*.[38] Nider's *Consolatorium timoratae* also addresses two typical and interrelated Gersonian issues: too scrupulous a conscience and moral certainty.[39] Although the term *scrupuli*, meaning excessive moral scrupulosity, was used in the Middle Ages in reference to exaggerated anxious agitations of the soul caused by the idea of a moral or religious insufficiency of its bearer, the discussion of this subject attains an unprecedented intensity in Gerson's works.

[33] See Brogl 2013; Tentler 1977.
[34] Hobbins 2006, p. 193.
[35] Tentler 1977, p. 145.
[36] Grosse 1994, p. 170.
[37] Nider 1604, Oart 1, p. 23.
[38] Nider 1604, part 3, p. 110 & p. 118.
[39] Brogl 2013, p. 66: 'Nider draws on Johannes Gerson first in *Consolatorium* because the thematic of the scrupulous conscience is to be found not yet so virulent in Thomas, highlighted by how the term *scrupulosa conscientia* is to be found neither in Thomas nor in Bonaventura'.

It culminates in book three of *De consolatione theologiae*, where the word 'anxiety' or its synonyms abound, beginning with the declaration of Gerson's alter ego Peregrinus: *[...] sollicitam enim super hoc auiditatem ex peruigili cordis mei cura quae te loco temporeque praeuenit, intellegis.*[40] While Gerson's precursors suggested various therapeutic exercises meant to relieve excessive scrupulosity, he was the first to choose an approach that implied a change in the doctrine itself. Applying his characteristic circumstance-based reasoning, the French doctor asserted that when absolute moral certainty is impossible to attain, one should settle for a relative or probable certainty, which is sufficient for peace of mind. He coined the term moral certainty (*certitudo moralis*), according to which *[...] sufficit tertia certitudo qualis non semper scrupulos omnes abiicit, sufficit ut contemnat uel superet sic operando quasi non sint.*[41] Through this step, pregnant with major future developments in theology, commerce and jurisprudence, irrational anxieties and fears were to be mitigated,[42] and Gerson's ultimate goal of 'inner calmness',[43] could be achieved. This innovative approach has been referred to as 'probable certainty'[44] or Gerson's probabilism,[45] although probabilism as a doctrine appeared only in the 16th century, well after the chancellor's death.[46]

Even though Nider's arguments derive from Gerson, his focus almost imperceptibly shifts from the more introspective, personal and spiritual one in *De consolatione theologiae* to a more legalistic and pragmatic one in *Consolatorium*. Gerson's offer of consola-

---

[40] *De consolatione theologiae*, OC: 9, p. 215. 'You see my anxiety and eagerness and my sleepless heart's care, for I arrived here before you' (Miller 1998, p. 215).

[41] Based on *De consolatione theologiae*, OC: 9, pp. 231–32. 'The third kind of certainty which, although it does not always remove all scruples, suffices to disregard or overcome them [scruples] operating as if they were not there'. Also in *Regulae morales*, OC: 9, p. 123: *Et haec uocatur certitudo moralis uel ciuilis, quod homo sufficienter probatus est.*

[42] Schüssler 2011, p. 452.

[43] Suzanne 1981, p. 238.

[44] Maryks 2008, p. 67.

[45] Schüssler 2011, pp. 450–52.

[46] Suzanne 1981, p. 235: 'This moral uncertainty was understood as concerning the sinfulness of actions, which was due to the often-disputable validity of precepts in concrete cases'. Also see Fleming 2006.

tion is unconditional. It does not depend on whether a person is or is not in the state of grace, since God's love is not completely withdrawn even from mortal sinners.[47] Nider's itemized scholastic analysis of moral certitude verges on an explicitly probabilistic approach. He writes:

> [...] certitudo non remouet omnem improbabilitatem uel opinionem alterius partis: licet magis declinet ad ista qua ad alia. Quod sufficit. Verba sunt pene totum cancellaru i tractatu de contractibus.[48]

The *pene* ('almost'), which Nider allows himself as a divergence from his French mentor, consists in his merging, in a convoluted and labyrinthine manner, words from Gerson's most personal work *De consolatione theologiae* with arguments taken from more canon-law related texts *De contractibus* and *De uita spirituali animae*. Yet, in doing so, the German theologian restates again and again that *verba sunt per totum Cancelarii*, 'the words are all the Chancellor's'.[49]

Following the chancellor, Nider also admits that *certitudo naturalis*, achievable in mechanics and mathematics, is not possible in civil and spiritual laws forming *lex humana*. In human affairs one must use a more flexible approach, derived from Aristotle and tirelessly promoted in Christian context by Gerson:[50]

> *Necessaria est praeceptorum discrete epikeysatio, seu interpretatione uel deductio. Equitas dicit Cancellarius est igitur Epikeyae*

---

[47] Grosse 1994, p. 132.

[48] Nider 1604, p. 110. '[it ...] certainly does not remove all the improbability or the position of the other party, even if it leans more to one position or the other. This is enough. The words are almost entirely those of the Chancellor's *De contractibus*'. De contractibus, OC: 9, p. 402: '[...] quae certitudo non remouet in una parte omne probabilitatem uel opinionem alterius partis, licet magis declinet ab istam quam uel ad illam, quod sufficit.

[49] Nider 1604, p. 111. Also, Nider 1604, p. 120: *Unde Cancellarius super eadem auctoritate dicit [...]* 'Whence the Chancellor spoke more about the same with authority'.

[50] The Greek term ἐπιείκεια was first proposed by Aristotle. Applied to Greek and Roman law, it was further developed by Thomas Aquinas in *Somma theologica*. 'Epikeia or equity 'consists of the principles of natural justice so far as they are used to explain or correct a positive human law if this is not in harmony with [...] positive law in its literal interpretation'. *Catholic Encyclopedia*, 1 Law, Concept of, V. Cathrein.

> *uirtutis considerare non nudum praeceptum, sed circumstantias omnes particulariter ipsum uestientes.*[51]

We will return to the concept of *epikeia* and to the Nider-Gerson connection a little further on.

Carthusian Tradition

Gerson's sojourn in Austria was one of several parallel and interconnected elements that assured his omnipresence in the Empire after his death.[52] Another was his connection, also personal, to the Carthusian tradition, which was particularly strong in what is now Austria. The chancellor's ties with this Order had developed already during his lifetime. He regularly sent his works to the Grande Chartreuse from Lyons, while Carthusian monk Johannes Huiklene or Hinklene translated several of his treatises.[53] The Carthusian connection was further reinforced by Vienna University's historical bonds with the same Order. By 1458, former professors and students of the University of Vienna constituted more than a half of the nearby Carthusian community of Gaming, located in the foothills of the Austrian Alps.[54] The most renowned monk of this monastery, the former Vienna university professor Nicolas Kempf (*c.* 1415–1497), espoused several features of Gersonian spirituality, such as emphasis on discretion and moderation, and the use of the vernacular for religious purposes. Kempf was particularly impressed with *De consolatione theologiae*, which he strove to emulate. The geographical proximity of Melk, where *De consolatione* was written, must have reinforced the connection. Making use of *De consolatione* as well as of another of Gerson's texts, *De uita spirituali animae,* Kempf hoped to move

---

[51] Nider 1604, p. 134. 'A descrete *epikeysatio*, or interpretation or deduction, of the precepts is necessary. The Chancellor says that equity is therefore the virtue of Epikeya, to be considered not as the naked precept, but with all the circumstances that specifically 'dress' it'.

[52] Massaut 1968, p. 127: 'Toute l'histoire du siècle qui le suivit est dominée par cette figure complexe, et hantée par son souvenir. Gerson devait garder après sa mort 'l'omniprésence'.

[53] Sönke 2002, p. 43.

[54] Martin, 1992, p. 22. This work by Denis Martin constitutes the most extended existing study of Kempf.

from a theology of the intellect to the theology of the heart'.[55] Another famous Carthusian, who explicitly cited Gerson as an authority on mystical theology, was Denys van Leeuwen, mostly known as Denys the Carthusian (1402–1471).[56] His positions on the power of general councils and on mystical theology were 'almost identical with those of Jean Gerson'.[57]

The chancellor's Carthusian connection manifests itself in the sheer number of his works held in Carthusian libraries. Among them, the library of Basel holds a special place, for it became the third center of the distribution of his works after Constance and Vienna. The library's success in accumulating Gerson's editions was due to the Council of Basel (1432–1443), which became, after Constance, the most important event for 'the spread of late medieval texts of all kinds'[58] and of Gerson's works in particular. The Basel collection is indicative of the early stages of what might be referred to as 'Gerson's frenzy'. Basel's Moser catalogue, edited by Veronica Gerz-von Büren, contains 352 Gerson titles, all of Germanic origin, the majority of which belong to the second

---

[55] Martin 1992, p. 83. *De uita spirituali animae*, OC: 3, p. 127: *Vis ergo secretum cognoscere? Transfer te a theologia intellectus ad theologiam affectus, de scientia scilicet ad sapientiam, de cognitione ad deuotionem*. 'Do you want to know a secret? Take yourself from theology of the intellect to theology of the affectivity, that is, from knowledge to wisdom, from cognition to devotion'. The same idea is also found in *De consolatione theologiae*, OC: 9, p. 237: *[...] ita theologum nominamus bonum uirum in sacris litteris eruditum; non quidem eruditione solius intellectus, sed multo magis affectus, ut ea quae per theologiam intelligit, traducat per iugem ruminationem in affectum cordis, et executionem operis [...]* 'so we call a theologian a good man learned in the sacred writings, not in learning of the intellect merely, but much more of the heart. As a result, what he understands through theology he transfers through constant rumination to the affection of the heart and to the performance of good works' (Miller 1998, p. 253).

[56] Emery 1991, p. 21: *In quibus assidue, Deo laus, exstiti studiosus, et multos legi auctores: scilicet super Sententias Thomae, Alberti [...] Bonauenturae [...], Richardi de Mediauilla [...] Libros etiam sanctorum: Hieronymi, Ambrosii, Gregorii, Dionysii Areopagitae doctoris mei electissimi Boetii, Anselmi, Bernardi, Bedae, Hugonis de Sancto Victore, Gersonis, Guillelmi Parisiensis*. 'Thanks God, I studied assiduously, and read many authors, namely [the Commentary] on the Sentences by Thomas [Aquinas], Albert [the Great] [...] Bonaventure [...], Richard of Middleton [...] as well as books by saints: Jerome, Ambrose, Gregory, Dionysius Areopagitis, my beloved [most chosen] doctor Boetius, Anselm [of Canterbury], Bernard [of Clairvaux], Beda, Hugues of St Victor, Gerson and Guillaume of Paris'.

[57] Ewig 1936, pp. 60–61. Also see Stieber 1978.

[58] Hobbins 2006, p. 203.

part of the 15th century with the last ones dating to its very end. The corpus includes the five 'full' Gerson's editions existing at the time: that of Cologne, 1483; of Strasbourg, 1488; of Basel, 1488; of Strasbourg, 1518, and that of Basel, 1518.[59] As was the case at Melk, the vast majority of Gerson's writings accumulated in Basel deals with reforming monastic life, mystical theology or pastoral care.[60] Out of fifty-four volumes contained in the Basel library, eighteen are dedicated to spirituality, fifteen to religious life and pastoral duties, nine to doctrinal questions, seven to ecclesiology and five represent polemical treatises. Judging by the number of manuscripts of Gerson's works, his *Super Magnificat* appears to be of special meaning for the Carthusians.[61] Better known among musicologists, *Super Magnificat* reviews all contemporary musical instruments, their use and their particular effects on human senses.[62] It explores the mystical connection between five musical notes, five vowels of the French language, and the five fingers of the hand, developing a special technique of internal or spiritual singing.[63] It must also be noted that more works were acquired in time. Consequently, while Constance had given Gerson's works an international audience, Basel and the Carthusians 'gave readers the chance to collect his works systematically and on a great scale'.[64] Besides Basel, another Carthusian house with an impor-

---

[59] Gerz-von Büren 1973, p. 118.

[60] Gerz-von Büren 1973, p. 120.

[61] Sönke et al. 2002, p. 118.

[62] There were eight editions published in the Empire and in Switzerland, and one published in Paris in 1521 (See Vendrix 1997, pp. 1453–62).

[63] An article published in 1904 underlines the unique character of *Super Magnificat* facsimile published by Conrad Fyner of Esslingen (Southern Germany) because musical notes, printed in black, and lines, printed in red, were certainly printed 'at the same time and not punched in afterwards' (Crotchet 1904, pp. 432–33). Art historian Kathi Meyer-Baer offered a hypothesis that the expressions of the singing angels on the famous Ghent Altar panel might correspond to five affections/notes/vowels described by Gerson in *Super Magnificat*: two negative, *timor* and *dolor*, and two positive, *gaudium* and *spes*, while the angel at the center can be understood as representing *pietas* or *misericordia* (Meyer-Baer 2015, p. 359). Gerson develops a similar theory in *Tractatus de canticis*, where he speaks of the correlation between vowels and the emotions they express: *O timet, U que dolens odit, et esta notes. I uel Iota compassionem, O timorem, U dolorem uel odium* (*Tractatus de canticis*, OC: 9, p. 542). For more details see Anttila 2013, pp. 42–49. Isabelle Fabre analyzes both of Gerson's musical treatises (Fabre 2005).

[64] Hobbins 2006, p. 213.

tant assortment of Gerson's works was that of Erfurt in Thuringia. Its *Lektürkanon* contained, among others, Gerson's *De libris legendis a monachis*, as well as a summary of his *Exhortatio finalis ad stadium sacrae lectionis*.[65]

We should not, however, 'oversimplify a complicated picture'[66] of Gersonian collections in Charterhouses. Although the Carthusian selection of Gerson's works was 'broad enough to reflect the complexity and wide interests of Gerson himself',[67] its readers had little notion of him as a Latin orator and poet, and virtually nothing of him as the author writing and preaching in the vernacular. Of how much interest these aspects of his creativity would have been to the Carthusian monks is another question. What seems to be certain is that in this particular context 'his legacy was taking shape as a moral and spiritual authority and guide to the religious life'[68] both because of the nature of his readership and the nature of the supply to which his readers had access.

Nicolas of Cusa and Bernhard von Waging

The intellectual relationship between cardinal Nicolas of Cusa (1401–1464) — a brilliant Renaissance mind, theologian, mathematician and astronomer — and Gerson is too vast a topic to be addressed by this study in any detail,[69] but three important connections are necessary to mention. The first concerns Gerson's reputation as a mystical theologian, which was challenged by a Carthusian monk named Vincent von Aggbach (1389–1464) in 1453. Initially very much in favor of the French master, whom he venerated according to the already established Carthusian tradition, Vincent subsequently turned against him, accusing the late chancellor of fundamental infidelity to Dionysian mystical theology. This complex controversy centered on a question that Gaspard (Kaspar) Aindorffer (Ayndorffer), abbot of Tegernsee

---

[65] Wassermann 1994, p. 488.
[66] Hobbins 2006, p. 200.
[67] Hobbins 2006, p. 200.
[68] Hobbins 2006, p. 200.
[69] On this controversy and Gerson-Cusa connection see Vansteenberghe 1920; Hopkins 1996; McGinn 2005; Mazour-Matusevich 2002; Vial 2006 & Vial 2014.

Benedictine monastery, formulated as follows: 'whether without intellectual knowledge, or even any prior or accompanying thinking, a devout soul can attain God by *affectus* alone'.[70] Gerson's answer to this question is negative because even though he gave the priority to love — as so many other commentators had — he was also 'anxious to maintain a place for mental understanding',[71] making sure that *affectus* and *intellectus* kept each other in check.[72] This position provoked Vincent von Aggbach's charge against Gerson of willful misrepresentation of the true meaning of Dionysius' teaching. At Aindorffer's prompting, Nicolas of Cusa came to Gerson's aid, declaring that the chancellor did no violence to the Dionysian doctrine. There is no doubt that the cardinal knew Gerson's works, including both *Theologia Mystica Speculatiua* and *Theologia Mystica Practica*, which 'had popularity in learned circles', including Cusa's 'correspondents and opponents'.[73] 'Displaying agreement with ideas from Gerson',[74] the cardinal rejected Vincent's position that the mystical ascent could be effectuated only by love without knowledge. Cusa's 'notion of the hunt for God',[75] reminiscent of Gerson's theology of spiritual quest — the middle ground between quietism and theology of merits, based on Hebrews 11:6: 'God rewards those who seek him' — might warrant further investigation.[76]

---

[70] Letter of Gaspar Aindorffer to Nicolas of Cusa, McGinn 2005 p. 452.

[71] McGinn 2005, p. 451.

[72] *La Montagne de contemplation*, OC: 7: 1, p. 37: 'Il est certain que la vie de créature raisonnable est plus en l'ouvrage d'entendement et de raison que ailleurs, c'est a dire en pensées raisonnables et en dilection voluntaire'. 'It is certain that the life of the rational creature concentrates more on the work of understanding and reason than on anything else. It is concerned with rational thought and voluntary love' (McGuire 1998, p. 103).

[73] Hopkins 1988, p. 15. McGinn 2005, p. 451.

[74] Hopkins 1988, p. 15 & 16: 'In mystical theology, he answered in a manner reminiscent of Gerson, knowledge must accompany love. For whatever is loved is loved under the aspect of the good — i.e., is loved as being a good. So if the soul did not deem God to be a good, it would not love Him; and if it loves Him, it deems Him a good. This judging, or deeming, is the intellectual, or cognitive, component that is necessary for love'.

[75] McGinn 2005, p. 456.

[76] For a detailed analysis of Gerson's theology of spiritual quest see Mazour-Matusevich 2004, chapter 5.

The second nexus is conciliarist. In 1434 Cusa published *De Concordantia catholica*, where he favorably presented the chancellor's views on the superiority of the council over the papal authority.[77] The third link pertains to what constitutes the greatest difference between these two late medieval minds. It has to do with the question of the relationship between intellect and affect in mystical theology. Gerson had a consistent preoccupation with simple believers, which was pastoral in nature. This concern was relevant, for example, to his evaluation of Ruysbroeck and some other mystics, whose language he deemed either too intellectually challenging or too dangerously unguarded for the general audience. The *doctor consolatorius* saw a likelihood that 'any necessity for cognitive abandonment would exclude simple believers from the *uia mystica* — since many such believers would be incapable of attaining the state of *pura intelligentia*' — as intolerable.[78] It contradicted his goal of opening contemplative life to all those who longed for it. Cusa, by contrast, was no moral theologian,[79] and he 'shows no signs of supposing that the pathway of mystical theology is available to all believers'.[80] While Gerson accommodated 'version of *theologia mystica* to the *uia deuotionis*',[81] open to all souls in search of God, no such concern is visible in Cusa.

Nicolas Cusa's friend and 'the most fervent admirer',[82] distinguished monastic theologian and Benedictine friar, Bernhard von Waging (1400–1472) valued Gerson as an expert on contemplative life, referring to him as *doctor insignis et emeritus* or just *cancellarius* in his major work *Consolatorium tribulatorum*, which is more or less a compilation of the chancellor's writings.

---

[77] See Watanabe 1993; Oakley 2015.
[78] Hopkins 1988, p. 97.
[79] Jacob 1953, p. 169.
[80] Hopkins 1988, p. 97.
[81] Hopkins 1988, p. 97: 'Gerson introduces his second route, the *uia deuotionis*. Through faith and love, he explains, the soul of the simple, fervent believer can attain unto the same heights as the soul of the erudite- i.e., can attain unto ecstasy and can do so without the precondition of intellectual detachment. For through the edifying quality of his devout love the simple believer can become released from attachment to the world in order to soar upward unto the Beauty of the Lord'.
[82] Jacob 1953, p. 166.

With entire passages inserted without acknowledgement, *Consolatorium*'s chapters one to four are taken from *De remediis contra pusillanimitatem*, chapters five and six from *Super Magnificat*, and chapter seven, for the most part, from Nider's *Consolatorium conscientiae timoratae*, which itself is a compilation of Gerson's texts. In the Prologue to *Consolatorium*, Bernhard openly and proudly states his dependence on Gerson's *De remediis contra pusillanimitatem*. To do so at the very beginning of his work, he must have expected his readers to recognize Gerson's name,[83] using it as an advertisement. It was an exceptional honor, since von Waging considered very few theologians, among either *veteri* or *moderni*, to be true witnesses of the contemplative experience.[84] Several of Bernhard's writings (*Laudatorium doctae ignorantiae*, *Defensorium laudatorii doctae ignorantiae* and *De cognoscendo Deum*) are part of the same Dionysian controversy discussed above. After reading Nicolas of Cusa, Bernhard identified *theologia mystica* with *docta ignorantia* and favored — against Vincent but with Gerson — a balanced relationship between *intellectus* and *affectus*. Von Waging also endorsed both Gerson's criticism of certain monastics, who wear the habit but whose life is corrupt and immoral,[85] and explicitly supported his views of the pope as being *seruum seruorum*.[86] Nevertheless, von Waging implicitly reversed some of Gerson's theological novelties, all the while exhibiting the

---

[83] Hohenadel 2015, p. 67.

[84] Treusch 2011, p. 101. On Bernhard von Waging also see Kaup 2013, pp. 23–24.

[85] Rieman 1985, pp. 264–66: *[...] inter haec monachis et claustralibus [...] testatur contra magis uidemus insolentes, magis carnales, magis tenaces, magis auaros [...] Quocirca monachi quidem sunt exteriori habitu, sed uita, sed operibus, sed internae conscientiae spurcitia a perfectione, quam habitus ille demonstrat longissime disiuncti.* 'Among these monks and those living in cloisters there are insolent, very carnal, very obstinate, very avaricious [...] Therefore indeed these are monks by exterior habit, but by life, deeds and corruption of internal conscience, they are most remotely disjoined from the perfection that this habit expresses'.

[86] Rieman 1985, p. 71: *Nempe ut ait doctor insignis et emeritus Iohannis de Gersona praetactus: omnis dominatio, primatus et praelatio est uerissimus seruitus, nec frustra nec ficte nec mendose dicit se summus pontifex seruum seruorum tamquam habens omnes homines impositos super caput suum redditurus de omnibus rationem.* 'Of course, like the already mentioned famous and venerable Jean Gerson said: all government, primacy and authority is most truly a servitude; the supreme pontiff says neither vainly nor insincerely nor falsely that he is servant of servants having people put on his head, giving an account of everything'.

most reverential attitude toward him. One of these reversals concerns, as in the case of Nicolas of Cusa, the chancellor's eagerness to open the contemplative life to the laity. Although for different reasons than Cusa (who was, like Gerson, a secular cleric), von Waging did not share the latter's enthusiastic program of contemplative life for all. Quoting Gerson's major work *De mystica theologia practica*, von Waging articulated his view of the contemplative life as a monastic prerogative:

> *Respondeo ex intentione doctoris praenominati olim Parisiensis cancellarii, quod claustralis deditus contemplationi et internae quieti multum proficit quam tam aliis quam sibi primo. Multum proficit sibi ipsi, cum ut sic in uita contemplatiua multo plus placeat deoquam in uita actiua.*[87]

Another theological novelty that Fra Bernhard chose to suppress was Gersonian notion of simultaneously maintaining active and contemplative modes of life: '[...] et qui porroit ensemble tenir l'une vie et l'autre parfaitement, ce seroit le meilleur'.[88] The focus of Fra Bernhard's works — despite their general titles *Speculum pastorum et animarum restorum* and *Defensorium specula pastorum et animarum rectorum*[89] — is inner reform and monastic contemplative life understood as one and the same thing.

Rhine Humanists: Geiler von Kaysersberg, Jacob Wimpheling and Johannes Trithemius

While monastics and academics were guardians and consumers of Gerson's works, the credit of printing and publishing them should be fully given to another group of people: Rhine humanists, the 'toujours et encore le relais rhénan',[90] whom Pierre Chaunu considered the most active and energetic intellectual community in

---

[87] Rieman 1985, p. 78. 'I respond on the basis of the intention of the previously mentioned doctor and formerly Parisian chancellor, that the monk devoted to contemplation and inner quiet greatly profits others as well as himself. He greatly profits himself since in the contemplative life he pleases God more than in the active life'.

[88] *La Montagne de contemplation*, OC: 7: 1, p. 36. 'The best would be if one could maintain both ways of life [contemplative and active] completely' (McGuire 1998, p. 101).

[89] Rieman 1985, pp. 70–268.

[90] Chaunu 1981, p. 92.

late medieval Europe. This milieu included professor, prior, and then chancellor of the Sorbonne, Johannes Heynlin von Stein, known in France as Jean Lapide (?1430–1496),[91] Strasbourg preacher Johannes Geiler von Kaysersberg or Keysersberg (1445–1510), Strasbourg printer Peter (Pierre) Schott (1427–1504), the already-mentioned humanist Jacob Wimpheling (1450–1528), Bishop of Basel Christoph von Utenheim (*c.* 1450–1527), poet and satirist Sebastian Brant (1457–1521), Basel publisher Johann Amerbach (1444–1511), poet laureate Thomas Murner (1475–1537), brilliant humanist Beatus Rhenanus (1483–1547), scholar of Greek and Hebrew and Melanchthon's future tutor Johannes Reuchlin (1455–1522), humanist monk Johannes Trithemius (1462–1516) and others. These remarkable men, who belonged to what Brian McGuire christened 'the last medieval reformation',[92] were united 'in their mutual effort at ecclesiastical and educational reform, and in their unanimous esteem for the unofficial fifth 'church father', Jean Gerson'.[93] While Gerson's pastoral theology and pedagogical objectives corresponded to the *reforma perpetua* program of 15th century German mystical humanists both in and outside monasteries, subjectivist and moralistic aspects of his religiosity resonated with their 'immense appétit du divin'.[94] A double process took place: on the one hand, the reception of Gerson was one of the central points of a 'distinctly religious revival'[95] in the late 15th century Germanic Europe, on the other, it is this very revival that allowed Gerson's ideas *laßten weiter*[96] in this geographical and cultural milieu.

---

[91] The countless spellings of names under which he was known creates confusion: Heynlein, Henelyn, Henlin, Hélin, Hemlin, Hegelin, Lapierre, de la Pierre, Steinlin, Lapidanus. The date of his death varies from 1496 to 1505. He is also often understandably confused with another Johannes de Lapide from England, who, besides having exactly the same name, also studied in Paris at the same time (1418). For Heynlin's other works, see Tilly 1990, col. 810–12.

[92] This is the title of McGuire's biography of Gerson.

[93] Oberman 1981, p. 38. Gerson's works were printed continuously: *Monotessaron, Ars moriendi*, Cologne, 1468 & 1482; *Modus uiuendi omnium Christi fideliu*, Cologne 1470; Marienthal, Urach 1480 & Cologne, 1510; *Sermo de uirginis marie*, Cologne, 1480; *Sermo de passione in latinum traductus*, Strasbourg, 1509 & 1510; Basel 1515, to name just a few.

[94] Fèvre 1957, p. 37.

[95] Holt 2005, p. 14.

[96] Smolinsky 2005, p. 261 & p. 362.

Nowhere else in the Empire was Gerson's spiritual presence more pronounced than in the imperial city of Strasbourg,[97] and no one in Strasbourg was more receptive to it than this city's celebrated preacher Johannes Geiler von Kaysersberg, who 'venerates Gerson to the point of being called his *illustrator*'.[98] The Strasbourg preacher played a crucial role in the preservation of Gerson's written legacy, as some of the latter's texts are only known to us thanks to Geiler's edition.[99] It opens with the epitaph, which expresses Geiler's distinct perception of the Parisian master as *fortis in ecclesia bellator maxime Gerson, armatus gladio* ('a strong warrior in the church armed with a sword').[100] It is a militant image, likely to please someone like Ignatius of Loyola less than fifty years later.

The chancellor's impact on Geiler was profound, manifold and vast, and his dependency on Gerson's ideas is well known.[101] It seems to permeate not only Geiler's ideas but his personality, preaching style and active civil position. Having 'adopted Gerson as his model'[102] as 'more than a theologian, but an engaged pastor of Saint-Jean-en-Grèves',[103] Geiler became 'the religious and political conscience of the city council of the Free City of Strasbourg'.[104] Characteristically, one of his first pastoral struggles, at the beginning of his service in Strasbourg, was his unconditional opposition to the common custom of refusing confession, communion and Christian burial to those condemned to death.[105] This was one of Gerson's concerns as well. In *Requête pour les condamnés à mort* the chancellor pleaded for compassion even for the worst of criminals.[106] Geiler picked up the battle where Gerson

---

[97] Kraume 1980 p. 82: 'Hatte der Straßburger Kreis wesentlichen Anteil daran, dass Gerson gegen Ende des 15. Jahrhunderts in Deutschland besser bekannt war als in Frankreich selbst'. On Gerson's influence among German humanists see Posset 2005; Ritter 2010.

[98] Arnaud 2006, p. 251, citing Herding 1970, p. 51.

[99] Ouy 1998, p. x.

[100] Wimpheling 1514. This edition does not have page numeration.

[101] See Dacheux 1876; Douglass 1966; Kraume 1980.

[102] Hamm 2004, p. 55.

[103] Arnaud 2006, p. 251.

[104] Hamm 2018, p. 353.

[105] Hamm, 2018, p. 355.

[106] *Requête pour les condamnés à mort*, OC: 7: 1, p. 341: 'La loy de Dieu commende que chascune personne [...] face avant sa mort confession a prestre [...]

had left it, and, unlike the Parisian theologian, prevailed over the tenacious resistance from both ecclesiastical and secular authorities. The custom was abandoned, and the clergy was allowed to regularly administer communion to condemned criminals.[107]

An outstanding orator famed for his capacity to attract crowds, Geiler largely based his preaching on Gerson's sermons, which he sometimes followed verbatim.[108] He appealed to his spiritual guide under a variety of names: *christenlich Lerer Joannes Gerson, Gerschon, Cancellarius, der grosse lerer Gerschon, cancilarius, kancelarius Barydietzis, kanzelar Baridientziss, kanzelar Baridyenßyß, kanzelar Barydienziss, kanzelar Barydyentziss, Johannes Canciliarius, kanzelar* and *kantzeler*. Even when Geiler was not quoting Gerson directly, he took over his spiritual mentor's 'subjects and positions, which he then handles and presents to his audience in an easily accessible form'.[109] For example, out of twenty-five of his Augsburg sermons, where Gerson is directly mentioned at least twenty-two times, nineteen represent close reworking of Gerson's texts, and specifically the *Mountain of Contemplation*, while in the remaining six 'die frommigkeittheologischen Grundpositionen des Pariser Kanzlers' can be clearly perceived.[110] Among these theological *Grundpositionen* are 'fundamental relationality in an older mystical tradition',[111] death preparation, psychological insights on dealing with contemplative practices, evangelical harmonization, confession, consolation of the Holy Cross, mental pilgrimage and spiritual begging. Theological relationality, meaning a spirituality centered on a personal relationship or even a friendship with God, found expression in Geiler's reworking of Gerson's *Mountain of Contemplation* in the cycle of sermons appropriately called *Der Berg des Schauens* and published in 1492.[112] In this cycle, where he creatively combines segments from *Mountain of Contempla-*

Toute loy ou estat au contraire des vérités dessus dittes est injuste, desraisonnalble et non a tenir pour quelconque proffit ou dammaige qui en doye venir a la chose publique'.

[107] Backus 2004, p. 119.
[108] Lieberman 1965, p. 294. Also see Dacheux 1876.
[109] Freiehagen-Baumgardt & Williams-Krapp 2015, p. xxxiii.
[110] Freiehagen-Baumgardt & Williams-Krapp 2015, p. xxxiv.
[111] Faesen *forthcoming*.
[112] McGinn 2005, p. 340.

tion and Gerson's vernacular text *La mendicité spirituelle*, with the chancellor's letter to his sisters entitled *Traité Enhortant a prendre l'estat de virginité plus que de marriage*,[113] and with the treatises *De exercitio deuotorum simplicium, Contre conscience trop scrupuleuse* and *Remède contre les tentations de blaspheme*,[114] one finds, among other borrowings, Gerson's lyrical rendition of the Pater Noster:

Gerson: Doncques nostre pere, puis qu'ainsy vous commandés nommer, vostre commandement soit fait; mais je vous supplie par ycelluy nom qu'il soit sanctifié en moy telement que ie ne mente en vous nommant pere.[115]

Geiler: Als ain kind sein vater halten sol, spricht der Gerschon. Vnd dar umb sprechen wir jm pater noster nit gemachel oder herr, sonder: Vater noster [...][116]

However, while introducing the work of 'der kantzelar Barydyentziss' as written for 'sein leiplich schwostren' ('his beloved sisters'), who were 'die junckfrawen' (young women), whom their brother let stay together 'jn ain hauss vnd nit ain closter' (at home and not at the cloister),[117] Geiler chooses to skip Gerson's confidence in his sisters' *entendement* (understanding).[118] Instead,

---

[113] McGuire 1997.

[114] Freiehagen-Baumgardt & Williams-Krapp 2015, p. xxxiv.

[115] *La mendicité spirituelle*, OC: 7: 1, pp. 316–17.

[116] Freiehagen-Baumgardt & Williams-Krapp 2015, p. 198. '[God] should be beheld as a kind father, says Gerson. And this is why we speak to him as our father and not as our consort or lord but rather: Our Father.'

[117] Freiehagen-Baumgardt & Williams-Krapp 2015, p. 40: 'der kantzelar Barydyentziss der schryb dise wort seinen schwostren. Er hot fier schwostren, waren und sein leiplich schwostren. Die tot er zusamen jn ain hauss vnd nit ain closter'. 'The Parisian chancellor who wrote these words to his sisters. He had four sisters, who were his beloved sisters. He put them together at home and not in a cloister'. *Sur l'excellence de la virginité*, OC: 7: 1, p. 419: 'car a vray dire — et sans blasme de religion — je navoye pas inclinacion grande que vous fucies mises en religion que je cougneusse, pour causes plusieurs qui a ce me mouvoyent'.

[118] *La Montagne de contemplation*, OC: 7: 1, p. 16: 'Si n'est chose plus convenable pour escripre a mes dictes sueurs qui par le don de Dieu ont entrepris pieca vivre sans mariage, que de les enseigner comment elles plairont a Dieu [...] Et ne me retarde point de ce faire la simplesse de mes dittes seurs car je n'ai entencion de dire chose qu'elles ne puissent bien comprendre selonc l'entendement que j'ai esprouvé en elles'. 'Therefore, nothing is more fitting, in writing to my sisters, who by God's gift set out some time ago to live without marriage, than to teach them how they will please God [...] The lack of learning of my sisters cannot keep them from going ahead, for I intend to speak only about what they can fully grasp according to the understanding that I have found in them' (McGuire 1998, p. 75).

he indulgingly stated that the given material is 'nit zu schwer say noch zu hoch zu verstan' ('is not too difficult and nor too lofty to understand') anyway.[119] Anyone who has read *The Mountain of Contemplation* would find Geiler's statement inaccurate, and Gerson's faith in his sisters' intellectual abilities impressive. Indirectly revealing his misogyny that would influence his exceptionally harsh stance toward witches, Geiler also leaves out Gerson's explicit intent to write about spiritual matters more to women than to men.[120] One also cannot help noticing that in these series of sermons, Gerson's nuanced attitude loses sophistication and subtlety in Geiler's over-simplified rendition of the chancellor's psychological insights on dealing with contemplative practices:

Gerson: [...] la maniere de tenir son corps pourfite a avoir ferme pensée, et que la personne se mette en tele disposition qu'il luy plaira mieus, soit a genolz, soit en estant, soit au séant, soit en s'enclinant ou apuyant, ou soit en gisant. Et c'est ce a entendre quant la personne est seule [...][121]

Geiler: Der kanzler Baridyenßyß der schreibt von ainem, aber er maint sich selb, der testu sprechen: wann jch schon allain pin, weiß jch doh gar nichtz, wye jch mich halten soll oder sain umb gaun oder ob jch kniegen sol. [...] Doch so kan man dir nit all wegen sagen, wye du dich halten solt. Du solt auch

---

[119] Freiehagen-Baumgardt & Williams-Krapp 2015, p. 40.

[120] *La Montagne de contemplation*, OC: 7: 1, p. 16: 'Aucuns se pourront donner merveille pourquoy, de matiere haulte comme est parler de la vie contemplative, je vueil escripre en francois plus qu'en latin et plus aux femmes que aux hommes, et que ce n'est pas matiere qui appartiengne a gens simples sans lettre'. 'Some persons will wonder and ask why, in a matter so lofty as that of the contemplative life, I choose to write in French rather than in Latin, and more to women that to men. They will say that such a subject is not appropriate for ordinary people who have no Latin' (McGuire 1998, p. 75). Geiler's fanatical misogyny and his extreme stance toward witches, which cannot be discussed here, are hard to reconcile with Hamm's opinion of Geiler as an example of a 'moderate, accommodating, balancing mediation of God's severity and mercy' (Hamm 2018, p. 337).

[121] *La Montagne de contemplation* OC: 7: 1, p. 34. 'the manner of bodily posture contributes to our having clarity of thought. A person should prepare herself in the manner that will serve her best, whether kneeling, standing, sitting, bowing, or leaning up against something, or perhaps lying down. I refer to the situation when the person is alone' (McGuire 1998, p. 98).

it söllichen dingen nit ton, das wyder dein natur sey. [...] du sytzest oder standest oder knyegest oder ob du joch auf der erd ligst, das jst vor got alles gleich.[122]

Geiler's interpretation of Gerson's *Scientia mortis*, although very close to the original, also displays a stylistic move downward, his style being much more folkloristic, with metaphors and examples lying well outside the scholarly spectrum. Geiler thus likens the man longing for his heavenly home to 'einem Hündehen, das keine Ruhe hat, wenn es nicht bei seinem Herrn ist' — ('a doggy, which has no peace, when it is not with its owner').[123]

While it is not readily evident whether Geyler's collection of sermons, *Der Passion oder das lyden Jesu Christi vnsers herren/noch dem text der fyer Euangelisten*, which he 'zu Strassburg järlich geprediget hatt',[124] is directly inspired by Gerson, his written *Passion des herrn Jesu [...] geteilt in stückes weiß eins süßen Lebkuchen ußgeben*, published in 1514 by Johanes Grüninger, relies on the chancellor's template in a more obvious manner. Even though Geiler does not mention the words 'evangelical harmony' or the title of Gerson's *Monotessaron*, which will be discussed in detail further on, he quotes the chancellor twelve times in direct relation to his rendition of the *Passion*: 'item Gerson in seinem passion spricht', 'Dies sprichet Gerson mitt weitern worten',[125] 'dann nach Gerson oben sagt',[126] 'wie solten wir lernen und mit Gerson sagen',[127] 'Dies sagt Gerson im seinem passion',[128] or 'darum spricht Gerson uber das magnificat/tractatu. ix. particolae. Iiif'.[129]

---

[122] Freiehagen-Baumgardt & Williams-Krapp 2015, pp. 114–15. 'The Parisian chancellor wrote about others but he meant himself when he said the following: when I am alone, I know not how I should hold myself, standing or kneeling. One cannot tell you all the manners how you should hold yourself. You should not do such things that are against your nature. [...] whether you sit or stand or kneel or lies on the ground, to God is all the same'.
[123] Hoch 1901, p. 36.
[124] Geyler von Keysersberg 1522. 'He had preached yearly in Strasburg'.
[125] Geyler von Keysersberg 1514, p. xi.
[126] Geyler von Keysersberg 1514, p. xxv.
[127] Geyler von Keysersberg 1514, p. xxvi.
[128] Geyler von Keysersberg 1514, p. xlvii.
[129] Geyler von Keysersberg 1514, p. lxxxv.

Subject to excessive anxiety in his role as a confessor, Geiler was particularly responsive to Gerson's efforts to address the problem of scrupulous conscience in relation to confession.[130] Wanting 'his listeners to develop *l'homme intérieur*',[131] the Strasburger concurred with Gerson's understanding of confession as an act of both penance and consolation, with purification and comfort going hand in hand, leading to an overall improvement of the penitent's spiritual well-being. Following the chancellor, Geiler was convinced that no other form of consolation is as efficient as the meditation on the Holy Cross, for it sweetens and softens the bitterness of penance.[132] The Strasbourg preacher also replicated the idea of mental pilgrimage, which Gerson developed in *Modus quidam, quo certis ex causis Romam ire non ualentes in anno iubileo spiritualiter peregrinationem eamdem perficere possint* (*A way, so to speak, in which those who, for certain reasons, are not able to go to Rome might in the Jubilee Year make the same pilgrimage spiritually*).[133] Geiler's creative rendition of this text, entitled *Peregrinus*,[134] but also known as *Geistliche Ronfart*, describes an imaginary mystical pilgrimage, which is illustrated, timed and commented upon as if it were real.[135] While Gerson's text was timed for the jubilee of 1400, Geiler's *Peregrinus* was composed on the occasion of the jubilee of 1500: 'Also mag eyn yetlicher cristen mensch thuon der nit mag gen Rom kummen. ursachen halb. und also gefangen und geirret ist an der Romfart ym ein geystlich Romfart machen und für sich nemen'.[136] Considering that Geiler's work is a close reworking of

---

[130] Douglass 1966, p. 153.

[131] Arnaud 2006, p. 251.

[132] Douglass 1966, p. 182: *Dicit Gerson super Magnificat, nihil enim efficatium cruce et crux Christi dulcorat amaritudinem [...]*.

[133] *Modus quidam*, OC: 4, p. 942.

[134] Geiler von Kaysersberg 1494. There is a long tradition of metaphorical pilgrimage, starting at least with the allegorical text of *Le pèlerinage de la vie humaine*, composed circa 1330-1332, by the French poet Guillaume de Digulleville. On this subject see Herbers 2016. Kathryne Beebe affirms, without explanation, that *Modus quidam, quo certis ex causis Romam ire* is not Gerson's work (Beebe 2014, p. 209, n. 130).

[135] Geiler von Kaysersberg 1494.

[136] Frey 2000, p. 437. 'Every Christian, who cannot make a pilgrimage to Rome, can do as follows. Because of this reason, and thus imprisoned and impeded from going on a Rome pilgrimage, he can instead make a spiritual trip for himself'.

Gerson's text, the fact that Geiler refers to the spiritual pilgrim as *mendicans* or a beggar [137] probably indicates another Gersonian feature.[138] The concept of spiritual begging developed within the framework of Gerson's theology of spiritual quest inspired by Ier. 33. 3 ('Call to Me and I will answer you'); and Lc. 11. 9–10 ('Seek, and you will find'). This notion is one of the most characteristic and original elements of Gerson's theology. One interesting thing about finding this idea in Geiler's work is that it can be further traced to the writings of French 16th century humanists of the Meaux Circle, Jacques Lefèvre d'Etaples, Guillaume Briçonnet and Marguerite de Navarre, in whose correspondence explicit references to spiritual mendicancy can be found.[139] Geiler's adoption of this concept might be one of the links between Gerson and Meaux humanists who became acquainted with the chancellor's ideas — among other sources — through Geiler's published sermons.

Although Geiler's affinity with Gerson was mostly pastoral, the Strasburg preacher was also receptive to humanist aspects of Gerson's legacy. It is quite plausible that it was his admiration for the chancellor's moral integrity that made him more open to the new humanist stimuli. Indeed, although not a humanist himself, Geiler wasn't opposed to the nascent Strasbourg humanist society,[140] whose prominent members Jacob Wimpheling and Peter Schott were his close associates and friends. Gerson's two-fold legacy of humanism and devotional theology rendered the choice between the two unwarranted. As shall be demonstrated further on, the 'prominent German humanists [...] were all fervent Gersonians'.[141]

---

[137] Dacheux 1876, p. 275: *Hanc ciuitatem in spetem uicos diuide et singulis diebus uicum unum pertranseas mendicans oratione deuotissima.* 'Divide this city into seven streets and pass through one street every day, begging with the most devout prayer'.

[138] This idea appears in vernacular treatises *La mendicité spirituelle* and *Dialogue Spirituel*, and is also found in sermons such as *Pour le 1er dimanche de carême*, OC: 2, p. 743: 'demander conseil et croire a l'example du poure mendiant qui demande ailleurs du pain quant il ne le puet avoir de soy meismes'.

[139] Geiler von Kaysersberg's friend Johannes Pauli (d. 1455) published Geiler's sermons in the book entitled *Die Brosämlei* in 1517.

[140] Rapp 1982.

[141] Lieberman 1965, p. 295.

Among them two, Jacob Wimpheling and Johannes Trithemius (1462–1516)[142] were humanists of international standing. They met as students at Heidelberg University, the most ancient institute of higher learning in Germany proper. Wimpheling went on to become professor of poetry and rhetoric at Heidelberg from 1498 to 1500, when he left for Strasbourg. Trithemius chose monastic life and became the abbot of Sponheim at the age of twenty-one. Both were members of the Heidelberg learned society *Sodalitas litteraria Rhenana*, which was founded by the central figure of German humanism, poet Konrad (Conrad) Celtis (1459–1508), when he moved from Vienna to Heidelberg fleeing the plague. The initial sodality was inspired by Celtis's experience in Florence — where he met Marsilio Ficino between 1487 and 1489[143] — and was modeled upon the Italian *Academia Platonica*.[144] The sodality was led by the bishop of Worms Johannes von Dalberg (1455–1503), and besides Trithemius and Wimpheling, its most prominent members included a distinguished classicist Rudolf Agricola (1442–1485), Carmelite theologian Arnold de Bosch or Bostius (1450–1499) and Johannes Reuchlin (1455–1522), a humanist celebrity second only to Erasmus. Out of the sodality's nucleus of six principal participants three — Wimpheling, Trithemius and Bostius — were lifelong Gerson's enthusiasts. Bostius was a proponent of Immaculate Conception, and, together with the theologian and bishop of Sisteron Laurent Bureau (1499–1504)[145] and monastic humanist Pierre Bury (1427/1430–1504) made efforts to establish Gerson's official cult as a saint.[146] Reuchlin also knew and quoted the chancellor's work.[147]

---

[142] Trithemius has been and still is commonly associated with black magic because of his manual on necromancy *Steganographia*. Jim Reeds and Thomas Ernst, completely independently from each other, decoded this book, discovering Trithemius's codification method, which became known as the 'Enigma machine'. This method, used by Nazis during the Second World War, has been expended by modern mobile phone companies. For more detailed information on this amazing story see Ernst 1996. For Trithemius's biography and humanist contribution see Chacornac 2005, pp. 43–44.

[143] See Bauch 1903, p. 67. On Celtis see Spitz 1957.

[144] Bauch 1903, p. 73.

[145] Debongnie 1980, 5, col. 893.

[146] Renaudet 1916, p. 259.

[147] There is enough evidence that Reuchlin was familiar with some of Gerson's writings, particularly with his book *De laude scriptororum*, which Reuchlin

Enthusiastic, immensely productive and intensely driven, Jacob Wimpheling represented a real engine of Gerson's promotion in the Empire, and his work was instrumental in the perpetuation of the chancellor's legacy. After moving to Strasbourg in 1501 he befriended Geiler von Kaysersberg and invested his frantic energy into dissemination of Gerson's writings, which he considered *puras, solidas, ueraces deuotas et animi penetratiuas*.[148] Eventually replacing Schott as Geiler's secretary, Wimpheling published his predecessor's collection of all Gerson's writings available at the time — the project that Schott was unable to finish because of an untimely death from the plague. He also perfected this edition (published in 1502 in Strasbourg with Martin Flach) by adding the table of contents, and taking particular care to list groups of potential readers who, according to his judgment, were to profit from Gerson's writings. As Kraume keenly observed, this list ended up including 'fast die gesamte kirchliche Hierarchie':[149] priests, confessors, prelates, jurists, teachers, monks, inquisitors, young people (*adolescentes*), advisers, etc. Remarkably, this list corresponds almost exactly to the recommendations given by French humanist bishops in the early 16th century, a parallel that testifies to the lasting pan-European appeal of Gerson's ideas for the reformed-minded clergy.

Believing, as Gerson did, that the reform of the Church is primarily a question of proper education,[150] Wimpheling was above all interested in Gersonian pedagogical insights. Although the French theologian was far from Rousseauian belief in the innocence of infants, he had faith in a basic natural goodness in children, which makes instruction possible. In his work with the telling title *De innocentia puerili* Gerson preferred speaking of an inclination toward evil, which can be corrected with time, rather than of an innate depravation. 'As a pedagogue, who he was with a passion'[151]

---

used to advocate for tolerance of Jews and for his studies of Talmud. According to Reuchlin, Gerson did not want to mandate that all books containing errors were to be banned. Rather, inquisitors and prelates should be allowed to conserve such books for future references (Posset 2015, p. 390).

[148] Kraume 1980, p. 85.
[149] Kraume 1980, p. 84.
[150] Kraume 1980, p. 89.
[151] Strauss 1993, p. 73.

— Gerson hoped to build a child's educational foundation on the seeds of reason already present which, with careful cultivation and protection, could eventually grow into virtues.[152] Based on this foundation, Wimpheling worked the chancellor's ideas into a comprehensive pedagogical theory,[153] which he presented in two major treaties: *Isidoneus germanicus* (1497) and *Adolescentia* (1500). Promoting the unity between theology and classical learning, he valued both logic and rhetoric, praised the benefits of studying poetry and, joining the eternal choir of professors from all times, he lamented university students' poor writing skills. In addition to authoring pedagogical books, the German humanist also sought to implement his ideas into the actual university curricula. In 1521 or 1522, he submitted a report to the chancellor of Heidelberg University Florentius von Venningen pleading for the reform of the departments of theology and the arts. In this report, he directly referred to Gerson's writings, providing concrete quotations in his edition.[154] Wimpheling's concept of a balanced early education later found a receptive ground in Philipp Melanchthon, who would later apply the same basic principles to reforming the Saxon educational system.

The German humanist's enthusiasm for the Parisian chancellor is all the more remarkable as he was known for his open francophobia, which greatly offended French humanist Robert Gaguin (1433–1501),[155] who engaged in vivid polemics with him in 1492. Wimpheling's book *Germania* (1501) angered even German *poeta laureatus* Thomas Murner, who mocked it in his 1502 work *Noua Germania*.[156] This passionate German patriot, determined to 'demonstrate that the customary division between the cultured southern and barbarian northern mentalities is a complete figment of the imagination promoted by Italian propaganda',[157] appears to

---

[152] Strauss 1993, p. 73.
[153] Strauss 1993, p. 73.
[154] Kraume 1980, p. 90.
[155] On Robert Gaguin see Gaquoin 1901; Collard 1996; Charrier 1996.
[156] For the Wimpheling-Murner debate, see Borries 1926 and Leitch 2010. During his stay in Strasbourg, Murner had a chance to personally hear Geiler's sermons, which, according to Heribert Smolinsky, greatly influenced his personal style (Smolinsky 2005, pp. 240–41).
[157] Brann 1981, p. 249.

be the one to have contributed the most to Gerson's posthumous prestige in the Empire, having generated all the major elements of his *rerum germanicarum* that emphasize a unique and special bond between the exiled chancellor and the Germanic lands. His 1514 edition of Gerson's *Opera* contains several poetic and prosaic panegyrics of a nearly hagiographic character, such as the following *Epithaphium*:

> Si gist le grand et vray contemplatif Gerson
> Docteur digne de grand memoire
> A tous pescheurs feruant demonstratif
> Le seul chemin de leternelle gloire.
> En ce cloustre a moins saincte volumes faicts
> Specia lament de bien vivre et mourir
> Dictez les a et complis se parfaits
> Que ung chun desire les ouyr [158]

Wimpheling also authored Gerson's first biography, with an equally hagiographical title *De uita et miraculis Iohannis Gerson*, published in Strasbourg in 1506. It contains the first version of the tale concerning Gerson's exile in German lands when *Ducis Austriae [...] omnia necessaria humaniter Cancellario suppeditauit*.[159] In this story Wimpheling skillfully used the conventional trop of *translatio studii* by presenting *studium Parisii*, incarnated in the figure of the persecuted chancellor of the University of Paris, passing from his ungrateful homeland, unable to appreciate its brightest mind, to the welcoming lands of the Empire. Echoing Gerson's similar proclamation,[160] the biographer takes care to designate Sorbonne as the 'Alma Mater of all German universities',[161] creating the political myth of a special German connection to this center of learning. Wimpheling's choice is significant considering that '[t]heology as a public study practiced in the matter of a guild

---

[158] Wimpheling 1506, no pagination.

[159] Wimpheling 1506. 'The Austrian prince provided the chancellor with all necessary things'.

[160] *Josephina*, OC: 4, p. 31: [...] *o studiorum Mater Parisius paris expers/ maior Athenis Maior et Aegypto prior est tua philosophia/ Pura nec errorum coeno permixta nocenti*. 'O Paris, Mother of learning without equal / your philosophy is greater than Great Athens and superior to Egypt / pure and not mixed with nefarious filth of errors [heresy]'.

[161] Oberman 1981, p. 264.

was, as it is well known, transplanted from Paris to German soil only at the end of the fourteenth century'.[162] Consequently, Gerson being the most influential theologian of the late Middle Ages, his thought reached the Empire at the same time as theological studies themselves did.

Some other elements of Gerson's story also appear to have derived from Wimpheling's excited mind. One is a poignant account about the chancellor devoting the last years of his life to 'teaching the fundamentals of Christian faith to the poor every day'.[163] Another concerns a rather cute attribute of his legend: an emblematic illustration, which traveled from one edition to another, depicting the exiled chancellor, dressed as a pilgrim and walking the countryside accompanied by a small dog on his right and an angel on his left.[164] The image of the little dog, originated from an earlier manuscript illustration, gives humanity and charm to Gerson's persona, and might have been inspired by a four-legged friend, *Hündehen*, of the chancellor's ardent follower and alter ego, Geiler von Kaysersberg.[165] Indeed, Geiler's little pooch still greets visitors of Notre Dame de Strasbourg cathedral, carved on the tall chair once occupied by his famous master. Thus Germanic passage became such an integral part of the late chancellor's biography that a proud Frenchman Edmond Richer (1559/60–1631), whose passion for the University of Paris could only equal his passion for Jean Gerson,[166] copied it in its entirety, including Wimpheling's epitaph and the iconic print, in his 1606 edition of Gerson's works.[167] Only the picture was altered: while in Wimpheling's edition the little dog dawdles on Gerson's right and the angel hangs on his left, in Richer's version they traded places.

Wimpheling's associate, rival and friend Johannes Trithemius also played an important role in the Empire's reception of Ger-

---

[162] Ritter 2010, p. 20.

[163] Wimpheling 1506: *Paruulos in fidei Christinae rudimentis quotidie informando*.

[164] Lieberman 1963, p. 328.

[165] An indirect confirmation that Geiler did have a dog comes from his own writings, as, for example, in the already cited description of a little dog (Hoch 1901, p. 36).

[166] Denis 2019a, pp. 106–07.

[167] Geiler is mentioned directly in Richer 1607 and Richer 1676, p. 315: *Ioannis de Gerson, hortatu Ioannis Geileri Keiserspergii*.

son and greatly contributed to the association of the chancellor's name with the idea of *translatio studii* from France to Germany. His appreciation of Gerson is known thanks to his 1494 epitaph where he praises the chancellor as *uir in diuinis scripturis eruditissimus*.[168] The abbot closely imitated the text of Gerson's *De laude scriptorum* in his treatise *De laude scriptorum manualium*, and inserted the French theologian's name into his *Calalogus illustrium uirorum*, where he listed the greatest men of learning. Peculiarly, Trithemius also included the French chancellor in his subsequent *Catalogus illustrium uirorum Germaniae* or *De liminaribus seu de uiris illustribus Germaniae*, which largely repeats *Catalogus illustrium uirorum*, except for retaining only the names of 'berühmter Männer Deutschlands'.[169] In *Catalogus illustrium uirorum Germanae*, written between 1491 and 1495, and containing information about one hundred illustrious German men (including, out of sheer modesty, Trithemius himself) and three women, Gerson's name stands close to that of Geiler von Kaysersberg (thanks to the alphabetic order), whom Wimpheling, in the foreword, calls *amantissime*.[170] The significance of the Frenchman's presence in this 'exclusive' catalog is hard to overestimate. The initiative to include him belonged, once more, to Jacob Wimpheling, whose zeal to promote Teutonic greatness and to prove that 'the German contribution to Christian literature is at least equal to that of Italy if not actually superior to it',[171] pushed him to declare 'Teutonic' (Teutsch) not only all prominent speak-

---

[168] Trithemius's epitaph is found in OC: 1, p. 146: *Ioannes Gerson natione Gallus, cancellarius Parisiensis, uir in diuinis scripturis eruditissimus, saecularis philosophiae non ignarus, ingenio subtilis, sermone scholasticus, scientia certus ac stabilis, consilio cautus et dubiorum clarissimus interpres; scripsit metro et prosa multa praestantissima opuscula quibus nomen suum apud posteros immortalitatem semper obtinebit; quorum lectio deuotis religiosis non minus utilis quam iucunda est.* 'Jean Gerson, of the Gallic nation, chancellor of Paris, man versed in divine scriptures, not ignorant of profane philosophy, subtle in intelligence, schooled in oratory, certain and dependable in learning, cautious in counsel and a most lucid interpreter of doubtful matters; he wrote many most distinguished works in verse and prose, which will forever obtain for his name immortality in posterity; reading them is no less useful than gratifying for the devout and religious'.

[169] Schmitt 2001, col. 1446–54. *De laude scriptorum manualium* was first published in 1494 in Mainz. Trithemius's other works were published by Marquard Freher in *Opera historica*, Francfort, 1604.

[170] Douglass 1966, p. 18.

[171] Brann 1981, p. 246.

ers of Germanic languages, but also all the celebrities whose works were either 'copied by German scribes, placed under German care or else were transported to Germany from foreign parts'.[172] Surely Gerson, whose legacy Wimpheling reworked 'mit außergewönlicher Intensität und under einer Vielfalt von Aspekten',[173] fitted into all three categories.

Considering the tendency of nationalistically inclined early German humanists to display their patriotism as an aversion to anything that was not German, and by contrasting Germany to 'the loquacious Greece, the presumptuous Italy, and the quarrelsome France',[174] the Frenchman's insertion in such a catalog ought to be viewed as their highest tribute to him. Yet, in the complex politics of North-South scholarly rivalries, claiming Gerson as their own served the purpose of German humanists' cultural war against the main target of their admiration and jealousy: Renaissance Italy. Counterposing the *christianissima Germania* to blasphemous, gluttonous and corrupt Italy,[175] German humanists staged their provincial resentment as a moral indignation at the service of true Christianity: 'die Humanisten hätten die nationale Konkurrenz in den Dienst der Christenheit gestellt'.[176] Conrad Celtis went so far as to declare that Italian men were no real men at all, and that pederasty, completely foreign to valiant Germans, was an especially Italian thing. The very roots of Roman greatness had to be undermined, with Romulus himself presented as a *Hurensohn*.[177] In this context the association with Gerson, whose scholarly prestige was universally acknowledged, represented a strategic and essentially opportunistic move on the part of Wimpheling and Trithemius, who, despite their 'antifranzösische Spitze',[178] aimed at incorporating in their supposedly purely

---

[172] Brann 1981, p. 249. Gerson's popularity with German humanists is not due to the popularity of *De Imitatione Christi*, since Trithemius considers Thomas à Kempis as its author. See Wheatley 1891, pp. 133–35.

[173] Kraume 1980, p. 85.

[174] Posset 2005, p. 13: 'However, the use of 'nation' (*natio*) in the period of the Renaissance around the 1500s is rather complex and in need of further clarification'.

[175] Hirschi 2005, p. 273 & p. 249.

[176] Hirschi 2005, p. 278.

[177] Hirschi 2005, p. p. 334.

[178] Hirschi 2005, p. 273.

Teutonic catalog as many allies as possible. Significantly for the near future, *Catalogus illustrium uirorum Germaniae* later served as an inspiration for the first Lutheran historiographer Matthias Flacius who, probably motivated by rationales quite similar to those of his late medieval compatriots, also included a large article on Gerson in his highly influential and heavily ideological *Catalogus testium ueritatis* of 1556.[179]

Gerson's legacy was not only part of the bond uniting the two friends Trithemius and Wimpheling. It also became the ground for their major falling out. Their quarrel concerned the question of compatibility of humanistic scholarship with monastic life. Attacking monastic learning in his book *De integritate*, Wimpheling maintained that the best *scientia* had always been developed by secular scholars, among whom, in a rather odd assortment, he cited Giovanni Boccaccio, Giovanni Pico della Mirandola and Jean Gerson.[180] The abbot of Sponheim answered by citing Gerson as precisely a perfect model of a mystical humanist who, although he never became a monk, had always subordinated his humanist interests to spiritual pursuits and personally longed for the contemplative life of a cloister, which he would have embraced given the chance.[181] Trithemius's point of view was shared by many monastics, including aforementioned Nicolas Kempf and Bernhard von Waging, as well as Johannes Altenstaig (*c.* 1480-*c.* 1525), who, after studying poetry and rhetoric at the university of Tübingen, joined an Augustinian monastery, where he composed his famous *Vocabularius Theologiae*.

Heidelberg, Vienna, and Strasbourg were not the only cities with bustling intellectual life. Sodalities similar to theirs appeared in Augsburg, Freiburg, Leipzig, Linz, Ingolstadt, Nuremberg, and others. Strasbourg humanists had particularly close ties with the Augsburg group, *Sodalitas Litteraria Augustana*, which was initially formed around bishop Peter von Schaumberg (1388–1469), and had a strong religious tendency. A prominent member of this group, theologian Sigmund Gossenbrot (1417–1488) was a close friend with a cousin of the already mentioned Peter Schott, the

---

[179] Flacius lists Geiler in *Catalogus testium ueritatis*.
[180] Lieberman 1965, p. 295.
[181] For the detailed analysis of this debate see Brann 1981.

first editor of Gerson's works in Strasbourg.[182] In a fashion typical of German humanists, Gossenbrot saw theology and poetry as naturally united, with Gerson and Petrarch belonging to the same 'wesentliche Kontinuität zwischen Patristik, mittelalterlicher Klosterkultur und Humanismus'.[183] The sodality's interest in Gerson remained strong under the subsequent leadership of Konrad Peutinger (1465–1547), a diplomat, politician and counselor to the Emperor Maximilian I.[184]

In Freiburg, the local humanist sodality was led by Johannes Brisgoicus (d. 1539), an influential theology professor and the rector of Freiburg University, who edited Wimpheling's letters and translated Gerson's writings from French into German.[185] Two other Freiburgers, Dietrich Ulsenius and Thomas Wolff published Gerson's *De misera humana epistole consolatorie* in 1505. Hartmann Schedel, a member of *Sodalitas Polychiana* and medical student at Leipzig from 1456 to 1460, composed an index *Sacri codices historiae sancte theologice ueritatis*. Reflecting the middle 15th century shift toward affective theology in university curricula, *Sacri codices* contained no Peter Lombard or Thomas Aquinas, but kept Hugh of Saint Victor and Gerson.[186] Gerson's texts were also used at Leipzig University along with Cicero's for the study of rhetoric, which was traditionally mixed with studies of music.[187] Gerson's text *Carmen de laude musicae*, written in praise of the spiritual benefits of music, appears in the handwritten summary of the *musica choralis*, under the heading *De laude musica*, with the title *Statuta scholarum*, and in the group entitled *Carmina scolarium* — works composed with the intention of influencing students' behavior.[188] The notes of another Leipzig alumnus Johannes Mickel (d. 1508), the future Carthusian monk and humanist, who studied in Leipzig right after Schedel, from 1460 to 1466, contain a German translation of Gerson's *Alphabetum diuini amoris*, published in 1493 under the German title

---

[182] Schädle 1938, pp. 45–46.
[183] Worstbrock 1981, p. 107.
[184] On Augsburg humanists see Müller 2010.
[185] Smolinsky 2005, pp. 261–62.
[186] Worstbrock 1994, p. 711.
[187] Metzler 2008, p. 42.
[188] Henkel 1988, pp. 291–92.

ABC der göttlichen Liebe.[189] Mickel was also interested in Gerson's treatises *De ualore orationis*[190] and *De probatione spirituum*,[191] and claimed to have discovered Seneca thanks to Gerson's enthusiasm for this author in yet another treaty, *De simplicatione cordis*.[192] Another example of Gerson's presence in Leipzig is found in the personal library of Stephan Roth (1492–1546), a statesman and a distinguished citizen of the city of Zwickau, who studied and taught at Leipzig University from 1512 to 1517. Roth was unconcerned with censorship or ideological issues then, because a person's position toward Luther played no role yet during his tenure.[193] The books which he cared to buy for himself reflect his own interests and those of his professional milieu. The majority among them were monographs written by renowned Leipzig professors of his time, with a small quantity of books by Thomas Aquinas, Duns Scotus, Jean Gerson and Thomas à Kempis. Later, after embracing Lutheranism, Stephan Roth became rector of the Zwichau Latin school. As an educator, Roth was interested in innovative, Gerson-inspired pedagogy, and bought new books for his school from none other than Gerson's biographer and editor Jacob Wimpheling.[194]

University of Tübingen: from Gabriel Biel to Conrad Summenhart

The University of Tübingen holds a special place in the story of the reception of Gerson in the German lands largely through the agency of Gabriel Biel (1425–1495) — professor of theology and Brother of the Common Life known as the 'the last of the scholastics'. Biel honored and quoted the French theologian as the first-ranked 'systematic and mystical authority' not only from his

---

[189] Sönke et al. 2002, pp. 353–55.

[190] *De ualore orationis*, OC: 2, pp. 175–91.

[191] *De probatione spirituum*, OC: 9, pp. 177–85. *De probatione spirituum* is a scholastic treatise listing cases when *probatione spirituum* (testing of the spirit) is required, such as, for example, cases of visions.

[192] Gerson's love affair with Seneca deserves a separate and extended study. He quoted Seneca very frequently both in Latin and vernacular works, as, for example, in *The Mountain of Contemplation*, in *Claro eruditori* (OC: 2, p. 206) and in *Viuat rex* (OC: 7: 1, p. 1175).

[193] Metzler 2008, p. 48.

[194] Metzler 2008, p. 63.

university in Tübingen but also from his pulpit at the Cathedral of Mainz.[195] His double appreciation of Gerson as a systematic theologian and a mystical writer is rather exceptional, and corresponds to his own twofold identity as an academic scholar and a Brother of the Common Life. Indeed, unlike Bernhard von Waging, Biel endorsed Gerson's suggestion of extending contemplative life to the laity referring to it 'for proof that limiting the term *religiosi* to monastics and *religio* to a monastic order was nothing short of semantic scandal'.[196] Having translated Gerson's *Opus tripartitum* into German around 1470 — twelve years earlier than Geiler[197] — Biel took advantage of the invention of printing to publish it, contributing to its vast distribution among *devotio moderna*'s houses.

Biel's theological dependence on the French master is so pronounced that, as Heiko Oberman has put it, he often even 'disappoints us by merely referring back to the mystical opus of Gerson',[198] instead of offering original thoughts on a given subject. His reliance, sometimes verbatim, on Gerson's authority have been characterized as 'pervasive' and 'striking'.[199] Thus, using direct and indirect quotations, sometimes without acknowledgment, 'particularly in respect to Mariology, the authority of the Church, the true sacrifice of the Mass, and the mystical aspects of the Christian existence',[200] Biel drew from *Monotessaron*, *Super Magnificat*, *De simplificate cordis* and especially from *De mystica theologia speculatiua*.[201] His attention to the latter is a significant detail, since Biel belonged to a small number of authors (including Nicolas of Cusa and Bernhard von Waging) who were interested in the French master's systematic theology. In this respect, Biel's own doctrine of the security or certitude of hope is doubly based on two of Gerson's

---

[195] Oberman 1963, pp. 331–32.

[196] Brown 1987, p. 47.

[197] Kraume cites at least nine editions of *Opus tripartitum* prior to Geiler's translation (Kraume 1980).

[198] Oberman 1963, p. 341.

[199] Burns 1991, p. 139.

[200] Oberman 1963, p. 6 & p. 282. Oberman bases his arguments both on direct citations and, more often, on comparative analysis, detecting unacknowledged Gerson quotations, and providing the corresponding sources.

[201] Oberman 1963, p. 330.

fundamental teachings. One is his theology of the spiritual quest, according to which 'salvation essentially rests on the authenticity of the viator herself and the genuineness of her search for God'.[202] The other is the principle *per desperationem enim ad spem uenire docuisti* ('through despair we come to hope').[203] This dynamic theology is characteristic of Gerson, Cusa, Geiler and Biel, who put enormous efforts toward safeguarding the balance between man's freedom of will and God's omnipotence.

Biel's unique position as both an academic and a Brother of the Common Life enabled him to transform the University of Tübingen into an especially welcoming center for the reception of Gerson in the 15th and 16th centuries. This very Gersonian combination of devotional piety and academic training made Tübingen a fusion point of these major late medieval legacies, and provided a crucial element in Gerson's reception by both Catholic and Protestant reformers who studied and taught there in the 16th century. Those included Biel's replacement, Luther's future mentor and opponent, Johannes von Staupitz and Luther's right hand Philipp Melanchthon.

Another illustrious Tübingen alumnus and Biel's colleague, German theologian Conrad (Konrad) Summenhart (1458–1502),[204] represents a particularly complex and complicated case of reworking of Gerson's legacy. Even though already Philipp Melanchthon viewed Summenhart as *Gersonis imitator*,[205] the degree and details of his actual indebtedness to Gerson are still a matter of an on-going debate among legal scholars.[206] There is, however,

---

[202] Fisher 2006, p. 235.

[203] OC: 9, p. 234. Miller 1998, p. 237.

[204] Before obtaining his doctorate in theology from Tübingen, where he remained for the rest of his career, Summenhart studied in Paris and Heidelberg. See Brett 1997, p. 43 & p. 45. 'Conrad Summenhart (d. 1502) outlived Biel and had preceded him at Tübingen. Like Heynlin he had gone there from Paris, where his studies were pursued during the ban on nominalist teaching; and his earlier formation, at Heidelberg, had been in the realist *uia antiqua*' (Burns 1991, p. 138).

[205] Oberman 1981, p. 62.

[206] Richard Tuck (Tuck 1979) and Burns (Burns 1991) consider this degree high. 'In Summenhart's case the debt to Gerson in respect of the theory of dominium is clear enough' (Burns 1991, p. 145). Also see Brett 1997; Varkemaa 2005; Tierney 2005; Varkemaa 2006; Varkemaa 2012.

a relative consensus to credit Summenhart with establishing some of our modern legal terminology, which, incidentally, originated from his interpretation of Gerson's legacy. Summenhart used the language that 'had formerly been employed by Gerson', while his extended discussion on the nature of rights 'was firmly and openly based on Jean Gerson's writings on the subject'.[207] For example, Summenhart's concept of the subjective right, which is sometimes considered as a precursor to the modern concept of individual right, was based on two parallel descriptions of *ius* in Gerson's *De potestate ecclesiatica* (1417), where the chancellor made a connection between right and justice. Summenhart's formulation of right in his massive *Septipertitum opus de contractibus pro foro conscientie atque theologico* is based on Gerson's differentiation between *ius* — understood as a subjective right — versus *lex* — understood as an objective or external law, a distinction typically credited to Hobbes.[208] According to this distinction humans — unlike the rest of God's creatures, for whom the natural right to do something follows from a natural ability to do it[209] — must measure their *ius* against *lex*, as Gerson defined them.[210]

Furthermore, Gerson's definition of *ius* (which in English problematically translates into only one word 'right'), is twofold. The first, general meaning is *ius per se*, as it belongs to all creatures (humans as well as animals) 'in so far as they have faculties and being',[211] and not as far as they have reason.[212] Since all being

---

[207] Varkemaa 2005, p. 185. 'His [Summenhart's] main work [...] was an extensive discussion of Gersonian terms of all the problems associated with contracts and the transfer of *dominium*. In the preliminary material, he systematized Gerson's insights into the nature of *ius* and *dominium*, but he also tried to deal with a number of obvious objections' (Tuck 1979, p. 27).

[208] Mäkinen 2006, p. 71. The distinction between *ius* and *lex* is not unique to Gerson, however. It is typical of the medieval canon law tradition. On this subject see Pennington 2008. 'He [Gerson] was thus even able to make that distinction between *ius* and *lex* which seventeenth-century natural rights theorists thought they had invented' (Tuck 1979, p. 27).

[209] Varkemaa 2005, p. 188.

[210] Varkemaa 2006, p. 130: 'Summenhart applied Gerson's concept of natural right to the concept of liberty (*libertas*), according to which man has a natural right to do whatever he is able to do, unless this action is prohibited by law'.

[211] Varkemaa 2005, p. 188.

[212] This 'naturalistic aspect' (Tuck 1979, p. 27) sounds surprisingly relevant to contemporary animal-rights debate and environmental concerns, which seek

comes from God, all creatures 'could be credited with having rights'.[213] In other words, being itself confers 'rights of a kind'[214] to all creatures:

> *Erit igitur naturale dominium donum Dei quo creatura ius habet immediate a Deo assumere res alias inferiores in sui usum et conseruationem, pluribus competens ex aequo et inabdicabile seruata originali iustitia seu integritate naturali.*[215]

Summenhart embraced the same position, which he called the justification through being:

> From the very fact that God has communicated [...] existence to a being, such a being has the right to resist those who want to take the gift [of existence] away from it. Similarly, the right of animals to take in nourishment in order to preserve their existence is based on the same gift. In this way, the wolf has the right to attack other animals, and birds have the right to collect grain and seeds [...] for their sustenance [...] they have right to nest in our gardens because God gave them potency to engender fledglings [...] he therefore also gave them the right to the instruments by means of which they can do it properly [...][216]

The second definition is more specific: *ius* as a right that belongs only to beings who possess rational capacity: *[...] Ius est facultas seu potestas propinqua conueniens alicui secundum dictamen rectae rationis.*[217] Summenhart appears to say exactly the same.[218] The

---

to include all creatures into the protective sphere of universal jurisprudence. It also offers a theological argument for those Christians who wish to support this effort.

[213] Varkemaa 2005, p. 188.

[214] Tuck 1979, p. 26.

[215] *De uita spirituali animae*, OC: 3, p. 145. 'There is a natural *dominium* as a gift from God, by which every creature has a *ius* directly from God to take inferior things into its own use for its own preservation. Each has this *ius* as a result of a fair and irrevocable justice, maintained in its original purity, or a natural integrity' (Tuck 1979, p. 27).

[216] Conrad Summenhart, *Opus septipartitum de contractibus pro foro conscientiae et theologico*, Varkemaa 2005, p. 188.

[217] *De uita spirituale animae*, OC: 3, p. 141. '*Ius* is an immediate faculty or power pertaining to anyone according to right reason'.

[218] Tellkamp 2013, p. 129.

chancellor characterizes *dominium* or right to something as *potestas propinqua assumendi res alias aut tamquam alias in sui facultatem aut usum secundum regulas politicas et ciuiles iuris humani*,[219] and Summenhart espouses this characterization too.[220] Although Gerson did not claim that the concepts of *ius* or *dominium* were equivalent,[221] he used them interchangeably. Thus, he used both words to explain natural right as pertaining to all: *Erit igitur naturale dominium donum Dei quo creatura ius habet immediate a Deo assumere res alias inferiores in sui usum et conseruationem [...]*.[222]

Summenhart also used the terms *ius* and *dominium* mostly as synonymous,[223] but put a somewhat stronger emphasis on the *dominium*. The latter gradually ceased to mean the same as *ius*, and eventually acquired the meaning of *dominium* as 'property right'.[224] The relation between *ius* and *dominium*, and its interpretation by Gerson and Sommenhart, would become the focus of heated debates in the 16th century. Sommenhart also adopted Gerson's idea of *ius* as a *facultas* or power/ability to do something.[225] Based on Gerson's idea that right derives from being

---

[219] *De uita spirituali animae*, OC: 3, p. 144. '[t]he adjacent power to take foreign things either into one's own command as if they were foreign or to use them according to political rules or human civil laws'.

[220] Summenhart 1580, 1a: *dominium est potestas uel facultas propinqua assumendi res alias in sui facultate uel usum licitum secundum iura uel leges rationabiliter institutas*. '*Dominium* is a proximate power or ability of assuming other things into someone's command or licit usage according to reasonably instituted rights or laws'. 'Summenhart agreed with Gerson's definitions of *ius* as a proximate power or faculty of individuals according to the dictates of right reason, and *dominium*, as a proximate power or faculty of appropriating things for licit use' (Depew 2016, p. 34) Finnish legal scholars Mäkinen and Varkemaa have argued that *libertas*, or the right to act freely unless it is prohibited by law or is contrary to reason, is associated by Gerson with the self-dominion that takes the form of (a moderate) self-ownership. British researcher Annabel S. Brett criticized this suggestion, arguing that the equivalence of *ius* and dominion is nowhere to be found in Gerson's *De uita spirituali animae*. See Brett 1997, p. 40.

[221] Varkemaa 2005, p. 81.

[222] *De uita spirituali animae*, OC: 3, p. 145. '[n]atural dominion [*dominium*] is a gift of God by which a creature has the right [*ius*] immediately from God to take inferior things for its use and preservation'.

[223] Summenhart 'took Gerson quite rightly, to have implied that all *iura* are *dominia*, that the categories of *ius* and *dominium* are identical' (Tuck 1979, p. 28).

[224] Schüssler 2014, p. 365.

[225] 'it was the first time that an account of a *ius* as a *facultas* had been given [in Gerson *De uita spirituali animae*)' (Tuck 1979, p. 26) *Ponitur facultas seu*

and that beings have a right to support their existence with available means, Summenhart concluded that men also have a right to freely exercise their rights as God's creatures. However, since man alone has reason, this right is limited to acts that are not aimed against the law of reason.

Devotio moderna: Wessel Gansfort, Jan Standonck and Johannes Mombaer

The chancellor came in direct and personal contact with the modern devotion during his sojourn in Bruges, and his works were already circulating among the communities of *devotio* during his life.[226] Gerson's manual *Opus tripartitum* — with the first part on the Ten Commandments, the second on the art of confession, and the third on the ministry to the dying — was the first product of the only printing press owned by the Brothers of the Common Life in the city of Brussels.[227] His reputation as 'the defender of the *devotio moderna* at Constance'[228] elevated him, in the eyes of the devotees, to the status of a Father of the Church.[229] According to some researchers, he inspired 'la *devotio moderna* toute entière'.[230]

---

potestas, quoniam multa conueniunt secundum dictamen rectae rationis aliquibus quae non dicuntur iura eorum [...] (*De uita spirituali animae*, OC: 3, p. 141) 'This definition includes *facultas* as power, since many things are in accordance with right reason which do not count as *iura* of those who have them' (Tuck 1979, p. 25). Tuck also refers to Gerson's *Definitiones Terminorum Theologiae Moralis*, where he writes: *Ius est facultas seu potestas competens alicui secundam rectae rationis. Libertas est facultas rationis, et uoluntatis ad utrumlibet oppositorum. [...] Lex est recta ratio practica secundum quam motus et operationes rerum in suos fines ordinatae regulantur* (OC: 9, p. 134). '*Ius* is a *facultas* or power appropriate to someone and in accordance with the dictates of right reason. *Libertas* is a *facultas* of the reason and will towards whatever possibility is selected [...] *Lex* is a practical and right reason according to which the movements and workings of things are directed towards their original ends' (Tuck 1979, p. 27) By claiming that right was faculty, Gerson was able to assimilate right and liberty as a kind of *dominium*. According to Tuck, these terms announce the idea of a right in the subjective sense introducing a theory of rights as liberties, sovereignties and property. Also see Burns 1991.

[226] See Hobbins 2006; Mazour-Matusevich 2006.

[227] Habsburg 2002, p. 78.

[228] Oberman 1981, p. 62. On Gerson's defense of *devotio moderna* see Debongnie 1928; Staubach 1997.

[229] Oberman 2008, p. 29.

[230] Combes 1963, 2, p. 668.

Dutch theologian Johannes Wessel Gansfort (1420–1489) is one of the most famous members of the Brethren of the Common Life, whose dependence on Gerson is undeniable. Like Gabriel Biel, he was also able to combine his adherence to the *devotio moderna* with his academic duties as a professor of logic and Latin first at Heidelberg (1456–1457) and then at Paris (1458–1473). Gansfort left a collection of works, which were published posthumously in Zwolle in 1521 and in Wittenberg in 1522 under the title *Farrago rerum theologicarum*, thanks to Martin Luther's efforts.[231] It is indeed the Wittenberg reformer himself (although not he alone) who is responsible for the association of Gansfort's name with the Lutheran Reformation, which has become traditional. In his preface to the 1522 edition of Gansfort's writings Luther famously declared:

> *Prodiit Vuesselus (quem Basilium dicunt) Phrisius Groningensis, vir admirabilis ingenii, rari et magni spiritus quem et ipsum apparet esse vere Theodidactum, quales prophetauit fore Christianos Esaias, neque enim hominibus accepisse indicari potest, sicut nec ego. Hic si mihi antea fuisset lectus, poterat hostibus meis uideri Lutherus omnia ex Vuesselo hausisse, adeo spiritus utriusque conspirat in unum.*[232]

This declaration should be taken with caution, however, given Luther's incentive to root his theology in the past, thereby securing it with historical precedents. This approach represented a strategy, which was initially endorsed by Philipp Melanchthon and later adopted, enriched and developed by Matthias Flacius Illyricus (1520–1575) in his 1556 *Catalogus testium ueritatis*. It was based on the model of historical writing first developed under the emperor Constantine by Eusebius (314 AD), and it aimed at two main objectives. The first consists of demonstrating that all

---

[231] Ferrago was a very popular book. At least seventeen editions were published between 1522 and 1524.

[232] *WA* 10. 337. 'For behold! A Wessel has appeared whom they call Basil, a Frisian from Groningen, a man of remarkable ability and of rare and great spirit; and it is evident that he has been truly taught by the Lord, even as Esaias prophesied the Christians would be. For no one could think that he received these doctrines from men, any more than I have. Had I read his works earlier, my enemies might think that Luther has absorbed everything from Wessel, his spirit is so in accordance with mine' (Miller 1917, p. 239). Miller based his translation on several editions of Gansfort's works, which he combined in one book.

events form a single pattern, beginning with the creation of the world and leading up to the moment of the triumph of a true Christianity — the Lutheran Reformation. The second amounts to presenting history as a long period of darkness, corruption and apostasy, where, before the luminous appearance of the Wittenberg prophet, there happened to be some witnesses to God's truth.[233] Gansfort's election as such a witness became a major factor in the Dutch theologian's 'rise in celebrity'[234] in the Protestant camp. Following Luther's enthusiastic assessment, Protestant scholars (as practically all studies of Gansfort belong to them[235]) have continued to brand Wessel's theology as a 'reformatory way of thinking',[236] in the specific sense of reformers before the Reformation. Since then, this assumption carried on uninterrupted, repeated both in academic publications as recent as 2006,[237] and in popular sources, such as contemporary websites by various Protestant denominations,[238] where Gansfort has been labeled a 'trailblazer of Martin Luther'.[239]

However, the connection between Gansfort and the French theologian exceeds the traditional presentation of the former as a transitory figure, filling up 'the interval between Gerson and Luther',[240] and goes beyond the general context of *devotio moderna*. Indeed, while the Dutchman was 'in harmony with the moral and religious ideas of the *devotio moderna*',[241] he did not necessarily always share all its opinions — especially with reference to scholastic methods, learned disputations and the merits of the study of logic and mathematics. In sharp contrast with *devotio*'s sensibility and in agreement with the chancellor's opinion that without logic men can hardly claim to be human,[242] Wessel

---

[233] Augustijn 1997, p. 15.
[234] Augustijn 1997, p. 14.
[235] Rupp 1972, pp. 155–70; Oberman & Caspers 1999; de Kroon 2009.
[236] Ullmann 1863–1877, p. 556.
[237] Mansch & Peters 2016.
[238] Needham 2017, online.
[239] Woods 2016, online.
[240] Ullmann 1863–1877, p. 382.
[241] Jacob 1953, p. 130.
[242] *Collectorium Super Magnificat*, OC: 8, p. 182: *Hanc opinor esse causam erroris hominum deuotioni se dare putantium, sine logica et metaphysici, sint homines [...]* 'I think this to be the cause of error of the devout men to give themselves

affirmed that theologians 'need logic, and in large doses, as proved by the example of Gerson who prevailed thanks to training in logical argumentation'.[243] The Parisian master's broad spiritual profile, which united devotional piety, scholarly learning and the zeal for 'pastoral counter-conduct'[244] in one person, afforded Gansfort the intellectual flexibility he craved. His motivation was mostly theoretical when he appealed to the medieval master in order to validate certain contended points of his arguments, but Gansfort also needed the *auctoritas* of the 'distinguished and venerable doctor'[245] on a more personal level in order to deal with his own spiritual and social challenges. Indeed, if the nickname 'Master of contradictions' — which was 'not an honorific title'[246] — applies to the 'illusive' Dutchman in three main respects: 1) 'as contradiction to untested knowledge; 2) as contradiction against unauthentic authority; 3) as contradiction against his own inner confusion, which indeed lends his work its highly personal and even psychotherapeutic dimension',[247] all three of these aspects are also found in his relation to Gerson's thought. Gansfort's conscious choice to present the Parisian master as his model for both thought and behavior is indeed both theologically and personally motivated.

Wessel's kinship with the chancellor has a solid foundation in his close knowledge of his writings. He relies, albeit implicitly and mostly without listing them, on *De consiliis euangelicis*, *De potestate ecclesiastica*, *Collectorium Super Magnificat*, *Contra Matthaeum de Fussa*, *De indulgentiis* and, most likely, on *Contra Sectam Flagellantium*, as well as on the on vernacular *The Mountain of Contemplation* and sermons. 'There can be no doubt whatsoever'[248] that 'Wessel war ein Rezipient des Werkes von Gerson'.[249] Gansfort's writings abound with explicit references to the chancellor, whom

---

an idea that, without logic and metaphysics, they are people.' Oosterhoff, on the contrary, argues that Gerson 'played a central role in the demise of the 14th century mathematics' (Oosterhoff 2018, p. 45).

[243] Oberman 1981, pp. 97–121.
[244] Depew 2016, p. 31.
[245] *A Letter Concerning Indulgences by the Venerable Master Wessel of Groningen in Reply to Master Jacob Hoeck, Dean of Naeldwick*, Miller 1917, p. 294.
[246] Oberman 1981, p. 97.
[247] Oberman 1981, p. 98.
[248] de Kroon 2009, p. 29.
[249] Oberman & Caspers 1999, p. 92.

he extols for having single-handedly ended the Western Schism.[250] His *Letter Concerning Indulgences by the Venerable Master Wessel of Groningen in Reply to Master Jacob Hoeck, Dean of Naeldwick*, comprising eight chapters, is all about Gerson. His reliance does more than make references to specific issues, such as indulgences,[251] papal jurisdiction[252] or Purgatory;[253] it also validates both the chancellor's personality and his theological approach.

One theme is clearly prevalent in Gansfort's dealing with Gerson's legacy. The Dutchman refers to it as the chancellor's tendency for 'moderation', be it in relation to his theological opinions, his personality or his choices as an ecclesiastical leader. Although generally full of praise *ad venerabilis Gersonis moderationem* ('[w]ith regard of the moderation of the venerable Gerson'),[254] Wessel seems to be both admiring and puzzled by it. When this quality appeals to him as appropriate, he fully supports it, as in the case of Gerson's advocating for moderation against extreme asceticism and self-imposed suffering in order to commend oneself to God. The chancellor was consistently weary and suspicious of extreme forms of devotion, such as flagellation, sleep deprivation

---

[250] 'The entire community of the faithful has to adhere to the wise man [...] as it was done during the Council of Constance, when the community of believers disagreed with pope John XXIII and consented with the theologian Jean Gerson'. (Weiler 1999, p. 313).

[251] Wessel Gansfort 1522, p. 107: *Venerabilem illum Gersonem alleges dognum allegatu, dignum considerate. Qui multa ualde in abusu indulgentiarum reprobat.* 'You cite the distinguished and venerable Gerson, who is worthy to be cited and to be considered, for he strongly condemns many things in the abuse of indulgences' (Miller 1917, p. 289). See Shaffern 1988, pp. 643–61.

[252] Gansfort 1522, p. 114: *Sic puto sensisse uenerabilem illum Gersonem, quia scio de menre sua esse uniuersam autoritatem Apostolicae fedis ex canonicarum scripturarum ueritate pendentem, debere moderatis aestimari, non scripturae ueritatem ex papali uoluntate aut autoritate, etiam si non deliret aut erret.* 'For I know that it was his [Gerson's] understanding that the universal authority of the apostolic see ought to be regulated by and be regarded as depending on the truth of the Canonical Scriptures; and by no means that the truth of the Scriptures depends on the will or authority of the pope, even if he is not deranged or mistaken' (Miller 1917, p. 308).

[253] Gansfort 1522, p. 114: *Quia timor habet, ideo timor not est in perfecta charitate. Purgandi in purgatorio habent poenam & timorem, ergo non sunt perfecti in caritate. Sic puto sensisse uenerabilem illum Gersonem [...]* 'Those who need to be cleansed in purgatory have punishment and fear; hence they are not perfect in love. I think the venerable Gerson was also of this opinion' (Miller 1917, p. 308).

[254] Gansfort 1522, p. 113. Miller 1917, p. 306.

and severe fasting, and he was strictly opposed to self-mutilation, castration and even 'baptism by fire' with hot iron, arguing against them in his Latin works such as *Contra Sectam Flagellantium*,[255] and in vernacular sermons such as *De la chasteté conjugale*.[256] Gansfort's opinion on the matter is very similar:

> [T]here is no necessity for severe fasts or the wearing of a rough goat's-hair garment. The worthy fruit of repentance requires no bodily severities, but only that which is necessary for us all, the piety that avails for all things. Be regular in the observance of your duties [...] and that will suffice for bodily discipline.[257]

Like Geiler and Biel, Gansfort also espoused the middle way in theology, following Gerson's *theologia media* — the medium ground between presumption of merits and quietism, which encourages the Christian soul to call, beg and cry loudly to God[258] while, at the same time, opening up to accept divine initiative. In

---

[255] *Contra Sectam Flagellantium*, OC: 10, p. 50: *Immo sicut non licet hominem seipsum propria auctoritate mutilare uel castrare nisi pro sanitate totius corporis consequenda, sic non licet, ut uidetur, quo a seipso quis sanguinem uiolenter eiiciat nisi causa medicinae corporalis; alioquin simili ratione posset se homo cauterizare per ignitum ferrum, quod adhuc nemo posuit uel concessit, nisi forsitan idolatrae uel falsi christiani, quales reperiuntur in India, qui se putant baptizari debere per ignem*. 'Indeed, like it is not lawful for a man to mutilate or to castrate himself of his own authority, unless it is for the sake of health of the whole body, it is not lawful, as it seems, for any man to violently extract blood by himself except for the medical reason. Otherwise, for the similar reason a man can brand himself with hot iron, which thus no one ordered or granted, except perhaps idolaters or false Christians, such as are found in India who think they ought to be baptized by fire'.

[256] *De la chasteté conjugale*, OC: 7: 1, p. 861: 'Ou les abstinances sont legieres et sans grande singularite; et lors elle se peuent faire'. See Mazour-Matusevich 2000.

[257] Letter to a Nameless Nun, Miller 1917, p. 245. This letter is included only in 1614 edition by Peter Pappus (Miller 1917, p. 168). As Miller states in his Introduction, 'no two editions of the Farrago contain exactly the same letters, nor is there any explanation offered as to the basis of their selection' (Miller 1917, p. 167). For Gerson's opinions on this subject see *Contra Sectam Flagellantium*, OC: 10, pp. 46–51 and vernacular works such as *De la chasteté conjugale*, OC: 7: 2, p. 861.

[258] *Sermon pour la Pentecote*, OC: 7: 2, p. 688: 'Appelle maintenant, je te prie, ô ame crestienne, appelle et huche a haulte voix.' The theology of spiritual seeking is omnipresent in Gerson's works. For example, see *Pour le mercredi des Cendres*, OC: 7: 2, p. 577: 'Pourtant se nous ne donnons nostre consentement a sa grace et misericorde que ainsy nous promet, et se nous ne l'ensuyons, se nous ne nous donnons nous meismes se nous ne metons la main a nous aidier comme il soit ainsy que il veut.'

an explicit agreement with the French theologian, and in a complete disagreement with Luther's views, Wessel believed that *deus facit nos cooperari [...] in illa cooperatione nostra, [est] nostrum peccatum uel nostra pietas*.²⁵⁹ Gansfort not only affirms that *et ad haec tria minister Christi quantum cooperator [...] quia scilicet uerbo uel ministerio concurrit*.²⁶⁰ He also believed that we, as humans, *consentimus enim operanti deo*.²⁶¹ He is careful, however, to make sure not to embrace another extreme, that of human self-sufficiency, mindful to leave the initiative to God: *Vult Gerson expresse que in peccatorii remissio naturaliter prior sit gratiae infusion, quia culpae remissio, quia nihil aliud est culpae remissio quia gratiae infusio*.²⁶²

Yet, the same wise moderation that Gansfort admired 'as opposed to blind subservience to the letter of the law',²⁶³ seems to have baffled him when it clashed with his own strong opinions. In his letter to Dean of Naeldwick Jacob Hoeck, Wessel advanced the following explanation of the chancellor's 'mildness': *mitius aliquando quam theologica pura ueritas habeat, puto pietati magis tacentem condescendere, quo non ueritas malicia quorundam pusillis scandalum pariat*.²⁶⁴

Obviously, what the Dutch theologian calls *Theologica pura ueritas* (the plain theological truth) corresponds to his own point of view, which Gerson chose, on political, spiritual, or pedagogical grounds, not to formulate as bluntly as Gansfort would have done:

> *Puto igitur prudentem illum uirum postque diligentibus lectoribus oculos per eas propositiones quae indubitatam ueritatem*

---

[259] Gansfort 1522, folio 1 & 2. Miller 1917, p. 209: 'God makes us cooperate [...] in that cooperation lies the opportunity for our sins or our godliness'.

[260] Gansfort 1522, p. 113. Letter to Jacob Hoeck, 'And, according to him [Gerson] [I]n so far as the minister of Christ cooperates with Christ [...] of course he concurs with him in word or ministry' (Miller 1917, p. 306).

[261] Gansfort 1522, folio 2.

[262] Gansfort 1522, p. 113. 'Now Gerson is clearly of the opinion that in the remission of sins the bestowment of grace necessarily precedes the remission of guilt, because the remission of guilt is nothing else than the bestowment of grace' (Miller 1917, p. 306).

[263] de Kroon 2009, p. 28.

[264] Gansfort 1522, p. 114. 'milder than what accords with the plain, theological truth, he [Gerson] is silently making a concession in the interest of piety, in order that the truth may not become a barrier for the unprepared 'little ones' through the malice of certain men' (Miller 1917, p. 308).

continent aperuit, consulte remissius rigorosam abditam ueritatem, pro tardioribus, propter contentiosos tacuisse. Quomodo enim aliter tam discrepantes, uenerabilis illius uiri sententias concordabimus? Cun sint quaedam earum tam euidenter pro me, ut in eis meam ego intentionem fundare putem. Sed id interim apud te. Quaedae uero tam remisse atque quiete pro populare assertione, quo tu in eis contra me neque id ab re, quia parite & illum studio communis pietatis allegare puto quo illum scripsisse, cum utrosque par procella iactauerit. Et ego consilium tuum laudo si ita facias doceas & praedicas.[265]

The above quote exudes a certain degree of frustration, reflecting Gansfort's ambivalent attitude toward what he perceives as the chancellor's strategy. On the one hand, he valued Gerson's restraint, which allowed him to act in wisdom and according to *studio communis pietatis*, 'in the spirit of zeal for piety'.[266] On the other hand, the Dutch theologian finds it somewhat upsetting, hard to comprehend and especially hard to emulate for himself, due to differences in their respective temperaments. Indeed, his description of Gerson's personality sounds almost condescending:

Nosti studiosam & officiosam uiri illius pietatem, quam saepe suam opinionem aliis contra sentientibus deferat. In quo tamen ualde mirandum uidetur tam diuersum a uero & recto consilium.[267]

---

[265] Gansfort 1522, p. 115. 'I think, therefore, that the prudent Gerson, after opening the eyes of careful readers by propositions which contain undoubted truth, purposely relaxed his strictness somewhat on account of contentious men, and was silent respecting the exact truth hidden within, for the sake of those who were of slower apprehension. Indeed, how shall we otherwise reconcile the great discrepancies we find in the opinions of this venerable man? For certain of these opinions so clearly support me, that I think of basing my premise upon them. Yet sometimes he agrees with you. Indeed, in statements intended for the people he expresses his opinions so mildly and gently that you can build on them opposing me. [...] Nor is this without value. For [...] if you act, teach, and preach in that spirit, I praise your wisdom' (Miller 1917, p. 310).

[266] Gansfort 1522, p. 115. Miller 1917, p. 310.

[267] Gansfort 1522, p. 114. 'You know intense and deep piety of this man, and how often he abandons his own opinion when others disagree with him. Nevertheless, in this it seems very strange that this judgment is so far removed [different] from what is true and correct'. Here translation is mine.

Taken out of context, it would imply that Gerson was moderate in his opinions due to the weakness of character and lack of solid principles. Yet, displaying an interesting case of introspection, Gansfort also admitted regretting his own lack of Gerson-like prudence during his tenure in Paris, expressing the wish that he be more circumspect himself: *Unde crebro & illum ac te beatos iudico, quibus officiosior in talibus moderatio est.*[268] A master of contradictions indeed!

Wessel's seemingly conflicting attitude toward Gerson finds explanation in his own unusual situation. Halfway between cloister and academia, spending his last years alternately in several monasteries, while remaining a layman, controversial without falling into heresy, he based his ability to stay out of trouble without sacrificing his ability to negotiate his dissent, on his reliance on Gerson as the main theological authority of his time, his personal hero and, very importantly, a precedent. By endorsing and contextualizing the chancellor's positions, the Dutch theologian justified and defended his own. Thus, he approved of the Frenchman's efforts to avoid, in dealing with complex theological questions, a 'widespread scandal' among 'those who were of slower apprehension', following Gerson's argument found in *Contra Matthaeum de Fussa*, where he spoke about situations when *populus non est capax, nec inde aedificationem sumeret sed scandalum* ('people incapable [of grasping the intricacies of an argument] would assume scandal from it, not edification').[269]

> *Puto igitur illu studiosum pietatis & aedificationis latissimi in Ecclesia dei scandala ex pertinaci scholasticorum contentione expertum, elegisse magis errorem sustinere ueritatis in pusillis, que scissura & scandala charitatis. Et hinc mitiora sua dicta in hanc partem accipienda, uti uidemus consilium naufragi suas & caras merces in tempestate iactantis, quo uitam & animam salute, natura duce & lucent, quanon intrunsque quod minis*

---

[268] Gansfort 1522, p. 115. Miller 1917, p. 309: 'I often consider you and those persons to be happy, who possess a more complaisant moderation in such questions'.

[269] *Contra Matthaeum de Fussa*, OC: 10, pp. 138–39: *[...] talis assertio non est deducanda ad populum, similiter nec opposita tamquam declarando uel elucidando; sic capiendo enim habet uel non habet ueritatem cuius [= quoniam] populus non est capax, nec inde aedificationem sumeret sed scandalum.*

malum subimis, quo maius declinemus. Unde & ergo saepius Parisius & hodie quandoque meipsum reprehendo, que aliquando cum non capacibus materiam istam confero, atque utinam solum sine fructu.[270]

Consequently, whenever Gerson appears to differ from Gansfort's position, it is not due to substantial differences of opinion between the mentor and the mentee, but to the chancellor's superior ability to adjust his message to his audience and to a specific purpose. As a learned theologian, the great chancellor had to condescend to the general imperfection of men who, in this life, act in darkness illuminated only as if by a lamp. Truly, in different contexts, *in disputationibus dico ubi discussionis dente opus est, in sermonibus ad populum, neque in contemplatione ad deum*,[271] to use the same approach would be both ineffective and inappropriate. Consequently, Gerson's seemingly 'milder' statements must be interpreted 'in the light of this purpose',[272] and not in the light of their relationship to an essential theological truth as Gansfort understood it.

It is also clear that through a close association with Gerson's universally recognized authority, Gansfort sought to avoid crossing the red line in his criticism of the Church, protecting himself from potential accusations of heresy. Fearful of the Inquisition, he reproached his superior and former friend, Dean of Naeldwick Jacob Hoeck, for reporting Wessel's theological 'faults' to

---

[270] Gansfort 1522, p. 115. 'I think, therefore, that Gerson in his zeal for piety and edification, knowing by experience what widespread scandal arose throughout the Church of God from the obstinate contentions of Scholastics, preferred to maintain a perversion of truth among the 'little ones' rather than cause a schism or any stumbling block to love in the Church. And therefore his milder statements must be interpreted in the light of this purpose; just as we see the wisdom of a shipwrecked man in throwing his precious wares overboard in a storm, in order that he may save his life. In so doing he is evidently led by nature, since we do not at any rate suffer both evils, when we undergo the lesser in order to avoid the greater. Hence also I sometimes blame myself today, as I used to more often in Paris, for discussing this subject at all with those who are not fitted for it, and I only hope that at any rate it did no harm [had no effect]' (Miller 1917, p. 309).

[271] Gansfort 1522, p. 114: *In disputationibus dico ubi discussionis dente opus est. Non in sermonibus ad populum. Neque in contemplatione ad deum.* Miller 1917, p. 308: 'I am speaking of disputations, where there is need of the sharp tooth of discussion; not of ser-mons to the people, nor of meditation Godward'.

[272] Letter to Jacob Hoeck, Miller 1917, p. 309. Gansfort 1522, p. 115.

Cologne's authorities instead of keeping his disapproval *primo inter te & me* and directly tell his brother about his misgivings.[273] Hoeck's stern warning clearly demonstrates why Gansfort, who had little to none of Gerson's famous discretion, had indeed a great need for the latter's retroactive theological back up:

> *At unum duntaxat ex literis tuis colligo, quod uirum grandem, mea opinione, uehementer dedecet. Id est, quod dura te iactas cervice, qua cunctis in dictis tuis quondam niteris inueniri singularitatem, adeò ut plurimorum iudicio Magister contradictionis meritò ualeas appellari. Et, ne dubites, tua doctrissimi uiri singularitas plurosque, scandalisat.*[274]

Reprimands of 'obstinacy' and 'singularity', repeated by Hoeck twice in one paragraph, are alarming, since 'singularity is not a virtue but a vice'.[275] Thereupon Wessel fiercely defends himself in his answer to Hoeck:

> *Numquam pertinax sui, etiam in certaminibos uanitatis. Circumiui multas uniuersitates, & certamina quaerens, multos reperi contradictores, uerum numquam in scandalis dimissos; quia rationibus meis auditis, & perspicaciter consideratis uel consentientes, uel saltem non irrationabiles confitentes, quietos redditi, ut nemo finaliter de me conquereretur.*[276]

---

[273] Gansfort 1522, p. 98: *Accepi ex ore tuo nonnullis meis doctrinis te scandalisatum, & ea re per motum, scripsisse de super Coloniam. Neque reprehendo, commodious tamen, & ad normam euangelicae rectitudinis uicinius puto, ut me peccantem in te fratrem tuum, primo inter te & me corripuisses.* 'I learned from your own lips [mouth] that you had been displeased at some teachings of mine and that you in alarm had written about the matter to Cologne. For this I do not find fault with you. And yet I think it would be have been more obliging and — by the standard of gospel rectitude — more neighborly, if, when I, your brother, sinned against you, you had shown me my fault, between you and me alone' (Miller 1917, p. 266).

[274] *Epistola M. Jacobi Hoeck ad M. Wesselum*, Gansgort 1614, p. 871. 'From your letters, however, I gather that you have one characteristic which in my opinion is extremely [vehemently] unsuited to a great man. This is that you pride yourself on your obstinacy [literally 'stiff neck'] and are bent upon having men find a certain singularity in all your statements, so that in the judgment of many persons you are rightly called 'The Master of Contradiction'. And unquestionably, in view of your being a most learned man, your singularity your singularity gives offense [scandalizes] to many' (Miller 1917, p. 267).

[275] Oberman 1981, p. 97.

[276] Gansfort 1522, pp. 98–99. Miller 1917, p. 267: 'I have never been stubborn, even in idle discussions. I have been to many universities, seeking discussion, and I have found many opponents. Sometimes, too, they have been offended by

At the end of this letter of self-defense Wessel takes out and wields, like a shield, the irrefutable argument of Gerson's authority:

> *Sed nunquid igitur Gerson haereticus quitam grauiter & fundamentalibus uerbis hodiernun cursum inussit. Video quorsum ista tendent, quia si uerum illi dicerent, omnis qui contradiceret in regulam fidei, quia contra traditionem apostolorum impingeret & si pertinaciter insisteret, hereticus esset.*[277]

Even though Wessel's reliance on Gerson might be qualified as 'pre-ideological', in a sense that it does not express an agenda of a particular denomination or party, it is not exactly non-partisan for two main reasons. The first is the above-illustrated need for personal protection that relied on Gerson's authority as a safeguard. The second has to do with the fact that Gansfort, like Gerson, Geiler von Kaysersberg, Nicolas Kempf, Nicolas of Cusa and many other historical characters to yet appear in this book, belonged to the *reforma perpetua* movement that attempted to improve the Church from within, without questioning its sacramental authority. Even if Gerson affords Gansfort 'the extraordinary latitude to the individual conscience in determining the limits of civil and ecclesiastical authority',[278] he does so in a way opposite to what we understand as individual conscience today. Via Gerson, Wessel affirmed his ability to remain different within the *reforma perpetua* movement, which sought, through criticism, no matter how severe, to amend, recover and uphold traditional Catholic values, of which love for the Church reigned supreme. Although 'caustic and extreme, often shocking his listeners with paradox and violent opinion',[279] Gansfort, who never denied the value of traditions, church sacraments or the freedom of will. He defended his right to remain in the Church, not to break with it.

---

my belief. But never have they parted with me in offense. For when my reasons had been heard and carefully considered, I left them quieted, either agreeing with me, or at least admitting that my statements were not unreasonable; so that in the end no one made complaint concerning me'.

[277] Gansfort 1522, p. 111. Miller 1917, pp. 299–300: 'But is Gerson who so forcibly and fundamentally branded the present system on this account [of indulgences] a heretic? [...] then everyone [...] who persists [in it] must be a heretic'.

[278] Oakley 2015, p. 206.

[279] Jacob 1953, p. 130.

It worked. He suffered no personal persecution by the Inquisition and died peacefully as a good Catholic. The fact that his writings were placed on the *Index of Prohibited Books* in 1529, forty years after his death and twelve years after the beginning of Luther's revolt, is more a comment on the change of times than on his actual theology.

Two other prominent members of *devotio moderna*, Jan Standonck (1453–1504) and Johannes Mombaer (1460–1501) similarly considered themselves Gerson's spiritual children.[280] The first, Jan Standonck, was a Parisian preacher and college administrator born in the Dutch-speaking Brabant. Like Biel and Gansfort, he was a university educator, although of a very special kind. As a preacher, he valued and pursued Gerson's use of the vernacular in spiritual matters and preached exclusively in French.[281] As an educator, best known as the principle of the Parisian College of Montaigu and its reformer, he conscientiously followed Gerson's ideal of *bonus pastor* by offering the best education to economically disadvantaged students. Yet, his handling of Montaigu hardly agrees with Gersonian pedagogical and pastoral legacy for several reasons. Although the moral purity of Standonck's intentions is incontrovertible, the harshness of his pedagogical methods stands in contrast to Gerson's milder approach. Furthermore, Standonck's pronounced anti-intellectualism, representative of *devotio moderna*, is uncharacteristic of Gerson, whose quest for affective theology was balanced by his humanistic and intellectual pursuits. Standonck paid almost no heed to such concerns. Finally, the Fleming's personal propensity toward extreme austerity and frequent self-imposed (and imposed on others) acts of severe penitence do not quite agree with the late chancellor's known dislike for such manifestations of piety. Amid the cohort of celebrities undeniably produced by Montaigu's excellent education — Erasmus of Rotterdam, Montaigu's future principal Noël Béda (1470–1537), an influential Scottish philosopher John Mair or Major (1467–1550), the brilliant scholar Jacques Almain

---

[280] On this subject see Godet 1912; Debongnie 1927, pp. 392–402; Debongnie 1928; Combes 1963, 2; Rapp 1994, VII, pp. 215–308; Giraud 2016, pp. 265–79.

[281] See Godet 1912.

(v. 1480–1515), significant Louvain theologian Jacobus Latomus (1475–1544), Jean Calvin and Ignatius of Loyola — some, like Erasmus and Almain, loathed Montaigu's atmosphere and Standock's methods, while others, like John Mair, were grateful for the opportunities they provided. Despite disparities in appreciation, however, this extraordinary group of alumni, which accounts for all the major novelties and conflicts of the 16th century, illustrates two certainties concerning Standonck's performance as Montaigu's principle. The first is that all the people on this list were influenced, to some degree or another, by Gerson's legacy. The second, determined by the first, and reflecting the complexity of this legacy, consists in the impossibility of aligning it with any one of these names, associated with a particular tendency or group, since they largely represent conflicting trends and sensibilities: Béda was a bitter enemy of Erasmus, Loyola of Calvin and Almain of Standonck himself.[282] Gerson's 16th century spiritual children had torn their late medieval inheritance into separate, although often brilliant, shreds.

Unlike Biel, Gansfort or Standonck, John Mombaer or John of Brussels had no university affiliation. A mystical writer à part entière, he played a key role in diffusing Gerson's thought in France and Spain, and is mainly known as the author of *Rosetum exercitiorum spiritualium et sacrarum meditationum (Rose Garden of Spiritual Exercise and Sacred Meditation)*, for which Gerson was 'la source des méditations les plus inexorablement méthodiques'.[283] Written shortly after the death of Thomas à Kempis, *Rosetum* quotes several sentences from *De Imitatione Christi*, but 'Gerson's influence and example definitely prevail

---

[282] The conflict between Standonck and Jacques Almain, who taught at Montaigu during Standonck's tenure, took place during an acute crisis between the University of Paris, which supported the king, and the papal power represented by the same cardinal Cajetan who had called Luther *Gersonista*. Having thought to have found roots of Gallicanism in the chancellor's treatises on the supremacy of general councils, Almain took upon himself the mission of 'defending Gerson and the old doctrine of the Church and tradition'. Almain ended up being so closely associated with Gerson's ideas that their treatises kept being published together in editions of Gerson's works up until 1706. See Burns & Izbicki 1998, p. 199, n. 120.

[283] Combes 1963, 2, p. 668.

over all others'.[284] Indeed, Mombaer's special bond with the Parisian master, whom he confessed to have often studied through the night,[285] is not conditioned by his supposed authorship of *De Imitatione Christi*, as he considered Thomas à Kempis and not Gerson to be its real author.[286] Mombaer's *Tabula librorum* lists nearly all of Gerson's works known at the time, and *Rosetum*'s borrowings from Gerson are numerous. They involve a variety of topics — ranging from the devotional practice of spiritual mendicancy to the use of mnemonic verses in prayer — and a great assortment of texts: Gerson's letters to his sisters,[287] *Mystica theologia practica, Monotessaron*,[288] *Monochordum Jesu Christi* (also called *Solatium peregrini*) and *Figura scacordi musicalis simul et militaris*. Most of these works, including the enigmatic *Figura scacordi musicalis simul et militaris*,[289] represent highly sophisticated attempts at systematization of contemplative practices, music, although critically evaluated, being one of them.[290] Most importantly, Mombaer's meditative techniques for reshaping the self were 'secured through the practice of engaging in daily exercises', which included Gerson's contemplative writings listed above.[291] An example of Mombaer's close reworkings of Gerson's text in *Rosetum* is his treatment of the image of the dove from *Mystica theologia practica*. The figure of mystical dove is offered for the purpose of meditation:

> *Meditabor, ut columba. Haec binis alis, dextera spei et sinistra timoris, uolat sursum, et cauda dirigitur discretionis. Utroque*

---

[284] Debongnie 1927, p. 397 & Debongnie 1928, p. 31.

[285] Debongnie 1928, p. 8: *Aliquas partes Gersonis dicitur paene perlustrasse nocte una*.

[286] 'Brother Thomas a Kempis, among other works which he made, composed the little book, qui sequitur me, which some attributed falsely to Dominus Gerson' (Habsburg 2002, p. 66).

[287] Debongnie 1928, p. 186.

[288] Debongnie 1928, p. 35.

[289] OC: 9, pp. 704–05 & p. 708, respectively. Mombaer seems to be unique in his interest for this work.

[290] Giraud 2016, p. 277: 'Ce contre quoi entend lutter le chanoine réformateur (Mombaer) à la suite de Gerson, c'est un recours jugé excessif à des prières vocales que leur attribution à des saints et la coutume de les indulgencier dotent parfois d'un pouvoir quasi magique'.

[291] Ritchey 2013, p. 162.

> *demum ala uelut aequo libramine sustentat hanc columbam, ut nec ala timoris nimis deprimat desperationem, nec ala spei sursum plus attolat praesumptionem.*[292]

In *Rosetum* Gerson's dove undergoes a curious transformation, as it retains only the wings, the right for virtues, the left for vices, and is tailless. The wings, sufficient for living a simple existence, are insufficient for flying, however. Otherwise people would be like ostriches, with big, useless wings.[293] In order to be like a dove, men need to balance intellectual effort with affectivity. A psychological metaphor of the delicate labor of the soul in its spiritual quest, characteristic of Gerson's theology of seeking, has been replaced by a didactic allegory with a strong emphasis on affectivity, central to *devotio moderna*'s mystical pursuit:

> *Hoc tamen praemonitum uolumus nos hic nolle sublimia tradere et contemplationis materiam explicare, sed tantum de rudi affectiue meditatione qua citius peruenitur ad mysticae theologiae arcem quam si sublimia dixerimus et altiora.*[294]

By 1495 Mombaer's meditations had been incorporated into the library at the College of Montaigu, where they were used by Standonck, his colleagues and pupils. They were subsequently copied throughout western continental Europe and 'practiced by

---

[292] OC: 8, p. 42. 'I will meditate, like a dove. This with two wings, the right of the hope and the left of the fear, flies on high, and it is directed by the tail of discernment. At last, both wings sustain this dove in equilibrium, so that nor the wing of fear would depress it too much with despair, either the wing of hope would lift it aloft to overconfidence'.

[293] Debongnie 1928, p. 167, n. 2: *Sed hoc notatu dignissimum, quod quamuis has alas quis habeat plumis et pennulis ornatas, et si cogitauerit ista intellectu, se non in alta librare studuerit affectu, non uolare dicendus est, sed struthioni comparandus magis; habet nempe, ut aiunt, struthio magnas alas, sed paucos uel nullos exercet uolatus [...]* 'But this is well worth mentioning that, although whoever has these wings adorned with feathers, if he will think about them through intellect only, and does not apply himself to balance it with love in the skies, he cannot be said to fly. Rather, he should be compared to an ostrich for ostrich has, as they say, big wings, but few or none of them [ostriches] are able to fly.'

[294] Debongnie 1928, p. 260. 'One should be aware that here we intend to deal with neither sublime matters nor with explanations about contemplation, but only with basic affective meditation, through which one can reach the summit of mystical theology faster than if we were talking about sublime and elevated things'.

hundreds of students' in the late 14th and 15th centuries and probably beyond.[295]

Ars moriendi

The popularity of Gerson's aforementioned *Opus tripartitum* was 'so uncommonly great'[296] that it deserves special and separate attention. This manual on Ten Commandments, confession and care for the terminally ill, underwent its first partial translations at Melk during the author's lifetime, and circulated under the title *Tres ueritates Gersonis* in a number of manuscript and printed late medieval editions, with its distribution soon surpassing that of any other of the chancellor's works.[297] Different parts of the *Opus* surged in popularity at different times, and were often published as separate works, responding to the changing demands of the reading public. Even though it was destined to acquire pan-European fame, it proved to be of the utmost importance in the Empire.[298] It was Johannes Geiler von Kaysersberg who was the first to translate it into German in 1481, under the title of *Dreieckecht-Spiegel*, making it available, for the first time, to Strasbourg's prosperous middle class, literate but ignorant of Latin. Geiler also pioneered the use of *Opusculum*'s second part as a separate work. This text, published as a treatise on the art of confession, enumerates three conditions necessary to continue in a state of grace: the acknowledgement of sin, the desire for amendment, and a willingness to make a full confession. Geiler also reworked *Opus*' third part — from the beginning written both in Latin and in French (under the titles *La médicine de l'ame* or *La science de bien mourir*) — into

---

[295] Ritchey 2013, p. 165.

[296] O'Connor 1942, p. 22.

[297] According to Daniel Hobbins, there are more than two hundred manuscripts of *Opus tripartitum* (Hobbins 2006, p. 148). Four were published in 1467, one in 1470, two in 1474, one in 1475, three in 1477, one in 1478, five in 1481, one in 1483, one in 1486, two in 1487, one in 1488, one in 1493, one in 1495 (Coates, Palmer & Schaepe 2005). Leipzig University Albertina Library alone has several editions, including those of 1475, 1477, 1493 and 1514.

[298] Bossy 2002, p. 225. The category of 'manuals for priests' was not limited to Gerson's booklet, but included dozens of titles. Thus, the *Manipulus curatorum* by Guido de Monte Rocherii or Monterochen or Monterocher was printed in 119 editions all over Europe during the second half of the 15th century (Dykema 2000, p. 145).

his Sterbebüchlein or Todtenbüchlein of 1482, titled *Wie man sich halten soll bei einem sterbenden Menschen*, the 1497 *Ein ABC, Wie man sich schicken sol*, and his 1496 sermoncineis on the death preparation.[299]

From Strasbourg, *Opus*' third part began its triumphant march across southern Germany and what is now Austria, Bohemia, Hungary, Northern Italy, Netherlands, Belgium and Poland.[300] Its first German editions diverged little from Gerson's original, and for the entire 15th century its basic structure and content remained practically the same. It became a lasting prototype for a new and popular genre, with its thoughts on the right way to die making their way in almost all German *Sterbebüchlein* from Bavaria to Denmark. The work's success also engendered a tidal wave of imitators, the most popular and most influential of which was *Speculum artis bene moriendi*. The authorship of this text remains unclear, but it explicitly refers to *Cantzler von pariß*[301] as its predecessor.

Another popular version of *Opus*' third part belongs to aforementioned theologian Thomas Peuntner,[302] who, in both versions of his work, one in Latin and one in German, entitled *Kunst des heilsamen Sterbens*, directly refers to Gerson by his name and by

---

[299] Hoch 1901, pp. 2–3: 'unter denen ist ein erleüchteter und tröstlicher doctor gesein, hat geheissen Johannes Gerson, etwan Cantzler zu Paryss. Der hatt für das gemein volck in Frantzosischem welsch, kurtz und lauter geschriben ein dreygeteilt wercklin, dz er genannt hat den spiegel der seelen [...] hab ich understanden, das in oberlendisch oder hoch teütsch zu bringen, auff das sie auch ein spiegel haben, darin sie sich besehen' 'among them is one most enlightened and consoling doctor, referred to as Jean Gerson or sometimes Chancellor of Paris. He had written a short and clear small work in three parts, called *The Mirror of the Soul*, for simple people in the French tongue [...] I have undertaken to render it in the upper or high German, so that you too could have a mirror in which to see yourself'. Berndt Hamm is silent about the fact that Geiler copied Gerson in his work on death preparation, presenting it as an original work by the Strasbourg preacher' (Hamm 2014, p. 113). Tarald Rasmussen and Jon Øygarden Flæten clearly demonstrate that *Wie man sich halten sol byeym sterbenden menschen* of 1480/81 is nearly a translation of Gerson's *ars moriendi* (Rasmussen, Flæten 2015, p. 18, n. 18).

[300] According to Chartier, there are 234 15th century manuscripts of different *ars moriendi*: 126 in Latin, 75 in German, 11 in English, 10 in French, 9 in Italian and 3 others (Chartier 1976, p. 53). 'Den Urtypus aber der *ars moriendi*-Literatur schuf Johann Gerson (1363–1429) um 1400' (Jäger 2010, p. 17).

[301] Rudolf believes it to be that of Nicholas Dinkelbühl (Rudolf 1957, p. 75).

[302] Rudolf 1957, p. 86.

his title of the chancellor of the University of Paris. Peuntner's book was followed by an anonymous German treatise *Ein gut kunst, darjnn man mag gar hailbartishlich lernen sterben*, also explicitly written 'nach der lere des cannczlers von Paris'.[303] The aforementioned Bernhard von Waging relied on *Opus*' questions to the dying person in his 1458 *Tractatus de morte nec non de praeparatione ad mortem siue Speculum mortis*, as did the Benedictine monk, mystic, and a Church reformer Johannes von Kastl (died after 1426) in his *Hortulus animae*. *Ars moriendi* also found numerous visual representations in the so-called Bilder-Ars, created between 1450 and 1460, of which the most famous is *Sterbebüchlein der Fünf Anfechtungen*.[304] Famous for its eleven beautiful woodcuts, it became a model for block-books for the death preparation, popular not only in Germany and all over Europe.[305] Other lavishly decorated *Ars moriendi* followed. According to Heiko Oberman and Neil Leroux, Gerson's guide for ordinary Christians facing death was also available in the cellar of Luther's monastery in 1513, serving as an inspiration for the latter's 1519 *Ein Sermon von der bereitung zum sterben*, an unquestionable bestseller with twenty-two German, two Latin, one Dutch and one Danish editions.[306]

A particular interest of Gerson's approach to death preparation consists in his attentiveness not only towards the dying, but also towards those who care for them, in other words in his aspiration to offer assistance to the assistants. His *ars moriendi* is one of the earliest attempts at training caregivers for the dying, by providing them with basic guidelines, a sort of a simple protocol or 'procedural manual'[307] divided into four parts intended to organize the process of the death preparation: 'exhortations, interrogations, oroysons et observacions'.[308] This *modus operandi*,

---

[303] Rudolf 1957, p. 88.
[304] 'Diese Sterbebuchlein bringt inhaltlich nicht viel Neues, es knüpf an die Fragen von Anselm und an das Sterbebüchlein von Gerson an' (Jäger 2010, p. 19).
[305] Rudolf 1957, pp. 69–70. See also Hannemann 2004.
[306] Leroux 2007, pp. 40–45.
[307] Ruys 2014, p. 67.
[308] *La médecine de l'ame*, OC: 7: 1, p. 404. The text has four exhortations, six questions, four prayers, and ten obsevations.

although influenced by earlier rituals,[309] is undoubtedly rooted in Gerson's own pastoral experience of assisting people in death. As a supervisor of the Hotel-Dieu, which used to combine the functions of a hospital and a hospice, he knew the matter first hand and asserted that 'nul ne le scet qui ne l'assaye'.[310] His description of the daily reality of the Hôtel-Dieu leaves no doubt as to his familiarity with it:

> On seult avoir misericorde poures chartiers langoureux, angoisseux et douloureux qui n'ont de quoy gairir ne de quoi vivre; telz sont ycy en multitude. On souloit avoir misericorde de poures pucelles ou de poures femmes veuves, honnestes, et puis de celles qui ont garde chastete sans marriage jusques a la fin, et autre plus quant elles labourent diligemment pour faire leur devoir envers Dieu et acquerir leur poure de vie. Pensons se en l'Ostel Dieu de Paris a grant foison de telles qui doresnavant tout cest yver seront en boue de Seine toute gelee jusques aux genoux par laver les drapeaulx poures. Considerons quants dures paines, de nuit et de jour, convient avoir pour soigner et coucher, relever, vestir, paistre, consoler tant de poures de diverses maladies et de si estrange condition [...] Se a bien gouverner ung malade a telle peine, quell labeur est ce de bien gouverner telle multitude presque innumerable de tant de maladies qui surviennent de jour en jour.[311]

This poignant text, which is of a great interest to the historians of medicine and public health, emanates a genuine emotion and a sincere compassion not only for patients, but also for those, especially women, who care for them in terms of their physical or moral well-being. It has an advantage of speaking directly for all those who have ever experienced caring for the seriously ill. With the same nuanced psychological insights that he displayed throughout his writings, the chancellor recognized, as an experienced pastor, that, one the one hand, for the majority of people the pursuit of

---

[309] O'Connor 1942, p. 23. 'This genre appears to have developed from two distinct textual traditions: the high medieval devotional texts of the formation of the self [...] and more emotionally sparse patristic and early medieval procedural manuals that advised pastors on the spiritual care of the sick and dying' (Ruys 2014, p. 55).
[310] *Pour l'Hôtel Dieu*, OC: 7: 2, p. 715.
[311] *Pour l'Hôtel Dieu*, OC: 7: 2, pp. 715–16.

a good death cannot be achieved in solitude. Such an expectation, advocated, among others, by the *devotio moderna*, and by the vast majority of contemplative religious practices, is simply unrealistic for average people who are untrained in 'building the spiritual muscle'.[312] The majority of people need to be accompanied by a spiritual attendant, 'who will fill-in for St Anthony's angel'.[313] On the other hand, knowing by experience that those who accompany the dying often experience an anxiety almost as intense as those whom they accompany, the chancellor attempted to offer assistance 'pour les personnes qui sont entre les maladies soit en hospitauz soit aillers ou ils ont conuersation'.[314] These words come from the *Lettre à un* inconnu, a short text written in correlation with the *ars moriendi* and explaining its audience and its aim. The letter is crucial for understanding some specific goals that Gerson had in mind in composing his *ars moriendi*,[315] which is part of his pastoral program of church reform that involved changes both among the clergy and among the laity. Thus, among *les personnes qui sont entre les maladies soit en hospitauz soit aillers* he especially wished to see bishops who should be like fathers for all the unfortunate and should go to the hospitals, houses of good women and leproseries to inquire about the way in which people are treated there:

> Qui orphano et pupillo et uidue et egenti et captiuo et egroto et aflicto et agricolis senebis et languoribus consumptis et onere puerorum aggrauatis etc., quia refugium esse debent atque patres, subueniant. Qui hospitalia Dei et probarum mulierum aut leprosorum domos aliaque pauperum Christi loca diligecius uisitent [...], ut sepe fit, in excessus uel abusus consumantur aspiciant.[316]

His approach to *ars moriendi* also is linked to his desire to encourage lay devotion. Indeed, although his advice for caregivers is

---

[312] Taylor 2007, p. 418.

[313] Taylor 2007, p. 418.

[314] *Gerson à un inconnu*, Paris 1404, Lettre d'envoi de l'*Opus tripartitum*, OC: 2, p. 75.

[315] Taylor 2007, p. 411: 'It is unreasonable to interpret Gerson's *Scientia mortis* without reference to the Chancellor's epistle [accompanying it]'.

[316] *Noua epistola pro instructione episcoporum et prelatorum ...*, in Vansteenberghe 1939 p. 40 and p. 42. This text, entitled 'Gerson à un évêque (Gilles des Champs?) nouvellement nommé', Paris, 1408, is found in OC: 2, pp. 108–16.

primarily aimed at clerics traditionally involved in such cares, it is by no means limited to them, as it includes all 'les vrays amys d'ung malade [qui] font grant diligence envers luy pour sa vie et sa santé'.[317] *Les vrays amys* refers to both men and women, as every exhortation in his *ars moriendi* begins with an inclusive 'mon amy ou mamye'.[318] The main motivation was to provide guidance for the attendants in order to lead the patient from 'souffrance à l'apaisement',[319] for the gift of consolation was available to all.[320] It is as a caring friend that Gerson sent *La médecine de l'ame* as a death preparation present to the famous writer Philippe de Mézières (1327–1405), who, although advanced in years, was by no means dying in 1404. The theologian expressed hopes that Mézières would 'y prendre plaisir et voulente dacomplir le contenu'[321] and 'bailler en bonne charite le conseil qui me semble a present profitable et presque necessaire a vous et a bien conduire vostre fin'.[322] The chancellor felt reassured specifically because Mézières was not alone, and had 'bonnes gens et devotes' to help him 'a toutes heures'.[323] This point is critically important, because his pastoral advice encourages lay people to take an active

---

[317] 'Si les vrays amys d'ung malade font grant diligence envers luy pour sa vie et santé corporelle et faillable, Dieu et charité requièrent que ilz soient plus soigneux pour son salut et vie espirituelle et pardurable, car a ce dernier besoing voit on qui vray ami est. Et n'est oeuvre de misericorde plus prouffitable; et est de si grant mérité souvent que ne serait service corporel a la personne de Nostre Seigneur s'il estoit sur terre' (*La médecine de l'ame*, OC: 2, p. 404). This pioneering aspect of Gerson's book was retained in its English version, *Crafte of Dyinge*, which is discussed in chapter four.

[318] 'Mon amy ou amie, veulx tu morir et vivre en la foy crestienne de nostre saulveur Jhesucrist, comme loyal et vray filz de sainte eglise? Responde oil. Mon amy ou mamye, pense la grace que Dieu te faist. Nous sommes tous et toutes en sa main' (*La médecine de l'ame*, OC: 7: 1, p. 405).

[319] Boquet & Piroska 2015, p. 287. 'Rädle ist der Ansicht, dass im Gegensatz zur anderen ars moriendi-Literatur, Gerson mit einem sehr persöhnlichen und menschenfreundlichen Ton versucht dem Sterbenden beizustehen' (Jäger 2010, pp. 18–19).

[320] 'Bei Gerson wird der Trost vor allem durch das Sakrament geschenkt' (Jäger 2010, p. 19).

[321] *Gerson à un vieillard*, OC: 2, p. 76.

[322] *Gerson à un vieillard*, OC: 2, p. 75.

[323] 'Et vous avez, Dieu mercy, aveuc vous bonnes gens et devotes pour vous ayder a ce et pour querir les pas des escriptures qui vous seront profitables a lire et pour vous dire au diner ou ailleurs semblable langage comme jay dit de vostre clerc' (*Gerson à un viellard*, OC: 2, p. 76).

part in the death preparation of their loved ones and emphasizes 'the communal nature of the passing-over'.[324] Faithful to himself, Gerson was seeking a practical remedy,[325] a model accessible to the laity that would serve to improve real and daily situations, a new norm for all Christians.[326]

This aspect of Gerson's *ars moriendi* stands in sharp contrast to Philippe Ariès's now famous assertion of the distinctively individual and solitary character of late medieval death as opposed to early modern communal attitudes.[327] Gerson considered solitary death as both unfortunate and dangerous with a view to salvation, and the immediate phenomenal popularity of his little book shows that his contemporaries were of the same opinion. Besides, if Gerson, together with other authors of similar texts, felt an urgent need for such recommendations in his society, this quite naturally means that the practice of accompanying the dying with friends or invited clergy already existed. Despite the fact that Ariès's opinion has maintained such an enduring currency among scholars that even Gerson's loving biographer Brian P. McGuire declared that 'Gerson's message can be interpreted as one of an isolated individual who abandons all hope',[328] the chancellor's take on this subject is hardly the individual death described by Ariès, Paul Binski, Alberto Tenenti or, more recently, Juanita Ruys.[329] Rather, it offers a compassionate, caring and practical approach to death and dying, seeking to confer to these experiences positive attributes of peace and affection through the loving support of a true friend, who does not leave the dying alone in the final isolation of death:

---

[324] Taylor 2007, p. 416 and Classen 2007, p. 77. This should not be confused with involving distraught family members, wife and children, who further distress and distract the dying person from the 'work of dying' (Ruys 2014, p. 72).

[325] 'Car vous trayes a vostre fin. si ne failles point a ce trait car le peril et la perte y seroit sans remede' (*Gerson à un vieillard*, OC: 2, p. 76).

[326] Neher 1989, p. 319.

[327] Ariès 1991, especially chapter 6.

[328] McGuire 2005, p. 347.

[329] Binski 1996; Tenenti 1989; Ruys 2014. The affirmation that 'Learning to die means learning to be self-sufficient in death' (Ruys 2014, p. 72) fails to stand up to criticism once one considers *Opus tripartitum* in conjunction with *Lettre à un inconnu*, *Gerson à un vieillard* and *Pour l'Hôtel Dieu*. Hospice priest Peter Neher finds that 'Durch den 'amicus' erhält der Sterbeprozeß eine menschliche Dimension, es ist die teilnehmende Liebe dessen, der den Sterbenden in der letzten Vereinsamung des Todes nicht allein läßt' (Neher 1989, p. 319).

> [...] cest que vous prennez aveuc vous ung [ami qui] sachent lire francois et latin, qui continue[le]ment soit pres vous de nuit et de jour en dormant et veillant, en buvant et mangent, a deux fins'.[330]

Does Gerson's lineage in this area have continuity in the innumerable 'descendants' of his *Opus tripartitum*?[331] The question remains to be explored. Among the texts that had retained the Gersonian approach there is the aforementioned anonymous *Speculum artis bene moriendi*, which, in its fifth part, focuses on providing advice not only to the dying, but also to those who accompany them. However, while in *Opus* such people could be monks, priests or members of the laity, *Speculum*'s author, who wraps Gerson's simple and practical language in layers of elaborated scholarly citations from Fathers of the Church and ancient philosophers,[332] appears to address the clerical audience specifically. This is yet another case when Gerson's innovation, which is orientated toward 'das einfache Volk zur Zielgruppe', was surreptitiously removed, reorienting his advice toward more traditional audiences. It is also a pertinent illustration of the situation where reworking of his text both greatly increased its circulation and influence, while simultaneously decreasing and altering its scope. Stephan von Landkron's (1412–1477) small book on the art of dying (Sterbebüchlein), *Die Hymelstraß* of 1472, based both on Gerson's *ars moriendi* and on the *Speculum*, is another example, where the author clearly puts 'the role of the friend in the foreground'.[333] Geiler von Kaysersberg's *Wie man sich halten soll bei einem sterchenchen Menschen*, of 1482, is a free translation

---

[330] *Gerson à un vieillard*, OC: 2, p. 76.

[331] 'Johannes Gerson jedoch gab den Hauptanstoß zur neuen Literaturgattung der Ars moriendi, auf ihn und sein Werk wird später noch genauer eingegangen. Es fand großen Beifall und wurde rasch verbreitet, um der Unterweisung von Klerus und auch von Laien zu dienen'. Marr 2010, p. 35.

[332] Marr 2010, p. 64.

[333] Neher 1989, p. 98: 'Stephan liegt damit wieder auf der Linie des Johannes Gerson [...] auch rückt er die Rolle des Freundes wieder deutlich in den Vordergrund'. Stephan von Landkron, *Das Buch genannt die Hymelstraß*, 1501, p. Cviij: 'Man so wirt recht erkannte em getreüwes mitleyden und ein rechte erbarmung und so wirt man warlich innen wer ein getreüwer freund ist'. 'This way one can recognize a true companion and a real mercy and thus will one really know who is a true friend'.

of Gerson's work, but his 1497 Volkbuchlein, entitled *Ein ABC, wie man sich schicken sol zu einem kostlichen seligen tod* (*An ABC, how one must prepare for a blessed and holy death*) fundamentally departs from the Gersonian text in relation to the role accorded to friends and family. Even though Geiler also proposes 'vnd dine lypliche fründ me des güts weder dyner selen pflegen warden',[334] the book is much less, as its title indicates, centered on the role of the *amicus*, but stresses the need for celestial support instead:

> In deiner Todesstunde hast du gegen schlaue und grausame Dämonen zu kämpfen, wobei es sich um die höchsten Güter für ewig handelt. Bitte auch du deine Freunde um Beistannd. 2. Ist es möglich, solche Freunde zu finden? Hier auf dieser Welt allerdings nicht. Suche sie dort, wo dein Vater ist, gemäss den Worten: 'Vater unser, der du bist im Himmel. Es werden aus Gerson (*Testamentum quotidianum*) Gebete angefügt, die als Muster für den Betenden dienen können.[335]

In the majority of visual representations, intended for death preparation of the illiterate and popular throughout Europe, *amicus* seems to have been replaced — with a few exceptions — by consoling angels or holy characters appearing between God and the sick person. Some examples of the continuation of the *amicus* tradition in the English and Catholic *ars moriendi* will be analyzed further on.[336]

Gerson's *Scientia mortis* has recently also been credited with an innovative attitude toward old age as a special time of spiritual harvest. The French theologian's thoughts on the challenges of senectitude [old age] exhibit the same balanced and balancing approach as his theology of spiritual quest: he believed that just as

---

[334] Hoch 1901, p. 80.
[335] Hoch 1901, p. 41. 'At the hour of death, you must fight against evil and cruel demons, for the greater eternal good. Pray also your friends to be with you. 2. Is it possible to find such friends? Not here in this world. Look for them where your father is, in these words: 'Our Father, who is in heaven. Gerson (*Testamentum quotidianum*) adds prayers that can serve as a model for the faithful'. In 1503 Geiler published *Trostspiegel so dir Vatter, Muter, Kynd oder Freünd gestorben synt* (*The mirror of consolation in case your father, mother or your friend died*) which treats, as the title indicates, of the spiritual consolation in case of a loss.
[336] It wasn't until 1942, however, that Gerson's *Ars moriendi* was rediscovered in the heavily bombarded England, to be 'a sort of layman's ritual to be used at the bedside of a dying friend' (O'Connor 1942, p. 23).

despair can serve to prepare for spiritual renewal, the terror of old age and impeding death, when accompanied with necessary support and assistance, might deliver the greatest spiritual benefits.[337] Consequently, instead of being a dreaded time, Gerson viewed old age and even grave illness as rare opportunities, never experienced by the majority of people, to lay aside earthly obligations and profit from the luxury of leisurely contemplation for some introspective reflection. When he wrote to his friend 'sire, pansez a vous, pansez a vostre fin, a vostre salut, a vostre mort'[338] the chancellor did not aim to terrify him into repentance. Rather, his aim was to reassure, console and instill confidence.[339] Gerson's motivation for composing *ars moriendi* was clearly conditioned by his historical and religious background and his principal aim was obtaining salvation for those facing immediate death, but great number of his insights and concerns still speak to a modern audience, and even become increasingly relevant to people living in a society which is collectively both obsessed and terrified by death. Among all of his works, *La médecine de l'ame*, accompanied by *Lettre à un inconnu* and *Lettre à un vieillard* and *Pour l'Hôtel Dieu* are probably the most approachable for 21st century readers, who will find little difficulty, upon reading them, to understand why the Parisian theologian earned the reputation of *doctor consolatorius*.

Early Catechization

The first part of *Opus tripartitum*, dealing with the Ten Commandments, also acquired an independent existence of its own. Although the literature concerning the Ten Commandments has its own history, including Bonaventure's *De decem preceptis*, the chancellor advanced the cause of the Decalogue by giving it effective vernacular expression and integrating it into a general scheme of late medieval piety, together with the practice of confession.[340] Also, while Thomas Aquinas and Bonaventure addressed their reflections on the Decalogue to 'Franciscan and Dominican

---

[337] See Classen 2007.
[338] OC: 2, p. 77.
[339] Taylor 2007, p. 416.
[340] Leites 1988, Introduction, p. 9.

preachers',[341] Gerson aimed at the moral instruction of the laity. Among the earliest examples of his impact in this area is the educational program composed by Johannes Wolff (or Lupi), chaplain of the St Peterskappelle in Frankfurt from 1452 to 1468,[342] who was directly inspired by *De mente cancellarii Parisiensis: Quilibet tenetur scire et intelligere decem precepta, sed nullus potest ea intelligere, nisi discat.*[343] Another important work, *Die collacien vanden eerwaerdigen vader broeder henricus van santen Gardiaen van Mechelen* by Henrik von Santen (d. 1493), a provincial minister of the Cologne province from 1487 to 1488, exhibits 'an intriguing aspect' of targeting 'female religious and literate lay people who were in search for a more fulfilling religious life', reflecting the fact that it 'was heavily indebted' to Gerson's *The Mountain of Contemplation*.[344] In 1438 the aforementioned Vienna theologian Johannes Nider also published his own version of Gerson-inspired catechism, *Preceptor of Divine Law* (*Preceptorium diuini legis*). His colleague, rector of the University of Vienna, historian, professor, and statesman Thomas Ebendorfer von Haselbach (1387–1464), also produced a Gerson-influenced *De decem preceptis* in 1438/39. The Church hierarchy widely distributed *Opus*' part on the Ten Commandments as well. In 1493 Archbishop of Mainz Berthold von Henneberg (1442–1504), a follower of Nicolas of Cusa and leader of the reform faction within the Empire, published a decree that extended a forty-day indulgence to any priest who recited Gerson's catechism from the pulpit of the parish church.[345] The impact of *Opus tripartitum* 'in German-speaking lands through the end of the sixteenth century is almost beyond calculation',[346] with even Luther's famous Catechism resembling Gerson's more than it differed from it.[347]

---

[341] Bast 1997, p. 110.
[342] Bast 1997, p. 23.
[343] Falk 1907, p. 70. 'The spirit of the chancellor of Paris: Everyone is bound to know and understand the ten commandments, but no one can understand them, unless the person learns them'.
[344] Roest 2004, p. 82.
[345] Bast 1997, p. 20.
[346] Hobbins 2006, p. 196.
[347] Leites 1988, p. 225 & p. 227.

Part II. Early Reception in France

In all three areas of influence — the monastic milieu, humanist circles and academia — Gerson's early reception in France, compared to the abundance found in Germanic lands, appears to be less significant.[348] However, several traits of his initial reception in the Empire are also present. The initial preservation of Gerson's manuscripts, for example, also took place in the monastic milieu, with his works being copied and promoted mostly by those who knew him personally. In the Empire these were people who met Gerson at Constance and at Melk, while in his native land these were members of his own family: his younger brother Jean the Celestine and his nephew Thomas Gerson, who worked diligently to safeguard their famous relative's legacy.[349] Thomas donated copies of his uncle's manuscripts to the Abbey of Saint Victor's library, as did Simon de Plumetot (1371–1443), the scholar, jurist, humanist, and book-collector who owned a great number of Gerson's writings,[350] and so did Guillaume Tuysselet (1403–1456), Saint Victor's learned monk who 'knew the chancellor's hand'[351] and copied numerous Gerson's originals.[352] St Victor consequently became a major depository of Gerson's works, where many future celebrities such as Josse Clichtove and Jacques Lefèvre d'Etaples would have a chance to consult them.[353] The aforementioned Laurent Bureau (1449?–1504), Bishop of Sisteron and confessor of Charles VIII and Louis XII, apparently considered Gerson a saint, and even tried to obtain his canonization. He solicited assistance from Charles VIII to this end and proposed the construction of Gerson's funeral chapel at the Church of Saint Laurent in Lyons.

---

[348] See Dagens 1952.

[349] Ouy 2003, pp. 281–308.

[350] On Simon Plumetot see Ouy 1979, pp. 353–82; Delsaux 2014, pp. 273–349.

[351] Calvot & Ouy 1990, p. 28. Also see Ouy 1961, p. 281. According to Ouy, a high percentage of Gerson's manuscripts was later stolen.

[352] Ouy 1970, pp. 276–99.

[353] Jeudy 1995, p. 89. *Le catalogue de l'abbaye de St Victor de Paris de Claude de Grandrue 1514* contains seven collections of Gerson's Latin and vernacular works including *De consolatione theologiae, De paruulis trahendis ad Christum, De practica mystice theologie* etc. B.N. Lat 14908 contains *Super Magnificat*, sermons on *Penitemini e credite euangelio* and *Ad Deum uadit*.

However, because of the chancellor's conciliarist position, Bureau met with resistance in Rome.[354]

First Printed Editions

The fact that French humanists and theologians depended on Rhinish publishers for a long time, not fully catching up with German publishing houses well until the years 1530–1540, affected the fate of Gerson's legacy in France.[355] French men of letters were well aware of the situation. So much so that the distinguished French humanist Robert Gaguin, while traveling on a diplomatic mission between the years 1491 and 1493, undertook what we would now qualify as research trips in order to personally assess the technological and humanist advancements of his German counterparts. He met with Jacob Wimpheling, who outraged him with his Germanic pride,[356] and with Johannes Trithemius, whom he praised as 'adorned by very noble virtues and effulgent not only among monks but also among the most diffuse people of Germany'.[357]

Notwithstanding the delay in production, Gerson's works were among the first to be printed in France, even though they were initially published thanks to the efforts of German printers. The printers came upon the invitation from the aforementioned chancellor of the Sorbonne Johannes Heynlin von Stein (Jean Lapide), who introduced printing in France and brought the first typographical workers to Paris. Whether first publications of Gerson's works can be fully considered French is another question, since German patrons and printers brought their fondness of Gerson with them.[358] On the other hand, considering the remarkable

---

[354] Monfalcon 1866, 4–5, p. 92.

[355] See Aquillon 1979, pp. 45–81 Gerson's first edition (Cologne, 1483–1484) is preserved in 150 copies, majority of them in Germany, but also in Spain, Poland and Italy. Basel 1484 edition survives in 212 examples, and the Nuremberg one in 208. The Strasbourg edition of 1494 survives in 362 copies found in England, Austria, Hungary, Poland and Switzerland. In Italy, Germany and France, 70–75% of Gerson's published works are in Latin. In Portugal, Spain, Bohemia and England vernacular editions dominate (Barbier 2006, pp. 218–20).

[356] Collard 1996.

[357] Brann 1981, p. 22, citing Gaguin's Letter to Trithemius, May 1, 1491.

[358] For example, *De ecclesiastica potestate*, *De contradictibus* and *De pollutione nocturna* were published by Ulrich Gering, Martin Crantz and Michael Friburger in 1473–1474.

mobility and connectivity of late medieval-early modern academics, one wonders whether someone like Heynlin — a fully humanist figure, who continued his career at the Sorbonne after studying at Leipzig University (1448–1452) and after being the chancellor of the Tübingen University — should be considered a German or a French scholar. While German printers and humanists might have viewed him as their compatriot, his friend, Sorbonne colleague and distinguished humanist Guillaume Fichet (1433–1480) regarded him as a Parisian academic. In any case, it seems to have mattered very little to Heynlin himself. The same can be said about the aforementioned reformer of the College of Montaigu, Jan Standonck, who was Flemish (Brabant) by origin and lived his whole life in France (except for his last years), and even preached in French. Also, there were a number of German printers who were active in France, having been granted letters of French naturalization by Louis XI in 1475. The most famous of them, Ulrich Gering, lived and worked in Paris from 1469 and died in Paris in 1510, never returning to Germany. The cases of Heynlin (a German, with an academic degree earned abroad, who ascended to the highest office of the most prestigious French university) or of Ericus Nicolai (a Swedish novice who became the chancellor of Leipzig University) demonstrate an academic openness quite unmatched in the much more compartmentalized Europe of today. One might also think of Thomas Murner, whose German nationality did not prevent him from challenging Wimpheling's nationalistic position regarding Alsace. Indeed, although Europe was entering the age of nationalism at the end of the 15th century, the men mentioned above did not feel the need to choose their national identities once and for all as something immutable and rigid. Their examples show identities in flux, and the boundaries still fluid and permeable. One of the many factors contributing to such fluidity was the fact that European scholarly elites shared the same common language, the same university system, and the same values characterized by the dual loyalty to Christian piety and classical learning. A distinguished humanist Guillaume Tardif (1436/40–1492) formulated this program in his letter to King Charles VIII: 'now, Sir, I return to my studies of humanities and theology'.[359]

---

[359] Collard 1996, p. 57.

This program was shared by both academics and monastics, and the gate between these two worlds remained open. Thus did Heynlin, after an international academic career, in 1487 become a Carthusian monk.

In any case, the German printing monopoly did not last very long, and already by 1477 Guillaume Le Roy published Gerson's *De contractibus* in Lyons. It was followed by editions printed in Paris in 1484 by Louis Martineau and Guy Marchant, and two editions of *Donatus moralisatus* published in 1486 by Jean Bouyer in Poitiers. Other editions by Pierre Levet, Philippe Pigouchet and many other French printers, mainly in Paris, quickly ensued. During this period, the most popular of Gerson's works were *De consolatione theologiae* and the *Super magnificat* — major, complex and personal works, revealing the taste for interiority and contemplation at the Sorbonne theology department. This current also represented the return to the affective mystical traditions of Bernard and Bonaventure, which Gerson worked to revive.[360] Sorbonne's theological faculty was not the only consumer of Gerson's works, however. The College of Navarre also cherished the chancellor's memory thanks to the efforts of his younger friend Nicolas Clamanges (1360–1437), who taught there from 1425 until his death.[361]

Reform-minded Clergy and Implementation of Gerson's Pastoral Program

Gerson was neither alone nor the first in his effort to improve pastoral care. His program was part of the general, continuous and widely shared movement inspired by the Fourth Lateran Council.[362] Yet, his way of formulating this program must have been particularly attractive, as he was clearly 'très lu au début du XVIe siècle'.[363] Thus, at the end of the 15th century when humanist Guillaume Pepin (*c.* 1465–1533) sought to recover the ideal of

---

[360] See Mazour-Matusevich 2004.

[361] Ouy 1998, p. xlvii: 'On sait que, nommé en 1418 secrétaire du nouveau pape Martin V, Nicolas de Clamanges, au lieu de le suivre à Rome, choisit de s'installer à Paris occupée par les Anglais, de s'inscrire à la Faculté de Théologie et de reprendre son activité d'enseignement depuis longtemps interrompue'.

[362] Dykema 2000, p. 144.

[363] Lemaitre 2018, p. 12.

early Christian bishops, he found it in Gerson's *De statibus ecclesiastias*.[364] For the reform-minded clergymen, such as the head of College de Navarre and later reformer of Cluny monastery Jean Raulin (1443/1444–1514/1515), or his student Louis Pinelle, who succeeded to him as the bishop of Meaux, Gerson's pastoral program, concisely formulated in *Opus tripartitum*, was part of a larger body of devotional literature, aimed at improving church practices in the kingdom.[365] *Opus* or its parts, under different titles but mostly as *Instruction des curez*, appear constantly: in 1481, 1486, 1489, 1490, 1492, 1495, 1503, 1506–1510, 1512 and 1515–1518, representing the vast majority of all Gerson's publications. Pinelle promoted Gerson's *Opus tripartitum* in *Les statuts synodaux meldois* of September 18, 1511.[366] *Opus*' second part, on the art of confession, was published, under varied titles, as confession manuals in 1483, 1485, 1490, 1498, 1500, 1515, 1537–1539, 1547, 1548.[367] *Opus*' first part, the exposition of the Ten Commandments, also circulated widely under titles of *ABC des simples gens, Le miroir de l'ame* or *Ung seul Dieu*. Similar to the Germanic lands, these works were not always published in their original form, but were often given in a reduced format or as rewordings and renderings by other authors.[368] An example of a shortened version is *Compost et kalendrier des Bergers* published in 1491, 1497, 1503, 1510, 1529 et 1541, which also acquired a tune, so that children could learn it by singing.[369] Such alterations make clear identification rather difficult. It is also uncertain whether works imitating Gerson's *Opus* were direct responses to

---

[364] Piton 1966, p. 107.

[365] Amalou 2007, p. 197.

[366] Veissière 1967, p. 36: *Habeant etiam conformiter ad Mandatum praedecessoris nostris Opus tripartitum uenerabilis Cancellarii Parisiensis Domini Iohannis de Gersonno, quod nunc uulgo dicitur Instructio Curatorum, tam Latine tam Gallice.* 'They must also conform to the mandate of our predecessor, *Opus tripartitum*, by Chancellor of Paris Jean Gerson, which is now commonly called the Instruction for the Priests, both English and French'.

[367] There are 96 editions of Gerson's works (unrelated to *De Imitatione Christi*) mostly pastoral in nature, published before 1601, of which 57 are printed in Paris and eight in Lyons. Others were printed in Bordeaux, Poitiers, Nantes, Toulouse, Limoges, Rodez, Anwerpen, Vienna and Geneva (Pettegree, Walsby & Wilkinson 2011, pp. 674–76).

[368] Bossy 2002, 224–25.

[369] Bossy 2002, p. 223.

his input or were rather products of a general Zeitgeist favorable to catechization. Along with catechetical works, Gerson's *De uita spirituali animae* and *De perfectione cordis* were almost as popular, closely followed by *Regulae morales*.[370]

Gerson's pastoral program was also disseminated at local parishes through sermons (these 'assemblages', according to the expression of Hervé Martin)[371] of many genres and sources, in which famous 'popularizing' preachers Observant Dominican Jean Clérée (1450–1507) and Franciscan Michel Menot (d. 1518),[372] sometimes reproduced Gerson's hominies 'mot par mot'.[373] The case of the energetic preacher, Observant Franciscan Olivier Maillard (1430–1502), who professed to be disciple of *maistre Gerson* in his *Histoire de la Passion de Jesus-Christ*, is telling, as 'both times when Maillard claims to cite Gerson as his authority, the cited passages are inaccurate'.[374] Maillard obviously knew that simply mentioning the chancellor's name would give weight to his sermons.[375]

Gerson's pastoral impact went further than words, however. According to historians of criminal justice, the diffusion of Gerson's pastoral ideas in France produced some practical results as well. One outcome is particularly interesting, as it defies current scholarly expectations pertaining to ecclesiastical gender policies. It concerns the issue of the gendered punishment for adultery, which underwent radical change under the impact of the rarely discussed and little known Gerson's position on matrimonial matters.[376] Being 'one voice which stood out from the

---

[370] Pettegree, Walsby & Wilkinson 2011, pp. 674–76.
[371] Martin 2011.
[372] Brown 1987, p. 266, n. 95.
[373] Schmidt 1989, p. 125.
[374] Peignot 1835, p. 50 & p. 53: '[...] car maistre Jehan Gerson dict quilz le firent rebattre, revestir de pourpre et recouronner despines, et comme devant adorer mocquerie, cependant que les sergens criouent par les rues que chacun se rendist en la montagne de Calvaire'. See Carnahan 1916, pp. 144–70 & pp. 148–49.
[375] Carnahan 1916, pp. 148–49.
[376] McDougall 2014, pp. 518–19. McDougall bases her article upon various kinds of sources: 'In addition to law and legal commentary, it is based on archival research conducted in local court records, usually registers of cases or fines, records primarily from Northeastern France [...] particularly of Troyes, in North-

crowd in defense of women',[377] the chancellor's writings testify to his deep involvement with women's welfare, ranging from domestic violence, abuse, childbearing, freedom of confession, etc. to practical measures aimed at decreasing child and mother mortality, healthier nutrition, improved training of midwives, better sleeping arrangements, special cloths, lighter workloads for pregnant women, etc.[378] His opinion of men as husbands was exceptionally and consistently low. Judging from his sermons, he viewed them as main aggressors rather than protectors of the family:

> [...] le mari ne doit point empescher sa femme a bien faire [...] Doit une femme mariée obeir a son mary en quelconque chose qui soit contre Dieu? Je di que non, jusques au mourir [...] et le remede est premierement par secrete monicion. [le mari] se traitera par divers autres femmes pour le temps de ta maladie quant il ne pourra avoir compagnie charnelle avec toi. [...] Notez ceulx qui vendent leurs femmes.[379]

eastern France, and makes use of court records from neighboring regions as well' (McDougall 2014, p. 497).

[377] Prosperi 2016, pp. 56–57: 'The Chancellor of Paris was concerned to avoid adding pain to pain, and advised ecclesiastical authorities to adopt an attitude of respect and understanding towards these women, in such a way as to reunite the bonds of affection within the family. The long series of suggestions show the new sensitivity of a man of the church towards the condition of women and the problems of pregnancy and child rearing'.

[378] Gauvard & Ouy 2001, p. 51: *In tantum quod pauperes mulieres uolentes hec implere, eciam dum grauire sunt uel infirme, pereclitantur in corpore, uel eciam fetus earum moriuntur in uentre uel extra propter debiti nutrimenti defectum*. 'To the extent that these poor women want to accomplish [the fasting], even while they are pregnant or weakened, ruin their health and risk, due to lack of nourishment to abort or lose their children the womb or outside of it'. Also, Gauvard & Ouy 2001, p. 52: *Moneantur denique cauere sibi diligenter ab aliis occasionibus et negligenciis, eas particulariter ex quibus solent peruenire infancium mortes, tam in utero quam extra, ut sunt strictura uestium [...] labor nimius, ira uehemens et percussio pregnantis, et quandoque indiscrecio obstetricum*. 'Finally, be advised to protect yourself carefully because of other circumstances and neglects, in particular those which tend to lead to child mortality, both inside and outside of the womb, such as too tight clothes [...], excessive labor, and beating of pregnant women with violent rage and sometimes a midwife's carelessness'.

[379] *De la chasteté conjugale*, OC: 7: 2, pp. 860–61. 'The husband should not prevent his wife from doing good. [...] Should a married woman obey her husband in something that is against God? I say no, even to death [...] and the only remedy [to this situation] is secrecy. [...] During the time of your illness, when he is unable to have intercourse with you, the husband will have intercourse with different other women. [...] Note those who sell their wives'. Advocacy for moderation

Historians happen to corroborate with Gerson's opinion: 'A la fin du XIVe siècle, le tiers des cent vingt-quatre demandes en séparation émanant de l'officialité de Paris se réfère à la 'dureté' du mari ou aux sévices qu'il exerce'.[380] It is to counterbalance this situation that the chancellor elevates St Joseph as a model husband of a Christian household. Although he campaigned for the feast of St Joseph during the Council of Constance,[381] 'in the environment suffused with Gerson's influence',[382] his promotion of Jesus's earthly father was neither an unintentional consequence of his political priorities, nor a simple projection of his macro political ambitions on the private micro level of everyday life, as some scholars have suggested.[383] Whereas it was exceptional 'in medieval documentation to meet portraits of ideal husbands',[384] the Chancellor first addressed the question of Joseph through the prism of marriage,[385] not politics, and did so well before the Council of Constance:

> A honnourer et celebrer la desponsacion sainte et sacree de Nostre Dame la vierge Marie avec son virginal et très loyal

and mercy in regards to women's issues seems to be a rather consistent theme in Gerson's oeuvre. Thus, in *De potestate absoluendi*, he argues that *Casus carnalium lapsuum, praesertim in sexu muliebri ac puerile, qui secreti sunt, uideantur curatis dimittendi sub terrore future iudicii [...]* (OC: 9, p. 422) 'The case of carnal sin, especially in female sex and in children, when they are secret, seem to be better dismissed by bishops pending the terror of future judgment.' Ouy speaks of exceptional care and compassion that Gerson demonstrates toward women as a pastor (Gauvard & Ouy 2001, p. 45).

[380] Lett 2000, p. 177.

[381] On 17 of August 1413, Gerson wrote an open letter addressed to 'all churches and especially those dedicated to Our Lady' on the cult of St Joseph (OC: 8, pp. 61–66). For Gerson's promotion of St Joseph see Richardson 2011.

[382] Appleford 2015, p. 164.

[383] See Richardson 2011. Gerson dedicated over fifteen works, most of them poetic, to St Joseph, among them *Prosa pro honorem sancti Ioseph, Carmen de matrimonio Mariae et Ioseph, Introductio altera ad Iosephinam, Introductio ad Iosephinam, Ut festum Ioseph celebratur, In honorem sancti Ioseph, Iosephina, Carmen de sancto Ioseph, Cor Iosephina reple, Carmen de annuntiatione dominica et Ioseph, Prosa de matrimonio Mariae et Ioseph, Carmen de annuntiatione dominica et Ioseph, Carmen in honorem sancti Ioseph, Considerations sur Saint Joseph* and *Prosa super epithalamium Ioseph. Carmen de matrimonio* (OC: 4) is also about Joseph. There are also sermons *Sur la fete de St Joseph* and *Sur le culte de St Joseph*.

[384] Lett 2000 p. 169.

[385] Payan 2006, p. 147.

espous saint Joseph juste, doit estre esmeu chascun cuer devost et religieux pour les consideracions ensuians et pluseurs autres.[386]

It is only later that St Joseph, as a family and marriage model, will give way to the more global project, symbolizing recovered peace and unity. Although Gerson's major texts in favor of Saint Joseph appear after 1413,[387] 'the only moment where Gerson quite clearly evokes Joseph as a figure of the pope intervenes at the end of his sermon at Constance in 1414'.[388] Yet, it is at the turning of the century that he affirmed that husbands 'Sy doivent tous espous y prendre veneracion et exemple pour avoir telle amour, telle foy et loyaulte envers leurs espouses, et les amer, les nourrir et garder'.[389] This program was articulated not only in his scholarly writings, but also in his vernacular sermons addressed to regular parishioners.[390] Presenting Joseph in his historical role as the most faithful, vigilant, and diligent guardian and nurturer of both Mary and Christ,[391] Gerson describes him as a contemplative man of the utmost discretion, 'quiet, obedient and willing to follow God's will'.[392] One cannot imagine such a husband to be a violent and angry brute Gerson refers to in his own vernacular sermons and warns his unmarried sisters about in his treatise *Enhortant a prendre l'estat de virginité plus que de mariage*.[393]

---

[386] *Pour la feste de la desponsation de notre dame*, OC: 7: 1, p. 12.

[387] Payan 2006, p. 326.

[388] Payan 2006, p. 184.

[389] *Pour la feste de la desponsation de notre dame*, OC: 7:1, p. 12.

[390] *De la chasteté conjugale*, OC: 7: 2, p. 858: 'Toute l'évangile, en especial celle du jour dui est plaine de haulx misteres incomprenables; si ne les pouons nous mie tous savoir ou tous dire; souffise nous d'en dire aucuns. Et quant a mon present propos je regarde en ceste evangile la belle couple de mariage et le precieulx message qui estoit de Marie et de Joseph et de l'enfant Jhesus. Et me samble que mariage est ycy grandement loe et endoctrine'. Glorieux gives dates this sermon as of 1403. The question of Gerson's Mariology, which balanced his Josephology, and its impact in the 16th century, represents a topic in and of itself.

[391] *Prosa super epithalamium Ioseph*, OC: 4, p. 111: *[...] Hic [Ioseph] aderit bonum triplex cara proles, fides simplex, et sacra signatio*. 'This man [Joseph] will support a threefold good: beloved offspring, simple faith, and the sacred signing'. *Iosephina*, OC: 4, p. 44: *Exemplum tibi sint Christus, Ioseph atque Maria*. 'Example for you are Christ, Joseph and Maria'.

[392] *Considerations de Saint Joseph*, OC: 7: 1, pp. 73–74, Richardson 2011, p. 263.

[393] McGuire 1997.

The chancellor's compassionate stance toward women's situation, his critical assessment of married men's behavior and his enthusiastic advancement of the cult of St Joseph as the head of Jesus's earthly household, had a tangible impact on lives of men and women who lived in the 15th century Northern France and on Burgundian lands. Acting upon Gerson's idea that men are more unfaithful and carnal than women, church courts in Northern France, which generally claimed jurisdiction over adultery, and punished offenders, took it upon themselves to turn their attention to male marital behavior, charging men with responsibility for their own moral and sexual behavior as well as that of their wives and children.[394] Being cast as the accountable authority figure in marriage began to have legal consequences for husbands, who now were held to standards similar to those applied to clergy. This new emphasis led to the situation where judicial officers of North-Eastern French-speaking territories regularly charged men with marital infidelity, punishing them far more often than their female partners.[395] In fact, Gerson should be credited for a decisive push (*un apport*, according to Jean Delumeau's expression) toward the modification of the fatherly image, which deserves to be emphasized in *une histoire des mentalités*'.[396] Unfortunately for women, this situation did not last as the power of French royal justice took precedence over the church. With an increased supremacy of royal courts and the transfer of adultery prosecu-

---

[394] McDougall 2014. Also see Lefebvre-Teillard 1973; Donahue 2007; Daumas 2007.

[395] McDougall 2014, pp. 495–96. Also, McDougall 2014a, p. 208: 'When prosecuting illicit sex, these courts, most clearly the church court in the north-eastern French diocese of Troyes, treated laymen like clergy. Just as a priest had responsibility for his parishioners' salvation as well as his own salvation and had to live as a celibate, so too did a husband have responsibility for his wife and himself. Whether a husband committed adultery or his wife did, the blame lay with the husband'. Also see McDougall 2014a, p. 223: 'We know of the popularization of Gerson's ideas across northern France in sermons and in devotional tracts. Writers of romance at the Burgundian court appear to have adopted Gerson's ideas about marriage and the appropriate behavior of spouses. Many of the church court officials of Troyes studied theology under Gerson and his successors at the Sorbonne. What my findings indicate, then, is that court officials in northern France implemented the strict moral code for husbands preached by Gerson and his followers'.

[396] Delumeau 1983, p. 11. Jean Delumeau does not mention the major contribution of Gerson in this domain even though his name is otherwise well present in *L'aveu et le pardon*.

tion over to secular control, methods of prosecuting adultery, as well the gravity of the offense, including who should be punished for adultery and how, have not changed to women's advantage.[397]

A similar evolution took place in dealing with infanticide,[398] representing two more cases of discontinuity of Gerson's legacy in modern times. While the chancellor opposed public penance for women accused of infanticide as *enormitatem et inhumanem ac bestialem crudelitatem [...] ut quid igitur afflicto superaddatur afflictio*,[399] the transfer of infanticide cases to the royal justice led to a far less nuanced approach, with the cruelty of public penance eventually replaced by speedy trial and painful death.[400] In another interesting twist of Gerson's legacy, royal jurists claimed to base their efforts in promoting the preeminence of royal justice in France on his authority. In doing so, they disregarded Gerson's moral and pastoral teachings, which were in their way, in favor of his political theory as taught by the canon law faculty of the University of Paris. In their attack on papal power in France the new generation of later 16th century jurists sought to decrease and limit church's jurisdiction. Gerson's innovative approach to family matters and female issues was no more.

Besides pastoral theology, Gerson's early reception in France took a curious turn associated with the interpretation of the famous tapestry *La Dame à la licorne*, now at the Cluny Museum in Paris. The tapestry is made of six segments, five of which are easily identifiable with five senses: sight, smell, touch, taste and hearing. The sixth segment, entitled *Mon Seul Desire*, remained an

---

[397] Lett 2000, p. 174.

[398] Gauvard & Ouy 2001. Prosperi 2016, p. 59: 'Between the 15th and 16th centuries infanticide became an 'unspeakable' (*nefendum*) crime. If before 'there was a clear awareness of the social causes which led to the crime [...] the process of criminalizing infanticide was rapidly to take giant steps'.

[399] Gauvard & Ouy 2001, p. 51: 'enormous, inhumane and bestial cruelty' [...] 'to add further affliction to those who are already afflicted enough'. In fact, Gerson also formulates his policy on the ever-tricky question of infanticide and abortion in his treatise *De potestate absoluendi*, OC: 9, p. 422: *Casus abortuum, uel in uentre uel extra, qui ueniunt omnino praeter intentionem parentem, dimittendi sunt curatis, maxime si sunt secreti, nec proximos scandalizant [...]* 'The case of abortions, whether in the belly or outside of it, which occur completely unintentionally from the part of the parent, should be dismissed by bishops, and maximally if they are secret in order not to scandalize other people'.

[400] See Wrightson 1982; Laurent 1989.

enigma for a long time, until it was finally interpreted in the light of Gerson's concept of the heart as the sixth sense. He developed this notion in two morality plays, with almost identical sets of characters, *L'école de la conscience* and *L'école de la raison*, where the allegorized senses and 'le coeur volage' lead man astray but finally submit to God led by Reason.[401] Gerson's description of a 'feeble and unfaithful Heart' is believed to be the key to the secret of the *Mon Seul Desire*'s interpretation.[402] Interestingly, this concept of the heart does not seem to reappear until Shakespeare, 'skipping' François Villon:[403]

> But my five wits nor my five senses can
> Dissuade one foolish heart from serving thee;
> Who leaves unsway'd the likeness of a man
> Thy proud heart's slave and vassal wretch to be.[404]

Part III. Early Reception in Spain

A large number of Gerson's works was translated into Castilian already in the 15th century, and they were often reprinted, clearly evidencing his popularity in Spain.[405] For example, University of Salamanca alumnus Antonio de Baeza translated *De probatione spirituum* already in 1492.[406] Among those who absorbed Gerson's spiritual legacy and communicated it further on, Garcia Jimenes (Ximenes) de Cisneros (1455–1510) deserves special attention. The future abbot of Montserrat, a monastery located on the mountain of Montserrat west of Barcelona, Garcia de Cisneros first studied at the University of Salamanca, which was to become a center of Gersonian influence of its own right, and then in Paris. There he met leading representatives of *devotio moderna*, Standonck and

---

[401] Davenport 2011. On the subject of Gerson's morality plays see Mazour-Matuseivch, 2016.

[402] See Boudet 2007. *L'école de la raison*, OC: 7: 1, p. 106: 'Cuer tres faintifs et tres volage; a tous maulx penses et ordure; a l'escole tu fais la rage; si te donray ceste bature'.

[403] Villon 1982, p. 213: 'All my five senses — sight, sound, taste, and smell, and you too, my sense of touch'.

[404] Shakespeare, sonnet 141.

[405] Luttikhuizen 2016, p. 55.

[406] Luttikhuizen 2016, p. 62.

Mombaer, who must have sparked his interest in Gerson. Deeply impressed by their piety, Cisneros felt particular closeness with Mombaer, whose writings he studied and later introduced in Spain. Upon his return to his native land in 1500, the Spanish abbot composed, imitating both Mombaer and Gerson, his own version of *Rosetum exercitiorum spiritualium et sacrarum meditationum*, which he entitled *Exercitatorio de la vida spiritual*.

Cisneros's reception of Gerson bears similarities with that of Mombaer and *devotio moderna* in general, as he also favored pastoral and devotional aspects of Gerson's theological legacy. However, while it is generally accepted that 'Cisneros's exercises were themselves shaped by Modern Devotion',[407] his dependence on Gerson is less known. Yet, in *Exercitatorio de la vida spiritual* Cisneros directly quotes Gerson over fifty times,[408] borrowing from the treaty *De mystica theologia practica*, the evangelical harmony *Monotessaron* and, most heavily, the vernacular *The Mountain of Contemplation*, which provides the very foundation for *Ejercitatorio*. The Spaniard's decision to write in Castilian, 'in order to be accessible to simple and devoted people, with limited knowledge of spiritual matters',[409] repeats Gerson's arguments for the use of vernacular language in *The Mountain of Contemplation*.[410] *Ejercitatorio* closely follows all major themes of this treaty: the teaching describing progression toward a contemplative life — 'Porque segun dice Gerson en su Monte de contemplacion de lo imperfect á lo perfecto podemos pasar ni sùbitamente';[411] three stages of contemplation — 'Purgativa,

---

[407] Maryks 2014, p. 219. See also Rodriguez-Grahit 1957 and McGinn 2017.

[408] Tyler 2018, p. 257. Before Tyler's article, Cisneros's extensive borrowings from Gerson had been brought to attention by Fr. Watrigant in his 1897 book *La genèse des exercices de saint Ignace*. Joseph de Guibert does not mention Gerson as one of Cisneros's influences though (Guibert 1953). Terence O'Reilly comments on Cisneros's debt to Gerson only in passing (O'Reilly 1995, p. 288).

[409] Rodriguez-Grahit 1957, p. 490.

[410] *La Montagne de contemplation*, OC: 7: 1, p. 16: 'Aucuns se pourront donner merveille pourquoy, de matiere haulte comme est parler de la vie contemplative, je vueil escripre en francois plus qu'en latin et plus aux femmes que aux hommes, et que ce n'est pas matiere qui appartiengne a gens simples'.

[411] Cisneros 1857, p. 15. 'And, as Gerson truly saith, in his book called the Mount of Contemplation, we cannot go from a faulty life to a perfect one instantly (based on Cisneros 1876, p. 5).

Iluminativa y Unitiva';[412] insights on the diversity of human types and temperaments in relation to their suitability for the life of meditation,[413] the possibility and advantage of combining active and contemplative lives,[414] emphasis on the importance of finding times and places suitable for spiritual concentration,[415] and other topics. In fact, citing all Cisneros's borrowings from Gerson would necessitate quoting *The Mountain of Contemplation* practically in its entirety, as it constitutes two thirds of *Exercitatorio de la vida spiritual*. The Spanish abbot mostly sticks to *The Mountain of Cotemplation*'s textual progression, and when he diverges from it, it is in order to quote from other Gerson texts, *De mystica theologia practica* or *Monotessaron*, the latter occupying the middle section of *Exercitatorio de la vida spiritual*. Even when he appears to be citing other authorities, such as Bernard, Bonaventure or Augustine, Cisneros actually quotes Gerson's references to them:

Gerson: Dist saint Gregoire au sixiesme livre de ses Moralitez que aucunes gens sont qui de leur nature et complexion ou coustume sont enclins a ouvrer par dehors et a se occuper en choses terriennes qu'elles ne se peuvent donner ou mettre ou eslever a la vie contemplative et valent trop mieulx a l'active [...][416]

---

[412] Cisneros 1857, p. 25. OC: 7: 1, p. 26: 'Ci commence parler de l'eschelle de contemplation et de ses trois degrés qui sont humble penitence, secret lieu et silence, et forte perseverance; ainsi les met saint Bernard sus Cantiques'.

[413] Cisneros 1857, p. 227: 'ni aun á todos es dada tal grazia de vivir en la vida contemplative por ciertas causas ya asignadas' 'Neither is the grace of contemplation granted to all men, for sundry reasons' (Cisneros 1876, p. 159).

[414] Cisneros 1857, p. 223: 'pues el que pudiese tener la una vida y la otra juntamente y perfectamente, este seria major, como la tuvieron san Gregorio y san Bernardo, y otros'. 'but could a man be found able to live perfectly both kinds of life at one and the same time, like St Gregory and St Bernard, such a kind of life would be better than either' (Cisneros 1876, p. 157).

[415] Cisneros 1857, p. 217. 'Segun la diversidad de los estados y variedad de las condiciones de los hombres, puede elegir cada uno para si lugar secreto, para que allí en paz y en silencio huelgue'. 'According to the several varieties of states and conditions of men, each one may single out for himself a secret hiding-place, where he may abide in peace and silence' (Cisneros 1876, p. 152). *La Montagne de contemplation*, OC: 7: 1, p. 33: 'Comment on puet ordonner son corps en voulant contempler, et des empeschemens que ont aulcuns'.

[416] OC: 7: 1, p. 17. 'Saint Gregody says in the sixth book of his *Moralia* that some people are by their nature or complexion or custom inclined to concentrate on externals [...] They cannot give themselves over to lift themselves up to the

Cisneros: Asi como, dice san Gregorio en el sexto libro de los Morales, son algunos naturalmente ó por la complexion ó por costumbre tan inclinados á las cosas exteriors y ocupaciones terrenas, que non pueden levantarse á la contemplacion, y son hallados mucho mas habiles para la vida active.[417]

Consequently, most of *Exercitatorio* amounts to a paraphrase, as Cisneros makes use of Gerson's ideas and examples sometimes verbatim or in close rephrasing, as, for example, in two following quotes:

Gerson: On récite d'un philosophe nomme Archimendes, qui estoit grant geométrien [...] avant que la cité où il estoit fut prise; et avoit commandé le prince que on ne le tuast mie. Ung d'aventure le trouva qu'il portraioit en terre ses figures et li demanda comment on le nommoit. Il estoit si fiché en faire ses figures qu'il ne sceut que dire fors que on ne l'empeschast mie. Pour quoy il fu occis.[418]

Cisneros: Léese de un filósofo llamado Arquimedes, excelente geometrico, que deliberó imaginando hacer sutiles ingenious para batallar y defender y tomar ciudades; y como aconteciese que la ciudad donde el dicho filósofo moraba fuse [...] el principe del ejercito mandó que no fuse muerto el dicho filósofo. Y acaso como uno entrase á él y lo hallase puesto en aquellas imaginaciones, preguntóle como se llamaba; y él estando fijo é intent en sus imaginaciones no subia ni entendia lo que le preguntaba, solo hacia señal al otro no le impiedise, no respondiendo otra cosa alcuna, y por eso perdió la vida.[419]

---

contemplative life, and they are much more effective in the active life' (McGuire 1998, p. 77).

[417] Cisneros 1857, p. 199. 'Blessed Gregory says, in the sixth book of his *Morals*, that there are some men, naturally or through bodily habit or custom, so strongly inclined to exterior things and worldly employments that they cannot raise themselves up to contemplation, but are much better suited to an active life' (Cisneros 1876, p. 138).

[418] OC: 7: 1, p. 39. 'It is said of a philosopher names Archimedes that he was a great mathematician and made complex machines for warfare [...] until one day the city where he resided was captured. The prince had ordered that no one should ever kill him. Someone by chance found him drawing his models on the ground and asked him who he was. He was so caught up in making his drawings that he did not know what to say except that no one should bother him. Therefore he was killed' (McGuire 1998, p. 105).

[419] Cisneros 1857, pp. 233–34. 'There is a story about Archimedes, a skillful mathematician, that he was wont to plunge deep in thought about the contriving

The section on the spiritual climbing of the *Mountain of Contemplation* emphasizes Gerson's favorite themes of perseverance, prudence and humility:

Gerson: Pareillement, di je, qui voet venir a parfaite contemplation il ne se doibt point arrester ou reposer, car reposer est descendre ou reculer aval. Et ne doibt mie aussi tousiours recommencer dou bas, mais dont il est parti. Et pour ce deffault de ceste perseverance sont tant peu de gens qui viennent a parfaite contemplation.[420]

Cisneros: Por semejante manera, el que anhela poseer la perfeccion de la contemplacion no ha de descandar ó detenerse [...] Y asi por la ausencia de esta perceverencia son hallados tan pocos que alcancen la perfecta contemplacion.[421]

Cisneros also takes heart in the chancellor's reassuring and optimistic attitude, which strikes a balance between human effort and God's freely given grace. To people who lose heart in their spiritual enterprise and feel that they 'do wrong and fail':

> Sobre lo cual dice Gerson: Que si los tales se esfuerzan y hacen en elio lo que es en si, trabajando rn la pugna continua y batailla contra sus cogitaciones con desplacimiento [...] mayor mericimiento por entonces alcanzan, que si algunas veces les viniese la devocion súbitamente sin la tal batailla.[422]

---

of military engines for the defense and storming of fortresses; and when the city in which the philosopher lived was stormed, the besieging general gave orders that the philosopher should not be killed. It so happened that a soldier found him at his studies, and asked his name; but he, fixedly intent on his own thoughts, neither understood nor answered what was asked of him, except by a sign of dislike at being disturbed, and so lost his life' (Cisneros 1876, pp. 164–65).

[420] OC: 7: 1, p. 41. 'I say that he who wishes to come to perfect contemplation should not cease or rest. It is because of this lack of perseverance that so few people come to perfect contemplation' (McGuire 1998, p. 109).

[421] Cisneros 1857, p. 323. 'In like manner, he that desires to perfect himself in contemplation, should he have halted on his march, must never turn back [...] For want of this perseverance so few are found to reach the perfect state of contemplation' (Cisneros 1876, p. 233. This section corresponds to pages 231–45 in the given edition).

[422] Cisneros 1857, p. 335. 'To them Gerson replies that if thy work and strive to be devout, and wage a constant war against evil thoughts, being sorry [...], they will often gain more than if the grace of devotion were at once granted to them without an effort [war]' (Cisneros 1876, p. 241).

The Spanish abbot equally faithfully adheres to the chancellor's position on several interrelated pastoral issues, which assume fundamental importance for the early Jesuits: emphasis on proper confessionary practices, the problem of scrupulous conscience and the question of moral certainty. On confession, contrition and communion he advises the following:

> Despues de esto se sigue la confesion de todos los pecados de los cuales la conciencia te acusa, mayormente de los notables, los cuales todos conviene que confieses, y de los pecados no conocidos acúsate por culpable delante del sacerdote. Con estas dod cosas, esto es, contricion y confesion, lavas la conciencia de la impuridad'.[423]

This is Gerson-based description of the general confession, which is the 'form of the sacrament [when] the penitent looked back over the course of the whole life in order to uncover sinful habits and inclinations, [fostering] a higher degree of self-knowledge as well as deeper contrition'.[424]

Exercitatorio's entire chapter is dedicated to the subject of 'harassing scruples' of conscience, Gerson's preoccupation par excellence: 'Como el varon devote y contemplative no debe dejar de recibir el santo Sacramento por razon de algunos escrúpulos que algunas veces le nacen'.[425] In the absence of an absolute moral clarity, the chancellor suggested assuaging such painful doubts by allowing all moral agents to adopt an opinion that they regarded as the most reasonable in given circumstances to avoid sin.[426] This

---

[423] Cisneros 1857, pp. 267–68. 'After this, confess all the sins whereof thy conscience doth accuse thee, and chiefly thy more notable faults, all which thou shouldst confess, and acknowledge thyself before the priest guilty of such also as thou canst not call to mind. And by these two means, by contrition and confession, shalt thou wash away the uncleanness of thy conscience. confess all the sins whereof thy conscience doth accuse thee, and chiefly thy more notable faults, all which thou shouldst confess, and acknowledge thyself before the priest guilty of such also as thou canst not call to mind. And by these two means, by contrition and confession, shalt thou wash away the uncleanness of thy conscience' (Cisneros 1876, p. 192).

[424] Bireley 2018, p. 34.

[425] Cisneros 1857, p. 272.

[426] Schüssler 2011, pp. 450–52. Schüssler argues that Gerson's moral probabilism was the result of the Great Schism. See Gerson's *De praeparatione ad missam*, OC: 9, p. 37.

opinion, which came to be known as a relative or sufficient moral certainty, is clearly retaken in the following passage from Cisneros's book:

> Hay otra humana ó moral certidumbre que para nuestro propósito se require y basta, conviene á saber, cuando alguno en el propio escrutinio y examinacio de su conciencia hizo aquell que entonces su discrecio y el buen consejo de otros
>
> Juzgó deber hacer, y esto por el tiempo suficiente para esto comunmente quardado y acostumbrado. Y si entonces, segun el proprio juicio, novea hallarse en pecado mortal, seguramente y sin peligro di Nuevo pecado mortal puede llegar á la santa comunion.[427]

However, despite obvious similarities and easily demonstrable dependence, Gerson and Cisneros belong to two distinct, although interconnected, worlds of academia and monastery, with their treatises targeting different audiences. Thus, even though Cisneros copied the opening lines from *The Mountain of Contemplation*, declaring his intention to write for ordinary people 'por simple que sea, aunque sea un labrador, ó una simple vejezuela' ('however simple and unlearned they might be, even like a peasant or an ignorant countrywoman'[428]), in reality his treatise is addressed to his fellow monks:

> Por esta causa, las repetidas instancias de algunos de nuestros hermanos y no una audacia temeraria y discola, me decidió á escribir una especie de compilacion de los Ejercicios espirituates.[429]

---

[427] Cisneros 1857, p. 274. 'There is another kind of human or moral certainty which we need and is enough for our purpose, and is when a man, upon recollecting himself and looking into his own conscience, has done all that his own prudence and other man's wholesome and wise counsel lead him to think he ought to do, and has given enough time to it, such as is usually set apart for that end; and if after this he is not aware of being in mortal sin, he may then securely and without danger go to holy communion' (Cisneros 1876, pp. 196–97).

[428] Cisneros 1857, p. 183.

[429] Cisneros 1857, p. xii. 'And for this reason, at the earnest wish of some of my brethren, and not out of any rash eagerness of mine, have I been led to put together this book of ghostly exercises' (Cisneros 1876, p. 1).

When the abbot uses 'us' and 'our' he means monastic community in general, and his own monastery in particular. Therefore, the following passages, although practically identical, do not carry the same meaning:

Gerson: Or est ainsi que l'omme qui va la teste levée, c'est a savoir en grant réputation de son entendement et de sa science et qui ne se veult encliner en guise d'ung petit enfant ou d'une simple femmelette, jamais ne porroit entrer a entrée si humble, mais se blesse et retourne arriere comme aulcuns des disciples Nostre Seigneur Jhesucrist quant ilz l'oyrent preschier du sacrement de l'autel. De quoy est advenu que plusieurs grans clers ont souhaitié aucune fois qu'ilz fussent demourer en leur simplece comme leur mere sans scavoir lettres [...] [430]

Cisneros: El que anda con la cabeza alta en vanidad de su seso, conviene á saber, en gran reputacion de su entendimiento y ciencia, y menosprecia el hacerse come pequeño, nunca por aqualla puerta humilde podrá entrar, antes tropezando tornará atrás [...] lo cual asimismo ha acontecido á algunos varones muy doctimos, y pluguiera á Dios que á tanta ciencia nunca hubieran llegado, mas antes hubiesen quedado en su simplicidad, así como sus madres sin alcuna literatura.[431]

Also, while in Gerson's text great scholars themselves wish for more simplicity, in Cisneros's version, the wish is applied to them. The perspective changes from one of an insider to that of an outsider. In other words, where Gerson includes himself among scholars wishing a state of simplicity for themselves, Cisneros,

---

[430] OC: 7: 1, p. 17. 'But whoever does not enter this gate, which is quite humble and low, he is a thief and his efforts are in vain, as Jesus says. [...] if a man walks with his head erect, that is, with a great conviction of his understanding and knowledge [...] he will never be able to enter a gate so humble. Instead he will harm himself and regress [...] That is why many great scholars have wished at times that they had remained in a state of simplicity, like their mothers, without knowing Latin' (McGuire 1998, p. 76).

[431] Cisneros 1857, p. 198. 'In the emptiness of his own conceit, while he walks with uplifted head — to-wit, with a high opinion of his own understanding and of his own knowledge — and while he scorns to be humbled and become as a little child, he will never be able to pass through this lowly gate but will stumble and turn back [...] the same thing has often happened to learned men for whom it were well indeed if they had not had much learning, but had remained simple and unlearned as their own mothers were' (Cisneros 1876, p. 137).

who, unlike Gerson, was not a professional academic, but an abbot, speaks of 'those scholars' as a category of people separate and dissimilar from himself:

> Pues vemos y vimos por experiencia en los ermitaños y en algunas mujeres, que mas approvecharon en elamor de Dios por esta vida contemplative, que no lo hacen muchos grandes cléricos y religiosos segun dice Gerson, porque esta vida contemplative major se alcanza por buna y simple humilidad que por gran literature [...] [432]

Here again, like in the case of Bernhard von Waging, Gerson's theological innovation had been reversed, by redirecting his theological insights back toward professional religious milieus.

Interestingly enough, Francisco Jimenes (Ximenes) de Cisneros (1436–1517), a much more famous Cisneros, the cousin of Garcia Jimenes, 'the stern Franciscan archbishop of Toledo' [433] and confessor of Queen Isabelle, also appears to have been interested in Gerson's legacy. In his case, it concerns reformist ecclesiastical and educational policies, which the chancellor had formulated in *De potestate ecclesiastica* and in *Bonus pastor*,[434] which Francisco de Cisneros was successful in implementing. The chancellor's reform program emphasized obligatory residence of the prelates in their parishes, regular visitations and close involvement in charitable institutions, such as hospitals and shelters for the poor. It also formulated the requirement for the prelates to execute their pastoral duties in person. Influenced by Gerson's pedagogical thought, Francisco de Cisneros also published, well before Martin Luther did the same in 1529, a small catechism for children to be used in classes every day.[435]

---

[432] Cisneros 1857, p. 201. 'For we have seen, and do often see by experience, among holy hermits, and even devout women, that some make greater progress in contemplation than many learned clergymen and religious men. Gerson gives a reason for this in his Mount of Contemplation: which is, that this contemplative life is better gained by a good, simple, and humble way of living than by great learning' (Cisneros 1876, p. 140).

[433] O'Malley 2013, p. 40.

[434] Vansteenberghe 1939, pp. 39–47; Pascoe 1973; Venard 2000.

[435] O'Malley 2013, p. 41. Gerson formulated his ideas about catechization in several works, including his letter of 1 April 1400 to Pierre d'Ailley (OC: 2: p. 28): *[I]n tanta angustia temporis et inter tot animarum pericula [...] quarumdam pestilentiarum facultas medicorum composuit tractatulum ad informandum singu-*

Part IV. Early Reception in Italy

Despite the fact that Gerson lived among the Celestine monks at the end of his life, when he took refuge in Lyons after the Council of Constance (1414–1418), his works apparently never crossed the Alps to the numerous, important (and older) Italian Celestine houses.[436] However, the lower impact of Gerson's legacy in Italy can be blamed neither on geography, nor on the lack of scholarly output, since Italian production of manuscripts and later printed editions was the greatest after that of the Empire, and the intellectual exchange was not less lively than in Germany. The reasons for the smaller distribution of Gerson's works in Italy lie elsewhere: in different cultural and political sensitivities and tastes. One significant factor is the chancellor's conciliarist position, which made him undesirable in Rome. The other is the vivid rivalry between Italy's newly found glory and the established authority of medieval learning incarnated in Sorbonne University and, by association, in its most famous chancellor. Italian prestige had been built at France's expense, and early French humanists naturally resented it. French humanist Robert Gaguin (1433–1501) proudly wrote in his 1498 *Epistolae et orationes*:

> *Nostros reges, quorum non est laus inferior Cesaribus, uel in omni fortuna probatissimos homines quibus Francia non orba est, nemo in lucem tollit splendore littererarum.*[437]

Such pretensions could not be to Italian taste.[438] Already in the 14th century, Francesco Petrarch, using the Psalms verse, directly

---

los, ita fieret per facultatem uel de mandato eius aliquis tractatulus super punctis principalibus nostrae religionis, et specialiter de praeceptis, ad instructionem simplicium [...] '[I]n these constricted times, so dangerous to souls, [...] just as the schools of medicine once wrote pamphlets to instruct people how to manage in times of plague, so now it would be good if a short work were written [...] dealing with the chief points of our religion, and especially the Ten Commandments, for the sake of the simple folk' (trans. in Bast 2009, p. 2).

[436] Hobbins 2006, p. 203: 'I have not identified a single Gerson text in any Celestine house in Italy'.

[437] Gaguin 1498, 1903, p. 280. 'Our kings among whom none is praised in a manner inferior to that of [Roman] Caesars, or our men, of whom France is not depraved, who had proven themselves in every circumstance, no one can take away the light from the splendor of [our] letters'.

[438] On the subject of the relationship between Italian and French humanist traditions see Gilli 1997; Buck 1993; Billanovich & Ouy 1964.

called all non-Italians, including the French, Barbarians: *In exitu Israel de Aegypto, domus Iacob de populo barbaro*.[439] Why should the Italians listen to Barbarians, in other words to anybody other than themselves? Also, unlike German humanists of the first two generations,[440] who had remained faithful to the religious aspirations of their predecessors, which they firmly associated with the mystical humanism inherited from Gerson, their Italian counterparts had no such inclinations. In fact, they had as many reasons to distance themselves from the French scholarly tradition as Germans had to associate themselves with it. If for emerging German humanism Gerson became the vehicle of *translatio studii*, Italian humanists, who took upon themselves the role of European cultural leaders, felt that they had no need to prove their obvious superiority. Thanks to the efforts of cultural giants such as Francesco Petrarch, Coluccio Salutati (1331–1406) and Leonardo Bruni (1370–1444), they firmly believed that all *stadium* belonged to their land already: *Mundi caput est Roma [...] terrarum caput omnium Roma est*.[441] Also, while in Italy humanism was essential to the formation of the Italian cultural identity, in the Empire, in spite of the efforts of Germany's *Erzhumanist* Conrad Celtis, to establish and develop literary movements *in aemulationem Italicatum litterarum academiam illam Platonicam*,[442] 'even in its brightest days, [German] humanism never became a sweeping movement able to grasp the whole nation in its deeper conscience'.[443] Consequently, while the late medieval chancellor

---

[439] Petrarch 1581, n. 89, 1, p. 844. On Italian humanism and nationalism see Cecchetti 1966; Cecchetti 1982; Roccati 1995; Cecchetti 1992.

[440] Spitz 1996, p. 208: 'Die Nationalisierung des deutschen Humanismus setzte mit der so genannten zweiten Generation, 'the high-tide of German humanism' ein'. Hirschi 2005, p. 269: 'Ihre literarische Produktion fiel etwa in die Zeit von 1490 bis 1530'.

[441] Petrarch 1975, XI, 7, pp. 694, 6: 'Rome is the pinnacle of the universe [...] the center of the earth'.

[442] *Libri epistolarum et carminum Sodalitas litterariae ad Conradum Celten* in Bauch 1903, p. 68. Hirschi 2005, pp. 307–08: 'Das Programm, in Deutschland 'Regionalvertretungen' der neuen Building zu gründen, ging auf Celtis zurück, der von seiner Italienreise die Anregung nach Hause genommen hatte, eine platonische Akademie zu gründen. Diese 'Sodalität litteraria per Germaniam' stellte die frühe Projektion einer Gelehrtengemeinschaft dar, die eine Nation repräsentierte'.

[443] Willy 1948, p. 504.

remained exceptionally popular in German-speaking humanist sodalities of Vienna,[444] Heidelberg, Strasbourg, Augsburg or Tübingen, he hardly played any role in the Italian humanist movement. As Franz Josef Worstbrock put it, 'Konstitutiv für die Renaissanceidee ist das Vergangenheitsbild'.[445] Unlike the Italians, whose image of the past was readily available in the incontestable prestige of the ancient Roman civilization, German *Vergangenheitsbild* had to be quickly patched together, and entailed digging for 'national' roots in pre-Christian history, such as Tacitus's *Germania*, as well as 'adopting' useful cultural authorities from neighboring ethnic entities. Therefore, whereas German scholars such as Johannes Trithemius or Jacob Wimpheling Germanized and adopted Gerson in order to build their new literary and cultural identity, Italians already had, if not their national and political identity, which would take centuries to form, their status as a Europe's literary and cultural leader. Italy also enjoyed a very different reading public: increasingly sophisticated and secular, full of national pride and rather ill-disposed toward the ideas coming from across the Alps. Hence, by the end of the 15th century Italy had a very different intellectual climate and cultural priorities.

However, even though the reception of Gerson in Italy might be rather limited, it should not be discounted altogether, as it touched upon some important intellectual and artistic developments on the peninsula. His *Opus tripartitum* was known, Basel 1489 edition of his works was available in some Italian cities,[446] and his other texts were published by German printers living in Venice.[447] Not all Gerson's publishers were German though. A prolific Italian printer Simone da Lovere published *Tractatulus de remediis contra pusillanimitatem, scrupulositatem, contra deceptoria inimici consolationes et subtiles eius tentationes* in Latin in 1503 and in Italian in 1510, under the title *Gioanni Gerson de gli remedij contra la pusillanimità, scrupolosità et deceptorie consolationi et suttile tentationi del'inimico*. The attribution to Gerson of *De Imitatione Christi*, as well as the indirect reception through his

---

[444] See Bauch 1903; Hamm, 1977.
[445] Worstbrock 1972, p. 516.
[446] Toussaint 2011, p. 113.
[447] Oglaro 2012, pp. 21–34.

imitators, played a role in his continual relevance for 15th century Italian cultural history.

Antoninus of Florence

There is little doubt that Saint Antoninus of Florence (1389–1459), the leader of Dominican Observant movement and founder of the convent of San Marco, was dependent on Gerson in his views on scrupulous conscience, as expressed in his *Summa theologica moralis*.[448] Indeed, *Summa theologica*, printed in Venice in 1477, focuses on a subject of quasi obsessive preoccupation for Gerson: the problem of excessive moral scruples. According to the majority of researchers, who looked into Antoninus's treatment of this issue, it does not appear original and mostly represents a compilation of passages from Gerson, copied by the aforementioned Observant Dominican friar Johannes Nider.[449] Whether Antoninus's link to the chancellor is direct or passes through Nider is of a secondary importance, since Nider's *Consolatorium timoratae conscientiae* has been shown to be heavily reliant on Gerson's works in regards to the challenges of too scrupulous a conscience.[450] In fact, the Archbishop of Florence might have helped popularizing the term 'scrupulosity'[451] by reinforcing the association between his name and this concept. *Summa theologica* being a consistent treatment of the problem of scrupulosity condensed in one book, however large, compared with the French theologian's dealing with this question in several places, had a clear advantage, which

---

[448] See Neddermeyer 1998.

[449] Gregorová 2014, p. 35. Rudolf Schüssler calls Antoninus 'diese Kanale' through which the impulse generated by Gerson reaches early modern times (Schüssler 2006, p. 43). Sigrid Müller and Cornelia Schweiger call Anthony of Florence a 'transcriber of Nider's *Consolatorium*' (Müller & Schweiger 2013, p. 62). Paolo Astorri also maintains that 'two of the greatest Dominican moral theologians of the 15th century, Johannes Nider (1380–1438) and Antonino of Florence (1389–1459), followed Gerson's positions' (Astorri 2019, p. 43). On Nider's and Antoninus's dependence on Gerson, see Grosse 1994; Izbicki 2012; Tentler 1977.

[450] The question of Nider copying Antoninus does not come up, for not only was Nider older, but also Antoninus had begun his *Summa* two years after Nider's death (Grosse 1994, p. 161).

[451] Decock 2012.

led to Antoninus's contribution to the issue of scrupulosity overshadowing Gerson's.[452]

Antoninus refers to Gerson with approval in rules five and six of *Summa theologica moralis*. In rule number five he advises that in order to heal excessive scrupulosity, one should walk humbly in the path of obedience, conforming to the dictates of wise counselors and bending in obedience to superiors. Adopting typically Gersonian pragmatism, the Italian Archbishop suggests approaching the issue of scrupulosity by first evaluating possible external and natural causes of moral discomfort. Since causes of scruples, says Antoninus, are often physical, it falls to the spiritual director or the confessor to recommend medicine or other physical remedies that the afflicted person should faithfully follow. Yet, a prolonged and strong dependence on a spiritual adviser is neither beneficial nor normal or desirable.[453] In dealing with the psychological issue of 'black melancholy' (depression), Antoninus embraces Gerson's advice of paying no heed to painful doubts, however insistent they might be. Addressing the issue of excessive pusillanimity (anxiety) in rule sixth, Antoninus employs Gerson's metaphor, which compares fears to dogs barking and snapping at passers-by. The more one pays attention to them, the angrier they get, while the best way to avoid being bitten is to ignore them and treat them with contempt. In the same rule number six Antoninus refers to Gerson directly: 'it is a good thing, he [Gerson] says, to act frequently against foolish and fearful scruples, avoiding them in accordance with advice from others'.[454] He then adds an illustration of his own: if a piece of wood is bent and one wishes to straighten it, one must bend it back in the opposite direction.[455] The Italian thinker also explicitly refers to *cancellarius Parisiensis* when attempting to solve the moral problem of trading in interest-bearing municipal debt securities,[456] and relies, among other sources, on the 'Gersonian position' that '*dominium* and *ius* mean the same thing'.[457]

---

[452] Gregorová 2014, pp. 35–36.
[453] Rule 5, Collins 1961, pp. 10, 13 & 15–16.
[454] Rule 6, Collins 1961, pp. 26–29.
[455] Rule 6, Collins 1961, pp. 26–29.
[456] Schüssler 2006, p. 43, n. 59, citing Antoninus of Florence, *Summa theologica*, I, lib. I, cap. 11, p. 189.
[457] Tuck 1991, p. 141.

Pietro Ritta da Lucca

Pietro Ritta da Lucca (d. 1522), canon regular of St Frediano da Lucca, and the spiritual director for the famous Italian mystic Beata Elena Duglioli (1472–1520), published several treatises inspired by Gerson's works. One is *Doctrina del ben morire*, modeled after *Opus tripartitum*'s third part on the art of dying. The other is *Theologia secreta*, printed in Bologna by Giovanni Antonio de Benedictis in 1504, 1507 and 1514 and reprinted in Venice by Simone da Lovere in 1514.[458] In the latter work the Italian refers to the French theologian as 'Giovanni Gerson Cancelliere Parisiense', 'il devoto doctore' and 'el Christianissimo dottore'.[459] The third is his *Regole della vita spirituale*, where Pietro speaks of Gerson as 'devotissimo et christianissimo dottore Giovanni Gerson canciclliere parisiense'.[460] Unlike Gerson's German distribution, mainly centered on his shorter and practical writings on devotional theology, da Lucca, 'a leading popularizer of Gerson's mystical theory in Italy',[461] was interested in more systematic theological works, such as *De mystica theologia speculatiua*. The Italian mystic, who, unlike many 15th, 16th, and even later centuries authors, did not attribute *De Imitatione Christi* to Gerson, explicitly based his *Regole della vita spirituale* and *Secreta theologia* on *De meditatione cordis*, which in Italy was customarily published in concert with *De Imitatione Christi*. While da Lucca privileged *De meditatione cordis* for the edification of the *docti*, he appreciated *The Mountain of Contemplation* for the use of *simplici et idioti*.[462] In this sense, da Lucca's use of Gerson's texts corresponds to the chancellor's own twofold intention of addressing two different audiences, the learned and the unlearned, by means of two linguistic media, Latin and the vernacular.[463] Indeed, da Lucca, who saw in Gerson the central figure for the renewal of religious life, used his theological texts precisely as the chancellor intended.

---

[458] Faini 2019, p. 312.
[459] Bussi 1987, pp. 144–45.
[460] Connolly 1994, p. 123.
[461] Brann 2002, p. 42.
[462] Bussi 1987, pp. 144–45.
[463] It is important to note, however, that at the time of da Lucca, Gerson's vernacular writings were not yet published and therefore this author's knowledge of these works could only be indirect.

Da Lucca might not be the only Italian writer to appreciate Gerson's efforts to reach out to uneducated laity and even unlearned women. An unknown author of a short early 16th century treaty addressed to young women and entitled *Capiati figliola*, suggests spiritual exercises, such as reading, meditation and prayer, in accordance with capacities and spiritual readiness of practitioners, in a manner reminiscent of Gerson. The author refrains from giving advice on prayer or meditation, however, since these subjects have already been treated by 'our reverend father Dom Peter from Lucca'[464] in *Regula de la uita spirituale et secreta theologia*, reprinted in Venice in 1514 by Simone da Lovere, who also published Gerson's works.[465] The reference to da Lucca's works, themselves based on Gerson's *De meditatione cordis*, and 'certain affinities' of *Capiati figliola* with Gerson's *Tractatulus de remediis contra pusillanimitatem*, translated into Italian in 1510, deserve further investigation into the French theologian's place in Italian devotional literature.

Pietro de Lucca was also reportedly interested in Gerson's little-known musical theory, which the latter developed in the already mentioned *Tractatus de canticis*. Instead of two traditional zones customarily applied to music, secular and sacred, *Tractatus de canticis* distinguishes three: sensual/animal/secular, mental/divine/heavenly, and intermediate/rational/moral. The latter is 'the mixed song of pilgrims'[466] — the living, whose salvation has not yet been decided — balancing between hope and fear, and another expression of Gerson's predilection for the midpoint, as in his *theologia media*. While sensual and rational types of music are audible, heavenly harmonies are not. Among musical instruments only organ fully belongs to the higher, rational category.[467] Gerson's threefold division of music, copied in Pietro da Lucca's writ-

---

[464] Faini 2019, p. 312.

[465] Faini 2019, p. 312.

[466] Connolly 1994, pp. 142–43. Stanislaw Mossakowski remarks that although 'la musica è stata presentata nell'opera di Raffaello conforme alla classificazione di Gerson', Connolly's hypothesis concerning Gerson's influence on Raphael's painting of St Cecilia is not easy to confirm (Mossakowski 2004, p. 275).

[467] Irvin 1981, p. 193: 'Gerson notes that the organ is the principal instrument used in churches, joined occasionally by trumpets and very rarely by bombards, reed-pipes, or cornemuses'.

ings, might be relevant to the interpretation of Raphael's painting *The Ecstasy of St Cecilia*.[468] On this famous painting Cecilia, the patron saint of music, is so absorbed by heavenly singing of the angels (*chorus angelorum*) from above (level 1) that she can barely hold her organ, the liturgical (and 'rational') instrument par excellence, in her hands (level 2), while her feet trample upon broken 'lowly' and sensual earthly instruments customarily used for entertainment (level 3). Cecilia's facial expression, symbolizing her complete detachment from earthly cares, corresponds to Gerson's belief, expressed in *Tractatus de canticis*, that 'songs of the mouth may be heard even against one's will, so long as the ears are open; the song of the heart is not perceived directly by the senses and can only be conjectured through the face, eyes, or gestures'.[469] The chancellor also directly mentions St Cecilia as a patron saint of church music, while her silent song leads him to reflect on the difference between music in patria/heaven and in via/on earth.[470] Besides possible connection to St Cecilia, Gerson's impact in the domain of music in Italy is also traceable in Sabba da Castiglione's 1560 book *Recordi*, where the French theologian's description of an instrument named *chorus*, as a 'hollow piece of wood with two or three strings much thicker than those of a harp, which were struck by a stick',[471] still serves as a reference.

Josephology and Mariology: Bernardino di Busti

Gerson's imprint in the visual arts also concerns the appearance of the image of Jesus's earthly family, which he so energetically promoted. While the public veneration of St Joseph began in the 10th century, the Parisian chancellor, with fifteen works explicitly dedicated to the saint, can be considered the father of Josephology. He also appears to be one of the first, if not the first, to question the traditional representation of Joseph as an elderly man. Probably referring to the mystery plays of the 14th century, where the figure of St Joseph sometimes approaches a caricature, Gerson

---

[468] Hobbins 2006, p. 183.
[469] Irvin 1981, p. 195.
[470] Anttila 2013, p. 48.
[471] Gifford 2001, p. 19, n. 64.

protested against the tendency to present saint Joseph as 'viel, lait, deffectueux et febble et comme impotent au labeur et qui eust eu gregneur besoing d'estre servi que de server; si eust esté plus a la charge de Notre Dame que a son aide ou consolacion.'[472] Using biblical references and especially Luc, Gerson not only frequently referred to Joseph as *vir*,[473] but also complained about the visual art tradition wrongly depicting the saint as 'un moult veiillart homme':

> Et peut estre que pour ceste consideracion les peintres au commencement paignoient saint Joseph comme un moult veiillart homme, a la barbe flori, ja soice fust plus josne comme nous dirons cy apres et proverons.[474]

Besides physical qualities, the chancellor insisted on Joseph's historical role as the most spiritual, faithful, vigilant, and diligent guardian and nurturer of both Mary and Christ.

This approach must have quickly traveled to Italy, succeeding in imposing a new Saint Joseph's image there. It is found in the writings of Franciscan Observant friar Bernardino de Busti (*de' Busti, de Bustis, de Bustis*, da Busto, 1450–1513),[475] who fully shared Gerson's passion for the saint.[476] He incorporated Gerson's ideas about the holy family into his sermons, and transmitted the chancellor's opinion concerning Joseph's supposed nobility.[477] The chancellor's views on Joseph and his marriage with Mary, channeled by de Busti, could potentially have an impact on Michelangelo's enigmatic painting *Tondo Doni*, where Jesus's father,

---

[472] OC: 7: 1, pp. 75–76. On this subject see Payan 2006, 2008 & 2012, p. 30; and Stefaniak 2008.

[473] *Prosa super epithalamium Joseph*, OC: 4, p. 111: *[...] homo noster spiritualis, Lucas uirum te nominat, iuentutem uir terminat* [...] 'our spiritual man, Luke, calls you a man, man at the end of his youth'.

[474] OC: 7: 1, p. 72, but also OC: 5, p. 353.

[475] See, for example, Sermo XII *De desponsatione Marie* in Lemire 1971.

[476] Conti 2011, p. 26.

[477] Stefaniak 2008, pp. 38–39 & 45. Richardson 2011, p. 246: 'Sixtus IV (1479–83) issued two liturgies for Joseph. In doing so the pope permitted the wider adoption of a feast, without making it compulsory, furthering the cause through his patronage of the cult of the Virgin's wedding ring at Perugia, a relic with particular contemporary relevance for the pope as vicar of Christ, the Church's spouse'.

although not young and gray-haired, is depicted as a strong, muscular and protective figure.[478] After di Busti, St Joseph's new image found an enthusiastic promoter in the writings of professor of theology and philosophy Isidore Isolano or Isolani (1480?–1528), who, in 1522, composed the first theological synthesis of Gerson's ideas concerning Mary's earthly husband entitled *Summa de donis sanctis Ioseph*.[479] As the idea of St Joseph's intercession on 'behalf of the Church, which had obvious potential for the current Florentine political and social situation',[480] gained ground, the saint's raise in popularity brought about an array of other significant developments: the emphasis on masculinity as protective rather than aggressive, the endorsement of man's role in marriage as the benevolent and caring dominance over his wife and child, as well as profound changes in the social ideal of fatherhood 'révolutionnaire pour son temps'.[481] Theological attention to St Joseph would only increase with time.

Besides St Joseph's connection, Bernardino de Busti's writings reveal a significant presence of Gerson-inspired Mariology. 'This concerns a uniquely Gersonian linkage between the close bodily association of Mary and Christ in the Passion',[482] the accent on the perfection of Mary's compassion, resulting from their 'shared flesh' as mother and son,[483] and perception of Mary as a second Eve. For Gerson, 'instrumental in establishing the official Parisian law requiring all doctors there to teach the Immaculate Conception',[484] 'the Virgin's ability to suffer with her son meant that she was a partner in the suffering that redeemed the world',[485]

---

[478] Stefaniak 2008, p. 9, n. 23 & pp. 55–57. Paul Payan, however, does not believe that Gerson's new perception of St Joseph as a younger and vigorous man had any impact on Italian artists (Payan 2012, p. 17): 'Même si les artistes du xve siècle s'intéressent particulièrement au père terrestre du Christ en renouvelant profondément le schéma iconographique de la Nativité, ils ne tiennent aucun compte du vœu de Gerson de le représenter dans la force de l'âge. L'image de Joseph reste pour longtemps celle d'un vieillard'.

[479] Isolano 1887, 1, I, c. X.
[480] Stefaniak 2008, p. 47.
[481] Delumeau & Roche, 1990, p. 63.
[482] Ellington 2001, p. 94.
[483] Ellington 2001, p. 94.
[484] Oberman 1963, p. 284.
[485] Ellington 2001, p. 78.

and therefore Jesus's partner in redemption itself. Bernardino de Busti and Gerson were two theologians who most explicitly emphasized the connection between the sufferings of Jesus and Mary, her pain and compassion directly attesting to her powers of salvation. The Mariological connection between the Parisian master and Italian spirituality appears to persist in the next century in the Mary-related writings of the aforementioned Isidore Isolani and Saint Lawrence of Brindisi (1559–1619).[486]

Sylvestro Mazzolini

The part of Gerson's *Opus tripartitum* concerned with the art of hearing confessions also attracted interest in Italy. This topic held central importance for the chancellor who produced, besides *Opus*, some thirty tracts on confession, which were copied and recopied throughout Europe and cited as authoritative.[487] In these works he addressed the plethora of reasons and abuses that deterred people from attending confessions:

> the lack of good confessors with adequate knowledge and moral conduct; numerous reserved sins, which limited priestly power of absolution; some inner motives of a penitent, for example shame at revealing personal sins; excessive hope or hopelessness, [...] a fear of a heavy penance.[488]

Among those who found inspiration in Gerson's confessional advice was one rather unlikely adherent: a stout supporter of the primacy of popes over the councils, the Dominican inquisitor of the Congregation of Lombardy Sylvestro Mazzolini (another name Sylvester Pririas, 1456/1457–1527).[489] His 1514 theological encyclopedia for confessors, entitled *Summa Syluestrina quae summa summarum merito nuncupatur*, adopts the basic structure of Gerson's *Opus tripartitum*, greatly expanded.[490] In his manual the austere Dominican, otherwise 'scarcely ever in doubt',[491]

---

[486] Ellington 2001, p. 145.
[487] McDonnell 1993, p. 414.
[488] Popelyaskyy 2018, p. 202.
[489] On Sylvestro Mazzolini see Tavuzzi 1997.
[490] Lochrie 2012, p. 37.
[491] McDonnell 1993, p. 422.

shares Gerson's opinions on at least four major confession-related topics: absolution, qualities desirable in a confessor, excessive scrupulosity and probable moral certainty. The first concerns the practice of reserving the absolution of grave sins to the higher office of bishops. Gerson believed that this procedure needlessly restricted the power of ordinary confessors, impeded the forgiveness of sins, took consolation away from penitents, and could even lead, because of the public knowledge of the penitent's journey to a higher authority for absolution, to the breach of the secret of confession. In general, instead of being

> *Denique quid prodest et certe obest plurimum addere uerecundiam super uerecundiam, onera grauia super onera et difficultatem confitendi talia peccata super difficultatem quae tanta est ut uix credi possit.*[492]

Mazzolini endorsed the chancellor's view that delaying the confession and absolution of a spiritually suffering person is equal to committing an injustice, and argued for the abolition of this custom. As to confessor qualities, the Dominican inquisitor, otherwise known for his investment in demonology and encouragement of witch-hunt, retains Gerson's accent on the gentleness of a confessor and his consoling role,[493] arguing that excessive questioning of the confessant should be omitted, 'lest the confessor 'molest' the penitent unnecessarily',[494] or there is a good reason for suspecting negligence or willful concealment of sin. On the question of moral certainty Mazzolini quotes the French theologian almost verbatim, with the entry 'probable' directly referring to Gerson: 'Aristotle (*Topics* I) says that the probable is what seems

---

[492] *Lettre à un évêque*, Paris, avant 1408, OC: 2, p. 92. 'And so what good does it do — certainly it does great harm — to add one source of shame to another, one more heavy burden upon the burden and difficulty of confessing such sins?' (McGuire 1998, p. 241). Also, further on: *Consulendum est insuper uerecundiae et famae mulierum uel parentum, si crebro uel publice uel de longinquo ad poenitentiarios mitterentur*. 'We must take into account also the sense of modesty and concern for reputation in women or their relatives, if women frequently either publicly or from a great distance are sent to confessors' (McGuire 1998, p. 243) On the issue of reserved sins see de Boer 2000.

[493] The theme is found in Latin and in vernacular works. For example, in *Note sur la confession*: 'Que les curés et gens d'Eglise qui a ce sont ordonnez, mettent diligence a traiter doulcement tous ceux qui se confessant' (OC: 7: 1, p. 412).

[494] McDonnell 1993, p. 422.

to be to all, or most, or the wise [...] According to the Chancellor [Gerson], what is thus probable is called morally certain'.[495] In the part of the *Summa* dealing with scrupulous conscience, Pririas directly advises his readers to consult Gerson's *De preparatione ad missam*.[496] Besides moral and pastoral theology, Mazzolini's position in legal matters qualifies him as 'Gersonian', for he accepted the chancellor's theory of rights, 'modified and presented by Summenhart'.[497] He 'argued that free men were free (among other things) to enslave themselves *ad libitum* and unconditionally'.[498] Considering that *Summa Syluestrina* had an enormous impact, being reprinted forty times during the 16th century, Gerson's insights, contained within it, also carried on.

Gianfrancesco Pico della Mirandola, Girolamo Savonarola, Marsilio Ficino and Christopher Columbus

Gerson's textual presence awaits its full evaluation in the writings of some of the most prominent Italian Renaissance figures. Girolamo Savonarola (1452–1498), Florentine preacher known for his *terrifica praedicatio*,[499] quoted the chancellor in his sermons, customarily referring to him as *doctor christianissimus*. He evoked Gerson when criticizing various Church abuses, such as simony, and appealed to his authority for self-defense in a manner similar to Wessel Gansfort. One instance of such a defense is Savonarola's letter of June 1497, addressed to Pope Alexander VI, and entitled *Against the Recently Imposed Sentence of Excommunication*. The fiery preacher draws on Gerson's treaty *Resolutio circa materiam excommunicationum et irregularitatum*:[500]

> I am not bound even in public to observe it [excommunication], nor can anyone be scandalized, unless he would obstinately profess himself a Pharisee. This can be even better

---

[495] Franklin 2001, p. 71.
[496] Tutino 2018, p. 13.
[497] Tuck 1979, p. 29. On legal aspects of Gerson's influence on Mazzolini also see Tierney 1997.
[498] Tuck 1979, p. 49, citing Mazzolini 1539, p. 256[v].
[499] Hamm 2018, p. 325.
[500] OC: 6, pp. 294–96.

understood in the words of Jean Gerson, a very learned and religious man, who is acclaimed as a most Christian doctor by the Parisians [...] Otherwise prelates would be able to introduce whatever servitude they might wish on others, if obedience is always owed to their unjust and erroneous judgments. [...] Behold how well to our purpose Jean Gerson speaks! To believe, therefore, that all censures ought to be observed proceeds from ignorance, which is especially inappropriate and injurious in priests and religious who have undertaken the office of reading and teaching in public.[501]

Savonarola's conciliar sympathies, which are evident from his letters to the King of France, the Emperor and the King and Queen of Spain, might be yet another connection between him and the Parisian theologian.[502] It remains to be seen whether Savonarola's sermon on the art of dying well, delivered on November 2, 1496, might, to some degree, have been influenced by Gerson's widely known *ars moriendi*. It is not very likely, however, for Savonarola's spirit in this work is quite different from Gerson's. Hardly a work of consolation, Savonarola's piece insists on the use of explicit terrifying images in order to make the reality of death more vivid, and pressure the dying person to repent.[503]

Another famous Italian, whose familiarity with Gerson might be quite extensive, was the famous Renaissance Neoplatonic philosopher Marsilio Ficino (1433–1499). Although more data is needed to elucidate this 'fresh new source for Ficinian studies',[504] the Italian thinker likely read at least one Gerson's treatise, *Sermo de sancto spiritu*, also known as *Spiritus domini repleuit orbem terrarum*, found in one of the three Gerson's editions available in Florence at the time.[505] Some of Ficino's images might have origi-

---

[501] Savonarola 2008, p. 304.
[502] Meier 1836.
[503] Terence 1967, p. 5.
[504] Cave 2011, p. 113.
[505] According to Toussaint, Ficino used the Basel 1489 edition of Gerson's works. According to Noel Brann, Savonarola's disciple and follower, Italian philosopher Gianfrancesco Pico della Mirandola (1470–1533), used the Parisian chancellor's descriptions of what we would currently qualify as mental illnesses in his book *De imaginatione* (1501). One of these illnesses, traditionally called the 'melancholy', is now commonly understood as depression, and the other — the person's complete absorption into perceptual fantasies leading to his or her

nated from Gerson. The first image, from a passage of Marsilio Ficino's *Theologia Platonica*, is that of a pilgrim, which the chancellor used as a personal emblem and even identity: 'Since man's mind is never at rest, his body is frail and he is totally without resources, the life he leads on earth is harsher than that of the beasts.'[506] This figure gained general popularity at the end of the 15th century, and appeared in different works of art, from woodcuts attributed to Dürer to paintings by Hieronymus Bosch. Another is Ficino's metaphor of human soul as the double-faced head placed on the horizon, which was employed by Gerson more than half a century earlier in his sermon *A Deo exiuit*. The two-faced figure placed on the horizon is a visual metaphor of the soul divided between two separate worlds, human and divine.[507] The third is Gerson's comparison, found in the same sermon *A Deo exiuit*, of human soul's attachment to these two worlds as two chains, one silver and one gold, which Ficino takes up in a passage in his *Commentary to the Divine Names* of the Pseudo-Dionysius the Areopagite:[508]

> *Ceterum anima humana praecipue illa est inter omnes rationales spiritus que non solum regredi ad Deum sed omnia alia in eum referre debet. Propterea enim ipsa corpori cuniuncta est et neruis certis ligata secundum Platonicos; propterea nexum duplicis mundi tam spiritualis quam corporalis operatur, quasi duas illas catenas causarum, auream et argenteam, nectens. Deinde in horizonte duplicis mundi statuitur facies sua, prout diuini theologi et eleuati metaphysici docuerunt, quatenus per ipsam ea omnia referrentur in Deum, cognoscendo et utendo quae ab eo egressa sunt in creando.*[509]

---

inability of controlling imagination — identified by modern psychology as Fantasy Prone Personality (FPP). Brann 2002, p. 185.

[506] Ficino 2001, I, 1, p. 15.

[507] Poncet 2010, p. 264, citing Ficino 1990, 1, p. 186: *Anima rationalis, quemadmodum omnes ibi conuenimus, in orizonte, id est in confinio eternitatis et temporis posita est [...]* On Ficino's reception of Gerson see Toussaint 1999 and Kristeller 2005, pp. 426–37.

[508] Poncet 2010, p. 265.

[509] *A Deo exiuit*, OC: 5, pp. 14–15: 'Finally, the human soul in particular is, among all rational spirits, the one who not only returns to God, but has to bring all other things to Him. Because of this, in fact, it is conjoined with the body, and, according to the Platonists, is attached to it by solid chains. Because of this, it forms the bond of the double world, spiritual as well as bodily, as if it knotted these two chains of causes, one gold and one silver. Then her face is placed

As in Gerson, Ficino soul's attachment to two worlds is not just bondage, but also a connection through which these worlds communicate and unite:

> But between the things that are purely eternal and those that are purely temporal is soul, a bond as it were linking the two. Even more must we postulate such bondage of parts in God's universal work, in order for the one God's work to be one too.[510]

Christopher Columbus (1436–1506), who was mainly interested in astrology and divination,[511] read a compilation of works by Pierre d'Ailly and Jean Gerson in the Louvain edition of *Ymago mundi*, published by John of Westphalia in 1480 or 1483.[512] Columbus's copy of *Ymago mundi*, which contains sixteen texts by d'Ailly and five by Gerson,[513] is preserved and displays Columbus's 898 annotations. According to Bartholomé de Las Casas's commentaries on Christopher Columbus:

> The first of three (Columbus's) authorities of a more recent date is Cardinal Pierre d'Ailly, a man of our era most learned in philosophy, astrology and cosmography, chancellor of the University of Paris, the teacher of Jean Gerson who, according to Jan Trithemius in his *De scriptoribus ecclesiasticis*, attended

---

on the horizon of the double world, as taught by the divine theologians and the high metaphysicians, because thanks to her, through knowledge and application, all things that come from Him through Creation are brought back to God'. The metaphor of the chain is also found in *The Mountain of Contemplation*: OC: 7: 1, p. 22: 'C'est comme mortier tenant qui tient les piés de l'ame tellement qu'elle ne s'en puisse franchement départir; et est comme une chayne qui tient l'ame enlassée et atachiée au corps qu'elle ne puet soi esloigner de lui, en figure d'un ours ou d'un singe qui tourne et va environ l'estaige ou il est lié sans passer oultre'. 'Or it is like a chain that keeps the soul tied up and connected to the body so that it cannot get any distance from it, like a bear or a monkey that [...] is tied' (McGuire 1998, p. 83). Neoplatonic elements in Gerson's thought are surely not limited to these instances. For example, the Neoplatonic origin of the idea of participation in the divine transpires in *De consolatione theologiae*: *[...] nam participatione diuinitatis dii fiunt*; 'through participation in the divine, they are made gods' (*De consolatione theologiae*, OC: 9, p. 225).

[510] Ficino 2001, 1, 3, pp. 233–35.

[511] Smoller 2017, pp. 3–4; Flint 1992, p. 45.

[512] Johannes of Westphalia also published *De Imitatione Christi*, attributed to Gerson, in the years 1484–1487. Barbier 2011, p. 37.

[513] Grant 1974, 1, p. 630. This edition was entirely translated into French in d'Ailly 1930.

the Council of Constance around the year 1416, [...] and I believe that d'Ailly was the most influential single authority in persuading Christopher Columbus to do what he did: he had read his work so often that the margins of it were, from beginning to end, covered in annotations and glosses in his own hand in Latin.[514]

Besides *Ymago mundi* Columbus was familiar with Gerson's *De sensu litterali Sacrae Scripturae*, which he found useful for naming new geographic locations.[515] He cites this treaty in his *Libro de las profecias*, written in Granada in 1502, where he borrows from Gerson four ways of interpreting Holy Scriptures — literal, allegorical, moral and anagogical (symbolic) — when choosing a geographical name.[516]

When talking about the reception of Gerson in Italy, it is impossible not to mention the consistent attribution to him of *De Imitatione Christi*. The very first Italian edition of *De Imitatione*, published in Venice by a German publisher Peter Löslein and attributed to Gerson, dates from 1483.[517] Different religious orders appear to have their own preferences in this matter. Benedictines favored Gerson. Augustinians privileged Kempis.[518] Another feature awaiting explanation is the fact that Italian sources frequently, almost always, included Gerson's *De meditatione cordis* alongside *De Imitatione Christi*, both under the chancellor's name. This combination is not necessarily unusual and is observable, although to a lesser degree, in similar editions published in France and in the Empire.[519] Some late 15th century Gerson editions also combined *De Imitatione Christi* with *De con-*

---

[514] Las Casas 1999, p. 32.

[515] Guzuskyte 2014, p. 40.

[516] *De sensu litterali Sacrae Scripturae*, OC: 3, pp. 333–40.

[517] Oglaro 2012, pp. 21–34. Habsburg 2002, p. 258: 'While it is difficult to determine precise geographical trends for the attributions of authorship, Kempis' name appeared more frequently in the German-speaking lands and in the Low Countries, while Gerson was more prominent in Spain, France and Italy'. Frédéric Barbier in confirms this observation: 'attribution à Gerson [...] dans nombre d'éditions imprimées [...] surtout en Italie, en France et en Espagne — de sorte que l'attribution à Thomas à Kempis semble être alors moins fréquente' (Barbier 2011, p. 47).

[518] Habsburg 2011, p. 3.

[519] Nuremberg, 1493; Paris 1498; Ulm 1487; Strasburg 1498.

temptu omnium uanitatum mundi.[520] What appears to be rather clear is that the ascription of *De Imitatione* to Gerson signals that his spirituality, carefully tuned to appeal to lay ears, seems to have struck a particularly resonant chord mostly within the Italian monastic milieu.

Indeed, the reception of Gerson in Italy seems to be significantly stronger among monastics, especially among Observant friars, while universities and humanist circles remained far less receptive to his thought. While secular Renaissance humanists had very little use for a 'barbarian' thinker representing a rival culture, monastic milieu, less susceptible to Renaissance arrogance, remained more faithful to the medieval spiritual heritage, and consequently more open to and interested in Gerson's legacy. His better reception among Italian monastics also seems to be related to his popularity within the Franciscan Order, whose social orientation and pastoral goals coincided with his. The Observant movement (Latin *obseruantia*), which was a very energetic part of the *reforma perpetua* phenomenon, channeled itself toward improvements not only within the monastic orders, but also in the society at large by means of invigorated public preaching, seeking, like Gerson, to reach out to more democratic layers of a society. Finally, Gerson's staunch defense of Mary's immaculate conception might be another trait that he and Franciscans had in common.[521]

Part V. Early Reception in Sweden

Gerson's glory reached even the Northern Germanic tip of Europe, in Sweden. Already in the early 15th century the convent of Vadstena held several of Gerson's writings, possibly brought from the Council of Constance by Thorer Andersson.[522] The first book ever printed in Swedish was none other than Gerson's *Traité des diverses tentations de l'ennemi* (*Tractatus de diuersis diaboli temptationibus* or *Aff dyaffwulens frastilse*).[523] This by itself

---

[520] Cancellieri 1809, p. 301.
[521] Lesnick 1989, pp. 134–35 & pp. 162–63.
[522] Härdelin 2009, p. 278.
[523] Warme 1996, p. 57. Also see Mornet 1995.

constitutes a national event. In Sweden this book is preserved in a unique copy at the Uppsala University Library and is considered a philological monument. Its first leaf is missing and is replaced with a colored copy of a woodcut depicting the Last Judgment. The title, *Mester Johans Gerson Bok Aff dyäffwlsens frästilse*, is followed by a short explanation: 'The work thus given in Swedish is one of the many treatises written in Latin by the famous Johannes Gerson, the pious and learned Chancellor of the University of Paris, who died in 1429'. The work's status as the first and only book printed in Swedish before 1500 gives Gerson an extraordinary place of honor in the country's history. The first book was followed by the second, which was nothing other than the Swedish translation of Gerson's *ars moriendi*. Both translations were completed by the Leipzig University alumnus and professor Ericus Nicolai (1485–1489). This is not surprising as Leipzig University, which received a strong current of Swedish students, had long become the channel through which Gerson's popularity reached this country. According to the Leipzig university register, Ericus matriculated at Leipzig, with pauses, from 1466 to 1489, under different names of Doctor Ericus from Upsalia, Ericus the Swede or Doctor Ericus Nicolai. After a distinguished academic career in Leipzig, where he was promoted to a rector, he returned, in 1488, to his native Sweden and became Uppsala's first known Doctor of Theology. It was Uppsala's Archbishop and the founder of Uppsala University Jacob Ulfsson (d. 1521), characterized by the Swedish researcher Gösta Kellerman as a Gersonian, who asked Ericus Nicolai to translate *Tractatus de diuersis diaboli temptationibus* and *Ars moriendi* into Swedish. Ulfsson's choice of the third part of *Opus tripartitum* is hardly surprising. The future archbishop completed his master degree in Paris in 1460, and was likely attracted to Gerson's theology already while being a student at the chancellor's alma mater.[524] Also, *Opus*' third part, known in Swedish as *tröstebok* (the book of consolation), was popular in Sweden even before Nicolai's translation. It already existed in two earlier Swedish manuscript translations,

---

[524] Kellerman 1953, p. 212: 'Jacob Ulfsson was interested in Paris theologian Gerson (d. 1429), who represented pastoral theology with a strong emphasis on practical piety. Kellerman characterizes the Archbishop's views as a Gersonian type nominalism'.

with which archbishop Ulfsson must have been dissatisfied. Why, out of all of Gerson's works, Ulfsson was attracted to the treaty on the temptations of the devil, is an interesting question. Whatever it might be, Nicolai completed the translation of this treaty before 1493, and Johannes Smedh printed it in Stockholm in 1495. *Ars moriendi* was published in Uppsala on October 19, 1514, under the title *Lärdom huru man skall dö*, and it is preserved in Sweden in five original copies. What happened to Gerson's legacy in Sweden later on is hardly known, and his 'Scandinavian passage' still awaits its historians.[525]

Conclusion

Multiple case studies of the 15th century receptions of Gerson reveal that his influence traversed it uninterrupted, progressively making its way into different lands and cultural spheres of Europe. Absorption and reworking of his ideas reflected motivations and personalities of those who appealed to them, and varied from candid emulation, verging on worship, as with Johannes Geiler von Kaysersberg or Garcia Jimenes de Cisneros, to the adoration mixed with political opportunism and cultural agendas, as in the cases of Jacob Wimpheling and Johannes Trithemius, to the commonality of interests as with Bernardino di Busti and Gabriel Biel and even self-defense as in the cases of Wessel Gansfort or Savonarola. His reception reveals some consistencies as well as differences from region to region, depending on the local situation. Spiritual needs of the late medieval clergy and of the growing numbers of the secular educated public determined the demand for certain recurring themes and particular writings. Amid consistencies are clerical receptivity to Gerson's pastoral innovations, and both clerical and lay responsiveness to his mystical theology, understood as affective and even affectionate spirituality. Clearly, it was not Gerson's speculative interest in mystical theology,[526]

---

[525] See Isnardi 2015.

[526] Vial 2006, p. 33: 'l'intérêt de Gerson pour la théologie mystique a été primordialement un intérêt spéculative'. By 'spéculative' Marc Vial means that when Gerson approaches the problem of mystical theology, even when he calls it *practica*, he bases his arguments on the text and not on personal supernatural experience, which he apparently never had (Vial 2006, pp. 34–38).

with some notable exceptions of Nicolas of Cusa, Gabriel Biel or Pietro da Lucca, that made him attractive to the majority of his 15th century admirers. Between what Marc Vial describes as Gerson's double contemplation, intellectual and affective,[527] it is no doubt the second that found more followers after his death. Not the least important explanation for this is the intent that the chancellor himself attached to his interpretation of affective theology: he wanted to open contemplative life to larger audiences, and he was heard. His suggestion of the possibility of a mutually beneficial balance between active and contemplative lives,[528] and his observation that one can love God while living an active life just as much as those who chose the cloister',[529] endeared to him many pious souls among both active clergy and laity. If his pastoral teachings were 'what a fair number of the laity, in France and Germany at least, were hearing and reading in the fifteenth and early sixteenth centuries',[530] while in Italy and Spain his reception was mostly limited to monastic milieus,[531] his reputation as a mystical author constituted one of the major draws for his 15th century readership both in and outside of monasteries. Such was the case of Benedictines at Melk, Carthusians at Gaming, *devotio moderna*, Bernardino di Busti and Garcia de Cisneros. Gerson's main treatise on affective theology, *De mystica theologia practica*, was appreciated by monks Bernhard von Waging and Garcia de Cisneros, modern devotee Johannes Mombaer, and an intellectual cardinal Nicolas of Cusa, while his highly personal *De consolatione theologiae* inspired Johannes Nider and Nicolas Kempf. Evangelical harmony *Monotessaron*, which, after *Opus tripartitum*, *De mystica theologia practica*, *De mystica theologia speculatiua* and *The Mountain of Contemplation*, emerges as one of the most

---

[527] Vial 2006, p. 42.
[528] McGuire 1998, p. 99. *La Montagne de contemplation*, OC: 7: 1, p. 17.
[529] *La Montagne de contemplation*, OC: 7: 1, p. 22: 'Vrai est qu'aucune personne puet aucune fois plus amer Dieu en sa vie active que ne fait l'autre en sa vie contemplative'.
[530] Brown 1987, pp. 1–2.
[531] Giraud 2016, p. 255: 'En effet, alors qu'en Italie les traductions sont destinées avant tout aux religieux et aux religieuses illettrés, en France, elles ambitionnent de toucher le plus vaste public [...] en raison d'une innocuité doctrinale dont Gerson se fit le chantre'.

popular of Gerson's works, will assume primary importance in the 16th century.

The double attraction of Gerson's pastoral and contemplative legacies in the long 15th century is evidenced by the pan-European popularity of two of his texts: *Opus tripartitum* and its parts and *The Mountain of Contemplation*. *Opus*' reception was quasi universal, in the Empire, France, Italy and even Sweden, in monasteries and among modern devotees, and attracted all categories of clerics: monastics like Bernhard von Waging and Sylvestro Mazzolini, canon regular like Pietro Ritta da Lucca and secular preachers like Geiler von Kaysersberg. In Sweden and in France Gerson's early reception is narrowly associated with the adoption of *Opus tripartitum* by the reform-minded clergy in order to promote changes not only within the Church, but also among the laity. This tendency, embraced by a growing number of French prelates, would significantly increase in the 16th century, determining Gerson's special place in the history of the Catholic reformation. Yet, some progressive aspects of his pastoral approach, such as the handling of marital matters and women-related issues, would be lost in the coming century, attesting to both continuity and discontinuity of his legacy in France. His ideal of 'la vie mixte', combining contemplative and active lives, will find its truest appreciation among the Jesuits.

The Mountain of Contemplation's user-friendly exposé of affective theology held fundamental importance for *devotio moderna* and for theologians influenced by it, such as Wessel Gansfort and Garcia Jimenes de Cisneros. Yet, the same people who relied on *Opus* could also appreciate *The Mountain of Contemplation*, as was the case for Pietro da Lucca or Geiler von Kaysersberg. An example of two sisters of a renowned humanist and Albrecht Dürer's friend, Willibald Pirckheimer (1470–1530),[532] Caritas (1466–1532) and Euphemia (1486–1547) Pirckheimer, illustrates the interest for both pastoral and mystical contributions of the Parisian chancellor among female monastics. Euphemia, the abbess of a Bavarian Benedictine house of the Holy Cross at Bergen in Neuburg an der Donau, held and worked with an edition

---

[532] Willibald Pirckheimer was a member of Nuremberg's humanist sodality. Suspected of Lutheran sympathies, he was later placed on the papal bull of 1520.

of a wide-ranging collection of prayers and meditations entitled *Liber specialis gratiae*, which contains *Opus* under the commonly used title the *Tres ueritates Gersonis*, both in German and in Latin. Her sister Caritas, abbess of St Clara convent in Nuremberg and a prominent humanist in her own right, referred to *The Mountain of Contemplation* in her bilingual letter to the founder of the Heidelberg sodality, the already mentioned poet Conrad Celtis, on April 25, 1502, as she defined the essence of mystical theology:

> *Humilis itaque oboedientia excuset, quaso, errorum [...] quia ut Iohannes Gerson doctor Pariensis testatur, mystica theologia nihil aliud est nisi ars amoris uel charitatis ut scientia Deum amandi [...]*

> 'als doctor Johann Gerson von Paris bezeugt, die heimlikeyt der heiligen geschrift ist anders nichts, dann ein kunst der lieb, oder ein wissenhait got zu lieben'.[533]

Thus, German-speaking people in the 15th century were comforted [tröstet] by Gerson's major theological opus *De consolatione theologiae* much less than by his 'kleine Traktaten'.[534]

With reference to geographical variations in the 15th century reception of Gerson, Germanic passage definitely holds a special place both from quantitative and qualitative points of view. Although German 'did not develop any genuine ideal of piety but took over its ideas from a variety of sources — German mysticism, the *devotio moderna*, and the reform theology of Jean Gerson who was universally revered',[535] it constructed the post-mortem legend of the French theologian's role in *rerum germanicarum*, which was to play such a major role in his later reception by the Lutherans. The story of the chancellor of the University of Paris, who, persecuted at home, finds a warm welcome among pious German men of learning, was reiterated from edition to edition, until Gerson's biographer Brian McGuire, who himself previously retold

---

[533] 'Thus, humble obedience excuses of errors [...] as Johannes Gerson, the Parisian doctor bears witness, mystical theology is nothing other than the ability of love or charity aimed at loving God'. Rupprich 1934, p. 488 & p. 493.

[534] Hohenadel 2015, p. 51.

[535] Volkmar 2018, p. 91.

it,[536] came to the conclusion that there might not even be enough historical evidence to support the moving tale about the supposed encounter between the exiled chancellor and the Austrian prince.[537] However, whether it is true or not might be of a lesser importance than the sheer fact of the appearance of the 'Austrian anecdote' in Gerson's official biographies. In a sense, it would have been even more significant if the whole story of Gerson's invitation to Vienna were fictional. Indeed, the German flavor in Gerson's legend has a profound meaning even if historical facts do not sufficiently corroborate with the Northern humanists' claim on the chancellor. Regardless of whether the Austrian episode took place in reality or not, the trajectory of his legend definitely corresponds to the path of Gerson's legacy in the 15th century. It tells us that at this particular moment German humanists needed this legend, and whether history helped them or they helped history is of secondary importance. Wimpheling's and Trithemius's enthusiasm for Gerson was powered by their frustration of being left out of the Renaissance prestige, and by their nascent national pride and patriotism, which in German context meant something quite different from what it meant in Italy. Indeed, while in Italy *patria* meant, in the vast majority of cases, a city and its adjoint territories,[538] the very size of the Empire and its loose organization predisposed nationalistically leaning German humanists toward creation of mental abstractions such as 'Deutschland'. Indeed, the tale of Gerson's 'asylum in German-speaking parts of Europe'[539] stresses a unique and original bond between the banished chancellor of the University of Paris and the welcoming Germanic lands, while his sojourn at Melk becomes the point of *translatio studii* from Paris, the capital of medieval learning, to a new, fertile and eager to excel humanist environment of Vienna, and, consequently, of 'Germany' as a whole. Pious Gerson and his story provided a perfect occasion for the German humanists to assert their presence in Europe since they, or 'Eastern Franks', as Trithemius

---

[536] McGuire 1998, p. 20.
[537] McGuire 2005, p. 288.
[538] Hirschi 2005, p. 109.
[539] McGuire 1998, p. 20.

preferred to be called,[540] knew how to appreciate *christianissimus doctor diuus*,[541] because they were both learned and pious men themselves. This is particularly important considering the German humanists' strong and contradictory feelings toward Italy, which combined painfully resented cultural inferiority with combative rivalry and moral condemnation of the corruption and supposed paganization perpetrated by their Italian counterparts. These complex feelings found expression in literary productions. Conrad Celtis in his 1494 *Ode to Trithemius* praised abbot Trithemius for the revival of 'our German nation [...] so that it might resurge and become the full equal of the Italian and Gallic genius',[542] while the same Arnold Bostius of Gent who considered Gerson a saint 'placed Celtis in the ranks of Virgil as well as of Cicero'.[543] The combination of the German humanists' claim to the monopoly in Christian piety with the resentment against Rome's cultural dominance, portrayed as 'an Italian instrument for the plundering of Germany and the satisfaction of Italian money',[544] provides context for Gerson's adoption by German intellectuals. The chancellor's pious reputation and his conciliarist position made him a perfect candidate for German 'Emanzipation vom italienischen Barbarenverdict',[545] which would soon take the form of Lutheran revolt against Rome.

In their strategy, German humanists reproduced the typical pattern of an emerging nation hastily securing for itself a place of

---

[540] Brann 1981, p. 237.
[541] Lyons chapter, 1504, OC: 1, p. 147. *Ibid*: *Vidimus et legimus quod diui Ioannis Gerson doctrinam solidam, omni statui consentaneam, affectu maximo complectimini, in eaque hactenus legenda sancta uoluptate tenemini, dignissimi et optimi antistitis et qui de litteraria doctoris sancti sapientia bene sentiat, officium habetis. Est profecto eius doctrina sana, clara, salubris et deuota; et inter ceteras ad pellendos animi morbos aptissima usque adeo iam christianissimus doctor diuus Gerson passim nominetur.* 'We have seen and read that you embraced with greatest affection the firm teaching, suited for any state of life, of the saintly Gerson. You have until now been bound to him in the enjoyment of his holy legend. You have the office of the most worthy and outstanding bishop, you who think so highly of the learned wisdom of the holy doctor. Certainly, his doctrine is healthy, clear, salutary and devout; amid other matters the saintly Gerson is commonly named, until now, as a most Christian doctor for purging illnesses of the spirit'.
[542] Brann 1981, p. 242.
[543] Brann 1981, p. 244.
[544] Hirschi 2005, p. 249.
[545] Hirschi 2005, p. 302.

honor among its more established neighbors, and thus looking for historical legitimacy. This pattern usually involves four main stages. First, the newcomer needs a solid genealogy in order to prove its 'noble' origin, be it great legendary ancestors, heroes or/and gods, an ancient center of learning, mythical source and so forth. Second, it needs a special, privileged connection with this ancient authority. At the third stage the now more confident candidate for greatness must acquire certain independence from the authority, which it had only recently sought out for its support. Finally, upon attaining a certain level of acceptance, the full detachment from the established authority is required, the process, which is often accompanied by a more or less sharp criticism of the very power on which the former newcomer initially depended.[546] German humanism quickly moved through these stages, progressing from humble 'pupils and admirers'[547] of their Italian and French masters to self-assured and contentious patriots proud of their newly found ancestry and achievements. Thus, Trithemius went so far as to proclaim that 'at least one line of German princes can locate its origin in pre-Trojan history.[548] Gerson's initial popularity in German lands may be associated with the first and second stages of the above-mentioned process, while the third and fourth stages became complete with Luther's reformation.

Gerson's exceptional reception in the Empire resulted not only in the presence of his works in university and grammar schools' curricula and his impact on pastoral care, but also in his rise into the status of 'a must have' author among the literate public. By the end of the 15th century educated city dwellers in the Empire typically read and owned the Bible, texts by Geiler von Kaysersberg, German mystic Johannes Tauler, and Gerson.[549] For example, the personal library of Johannes Roth (1426–1506), dean of the cathedral in Passau (1460–1466), and then in Wroclaw

---

[546] Trotsky 1965, p. 24: 'A backward country assimilates the material and intellectual conquests of the advanced countries. The backward nation, moreover, not infrequently debases the achievements borrowed from outside in the process of adapting them to its own [...] culture. In this the very process of assimilation acquires a self-contradictory character'.
[547] Kristeller 1962, p. 87.
[548] Brann 1981, pp. 240–41.
[549] Smolinsky 2005, p. 300.

(until 1468), bishop of Lavant and then an emissary to Rome and Venice, included the Bible, collection of homilies and theological works by only three authors: Augustine, Gregory the Great and, of course, Gerson.[550]

Even though Gerson's 15th century reception was truly exceptional in Germanic Europe, its span was pan-European. Shaping 'catechetical instruction throughout Europe in the fifteenth century', his treatment of the Ten Commandments 'was printed twenty-three times in five languages before 1500'.[551] His use of the vernacular in spiritual matters, as well as pedagogical, psychological and consolatory dimensions in his pastoral theology attracted representatives of the Europe-wide movement of devotional theology, which found expressed in *devotio moderna*, the Vienna school of *Trosttheologie* (consolatory theology), Carthusian monasticism, various humanist sodalities in the Empire, and was taken over by French, Italian, Spanish and Swedish reform-driven clergy. 'A wave of devotional literature [...] swept over the Continent and united Europe spiritually as it had never been [...] For his role in fostering and disseminating that devotion, Jean Gerson was recognized as the father of the Church'.[552]

Finally, summarizing the 15th century the reception of Gerson, one word, which also expresses his very 'way of life',[553] emerges as the best characteristic of this period in European history, and this word is conversation. The degree of connectivity, the vividness of intellectual exchanges and the boiling energy of the 15th century scholars are truly astonishing. Despite their often-nomadic way of life, continuous plague epidemics and a relatively short (although

---

[550] Bott 1983, p. 116.

[551] Hobbins 2006, p. 148. The *Catalogue of Books Printed in the German-speaking countries and German books printed in other countries, 1455–1600*, 1962, lists the following editions of Gerson-related books (by him, attributed to him and about him): *Donates ethimoloyzatus or moralisatus* 1470, 1472, 1475, 1475, 1477, 1485, 1486; 1488, 1498; *Modus uiuendi omnium Christi fideliu*, 1510; *Monotessaron*, 1510; *Ars moriendi*, 1468, 1470, 1475, 1480, 1482; *Sermo de passione in latinum traductus*, 1509, 1510, 1515; *Tractatus i trilogio astrologiae*, 1475; *Alphabet diuini amoris*, 1466, 1475; *Sermo de uirginis marie*, 1480; *De uita et miraculis Ioannis Gerson* (Wimpheling 1506).

[552] Oberman, 2008, p. 29. On the genre of *Trostliteratur* (consolatory literature) see Hohenadel 2015.

[553] McGuire 2005, p. 491.

not nearly as short as historians would lead us to believe) lifespan, our distant colleagues found time to read voraciously, write profusely and, what is most important, discuss passionately, while being keenly aware of each other's opinions. The 15th century reception of Gerson leaves an overall impression of a continent-wide, open and intense conversation among educated elites not yet sure of their own place and power, probing their intellectual muscles and experimenting with new humanistic methods and theological approaches. Gerson's voice, which had played a leading role in this discussion during his lifetime, remained just as audible after his passing.

CHAPTER 2

THE PROTESTANT RECEPTION OF GERSON

Introduction

'Awakened, conscience is a personal discomfort; activated toward a goal, it can be a disruptive force in society'.[1]

When evaluating the Protestant reception of Jean Gerson in the 16th century, one must consider two conflicting and equally reductionist assumptions. One is that 'with the coming of the Protestant Reformation, Gerson and his works lost some of their attraction'.[2] The other is the continuous, centuries-long attempt at presenting him as a 'forerunner of the Reformation'.[3] The second tendency is particularly strong, for it has a long history of its own. Indeed, though the master narrative of Gerson's legacy has not yet been written, the subject was certainly shaped by Protestant, and especially by Lutheran researchers long before it was even approached by Catholic historians. This chapter aims to counter both conventions by examining some of the ways in which Protestant thinkers of different personal convictions interacted with Gerson's theological legacy, including pastoral, mystical and systematic dimensions.

The major difficulty of such an assessment involves an unprecedented variety of theological opinions that the Reformation unleashed practically from its beginning. These opinions contin-

---

[1] Kelley 1983, p. 63.
[2] McGuire 2005, p. 327.
[3] Oberman 1981a.

ued to multiply, even before the rise of Protestant orthodoxies, throughout the 16th century. When theologians as different as Philipp Melanchthon (1497–1560), Andreas Bodenstein von Karlstadt (1486–1541), Andreas Osiander (1498–1552) or Martin Bucer (1491–1551) — to name only the major ones — turned to Gerson's authority in their writings, their motivations differed significantly, sometimes drastically, and could be spiritual, pastoral, polemical or historical, with various combinations thereof. For better or for worse, depending on one's point of view, the Reformation let loose a great number of powerful personalities, who, thanks to a new emphasis on personal faith, now expressed themselves through their religious views, which more often than not clashed with one another. Gerson's legacy was caught in this chaotic swirl, further complicating the task of presenting a coherent picture of his reception amongst Protestant theologians.

The explosion of spiritual creativeness, which followed Luther's revolt, warrants a mosaic exposé, composed of a combination of diverse elements, which, nevertheless, is more truthful and consistent with reality than a forced generalization. This carnival of personalities and opinions dictates the necessity of organizing the chapter, unequally divided into Lutheran and Reformed (or, in France, Huguenot) parts, not by movements or regions, but by individual theologians — mostly proceeding according to the criterion of Gerson's relevance for each of them. Therefore, this mosaic would not be made of equally-sized pieces, but rather of several central slices surrounded by smaller but theologically relevant fragments. The only exception from the 'individual approach' will be made, in part, for the collective phenomenon of evangelical harmonies, which bring together a wide variety of sources, ranging from influential works by Johannes Bugenhagen and Andreas Osiander to less known and even anonymous texts. Gerson's place in the emerging Lutheran and then Reformed historiography is evaluated in the writings by Matthias Flacius Illyricus, Jean Crespin and Simon Goulart.

Part I. Gerson's Lutheran Reception

Martin Luther

Although Luther's attitude toward Gerson has attracted scholarly attention before, this notice almost exclusively came from Protestant scholars, who invariably presented the French theologian as a forefather of the new religion. Fitting Luther's opinion of Gerson into a preset mold of specific teleological and theological expectations was meant to reflect the German reformer's spiritual evolution or 'progress' from a more traditional late medieval cleric toward a radically new religious thinker. This perspective led to a general, continuous and so far unbroken consensus that Luther formed the most favorable opinion of Gerson in his youth, but later abandoned all association with him.[4]

The German reformer appears to have read many of Gerson's works, from pastoral *Opus tripartitum*, *De modo uiuendi omnium fidelium* and various sermons, to highly sophisticated *De uita spirituali animae*, *De mystica theologia practica* and *De consolatione theologiae*. It is important to mention that Gerson and Luther seem to share certain mental features: an acute existential anxiety, and an obsessive preoccupation with the question of scruples of conscience. The latter sparked young Luther's initial interest in the French theologian. Luther's idea of being a mystic was close to Gerson's as far as it implies the theology of Praxis, and not theory.[5] Tormented soon after 1516 by a growing awareness of human beings' absolute and innate depravity, young Martin turned to the chancellor at the moment of a severe spiritual crisis. The latter's frankness in relating what he called 'une tristesse mortelle', when, *Visam est tamen michi nonnumquam meditanti in secreto cordis mei cubiculo per noctes, heu, presentis ubique calamitatis [...]*[6] must

---

[4] Such are the opinions of Jaroslav Pelikan, Walther Köhler, Berndt Hamm and Heinrich Denifle. 'Gerson, held in high esteem by Luther though rebuked by him [later]' (Denifle 1917, p. 407).

[5] Saarinen 2016, p. 444.

[6] *Tractatus de canticis*, OC: 9, p. 546. 'It seemed to me sometimes, while meditating in the secret of my heart [lying] in bed during the nights — alas — the present calamity was everywhere'. Also, Gerson, *Canticordum au pelerin*, OC: 7: 1, p. 421: 'Celui cuer sentoit souvent tristesse en soy et ne savoit souvent pourquoy. Entens et oy qu'il faisoit souvent pour vaincre ou oster ceste tristesse. Il commen-

have greatly appealed to the restless Augustinian friar. In fact, Gerson's candor about his spiritual afflictions gave Luther the courage to openly speak about his own.[7] Aside from courage, reading the works of Gerson also offered consolation. In this respect, 'Luther was particularly influenced by two of Gerson's tracts, *Contra nimis strictam et scrupulosam conscientiam* and *Contra foedem tentationem blasphemiae*'.[8]

According to the Leipzig researcher Friedemann Pannen, who conducted a quantitative study of Luther's direct references to Gerson, there are at least eighty-seven direct quotes, with fifty-seven in the Weimarer Ausgabe, twenty-eight in *Table Talk* and two in *Letters*.[9] Unambiguous references are found in nineteen different texts, ranging from sermons to disputations, beginning in 1516 and continuing until 1545. The French chancellor is mentioned by name or simply as *der Kanzler von Paris* or *der alte Lehrer zu Paris*. However, at times he is not acknowledged at all. This latter circumstance represents one of the major difficulties in evaluating Gerson's presence in Luther, since he relied on the French chancellor's ideas and works more than he was ready to admit.[10] For example, there is no doubt as to the reformer's reliance on *Opus tripartitum*, and yet he gives no explicit mention of this text. Another example is an unstated dependence on *De modo uiuendi omnium fidelium*, which served as a model for Luther's so-called *Haustafel*[11] — a commentary on family member duties as prescribed in the Scriptures and particularly in Paul's and Peter's letters — which he had attached to his 1529 *Small German Catechism*. Luther's close associate, the Saxon theologian

---

çoit tantost penser a sa mort et a la briefté de ceste vie, puis a ses pechez, puis aux peines d'enfer'.

[7] Rittgers 2012, p. 220.

[8] Pietsch 2016, p. 18.

[9] Pannen 2000, pp. 7–25.

[10] Bubenheimer 1971, p. 92. This is the case not only with Gerson but with other medieval thinkers, such as Gabriel Biel. On Luther's use of Biel's methods see Haga 2012.

[11] Behrendt 2009, p. 83. *De modo uiuendi omnium fidelium* is found in OC: 8, pp. 1–5. Another example of Luther's tacit reliance on Gerson concerns his application of the concept of *epikeia* in a Christian context. See Haile 2014, p. 346; Montover 2011, p. 91. Büttgen (Büttgen 2011) presents Luther as the sole inventor of Christian *epikeia*, and does not mention Gerson.

and the librarian of Saxony's elector Frederick the Wise, Georg Spalatin (real name Georg Burkhardt, 1484–1545), translated *De modo uiuendi omnium fidelium* into German. Whether Luther knew Spalatin's rendition of Gerson's *De modo uiuendi* or was directly inspired by the Latin original is unknown, but the structure of Gerson's text, consisting of twenty-three concise *regulae* for practicing religion in different circumstances, as well as the brevity of its style, looks like the template for Luther's *House panel*.[12] Luther's own reading of the Ten Commandments in his catechism also differs little from the catechistic section of Gerson's *Opus*.[13] It must be noted, however, that with time the heavy emphasis on this portion of *Opus tripartitum* resulted in giving the Ten Commandments far more prominence than Gerson and even Luther intended. Transforming the Ten Commandments into the main mechanism for revealing sin[14] deemphasized the initial stress on divine grace and faith in Christ's sacrifice in later Protestant catechisms.[15]

Although existing studies and opinions tend to agree that Luther's initial appreciation of Gerson peaked in his youth and drastically declined in his more mature years, there is less consensus about the exact timing of his disengagement. Some scholars place the reformer's rupture with Gerson as early as 1517.[16] If this indeed happened, it is not reflected in Luther's continuous quoting of the French theologian as the 'most zealous for the truth'[17] in the years 1518–1519, when Luther praised him in a lengthy citation from the *Explanations of the Ninety-Five Theses*:

> Gerson dared to condemn indulgences, which were bestowed as being valid for many thousand years. And I cannot help wondering what happened to the inquisitors of heresy that

---

[12] Spalatin's translation was never printed and remained in manuscript form, surviving in only one copy. Whether Luther was aware of the source of his inspiration is unclear, since he never mentioned Gerson's text.

[13] Bossy 2002, p. 227.

[14] Bossy 2002, p. 227.

[15] Rittgers 2012, p. 340.

[16] Cummings 2009, p. 40.

[17] *WA* 2. 345: *Gerson quem reuerendus pater illustrem theologum appellat, sicut fuit ueri et honesti studiosissimus [...]*. 'Gerson is called the illustrious theological father because he was truly and honestly the most knowledgeable'.

> they have not burned this heretic even after his death, for he condemned indulgences which entitled recipients to many thousand years and he spoke out confidently against the custom of every pilgrimage station in the city [Rome]. He spoke out also against the practice of that squanderer of indulgences, Sixtus IV, as a result of which the latter warned his prelates that it was their duty to correct and give careful attention to these indulgence practices. He referred to the claims of these indulgences as foolish and superstitious etc.[18]

In the same *Explanations of the Ninety-Five Theses* Luther also recommended Gerson's approach to death preparation, as found in *Opus*' third part:

> Therefore, absolutely nothing should be imposed upon those about to die [...] but rather as [Gerson] asserts more correctly elsewhere), they should surrender to death with steadfastness and resignation according to God's will.[19]

Opus' third part is also likely to have served as an inspiration for Luther's 1519 *Ein Sermon von der bereitung zum sterben*,[20] composed in High German and 'probably written in the first half of October 1519 and published before the end of this month'.[21] It presents all the main elements found in the *Opus*: concentration on the deathbed scene, pragmatic brevity, clear structure, a simple manner of speaking, elementary pastoral and catechetical theology and successful use of the vernacular.[22] In 1519 the Wittenberg reformer appealed to the chancellor's authority to back the very heart of his own theology — the *sola scriptura* principle — during his disputation with Johannes Eck: *Non potest fidelis Christianus*

---

[18] *LW* 31. 116.
[19] *LW* 31. 116.
[20] Cubillos 2009, p. 59.
[21] Hamm 2014, p. 110.
[22] Hamm 2014, pp. 112–13. Leroux believes Gerson's *ars moriendi* texts to be the direct source for Luther's sermon (Leroux 2007, p. 46). Oberman considers it 'inconceivable' that the reformer knew them (Oberman 1986 p. 143. n. 78); Arnaud qualifies German reformer as an heir of Gerson's pastoral tradition (see Arnold 2017). However, Haas (Haas 1997, p. 28) and Goetz (Goetz 1981) maintain that Gerson's influence is absent from Luther's sermon.

ultra sacram scriptoram, quo est proprie ius diuinum [...] ut Gerson etiam etsi recentior in multis locis asserit [...][23]

It is logical to think that Luther's opinion of Gerson would take a sharp turn for the worse once he heard, probably for the first time (although the *Acts of the Council of Constance* were available in print since 1500),[24] the story of Jan Hus's trial in Constance from his mentor Johannes Staupitz.[25] From the time of Leipzig Disputation (June 1519) 'it seems that Luther [...] read the *Acts of the Council of Constance* carefully and had also retained passages from Hus's *De ecclesia* not contained in the condemnatory decrees of the Council'.[26] Indeed, he expressed an open criticism of the Council of Constance in his 1519 *Disputatio et excusatio*, after which his opponent Johannes Eck (1486–1543) accused Luther of catching the 'Bohemian virus'.[27] Initially taken aback by this association, the Wittenberg reformer would ultimately fully embrace it, defending the Bohemians as being unjustly persecuted and murdered.[28] Duke George of Saxony registered Luther's change of position in his letter to him of 28 December 1525: [...] you were accused by Dr Eck of being a supporter of the Bohemian sect. At the time:

> you very vocally and energetically refuted that accusation. [...] A short time later, however, you did in fact release a text praising and validating all the fallacies of the Hussites [...][29]

---

[23] 1519, *WA* 2. 279: 'No faithful Christian can be forced beyond the Sacred Scripture, which is above the divine law [...] This principle was lately supported by Gerson in many places'.

[24] Polman 1932, p. 193.

[25] Pelikan 1948, p. 750. Strasbourg and Heidelberg educated historian Johannes Stumpf (1500–1578) also published *Acta scitu dignissima* in Hagenau in 1514.

[26] Pelikan 1948, p. 750.

[27] Bainton 1995, p. 116: 'But this', said Eck, 'is the Bohemian virus, to attach more weight to one's own interpretation of Scripture than to that of the popes and councils, the doctors and the universities.'

[28] *LW* 2. 21: 'Then [after Christ's second coming] it will be revealed that the holy martyrs of God, John Hus, and Jerome of Prague were true and holy members of the holy church.' *LW* 2. 87: 'Whenever I think of those saintly men, John Hus and Jerome of Prague, I reflect with the great admiration on their great courage'.

[29] Volkmar 2018, p. 455.

With time other people, both his followers and his enemies, began identifying Luther as Hus's successor and redeemer, or as a Saxon Hus. Thus, Georg von Zediltz, son of Sigismund von Zediltz, who was an eye-witness to the burning of Jan Hus, had sent two men to personally ask Luther whether he was the swan that Hus ('hus' meaning goose in Czech) had promised would succeed him.[30] It seems indeed logical that Luther's affinity with Hus and his subsequent espousal of his own role as a leader of a new faith would result in disavowing Hus's slayer. Yet, textual evidence does not support this assessment. Luther not only continued to cite the French master with reverence, but he also repeatedly put Gerson and Hus literally on the same page, without mentioning any connection between them or simply stating the fact that Hus and Jerome of Prague were burned in Constance.[31]

A year later, in 1520, Luther mocked the chancellor for 'die Fantastik der Allegorie im *Donatus Moralisatus*',[32] calling him 'weak a mind',[33] and after 1521 predominantly appealed to him as his support (*Stütze*) in his *Kirchenpolitik* and his fight against Rome for which the reformer needed 'immer neue Waffen'.[34] Although this is certainly true, the years 1520–1521 do not mark a major falling-out with the late medieval master 'wie ein übriger Mystiker'.[35] In 1520 Luther continued referring to Gerson in the most laudatory terms, and in relation to such heavy subjects as confession or the relationship between religious and secular authorities.[36]

---

[30] Olson 2002, p. 41.

[31] *LW* 39. 211. Dated according to Gritsch, Introduction *LW* 39. 140.

[32] Köhler 1900, p. 343. Köhler thought that *Donatus moralisatus* 'ist nicht von Gerson' (Köhler 1900, p. 343, n. 2). I agree with this opinion.

[33] *The Babylonian Captivity of the Church*, 1520, *LW* 36. 110: 'Gerson even converted the smaller *Donatus* into a mystical theologian. Who has so weak a mind as not to be able to launch into allegories?' Most likely *Donatus* is not by Gerson. See Mazour-Matusevich 2010.

[34] Köhler 1900, p. 344 and p. 347.

[35] Köhler 1900, p. 341: 'Luther citiert Gerson als Mystiker in der Zeit bis 1521'. Julius shares Köhler's opinion (Köstlin 2017, 2, p. 71).

[36] *Discussion of How Confession Should Be Made*, *LW* 39. 40: 'I advise, as Jean Gerson advised several times, that a man should at times go to the altar or to the sacrament with a scruple of conscience, that is, without confessing, when he has been drinking too much, or talking, or sleeping, or has done anything else, or has not prayed a single one of canonical hours. This advice [by Gerson] is given so that man learns to trust God's mercy more than his own confession or effort'.

In 1521 he praised 'Gerson, eyn man (alß scheynet) voll Christus geyst'[37] and as an expert on spiritual comfort:

> Why were we born? Why is not our lot the same as that of animals? Even the saints are troubled by this temptation [...] The monks called it the spirit of blasphemy. In various ways Gerson comforts the brothers when they feel the sting of this temptation.[38]

These positive endorsements do not mean, however, that Luther had no significant ontological differences with the French theologian at this time. One of these early divergences concerns Luther's position on the subject of *synderesis*.[39] His initial understanding of this concept, found in his biblical commentary the *Dictata Super Psalterium* (1513–1515) and some earlier sermons, was rather conventional,[40] and fully consistent with Gerson's position, which was widely deliberated upon in German universities both before and after the Reformation, and which 'an avid reader of Gerson'[41] such as Luther is unlikely to have missed. He believed, for instance, that 'the *synderesis* of the reason pleads inextinguishably for the best, the true, the right, and the just' in men, and, repeating Gerson's argument that *synderesis* provides the major premise in the moral syllogism,[42] spoke of 'the worm of *synderesis*' present in every man as 'a preservation, a remain-

---

LW 39. 44: 'Therefore, as Gerson correctly thinks, one should know that oaths or vows usually taken at universities, or made to secular lords, are not to be regarded so highly that we should judge every violation of them to be a violation of a vow or an act of perjury'. *Discussion of How Confession Should Be Made* was written in 1520 (Gritsch, Introduction to *LW* 39. 26).

[37] *Handschrift von Ein Urtheil der Theologen zu Paris*, 1521, *WA* 9. 744. 'Gerson is a man full of Christ's spirit'.

[38] Psalm 90:7, *LW* 13. 113. 'He lectured on Psalm 90, using Latin predominantly, [in Fall] 1534 and in Spring 1535' (Pelikan, *LW* 13. xi).

[39] Sometimes moralists translate *synderesis* as 'conscience', and sometimes as 'pre-conscience'. The term *synderesis* was introduced by St Jerome but derives from the Greek term (syntéresis) and means 'preservation', 'safekeeping', 'keeping something in mind' and 'warning'. The term was popular in the ethics of the scholastics to mean human ability (*habitus*) to know the first moral principles as the foundation for the judgements of conscience (Stepien 2014, p. 377). For a detailed study of *synderesis* in Gerson, see Vial 2007.

[40] Greene 1991, p. 203.

[41] Cummings 2009, p. 40.

[42] Greene 1991, p. 203.

der or a left-over portion of our nature in the corruption and faultiness of perdition'.[43] This position must have changed considerably in the years immediately preceding his revolt of 1517, as he stopped using the word *synderesis* altogether after 1516.[44] Luther dealt the most significant blow to the concept of *synderesis* when, in total opposition to Gerson and to the medieval theological tradition, he perceived in it not the point of connection between human and divine intelligences, but 'the point of absolute separation between the sinful man and righteous God'.[45] This 'maximum dissimilarity between him [man] and his Lord'[46] had a major consequence of leaving no room for Gerson's theology of spiritual quest. There was no longer any point in *ad gratiam praeparatorii*[47] by arranging, within one's soul, 'le petit logis [...] pour le [Saint Esperit] dignement recevoir'.[48] Total human wickedness was the very foundation of Luther's total faith in Christ's undeserved mercy, which no preparation can anticipate. This 'holistic' approach to humankind turned *synderesis* into a loophole allowing man some existential dignity, and, therefore, into a perilous fallacy and a devilish trick. Completely lacking, in his theological thinking, the sense of extenuating circumstances,[49] so central for Gerson, the German theologian moved from judging sins to judging the sinner, condemning the whole person.[50] For Luther, absolute depravity of humans could only be matched by the Lord's absolute mercy, with no compromise, nuances or gradations in between.

Yet, this disagreement did not prevent Luther, in 1527, from qualifying the chancellor as *qui solus ex recentioribus de consolandis aegris animis et infirmis conscientiis cogitauit*.[51] Neither the

---

[43] Greene 1991, p. 203. For the discussion of *synderesis* in Luther, see also Ojakangas 2013, pp. 65–74.

[44] Langston 2008, p. 76.

[45] Ojakangas 2013, p. 66.

[46] Ojakangas 2013, p. 66.

[47] *De uita spirituali animae*, OC: 3, p. 117.

[48] *Sermon pour la Pentecote*, OC: 7: 2, p. 680.

[49] Delumeau remarks that Luther and Pascal both rejected casuistic developments because they were Augustinians (Delumeau 1983, p. 87).

[50] Baylor 1977, p. 210.

[51] *Vorlesung über Iesaia*, 1527/29, *WA* 25. 232. 'The only one among the recent [theological authorities], [who] had knowledge about consoling weak souls

year 1528, with its polemical lectures on Timothy,[52] nor 1529, signal a cardinal shift in Luther's attitude toward Gerson.[53] In 1528 he approvingly cited the chancellor's moderation in relation to bodily needs: 'Treat your body in such a way that it does not waste away. Both are sins — to go to excess in drinking and in fasting. Gerson says this well'.[54] Though 1528 witnessed Luther's highly critical reflection on Gerson in relation to Hus,[55] in 1529 the Wittenberg prophet not only renewed the tendency of suppressing all information concerning the former's role in the fate of the latter, but went as far as praising both Hus and Gerson as *patres nostri*: *Nostri patres Iohannes Gerson, Hus fecerunt max[imam dilig]entiam, laborarunt und groebelet*.[56] Despite what happened in Constance, and against what seems to be common sense, Luther continued to see Gerson as someone who preceded Hus in the return to Scripture, even though the latter was the one who had given his life for the evangelical light.[57] Indeed, in *Katechismuspredigten* Luther went on to say that Hus and Ger-

and sick consciences'. Jean Delumeau considers 1525 as 'cette année charnière', when Luther would become inferior to himself (Delumeau 1983, p. 83).

[52] Oswald, Introduction, *LW* 28: xi. *Lectures on 1 Timothy* (1527-28), *LW* 28: 355–56: 'But you who mingle with people and are involved with the common crowd, if you were to restrain yourself there, you can [...] gain others for Christ, that they may live soberly, etc. Gerson wrote about this. He comforts those sects with this statement'.

[53] Luther brings up Gerson's authority in order to support his own opinion of monastic seclusion as unserviceable and socially useless: 'If a monk lives in a monastery, to whom is it useful? Whom does he serve? No one. What if they [monks] pray and fast so often, if in the meanwhile no one is providing any service? The anchorites, therefore, are quite a troublesome crowd. But you who mingle with people and are involved with the common crowd, if you were to restrain yourself there [...] and gain other for Christ, that they may live soberly, etc. Gerson wrote about this' (*LW* 28. 322–23).

[54] *LW* 28. 355. Also: 'Gerson says this well: 'Which one is to be thought of as pure, excess in eating or in fasting? Here we ought to compliment no one' (*LW* 28: 356).

[55] Predigten des Jahres 1528, *WA* 27. 154: 'Wie fern ist Gerson, Hus er fur komen prae [] ceteris in *uniuersitatibus*'. 'How far-off is Gerson, it was Hus who came in advance of others in the universities [academia]'.

[56] *Predigten des Jahres* 1529, *WA* 29. 523. 'Our fathers Johannes Gerson and Johannes Hus, applied maximum diligence, labored and investigated'. 'Groebelet' is a derivative of the verb *graben* meaning to 'dig' and is most likely a 16th century variation of *grubeln* meaning to 'think, meditate, examine'.

[57] Headley 1963, p. 225.

son (in this order) had labored together for the sake of truth: *Vide sudorem Ioannis Huss, Gersonis: quantis uigiliis laborarunt ad hunc thesaurum adipiscendum*.[58] In the same year 1529 Luther included Gerson, together with Hus, Bernard and Bonaventure, among those rare people to whom Christ *dat spiritum sanctum certissime*.[59] He repeated the same idea in *Der große und kleine Katechismus* of 1529,[60] naming Gerson and Hus 'in einem Atemzug' (in 'one breath').[61] Obviously, at this moment the ideological benefits of lining up with both Hus and Gerson in one destiny must have been greater than the potential profit of condemning the latter. Regardless of Luther's motivations behind this move, it is clear that the practice of Lutheran historiography to routinely put Gerson and Hus on the same page (alphabetical order notwithstanding), as witnesses to both the eternal truth of the Gospels and the new reformed faith, originated neither from Matthias Flacius's *Catalogus Testium Veritatis* nor from Melanchthon's conciliatory position, but from Luther himself.

A careful tracking of Luther's references suggests an extensive reliance on Gerson not only in later 1520s, but also in 1530s. The years 1530–1532 saw increasingly critical evaluations of the late medieval chancellor: 'Though Gerson and others say that you should do this (hear your brother who brings the Word of the Gospel in such perils of conscience), they still were unable to base the

---

[58] *Predigten des Jahres 1529, WA* 29. 523. 'Look at the sweat of Jan Hus and of Gerson: how many sleepless nights they labored for this treasure to be obtained'.

[59] *Katechismuspredigten, WA* 30. I. 114: [...] *nullus homo in terris esset, qui uere de Christo unum uerbum diceret. Cum autem Christus dat spiritum sanctum certissime, ut Bernardus, Bonauentura, Gerson, Iohannes Hus eum habuerunt* [...]. 'There is nobody on earth who has said one word about Christ truthfully. But when Christ really [most certainly] gives the holy Spirit, such as Bernard, Bonaventure, Gerson, John Hus had it'.

[60] *Der große und kleine Katechismus Luthers, WA* 30. 218: 'Weil nu Gott die Tauffe bestetigt durch eingeben seines Heiligen geists, als man ynn etlichen Vetern als Sanct Bernard, Gerson, Johan Hus und andern wol spueret, und die Heilige Christliche kyrche nicht untergehet bis ans ende der welt, so muessen sie bekennen, das sie Gotte gefellig sey'. 'Because only God confirms the baptism by giving his Holy Spirit, as one fully feels [him to do] in some Fathers such as St Bernard, Gerson, John Hus and others, and the Holy Christian church does not perish until the end of time, then they must recognize that they are pleasing to God'.

[61] Pannen 2000, p. 120.

advice of a good man on the Word alone'.[62] This reproach recurs several times, both in Latin and in German. In 1532 Luther also pronounced his famous judgment *Fuit autem Gerson uir optimus, qui non fuit monachus, non eo peruenit, ut conscientias Christo et promissione consolaretur [...]*[63] For many evangelical scholars this statement represents *die Grenze* or the dividing line in Luther's attitude toward Gerson, and this line passes through Scriptures.[64] Yet, 1531 sees the Wittenberg rebel place the late medieval chancellor, once again, amid 'the fathers'.[65] The same year, in *Lectures on Galatians*, the reformer still finds the chancellor's opinion relevant,[66] and in 1533–1536 affectionately speaks of him, in concert with Johannes Nider, as 'zween frome, troestliche lerer' ('two most pious, consoling teachers').[67] In 1532 Luther praises Gerson's 'supreme wisdom'[68] in *Two Rules for translating the Bible* and appeals to his works when affirming the preeminence of the Scriptures over any other authority: '[We] conclude that the pope is under the Scriptures and with that he is defeated. Gerson wrote three books to show that by divine authority the pope is subject to the Scriptures'.[69]

---

[62] Commentary on Psalm 45:10, *LW* 12. 270.

[63] *Tischreden*, *WA* 48. 478. 'the most excellent man who, although he was not a monk, did not succeed in consoling consciences through Christ and his promise'. This quote can be relatively safely placed between 1531 and 1532, since the witness who recorded it, Johannes Schlaginhaufens, was present at Luther's house during this period.

[64] Pannen 2000, pp. 124–25.

[65] *LW* 54. 133: 'Then I spoke about my temptation when I was approaching [the sacrament] of the altar. He [Luther] responded, 'Gerson and other fathers have said the one should adhere to one's original intention'.

[66] Lectures on Galatians 5:19, *LW* 27. 81: 'It admonished us not to act like the men of whom Gerson writes, who labored to rid themselves of any awareness of temptation or sin, in other words, to become nothing but stones'. These lectures are usually dated to 1535, the year of their publication. According to Pelikan, Luther worked on his commentaries on Galatians since the early years of the Reformation, but his actual lectures took place in 1531 (*LW* 27. ix).

[67] Schrifften 1533/36, *WA* 38. 160: 'Die fromesten unter jnen lereten also, auch Gerson und Johannes Nider, zween frome, troestliche lerer'. 'But the most pious among teachers, also Gerson and Nider, two pious, consoling teachers'.

[68] The Table Talk, *Two Rules for translating the Bible*, *LW* 54. 42: 'This is (and Gerson said it is supreme wisdom) to reduce all things to the first principle'.

[69] *LW* 54. 142.

Despite rather opportunistic exploitation of Gerson's theological prestige in relation to 'the meat question', to which Luther returned, in a rather zigzag-like fashion, in 1529, 1535 and 1539,[70] the early and middle 1530s actually mark Luther's particular appreciation of his favorite *Trostvater* as an expert in *perplexis conscientiis*:[71]

> *Solus Gerson scripsit de tentatione spiritus, alii omnes tantum corporales senserunt, Ieronimus, Augustinus, Ambrosius, Berhardus, Scotus, Thomas Richardus, Occa, nullus illorum sensit, solus Gerson de pusillanimitate spiritus scripsit. [...] solus Gerson ualet ad mitigandas conscientias.*[72]

This quote is of particular significance, since here Luther juxtaposes the chancellor to all theological authorities of the past, including Augustine himself, and links the issue of the 'frightened spirit' to the emerging concept of conscience. In May of 1532 the German reformer affirms once more that *Gerson primus est, qui rem aggressus est, quod attinet ad theologiam; ille etiam expertus est multas tentationes.*[73] When dealing with psychological issues of anxiety and depression, on account of which he was often solicited by his parishioners and peers, Luther explicitly states that

---

[70] Lectures on Isaiah 42:3, 1529, *LW* 17. 65: 'Gerson recommended that one must rather die than eat meat'. Date established according to Hilton C. Oswald, *LW* 17, Introduction, ix. Lectures on Genesis 13:8, 1535, *LW* 2. 339: 'the purpose of all laws is love. Therefore, Gerson and others have correctly disapproved of this severity'. The year 1535 is the year of the publication. *On the Councils of the Church*, 1939, *LW* 41. 129: 'Gerson writes that Carthusians are right when they apply their rule so rigorously that they eat no meat even if they should have to die'. The date 1539 is established by Gritsch, *LW* 41. 8.

[71] 'I have also seen how much the doctors, especially Gerson, had to deal with *perplexis conscientiis* or confused consciences' (*LW* 46. 318). The date 1530 is established according to Schultz (*LW* 46. 263).

[72] *Tischreden, WA* 2. 64, n. 1351, January to March 1532: 'Gerson is the only one who wrote about the temptation of the spirit, all others were concerned with physical temptations only. Jerome, Augustine, Ambrose, Bernard, Scotus, Thomas [Aquinas], Richard [of St Victor], Occam, none of them recognizes it, only Gerson wrote about the pusillanimity of the spirit. [...] only Gerson was effective in alleviating consciences'. Gerhard Ebeling dates this reference to January-March 1532 (Ebeling 1977, p. 252), and so does Erich Vogelsang (Vogelsang 1932, p. 15).

[73] *WA* 2. 114, n. 1492 (1532). 'Gerson is the first who addressed this subject [of the troubled conscience], which belongs to theology. He also experienced many trials'.

'[Gerson's] advice is the best'.[74] Luther reiterates the chancellor's suggestion when he advises Jerome Weller and Jonas von Stockhausen to treat depressive thoughts as 'one treats the menacing hiss of a goose' — by simply ignoring them and letting them pass.[75] In 1533 he still quotes the French theologian as a mystical authority,[76] and on October 7, 1534 advises Matthias Weller to alleviate depression by playing music, adopting, once again, Gerson's recommendation.[77] While in sermons of 1533–1536 the reformer declared that both Bernard and Gerson were witnesses to despair and sinfulness inherent to monastic life,[78] in his 1535–1538 lectures on Genesis the latter is praised as a promoter of benevolent justice: *Hoc quidem est sine dispensatione urgere legem, et obliuisci, quod omnium legum finis sit dilectio: Igitur Gerson et alii hanc seueritatem merito improbarunt*.[79] Even 'a growing number of [Luther's] attacks on past councils, especially the Council of Constance, and on the Catholic conception of a council in general',[80] as in his 1536 virulent *Disputatio de*

---

[74] Letter of 17 November 1532 to Jonas von Stockhausen, in Pietsch 2016, p. 279.

[75] Pietsch 2016, p. 90.

[76] Predigten 1533/34, *WA* 37. 475: *Isti patres dicunt, quod T\euffel sol so andechtig kunnen machen homines, ut prae gaudio lach\rimentur. Gerson hat dafur gewarnet, ut multa exempla leguntur, quidam e terra embor gehoben, quidam mit gulden kl\eid\ern geschmuck\t, sed fuit kue treck*. 'These fathers said that the devil can render men so pious that they weep for joy. Gerson warned, so that many examples are read, about someone lifted up from the earth, adorned with golden cloths that it was nothing else but it was nothing else but cow shit!' The same quote appears in Nicolas of Cusa and Juan Cazalla.

[77] Luther offers Gerson's example about 'the nagging wife who is eventually exhausted and gives up, because the husband ignores her and merrily plays the flute' (Mennecke-Haustein 2003, p. 218; Pietsch 2016, p. 99). In *WA* 7. 104–06.

[78] 1533/36, *WA* 38. 154: 'Muste doch Sanct Bernhard, der aller frömest Münch, da er lange jnn der Münchtauffe gelebt und ein mal tödlich kranck war, an aller seiner Muencherey verzweiveln und widderumb? ein Christ werden und also sagen (wie es auch Gerson an zeucht): Jch habe verdamlich gelebt und mein leben verloren' 'So St Bernard, of all monks the most pious, who lived a long time as a monk and, one time when he was deadly ill, must have despaired of his monastic state and turned to Christ and said (like Gerson also showed): I have lived sinfully and lost my life'.

[79] Genesisvorlesung (cap. 1–17) 1535/38, *WA* 42. 504. 'When this law is advocated without dispensation, and it is forgotten that the end of all laws should be happiness (*delectio*): this is why Gerson and others rightly disapproved of such severity'.

[80] Campi 2018, p. 280.

potestate concilii (*On the Power of a Council*),[81] did not provoke his disengagement from the Parisian chancellor. 'Jch dencke offt an den guten Gerson', writes Luther affectionately in late 1530s.[82] In 1539 his praise for Gerson's promotion of contemplative life, as found in *The Mountain of Contemplation*,[83] is interspersed with warnings about the danger of being deceived by contemplations as described in the same work.[84] As late as in 1538, while criticizing ideas of a controversial German theologian Caspar Schwenckfeld (1489/1490–1561), whom Luther expelled for his views from Silesia in 1540, the reformer was careful not to 'condemn Gerson as the spiritual father or ally of Schwenckfeld'.[85]

The late 1530s reveal one more highly interesting aspect of Gerson's influence on Luther. It concerns the German reformer's views on the use and status of liturgical music, which would play a crucial role in the future development of not only Lutheranism, but also Western European music in general. Although Luther never explicitly acknowledged his debt to the late-medieval understanding of music in general or to Gerson in particular, the overall consensus among scholars is that it was considerable.[86] Existing studies of Luther's views on music point to music theorist Adam von Fulda (1445–1505) as the main channel of late medieval musical influence in both Luther-associated centers of learning: Erfurt, where the reformer studied, and Witten-

---

[81] *Disputatio de potestate concilii*, WA 39/1. 184–97.

[82] 1536–39, *WA* 50. 194: 'Jch dencke offt an den guten Gerson, der zweivelt, ob man etwas guts solt oeffentlich schreiben. Thut mans nicht, So werden viel seelen verseumet, die man kundte erretten'. 'I often think about the good Gerson, who doubts that one ought to publish anything good. If one does not, then many souls will be lost, which could be saved'.

[83] Lectures on Genesis 19, 1539, *LW* 3. 276: 'Gerson, too, has written about the contemplative life. He gives it high praise'. Pelikan believes (*LW* 51: 276) that Luther probably refers to *The Mountain of Contemplation*. According to Pelikan, 'it appears safe to conclude that Luther was lecturing on chapter 19 of Genesis about March or April 1539' (Pelikan, *LW* 3. x).

[84] Lectures on Genesis 19, 1539, *LW* 3. 277: 'But that union of the soul and the body about which Gerson discourses in a grand manner is often fraught with great peril and pure mockery of Satan, who stirs up such devotions in the heart'.

[85] Oberman 1986, p. 138.

[86] See Schalk 1988; Guicharrousse 1995; Leaver 2007, pp. 27–30 & 34–35; Leaver 2009.

berg, where he taught.[87] Although the curricular requirements at Erfurt did not explicitly include the study of theorists such as Adam von Fulda, Luther's *Preface to the Symphoniae Iucundae* (1538) appears to be clearly 'dependent on Adam von Fulda's music theory'.[88] Fulda's 1490 treatise *De musica* was also certainly known in the Wittenberg academic community, and was used in the university curriculum in the early 16th century during Luther's tenure.[89] From 1502 Adam von Fulda also taught at Wittenberg as a professor of music, becoming one of Luther's closest collaborators. Adam von Fulda's connection is of particular importance here, since his book *De musica*, which was widely diffused in Saxony, is inspired by Gerson's treatises on music.[90] Besides Erfurt and Wittenberg, Gerson's poem *Carmen de laude musicae* was also known at Leipzig university, where it was used for studies of music both before and after the beginning of the Reformation.[91] As it has been mentioned earlier, *Carmen de laude musicae* was included in Leipzig curriculum for the improvement of students' behavior.[92]

Luther has commented on music in four songbook prefaces of 1524, 1533 (the 1529 edition is missing), 1542 and 1545, as well as in the already mentioned 1538 preface to Georg Rhau's (1488–1548) collective edition *Symphoniae Iucundae*.[93] This preface, which represents his most comprehensive text on musical theory, reveals familiarity with Gerson's *Tractatus de canticis*, especially in what concerns 'the *usus* of music'.[94] Despite his emphasis, in *Tractatus de canticis*, on the silent music of the heart or *canticordum* as the highest type of expression, Gerson

---

[87] On Wittenberg connection see Veit 1986; Leaver 2007, p. 71.
[88] Loewe 2013, p. 576.
[89] Leaver 2007, p. 72.
[90] In *De musica* Fulda 'quotes parts of Gerson's *Carmen super Recogitatione Mortis, Carmen de Laude Musicae* and *Carmen de Laude Canendi* in Chapter 2 of Book I' (Slemon 1975, p. 16).
[91] Metzler 2008, p. 42.
[92] Henkel 1988, pp. 291–92.
[93] *Praefatio zu den Symphoniae Iucundae*, 1538, WA 50: 364–74.
[94] Loewe 2013, p. 576 and Leaver 2007, p. 71.

never disavowed music of the mouth or *canticum oris*.[95] He would agree with Luther that Christians should practice singing to praise the Lord and his creation. Indeed, the French theologian's conviction that praising God is a reward in itself, as it is given freely and joyously,[96] found its ultimate advocate in Luther, who, unlike other Protestant reformers, such as Zwingli, never suggested that audible music should be removed from the church service. On the contrary, he famously declared *Musicam semper amaui*.[97]

The most noticeable trace of Gerson's presence in Luther's music-related writings is found in a rhymed *Vorrede* that the reformer provided for a theoretical treatise, *Lob und Preis der löblichen Kunst Musica*, written by his friend and Adam von Fulda's pupil Johann Walter (real name Johann Blankenmüller, 1496–1570).[98] The composer and editor of the first Lutheran hymnal for choir and author of the first German-language Mass, Walter adopted and applied Luther's ideas from the Preface to *Symphoniae Iucundae* in both his 1538 *Lob und Preis der löblichen Kunst Musica*, and in its second, slightly extended edition, entitled *Lob und Preis der himmlischen Kunst Musica*, published in 1564.[99] Probably written before 1538,[100] during the 'Tischreden years', Luther's poetic *Vorrede*, affectionately entitled *Frau Musica*, is highly reminiscent of Gerson's already-mentioned poem *Carmen de laude musicae*. Found in the second part of *Tractatus de canticis*, this poem was not only generally known in Saxony, but it was also extensively quoted by Adam von Fulda's treatise in his *De musica*.[101] Therefore, due to a complicated twist of prefaces, it is safe to say that when Luther followed Adam von Fulda as 'to

---

[95] Anttila 2013, p. 45: 'The song of the heart, *canticordum*, is not to be understood as an opposition of the outward song of the mouth, but rather as its fulfillment'.

[96] Anttila 2013, p. 46.

[97] *LW* 5: 557.

[98] On Walter see Blankenburg 1991 and von Siegmar 2012.

[99] Hendrickson 2006, p. 22 and Østrem, Fleischer and Petersen 2003, p. 171.

[100] Leaver 2007, p. 73. Also see Kristanto 2009, pp. 16–17.

[101] Leaver 2007, p. 72: 'Luther's known interest in and knowledge of the writings of Gerson, together with the Wittenberg awareness of Gerson's poem within Fulda's treatise, make it a strong possibility that Luther's knew of it'. Also see Veit 1986.

suggest that the gifts of the Spirit were conveyed through music to prophets' just as 'of all kinds of graces and good works is conveyed through music',[102] he actually adhered to Gerson's poem from *De canticis*. Indeed, the poem's first twenty-four lines bear strong resemblance to that of Gerson, particularly in regards to music's positive influence on human disposition, its ability to drive away evil, and its biblical references to Saul, David and Elisha as examples of such an influence (David playing the harp before Saul in 1 Samuel 16:23).

Luther: Vor allen Freuden auf Erden
Kann niemand keine feiner werden,
Denn die ich geb mit meinem Singen
Und mit manchem süßen Klingen.
Hier kann nicht sein ein böser Mut,
Wo da singen Gesellen gut,
Hier bleibt kein Zorn, Zank, Haß noch Neid,
Weichen muß alles Herzeleid;
Geiz, Sorg und was sonst hart an Leid,
Fährt hin mit aller Traurigkeit.
Auch ist ein jeder des wohl frei,
Daß solche Freud kein Sünde sei,
Sondern auch Gott viel bass gefällt
Denn alle Freud der ganzen Welt.
Dem Teufel sie sein Werk zerstört
Und verhindert viel böser Mörd.
Das zeugt Davids, des Königs Tat,
Der dem Saul oft gewehret hat
Mit gutem, süßem Harfenspiel,
Daß er in großen Mord nicht fiel.
Zum göttlichen Wort und Wahrheit
Macht sie das Herz still und bereit.
Solchs hat Elisäus bekannt,
Da er den Geist durchs Harfen fand.[103]

---

[102] Loewe 2013, p. 590.

[103] *LW* 53: 319. Of all the joys upon the earth// None has for us a greater worth// Then what I give with my singing// And with others sweetly ringing// Here cannot be an evil mood// Where there are singing follows good// Here is no grudge, hate, rage, or row// Softened in all grief and sorrow// Thus is everyone well and free// Since in such a joy no sin can be.// The devil's works are confounded// Evil murderers are avoided// Witness King David's actions good//

Gerson: *Cor recreat, curas abigit, fastudia mulcet*
Fitque peregrinis quos uehit apta comes
Per medias hyemes, per soles carmine fisus
Ibo spe patiens, laetus alacris ouans
Nam fugiunt tristes canu per inania curae
Omnis et insidians hostica pestis abest
Vertitur occusu psallentium Saul uelut alter
Factus homo, psallit fitque propheta novus
Exagitat nemquam dum spiritus hunc citharaedus
Pastor per numeros cogit abire David
Vatidicus deerat Elisaeo spiritus olim
Dum cecinit psaltes protinus implet eum.[104]

Both Gerson and Luther clearly had a weakness for the art of music, and for both it was more than an entertainment. Both believed that music exercises a positive moral influence, promotes goodness and creates a sense of therapeutic well-being for people.[105] Moreover, they share the view of music as a consolatory and healing practice for soul and body. Luther would surely endorse Gerson's enthusiastic statement that music can even cure bodily afflictions — *corporibus curandis musica prodest*.[106]

One cannot, however, help remarking several manifest differences in Gerson's and Luther's treatments of music and its role

---

Who often quelled Saul's evil mood// By sweetly playing on the lyre// And thus escaped the murderous ire// Such did Elisha once propound// When harping he the spirit found' (Leaver 2007, p. 74).

[104] *Carmen de laude musicae*, OC: 4, p. 135. 'It [music] refreshes the heart, drives away cares, and soothes ennui //And is a congenial companion to the travelers [*peregrinis*] whom it bears along. // Through the midst of snows and through [blasting] suns, in reliance on song [*per soles carmine*] // I shall go, patient in hope, happy, eager and cheerful// For miserable cares flee at [the sound of] song through the empty air, // And every hostile plague that might lie in wait is dispelled. // On encountering the string-players Saul is turned as it were//Into another man, he plays the strings and becomes a prophet. // While evil spirit torments hither shepherd David who sings to the cithara // Forces it to depart through song. // At one time Elisha lacked the prophetic spirit; // As string-player sang the spirit filled him' (trans. L. Holford-Strevens in Leaver 2007, Appendix 2, pp. 307–08). The translator chose to interpret the word *cor*, which literally means 'heart', as spirit. However, considering Gerson's particular focus on and expansion of the concept of the heart as the center governing the emotions literal translation as 'heart' seems preferable.

[105] Leaver 2007, p. 71.

[106] *Carmen de laude musicae*, OC: 4, p. 135.

in the interpretation of the biblical episode in their reciprocal poems. The first difference concerns the manner or rather circumstances of singing. The chancellor praises solitary singing 'through the empty air' and in 'the midst of snows', plausibly referring to his own voyage as an involuntary pilgrim after the Council of Constance (1414–1418).[107] The poem, as it happens very often with Gerson, feels like a written testimony to an actual experience, making it easy to picture our theologian traveling on foot and singing in order to lift his own spirit. Luther meant collective choral singing in the midst of a congregation rather than the solitary experience evoked by Gerson. Although this dissimilarity might reflect a basic contrast between Gerson's rather self-contained disposition and Luther's gregariousness, it perhaps signals the chancellor's belief, conveyed in the same *Tractatus de canticis*, that a prayer is the most effective when it is carried through the intimate music of the heart or *canticordum*.

The second difference is Luther's emphasis on the preeminence of the human voice, which contrasts with Gerson's enthusiasm for musical instruments — *cithara, tympana cum chordis, organa, nabla* described in *Carmen de laude musicae*.[108] Technicalities found in *Tractatus de canticis*, such as a depiction of the materials from which strings could be made, or occasions for which the use of certain instruments would be appropriate, strongly suggest Gerson's personal mastery of musical instruments and a keen interest in music making.[109] For Luther, however, the physical human voice had a special, unparalleled value, because it could

---

[107] Indeed, in *Carmen de laude musicae* Gerson mentions being *peregrinus* or pilgrim in exile *Fitque peregrinis quos uehit apta comes* (OC: 4, p. 135) and *moribus et ritu degit in exilio* (OC: 4, p. 137).

[108] *Carmen de laude musicae*, OC: 4, p. 135.

[109] Christopher Page, who considered *De canticus* to be 'of the first importance to modern instrument makers', argued that, unlike usual medieval glosses, which typically repeated the same conventional depictions from manuscript to manuscript, Gerson appears to derive his descriptions and explanations from his personal experience as a musician, showing little use of the early fathers' (Page 1978 pp. 339–40). Jeremy Montagu confirms this assessment by crediting *Tractatus de canticis* to be the only remaining evidence of the 15th century usage of certain type of drums such as *abtusus* (dull) and *peracutus* (clear) (Montagu 2002, p. 28).

sing *uerbum dei* (the Word of God), while instrumental music was hardly of higher spiritual value than 'the song of the birds'.[110]

The third variance concerns Luther's use of the word 'devil', where Gerson has *spiritus*.[111] This is not a slip of the tongue for a theologian who believed in the existence of an entire church of Satan and preached that 'the Devil is beside you'.[112] Satan had a permanent presence in Luther's life and writings. Although Luther's apparent faith in music's ability to drive away evil drew, via Adam von Fulda, from Gerson, the rationale he intended to convey was of music as an actual supernatural power capable of fending off the Archenemy himself. Characteristically, when warning, at the end of his Preface to the *Symphoniae*, about music's capacity to be abused by depraved souls, Luther, once more, evokes the evil spirit in person.

> Impudent poets [...] whom the Devil carries off against nature [...] these bastards [*adulterini filii, Wechselbelge*] who then snatch away the gift of God [music], and cultivate it for the enemy of God, who is the enemy of nature and the enemy of this most joyful art.[113]

The fourth difference is the most substantial. For the French theologian music was a form of theology, as is attested, in *Tractatus de canticis*, by a striking resemblance between the power of theology, which *qua curae fugiunt mens hilarescit quae uirtute sua monstra trucidat [...]*,[114] and the power of music to chase away demonic thoughts.[115] For Luther, the art of music, although the most important of the seven liberal arts and the queen of sciences, was akin to theology, but deserved only a second rank 'next

---

[110] Kristanto 2009, p. 18.

[111] For a more detailed analysis see Leaver 2007, pp. 74–76.

[112] Gordon 2000, p. 89, citing Luther's *Sermo de angelis*. Loewe 2013, p. 590: 'Both Luther's interpretation of the ability of music to drive away evil and his identification of Saul's spirit as Satanic is adopted by Lutheran successors like Johannes Lippius who, in his *Synopsis Musicae* (1612), asserted that 'Satan is the enemy of God's beautiful and most delightful gift of music'.

[113] Loewe 2013, p. 44, citing WA 50. 374.

[114] *Carmen de laude musicae*, OC: 4, p. 28. 'theology [...] which, makes cares flee, gladdens the mind and kills monsters by its virtue'.

[115] Anttila 2013, p. 47.

to the Word of God'.[116] The Word had an absolute supremacy, and 'only in connection with the words can music attest praising God'.[117] For Gerson, one could sing without words, even without sound, and a wordless song of a mute child would be as valuable to God as a beautiful harmony mastered by an elaborate professional choir.[118] His attitude towards music is less anthropocentric and, therefore, less word-centric, and the song of the heart or *canticordum* requires no words in order to be heard.[119] Moreover, his validation of the silent music of the heart corresponds to his emphasis on the internal, mental prayer as the highest form of worship. For the French master, like for the author of *De Imitatione Christi*, silence was absolutely essential to prayer.[120] Inversely, Lutheran principle of *sola scriptura* led to music being bound to Scripture,[121] with *[...] uerbum dei uel cantu inter populus maneat* or 'das Wort Gottes auch durch Gesang unter den Menschen bleibe',[122] as its only purpose. Subsequently, mental prayer was to be privileged in the Catholic tradition of the Spanish Mystics such as Teresa of Avila and John of the Cross, while insistence on the benefits of vocal, audible and collective singing became an identifiable Lutheran feature. Thus, although Ger-

---

[116] Kristanto 2009, p. 17.

[117] Kristanto 2009, p. 18.

[118] For one of the most important medieval discussions about whether God should be praised with lips and songs, see Thomas Aquinas, *Summa theologica* (II–II. Q.91, Art. 2).

[119] The Reformation's strong accent on the verbal component of singing influenced the Catholic stance toward liturgical music. Although the Council of Trent offered 'la maigre substance musicale' in general, canon 12 of the 24th session emphasizes the necessity to celebrate the office by praising God 'respectfully, distinctly and devoutly', *Dei nomen reuerenter, distincte deuoteque* (Bisaro 2018, p. 147). After the Council, in 1565, pope Pius IV summoned cardinals Vitellozzo Vitelli and Borromeo to execute the Council's decision concerning music. The cardinals formed a special commission, which decided, among other things, that messes and liturgies, where words were mixed or overlapping, would no longer be sung (Fétis 1841, 7, pp. 142–43).

[120] Thomae Hemerken a Kempis, *Opera Omnia* in Habsburg 2011, p. 52, n. 105: *In silentio et quiete proficit anima deuota et discit abscondita scripturarum*. 'In silence and quiet the devout soul advances in virtue and learns the hidden truths of the scriptures'. On Johann Sebastian Bach see Rathey 2016.

[121] Raley 2012, p. 1085.

[122] *Briefe* WA 3: 220.

son's *musica extolli nulla laude satis poterit*[123] ('music can never be praised enough') strongly resonates with Luther's *[...] neque initium neque finem neque modum rationis inuenire queam*[124] ('I know neither where to begin or stop praising it [music], nor how to find ways to praise it'), what the two theologians meant was not the same thing.

Luther does not abandon his favorite medieval authority even in the 1540s. He revisits Gerson's *De uita spirituali animae* in his Commentaries on Genesis 30:1,[125] and refers to him in *Vorlesungen über Jesaja* and in *Table Talk* of the winter 1542–1543. Three years before his death, the reformer still calls the late medieval theologian 'the best':

> [...] Gerson was the best; he began [to attack papacy], although he was not altogether sure what he was about. He could not make up his mind to make the break [with the pope] complete. Yet what he said was comforting to people; therefore they called him the consolatory doctor. As a consequence, he was also condemned. Accordingly [Cajetan] called me Gersonista.[126]

Thus, 'not even in this late stage of his development does Luther put Gerson to the Index. To the contrary, he exhorts his audience to study Gerson'.[127]

Much more than a polemical tool or a prestigious theological reference, Gerson never ceased to be for Luther one of *christlichen Theologen*, whom God had chosen, at the time perceived as the end of times, to enlighten others.[128] For the Wittenberg reformer the Parisian master never ceased to be 'a prime example of a *uir conscientia* — in distinction from the scholastic *uir speculatiui* — and, therefore, the archetype of a theologian who reads, prays and

---

[123] *Carmen de laude musicae*, OC: 4, p. 135.

[124] WA 50. 368.

[125] *LW* 5. xi. M. Luther, Lectures on Genesis 30:1, *LW* 5. 323: 'and although he [monk] checks himself and abstains from the act, yet that flame causes pollutions for him not only when he is asleep but also when he is awake, as Gerson testifies'. Luther could be referring to *Poenitemini contre la luxure*, OC: 7: 2, p. 840.

[126] *LW* 54. 443.

[127] Oberman 1986, p. 138.

[128] Pannen 2000, p. 119: 'derjenige, den Gott auserwählt hat, die als Endzeit empfundene Zeit, zu erleuchten. Deshalb nennt Luther ihn 'hoch-erlaucht'.

consoles'.[129] Luther's apparent inability or unwillingness to disengage himself from the French theologian, that some Protestant scholars found so 'outrageous',[130] reveals an attachment strong enough to withstand criticism and disagreements without causing a complete breakup.

I could locate no references to the chancellor dating to 1546, the year of Luther's passing, and it is plausible that the thread from Gerson to Luther wore out at the very end of reformer's life. Furthermore, an in-depth study is needed to place Gerson's chronology within the broader context of Luther's thought and theological development at any given moment. Instances of Luther's indirect dependence on the French theologian also await scholarly attention. What can be safely affirmed now is that Luther's attitude toward Gerson did not evolve in a straight line of a measured and steady 'progress' from a pious medieval monk to an enlightened reformed theologian. Rather, it looks like an uneven and unpaved road of many detours, returns and halts, which reflects complexity and depth of Luther's attachment to *doctor consolatorius*. Furthermore, the German theologian's reworking of Gerson's legacy bears many important outcomes for the future.[131] Luther's predilection for *der grosse Pariser* secured for Gerson a special place of honor not only in the early evangelical dogma and early Protestant confession[132] but also in Lutheran historiography, musicology and pastoral care up to the most recent times.

Philipp Melanchthon

Philipp Melanchthon (Schwarzerd), Luther's right hand, 'the fusion of humanist and theologian',[133] was a grammarian and classicist of the Reformation, and a more moderate, balanced and cerebral thinker than Luther. He exhibited a far more poised and

---

[129] Brogl 2013, p. 61. See *LW* 2. 9–13 & 25–30. 'Luther était l'héritier de la théologie pastorale de Jean Gerson et des travaux des humanistes sur les sources bibliques' (Arnaud 2017, p. 80).

[130] Denifle 1917, p. 319.

[131] Köhler 1900, p. 346: 'Luthers Berufung auf Gerson ist nicht wirkungslos geblieben'.

[132] Köhler 1900, p. 346: 'in der ersten evangelischen Dogmatik und der ersten protestantischen Bekenntnisschrift.'

[133] Preus 2014, Introduction, p. 1.

consistent attitude toward Gerson than his passionate teacher. In fact, of all Reformers, Melanchthon appears to have had the highest degree of theological continuity with the late medieval chancellor, whose writings he knew well and of whom he maintained a consistently favorable opinion throughout his life, in spite of some mild criticism.[134] The future Wittenberg's Elisha,[135] Philipp was born lucky. His maternal uncle, his grandmother's brother, Johannes Reuchlin (1455–1522), was an outstanding humanist, second only to Erasmus. Reuchlin took a great interest in his extraordinarily gifted great-nephew, and became Philipp's dedicated tutor, preparing him from a very young age for his studies at the University of Heidelberg. There Philipp met professor of rhetoric and poetry and Gerson's admirer, Alsatian humanist Jacob Wimpheling. These encounters probably introduced him to the famous Parisian chancellor for 'to know Wimpheling and Reuchlin was to hear of Wessel and Gerson'.[136] Wimpheling, in his book *Isidoneus germanicus*, opposed scholastic methods, promoted humanist studies and insisted on the necessity of a new type of relationship between pupils and teachers. Meeting him must also have awakened Melanchthon's early interest in the reform of the educational system. Wimpheling's second pedagogical work, *Adolescentia*,[137] where 'Gerson's influence is palpable',[138] directly focuses on the reform of education,[139] and develops the idea of an ideal teacher as not only knowledgeable, but also kind, patient and caring. These new pedagogical ideas are based on Gerson's pioneering views expressed in his little book *On bringing children to Christ*, with which his Strasbourg editor was certainly familiar, as well as in vernacular sermons: 'douceur mieulx que rigueur; avoir cuer humain et oisel de proie [...] des enfans qui ne pouvainet proffiter pour ce que on les batoit trop'.[140]

---

[134] Melanchthon mildly criticized Gerson in the 1559 edition of *Loci communes* (II, p. 745).
[135] Preus 2014, Introduction, p. 1.
[136] Wilson 1897, p. 41.
[137] Wimpheling 1500.
[138] Smolinsky 2013, p. 193.
[139] Smolinsky 2013, p. 193.
[140] *De la chasteté conjugale*, OC: 7: 2, p. 865. 'gentleness is better than severity, and it is better to have a human heart than that of a bird of prey [...] as some

Following Gerson's conviction that 'virtues instilled in children represented reform',[141] Wimpheling believed that education, as the foundation for 'returning the Catholic Church to the old and holy mores', began with the young, just as degeneracy began 'with the poor and incorrect education of the same'.[142] Having popularized the account of the aging chancellor dedicating his last years to catechizing poor little children in Lyons, Wimpheling launched the idea of *quotidie* (daily) religious instruction free of charge for children. Melanchthon's interest in pedagogy is manifest already in his inaugural speech *De corrigendis adulescentiae studiis* (*On Reforming the Studies of the Youth*), delivered by the twenty-one-year-old professor of Greek upon his appointment at Wittenberg university in 1518. He would seek to implement quotidian religious instruction in primary schools in the 1520s. This practice became a part of educational reform in Saxony, where Melanchthon's plan for the creation of the first elementary school system, published in 1526 in his *Instructions for Visitors*, was enacted into law. This plan, in turn, was widely copied throughout Germany, where at least fifty-six cities asked Melanchthon's advice in founding schools. The impact of his pedagogical ideas extended far beyond German lands proper, to Scandinavia and the Baltic. Consequently, 'the general pedagogisation of the age with its goal of making everything teachable',[143] began with Gerson's ideas that were processed and promoted by Wimpheling and found their practical fulfillment in Melanchthon's reform of education.

Catechization was the main component of Melanchthon's educational reform. In 1549 he composed the first official *Evangelical Catechism*. It is based on Luther's 1529 *Small German Catechism*, in which the latter had abandoned the seven sins in favor

---

children could not profit [from education] because they were beaten too much'. *Sed absit omnis amaritudo reprehensionis; procul esto omnis substomachatio proteruiens, imitemur paruulorum simplicitatem, de paruulis locutari; nihil hic contentiosa animositate declamemus* (*De paruulis ad Christum trahendis*, OC: 9, p. 669) 'However, let us not, when we undertake to champion the cause of children, give way to any bitterness or severity of invective; let us rather imitate the gentle and simple ways of children themselves' (Gerson 2019, p. 2).

[141] Smolinsky 2013, p. 193.
[142] Smolinsky 2013, p. 193.
[143] Smolinsky 2013, p. 193.

of an ethics built on the Ten Commandments.[144] One Gersonian feature — a particularly strong emphasis on the fourth commandment to venerate your father and your mother — was retained in all Lutheran catechisms. However, without the balancing effect of the Virgin Mary and an army of female saints, Gerson's accent on fatherhood quickly morphed into a patriarchal approach of a recognizably Old Testament type, in a sense that the father 'replaced the priest'.[145] Moreover, this father-centrism also acquired a uniquely Lutheran political dimension of honoring and obeying not only fathers of the household but also secular authorities and 'fathers of the body politic, the *patres patriae*'.[146]

The pedagogical connection between Gerson and Melanchthon transcends catechization, however. Whereas Luther viewed education as a preparatory tool to the understanding of the Gospel, Melanchthon believed that learning, although always combined with an ethical foundation, had an end in and of itself. In his reflections on what is possible and impossible to achieve through education, Melanchthon followed the reasoning of *De theologia mystica practica* (1408), which he knew well. Using expressions 'faculty of knowing' and 'the faculty that is subject to the affections' or in German *die Erkenntniskraft* and *die Kraft der Affecte*,[147] which correspond to Gerson's concepts of *uis cognitiua* and *uis affectiua*,[148] Melanchthon asserted that 'moral education cannot be limited to the intellect, but must also aim at the *affectus*',[149] which he understood as an inner disposition or rather

---

[144] Bossy 2002, p. 222.

[145] Auke 1998, pp. 130–31: 'Time and again it was urged that a father should have his child baptized as soon as it was born. He should be present. He had to take the initiative. The mother's presence was not appreciated'.

[146] Bast 2009, p. 53.

[147] Müller 2017, pp. 127–28.

[148] *De theologia mystica practica*, OC: 3, p. 273: *Cognitio Dei quae est per theologiam mysticam melius acquiritur per poenitentem affectum quam per inuestigantem intellectum*. 'For mystical theology knowledge of God is better obtained via penitent love [affection] than through intellectual investigation'. For a critical edition see Combes 1958. 'Diese Zweiteilung des Menschen in seine *Erkenntniskraft* (*uis cognitiua*) und *Gefühlskraft* (*uis qua affectus oriuntur*) ist auf Gerson seine Schrift *De theologia mystica* von 1408 zurückzuführen. Gerson unterscheidet im Menschen den *intellectus* und *affectus*, and *potentia intellectiua* und *potentia affectiua*, *uis cognitiua* und *uis affectiua* genannt' (Pöhlmann in Melanchthon 1993, pp. 26–27).

[149] Golz 1998, p. 19.

as a combination of numerous conflicting effects, floating 'around people like a ball'.[150] Rejecting the concept of *apatheia* or the possibility of a complete emotional detachment, he believed that men were always affected by conflicting emotional impulses and 'cannot free themselves from the slavery of emotions except through the working of divine grace'.[151]

Studies at Heidelberg university mark only the first phase of Melanchthon's association with Gerson's legacy. The next chapter took place at the recently founded University of Tübingen, another of Gerson's hubs. 'Fifteenth-century addition to the church fathers',[152] Gerson was venerated, quoted, copied and edited by Geiler in Strasbourg and Wimpheling in Heidelberg, and became the patron of *uia media* at Tübingen. The esteem for the chancellor was initially fostered by Gabriel Biel, whose ideas the young Philipp was certainly familiar with, as they permeated Tübingen's atmosphere. In 1497 Biel was replaced, as the university prior, by another Gerson scholar, Johannes von Staupitz (1460–1524), who, although often at odds with his predecessor's views, was profoundly influenced by both Gerson and Biel. In fact, one can speak of a vertical line in transmission of Gerson's theological legacy from Biel to Staupitz and from Staupitz to Melanchthon. After familiarizing himself with Gerson's writings at Tübingen, Melanchthon would never lose his reverential attitude toward the chancellor, to whom he consistently referred as a champion of true spiritual life, 'full of Christian spirit', and 'great in all respects'.[153]

Melanchthon's predilection for Gerson is particularly interesting when placed in the context of his aversion to scholastics in general. As a young humanist and Reuchlin's pupil, he jointly condemned them all, including the greatest, as a useless gang: *Hinc prodiere Thomae, Scoti, Durandi, Seraphici, Cherubi, et reliqui proles numerosior Cadmea sobole*.[154] Yet, even in the first edition of his encyclopedic exposé of Lutheran theology, *Loci*

---

[150] Wollersheim 1999, p. 91.
[151] Wollersheim 1999, p. 91.
[152] Oberman 1981, p. 62.
[153] Melanchthon 1983, p. 14.
[154] *Declamationes*, CR: 11, p. 17. 'Thomas, Scotus, Durand, Francis, Dominic, and others, a gang more numerous than the descendants of Cadmus'.

Communes, where he rebuked the scholastic method and especially lambasted late medieval authors, Philipp took special care to spare Gerson by not including his name among the members of the scholastic 'gang'.

There are several reasons for this deliberate omission. Dr Philipp gave the chancellor credit for several issues that were close to his heart: the return to affective, as opposed to speculative, theology,[155] Christocentric perspective, centrality of Scripture,[156] as well as promotion of the introspective contemplation as opposed to exterior religious observances. He also constructed his vision of the role of law in society on the foundation built by Gerson in *De uita spirituali animae*, which he cites in all editions of *De Loci communes*. Thus, Melanchthon's explicit distinction between three types of law — divine law, natural law and human law — is based on Gerson's rendition of these concepts in *De uita spirituali*.[157] Dr Philipp continued to rely on Gerson in order to demonstrate the essential difference between the laws directed to the spiritual life and those directed to civil and political life. In *Philosophae Moralis epitomes libri duo* of 1546, he formulated the competency of civil law as the following:

> *Prima sumiter a causis effecientibus, seu iure potestatis, et hanc Gerson sequitur. Ciuilis magistratus auctoritate diuina ius habet condendi leges honestas et utiles de iis negotiis, quae ad defensionem uitae corporalis et societatem pertinent, ut de iudi-*

---

[155] *Mysteria diuina rectius adorauerimus quam uestigauerimus* (Melanchthon 1993, p. 18) 'We shall rather adore the divine mystery than investigate it'. As Horst Georg Pöhlmann remarks (Melanchthon 1993, p. 19), 'das Urmuster des Satzes in der Hauptthese der Gersonschen *Theologia mystica* zu suchen ist, die Melanchthon gut kennte: [...] *cognitione Dei* [...] *Melius acquiritur per poenitentem affectum quam per iuuestigantem intellectum* (OC: 3, p. 250).

[156] Melanchthon's view on vain curiosity, although based on a long ancient and medieval tradition, appears to be directly inspired by Gerson's *Contra curiositatem studentium* (OC: 3, p. 233).

[157] *De uita spirituali animae*, OC: 3, p. 136: *Secunda difierentia legis diuinae ad naturalem est quia lex diuina principalit respicit finem supematuralem; lex naturalis naturalem; humana lex potest ad utrumque dirigere [...]*. 'The second difference between divine law and natural law is that divine law aims at divine end; natural law at natural end; human law can lead to either direction'. For Melanchthon's interpretation of divine, human and natural laws see Astorri 2019, p. 57.

ciis, de poenis delictorum, de contractibus, de successionibus et similibus rebus, sicut Solomon inquit: Per me reges regnant, et iusta constituent.[158]

There is also exegetical connection. Melanchthon deduced the fundamental Protestant principles of interpreting Scripture from the Scriptures themselves — *sola scriptura* and *sufficientia scriptura* — from none other than Gerson and his harmony *Monotessaron* with which Melanchthon was familiar.[159] For 16th century Lutheran theologians, the question of their movement's legitimacy rested upon finding means of interpreting scripture in a consistent manner. Gerson's *Monotessaron* became an urtext for this purpose. The two earliest 16th century Gerson-based harmonies were printed in 1505 and 1506: *Passio Domini Nostri Iesu Christi*, edited by Adam Petri in Basel, and *Passio Domini Nostri Ihesu*, edited by Wimpheling's student Matthias Ringmann, in Strasbourg.[160] In *Loci communes*, where Dr Philipp developed tenets of scriptural interpretation, Melanchthon probably relied on the Strasbourg edition, which at times follows Gerson's *Monotessaron* verbatim. Via *Loci*, Gerson's methods of scriptural harmonizing (to which we will return further on) passed to and were preserved within Lutheran hermeneutical tradition.[161]

---

[158] CR: 16, p. 113. 'Let's first take the operative causes or the power of law, as followed by Gerson. Civil magistrate, by divine authority, has the right to enact laws about what is good and profitable business, concerning the protection of bodily life and society, procedures, penalties for wrongdoers, contracts, successions and similar things, as Solomon said: By me kings reign and princes decree justice'.

[159] *Monotessaron*, OC: 9, p. 246: *Ita narratum est de theologizante Cecilia quod semper euangelium Christi gerebat in pectore suo; cuius exemplo numquid non est utile sapientiae sectatoribus ut suum omne studium ad euangelicam referant unitatem? Prorsus erit hoc ad memoriam utile et ad pietatem proficiens cum in eo reconditus sit cultus Dei praecipuus [...]* 'So it is narrated of the theologian Cecilia, who always held the Gospel close to her heart. Isn't this example useful to those who pursue wisdom, so that they direct the entirety of their study to the unity of the Gospel? This would be certainly useful to memory and convenient for piety, since it is in it [the Gospel] that resides the primary worship of God'.

[160] Bieber 1993, p. 69. The full title of this harmony is *Passio Domini Nostri Ihesu ex euangelistarum textu quam accuratissime deprompta additis sanctissimis exquisitissimisque figuris*.

[161] See Preus 2014, p. 16.

Melanchthon's positive outlook on the French chancellor extends to the Lutheran profession of faith solemnly presented to the Emperor Charles V on the 25th of June 1530. By incorporating Gerson's name into *The Augsburg Confession*, Melanchthon secured for him a permanent place of honor in Lutheran tradition. Here, as in *Loci communes*, Dr Philipp brought Gerson into discussion, not only to back up Lutheran argument against monastic life,[162] but also to praise him for having spoken against the weight of tradition in favor of internal and personal religion:

Gerson scribit multos incidisse in desperationem, quosdam etiam sibi mortem consciuisse, quia senserant se non posse satisfacere traditionibus, et interim consolationem nullam de iustitia fidei et de gratia audierant. Videmus summistas et theologos colligere traditiones et quaerere 'epieikeias', ut leuent conscientias; non satis tamen expediunt, sed interdum magis iniiciunt laqueos conscientiis. Et in colligendis traditionibus ita fuerunt occupatae scholae et conciones, ut non uacauerit attingere Scripturam et quaerere utiliorem doctrinam de fide, de cruce, de spe, de dignitate ciuilium rerum, de consolatione conscientiarum in arduis tentationibus. Itaque Gerson et alii quidam theologi grauiter questi sunt se his rixis traditionum impediri, quominus uersari possent in meliore genere doctrinae.

[...] und schreibt Gerson, dass viele hiemitin Verzweiflung gefallen, etliche haben sich auch selbst umgebracht, derhalben, dass sie keinen Trost von der Gnade Christi gehoert haben. Denn man sieht bei den Summisten und Theologen, wie die Gewissen verwirrt, welche sich unterstanden haben, die Traditionen zusammenzuziehen, und *epieikeias* gesucht, dass sieden Gewissen huelfen, haben so viel damit zu tun gehabt, dass dieweil alle heilsame christliche Lehre von noetigeren Sachen, als vom Glauben, vom Trost in hohen Anfectungen und dergleichen, daniedergelegen ist. Darueber haben auch viel fromme Leute vordieser Zeit sehr geklagt, dass

---

[162] CR: 26, p. 319: *Et ante haec tempora reprehendit Gerson errorem monachorum deperfectione et testatur, suis temporibus novam uocem fuisse, quod uita monastica sit status perfectionis.* 'Es hat auch Gerson in Vorzeiten den Irrtum der Moenche von der Vollkommmenheit gestraft und zieht an, dass bei seinen Zeitendieses eine neue Rede gewesen sei, dass das Klosterleben ein Standder Vollkommenheit sein solle'. 'And before these times, Gerson rebukes this error of the monks concerning perfection, and testifies that in his day it was a new saying that the monastic life is a state of perfection' (Melanchthon 1921, online).

solche Traditionen viel Zank in der Kirche anrichten, und dass fromme Leute, damit verhindert, zu rechter Erkenntnis Christi nicht kommen moechten. Gerson undetliche mehr haben heftig darueber geklagt.[163]

The reference to 'sorely tried consciences' may be safely taken to speak about scrupulosity, Gerson's subject par excellence, while 'profitable doctrine of faith, of the cross, of hope' points at the *doctor consolatorius*' theme of *per desperationem enim ad spem uenire docuisti* (leading the believer from desperation to hope).[164] This function fits not only Melanchthon's psychological profile of an appeaser, but also the conciliatory nature of *The Augsburg Confession* itself, which was written in hope of reestablishing religious unity and peace in the Empire of Charles V. The use of the legal term *epieikeia*, so dear and central to the chancellor's moral theology, seems momentous, especially considering its placement between two mentions of Gerson's name. Although rendered in all official English translations as simply 'mitigations', Melanchthon's choice of a specific judicial terminology in both Latin and German texts of *The Augsburg Confession* is unlikely to be accidental, particularly in view of his keen interest in jurisprudence. Moreover, he had addressed the issue of *iustitia particularis* (circumstantial or interpretative justice) in the manner of the scholastic jurists like Gerson in his other writings. Thus, he believed that no right decision could be made before taking into account *collationes circumstantiarum [...] cum uerum postea pro diuersitate*

---

[163] Melanchthon, *Confessio Augustana ipsa*, CR: 26, pp. 306–07. 'Gerson writes that many fell into despair. Some even took their own lives because they felt that they were not able to satisfy the traditions, and they had all the while not heard any consolation of the righteousness of faith and grace. We see that the authors of *summae* and theologians gather the traditions and seek mitigations whereby to ease consciences, and yet they do not sufficiently unfetter but sometimes entangle consciences even more. With the gathering of these traditions, the schools and sermons have been so much occupied that they have had no leisure to touch upon Scripture and to seek the more profitable doctrine of faith, of the cross, of hope, and of the dignity of civil affairs of consolation of sorely tried consciences. Hence Gerson and some other theologians have grievously complained that by these strivings concerning traditions, they were prevented from giving attention to a better kind of doctrine' (Melanchthon 1921 online).

[164] *De consolatione theologiae*, OC: 9, p. 234: 'to be surely led through desperation to arrive at hope'.

circumstantiarum, nationum, temporum, poenae atrociores aut mitiores constituuntur.[165]

> *Ut enim medici in curationibus propter uarietatem circumstantiarum augent aut mederantur remedii formam probabili ratione, ita legumlatores propter uarietatem circumstantiarum exasperant aut mitigant generales notitias.*[166]

As was the case with Thomas More, Melanchthon's fondness for the late medieval chancellor increased with time, resulting in his desire to gradually unite his two favorites, Gerson and Luther. Already his 1521 *Defense of Luther* suggested that the Sorbonne has fallen since the time of the great chancellor.[167] In the 1540s Melanchthon refers to Gerson as *illustrius apud eos Theologus* (a more distinguished among theologians)[168] and declares, in a slight paraphrase from Luther, that *Solus Gerson de tentationibus spiritus scripsit, alii omnes externas tantum et corporales senserunt.*[169] In 1546, at Martin Luther's funeral, Philipp gave a speech, published the same year as the Preface to the second volume of Luther's works, which presented 'Canßler Parifienftsas' as the most recent prophet of the Reformation. The rapprochement with the French master culminated in Melanchthon's 1548 biography of Martin Luther, *De obitu Lutheri historia de uita et actis reuerendis*, where Dr Philipp straightforwardly affirmed the

---

[165] Melanchthon, *De iustitia particularis*, CR: 16, p. 67. 'More frightful or less aggressive penalties are decreed after truly considering the diversity of the nation's circumstances of the of the times'.

[166] CR: 16, pp. 71–72. 'Just as physicians in curing diseases increase or decrease the probable form of cure according to the variety of circumstances, so should the legislators increase or mitigate general rules according to the variety of circumstances'. See Berman 1989, p. 1643. *Errabant & Academici qui contendebant nihil esse certum, ac iubebant suspendere assensionem, seu epexeih etiam de principiis naturae notis, & de perpetua experientia. Ab his prodigiosis deliramentis abhorrere auribus atque animis omnis debent* (Appendix to Chapter 4: The *Disputatio* in Melanchthon's *Commentarius* De Anima, 1548 in Peterson 2009, p. 268) 'The academics, who have contended that nothing is certain, also erred and voted to suspend approval, or *epikeia*, even about known principles of nature and perpetual experience. All ought to shield their ears and souls from such prodigious ravings'.

[167] *Didymi Faventini versus Thomam Placentinum pro M. Luthero oratio*, Basel: Adam Petri, 1521. Oberman 1981a, p. 28.

[168] CR: 4, p. 56.

[169] CR: 20, p. 566.

German reformer's special indebtedness to Gerson, whom he *[Luther] diligenter et Gersonem legerat [...]*.[170]

Several factors are likely to have contributed to Melanchthon's increasingly favorable reception of Gerson in his later years. The first is the mere fact of Luther's passing. Now that the founding father was deceased, his closest associate could choose to take a distance from his mentor and articulate opinions that were truly his own. Secondly, Melanchthon's own opinions had changed. While both Melanchthon and Luther evolved as thinkers, they evolved in opposite directions. Unlike Dr Martin, who believed in his divine mission as a prophet of a new era, thus becoming more and more intransigent as he aged, Philipp grew milder and more appreciative of the intellectual treasures of the past, such as late medieval scholasticism, which he had so vigorously bashed as a young man. Nonbelligerent by nature, Melanchthon loathed open confrontations and clear cuts, leaning toward compromise and accommodation. Always careful to emphasize his agreement with Luther on the main doctrine, he liked to mention that he expressed the same religious truths *admodum amanter* ('in a more friendly fashion') and *minus horride* (less rudely) than his mentor.[171] Remembering Erasmus's letter of 1520, in which the Dutch humanist said that he would much prefer that [Luther] *illum quaedam ciuilius ac moderatius scripsisse*,[172] Melanchthon always tried to smooth rough edges. An inclusive approach toward the theological heritage of his immediate predecessors agreed much more with his temperament than revolutionary insolence. A careful reading reveals that he gradually eliminated his diatribes against the scholastics from *Loci Communes*' later editions, increasingly adopting their terminology and classifications for his own use. Moreover, even though Melanchthon kept rewriting *Loci Communes* through continuous editing (the last editions were almost four times the size of the initial text of 1521), he kept positive

---

[170] Melanchthon 1548. 'Luther read Gerson diligently.'

[171] *Scis me quaedam minus horride dicere de praedestinatione, de assensu uoluntatis, de necessitate obedientiae nostrae, de peccato mortali* (Melanchthon, CR: 3, p. 383) 'You know I say fewer alarming things about predestination, about the assent of the will, on the necessity of obedience, on the mortal sin'.

[172] Erasmus to Melanchthon, CR: 1, p. 206. See Melanchthon 2014.

references to Gerson in all of them.[173] Thirdly, the necessity to develop a formal Lutheran theology compelled Melanchthon to come to terms with medieval theological tradition. As a humanist and an academic, he never shared Luther's disdain for reason as the 'Devil's whore'[174] and, therefore, appreciated a carefully maintained equilibrium between affectivity and intellect, which Gerson strove to achieve in his theology.

This increasing moderation and inclusiveness are reflected in Melanchthon's changing theology. After first denying, with Luther, all freedom of will, Melanchthon began modifying his position on this issue as early as the 1530s, trying to find a middle ground between the Wittenberg reformer and Dr Philipp's beloved mentor and friend, Erasmus. Whereas the first 1521 edition of *Loci communes* sounded virtually identical with Luther's work *The Bondage of the Will*, by 1535 Melanchthon had made some major adjustments:

> *Haec particula exclusiua, non excludit nostram poenitentiam, et bona opera, sed tantum conditionem dignitatis excludit, & tota causam beneficii Christi transfert in misericordiam [...]*[175]

By 1543, three years before Luther's passing, Philipp expressed views, which were closer to Erasmus's (and Gerson's) position, that 'three causes concur in the conversion of a human being — the word of God, the Holy Spirit, and the human will':

> *[...] uidemus coniungi has causas, Verbum, Spiritum sanctum, et uoluntatem, non sane otiosam, sed repignantem infirmitati suae. [...] Deus anteuertit nos, uocat, mouet, adiuuat, sed nos uiderimus, ne repugnemus.*[176]

---

[173] Besides *Loci Communes*, Melanchthon positively mentions Gerson in his letters to King Francis of France and King Henry VIII of England (Meijering 1983 p. 14, n. 78).

[174] See Dragseth 2011.

[175] *Loci Communes* 1535, CR: 21, pp. 423–24. 'This exclusive function [of divine grace] does not exclude our penance and good works, but excludes only the condition of [our] dignity, and transfers the whole foundation of the benefit to the mercy of Christ'.

[176] *Loci Communes* 1543, CR: 21, p. 276. 'We see conjoined these causes, the Word, the Holy Spirit, and the will, which is certainly not idle but fights against its infirmities [...] God anticipates us; he calls, he moves, he delights, but we shall have seen and shall not have resisted' (Trans. in Osslund 1984, p. 28).

The expression *uoluntas non est otiosa*[177] makes a frequent appearance in his later writings, signaling Melanchthon's gradual dissociation from Luther's radical stance concerning freedom of the will. Softening Luther's crude language and uncompromising position, Dr Philipp attempted to achieve a certain balance between God's providence and human effort, discretely allowing for a degree of cooperation between the divine and human wills: *Fit autem uoluntas adiuuante spiritu sancto magis libera, id est, circumspectius et constantius agent, et ardentius euocans deum.*[178] However, although he moved somewhat closer toward Gerson's *theologia media*, the theology of spiritual quest remained utterly unacceptable to him.[179]

The dichotomous evolutions in Luther's and Melanchthon's attitudes toward the late medieval chancellor reflect differences in their respective theological journeys and in their respective personalities: from a close association to a more distant reverential regard in the case of Luther, and from a reserved deference to an outright fondness in the instance of Melanchthon. Still, *Loci Communes*, which grew from a simple guide to Scripture into the Lutheran book of systematic theology,[180] de facto became a vehicle of Gerson's legacy. Highly praised by Luther, who endorsed all of the editions, it had an enormous impact on the development of Protestant thought. Leading Lutheran theologians, such as Martin Chemnitz, used it both to teach their students the fundamentals of Evangelical theology and as a basis for their own dogmatic works.[181]

Andreas Bodenstein von Karlstadt

One can hardly imagine a personality more opposite to that of Melanchthon as Andreas Rudolph Bodenstein von Karlstadt (1486–1541), one of the most controversial and complex fig-

---

[177] CR: 21, p. 663. 'Will is not inactive'.

[178] CR: 21, p. 663. 'However, the will, with help of the Holy Spirit, becomes more free, that is, acting circumspectly and steadily, and fervently calling God'.

[179] Melanchthon's position is famously ambiguous, and his smooth formulations gave ground to much debate leading to even considering him seen as 'the father of synergism in the Lutheran Church' (Pieper 1953, p. 3122).

[180] Preus 2014, p. 15.

[181] Preus 2014, p. 16.

ures among the first generation of German reformers. At first opposed to Luther's views, then his passionate co-legionary, Karlstadt broke with the mainstream Lutheranism by 1524, forming a theology of his own. As a thinker deeply influenced by *theologia deutsch* and particularly by Johannes Teuler (1300–1361), he initially approached Gerson as a mystic, and his reassessment of the chancellor's theology acts as a means of defining his own views on traditional exegesis. Stages of Karlstadt's reevaluation of Gerson are traceable in his 1518 three-hundred-eighty theses, known as *Apologeticae conclusiones*, which were written in response to Johannes Eck's attack on Luther's ninety-five theses of 1517. These theses are a fascinating mirror of Karlstadt's rapid radicalization and his transformation into a biblical literalist and by 1521, an iconoclast. In the first set of theses, where Bodenstein mainly refuted the necessity of having church authorities, it was Gerson's conciliarist position at the Council of Constance that interested him the most for obvious strategic reasons. Out of words to describe the infamy of the Church that dares to 'condemn Gerson as a heretic', Karlstadt calls it *bestia Crocodilina*.[182] However, it soon appeared clear to him that rejection of *spurcum, sordidum et propudiosum animal Rome*[183] was only the first step, the next being dismissal of ecclesiastical councils, which he saw as being just as unnecessary as the pope. This step was quickly followed by the argument for absolute superiority of Scripture over all human authorities. Citing Gerson's text *De examinatione doctrinarum* in central theses twelve, fourteen and seventeen, Karlstadt ponders on the issue of *Irrtumsfähigkeit* or infallibility, which, since it cannot be attributed to any human institution — be it the Pope, the Council or even the whole church (*Gesamkirche*) — justifies the position that 'it is better to put faith in the Gospel than in any other human authority'.[184] However, what Karlstadt meant by 'the whole Church' and what Gerson meant by this notion no

---

[182] Sider 1974, p. 89: *Itaque noli bestia Crocodilina Gersonem quasi haereticum condemnare, quia non ex hominum sed ex dei uerbo et potestate pendemus.* 'Therefore, O crocodile, do not condemn Gerson as a heretic, for we judge according to the word and power not of man but of God'.

[183] Sider 1974, p. 89: 'swinish, sordid and infamous animal the Roman Church'.

[184] Thesis 12, Bubenheimer 1971, p. 73.

longer denoted the same thing. In traditional medieval understanding, which was that of Gerson and continued to be that of Luther, the whole Church or *ecclesia universalis*, was implicitly understood to mean the church as the bride and mystical body of Christ, animated by the Holy Spirit, and therefore infallible.[185] Karlstadt meant something different and theologically new. Due to his radical dualism, which, on the one hand, affirms the existence of a spiritual and universal church, while, on the other, rejects the idea of the church as a mystical body of the *Braut Christi*, the *ganze* or *Gesamkirche* began to mean simply *fidelium omnium congregatio*, or, in other words, church as a religious community. As such, the church can and even is bound to err. Therefore, while Gerson's and Luther's understanding of the universal church was still traditional, holistic and mystical, Karlstadt's notion, close to that of Zwingli, moved toward the idea of a community of people sharing similar beliefs, which is a precursor of the modern Protestant parish as an administrative unit.[186]

Bodenstein furthers the discussion of the absolute priority of Scripture as sole authority in all matters in thesis fourteen, where he continues to rely on Gerson's *De examinatione doctrinarum*. He cites the chancellor's statement that *in casu doctrinali* 'a doctor supported by canonical authority' *plusquam declarationi papae credendum est* — should be believed more than the pope.[187] Here again, however, what Karlstadt wanted to prove and what Gerson actually meant in his text is not the same thing. For Gerson, the expression *in casu doctrinali* did not refer to papal authority in general, which was not in question, but to professional expertise needed in particular cases, should difficulties concern-

---

[185] *WA* 1: 685: *[...] uniuersalis autem ecclesia non potest errare, ut doctissime etiam probat Cardinalis Cameracensis [...]* (it is unclear which Pierre d'Ailly's passage Luther had in mind here).

[186] F. Oakley maintains that when Gerson and Pierre d'Ailly described the universal church as 'a mystical body (*corpus mysticum ecclesiae*), they did so without evoking any spiritual connotations. Instead 'they used *cospus mysticum* as a synonym for the 'moral and political body' (*corpus morale et politicum*)' (Oakley 2015, p. 232).

[187] Bubenheimer 1971, Thesis 14, Part 1, consideration 5, in p. 73: *Praemissa in tantum procedit, quod dicto doctoris auctoritate canonica communito plusquam declarationi papae credendum est*. 'Having said that, the saying of a doctor supported by canonical authority must be believed rather than the declaration of the Pope' (*De examinatione doctrinarum*, OC: 9, p. 463).

ing the dogma arise. The chancellor firmly placed this expertise in people like himself, professional theologians with academic training, allowing only for some specific exceptions:

> [...] *aliquis simplex non auctorisatus esset tam excellenter in sacris litteris eruditus, quod plus esset credendum in casu doctrinali suae assertioni, quam Papae declarationi; constat enim plus esse credendum Evangelio quam Papae.*[188]

However, it could never cross Gerson's mind to juxtapose the Church and the Gospel. Taken out of context and generalized, the French theologian's statement acquires the meaning almost opposite to his original intent. By affirming that the Bible has sole and absolute authority in all matters, 'Karlstadt already positions himself apart from Gerson, with whom he concurs only to a limited degree'.[189] Indeed, while Gerson's position, as in most cases, is circumstance-based and relevant within a clearly defined context, Karlstadt's statement *Romanus pontifex omni auctoritate destitutus et uacuus esset,*[190] found in the next, fifteenth thesis, signals an unconditional antagonism to Rome.

Karlstadt's increasingly revolutionary opinions would lead not only to dissatisfaction with Gerson's position on the superiority of church councils, rejected as insufficiently radical, but also to the degradation of his opinion regarding the chancellor's authority and even his persona. Karlstadt ends up accusing Gerson of shamelessly plagiarizing Mattheo de Mattesilani (died in 1424), professor of canonical law at the university of Bologna.[191]

---

[188] *De examinatione doctrinarum*, OC: 9, p. 463. '[...] a certain simple person who is unauthorized [i.e., without theological license] would be so excellently learned in sacred literature that his assertion would be more believed in a doctrinal case than the declaration of the pope. For it is the case that the Gospel should be believed more than the pope.' (Flanagan 2006, p. 175) Gerson maintains a careful balance between authorities of the Church and Scripture by adding immediately after that 'it is not said [the Gospel is to be believed more] than of God [the authority] of the whole Church' (Flanagan 2006, p. 175). For further discussion of Karlstadt's use of medieval authorities, see Sider 1974.

[189] Barge 1905, p. 120: 'Er setzt sich bei dieser Gelegenheit mit Gerson auseinander, dem er nur bedingt zustimmt'.

[190] Thesis 15, Bubenheimer 1971, p. 110.

[191] Thesis 15, Bubenheimer 1971, p. 73: *Gerson tamen, non commemorato Matthaeo de Mathaselanis, qui prius in aliis terminis idem docuit, cuius et exemplum imitatus eum turpiter tacuisse uidetur.* 'Gerson, however, failed to mention

Through manipulation of Gerson's words he also attacks the legitimacy of church councils as bound to 'mislead [the people] and make a mistake both out of maliciousness and ignorance'.[192] In thesis twenty-five Bodenstein openly declares to be *contra Gerson* in the context of biblical exegesis: *Contra Gersonem negamus, esse sensum litteralem, qui ex intentione, et circumstantiis scribentis colligitur*.[193] Though he would still occasionally speak about Gerson in a positive manner as, for example, in theses nineteen and eighty-nine, Karlstadt makes sure to clearly distance himself from the chancellor's opinions. Disagreements turn into an open confrontation in theses sixty-eight to seventy-four, where Bodenstein condemns Gerson's idea of ecclesiastical power as an heir of the apostolic and early Christian church.[194] From that point onward the Pope, the Catholic Church, the general councils or Sorbonne theologians were all the same and equally guilty of *Euangelio non crederum*. 'For Karlstadt there exists an 'offence in faith', if something is objectively in conflict with divine Law. This state of things 'offends', in that it stands in the way of real faith, even though the erring believer may be unaware of this'.[195] Gerson had inadvertently become part of the 'material-spiritual circumstances that offend God and, consequently, Karlstadt himself'.[196]

After thesis eighty-nine Karlstadt discontinued referring to the French theologian altogether. A biblical fundamentalist, he believed that 'the standard of judgment and action came not from

---

Matthew de Mathaselanis, who had previously taught the same thing in other terms, and whose example he seems to imitate shamefully, while remaining silent about him'.

[192] Theses 18 and 20, trans. in Sider 1974, p. 53, note 33: *Quod restringit, si malicia (quod nota) uel ignorantia, ab euangelia auctoritate declinaret concilium.* 'He [Gerson] restricts that, in case of maliciousness (which is known) or ignorance, the council would digress from the authority of the Gospels'. *Concilium autem generale, iuxta Gersonem, et ex malice et ignorantia fallere ac falli potest.* 'According to Gerson, the general council, however, can mislead and be misled because of maliciousness or ignorance'.

[193] Thesis 25, Bubenheimer 1971, p. 131. 'We deny against Gerson that there is a literal sense, which is gathered from the intention, and the [historical] circumstances of the writer'. On Gerson's understanding of the literal sense, see Flanagan 2006, pp. 133–78.

[194] Bubenheimer 1971, pp. 148–49.

[195] Bubenheimer 1973, p. 287.

[196] Leroux 2003, p. 76. This article contains an exhaustive bibliography of Karlstadt's scholarship.

human authority, tradition, or institutions but from a transcendent 'Word' to be derived directly from the sacred text without any interpretation'.[197] An authority which violates God's standards, as they are spelled out in Scripture, is a false authority, and needs to be immediately dismantled, regardless of collateral damage. Such views set him apart from the mainstream Lutherans, for, projected into a social sphere, this position would unavoidably lead to the rejection of all human authorities, steering toward an open rebellion against civil and church powers, as it would happen during the Peasant War of 1525.

Although Karlstadt continued to express some solidarity with Gerson as one of the papacy's victims two years later, in his 1520 book *De canonicis scripturis libellus*, his numerous references to the chancellor rather illustrate the principle of 'an enemy of my enemy is my friend' than a genuine interest in the chancellor's thought. His attitude toward Gerson underwent a complete reevaluation, changing, within a short period of time, from reverence to detachment, then to manipulation, criticism, hostility and finally irrelevance. Unlike Melanchthon, for whom the French master's voice remained pertinent until the end, and Luther, who never completely disengaged himself from his spiritual father, Karlstadt demonstrated willingness to free himself from the sway of this or any other human authority, which, like the Church of Rome itself, he first loved and then scorned.

Martin Bucer

Although the sheer volume of Gerson's presence in the writings of the Strasbourg theologian Martin Bucer (1491–1551) does not compare to that found in Luther, Melanchthon or Karlstadt, his reception of the chancellor's legacy is relevant, as it concerns several issues of major importance: irenicism, as an attempt to find common ground in different Christian apologetical systems, Eucharistic theology, and ecclesiology. Second in influence only to Luther, Bucer left a mark not only on Lutheran, but also on Calvinist and Anglican doctrines and practices. Being, like Mel-

---

[197] Kelley 1983, p. 63.

anchthon, of a rather conciliatory disposition, the Strasbourg theologian spent most of his life looking for a possible compromise with Catholics, and his *Memorandum* (1534) has the twofold historical significance: it discusses the possibility of religious concord and helps to initiate interconfessional dialogue.[198] Even though Bucer reportedly declined to buy any of Gerson's or Geiler von Kaysersberg's works during his tenure in Strasbourg,[199] he relied on the chancellor's prestige as a unifying authority figure, which all parties knew and respected, during his initial attempts to mend ways with Catholics. It was his desire of rapprochement with Catholics that initially led him to Gerson, and it was his later disagreement with them that eventually brought about a fall out with his favorite late medieval theologian. The accord with Catholics concerned the central place of the Eucharist in Christian life, while the discord with them was about the manner of administering it. The stumbling block was the issue of the laity's communion of both kinds — the very 'battle cry of the Hussite movement'[200] — which was of primary importance to Bucer, who argued for the elimination of anything that could stand in the way between the Eucharist and the people. He particularly objected to the perpetuated belief in the sacrosanct powers of priests and harshly criticized the medieval practice of communion by bread only as an insolent deviation from the apostolic practice. There was no way around it: the chancellor's position at the Council of Constance was an embodiment of everything to which Bucer so passionately objected. Gerson presented his reasons for denying the communion of both kinds as primarily practical, even hygienic: the danger of spilling the wine, defilement to the sacred vessels from their contact with laymen's hands and lips, laymen's long beards, the possibility of the wine's turning to vinegar while it was being carried to the sick, or being corrupted by flies, or frozen by the cold; the difficulty of always purchasing wine, or the impossibility of providing cups for ten or twenty thousand communicants on

---

[198] Hazlett 2000, p. 143. Also see Bender 1975.
[199] Greschat 2004, p. 20. Greschat's book represents the latest assessment of Bucer's theological views.
[200] di Mauro 2005, p. 1.

Easter.[201] These reservations have no basis in Scripture, which for Bucer was the only gold standard. The chancellor's intransigent position on this issue, expressed in *De necessaria communione laicorum sub utraque specie*, should have, in all logic, resulted in Bucer's complete disavowal of the late medieval theologian. Yet, this did not occur, and Strasburger continued referring to Gerson as *uiro alioqui et doctissimo et sanctissimo* ('man otherwise the most learned and the most holy').[202] Moreover, in his *Retractiones*, written in 1537 in order to demonstrate to Luther 'that he truly had abandoned his former Zwinglian teachings on the Eucharist',[203] Bucer presents the chancellor as following:

> [...] der Gerson so ein gotsforchtig man und der gor fil mehr uff gotswort gehalten hat dann die Theologen zu seiner zeit zuthun pflegten, sich in diser sachen so gor kindisch erzeiget hat, die doch im Concilio zu Constanz durch den frommen Huss gruntlich und hell dargethon ware. Diser Gerson, als er sahe, das die gemeine ursach, die man zugeben pfleget, darumb man den laien billich die gemeinschaft des kelchs (chalice) Christi verholte [...] und dise ursach, meinet der gut man, seie gleich genug, dass die kirch den leien die gemeinschaft des kelchs verboten hatte.[204]

---

[201] Gerson, *De necessaria communione laicorum sub utraque specie* (*On the Necessity of Communion for the Laity Under Both Kinds*), OC: 10, p. 63: *[...] propter euitationem multiplicis periculi irreuerentiae et scandali, circa susceptionem huiusmodi benedicti sacramenti: primum periculum in effusione; secundum in deportation de loco ad locum; tertium in uasorum sordidatione quae deberent esse consecrate nec passim tractate uel tacta a laicis; quartum in barbis longis laicorum; quantum in conseruatione pro infirmis [...] aut muscae generarentur [...] aut fieret uelut abominabile ad Bibendum [...]* 'On account of the avoidance of the multiple risk of irreverence and scandal, regarding the reception of the blessed sacrament in this way, firstly the danger in spilling it; secondly in moving it from place to place; thirdly in the dirtying of the pyxes that should be consecrated, nor handled randomly or touched by laymen; fourthly in long beards of the laymen, fifthly because of the necessity to conserve it for the sick [...] or flies would be generated in it or it would become even as abominable to drink.' This position was upheld by the Council of Trent, which approved the teaching 'the whole body and blood of Christ are truly contained under each form. Therefore, the Eucharist cup could legitimately be withheld' (O'Malley 2013, p. 28).

[202] Hazlett 2000, 5, Appendix, p. 150.

[203] Bruening 2006, p. 79.

[204] Bucer 1960, p. 360. 'Gerson, a God-fearing man, and the one who trusted in God's Word much more than other theologians of his time ever cared to do, proved himself childish [kindisch] in this matter, even though it was so thor-

Bucer's choice to refer to the church official who was directly responsible for the martyrdom of 'fromme Huss' as 'kindisch' and 'der gut man' is, to put it mildly, rather odd, and betrays his earnest frustration with the late medieval theologian, whose position he was no longer able to comprehend. In the same year (1537) Bucer attempted, once more, to twist the chancellor's position in order to make it agree, at least partially, with his own. He asserted that 'the dignity of the laity in relation to the consumption of the body of Christ would be as great as that of the priests' by quoting Gerson's own words: *[...] primo, quod tanta esset dignitas laicorum circa sumptionem corporis Christi sicut et sacerdotum.*[205] However, when his hopes that Catholics would allow communion of both kinds for the laity and would abolish the private Mass did not materialize, his position hardened both toward the Church of Rome and toward Gerson: 'Wollen sie dann für wenden mit dem Gersone, es gepure sich, mit diesem halbieren des Sacramentes die Priesterlich wurde zu erhalten?'[206] And again:

> Wil man dan sagen, wie Gerson, diss Sacrament rauben diene darzu, das man den Priester Hoher halt dan die Leien, so geben sie doch den Kelch den Priesteren gleich so wenig als den Leien [...][207]

Not finding support on the issue of communion in his immediate predecessors, Bucer turned to Christian antiquity, and specifically to John Chrysostom, whose authority he used as a weapon against the late medieval chancellor who so badly disappointed him: 'Nun hat der Heiliger Chrysortomus sich etwas bass (besser) dan Gerson

---

oughly and clearly presented to him by pious Hus at the Council of Constance. This Gerson, as he saw the reason that one would give as to why the communion of the chalice was commonly denied to lay people [...] and the good man believes this reason to be sufficient enough for the Church to have forbidden the communion of the chalice to the laity'.

[205] Bucer 1960, p. 363. Gerson, *De necessaria communione laicorum sub utraque specie*, OC: 10, p. 63.

[206] Bucer 1543, p. 215. 'Do you want then to argue together with Gerson that it is right to maintain priestly honor through the breaking in two of the sacrament?'

[207] Bucer 1543, Band 11, 3, p. 355. 'Do you want to say then, like Gerson, that withholding this sacrament [from the laity] means that priest is held to be higher than the laity, then give the chalice to the priests just as little as to lay people'.

umb diese sachen verstanden.'[208] The theme of double or full communion remained central in Bucer's writings, resurfacing again and again, each time bringing references to Gerson, for whom Bucer continued to have mixed feelings of veneration and vexation. The Strasbourg theologian's final disenchantment with the late medieval master represents another case of a reversal of opinion, although more gradual and guarded than with Andreas von Karlstadt. As for many other theologians of the 16th century, the Eucharist became the dividing line and the limit beyond which Bucer was unable to compromise.

German Evangelical Harmonies, Johannes Bugenhagen and Andreas Osiander

The Lutheran principle of self-sufficiency of Scripture increased the demand for Biblical harmonies, making Gerson's *Monotessaron* into 'ein Stolperstein' for almost all subsequent authors who took upon themselves the challenge of evangelical harmonization. The French theologian apparently coined the word 'monotessaron' based on the beginning of Augustine's *De consensu evangelistarum*.[209] It would not be an overstatement to say that his unprecedented enterprise engendered a whole new genre, which 'widely circulated in pre-modern and modern Europe and played an impressive role, either directly or indirectly, in the flourishing of this literary genre in the 16th century and beyond, within the framework of biblical humanism and Reformation'.[210] *Monotessaron*'s popularity in the Empire surged in the 1520s, after an Alsatian humanist Ottimar Luscinius (1487–1537) published this

---

[208] Bucer 1543, Band 11, 3, p. 355: 'Now the Holy John Chrysostom has a slightly better understanding on this matter than Gerson'.

[209] According to William Lawrence Petersen's theory, Gerson derived this concept from the Tatian's (*c.* 160–175) gospel harmony entitled *Diatessaron* (Petersen 1994, p. 189). The terms *monotessaron* or *monatessaron*, as it can be seen in some spellings, possibly originate from the faulty translation of the Greek term *diatessaron*. As it was suggested by C. Arthur Lynch of the Brown University Department of Classics, both terms are just poor Greek, since 'dia' was incorrectly rendered as 'two' and replaced by 'mono' in an attempt to express the idea of creating one text out of four. Marc Vial contests Glorieux's dating of *Monotessaron* to 1420, suggesting a much earlier date. See also Vial 2004, p. 65.

[210] Masolini 2020, p. 2.

text in German, duly acknowledging the harmony's real author. From this point on Gerson's text, initially intended for the clerical audience, was open, at least in German-speaking lands, to quite a different reading public of cultured laity. It is no coincidence that this work was first translated and published in Alsace, as this region continued to play a special role in both *translatio studii* and *transmitii Gersonis*, which was one and the same at the time. Luscinius himself belonged to the Strasbourg's humanist circle, where he befriended Sebastian Brant and Jacob Wimpheling, before going to Paris to study Latin under Faustus Adrelini. Being particularly interested in music, Luscinius published, in 1515, a book on the elements of music called *Institutiones musicae*,[211] followed, in 1517, by *Musuragia seu Praxis Musicae*, where he appears to mention the same instruments as the ones described by Gerson in his treaty *De canticis*.[212] Whether Luscinius's interest in musical harmonies eventually led him to Gerson's *Monotessaron* remains to be seen, and the intriguing connection between musical and evangelical harmonies still awaits its researcher.

More than forty comprehensive harmonies survive from the 16th century, and all of them are direct or indirect descendants of Gerson's *Monotessaron*. Not all 16th century authors were as open and honest about their dependence on Gerson's model as Luscinius, however. In actuality, quite the opposite was the norm. Thus, Bamberg printer Georg Erlinger, who took Gerson's harmony for a coherent actual account of Christ's life, and candidly offered it to all Christians 'schwachen des glaubens'[213] under a rather dangerous title of *Euangelion Christi*, did not mention Gerson's authorship at all. Melanchthon, who wrote a short preface to the 1530 edition of Erlinger's book, attempted, in his typically tactful and diplomatic manner, to rectify the situation by crediting *Monotessaron* as a direct prototype for *Euangelion Christi*. In his preface, Philipp put forward three reasons as to 'darum ich diß monotessaron achte nutzlich zu lessen' ('why *Monotessaron* was useful to read').[214] First, Gerson's harmony

---

[211] Wünsch 1983, p. 16.
[212] Luscinius 1536, p. 74. On Luscinius see Virdung & Bullard 1993.
[213] Wünsch 1983, p. 61.
[214] Wünsch 1983, p. 63.

presents the entire story of Jesus's life. Second, it demonstrates the extent to which the Evangelists, even if they differ in their wording, complete each other. Finally, by putting all four texts together, Gerson made each Evangelist function as an interpreter [Ausleger] of the others, so that Scriptures can be better understood through juxtaposition.[215] Erlinger made his own conclusions though. He proceeded without mentioning Gerson's model in subsequent editions, dropped Melanchthon's inconveniently honest preface and wrote later prefaces himself instead.[216]

Some harmonies are anonymous, like *Die vier Evangelia in ainen formlichen ordnung*, which is a German reworking of *Monotessaron* combined with Luther's translation of the New Testament. Others bear famous names of Johannes Bugenhagen (1485–1558) or Andreas Osiander (1498–1552). A Biblical scholar, humanist and a prominent church administrator, Bugenhagen, known as Doctor Pomeranus, played a key role in the development of Lutheranism in Northern Germany. He began composing his first evangelical harmony as early as 1519, continually revising it through the years. Although his work is clearly based on Gerson's model, Pomeranus did not acknowledge his debt to *Monotessaron* until a later revised version of his harmony, titled *Harmony of the Passion of Christ* and published in 1566: *Gerson habe sein monotessaron in multis satis feliciter, praecipue usque as illud iter, quo Christus ex Galilaea toto tertio praedicationis suae anno pergit per Samariam in Iudaeam geschrieben.*[217] Bugenhagen's subsequent harmonies, expanded with the addition of Psalm 22 and Isaiah 53, two Old Testament texts that were considered as prefiguring the passion of Christ, were immensely popular, and had many later 16th century editions. Their popularity peaked in Saxony, where Pomeranus's harmonies were elevated to the status of alternative preaching texts, and served in this capacity up until

---

[215] Wünsch 1983, pp. 62–63.

[216] Dietrich Wünsch suggests that Erlinger's book, being nothing other than a simple German translation of Gerson's *Monotessaron*, does not deserve belonging to the history of German harmonies but rather to the *Wirkungsgeschichte* of Gerson's work (Wünsch 1983, p. 64).

[217] Wünsch 1983, p. 245. 'Gerson has written his *Monotessaron* quite successfully in many places, especially the way in which Christ continues his preaching during the year starting from Galilee, through Samaria to Judea'.

the end of the 18th century. During Johann Sebastian Bach's tenure at Thomas Church in Leipzig (1623–1750), the city's chorale collection, which he practiced with his pupils, included Bugenhagen's harmony of the Passion.[218] Two passages in Bach's St John Passion text 'occur in the same sequence as in Bugenhagen's harmony of the Passion',[219] possibly revealing traces of its influence on Bach. This is particularly likely since an edition of Bugehagen's harmony was available in the 1724 *Leipziger Gesang-Buch*, as well as in many other hymn books of the time.[220] Thus, a distant voice of Gerson's *Monotessaron*, whose structure Doctor Pomeranus borrowed in his harmony, appears to have reached the great Leipzig maestro himself.

Andreas Osiander's reworking of Gerson's harmony is of a completely different order. A highly controversial theologian, he was opposed by nearly all evangelicals in an ideological war, which produced over ninety tracts, pamphlets and theses, uniting such bitter enemies as Matthias Flacius and Philipp Melanchthon against him. A Biblical literalist and mystic, Osiander believed that Christ's righteousness is transferred to the faithful in this life through divine indwelling and not as a forensic declaration of forgiveness.[221] Taking Luther's principles of *sola fide* and *sola Scriptura* to their ultimate limits, Osiander held that if Christ is an incarnate Word, and the Word is Scripture, solely through faith in Scripture sinners unite with Christ's divine essence, and are *essentially* justified, with no need for grace.[222] 'Osiander added a dimension to the role of Christ as Mediator, which [...] united him to an individual who was in the process of being perfected, or deified'.[223]

It was only natural that his radically Christocentric position, focused almost exclusively on scriptural exegesis, would bring Osiander, who knew Gerson's work and used *Opusculum tripar-*

---

[218] Chafe 2000, p. 133.
[219] Leaver 1985, p. 8.
[220] Leaver 1985, p. 8.
[221] Kang 2006, p. 75. For further theological discussion of this subject see Horton 2012.
[222] See Wengert 2012, pp. 4–73.
[223] Matthews 2013, p. 44.

titum as the basis for his 1533 *Catechismus oder Kinderpredig*,[224] into close contact with *Monotessaron*. Osiander acknowledges Gerson's influence in the preface to the 1537 edition of his *Harmony of the Gospels*, where he borrows *Monotessaron*'s overall text presentation and the abbreviation system, without which his endeavor would have been impossible. He begins his harmony by proclaiming that his objective is the same as Gerson's: 'to remove all conflicts between the gospels, by showing how the varying accounts were each correct'.[225] However, despite this declaration, his design was 'in direct contrast to Gerson's work',[226] because at the foundation of Osiander's harmony lies the principle diametrically opposed to that of *Monotessaron*. The latter is held together by the notion of *concordissima dissonantia*, which Gerson derived from Augustine's principle of *concordia diuersitas*. This principle holds together Augustine's *De consensu Euangelistarum*, where he first unified the four Evangelists into one narrative.[227] The tenet of *concordia diuersitas* is of principal anthropological importance, as it is an extension of the Augustinian theodicy, according to which discordances do not disrupt but rather enhance the beauty of the whole: 'I had come to see that though the higher things are better than the lower, the sum of all creation is better than the higher things alone'.[228] Gerson adopted this principle — according to which Gospels did not have to be absolutely consistent with each other in order to be considered truthful — as the foundation of his presentation of the Gospels, and called it *concordissima dissonantia*:

---

[224] Bossy 2002, p. 231.
[225] Petersen 2011, p. 298.
[226] Petersen 2011, p. 298.
[227] Gerson, Prohemium to the *Monotessaron*, OC: 9, p. 248: *Unum ex quatuor Euangeliis componere, diuinus aperuit Augustinus qui libro suo De consensu euangelistarum, subtilissimo quidem & operosissimo, compingit sub una serie narrationis euangeliorum uerba usque ad tempus, quo praedicare et baptizare Ioannes exorsus est [...]* (trans. in Haupt 1976, p. xlvii). 'In order to combine four Gospels into one, the divine Augustine, who launched his most subtle and indeed laborious book *On the Consensus of Scriptures*, joined together, under one sequence of evangelical narratives, the words until the point in time when John (the Baptist) began to preach and baptize'.
[228] Augustine of Hippo 1961, p. 149.

Sed cum magno sacramenti mysterio sibi placuit sub quadam concordissima, si ita dici possit, dissonantia, mentes fidelium commouere ad humiliorem uigilantioremque necnon multipliciorem inuestigationem ueritatis, palam fieret quatuor euangelistas non mutua conspiratione sed diuina inspiratione fuisse locutus.[229]

For Osiander, Gerson's concept of *concordissima dissonantia* was an oxymoron, and he does not hesitate to proclaim both he and Augustine to be simply wrong.[230] Considering that Osiander's theology is based on the understanding of the Word as comprising literally every word in Scripture, ambiguity or grey areas in interpreting the Gospels are no longer possible. Therefore, 'hermeneutics of both/and, indispensable for exegesis, given the multiplicity of meanings as well as the frequent contradictions to be found in Scripture'[231] must be rejected. Made of God's own words, Scripture cannot be composed of obscure statements, and Gerson's *probabile est*, frequently used in *Monotessaron* in relation to scriptural narrative, is unacceptable for the German literalist. Osiander aims at constructing a new, coherent type of harmony, which would be unified through elimination of all contradic-

---

[229] *Monotessaron*, OC: 9, p. 248. 'But, by means of the great mystery of the sacrament, He pleases Himself — if it can be said — by a dissonant harmony to move the minds of the faithful toward a humbler, more vigilant, and also a more complex search for truth, and it clearly happened that the four Evangelists have spoken not through mutual agreement, but [rather they have spoken] through divine inspiration'. Mathew Vanderpoel in his paper 'The Rhetoric of Sacred Scripture in Jean Gerson', presented at *Jean Gerson écrivain* Colloquium in Montpellier in April 2018, argues that Gerson's exegesis demonstrates the importance 'of asserting the indefinite, non-apophatic nature of most scriptural texts', which can only be understood as a whole'. David Z. Flanagan also insists on rhetoric as a 'crucially important factor in Gerson's exegesis', according to which Sacred Scripture 'should not be interpreted according to the power of logic and dialectic, which serve speculative sciences [...] as the moral sciences have rhetoric in the place of logic' (Flanagan 2006, p. 150).

[230] Osiander 1537, pp. 244–45: *Tertius, qui omnium fere manibus iam teritur, Iohannes Gerson Parisiensis tantum praestitit, ut post illos omnes laborem fortassis non frustra suscepisse existimari possit, uterum in iisdem fere logis omnibus haesit nauemque impedit, e quibus Augustinus enauigare non potuit*. 'The third, who amongst all already tried his hand at it, Jean Gerson of Paris so much excelled that perhaps after all of them (his) work cannot be considered undertaken in vain; nevertheless, he keeps close nearly all the same words and (further) deterred the ship, from which (words) Augustine could not sail forth'.

[231] Newman 2013, p. 13.

tory elements in accounts of Jesus's life. Fully conscious of his innovation, he proclaimed that only he, Andreas Osiander, had finally discovered the most exact accord, *exactissimam concordiam*, between four evangelical accounts, which no one *ante me*, before him, even suspected.[232] His need for consistency pushed him so far as to affirm that the Evangelists must have written their accounts in perfect chronological order, with the same transactions and discourses happening twice and more in Christ's life. This development has significance beyond the narrow topic of evangelical harmonies. Osiander's *exactissima concordia et consonantia* signals a mental break of tectonic proportions, since in his interpretation the concept of harmony acquires a new, modern meaning of total congruence, synchronization and coherence of all parts forming a whole. The *exactissima consonantia* reveals a new mindset centered above all on 'the values of unity',[233] for, if *concordissima dissonantia* allowed for the incorporation of discordant elements, *exactissima consonantia* seeks to unify within the 'same', that is, within the elements of the same order and nature. Osiander's versus Gerson's approaches to scriptural harmonization correlate as coherence versus juxtaposition, cleanness of line versus accretion, conversion versus addition, and purity versus totality.[234]

Although Osiander's *exactissima consonantia* model was followed by many early modern theologians, such as Polycarp Leyser (1552–1610), Johann Gerhard (1582–1637) and Kaspar Hermann Sandhagen (1639–1697), whose *Kurtze Einleitung in die Geschichte unsers Herrn Jesu Christi* was published in Lüneburg as late as 1684,[235] *Monotessaron*'s original prototype had prevailed. With the fancy for evangelical harmonies spreading beyond German-speaking lands, Gerson's model reached further North when Dutch theologian Wilhelm van Branteghem (unknown dates) published his Gerson-based Latin harmony *Vita Christi* in 1537, followed by two subsequent editions in French and in Dutch.

---

[232] Wünsch 1983, p. 110: *[...] exactissimam concordiam et consonantiam, quam ante me nemo ne suspicatus quidem est.*
[233] Simpson 2004, p. 1.
[234] Simpson 2004, p. 2.
[235] Marsh 1823, p. 33. See Sandhagen 1684.

Second-generation Lutherans: Martin Chemnitz

Gerson's influence resurfaces with an eminent second-generation Lutheran leader, Melanchthon's favorite student and the most important theologian in the history of Lutheranism, Martin Chemnitz (1522–1586), who is known as *Alter* or *Posterior Martinus*, about whom it is famously said *Si posterior Martinus non uenisset, prior Martinus non stetisset* ('If the second Martin had not come, the first Martin would scarcely have endured').[236] Considered by Lutherans as 'the father of normative Lutheran theology',[237] *Alter Martinus* played a key role in the creation of the *Formula of Concord*, which was meant to unite all Protestants.[238] Invested in education, he also implemented Melanchthon's pedagogical ideas by setting up a new, reformed curriculum in primary schools and supervising the educational reform in much of Northern Germany.

Gerson occupies a prominent place in Chemnitz's theology. The Second Martin cites him continuously in his major works *Harmonia Euangelica*, *Loci Theologici*, *Enchiridion* and *Examinis Concilii Tridentini*. Although he sometimes evokes Gerson in what has by now become a traditional Lutheran use of the past authorities — in order to support the Protestant ideal of the return to the primitive church[239] or to criticize monasticism[240]

---

[236] Campi 2018, p. 283.

[237] Chemnitz 1959, p. 14.

[238] 'His credentials as a leading orthodox Lutheran are without blemish, as demonstrated by his extensive publications on Church government, theology, and devotional literature, as well as his formative role in drafting the *Formula of Concord* in 1577 and compiling the Book of Concord in 1580. These are seminal documents which settled the many disputes' (Campi 2018, p. 283). The *Formula* constitutes the final section of the *Corpus Doctrinae* for the Lutheran Church, which was presented to the Elector August of Saxony on May 28, 1577. Although signed by three Electors and many lords in the Empire, it was rejected by several major congregations.

[239] Chemnitz 1875, pp. 147–48: 'So behauptet Gerson *de uita spirituali*, lectione 2, corollario 7, daß Urlebel der ersten Kirche sei in dieser Beziehung größer gewesen als jetzt sei. [...] Denn da nimmet er Kirche für die erste Gemeinde der Gläubigen, die Christum gesehen, gehört haben und seine Zeugen gewesen sind. So weit Gerson'.

[240] *Gerson agnoscit falsum elie illud axioma quod Monachi imaginantur, praecepta Legis ordinate esse ad uirtutes [...]* (Chemnitz 1653, p. 103) 'Gerson acknowledged as false this axiom that monks imagine to be ordained by principles of Law for the sake of virtue'.

and other *multos errores Pontificios* in general[241] — the late medieval chancellor meant much more to him than a useful reference. Unlike later Protestant writers, who would treat Gerson's legacy as a foil, selectively appropriating his ideas and writings in order to tell their preferred stories about late medieval Catholicism and the origins of the Reformation, Chemnitz's references to Gerson are usually theologically meaningful. The Second Martin quotes from some of the chancellor's most popular works, such as *De uita spirituali animae, De consolatione theologiae, Monotessaron, De contractibus* and *De examinatione doctrinarum*, as well as from lesser-known texts such as *De perfectione cordis, Tractatus de consiliis euangelicis, De unitate ecclesiæ, De schismate tollendo*, sermon *De quatuor Domibus*, and likely other works. What's more, Chemnitz was fond of the chancellor not only as a great master of theological guild but also as a gifted writer, who not only *uero tradit*[242] and *rectè dicit*,[243] but also *pulcherrimè describit*[244] and *eleganter inquit*.[245] His reliance on Gerson involves three main areas: evangelical harmonization, the *Trosttheologie* (consolatory theology) and the relationship between law and religion in a Christian society.

In *Harmonia Euangelica*, which enjoyed lasting popularity through many editions, Chemnitz returns to Gerson's *Monotessaron* as his model of harmonization,[246] rejecting Andreas Osiander's approach to evangelical harmonization as nonsense. In lengthy *Prolegomena* to *Harmonia Euangelica* Chemnitz directly states, at the very beginning, that he constructs his harmony *sicut Gerson recitat*.[247] He restates his intention to follow the chancellor's method throughout the volume: *Gerson & alii secunti sunt, Gerson & cum alii sequitur*.[248] *Alter Martinus* explicitly returns to Augus-

[241] Chemnitz 1653, p. 191.
[242] Chemnitz 1653, p. 169.
[243] Chemnitz 1653, p. 170.
[244] Chemnitz 1653, p. 16.
[245] Chemnitz 1653, p. 107.
[246] Although Chemnitz worked on his *Harmonia Euangelica* for several years, it was published only posthumously in 1593. Johann Gerhard completed Chemnitz's *Harmonia* in 1626–1627, and the whole work was finally published in Hamburg in 1652.
[247] Chemnitz & Gerhard 1645, 1, p. 5.
[248] Chemnitz & Gerhard 1645, 1, 540.

tine's and Gerson's principle of *concordissima dissonantia*, but credits the latter with creating the genre of evangelical harmony:

> *Tantem circa Ann. Dom 1409[...] Iohannes Gerson exemplo Augustini illud instaurare coepit [...] Gerson id, quod Augustinius inchoauerat, pertexuit. Totam enim historiam Euangelica ordine quodam in unam continuam narrationem redegit, atque ita Harmoniam ex quatuor Euangelistis contexuit.*[249]

Chemnitz's harmony not only bears close resemblance to *Monotessaron* in its overall structure, methodology and abbreviation system — (M) for Matthew, (R) for Mark, (L) for Luke and (J) for John, with no new divisions — it also directly mentions Gerson's name at least twenty times, and its second volume contains an entire section titled *Gerson de parabola*. Full of admiration, the Second Martin chose *Monotessaron* as his model for practical as well as for aesthetic reasons, for Gerson knows how to be eloquent.[250] Only once in the voluminous *Harmonia quatuor euangelistarum* Chemnitz cautiously and respectfully ventures to say *in io tamen a Gersone dissentimus*[251] ('In this, however, we differ from Gerson'), when discussing meanings of Jesus's name. However, in contrast to the late medieval chancellor, and reflecting new humanist scholarship, *Alter Martinus* provides parallel passages in both Greek and Latin to the harmonized text.

The Parisian theologian seems to be the only late medieval authority, with the exception of one mentioning of Nicolas of Cusa, whom Chemnitz brings up in *Examinis Concilii Tridentini* (*The Examination of the Council of Trent*). This four-volume monumental work was published between 1565 and 1573 and has been the basis for dialogue between Catholics and Lutherans

---

[249] Chemnitz & Gerhard 1645, 1, p. 8. 'About the year of the Lord 1400 Jean Gerson began to restore this following the example of Augustine [...] Gerson accomplished (interweaved) What Augustus inaugurated. For in this manner he compressed the entire scriptural story into one continuous narrative, and created this harmony from four Evangelists'. 'In Chemnitz's view the fact that there were four authors, not one, posed no fundamental problem since the Gospels differed without contradicting each other' (Jonge 1990, p. 156).

[250] *Ac Gerson eleganter dicit: debet credentes agnoscere & magnificare priuilegium illud* (Chemnitz & Gerhard 1645, 1, 540). 'As Gerson elegantly said: believers should acknowledge and magnify this privilege'.

[251] Chemnitz & Gerhard 1645, 2, p. 431.

for centuries. An evaluation of the Trent's decrees from Lutheran point of view, *Examinis* contains an entire section titled *Gerson de Scriptura autoritate*, and cites from four of the chancellor's works: *De examinatione doctrinarum* (repeatedly),[252] *De uita spirituali animae*, *De schismate tollendo* and *De unitate ecclesiæ*.

> *Ita Gerson de uita spirituali animae, lectione secondo, corollario septimo disputat, maiorem hac in re suisse auctoritatem primitiuae Ecclesiae, quam nunc sit. Et addit: Non est in potestate papae aut Concilii, aut Ecclesiae, immutare traditions datas ab Euangelistis & ab Apostolis. Subiungit & hoc. Et his aperitur modus intelligendi illud Augustini: Euangelie non crederem, nisi me auctoritas Ecclesiae compulisset. Ididem enim Ecclesiam sumit pro primitiue congregatione fidelium eorum, qui Christum uiderunt, audierunt and sui testes extiterunt. Haec Gerson.*[253]

Among pastoral issues discussed in *Examinis*, Chemnitz ponders the question of absolution. The chancellor's position on this matter found a positive reception in the Second Martin. Based on Gerson's treatises *De schismate tollendo* and *De unitate ecclesiæ*, Chemnitz praised the Parisian theologian for extending absolution to the vast majority of confessed transgressions, thus being merciful in the spirit of the Lord who took away our sins:

> *Hinc Gerson recte disputat, absolutionem non in optatiuo modo, sed propter certitudinem pronunciandam esse in indicatiuo modo, sicut hac forma absolutionis Nathan utitur: Dominus abstulit peccatum tuum*[254]

---

[252] *Gerson in prima parte de examine doctrinarum, citat glossam quondam super illud: apparuit Moses & Helias cum ipso: suspecta est omnis reuelatione, quam non confirmat lex & prophetae cum Eungelio* (Chemnitz 1875, p. 72) 'Gerson, in *Examine doctrinarum*, quotes the glossa on this: there appeared Moses and Elijah with Him (Matt 17:3): Every revelation, which the Law and the prophets, together with the Gospel, do not confirm is suspect'.

[253] Chemnitz 1875, p. 90. 'So Gerson argues in *De uita spirituali animae*, in this regard it was better under the authority of the primitive Church than it is now. And he adds: it is neither in the power of the pope, nor of the Council, nor of the Church to change traditions given by the Evangelists and Apostles. And he also adds this (and this reveals Augustine's understanding): I would not believe Scripture unless I was compelled by the authority of the Church. But by this Church he means the primitive congregation of the faithful who saw and heard Christ, and were his witnesses. This is according to Gerson'.

[254] Chemnitz 1875, p. 306. 'Gerson argues very correctly that absolution is not in the optative mood, but for the sake of certainty must be pronounced in the

References to Gerson abound in Chemnitz's major theological work *Loci Theologici*. Begun as the compilation of his lectures on Melanchthon's *Loci Communes* while still at the Wittenberg university, *Loci Theologici* became one of the founding texts of Lutheran tradition. Chemnitz, who often referred to his beloved mentor as Dr Philipp, continuously studied and lectured on Melanchthon's great work until his retirement in 1584.[255] Always suggesting Melanchthon's writings for consultation on all matters concerning Scriptures,[256] Chemnitz never completed his *Loci Theologici*, since he considered his own thoughts unworthy of recording. The book was finalized by gathering material from the notes of his listeners, and put together by his associates and family members to be finally published in 1591, five years after his death. The importance of this multi-volume work, which represents a bridge covering the darkest days of Lutheranism from the death of its founder to the Formula of Concord, is difficult to overestimate. It knew thirteen editions by the year 1699, was still cited in 1891, and excerpts from it were still included in the *Classical Lutheran Theology* published by Augsburg Publishing House in 1962.

It is tempting to think, considering Chemnitz's 'strict dependency'[257] on Melanchthon's work, on which he lectured for thirty years, that his references to Gerson would exactly correspond to those found in *Loci Communes*. This is, however, not the case. While it is probable that Melanchthon's high esteem for Gerson had some influence on Chemnitz's initial choice of authorities, his discussions of the chancellor's ideas in *Loci Theologici* appear to be unrelated to his mentor's take on the subject. As is often the case in *Loci Theologici*, the tactful and discrete Chemnitz sometimes totally differed with Melanchthon's opinions, while being careful not to bring his disagreements to public attention.

Despite Chemnitz's general respect for scholastic authors,[258] *Loci Theologici* contain fewer references to medieval authorities

---

indicative mood, according to the form of absolution used by Nathan: the Lord has put away your sin'.

[255] Chemnitz 1959, p. 13.
[256] Chemnitz 1959, 2, p. 66.
[257] Astorri 2019, p. 72.
[258] Campi 2018, p. 284.

than *Loci Communes*.²⁵⁹ Aside from his favorite Bernard of Clairvaux and Bonaventure, whom he cites with approval, and, to a lesser degree, Thomas Aquinas and Anselm, there are no other medieval authority figures in Chemnitz's work. As for late medieval scholastics, Gerson is, once again, the only 'survivor' of this period, which Chemnitz outright calls *tempore Gersonis*.²⁶⁰ As in *Harmonia quatuor euangelistarum*, Chemnitz displays a pronounced aesthetic appreciation of the chancellor's eloquence and style, which is repeatedly characterized as *eleganter* and *pulcherrime*:

> *Et fides edocta ex Euangelio prouocat, a throno seuerae iustitiae ad thronum gratiae (sicut Gerson pulcherrime hunc actum describit)*²⁶¹
> *Et Gerson eleganter inquit, Gloria humanitatem non tollit, sed extollit, non interficit, sed pficit [perficit]*.²⁶²

Chemnitz, unlike Melanchthon, was not an academic but rather a practical church official. He was less concerned with theological subtleties than with daily pastoral duties and preaching. His preoccupation with the psychological well-being of his parishioners led him to embrace the late medieval tradition of *Trosttheologie* with which Gerson was so closely associated, as well as to promote the role of law and legislature in Christian society. Concerning the former, *Alter Martinus* particularly appreciated Gerson's quality as *doctor consolatorius*, continuously referring to him as a 'comforting' theologian'.²⁶³ As in *Examinis*, Chemnitz

---

²⁵⁹ 'To Chemnitz, theology must not be contaminated with scholastic or philosophical terminology. Crucial attention is given to the Scriptures and the Church Fathers, which in his opinion have greatly contributed to the Church' (Astorri 2019, p. 72).

²⁶⁰ Chemnitz 1653, p. 157.

²⁶¹ Chemnitz 1653, p. 16. 'And the faith, informed about this from Scripture, calls forth, from the throne of strict justice to the throne of grace (as Gerson beautifully described this action)'. The official translation of this passage is the following: 'Gerson has some wonderful thoughts about the tribunal of God's justice and the throne of His grace' (Chemnitz 1959, 2, p. 482).

²⁶² Chemnitz 1653, p. 107. 'And Gerson put it elegantly, Glory does not take away humanity, but extolls it, not destroys it, but perfects it'. Nicolaus Selnecker also uses this phrase in *Operum latinorum: pars prima, continens formam explicationis examinis ordinandorum olim scripti a Philippo Melanthone of 1584*, but with *perfecit* spelled correctly.

²⁶³ Chemnitz 1971, 1, p. 510.

also shared Gerson's views on several pastoral issues that were debated within the Lutheran community at that time. Following the French theologian, the Second Martin maintains that conditional absolution is the best option in comparison to the situation when, if it is not given or is denied, the penitent is left to suffer spiritual loss, potentially leading him or her into the sin of mortal despair.[264] On the thorny issues of the human part in salvation and bondage of will, Chemnitz closely adheres to the position of his mentor Melanchthon. Thus, having emphasized that *uoluntas est captiua non libera [...] non potest sine Spiritu sancto efficere spirituales affectus*, he proceeds to say, paraphrasing Dr Philipp, *[...] cumque concurrant tres causa [...] Verbum Dei, Spiritus Sanctos, & homina uoluntatas assentiens, nec repugnans uerbo Dei [...] uoluntas non est otiosa*.[265] Sometimes Chemnitz's position sounds closer to Gerson's *theologia media* than he might have wanted it to be: *Agentes enim poenitentiam & credentes in Christum accipiunt, habent & retinent gratiam & remissinem peccatorii*.[266]

Chemnitz clearly relies on Gerson in the area of the relationship between law and religion in a Christian society, which concerns contractual law, usury and the responsibilities of a legislator. The chancellor has a strong bearing in the second part of *Loci theologici*, dedicated to the issue of poverty, where the Second Martin borrows from Gerson classifications of various types of contracts,[267] and asserts that

> *Theologus igitur non debet temere reprehendere contractibus, Legibus approbator qui fundamenta habent in Lege natura, sed potius debet obseruare, quomodo Scripture tales contractus*

---

[264] *Gerson recte disputat, absolutionem non in optatiuo modo, sed propter certitudenem pronunciandam esse in indicatiuo modo* (Chemnitz 1653, p. 258, trans. above). Gerson's support for absolution found little reception among early modern Catholics.

[265] Chemnitz 1653, p. 162. 'The will is captive, not free [...] it cannot without the Holy Spirit, bring spiritual love [...] whenever three causes concur: the Word of God, the Holy Spirit, and human will that accepts and not rejects the Word of God [...] the will is not inactive'.

[266] Chemnitz 1653, p. 103. 'Empowered by repentance and faith in Christ, they accept, have and keep grace and the remission of sins'.

[267] Astorri 2019, p. 138.

> *probet.*[268] *[...] Gerson enim recte laudat dictum Cameracensis: in contractibus humanes, qui praesupposito peccato sunt naturales and necessarii, non debet leuiter fieri reprobatio seu ad usurariam prauitatem reductio.*[269]

Concerning the roles and responsibilities of civil legislators, Chemnitz, once again, recommends Gerson's take on the issue: *Sed alia est explicatio simplicior, quae apud Gersonem extat. Deus in Veteri Testamento fuit & Theologus & Legislator [...] ordinat forum politicum & forum conscientiae.*[270] Therefore, the rules that exist for the civil legislator 'should only be considered in front of the magistrate and not in the *forum conscientiae*'.[271]

> Chemnitz keeps theology, philosophy and law separate. As a theologian, for him the point is not the legal or philosophical description of a contract, but the relation with God. Using the Aristotelian doctrine of causes, he writes that the matter and form of contracts is to be asked of philosophers and jurists. The theologian adds the efficient cause, which is the ordinance and approval of God. This perspective reveals a definite border between law and theology.[272]

One obvious commonality between Melanchthon's and Chemnitz's assessments of Gerson is their desire to present the latter's position as comparable and compatible with that of Luther and his legacy as part of historical momentum building toward the final triumph of the Lutheran cause:

> *Gerson tamen dicit, formam publicae promotionis Doctorum hanc esse: De tibi facultatem disputandi, docendi, legend hic ubique terrarium. Et Luterus testator, se saepius consolationem*

---

[268] Chemnitz 1653, p. 157. 'Therefore, theologian should not be afraid to inspect contracts, showing approbation to laws, which have foundation in the law of nature, but he must even more strongly observe how Scripture approves such and such contract'.

[269] Chemnitz 1653, p. 162.

[270] Chemnitz 1653, p. 159. 'But another explanation is simpler, which exists in the writings of Gerson. God in the Old Testament acted both as a theologian and legislator [...] regulating not only the *forum conscientiae* but also the *forum politicum*'.

[271] Astorri 2019, p. 381.

[272] Astorri 2019, p. 138.

hausisse ex tua promotione: quia ipsi publica potestas tradita fuerit docendi Euangelium & taxandi errores.[273]

That Gerson *mitigauit doctrinam de consiliis* ('changed the doctrine about the councils'),[274] and criticized *multos errores Pontificios* ('many papal errors') gave the medieval chancellor clearance to enter Lutheran pantheon, where he was to remain for centuries to come. Chemnitz's fondness of Gerson led him, just as it was the case with two other Martins of the Reformation, Luther and Bucer, to pass under complete silence his favorite theologian's involvement in Jan Hus's martyrdom. In fact, *Loci theologici* strategically injects Hus and Gerson right between *Wicleffus Anno Domini 1350 uidit commune tunc doctrinam de Libero arbitrio non conuenire cum Scriptura* and *annum Domini 1517* marking the appearance of *Domunus Luthero*.[275] In *Loci theologici* the eagerness to reinsert Gerson in the Lutheran narrative ends up being something of a macabre joke: *Huss anno 1416 Gerson, qui Concilio Constantiensi interfuit, and multos in doctrina Pontificia errores animaduertit.*[276] As a result, Gerson is presented as simply another delegate who, together with Jan Hus, 'was present' or 'attended' [*interfuit*] the Council of Constance and called attention to many errors in the papal doctrine'.[277] To a reader unfamiliar with historical circumstances, this description reads as if Gerson and Hus simply joined the Council as two delegates. While Chemnitz's discomfort in dealing with this episode is not unique, the strategy of ignoring or smothering the historical truth would become a cliché in countless Protestant catalogs and indexes, starting with the most important, *Catalogus testium ueritatis* by Matthias Flacius Illyricus.

---

[273] Chemnitz 1653, p. 125. 'Yet Gerson says that the formula for the public preferment of teachers is this: 'I give you authority to engage in disputation, to teach, and to lecture here and everywhere in the world. And Luther says that he very often drew comfort from his preferment because public authority was given him to teach the Gospel and to condemn errors' (Chemnitz 1959, 2, p. 703).

[274] Chemnitz 1563, p. 103.

[275] Chemnitz 1653, p. 191. 'In the year of the Lord 1350 Wycliff saw that the then common doctrine of free will did not agree with Scripture.'

[276] Chemnitz 1653, p. 191.

[277] Chemnitz 1653, p. 191. Trans. in Chemnitz 1959, 1, p. 256.

Lutheran Historiography

Along with the more traditional approach to a theological authority of the past, a new, rival and increasingly dominant tendency emerged in Lutheran polemical literature in the middle of the 16th century. This tendency consisted in relying on the past for historiographical and increasingly ideological purposes. While various Protestant movements of the 16th century eventually came to the understanding of historical writing as 'a powerful vehicle for the expression of ideology, shaping their histories by remembering and forgetting, by editing and deleting, by compiling and destroying',[278] it was Lutherans who pioneered it. They developed not only a reform program for the future, but came up with a new perspective on the past, which was even more important in social and political terms.[279] This perspective originated from Martin Luther himself, who, already during his 1519 Leipzig Disputation with Johannes Eck, designated history as *mater ueritatis*.[280] Since Rome had excommunicated him, forcing him out of the Catholic Church and its centuries-long continuum, Luther felt justified in reclaiming his legacy from history itself. The first Martin also formulated the division of history into three periods each lasting about two thousand years — from creation to the period of the Kings of the Old Testament, from the Kings to Christ and from Christ to the present (the last period being significantly shorter than previous two had eschatological consequences). This categorization, which eventually became traditional for Lutheran historiography, first appeared in his *Supputatio annorum mundi*, written between 1541 and 1545.[281] However, the critical need for Lutheran historiography came later, when the change in the political situation made the strict adherence to the principle of *sola fide* insufficient as the one and only denominational criterion. As soon as the initial apocalyptic feeling, characteristic of the early Lutheran thought, gradually subsided, Lutherans found themselves in urgent need of a new legitimacy in order to reinforce their

---

[278] Gordon 1996, p. 21.
[279] Kelley 1983, p. 26.
[280] *WA* 2. 289.
[281] Wriedt 1996, p. 40.

positions and win new adherents to the now diversified market of Christian faiths. This legitimacy was to be found in its past and in its most prominent characters. It was Melanchthon who developed the idea of historical writing as an important polemical tool of the Reformation, tracing Lutheran interpretation of faith from Christian antiquity, via Bernard, Gerson and Wessel Gansfort, up to his own time.[282] Philipp's inclusion of medieval authorities in Lutheran historical narrative, which differs with Luther's strictly biblical attitude, allowed this narrative to be 'more about coming to terms with the Middle Ages than making a break with them'.[283] Gerson's legacy became part of this complicated process.

Lutheran historical writing developed three key concepts, which remained constant throughout the 16th century, and were quickly adopted by other, although not by all, Protestant denominations: the connection between Word and history, the development of church history within a national context, and the emphasis upon the chain of witnesses.[284] The latter idea was also promoted by Melanchthon, who, unlike 'Luther [who] regarded history as the place where God's Word struggled with the opposing power of Satan',[285] perceived it from the angle of continuity maintained by witnesses of truth, *testes ueritatis*. This idea indubitably represents the Lutheran counterweight to the Catholic 'apostolic succession' of the unbroken chain of bishops, which can be traced back to the apostles themselves, guaranteeing that the faith remains intact in the process of handing it down through generations. The Catholic accusation that Protestants broke this chain and with it the integrity of the faith, demanded a response, and Melanchthon was not alone in coming up with one. Strasbourg theologian Johannes Pappus (1549–1610) formulated a similar principle of continuity, according to which medieval heretics would be seen as righteous proto-Lutherans, while 'regular' Catholics would be, in reverse, considered heretics. In this way 'there were never not enough witnesses of the true heavenly doctrine which opposed the heretics even in the face of mortal

---

[282] Oberman 1981a, p. 30.
[283] Gordon 1996, p. 15.
[284] Gordon 1996, p. 14.
[285] Bollbuck 2010, p. 240.

danger'.[286] These new concepts and ideological needs that they served impacted various ways in which Lutheran historiography would choose to represent Gerson: as a prominent critic of the Roman Church, a true reformer, a precursor of the evangelical movement or even a martyr for the Lutheran cause. These interpretations were, for the most part, not cynical manipulations, but rather results of a conviction that through faith of a few witnesses of truth, such as Gerson, God's word carried on until it finally shone forth in Wittenberg. The Lutheran emphasis on Rome as the source of all evils enabled a positive perception of all those who had been critical of this institution in earlier centuries.[287] In fact, criticism against the corruption of the Catholic Church expressed by such 'witnesses' became the indulgence for their future salvage by the Lutheran authors. Such was, for example, the initial perception of Gerson by Andreas Karlstadt. It was Gerson's dissatisfaction with church practices of his day that most endeared him to the Lutherans, who were quick to enlist him as a witness and then forerunner for their cause.

The strongest introduction of the theme of 'witnesses' is found in Matthias Flacius Illyricus's monumental *Catalogus testium ueritatis, qui ante nostram aetatem reclamarunt Pape*, composed between 1553 and 1555, published in Basel in 1556, and initially intended for Lutheran ministers who had mastered Latin. Croatian by origin (hence Illyricus), Matthias Flacius (Vlacich) was a colorful figure. A distinguished scholar of Greek and Hebrew, more Lutheran than Luther himself, he is firmly associated with the most uncompromising and militant wing of the Lutheran movement.[288] A close associate of Philipp Melanchthon in his youth, he, unlike peaceful Chemnitz, not only broke with his former mentor in later years, but also made him a target of continuous attacks. An enemy of moderation, unable, because of his confrontational nature, to hold an academic position for any prolonged period of time, Flacius, who shared Luther's eschatological

---

[286] Bollbuck 2010, p. 240.

[287] This is also the reason for the continuous popularity of the writings by Gerson's close friend, Nicolas de Clamanges. See Polman 1932, p. 194.

[288] A summary treatment of such a monumental figure as Flacius cannot do him justice. For a detailed and balanced study of Flacius's life and doctrine, see Olson 2002.

view of the world, perceived Melanchthon's attitude of compromise as a betrayal of true Lutheran thought. The following citation says it all:

> I truly attribute to Philip many virtues, as all rational people do, yet this I cannot attribute to him, that he is so wise that he is able to remove from the gospel the sword and fire that Christ sent with the gospel [...] into the earth.[289]

Yet, despite his antagonism, which made him persona non grata even within the Lutheran camp, and regardless of speculations about who else may have influenced Flacius's historical publications, the structure of his work, the concept of the chain of tradition, the succession of ages of the church, the point at which corruption began and how it gained ground, all came from Melanchthon.[290]

Moreover, without Melanchthon's fundamental work *Chronicon Carionis*, published in German in 1532, and subsequently republished several times with enlargements in Latin as well as in High and Low German, Flacius's work would not have been possible.[291] His special focus on the Middle Ages, even though the catalog opens with St Peter himself, also originates from Melanchthon's inclusive position. The *Catalogus* closely follows 'Melanchthon's principle of the continuity of evangelical doctrine from the early church through the Middle Ages to the Reformation',[292] with the Middle Ages represented as 'a connecting bridge between the times of the Church fathers and the sixteenth century'.[293] Indeed, Flacius, unlike Bucer, pays only limited attention to the fathers of the Church,[294] giving the lion's share of his *Catalogus* to the Middle Ages. This choice materializes in the *Catalog*'s structure and page distribution: while the first ten centuries after Christ occupy approximately two hundred pages, the later five hundred years are allocated twice as much space.

---

[289] Olson 2002, p. 93.
[290] Olson 2002, p. 45. See Scheible 1996.
[291] Bollbuck 2010, p. 242. Melanchthon published a completely revised version in 1558–1560.
[292] Pohlig 2010, p. 264.
[293] Frank 1990, p. 235.
[294] Polman 1932, p. 186.

Written in an attempt to defend Lutheranism against the charge of doctrinal innovation, *Catalogus* uses the concept of a chain of witnesses in order to reclaim periods of ancient and medieval past for Evangelical Christianity. This concept, 'regardless of inconsistencies', was crucial for this task: it proved to those who held to the evangelical faith that they were neither innovators nor alone'.[295] In fact, it allowed Flacius to demonstrate that it was Catholics who had innovated and altered the original Christian dogma, by introducing saints, purgatory, additional sacraments, etc. On the contrary, what Luther had taught, Flacius argued, had always been taught, beginning with the apostles.[296] Therefore, all that Lutherans wanted was to get rid of Catholic innovations in order to return to the original apostolic purity and 'stand in conformity with the ancient church'.[297]

The *Catalogus*' grounds for enlisting a historical figure into 'witnesses' to Evangelical truth were broad, as Flacius's goal appears to be quantity rather than quality. Without distinguishing between those who were simply not guilty of papist sins (*Unschuldigen*), and those who had the correct faith (*Rechtgläubige*)',[298] he sought to include and gather rather than analyze and define. His *Catalog* proceeds by presenting short descriptions of over four hundred individuals who had constituted, in his opinion, a true Christianity throughout centuries before Luther. Dante is listed as a witness for wanting to reduce the popes' political power, and Petrarch for calling the papal court in Avignon Babylon. Anybody who could be considered a victim of ill treatment for criticizing the *ecclesia papistica* won an entry in his catalog, and Gerson easily qualified. This sort of inclusiveness was not unique to Flacius, and rather represented a general tendency. It would reach the height of absurdity with Adam himself being presented as the first Lutheran martyr in the 1552 German martyrology *Historien der Heyligen* written by the Lutheran theologian Ludwig Rabus (1523–1592).[299]

---

[295] Gordon 1996a, p. 107.
[296] Olson 2002, p. 237.
[297] *LW* 41: 195.
[298] Frank 1990, p. 205.
[299] Polman 1932, p. 199.

While hardly any German work claiming to have anything to do with history failed to include Gerson,[300] Flacius's handling of the late medieval theologian in the *Catalogus* transcends the simple logic of maximum inclusion. His article about the chancellor, consisting of two pages, is one of the longest in the *Catalog* and reveals Flacius's poised attitude toward the late medieval chancellor:

> *Fuit omnino, meo quidem iudicio, uir pius ac eruditus: qui licet multis monachorum & sophistarum erroribus fuirit infectus, multos etiam errores & abusiis papatus animaduerit, eosque & taxauit, & tolli ex animo optauit, ut ex eius scriptis non uno in loco apparet. Aliquos tamen proculdubio metu phariseorum aut penitus dissimulauit, aut etiam lenius, quam tantum uirum decuisset, & res ipsa postulasset, reprehendit.*[301]

The article gives the impression of the author's goodwill toward his subject, as he attempts to mention as many positive sides of Gerson's personality and activity as possible, with 'positive' meaning compatible, helpful or useful for the Lutheran cause. Flacius begins with a matter crucial for Lutherans, the question of indulgences, against which the chancellor wrote *longa epistola*, plainly proving that he disapproved of them: *eos indulgentia plane abrogandas sinserit*.[302] Praising Gerson for chastising the negligence of the prelates, the author also pays tribute to him for gathering around him and teaching religion to the poor.[303] The chancellor is also credited with a special prayer that will be repeated from one Gerson biography to another: *Meus deus, meus creator, miseriaris*

---

[300] For example, German astrologer and author of some historical writings favored by Melanchthon, Johann Carion (1499–1537) included Gerson as *theologus doctissimus* in the appendix of his 1531 *Iannis Carionis mathematici*.

[301] Flacius Illyricus 1556, pp. 930–31. 'Overall, in my opinion, he was a pious and learned man who allowed himself to be infected by many errors of the monks and sophists, but who also called attention to many abuses and misdeeds of the papal office, which he criticized and sincerely (from his heart) tried to remove, which is apparent from his writings in more than one place. However, no doubt fearing Pharisees, he either dissimulated some (errors) completely or, as it would have been appropriate for such a man & as the thing itself demands, he condemned them rather leniently'.

[302] Flacius 1556, p. 931.

[303] Flacius 1556, p. 933.

tui miseri famuli Gersonis.[304] The chancellor's humility reveals him as a good man who, when thinking about his salvation and pious death, humbly asks for God's mercy instead of buying a multitude of masses, vigils, pilgrimages and *similium nugarum miryadas* ('myriads of similar toys').[305] Although Flacius names only two of Gerson's texts by their titles, *De potestate ecclesiastica* and *De defectibus ecclesiasticorum*,[306] he makes sure to mention all of his 'contributions' to the evangelical cause, such as his critical writings against the Roman Church *in quo corrupta spiritualium uita et neglecta officium accusat*,[307] his use of the vernacular in spreading the Evangelical message in sermons; and his teaching of the small children.[308] The article finishes on an almost hagiographical note, for, as good and pious a man as Gerson was, he could not fail to fall victim to persecution by the papist Antichrist:

> *Testantur autem quidem, eum ob ueritatem à spiritualibus & Sorbonistis in exilium è Parisiis pulsum, omnibus fortunis & dignitatibus expoliatum. Ideoque Lugduni, non Parisiis, ubi fuerat cancellarius, mortuus est.*[309]

Flacius also had to deal with the embarrassing issue of accommodating Hus's story into Gerson's narrative. An awkward alphabetical and chronological proximity of their names, combined with Hus's high profile in Lutheran circles, exacerbated the problem. The Czech's martyrdom was known since the 1500 publication of the *Acts of the Council of Constance*,[310] as well as through Johannes Sumpf's 1514 *Acta scitu dignissima*.

---

[304] Flacius 1556, p. 933. 'My God, my creator, have mercy on your miserable servant Gerson'.

[305] Flacius 1556, p. 933.

[306] This work it is not Gerson's.

[307] Flacius 1556, pp. 930–32. 'in which he accuses of corruption in spiritual life and ignoring the [ecclesiastical] service'.

[308] Flacius 1556, pp. 930–32: *In calce operum olim Parisiis impressorum [...] est adiectum solitu Gersonem paulo ante mortem congregare multos pueros in templo, quorum ueluti praeceptor erat*. 'At the end of the Parisian edition [...] it is added about Gerson that before his death he was accustomed to gather many children in the temple, for whom he was like a teacher'.

[309] Flacius 1556, p. 933. 'For his righteousness, he was exiled by the Sorbonne, stripped of fortune and dignities, and because of this he died in Lyon and not in Paris'.

[310] Polman 1932, p. 193.

Both Peter of Mladoňovice's eyewitness account of Hus's trial and execution, and Poggio Bracciolini's *Historia Iohannis Huss* were published in 1528. His fate attracted admiration and had been widely publicized by early Lutherans, who perceived him as a saint and martyr of their cause.[311] In 1525, a famous humanist scholar Johannes Agricula (1494–1566) published, with Nicholas Krumbacher, a book directly treating the subject of Hus's trial in Constance. It was followed by Agricola's 1538 five-act theater play,[312] which was based on the 1536 eyewitness account published by Ulrich von Reichenthal (1360–1437), *Das Concilium so zu Konstanz gehalten ist worden*.[313] What's more, Flacius's own sympathies clearly were with Hus. After discovering the Bohemian reformer's Latin writings, Flacius proceeded to produce, in 1558, an edition of his works, including a narrative of his life,[314] called *Iohannis Hus et Hieronymi Pragensis ... Historia et Monumenta*, 'which brought together many of the key Hussite letters and documents into a large-scale history'.[315] Subsequently he even presented Hus's compatriot Jan Blahoslav with a copy of the *Catalogus*, while promising to send him a copy of the celebrated Bohemian's Latin works.[316] Yet, in spite of all this, and totally out of his character, completely disinclined as it was to Melanchthon-like care for propriety, the fiery theologian chose to resolve this dilemma by diplomatically omitting the gruesome episode altogether. The article on Hus does not mention Gerson's role at all, solely blaming the pope John XXIII for his refusal to release the Czech reformer.

Eight years later Flacius's account of Hus's life and martyrdom appeared, although without giving him credit, in the 1563 edition of the highly influential, especially among the Puritans, *Acts and Monuments*, composed by the English historian and mar-

---

[311] The book's full title reads as *Historie und warhafftige geschicht, wie das heilig Evangelion mit Johann Hussen ym Concilio zu Costnitz*. Othon Brunfels dedicated an edition of several of Hus' works, especially his *De anatomia Antichristi*, to Martin Luther (Polman 1932, p. 196). Lutheran writers proclaimed Hus to have been 'like a morning star in the darkness of the papacy' (Polman 1932, p. 196).

[312] Kolb 1987, p. 762.
[313] Buck 2010.
[314] Hartmann 2001, p. 131.
[315] Tucker 2017, p. 27.
[316] Olson 2002, p. 244.

tyrologist John Foxe (1516/17–1587).[317] Foxe's connection to Flacius is interesting because the two collaborated on Flacius's most famous endeavor, the anti-papal compilation known as *Centuriae Magdeburgenses*. Published from 1559 to 1574, and tracing the church history up to 1300, *The Magdeburg Centuries*, albeit based on Melanchthon's ideas, was designed to contrast and correct the latter's *Chronicon Carionis*, by replacing elementary concepts of nationhood by those of confession.[318] Foxe, like the above-mentioned Strasbourg theologian Johannes Pappus, believed that heretics of the medieval period formed the very genealogy of the true church of Christ,[319] but, unlike Flacius, did not hesitate to openly blame Gerson for Hus's death in *Acts and Monuments*:

> Unto these articles above prefixed were other articles also to be annexed, which the Parisians had drawn out against Master John Huss, to the number of nineteen. The chief author whereof was John Gerson, chancellor of the university of Paris, a great setter-on of the pope against good men.[320]

An explanation for such a difference in judgment from two otherwise like-minded people probably lies in the very fact that one was English and the other German (Flacius self-identified as a German). While Foxe had no special affinities with Gerson, and, therefore, no inhibitions in his assessment of his deeds, Flacius was formed, particularly in Tübingen, by the generation of German preachers, theologians and humanists for whom Gerson was a pivotal figure. His prestige in German-speaking territories was enormous, and his legacy, as well as his story, became, thanks to the efforts of the patriotically-minded

---

[317] 'In my opinion, for as muche as Pope John feared that which in dede did after folowe, that he should be deprived of his dignitie, he thought to wyn the favour of these Herodian Cardinalles and byshops, by betraying the good man unto them' (Foxe 1563, p. 198, in Kolb 1987, p. 38). It has been proven that it was Foxe who copied Flacius and not another way around. See Olson 2002, p. 253 & Haller 1940.

[318] Bollbuck 2010, p. 245 & p. 250. As Irena Backus had shown, *Catalogus* does not represent a preparatory stage to the *Magdeburg Centuries*, which appeared in Basle in 1624. See Backus 2013, pp. 125–39.

[319] Cameron 1993, p. 203.

[320] Foxe 2009, p. 82.

German humanists like Jacob Wimpheling, part of *rerum Germanicorum*.[321] Gerson's 'adoption' as a 'Teutonic' celebrity was recorded by Johannes Trithemius in his *Catalogus illustrium uirorum Germaniae*, which served as a prototype and foundation for Flacius's work.[322] By the time the latter began his *Catalogus*, the Parisian chancellor had been firmly integrated into German historical narrative as one of the spiritual ancestors (literally *generator*) of the Teutonic nation. The chancellor continued to be presented in this manner up to the end of the 17th century and possibly beyond.[323] Gerson's exceptional status in German-speaking lands likely compelled Flacius to purge the chancellor's biography of all unwanted details in order to make him into a bearer of unbroken truth for the nascent Lutheran and, therefore, German historiography.

After the ambition of 15th century German intellectuals to bring German history from 'the shadows into the light of the day'[324] (as the most prominent among them, Johannes Reuchlin, put it) was accomplished by the second half of the 16th century, it merged with the new agenda of the Lutheran Reformation. In a new religious climate, the idea of early German humanists that their homeland had suffered injustice and misrepresentation because of Italian cultural hegemony, metamorphosed into the notion that Germany had been victimized throughout the centuries by ruthless, and, accidently, mostly Italian, pontiffs and other foreigners.[325] As a result, the model of humanist martyrdom was

---

[321] Brady 1992, p. 199: 'It is highly debatable that the classic point of origin of the German way lay in Martin Luther's *To the Christian Nobility of the German Nation* and his Reformation. Although Luther raised the flag of nationalism in his 1521 address against the ecclesiastical establishment and therefore against the Emperor, German national pride and patriotism were awakened way before Luther by German humanists'.

[322] Olson 2002, p. 270. Also see Hartmann 2001, p. 193.

[323] Flacius turns to Gerson once more, while citing his own catalog, in his 1568 book *Unchristliche Uneinigkeit und Einigkeit der Papisten, dagegen ware Christliche ... einigkeit dera auffrichtigen der Augsp. Confessions vermanten*.

[324] Strauss 1993, p. 199, citing Preface to Johann Nauclerus *Memorabilium omnis artatis et omnium gentium chronici commentarii*.

[325] One finds this idea in Sebastian Frank's *German Chronicle* of 1538, Johann Carion's *Chronicle* of 1532 and other works of this genre. See Strauss 1993, p. 684.

now transposed on the whole German nation.[326] Flacius was part of this movement, and wrote *De translatione imperii Romani ad Germanos* to argue his point:

> [...] *quando & qua ratione Imperium ad Germanos translatum fit* [...] *imperium transiit à Babylonis ad Persas, à Persas ad Macedonas, à Macedonas ad Romanos & à Romanis ad Germanos* [...] *natione Germanica amplissima & robustissima* [...][327]

Once again, Flacius develops what is already in place in Melanchthon's *Chronicon Carionis*: 'an imperial-patriotic profile'.[328] In search of their new, simultaneously national and religious identity, German *litterati* sought to explore possibilities of expansion both horizontally and vertically, synchronically and diachronically. Their horizontal quest spread to the neighboring countries with the exception of Italy — their main model, rival and object of jealousy. The vertical exploration aimed to absorb the past and portray it as related to German origins and history. Flacius's *Catalogus* was part of this double effort. By including Gerson as a prestigious ancestor in the newly written, and one may just as well say newly imagined German Lutheran history, Flacius had to be careful to structure the material so as to demonstrate Germany's divine mission, of which Gerson had already been made an integral part.

Flacius's *Catalogus* 'came to be used as a research guide'[329] by generations of authors and editors of subsequent catalogs, indexes and histories, such as, for example, *Lectiones Memorabiles* by Johannes Wolff or Wolf (1537–1616).[330] Flacius's successors also knew who burned whom and why, but continued to leave embarrassing parts of Gerson's biography out. This fact indicates

---

[326] Gordon 1996, p. 13.

[327] Flacius 1556, p. 35. 'when & for which reason the Empire was transferred to the Germans [...] the supreme power moved from Babylon to Persia, from Persia to Macedonia, from Macedonia to Rome & from Rome to Germans [...] with the ample & robust German nation'.

[328] Bollbuck 2010, p. 245.

[329] Olson 2002, p. 240.

[330] Johannes Wolf was familiar with Gerson's writings, particularly with *Opus tripartitum*, which inspired his own guide to confession (see Bast 2009, p. 4).

that cultural and national agenda still prevailed over bitter interdenominational feuds at this point. The time was not for reflection and discrimination but for action and debate, in which both Hus and Gerson had to be presented, a couple of pages apart, 'as godly witnesses to the truth in times of darkness'.[331] This last formula would become a cliché to the point of being immortalized in stone. The visual representation of Flacius's unbroken line of Evangelical witnesses is found at the Church of Saint Ulrich in Braunschweig, where the carvings of Jean Gerson, Jerome of Prague and Jan Hus, the persecutor and his victims, 'stand' side by side in choir stalls built in the closing years of the 16th century. The purpose for this controversial sculptural *voisinage* is the same as in Flacius's *Catalogus*. Saint Ulrich's forty-six key figures, representing post-biblical confessors from the ancient fathers of the Church, such as John Chrysostom and Gregory the Great, to medieval figures of Bernard and Bonaventure, were meant to celebrate the chain of witnesses to God's Word. Next to Bonaventure 'stands' Gerson, immediately followed by Jan Hus and Jerome of Prague, who visually lead to figures of Martin Luther and Philipp Melanchthon.[332] The series concludes with Johannes Bugenhagen for, after the peace of Augsburg, it was important to present all the Evangelicals as united.

Despite its ideological dimension, conditioned by Luther's triadic method of writing history as a revelation of God's Word, its propagation in the face of persecutions, and the eventual decline of the Church,[333] Flacius deserves full scholarly credit for his enormous and pioneering work. His good faith is beyond doubt, as he painstakingly worked to recover and include Latin sources pertaining to the medieval period,[334] and performed actual archival research in a manner foreshadowing what would eventually become a standard historical investigation in modern times.[335]

---

[331] Gordon 1996, p. 15.
[332] Kolb 1987, p. 147.
[333] Bollbuck 2010, p. 252.
[334] Backus 2013, p. 128.
[335] Hartmann 2001, p. 16.

Part II. Reception in the Reformed Tradition

The reception of Gerson by the most significant among the reformed theologians, John Calvin, is rather limited and unrelated to the idea of *testium ueritatis*. Unconcerned with either contemplation, affective theology or spiritual consolation, Calvin was more preoccupied with the problem of religion's place in a society and in the daily life of an individual.[336] He mentions Gerson once directly in his early and anti-Anabaptist work *Psychopannychia* (literally meaning 'all-night-vigil of the soul') of 1534 and several times in *Institutes of the Christian Religion* (1536) and in *Brieue instructione* of 1544. His quotations, from Gerson's Easter sermon and *De uita spirituali animae*, are precise and specific, leaving no doubt about Calvin's close knowledge of the chancellor's writings.[337] Yet his connection to Gerson appears to be of no great significance. Until an in-depth study takes place, there seems to be no reason to believe in any substantial consonance between Calvin's and Gerson's doctrines beyond 'des points tellement généraux qu'ils ne seraient être le Sondergut de personne'.[338] There might be one potential exception, and it concerns the content of Gerson's *synderesis* theory, much of which is to be found in Calvin's *Institutes*.[339] Indeed, though it is not certain that this content comes specifically from Gerson, it is hard not to hear his voice in Calvin's repeated affirmations, spread throughout different volumes of the *Institutes*, that there is 'a sense of deity inscribed in the hearts of all';[340] that 'in man's perverted and degenerate nature some sparks still gleam', that 'man's soul is so illumined by the brightness of God's light as never to be without some slight flame or at least a spark of it';[341] or especially that 'there is within the human

---

[336] Cave 1967, p. 2. Holt 2005, p. 22: 'The real significant departures from Luther, however, were not theological but social: specifically, in the practice and enforcement of doctrine [...] the emphasis on social discipline'.

[337] Oberman 1991, pp. 34–35.

[338] Vial rejects any substantial connection between Gerson's *Contra curiositatem studentium* (OC: 3, pp. 224–49) and Calvin's views on the subject of curiosity (Vial 2009, p. 40).

[339] Greene 1991, p. 204. Robert Greene makes a strong case of Gerson's influence on Calvin's subtle return to *synderesis* in the *Institutes*.

[340] Calvin 1960, I: iii: 1.

[341] Calvin 1960, II: ii: 12 and II: ii: 19, respectively.

mind, and indeed by natural instinct, an awareness of divinity'.[342] Puzzled by the fact that humans sometimes do perform righteous deeds in an apparent contradiction to the principle of complete human depravity, the stern reformer allowed for a loophole left by *synderesis* 'for whence comes such concern to men about their good name but from shame? And whence comes shame but from regard for what is honorable?'[343] This loophole is filled with the most contradictory element found in Calvin's theology built on the premise of avoiding contradictions: the concept of 'conscience, which God has engraved upon the minds of men'.[344]

Although the Geneva reformer uses the term 'natural instinct' in a generic and morally neutral sense of an innate need for all things to seek their proper ends and to preserve themselves, which is also found in Gerson, he develops an original idea of humans' natural inclination or instinct towards the preservation of society through laws:

> [S]ince man is by nature a social animal, he tends through natural instinct to foster and preserve society. Consequently [...] there exist in all men's minds universal impressions of a certain civic fair dealing and order. Hence no man is to be found who does not understand that every sort of human organization must be regulated by laws [...] Hence arises that unvarying consent of all nations and of individual mortals with regard to laws. For their seeds have, without teacher or lawgiver, been implanted in all men.[345]

Finally, there is a negative correlation between Gerson's ideas and Calvin's. It concerns the latter's rejection, regardless of his understanding of conscience, of the slightest suggestion of the possibility of cooperation between God and man in salvation. In direct reference to Gerson's *De uita spirituali animae*,[346] Calvin disal-

---

[342] Calvin 1960, II: ii: 26.
[343] Calvin 1960, I: xv: 6. Greene 1991, p. 204.
[344] Calvin 1960, IV: xx: 16.
[345] Calvin 1960, II: ii: 13.
[346] Calvin 1960, III: xiv: 12: 'They [Sophists] say: 'Good works are not as important in their intrinsic worth as to be sufficient to obtain righteousness, but their great value lies in 'accepting grace'. Gerson, *De uita spirituali*, in OC: 3, p. 118: *[...] nam si gratiam appellamus omne illud a Deo liberaliter datur sine meritis [...]* 'we call grace everything freely given by God without merit'. The same idea

lows even the idea of accepting God's grace, since only God, 'by his fatherly kindness and indulgence', can accept anything.[347]

Trained as a lawyer, the Geneva reformer was more sensitive to the interpretation of equity as permeated with Christian mercy or an 'Equity Wing', which 'bears upon Calvin's legal study'.[348] The extent to which his thoughts on this subject are similar to St Germain's, and, by extension, to Gerson's, is remarkable,[349] and calls for investigation. Already in his earliest published book *Treatise on Clemency*,[350] Calvin emphasized the necessity to moderate the strictness of written law by mercy in a way reminiscent of Gerson's approach.[351] He also promoted equity as a concept both accessible to the understanding of all men — 'For, while men dispute among themselves about individual sections of law, they agree on the general conception of equity', and as a universally applicable measure — 'Equity must be the rule and limit of all laws'.[352] Considering Calvin's familiarity with Gerson's texts, more indications of direct or indirect influence of the latter might still be discovered.

Gerson's impact in the Reformed movement was the strongest in evangelical harmonization, where *Monotessaron* continued to dominate for centuries.[353] Only Calvin broke with the consistency of the *Monotessaron* tradition with an interpretational shift of major significance. This shift concerns the Gospel of St John and the Revelation of John, known as *Johanine corpus*, and traditionally attributed, together with John's letters, to one and the same person, the apostle John. Calvin's 1555 *Harmony of the Evangelists Matthew, Mark, and Luke* differs from all previous harmo-

---

of man's consent to grace is present in Gerson's vernacular sermons: 'Pourtant se nous ne donnons nostre consentement a sa grace et misericorde que ainsy nous promet, et se nous ne l'ensuyons, se nous ne nous donnons nous meismesse nous ne metons la main a nous aidier comme il soit ainsy que il veut' (*Pour le mercredi des Cendres*, OC: 7: 2, p. 577).

[347] Calvin 1960, III: xiv: 16–18.

[348] Haas 1997, p. 28. Haas mentions neither Gerson nor Christopher St Germain, but rather French legal school in general.

[349] Brooks 2009, p. 68. On Gerson and St. Germain see chapter 4.

[350] Brooks 2009, p. 68.

[351] Brooks 2009, p. 68. Gerson, *Regulae morales*, OC: 9, pp. 95–96.

[352] Calvin 1960, II: ii: 13 and Calvin 1960, IV: xx:16.

[353] See Thompson & Robinson 1828.

nies, because it excludes the *Iohanine corpus*, focusing solely on three synoptic Gospels, as its title indicates. Whereas Calvin eventually added a separate translation and commentary of the Gospel according to St John, he never commented on the Revelation. This omission is meaningful. The importance given to the Revelation of John — the most mysterious, enigmatic and opaque of the New Testament's texts — is always an indicator of the prominence of mystical dimension in any given Christian movement, denomination, tradition or an individual theologian. The Revelation of John retains the central place in Eastern Orthodox or Coptic Churches, and exercised a strong attraction during Western mystical movement, in which Gerson played such a prominent role. On the contrary, the Apocalypse presented an unsurmountable challenge for Calvin, since this text, full of incomprehensible and frightening symbols, cannot withstand the tests of clarity, logic or order, which are inherent features of his thought. He 'may have considered that apocalyptic is foreign to the New Testament as if it involved a re-veiling of the clear and unambiguous Gospel'.[354] Since Calvin considered sinful and disorderly as synonymous, with order being tantamount to absolute good and chaos to absolute evil,[355] the Revelation of John inevitably ends up on the wrong side of the chaos-order dichotomy, making its integration into the evangelical harmony unworkable. With Augustine's and Gerson's notions of *concordia diuersitas* or *concordissima dissonantia*[356] having already lost all credibility in Calvin's eyes, he had no way to solve the issue of the Apocalypse but through a simple excision. His decision was so puzzling to his contemporaries that several pseudo-Calvin commentaries on the Revelation of St John were

---

[354] Parker 1993, p. 119.

[355] Calvin 1960, II: iii: 12: 'We teach that all human desires are evil [...] not in that they are natural, but because they are inordinate. Moreover, we hold that they are inordinate because nothing pure can come forth from a corrupt and polluted nature'. On the topic of chaos in Calvin see Mazour-Matusevich 2017 & Mazour-Matusevich 2018.

[356] Musical analogies are characteristic of Gerson. See, for example, his *Spiritus Domini*, OC: 5, p. 521: *Quia pleni sunt coeli et terra maieestitatis gloriae Spiritus Sancti, hinc coelum laudadibus intonat, mundus exultans iubilat, gemens infernus ululate*. 'Thus skies and earth are full of the shiny glory of the Holy Spirit, skies attune praises for him, the universe is exceedingly glad and the hell scrims groaning'.

produced in Geneva. One of them was titled *Familiere et briefve exposition sur l'Apocalypse de Sainct Jehan*, and another was used by French Huguenot preacher Augustin Marlorat (1506–1562), who made reference to a commentary by Calvin on the Revelation, which was most certainly not his.[357]

Despite Calvin's magisterial sway over his movement, his reductionist approach to scriptural harmonization did not endure even within Swiss Protestant tradition. In his zeal 'das Buch der Bücher popularisieren', Zürich Reformer Leo Jud (1482–1542) translated *Monotessaron* (which he found in Zürich's edition of Gerson's works) in its entirety.[358] His version remains very close to Gerson's original, except for some places, where the author borrowed from Johannes Bugenhagen's Latin *Harmonie* of 1524.[359] In order to make Gerson's text more legible for German 16th century readership, Jud succeeded in avoiding repetitions that are frequent in Gerson, smoothing over some of *Monotessaron*'s outdated expressions, but his changes are rather cosmetic. Jud's translation, perceived as his own work,[360] was republished twice in the 16th century. In addition to Jud, *Monotessaron*'s structure was retained by Huldrych Zwingli in his *Passionsharmonie*.[361] Zwingli's successor Heinrich Bullinger (1504–1575), who did not write scriptural harmonies himself, enthusiastically recommended Gerson's model as the best archetype for scriptural harmonization in his 1525 book *De institutione eucharistiaeae*.[362]

---

[357] See Parker 1993.

[358] Christ-von Wedel 2011, p. 30.

[359] Christ-von Wedel 2011, p. 31.

[360] Oskar Farner, who translated Jud's work into modern German in 1955, considered Jud as an original and independent author (Christ-von Wedel 2011, p. 28).

[361] Brown 1987, p. 316, n. 111.

[362] Stolz 2004, p. 45. Hausamann believes that Gerson and Bullinger have several exegetical convictions in common. One is the belief that the holy Scripture is the measure of Christian learning, without which the Church has no validity. The other is the view that the Scripture is the whole, where different parts enlighten and clarify each other. The third is that in order to interpret correctly, the interpreter himself should be filled with the Holy Spirit. Finally, that *sensus litaralis* is the sense of the Scripture to be understood not as a simple compilation of isolated words, but rather to be based on the vocabulary and syntax of the time. Therefore, the true meaning and importance of a particular scriptural term is always contextualized. See Hausamann 1970, pp. 128–29.

Radical Huguenot writer Charles Dumoulin (1500–1566), famous for his flamboyant rhetoric in *Conseil sur le fait du concile de Trente*,[363] also relied on *Monotessaron* in his 1565 book *De collatione et unio*, without, however, giving any credit to Gerson, whom he disdainfully called one of *homines obscuri, indocti [...] quos ingignos puto qui recitentur*.[364]

Huguenot Historiography: Jean Crespin, Simon Goulart

Neither *Catalogus testium ueritatis* nor *Magdeburg Centuries* had a significant impact on Protestant historiography immediately after their publication. The general unpopularity of Flacius's work among early Calvinists and other non-Lutheran Protestants is striking, especially considering his radical, Gnesio-Calvinist theological views, which should, in all logic, have made early Protestant reformers receptive to his work. Yet, no sympathy seems to have existed between them and the fiery Croatian. Such aversion might be explained by the quasi-unanimous dislike in which his name was held among all fractions of the Reformation movement. In addition to Melanchthon, he quarreled with Osiander, mainstream Lutheran theologian Johannes Pfeffinger (1493–1573), Melanchthon's follower (Philippist) Victorinus Strigel (1524–1569), fellow historian and radical reformer Sebastien Frank (1499–1543) and countless others.[365] More importantly, early reformed theologians, unlike Lutherans, were rarely preoccupied with the history of the Church, the only exception being Christian antiquity. In this sense, Swiss reformers were true to their humanist formation, with their fascination with antiquity coupled with the despise for the thousand years that separated them from it. Just like Italian humanists struggled to achieve par-

---

[363] Born in Paris, Dumoulin practiced as a lawyer at the Parlement before turning Calvinist, and fleeing in 1552 to Strasbourg, where he wrote *Commentaire sur l'édit du roi Henri II sur les petites dates*, which was condemned by the Sorbonne. Returning to France in 1557 he was imprisoned by order of the parlement until 1564 for writing *Conseil sur le fait du concile de Trente*, which aroused both Catholics and Calvinists against him.

[364] Wünsch 1983, p. 181: 'an obscure uneducated man whom I consider unworthy'.

[365] Polman 1932, p. 235.

ity with great ancient authorities, aiming to revive their literary brilliance after an unfortunate lapse into medieval 'barbarism', early Swiss Protestants sought to regain the purity of the primitive Christian church. Consequently, while they tried their best to achieve the complete agreement between their doctrine and that of the fathers of the Church,[366] they essentially abandoned and ignored the medieval period.[367] Moreover, militant Huguenot publications, such as the famous vehicle of Calvinist propaganda, the pamphlet *Reveille-matin* (1573–1574), considered that the true preaching of the Gospel originated only with Luther, Bucer, Zwingli, Oecolampadius, and Melanchthon,[368] and were not particularly interested in history. It is telling that Johannes Sleidan's *Commentaries on Religion and the State in the Reign of Emperor Charles V*, published in Latin in 1555 and in French in 1556, covered the events starting only from 1517 and up to 1555.[369] This attitude affected the fate of Gerson's legacy among the Reformed. Thus, Calvin's secretary, radical legal theorist and Monarchomach François Hotman (1524–1590) does not mention Gerson's name in his *Franco-Gallia* (written before 1570 and published in 1573), where he argues against tyrannies of popes and kings. The only exception to this general rule was, once again, Zwingli's successor Heinrich Bullinger, who adopted the idea of the chain of witnesses in his 1525 anti-Anabaptist work *De propheta*, naming, among non-Scriptural witnesses of truth, only Augustine, Hilarius, and Gerson.[370]

However, starting from 1570 the ideological landscape began to change. The Protestant ideological machine, which believed printing to be 'a divine gift which promised fulfillment of a divine mission',[371] discovered the use of historical narrative as a powerful polemical weapon for the *propaganda fidei*.[372] This discovery led to the adoption of the concept of *successio doctrinae* (as opposed to papal *seccessio personarum*), which is similar and compatible

---

[366] Polman 1932, 256.
[367] Kelley 1983, p. 26.
[368] Kelley 1983, p. 302.
[369] Watson 1997, pp. 11–12.
[370] Hausamann 1970, p. 125. Also see Campi 2004; Stolz 2004.
[371] Kelley 1983, p. 237 & p. 246.
[372] Kelley 1983, pp. 247–49.

with the idea of the chain of witnesses. This new type of historical narrative stemmed from a distinct, although related genre of martyrology, launched by Leuven alumnus, French Huguenot printer and 'pioneer in French language histories of the Church',[373] Jean Crespin (1520–1572). This 'patron of the martyrological tradition'[374] published his first *Book of Martyrs That Is, a Collection of Several Martyrs Who Endured Death in the Name of Our Lord Jesus Christ, From Jan Hus Until This Year* in 1554. It was followed by four other editions, revised and printed by the author himself, with a variety of titles: *Recueil de plusieurs personnes qui ont constamment enduré la mort pour le nom de N. S. J. C. depuis Jean Hus jusqu'à cette année présente 1554* (1555, 1556), *Actes de Martyrs* (1564) and finally *Histoire des vrays témoins de la vérité de l'Évangile depuis Jean Hus jusqu'à present* (1570). The fact that the first edition had 687 pages and 180,000 words, and the last 1,424 pages and over a million words,[375] obviously testifies to Crespin's numerous additions,[376] which consisted of new accounts of martyrdom that Crespin dutifully collected from all available French and European sources. Fluent in German, Crespin maintained strong ties with the 'German-speaking world, especially in Zurich, Strasbourg, Frankfurt and Basle',[377] and published Lutheran works in French. His collection of martyrs, which 'acted as a history of the Reformed Church, defined in the broadest sense'[378] was 'the most international' and 'pan-European'[379] in scope of all the 16th century Protestant martyrologies. As much as Lutheranism was a national movement, Calvinism was a cosmopolitan one. Its international character is clearly reflected in Crespin's martyrology, where he 'does not identify Lutheran martyrs as being in any way different from Reformed ones' but 'as essentially part

---

[373] Watson 1997, p. 11.

[374] Watson 1997, p. 151. Although John Foxe exerted influence on Crespin after 1559, Crespin was definitely the first to come up with an idea of an organized Calvinist martyrology as he began writing five years before the Englishman. Foxe himself acknowledged his debt to Crespin (King 2009, p. 44), although some researchers believe that Foxe could not read French (Watson 1997, p. 151).

[375] Watson 1997, p. 30.

[376] Watson 1997, p. 151.

[377] Watson 1997, p. 11.

[378] Tucker 2017, p. 11.

[379] Watson 1997, p. 161; King 2009, p. 43, respectively.

of the same movement'.[380] It was religious convictions, regardless of nationality and language, that mattered to Crespin, who tirelessly worked to make German authors available in French.[381] Consequently, his book, completely foreign to the patriotic agenda exhibited in Flacius's *Catalogus*, focused exclusively on martyrs, aiming at showing 'the parallel between contemporary martyrs and the godly champions of biblical eras'.[382] The preface to his 1570 edition states that 'tout mon but a esté d'escrire la vie, la doctrine, et la fin heureuse de ceux qui ont suffisant tesmoignage d'avoir scellé par leur mort la vérité de l'Evangile'.[383] The word choice of 'tesmoignage' is deliberate, and among the witnesses Jan Hus, 'un homme de vie saincte & hōneste',[384] and Jerome of Prague, 'le savant et bon personage' qui 'mourra sainctement' [385] are the first. With them, as the title indicates, Huguenot history truly begins. Correspondingly, Crespin's narration of the trial and execution of Hus, based on the *Relatio de Magistri Ioannis Hus* by the eye-witness Peter of Mladonovice, is reverential and lengthy. Clearly, the chancellor of the University of Paris, directly responsible for Hus's martyrdom, should be placed among those whom Crespin calls 'la chair pourrie des Ecclesiastiques assemblez en ce Concile de Constance'.[386] Yet, that is not where the reader finds him. 'Un homme plus excellent, ce monsieur le chancelier Gerson' [387] is introduced in a very long opening article on Jan Hus as the first evangelical martyr:

> [...] le venerable chancelier de Paris, nommé Jean Gerson, qui au nom de toute la Sorbonne apporta d'autres articles magistralement composes contre Hus [...] Ces articles ont esté faits sous correction, ainsi que Gerson passoit. Ainsi signé, Jean Gerson, Chancelier indigne de Paris.[388]

---

[380] Tucker 2017, p. 120.
[381] Watson 1997, p. 11.
[382] Parker 1993, p. 242 & p. 230 respectively.
[383] Crespin 1570, last page, unnumbered, of the Preface.
[384] Crespin 1570, p. 5.
[385] Crespin 1570, p. 39 & 33. Crespin added Jerome's last appearances before the Council of Constance in 1564 (Tucker 2017, p. 51).
[386] Crespin 1570, p. 36.
[387] Crespin 1570, p. 20.
[388] Crespin 1570, p. 26.

But the real surprise comes four hundred seventy pages later, with Crespin's final evaluation of Gerson, which reads like a tribute:

> Jean Gerson, Chancelier de l'Université de Paris au mesme temps taxoit plusieurs erreurs & abus de la Papauté, & desiroit qu'ils fussent ostez. Il fit un livre intitulé Défaillances des Ecclésiastiques, auquel il accuse leur vie corrompue, le mespris du vray devoir & predît leurs peines avenir. Il escrivit aussi de l'esproevue des esprits, De la molesse et pollution de la nuict & du jour, taxant le Celibat. Iceluy estant devenu povre & banni pour avoir beaucoup de choses veritables, mourut finalement a Lyon prive de toute dignité.[389]

How is one to explain such assessments? As it was stated earlier, national solidarity is out of question. What could have happened to Crespin's 'clear and essential criteria' that, in order to be included in his book, 'a person had to have been executed as a result of refusing to recant his or her beliefs'?[390] Was it the high esteem in which Heinrich Bullinger, Crespin's lifelong friend, held Gerson that influenced Crespin's judgment? Since the above quote comes from book VI on 'Persecution de l'Eglise de Paris', one could imagine that it might have to do with criticism of the Church of Rome, as it was the case in *Catalogus testium ueritatis*. Yet, Gerson's close friend Nicolas de Clamanges (1363–1437) did not earn a similar 'honorable mention' in *Histoire des vrays témoins*, despite the fact that Crespin knew and valued his writings, and even inserted an approximate French translation of Clamanges's virulent pamphlet *De ruina et reparatione Ecclesiæ* in the 1564 edition of *Actes de Martyrs* under the title *Escrit de Nicolas Clemangis docteur de Paris et archediacre de Bayeux touchant l'état corrompu de l'Église*. The most likely explanation is Crespin's desire to impress his readership with the shared tradition of suffering 'at the hands of the evil machinations of the Catholic Church'.[391] While Nicolas de Clamanges, although very critical of the Church, did not suffer persecution, Gerson, whom Crespin appears so eager to exonerate, suitably died exiled *devenu povre & banni*. Not quite a martyr but almost.

---

[389] Crespin 1570, p. 492.
[390] Tucker 2017, p. 11.
[391] Watson 1997, p. 107.

Jean Crespin died in 1572, and his work was taken up by one of the most prominent, prolific and influential figures among the third-generation Calvinists, the successor of Théodore Beza (1519–1605) and another Monarchomach, Simon Goulart (1543–1628), who published four editions of *Histoire des vrays témoins* in 1582, 1597, 1608 and 1619,[392] and had further enlarged it by a third. Goulart, an energetic but not original theologian, who generally made articles on the martyrs longer but did not add new names, retained all references to Gerson. In the late 16th century, when Swiss Protestants found themselves increasingly involved in controversies not only with their initial enemy, the Catholic Church, but also with Lutherans, the time came for consolidation.[393] Attempts at consolidation found expression in the joint efforts of several theologians, including Goulart, to create, in 1581, almost simultaneously with the Lutheran *Formula of Concord* (1580), one common Creed between Helvetic and other Protestant confessions. The creation of this Creed, known as *Harmonia confessionum fidei*, brought about the renewed interest in common historical narrative, and the 'mode of thinking that identifies almost all pre-Reformation opposition to the Catholic Church as belonging to a coherent movement, which would eventually make the Reformed Church its heir'.[394]

This new focus naturally drew attention to *Catalogus testium ueritatis* as a good model and a source of ammunition for polemical wars.[395] Its author's difficult character was now the thing of the past, while Melanchthon's theological school has prevailed.[396] Also, the brand new Jesuit challenge forced Protestants to reconsider their attitude toward the past, including the medieval sources, which Reformed theologians were now ready to use as a verbal sword.[397] Flacius's *Catalogus* found new life with the same Simon Goulart, who reworked it into a major piece of Protestant historiography. Just as he did with Crespin's *Histoire des vrays témoins* (which would also be surreptitiously added

---

[392] Racaut 2003, p. 39.
[393] Watson 1997, pp. 173–74.
[394] Tucker 2017, p. 19.
[395] Olson 2002, p. 240.
[396] Pohlig 2010, p. 266.
[397] Muller 2003, p. 55.

to his version of *Catalogus*), he made the new catalog deceptively indistinguishable, on the surface, from Flacius's original. Title, organization and format remained exactly the same.[398] In a move indicating his intention to rework Flacius's Lutheran narrative into a Calvinist one, Goulart dedicated his creation to a former Wittenberg student and prominent Calvinist, member of the ecclesiastical council of the Rhenish Palatinate, Otto von Grünrade (1545–1613). The need to bring Flacius's endeavor into line with Calvinism forced Goulart to overlook some substantial theological differences separating two denominations. Thus, in the dedication, which 'links Genevan and French Calvinism to Calvinism in the Empire',[399] Goulart characterizes Flacius as an 'inquisitive and careful researcher of the Church's antiquity', passing under silence the latter's militant anti-Calvinist position on the Eucharist.[400] Goulart's ability to 'recycle and purge'[401] the corpus of theological, poetic, philosophical and historical sources for the Huguenot cause, without bringing much attention to his technique, is remarkable. His reworking of *Catalogus* consists in a careful sifting through Flacius's book, keeping some elements in their entirety and modifying others. As in his adaptation of *Histoire des vrays témoins*, his changes have less to do with his choices of entries than with their extensions, many of which he borrowed from Flacius's *Magdeburg Centuries*.[402] Some additions are substantial, such as, for example, the insertion of an appendix with witnesses from 1517 to 1600, while eliminations are very rare.[403]

---

[398] Confusion between Flacius's and Goulart's catalogs persists to this day, with libraries listing them as one and the same text. For example, Raymond A. Mentzer and Andrew Spicer in their book *Society and Culture in the Huguenot World, 1559–1685* simply state that Goulart reprinted Flacius's catalog in Geneva (Mentzer & Spicer 2007, p. 39). Also, Goulart's catalog is not usually listed as his work in the majority of articles about him.

[399] Pohlig 2010, p. 270.

[400] Pohlig 2010, p. 270. 'Although Flacius opposed these theological elements vigorously and railed against the Calvinist theology of the Eucharist during ten years of polemics with Beza from 1565 on, his works were nevertheless read and used by Calvinists' (Pohlig 2010, p. 266).

[401] Pohlig 2010, p. 13.

[402] Pohlig 2010, p. 268.

[403] 'The French Reformed Church went so far as to formally acknowledge, at the 1572 Synod at Nimes, that the Albigensians, members of the medieval dualist heresy, had been ancestors of the Reformed Church' (Tucker 2017, p. 11).

Goulart's goals were, according to the notion of *successio doctrinae*, not very different from that of Flacius: to attach martyrs of all ages to the cause of the Reformation.[404] Consequently, he kept Flacius's conveniently 'blurry conception of who was a witness of the true faith'[405] when he expanded his *Catalogus*. Through his inclusive 'Melanchthonian' approach, Goulart introduced into the Reformed historiography Lutheran practice of presenting medieval heretics as martyrs of the True Church — the tactic whose relevance Huguenots failed to acknowledge until then, with the notable exception of Jan Hus and Jerome of Prague in Crespin's *Book of Martyrs*.

Through a complex process of assimilation and manipulation, Goulart created a different book, which is twice as long as Flacius's and embodies new Calvinist principles. One of these principles is 'a perceptible shift of emphasis from spiritual and individual ideals to worldly and social goals [...] to the secular interests of the congregation'.[406] The Reformed orientation toward community is reflected in the organization of Goulart's *Catalogus*.[407] Instead of Flacius's purely chronological order, Goulart gathered Christian centuries under four rubrics: theologians, ecclesiastical government, Roman pontiffs, and synods. The other novelty came from the need to develop a systematic Protestant theology and consisted in the large-scale appropriation of the Catholic tradition, which was already largely absorbed by Philippist (Melanchthon-inspired) Lutheranism.[408]

All these tendencies are observable in Goulart's seven pages long article on Gerson, which is, like in Flacius, one of the longest, if not the longest, in the catalog. It is twice as long as the one about Hus and more than three times longer than the corresponding article in Flacius's book. The first part of the article, unchanged,

---

[404] Polman 1932, pp. 199–200. Interestingly, Goulart never mentions Flacius's *Magdebourg Centuries*. 'Goulart's reedition of Flacius's text may thus be seen as a Calvinist confessionalisation of a historiographical text written by a Lutheran — rather than as a Calvinist confessionalisation of an intrinsically Lutheran text' (Pohlig 2010, p. 264).

[405] Pohlig 2010, pp. 265–66.

[406] Kelley 1983, p. 259.

[407] Pohlig 2010, p. 268.

[408] Goulart revises his catalog in 1608 (Jones 1886, p. 215).

comes from Flacius, while the second is entirely new.[409] Goulart cites far more of Gerson's works than Flacius does. Thus, in addition to *De potestate ecclesiae, De defectibus ecclesiasticorum* (which is not by Gerson) and the letter *De neglegentia prelatorum*, cited by Flacius, Goulart itemizes Gerson's letter *Contre Mattheus Grabon*, treatises *De examinatione doctrinarum, De distinctione uerorum uisionum a falsis, De uita spirituali animae, Declaratio defectum uirorum ecclesiasticorum* [410] and *An liceat in causis fidei*, as well as his sermons. His list of Gerson's contributions also exceeds the one by Flacius. The late medieval chancellor is praised for *errores pontifici detecti* (detecting papal errors), for being *uir pius ac eruditus*, for disapproving the practice of indulgences, for considering violating human traditions not to be a mortal sin, for admitting that both 'pope and the council could err',[411] for criticizing the Church in general, for his humble prayer *Mi Deus, Creator meus, miserere miseri tui famuli Ioannis Gersoni*,[412] for foretelling of the imminent ruin of the Church,[413] for urging simple people to believe Gospels more than Pope or the Council,[414] for disapproving of human traditions that often overshadow God's commandments,[415] for giving final authority to the Scriptures,[416]

---

[409] Goulart's *Catalogus* also includes Bernard for *A Deo excitatus corruptissimo seculo, ut uariis modis tyrannidem Pontificiam* (Goulart 1608, p. 1379), Hugh of Saint Victor because he was *à Trithemio laudatur* (praised by Trithemius, Goulart 1608, p. 1452), Francesco Petrarca for calling *Papae curiam Babylonem [...] matrem omnium idolatriarum & scortationum* (Goulart 1608, p. 1769) and Savonarola for being *monachus Dominicanus, uir eruditione ac pietate insignis* (Goulart 1608, p. 1914). Savonarola was also highly and lengthily praised in Crespin's martyrology.

[410] According to Trapp, (Trapp 1979 *CWTM* 9: 339), this treatise is actually written by the distinguished professor of the University of Vienna, Heinrich von Langenstein.

[411] Goulart 1608, p. 1805: *Papa & uniuersal concilium errare possint*.

[412] Goulart 1608, p. 1805.

[413] Goulart 1608, p. 1805: *Gerson [...] in sermoni recenset immonentis ruinae Ecclesiae*.

[414] Goulart 1608, p. 1805: *Plus credendum simplici non authorisato Euangelium alleganti, quam Pape aut Concilio. De examinatione doctrinum*, OC: 9, p. 463: [...] *plus est credendum Euangelio, quam alteri auctoritati humanae*.

[415] Goulart 1608, p. 1806: *Fit insuper frequenter irritum mandatum Dei propter traditiones hominum*.

[416] Goulart 1608, p. 1807: *Quia constat plus esse credendum Euangelio quam Papae*.

for criticizing abuses of the monks,[417] and, finally, for asserting of the urgent need for reform of the Church.[418] In short, Gerson appears as both a staunch opponent of *Pontificis Romani brutis*[419] and a representative of the new Evangelical religion. The attention that Goulart gives to Gerson's article, which is carefully and painstakingly researched, extended and systematized, demonstrates the degree of his importance for the late 16th century Swiss Protestants, who, in their desire to 'reform the diversity, to give a more systematic and orthodox (which is one and the same thing for Goulart) form to the fragmentation',[420] sacrifice their loyalty to Jan Hus in order to retain his executioner among their theological ancestors. Like all revolutionary movements that passed their initial eschatological phase, Protestants needed a solid foundation in order to build a long-lasting community, and the chancellor of the University of Paris, presented by Goulart as an all-around virtuous man and one of the forefathers of the new faith, was now wanted as an integral part of it.[421]

Not all Protestant historiographers, Lutheran or Reformed, felt as compelled to be inclusive, however. For example, Protestant scholar Nikolaus von Reusner (1545–1602), in spite of his patriotism, expressed in his 1565 poem *Germania ad Caesarem et Electores Imperii*, did not share German humanists' tendency to view Gerson as their ancestor. He does not include the French theologian in his 1587 *Icones siue imagines uirorum literis illustrium*, while dedicating considerable space to both Hus and Jerome of Prague. Another German patriot, Heinrich Pantaleon (1522–1595), author of *Prosopographia heroum atque illustrium uirorum totius Germaniae* (1565) and its German version *Teutscher Nation*

---

[417] Goulart 1608, p. 1805: *De monachis loquitur satis improprie & abusiue & arroganter, dictae sunt status perfectionis.*

[418] Goulart 1608, p. 1805: *[…] asserit Ecclesiam indigere correctione & emendatione & reformation.*

[419] Goulart 1608, p. 1806: *Addamus & duodecim Gersonis considerations circa materiam excommunicationum & irregularitatum tyrannidem Pontificis Romani brutis […].*

[420] Pot 2013, p. 37.

[421] Goulart also wrote an *ars moriendi* discourse *Remedies Against Satan's Temptations in our Final Hour*, which bears no recognizable resemblance to Gerson's. Written for pastors, it relies entirely on Scripture as a 'pharmacy' for wounded souls. See Matnetsch 2012, p. 297–98.

warhaffte Helden (1570), does not mention Gerson either, but includes large articles on Hus, Jerome of Prague and the military leader of the Hussites, Jan Ziska. Protestant historian, poet laureate and biographer Melchior Adam (1575–1622), who intended to 'celebrate the whole range of German cultural achievement beyond academic life',[422] and modeled his bio-bibliographies on Trithemius's *Catalogus*,[423] did not retain Trithemius's article on Gerson in his 1620 *Vitae germanorum theologorum*. Theodore Beza mentions neither Gerson nor Hus in his *Icones, id est Verae Imagines Virorum Doctrina Simul et Pietate Illustrium*, published in Geneva in 1580.

Nevertheless, Goulart's contribution became a major reference for dozens of subsequent publications. It played the most important role in presenting the entire ecclesiastical history, and framed interpretations of the French civil wars down into the 20th century. Concealed under Flacius's name, Goulart's *Catalogus testium ueritatis* became part of the new development in Protestantism, which was able to incorporate history into theology and dogmatics, and which would eventually be called Protestant orthodoxy.[424] Through Goulart, Flacius's exceptional reception of Gerson would find new takers in the second and third generations of Calvinist historiographers, essentially at odds with their predecessors, who would propel the chancellor's legend well into the 17th century.

Conclusion

Tracing Gerson's legacy in the 16th century Protestant thought yield two sets of interconnected outcomes. The first concerns tendencies in his reception by Protestant theologians; the second relates characteristics of his legacy, as revealed through their reception. In other words, while the first group of outcomes

---

[422] Weiss 1992, p. 343. Biographies by Melchior Adams include those of Hus and Jerome of Prague, as well as the one of Geiler von Kaysersberg.

[423] Weiss 1992, p. 346.

[424] Muller 2003, p. 74: 'the rise of Protestant orthodoxy and, within, the acceptance of scholastic method, are indications both of the fundamental catholicity of Protestantism and of the instituralization of the Reform movement as Church'.

tells us more about the reformers, the second sheds light on the chancellor himself. The most important outcome belonging to the first category is that his influence did not fade with the triumph of Protestantism. Although the reception of Gerson in Lutheran and other Protestant 16th century milieus entailed little direct distribution, reproduction and accumulation of his writings, Gerson continued to exercise a strong, although sometimes challenged presence, as he remained an important interlocutor for both those who favored him and those who contested his ideas. One trait that unites practically all theologians presented in this chapter is the fact that Gerson was consistently (with sometimes a notable exception of Nicolas of Cusa) the only late medieval authority cited in their writings. Melanchthon, Osiander, Chemnitz and Bullinger, although critical of scholasticism in general, made an exception for the French chancellor. Such was also the case, for example, of German patristic scholar and preacher Johannes Oecolampadius (original name Heussgen, 1482–1531), who, while greatly disliking scholastics, highly valued the French theologian:[425] *Gersonem triuit non indiligenter quod is uideretur ad alendam pietatem comparatior.*[426] Another theological celebrity, the twice apostate Friedrich Staphylus (1512–1564) also names Gerson, along with Cusanus, as the only late medieval witnesses of Evangelical truth.[427] The chancellor's 15th century adoption into German cultural narrative, when the 'texts preferred by bishops and reform theologians especially significant for the German 15th century were Jean Gerson and Nicolas of Cusa',[428] doubtless prepared his exceptional reception among 16th century German reformers.

The second conclusion is that Gerson's work, ideas, legend, and even his very person, were claimed as Evangelical or proto-Protestant (regardless of which concrete term was used) from the very beginning, with this tendency carried out, although unequally and not universally, by both Lutheran and Reformed authors, who

---

[425] Middleton 1816, p. 85.
[426] Backus 2008, p. 55, citing Capito 1592: 'He studied Gerson not negligently, as he seemed to provide the most suitable food for piety'.
[427] Mennecke-Haustein 2003, p. 304.
[428] Dykema 2000, p. 145.

were sometimes hostile to each other. This phenomenon is best illustrated in Protestant historiography, where the need of listing Gerson among their own proved to be strong enough to make the balance of judgment between loyalties to Gerson and Hus not only to remain still, as in the Lutheran *Catalogus testium ueritatis*, but even lean toward the former, as in the Calvinist version of the *Catalogus* by Simon Goulart.

The third finding suggests that the dynamics between the reception of Gerson and the evangelical thought are far more complex than the continuous, centuries-old efforts at presenting him as a 'forerunner of the Reformation' have attempted to demonstrate. Theologians as different as Luther, Melanchthon, Karlstadt, Bucer, and Osiander, time and again turned to Gerson's authority in moments of doubt and crisis, often with unpredictable results, ranging from a growing enthusiasm for scholastic thought, as in Melanchthon, to a complete rejection as in Karlstadt.

The case of Johannes Brenz (1499–1570) is a perfect illustration of this paradigm. Leader of the Reformation in Württemberg and influential church administrator, ranking just after Luther and Melanchthon, Brenz was solicited to theologically refute the Anabaptist position in May 1530. The difficulty of his situation was aggravated by Luther's position toward the Anabaptists, which was a complete reversal of his own declaration of the absolute priority of the individual conscience over any form of institutional authority nine years earlier at Worms. To uphold Luther's former views in relation to Anabaptists in 1530 would mean to openly go against him, and Brenz, who was Lutheran to the core, was fully aware of it. Faced with the issue of the relationship between those in power and moral conscience of an individual or a group of people, which 'will be the watershed [...] among reformers and defenders of established power even beyond confessional lines',[429]

---

[429] Prodi 2000, p. 182: 'La sua teoria che la legge umana in quanto tale non puo obbligare sotto pena di peccato mortale se non in quanto connessa con la legge divina, sara lo spartiacque nei secoli successivi, sino al Settecento, tra i riformati e difensori del potere stabilito anche oltre le separazioni confessionali'. 'His theory that human law as such cannot oblige under penalty of mortal sin, except as connected with divine law, will be the watershed in the following centuries, up to the eighteenth century, between the reformed and defenders of power established even beyond the confessional separations'.

Brenz appealed to Gerson's understanding of moral conscience as both knowledge and actualization.[430] Württemberg reformer chose to base his arguments in the memorandum 'Whether a Government Violates Conscience When It Forcibly Banishes False Teachers'[431] on the chancellor's 'theory that human law as such cannot be imposed, under the penalty of mortal sin, except if it relates to divine law'.[432] Although he failed to clearly delineate his position and prevent violence, when the Diet of Speyer (1529) passed the imperial law sanctioning the death penalty for rebaptism, Brenz's example demonstrates the multivalence and complexity of Lutheran theological response to and subsequent use of Gerson's impetus.

The fourth outcome, relatively unsurprising, consists in the observation that Lutheran theologians appear to be more engrossed in Gerson's legacy than their Swiss rivals. This is due to several interconnected factors. One is their preference, rooted in Luther himself, for the historical narrative, which, unlike that of their Swiss rivals, did not exclude their immediate predecessors. The other is their unwillingness, exemplified, among others, by Melanchthon, Flacius and Brenz, to completely disavow scholastics and the medieval period in general. Despite explicit negative statements regarding scholastics found in Luther, Melanchthon, Oecolampadius and other reformers, they continued to rely on scholastic distinctions and modes of argument when needed.[433] Another factor figuring in Lutherans' stronger attachment to Gerson is their interest in *Frommigkeittheologie*, which was firmly

---

[430] Klinck 2010, p. 33. Brenz 1974, p. 502: 'The little word conscience, as Gerson shows, comprises two things, namely knowledge and supposition, and then conscience [Gewissen] is when/if you put knowledge or what one knows into an actual deed ['wreck']'. Glorieux does not believe *Compendium Theologiae, De esse, natura et qualitate conscientiae* to be Gerson's work (OC: 1, p. 41), but Du Pin, whose edition is generally considered to be more trustworthy, lists *Compendium Theologiae* as Gerson's text in *Opera omnia*, 1, col. 290–91. Haga affirms that Brenz's descriptions of paradise and beatific visions also come from Gerson (Haga 2012, p. 143).

[431] Brecht 1966, p. 306: 'Das Problem ist, ob die Obrigkeit nicht mit ihrem Vorgehen gegen die Täufer diese in ihrem Gewissen tangiert'.

[432] For more details on Brenz's complicated and knotty arguments see Estes 2007, pp. 79–80.

[433] Both Lutheran and Calvinist theologies ended up using scholastic method of argumentation. See Erb 1989.

associated with his name. Finally, their perception of the Parisian chancellor as an integral part of their cultural history and German ancestry certainly played an important role. To minds formed by German humanists of the previous generation, Gerson's legacy was inextricably intertwined with their national identity, which, fused into the triumph of Lutheran Reformation, they naturally understood as one and the same thing.

In contrast to the majority of Lutheran theologians, who, regardless of their differences, still approached Gerson as not only a mystic, but a German mystic, early Calvinists, due to their persecution, migration and mass exile, did not view him as a particularly French thinker. In fact, his Frenchness does not seem to matter in Huguenot reception at all. However, by the end of the 16th century this difference between Lutheran and other Reformed attitudes toward the late medieval chancellor became less and less discernible, as earlier proto-nationalist appropriations were gradually replaced, at least for a while, by confessional divisions. While in the 15th century Gerson's presence in biographical collections seems to be situated on the line between broad humanist culture of the Renaissance and nascent national aspirations, in the 16th century his authority is placed against the background of 'the processes of reciprocal demarcation and internal homogenization of the confessional churches that took place in conjunction with territorial state-building'.[434] The new 'culture of clearly delineated rival orthodoxies' was now ready to use historiography as a very public function of identifying heroes of a specific group or region.[435] As the crossing of confessional boundaries was coming to an end, Calvinist reworkings of Flacius's *Catalogus testium ueritais* signaled the new era of covert ideological cross-fertilization and unacknowledged borrowings from fellow polemicists of different and sometimes opposite theological views. These indirect exchanges do not signify any form of real dialogue or openness toward one another. Rather, they imply the inescapability of contacts which all sides involved would have preferred to avoid.

Several characteristics of Gerson's thought appear to consistently appeal to early Protestant Reformers. The first and the most

---

[434] Wassilowsky 2018, p. 81.
[435] Weiss 1992, p. 349.

important is his attitude toward Scripture, in which he recognizes the rule of faith: *Scriptura sacra est fidei regula*,[436] and *totius diuinae legis fundamentum* — 'the foundation for all divine laws'.[437] *Poenitemini et credite euangilio* is the leading theme of his works.[438] This aspect is central for Luther's, Melanchthon's, Karlstadt's, Bucer's and Bullinger's reception of Gerson. However, while Gerson's view of the Scriptures was a point of connection and recognition for all these theologians, it had also become a major point of contention. The late medieval master considered post-apostolic tradition as an equally authoritative interpretational norm alongside the 'naked' text of the Bible. This conviction, being unacceptable to all Protestant theologians, formed one of the major demarcation lines between the Protestant and Catholic sides.

The second aspect concerns Gerson's pastoral theology, which found vivid response among Protestant clergy. By means of Luther's, Melanchthon's and Chemnitz's educational endeavors, the chancellor's contributions to catechization and elementary education among young children and the poor were transmitted to future generations. Aside from educational matters his pastoral influence is also found in Lutheran literature of *ars moriendi*, such as *Evangelisch lere und uermanung eines sterbenden menschen* (1523) by the Leipzig publisher Wolffgang Stoeckel,[439] *Christlich leben und sterben* (1528) by Geiler von Kaysersberg's personal secretary and Jacob Wimpheling's friend, Jacob Otter (1485–1547) or *Seelen arstedye vor de gesunden und krancken* (1529) by the 'bishop of Lower Saxony', Urbanus Rhegius (1489–1541).[440] While Otter's manual appears to have retained some remnants

---

[436] *De necessaria communione laicorum sub utraque specie*, OC: 10, p. 55: *Scriptura sacra est fidei regula, contra quam bene intellectam non est admittenda auctoritas [...]* 'Scripture is the rule of faith against which, when properly understood, no authority can be admitted'.

[437] *Monotessaron*, OC: 9, p. 246. De Lang 1991, p. 39.

[438] *Sermon contre l'envie*, OC: 7: 2, p. 906. The same motive is found in *Sermon contre l'orgueil*, OC: 7: 2, p. 933 and in *Sermon pour la fête de saint Antoine*, OC: 7: 2, p. 935.

[439] Reinis 2007, p. 156. *Pour le jour de la Pentecôte*, OC: 7: 1, p. 405: 'Mon amy, pense la grace que Dieu te faist [...] de te donner cognoissance en ce dernier trespass, et ne laisse pas mourir de mort soudaine'.

[440] Rittgers 2012, p. 329.

of Gerson's advice to care-givers,[441] *Ein kurtz unterricht der Sterbenden menschen* by Thomas V. Venatorius (real name Gechauff, d. 1551), published, with Luther's help, in 1526, almost exclusively focuses on the spiritual wellbeing of the dying person.[442] The dimension of Gerson's legacy in death preparation, which addressed needs and difficulties of those accompanying the terminally ill, seems to have been mostly lost to subsequent generations of Protestant authors, who focus primarily on patients themselves. Another major difference concerns an explicit fixation of Protestant and specifically Lutheran manuals for priests on the task of battling the Devil. Indeed, if 'the late medieval handbooks present the ideal priest [...] the *Pastorale Lutheri* sought to promote doctoral purity, beat back the Devil and prevent error'.[443]

The third Gersonian feature to persist in Protestant thought is his moral theology and specifically his development of the concept of *synderesis*. Although this notion itself did not know a long life similar to that which it had in England, it did stimulate discussion and eventual formulation of new Protestant approaches to ethics and the issue of conscience. This discussion was initially related to another characteristically Gersonian topic of scrupulous conscience, as seen in Luther and Melanchthon, then to the attempts at defining what conscience is, as in Luther, Melanchthon, and Calvin, and ultimately to testing the outside limits of the individual conscience, as in the cases of Luther, Karlstadt, and Brenz.

A somewhat personal character of Gerson's oeuvre, the fact that 'Gerson is chatty, not because he wrote more but because he speaks about himself',[444] also played a non-negligible part in his attractiveness to early modern reformers and especially to Martin Luther himself. The fact that the chancellor 'aimait se raconter et

---

[441] Reinis 2007, p. 235. *Ein kurtz Unterricht* follows Gerson's text very closely, making it appear as a simple German translation of the original text.

[442] Reinis 2007, p. 110. Already-mentioned Georg Spalatin also wrote his version of *Sterbebuch*.

[443] Dykema 2000, p. 162. This feature stands in contrast to Gerson's approach. 'Er habe vor allem selten den Teufel vor Augen und auch nicht den strafenden, sondern eher den gütigen Gott' (Jäger 2010, pp. 18–19).

[444] Kaluza 1988. Also see Mazour-Matusevich forthcoming.

à s'analyser'[445] could not fail to attract notice in the movement, which had transformed theology into a highly-personalized declaration of faith.[446] Indeed, the unprecedented degree to which personal factors — such as character, temperament and belief system of different theologians — could influence their reception of Gerson's legacy is obvious. Karlstadt's impatient nature, Luther's anxiety or Chemnitz's systematic mind had a significant impact on the way they treated Gerson's theological insights. However, despite this diversity, it is possible to make some more general observations. One reflection can be formulated as the following: the more radical were the views of a given Protestant thinker, the less inclination he had to validate Gerson's theological choice of *uia media*. Such was the case of Karlstadt, Zwingli[447] or Thomas Müntzer (1489–1525), who, besides once borrowing from *De non esu carnium* (and an odd coincidence that he married a former nun whose name was Ottilie von Gerson), has no affinity with the late medieval chancellor. On the other hand, the more conciliatory and moderate a theological position on the 'receiving end' was, the more inclined such theologians were to embrace Gerson's legacy. This was the case with Melanchthon, Bucer, Brenz and Chemnitz. The notorious exception is Matthias Flacius, who, although a fundamentalist theologian himself, showed an attitude of compromise toward Gerson due to specific historical and ideological motivations that determined his selections in the creation of *Catalogus testium ueritatis*. Confirming the rule, however, is the fact that his catalog won popularity with the next generation of reformed theologians precisely because of its inclusive, 'Melanchthonian' character.

Here another tentative premise might also be of relevance: it seems that theologians of intensely mystical leaning, such as Osiander, Karlstadt, and Luther himself, were attracted to Gerson for the very same reason that they would subsequently be disappointed by him. They initially perceived him as a mystic, which he was not, at least in the sense that these theologians understood

---

[445] Delaruelle, Laband & Ourliac 1964, p. 866.
[446] MacKim 1998, p. 104.
[447] Catherine Brown remarks that 'Gerson's democratic mysticism is analogous to the 16th century Zwingli's universalism' (Brown 1987, p. 316, n. 111).

a mystic to be. The chancellor had never reported mystical experiences and was rather suspicious of supernatural revelations, prophetic apparitions, transcendent ecstasies and the like. As he himself put it, 'Mais de ceste maniere ne suis je mie digne d'en ouvrir ma bouche; ie la laisse aux plus grans'.[448] Indeed, in spite of his promotion of affective theology, he always, and quite disappointingly in Luther's eyes, held on to reason. Even love, and Gerson meant the love of God, needs the safeguard of a rational judgment for *affectus singulus impellit* ('love alone impels [...])'.[449] Nothing could be more foreign to the chancellor's temperament, philosophy and legalistic mindset than Lutheran aversion to reason, which Luther famously called 'the devil's whore'.[450] In this sense, early Lutheran zealots were not mistaken in their ultimate dissociation from Gerson. Indeed, the late medieval theologian thought that hardly anything could be worse than unrestrained religious zeal, which, regardless of cause, is *recte comparaueris ipsum gladio bicipiti in manu furiosi, igni rursus et fulmini sine obice peruaganti*.[451] Considering what was about to unfold on the European scale in the 16th and 17th centuries, these words sound tragically prophetic.

---

[448] *La Montagne de contemplation*, OC: 7: 1, p. 55. McGuire 1998, p. 125.

[449] *De consolatione theologiae*, OC: 4, p. 107. Miller 1998, p. 165.

[450] On Luther's attitude toward Aristotle see Büttgen 2011 and Dragseth 2011.

[451] *De consolatione theologiae*, OC: 9, p. 216. 'zeal [...] may rightly compare to a two-edged sword in a madman's hand, or again to fire and lightning spreading without obstacle' (Miller 1998, p. 165).

CHAPTER 3
CATHOLIC RECEPTION OF GERSON

'[Is] not a 'theological politics' always nourished by
the impossible combination of a strategy and a cry?'
(Jean-François Lyotard)[1]

Introduction

Addressing the reception of Gerson in early modern Catholicism automatically requires dealing with the terminological problem of 'the never-ending debate over whether mid-sixteenth century Catholicism leaned more towards 'Reform' or 'Counter Reformation'.[2] Both commonly used terms, 'Catholic Reformation' and 'Counter-Reformation' have been deemed unsuitable, because they 'divert our attention from the more comprehensive reality of sixteenth-century Catholicism'.[3] Alternative terms 'Early Modern Catholicism', 'sixteenth-century Catholicism', 'Roman Catholicism' or a euphemism 'Rome' are also misleading because they all downplay the militant dimension of the Catholic movement or, as in the case of the latter two terms, are chronologically vague. These expressions are particularly problematic in relation to initial anti-Lutheran reactions in the Empire, such as the Sorbonne's conflict with followers of mystical humanism in France, persecution of *illuminati* in Spain and early Jesuit thought. Even if it is true that 'la spiritualité des jésuites n'est pas du tout une défense de l'orthodoxie',[4] it was from the beginning inextricably intertwined with Ignatius of Loyola's resolve to fight 'the plague of heresy' by means of a specific anti-heresy program,

---

[1] Lyotard 1999, p. 83.
[2] François & Soen 2018, p. 9.
[3] Lindberg 1996, p. 10.
[4] Bataillon 2009, p. 282.

that he spelled out in his letters as early as 1554.[5] In his letter to a fellow Jesuit, Peter Canisius, Ignatius appealed to his consorts ('the Ours') to expediently address the issue of 'the heretics writing a large number of books and pamphlets [...] so that they can be produced without delay and bought by many'.[6] Additionally, the Jesuit anti-heresy agenda was intended to be expanded into 'Northern countries' from a very early date.[7] Both Loyola and German anti-Lutheran theologian Johann Fabri explicitly spoke of the battle against the new invading heresy,[8] referring to Protestantism as a spreading infectious disease.[9] In this context it is hard to agree that the Catholic Reformation 'in Spain, as elsewhere, was an awakening and not a reaction'.[10] It surely was not only and not always a reaction, but the Protestant threat, perceived as existential, loomed large at all times. It colored, explicitly or implicitly, to a lesser or greater degree, the vast majority of Catholic religious expressions, including the reception of medieval theological authorities.

In fact, analysis of the sixteenth century Catholic reception of Gerson requires broadening the notion of reception beyond distribution, reproduction, accumulation and response. It includes a new factor, namely the Catholic reaction to Protestant, and especially Lutheran, reception of the chancellor's legacy. Since aspects of Catholic reception of Gerson varied considerably depending on geography and political circumstances, this factor also played out differently in different parts of Europe. In the Empire, both in the German-speaking world and in the Low Countries, reaction to the Lutheran reception of Gerson dominated. In France, distribution, reproduction and translation of Gerson's works was initially delayed in comparison to the German-speaking world, but it picked up speed in the early sixteenth century. In Spain, where the reception was massive and all aspects of it present, his legacy was implicated, in one way or another, in practically all of the sixteenth-century major movements and controversies.

[5] Young 1959, p. 345.
[6] Young 1959, p. 346.
[7] Young 1959, p. 345.
[8] Oberman 1981, p. 258.
[9] Young 1959, p. 345.
[10] Bataillon 2009, p. 282.

Regardless of local variations, however, it is safe to state that Gerson's legacy initially had less luck with the Catholics than with their Protestant counterparts. There are three main explanations for this situation, all related to the reception of Gerson by the Lutherans, who at this point clearly led the game, while the Catholic Church, still under shock, was on the defensive. The first factor concerns attitudes toward medieval scholasticism in general. Even though it already lost a lot of its prestige under Erasmus's humanistic blows, Thomas More's stylistic refinements and Rabelais' mockery, it was the Protestant Reformation that gave it a fatal blow. Knowing their adversaries' highly unfavorable opinion of scholastics, the vast majority of Catholic theologians elected to avoid referring to them as well. Luther's mighty opponent at Leipzig disputation, Johannes Eck 'understood that anyone fighting the new doctrine needed arguments other than those offered by medieval *Sommae*'.[11] By dismissing all scholastics as a block, Catholics actually ended up being more restrictive and less discriminating than Lutherans. This dismissal affected open references to Gerson. The second factor is defined by an overall positive reception of Gerson in the Lutheran camp, where medieval scholastics never completely lost footing. References to the late medieval chancellor became suspect among Catholics precisely because Luther and Melanchthon quoted him so often and so approvingly in their writings.[12] His popularity on one side of the religious divide warranted, to a certain degree, his unpopularity on the other. Thus, during 'the case Gerson', examined in this chapter, his 'fellowship' on the Lutheran side became a major consideration in the interpretation of *De uita spirituali animae* by leading Spanish theologians. The third factor has to do with the association of Gerson with the conciliar movement. Under the new circumstances of civil and religious strife, this movement made him a controversial figure in the eyes of the Church of Rome and, consequently, of all those who aligned themselves with it. The fact that cardinal Cajetan called Luther *Gersonista* — the accusation that the former considered as the most detri-

---

[11] Polman 1932, pp. 318–19.
[12] Bossy 2002, p. 233: 'Gerson became somewhat suspect among Catholics because Luther quoted from his writings'.

mental, and the latter as the most flattering — did not improve the chancellor's standing in the Catholic camp.[13]

Nevertheless, even though his legacy was caught in a highly complicated, dangerous and often spontaneous polemical game of action-reaction-action, in the later sixteenth century, when Catholic Reformation gradually gained ideological maturity and strength during and after the Council of Trent, interpretations and appreciations of Gerson's spiritual, intellectual and pastoral heritage began to emerge, unrelated to his Protestant reception.

In this chapter, various Catholic receptions of Gerson will be examined geographically, in the German-speaking Empire, France, Low Countries and Spain; thematically, in accordance with the main dimensions of his legacy, pastoral care, mystical humanism, legal thought and mystical theology; and by its collective or individual 'beneficiaries' on the receiving end, such as the first anti-Lutherans in Germany, the clergy, humanist and academic milieus in France, the Leuven University faculty in the Low Countries, the School of Salamanca, Francisco de Osuna, John of the Cross, Teresa of Avila and the *illuminati* in Spain and early days Jesuits.

Part I. Catholic Reception in the Empire

The state of mind of German Catholic theologians of the first half of the sixteenth century can safely be characterized as a reaction to what they perceived as a catastrophic event. The Lutheran Reformation should more appropriately be called a Revolution, because it brought an abrupt and 'violent disruption, rather than a natural fulfillment, of most of what was vigorous in late medieval piety and religious practice'.[14] As is the case with almost all revolutions, all those involved on both sides of the conflict were completely unprepared for it. Luther, from the very beginning, 'put great faith in the persuasiveness of the printed word',[15] but his opponents had difficulty finding an audience, especially in the early years. The public is always more inclined to listen to

---

[13] Cahill 2013, p. 168.
[14] Duffy 1992, p. 4.
[15] Volkmar 2018, p. 563.

something new, especially if it concerns 'the self-proclaimed new light of the Gospel', than to the old familiar message.[16] Moreover, early anti-Lutheran writers were met with suspicion from ecclesiastical authorities, who, failing to recognize the value of polemics, were not initially supportive of their efforts, either financially or otherwise.[17] The Roman establishment clung to the notion that there was no good in arguing with heretics, since any engagement with Luther was seen as a threat compromising the Church's authority in interpreting the Gospel. As a result, 'the wave of Evangelical pamphlets that swept from the printing presses throughout the empire went unanswered by dissenting voices', and 'there was no pamphlet war — it was a siege'.[18] Due to these factors, there was a lack of funding and coordination among defenders of the Catholic faith until the 1530s, when the attitude of the curia began to change. Ultimately, with no backing, the 'men of the Counter-Reformation's first hour'[19] felt like 'lonely fighters'.[20]

These first responders, Luther's contemporaries Kaspar Schatzgeyer (1464–1527), Johannes Eck (1486–1543), Johann Fabri (1478–1541) and Johannes von Staupitz (1460–1524), were, indeed, the least equipped for what was to come. The challenge they faced was, on the one hand, without a precedent and, on the other hand, emerged from their own milieu, from people they thought they knew, including their associates and even close

---

[16] Leipzig printers complained, in 1524, that 'their livelihoods were ruined [...] because they were not allowed to print or sell anything new that is made in Wittenberg or elsewhere. [...] but that which they have in large stacks, is desired by no one' (Letter from the Leipzig city council to Duke George of Saxony, 7 April 1524, in Volkmar 2018, p. 569, n. 42).

[17] Volkmar 2018, p. 566: 'However, both Cochlaeus and Emser hopes for financial and logistical support [...] were bitterly disappointed. Despite the fact that year after year the curia granted thousands of probents and financial awards, Rome was not prepared to contribute any resources or even the smallest German benefice to the media campaign against Luther'. The situation improved starting from the 1550s. For example, Cardinal Otto Truchseß von Waldburg, Prince-Bishop of Augsburg, (1514–1573), hired Sebald Mayer in 1550 in order to publish as many attractive Catholic authors as possible, among them Johann Fabri and Gerson (Gilmont 1990, pp. 39–40).

[18] Volkmar 2018, p. 560.

[19] Oberman 1981, p. 257.

[20] Volkmar 2018, p. 563.

friends. The split, which occurred between people who embraced the new faith and those who did not, was of tremendous proportions. It was not only ideological but also highly personal, especially in its initial phases, with former best friends becoming mortal enemies in a record short amount of time. The ideological rift cut through concrete individuals, who should not be seen as some sort of a group. Each individual chose which argument to support. It might never be possible, for example, to find out the exact reasons why Johannes Bugenhagen embraced the Reformation, while his bitter opponent, Johann Cochlaeus, did not. Both had the background of *reforma perpetua*, in which practically all historical characters mentioned in this chapter were engaged.

In the generation of lonely anti-Lutheran fighters, one name stands out, Kaspar Schatzgeyer. Appointed inquisitor for the Empire and an Observant Franciscan friar, he most energetically opposed Luther's innovations. It is in great part due to him and his confreres that the Catholic faith held its ground in southern Germany, and particularly in Bavaria. A prolific writer, he defended the Catholic position in twenty-three works published within ten years between 1517 and his death in 1527. As a Catholic controversialist, Schatzgeyer had a conciliatory approach to the new theology. He hoped to pacify the situation by offering a positive presentation of disputed doctrines instead of rejecting Luther's arguments directly.[21] He turned to Gerson when dealing with the concrete theological issues that were challenged by Luther, including the doctrine of grace, the veneration of saints, monasticism, Mass and purgatory. Aware of Luther's and Zwingli's anti-scholastic position, Schatzgeyer was 'holding fast to the safety of the biblical-patristic traditions',[22] preferring to stay away from all medieval authorities. Consequently, in spite of the fact that Gerson 'remained for Schatzgeyer a theological interlocutor, source of inspiration, as well as his main mystical authority',[23] he avoided the chancellor's name in his anti-Lutheran texts.[24] The combina-

---

[21] Smolinsky 2014, p. 507.

[22] Iserloh & Fabisch 1984, 5, pp. 10–11.

[23] Iserloh & Fabisch 1984, 5, p. 33: 'Die Auffassungen Schatzgeyers von Gesetz und Freiheit in der Kirche spiegeln Gadanken Gersons wieder'. See Schneider 1953.

[24] Gerson is not mentioned by name in Schatzgeyer 1554.

tion of Schatzgeyer's 'real dependency on Gerson's writings'[25] with his unwillingness to acknowledge it with textual references, conditioned by his attempt to firmly stay within the limits of Catholic orthodoxy, must all be taken into consideration when analyzing his texts. Instances of hidden influence abound. One example is found in *Scrutinium diuinae scripturae pro conciliatione dissidentium dogmatum* (1522), where the author praises the idea of *concilium generale* without mentioning Gerson. Another example belongs to *Examen nouarum doctrinarum* whose very title is inspired by Gerson's *De examinatione doctrinarum*. To mark his dissimilarity with the Lutheran position on *sola scriptura*, Schatzgeyer incorporates Gerson's argument into his own.

Schatzgeyer: *Additum est autem modo credulitas sua non discrepet ab instituto diuino et a sacrae scripturae regula. Fides equidem pro obiecto habet scripturam sacram, igitur aliter credens, quam scriptura sacra docet, erat in fide.*[26]

Gerson: *Attendendum est in examinatione doctrinarum primo et principaliter si doctrina sit conformis sacra scripturae, tam in se quam in modi traditione [...] nihil audendum dicere de diuinis, nisi quae nobis a scriptura sacra tradita sunt.*[27]

Schatzgeyer's use of Gerson 'als Vorlage'[28] also expresses itself through certain hints.[29] Relying on the French theologian's vocabulary from *De uita spirituali animae*, Schatzgeyer upholds the same division between *lex pertinens at diuinem legem* and *lex impertinens ad diuinem legem*,[30] and asserts, like Gerson, that purely human laws are not binding unless they are in accordance

---

[25] Klomps 1959, p. 161: 'tatsächliche Abhängigkeit von der Schrift Gersons'.

[26] Iserloh & Fabisch 1984, 5, p. 44, n. 8. 'In addition, a belief should not deviate from the rules of the divine institution and the Scripture. The object of faith is the sacred scripture. Whoever believes differently than teaching the Scripture, errs in faith'.

[27] *De examinatione doctrinarum*, OC: 9, p. 465. 'It must be attended to examine whether the doctrine conforms to the teachings of Sacred Scripture, both in itself and in the ways of tradition. None dare speak of divine matters unless they are delivered to us from Scripture'.

[28] Klomps 1959, p. 93.

[29] Klomps 1959, p. 161.

[30] Klomps 1959, p. 161. *De uita spirituali animae*, OC: 3, pp. 132–35.

with divine commandments.³¹ A further comparative textual analysis would most certainly reveal more hidden references.

Johannes von Staupitz, the Vicar-General of the German Observant order of Augustinians, professor of theology at Erfurt University and Martin Luther's once beloved mentor, had a very extensive and intimate knowledge of Gerson's writings and drew heavily on them.³² His connection to Gerson and his textual dependence on him probably were greatest among both Protestant and Catholic authors appearing in this study. Thus, his Tübingen sermons of 1497/98 are permeated with over a hundred of Gerson's quotes, demonstrating particularly careful reading of *De consolatione theologiae*, cited according to Cologne's 1483 edition,³³ and *De uita spirituali animae*. Besides these two profusely cited works, Staupitz quoted from *Centilogium de impulsibus, sermo St Bernardo, Super Magnificat, De passionibus animae, De simplificatione cordis, Regula mandatorum, De theologia mystica practica, Tractatus de canticis, Iosephina*, sermons *A deo exiuit, A deo uadit, Considernati mihi, Considerate lilia, Spiritus domini, De quatuor domibus, Fulcite me, Exsultabunt, Super uictu pompa praelatorum* as well as from Gerson's letters.³⁴ Sometimes the Erfurt professor explicitly referred to Gerson's works: *[...] unde dicit Gerson in tractatu de impulsibus, de secondo Gerson in*

---

[31] According to H. Klomps, Schatzegeyer also relies on *Declaratio ueritatum: quae credenda sunt de necessitate salutis* and on *De examinatione doctrinarum* (Klomps 1959, pp. 92–93, n. 8, and p. 159). Iserloh and Fabisch also argue that Schatzgeyer liberally paraphrases Gerson's *De examinatione doctrinarum* (Iserloh & Fabisch 1984, 5. p. 44, n. 8). Klomps argues that *Die Verpflichtungstheorie Gersons*, concerning obligations to human versus divine laws, was a dangerous subject because of its potential practical implications for the post-Reformation Catholic church (Klomps 1959, p. 162).

[32] There has been no consensus among Staupitz's scholars on the question of his theological affinities. Ernst Wolf, in his classical study *Staupitz und Luther*, emphasized Staupitz's association with *via antiqua*, barely mentioning his connection to late medieval theology (Wolf 1927). David Curtis Steinmetz stressed, to the contrary, the 'extent to which he was influenced by nominalist theology' (Steinmetz 1968, p. 27). A Catholic researcher Adolar Zumkeller OSA in his 1994 monograph criticized Steinmetz's analysis as too partisan, aiming at making Staupitz 'closer to Luther than to Gerson' (OSA 1994, p. 223). Franz Posset, in a more recent study affirms, in direct criticism of Steinmetz's opinion, that 'Staupitz was more of a Scottist than anything else [...] It appears Staupitz and Biel had little in common' (Posset 2003, p. 101).

[33] Hamm 2014, p. 61, n. 8.

[34] Graf zu Dohna & Wetzel 1987.

sermone de quatuor domibus, Hinc est, quod Gerson de consolatione the. Dici,[35] etc. Sometimes Gerson's quote was completely fused into Staupitz's text and requires a special expertise to be detected. In 1517 Staupitz published *Libelus de exsecutione aeternae praedestinationis*, where he quoted Gerson 125 times, relying on *Contra curiositatem studentium, Super Cantica, De consolatione theologiae, De contractibus, De directione cordis, De distinctione reuelationum, De impulsibus, De indulgentiis, De mystica theologia practica, De nuptiis Christi et ecclesiae, De potestate ecclesiastica, De primis motibus et consensus, Super Magnificat, Regulae Mandatorum*, sermo *in festo St Bernardi, De theologia mystica speculativa* and, once again, *De uita spirituali animae*.[36] Even quotes from other authors, such as Juvenal, Terence, Virgil and Bernard actually are Gerson's quotes of them.[37] All major themes of Gerson's theology — his 'humble reverence and loving faith in God's infinite, paternal loving kindness',[38] the advice to tirelessly seek God's grace and mercy, the emphasis on the certainty of hope, dangers of too scrupulous a conscience, the teaching of the soul's preparedness and receptivity to grace, and the consolatory mission of priests — are found in Staupitz. Indeed, the chancellor's voice is clearly audible in Staupitz's sermon:

> Therefore, every preacher, as a guide appointed by God, should direct his teaching toward showing the sinners a comforting right path so that, liberated from the burden of their consciences and scrupulous feelings [...] they may be receptive to God's grace and mercy [...].[39]

Among Catholic theologians of the next generation after Staupitz, Gerson found an admirer in the outspoken opponent of the Reformation, controversialist Johannes Cochlaeus (original name

---

[35] Buchwald 1927, p. 182, p. 238 & p. 257.

[36] Graf zu Dohna & Wetzel 1987. Staupitz also shared Gerson's position on the immaculate conception of the Virgin Mary, and composed *Ein büchlein von der nachfolgung des willigen sterbens Chrsiti*, published in Leipzig in 1523, which, although officially dedicated to the Countess Agnes of Mansfeld (1551–1637), was intended for spiritual consolation of a wide clerical and lay audience (Posset 2003, pp. 156–58).

[37] Graf zu Dohna & Wetzel 1987, p. 215.

[38] Hamm 2018, p. 337.

[39] Knaake 1867, 1, p. 27, trans. in Hamm 2018, p. 337.

Johannes Dobeneck, 1479–1552). Initially Luther's sympathizer, he turned against him from 1520 onward, famously calling him a seven-headed monster. Cochlaeus subsequently produced 'a veritable library'[40] directed against 'this terrible plot of the Lutherans'.[41] He was 'educated to his mission of saving Christianity from suckled apostates, through whom the whole world might be corrupted [...] unless the Church responded in a more effective manner than it previously had'.[42] He saw his opponent's fondness of Gerson as neither a blemish on the latter's reputation, nor as a potentially vulnerable point in his own polemics, but rather as a wrong to be rectified. Appealing to Gerson's authority was instrumental for his mission precisely because Lutherans so frequently did so. According to this principle, Cochlaeus constructed his dispute with Melanchthon, the Lutheran author who favored the French theologian the most, as a Gerson-based duel, and responded quotation by quotation. Attacking Melanchthon's *Loci Communes* on the question of free will, Cochlaeus widely cited Gerson both in support of his position and in condemnation of Melanchthon's views.[43] He also opposed Melanchthon's stance concerning human emotions, embracing Gerson's faith in the limited but nevertheless potent power of human reason. 'Where Melanchthon argued that our internal affections were not in our power [...] Cochlaeus replied that the actual situation was reversed'.[44] Even though Cochlaeus's reliance on Gerson represented a conscious strategy aimed to counteract that of his adversaries, evaluating his affinity with the late medieval theologian is not without problems. The degree to which he had absorbed Ger-

---

[40] Marius 1984, p. 310.

[41] Cochlaeus 1988, p. 48. Also see Cochlaeus 1549. Thomas More also 'seems to have used it [Cochlaeus's book against Luther] in composing his own polemics against the heretics' (Marius 1984, p. 310). The story of Cochlaeus's initial engagement into polemical warfare is indicative of the unstable and unpredictable situation in the sixteenth century book market. The city of Inglestadt had only one Catholic press, which was busy printing the works of Johannes Eck. After Eck's death, Cochlaeus, who feared that the printer, Alexander Weissenhorn, would give priority to Protestants, since he was now out of job, began to supply him with his own books (Gilmont 1990, pp. 39–40).

[42] Haberkern 2016, p. 238, citing Cochlaeus's Letter to Vergerio, July 1534. Cochlaeus produced a *Historia Hussitorium* in 1549 (Tucker 2017, p. 27).

[43] Bäumer 1980, p. 70.

[44] Wengert 2012, p. 81.

son's writings/theology sometimes rendered it difficult for him and consequently for those who read and interpret his writings, to pinpoint his exact sources.[45] For example, in the last pages of his 'small book' (*Büchlein*),[46] or in his letter to Herzog Georg von Sachsen,[47] where he defended the celebration of the traditional Catholic mass, he frequently mentioned Gerson, without, however, giving precise quotations.

Besides Schatzgeyer, Staupitz and Cochlaeus, Gerson's impact is present, although to a lesser degree, in the writings of Johannes Eck, Hieronymus Dungersheim (1465–1540), Kilian or Chilian Leib (1471–1553), Melchior Vattlin (Fattlin) (1489–1548), Georg (Georgius Wicelius) Witzel (1501–1573), Johann Fabri and Adam Walasser (1540–1581). Johannes Eck, one of the main protagonists of German Counter-Reformation and 'every bit as well educated and intelligent as Luther',[48] referred to Gerson as 'the most Christian chancellor of the University of Paris'.[49] Mainly interested in Gerson's pastoral theology, both in its confessional and catechismal aspects, Eck shared the chancellor's accommodating position concerning the question of suffering consciences,[50] and drew heavily on *Opus tripartitum* while composing his *Decalogue* of 1539.[51] However, it is rather difficult to differentiate between Gerson's direct and indirect (namely via Gabriel Biel) influences based on Eck's writings, since he often cited both Gerson and Biel as his primary authorities, as, for example, during his controversy with Karlstadt on the use of Christian images in churches.[52]

---

[45] Jedin 1957, p. 96. More in depth study of Cochleus' writings is likely to reveal more continuity with Gerson's thought.

[46] Jedin 1957, p. 96.

[47] Koch 1985, 3, pp. 128–29, citing *Ein Brief von Cochlaeus an Fürst Georg*, April 26, 1538.

[48] Gordon 1996, p. 12.

[49] Mangrum & Scavizzi 1998, p. 296. Also see Douglass 1966.

[50] Tentler 1977, p. 114.

[51] Bast 2009, p. 15. See, for example, Johannes Eck, *Predigt über das 9 und 10 Gebot, Schriften und Briefe 1539–1543*, in Osiander 1985, 7, p. 162: 'Diss (dafür) gibt Gerson ain guter bericht (unterricht) und spricht, dass die zehen gebott haben ein ordnung, die Moyses im buch Exodi beschriben'. 'For this Gerson delivers a good teaching, and says that Ten Commandments have an order, which Moses describes in the book of Exidus'.

[52] See Mangrum & Scavizzi 1998.

Hieronymus Dungersheim was a Conciliarist Catholic theologian and professor at Leipzig University on whose services Duke George of Saxony 'frequently drew'.[53] He was an ardent promoter of Gerson's *bonus pastor* ideal and 'played an important role as preacher in the episcopal visitations from 1522 to 1524 and in the 'Counter-Reformation' campaign in Mühlhausen in 1525'.[54] In his *Schriften gegen Luther*, Dungersheim praised Gerson as 'allerchristlichste Lehrer Johannes Gerson' and *praeclarissimus* (the brightest) *doctor*, referring to two particular works, *De consolatione theologiae* and *De uiagio regis romanorum*.[55] Kilian Leib, an accomplished humanist, historian and scientist'[56] and Bishop of Constance, Melchior Vattlin, appealed to the chancellor's legacy when dealing with theological and ecclesiological issues of primary importance. Leib turned to 'der wirdig' [the worthy]' Johannes Gerson in order to prove the central point of *theologia media* that 'Got wolle herren und pauren sein gnade mittailn [...] als der wirdig Johannes Gerson geschrieben hat'.[57] Melchior Vattlin brought up the the chancellor's authority when arguing an essential unity of the Catholic Church with Christ:

> Dann kirch redt durch Christum und Christus durch kirchen, die kirch, so do ist ein leib Christi und on underlasslich vom Heiligen geist regiert wirt [...] Darvon schreibt an vil orten der heilig Augustinus gar schon, und dessgleichen der trostlich lerer Gerson.[58]

Georg Witzel's connection to Gerson, like that of Staupitz and Dungersheim, was grounded in his longtime commitment to

---

[53] Volkmar 2018, p. 106.
[54] Volkmar 2018, p. 106.
[55] Freudenberger 1987, p. 73 & p. 100.
[56] Leib was one of the first meteorologists. He knew both ancient Greek and Hebrew and studied Aramaic, composed *Historiarum sui temporis ab anno MDII ad MDXLVIIII annales* (1513–1521), and observed weather and skies daily, leaving detailed weather observations in a series of diaries (*Tagebücher*).
[57] Laube 2000, pp. 146–47, citing Kilian Leib. 'God is willing to share his grace with lords and poor people [...] as the worthy Gerson has written'.
[58] Laube 2000, p. 324. 'Then the Church speaks through Christ and Christ through the Church for the Church is Christ's flesh and is directed by the Holy Ghost [...] On this subject the holy Augustine writes in many places quite beautifully and the pious teacher Gerson does likewise'.

reforma perpetua, while his anti-Lutheran strategy was reminiscent of Cochlaeus. In an effort to show that the reform does not have to be *unkatholisch*, Witzel turned to Gerson's writings critical of the Church. However, the text he most relied on, *De defectibus Ecclesiae*, that was used by Lutherans in order to prove Rome's inherent and irreparable corruption,[59] is not by Gerson. Finally, Johann Fabri or Faber, the leader of the anti-Protestant opposition nicknamed 'hammer of heretics', was one of the authors, together with Eck and Cochlaeus, of the 1530 *Confutatio* (refutation of the Augsburg Confession). He does not appear to have much use for Gerson even though the French theologian is, once again, the only late medieval author mentioned in Fabri's *Declamationes diuinae de humanae uitae miseria*.[60]

Duke George of Saxony (1471–1539) offered massive and practically unique support for almost all above-mentioned first Catholic responders. Stepping in where the Roman curia refused to contribute, Georg provided both subsidies for printing of Catholic books and income for the lonely fighters of the early Catholic Reformation. Thus, he offered appointments at the Dresden court to an anti-Lutheran theologian Hieronymus Emser (1477–1527), whose *Vita Bennonis*, the biography of the bishop of Meissen, was inspired by Gerson's ideas of *bonus pastor*.[61] After Emster's death George appointed Johannes Cochlaeus. Thanks to George's support, Leipzig and Dresden surpassed all other cities in the empire in the production of Catholic propaganda in Germany, accounting for almost half of the total production. A total of 219 anti-Lutheran pamphlets were published in Leipzig alone before 1539.[62]

> Of the six most productive anti-Lutheran authors in the empire before 1555, no fewer than four — Emser, Cochlaeus,

---

[59] Henze 1995, pp. 109–41, p. 249 & p. 285.

[60] See Braun 2006. There is an apparent confusion (as in Warme 1996, p. 57) between this Johann Fabri and his namesake, who published the first Swedish language book, which happens to be a translation of Gerson's *Tractatus de diuersis diaboli temptationibus*, in 1495 and 1496. The other, Swedish Fabri, was called Smed or Smit and was a professional printer. See Undorf 2014, p. 48.

[61] Volkmar 2018, p. 446.

[62] Volkmar 2018, p. 561.

Sylvius and Georg Witzel — were based in Albertine Saxony [...] closely connected to Duke George.[63]

Georg, 'whose actual reform in practice' 'corresponded to ideas of Jean Gerson',[64] also supported Johannes Staupitz as Saxony's leader of the reform movement.[65] Georg and those whom he supported struggled desperately to salvage whatever could still be saved of Catholicism in Germany. In all fairness, they largely succeeded in this endeavor. The Catholic Church owes its initial preservation, as the church most German-speaking people still identify with, to people like Johannes Eck, Johannes Cochlaeus and Kaspar Schatzgeyer.

In the next generation of Catholic German theologians, Adam Walasser (1540–1581), poet, translator, polemist and publisher, holds a particular interest.[66] His relation to Gerson's legacy is threefold. He retranslated Gerson's *De modo uiuendi omnium fidelium*, that by 1520 had been translated but not published by Luther's associate Georg Spalatin. Whether Walasser used Spalatin's earlier little-known manuscript translation or based his version on Gerson's original, which was often printed in the first decade of the sixteenth century, is unclear. He mentioned neither. Besides connection through *De modo uiuendi omnium fidelium*, Walasser also wrote his own variation of *ars moriendi*, the *Trostbüchlein für die kranken und sterbenden Menschen*, published in 1597 and loosely based on Gerson's text. Finally, reworking the Gersonian notion of spiritual pilgrimage, Walasser acknowledged quoting 'ein schön Gebettlein Gersonis dass täglich Testament des Piligrams genant' — 'a pretty little prayer by Gerson, which is called a daily testament of the pilgrim'.[67]

---

[63] Volkmar 2018, p. 570.
[64] Volkmar 2018, p. 219 & p. 446.
[65] Volkmar 2018, p. 270.
[66] Walasser authored *The German Mirror*, published in 1563, and several collections of poetry and a devotional book of old songs.
[67] Adam Walasser, *Kunst wol zusterben: ein gar nutzliches hochnothwendiges Büchlein*, 1585, 1572, 1579, reprinted in 1607 and 1612. Also, Adam Walasser, *Der Seelen Artzney*, 1571.

Part II. The Catholic Reception in the Low Countries

Jacobus Latomus and Godescale Rosemondt

Gerson had a significant and traditional following in the Low Countries. His reception by Wessel Gansfort, Standonck and Mombaer, and by *devotio moderna* in general, naturally reinforced his connection to this region, where this movement originated and was the strongest. His works had become known in this part of Europe during his lifetime,[68] with his *Opus tripartitum* and parts of *Collectorium super Magnificat* translated into Middle Dutch by 1435.[69] In the sixteenth century his influence was mainly associated with Jacobus Latomus (*c.* 1475–1544), the leading figure of the Leuven Faculty of Theology, and Luther's powerful opponent.[70] The Leuven theologian's reception of Gerson was threefold: pastoral, intellectual and exegetical. The Parisian master was Latomus's source of inspiration in practically all the questions concerning the care of souls and the core duties of Church officials.[71] Reacting to the widespread absenteeism among bishops, Latomus adopted Gerson's views on the responsibilities of prelates in his *Quaestio quodlibetica* of 1518, including the demand that they were to execute their pastoral duties in person. His academic training in Paris must have left a strong impression on the young scholar, as he remained oriented toward the French theological school during the rest of his career.[72] In his *De trium linguarum et studii theologici ratione Dialogus* (1519), Latomus recommended the study of scholasticism for the discipline of the mind, and respect for philosophy and the variety of topics covered, specifically referring to Gerson as a brilliant representative of the Parisian theological tradition.[73] In this sense what humanists like Erasmus or Thomas More considered Gerson's shortcoming constituted a splendid quality for Latomus.

---

[68] Caspers 1999, p. 89. For details see Schepers 2008.
[69] Caspers 1999, p. 89.
[70] As a student in Paris Latomus was closely associated with Jan Standonck, in whose house he lived. See de Boer 2017, p. 477.
[71] See François & Gielis, forthcoming.
[72] François 2020, p. 22.
[73] Latomus 1905, p. 70 & p. 83.

The most important dimension of Latomus's reception of Gerson is exegetical and concerns the theological issue of the relationship between tradition and Scripture. This issue was extremely troubling for the Leuven theologian, who faced the 'orality-scripturality' dilemma, when at first humanists and then Lutherans, elevated Scripture as the sole basis for the formulation of doctrine.[74] Since Gerson was one of the first theologians to be confronted with the very possibility of this opposition on account of what he perceived as the *sola scriptura* doctrine of Wycliff and Hus, it was only natural for Latomus to turn to the chancellor's authority a century later. Gerson's formulation of the *communis opinio* on this issue — later perceived as if it was always there[75] — is unambiguous. Any separation, let alone conflict, between two authorities — Sacred Scripture and the Church, written and spoken Word of God — is a heresy and an inconceivable nonsense. Building on this opinion, Latomus considered the authority of the Church equal to that of Scripture, especially when it comes to interpreting obscure biblical passages or managing the everyday life of the faithful, especially in relation to aspects of life that the Scriptures do not mention at all. Like his German contemporaries, Johannes Staupitz and Melchior Vattlin, Latomus believed that the same Spirit that had inspired the Evangelists continually dwells in the Church. Although he did not explicitly use the words 'tradition' or 'traditions', it was inconceivable for him, just as it was for Gerson, that Scripture and the Church could be in disagreement. However, his stand on this issue was more assertive than Gerson's because he 'is far more explicit in his acceptance of a group of liturgical and disciplinary customs and even some tenets of the faith that were orally handed down [...] without an explicit reference in Scripture'.[76] Considering the radical

---

[74] Latomus's views on the issue are found in *De trium linguarum, et studii Theologici ratione dialogus (Dialogue concerning the Three Biblical Languages and the Study of Theology)* published in 1519; Gerson's in *De sensu litterali sacrae scripturae (On the Literal Sense of Sacred Scripture* 1413/14 (OC: 3, p. 335).

[75] On this topic see François 2020, p. 13.

[76] François 2020, p. 13. Leuven theologian John Driedo (d. 1535) further developed the concept of the relationship between Scripture and Tradition in his work *De ecclesiasticis scripturis et dogmatibus* (1533). Unlike Vitoria and Soto, Driedo 'has no scruples making the identification of *ius* and *dominium*' (Tuck 1979, p. 51).

change in historical circumstances, his explicitness corresponds to the zeitgeist of the time, when just about all positions sharpened and hardened, and practically no theologian, on either side of the conflict, was any longer able to maintain any significant degree of ambivalence or compromise.

In addition to Latomus, Gerson's pastoral legacy found continuation in the writings of another Leuven theologian, Godescale or Godescalc Rosemondt (d. 1526), who relied on the chancellor's works *On the Art of Hearing Confession* and *On the Power of Absolution* (*De potestate absoluendi*) in order to protest an unreasonably great number of confession cases reserved for bishops.[77] In his *Confessionale* Rosemont deplored the negative effects that such practices tended to have on penitents and restated the chancellor's opinion that reserving cases for higher ecclesiastical authorities was scandalous and ineffective at best, since regular priests were perfectly fit to resolve them in a more discrete manner.[78] Directly naming the late medieval theologian thirteen times in elaborate and lengthy citations, Rosemondt relied on his authority regarding other pastoral matters such as definitions of capital, carnal and deadly sins, penance, punishment and preparation for the mass.[79] Besides Latomus and Rosemondt, Gerson's influence in the sixteenth-century Low Countries can be found in the evangelical harmony by the Leuven professor of theology, famous biblical scholar and bishop Cornelius Jansenius of Ghent (1510–1576). In the introductory epistle of his *Concordia euangelica*, that follows *Monotessaron*'s pattern,[80] Jansenius mentioned Gerson, and Peter de Rivo, as his models.[81] Published in Leuven in 1549, *Concordia euangelica* served as a model for the famous first English

---

[77] Brown 1987, p. 72.

[78] Gerson's consistent opposition to these cases has been discussed in Chapter 1. See, for example, his letter to a bishop in 1408, *EW* p. 240.

[79] Rosemondt 1553, fol. 8: *[...] Gerson Cancellarius Parisiensis que [...] fiat processus & distinctio secundum septe uitia capitalia, nam oia & sola mortalia necessario sunt confitenda'*. 'Gerson, chancellor of Paris, who proceeded according to the division of seven capital sins for only the mortal ones must necessarily be confessed'. *Confessionale*, initially written in the vernacular, was then translated into Latin. It has 288 leaves (folio) and is divided into 21 chapters. See Langholm 2003, p. 98.

[80] Wünsch 1983, p. 213.

[81] Masolini 2020, p. 92.

Gospel harmony, that was produced in Little Gidding in Cambridgeshire in the late 1620s.[82]

Part III. The Catholic Reception in France

Pastoral Renewal

By the end of the fifteenth and early sixteenth centuries, Gerson's reformist efforts, aimed at improving the pastoral care and educational level of the clergy, found an enthusiastic reception among the French bishops, particularly in the Northern part of France, in Senlis, Meaux, Bourges, Sens and in Paris itself.[83] Bishops Francois d'Estaing in Rodez (1504–1529), his brother Antoine d'Estaing (1506–1524), Etienne Poncher in Paris (1503–1519), Hugues des Hazards (1506–1517) and Louis Pinelle in Meaux (1511–1516) emphasized the need for the clergy to serve as shining examples of piety and virtue.[84] Francois d'Estaing regularly gathered his clergy from 1517 to 1529 in order to ensure their level of preparation and reinforce parish visitation.[85] In *Opus tripartitum* Gerson answered his own call to create 'a short work [...] dealing with the chief points of our religion, and especially the Ten Commandments, for the sake of the simple folk',[86] and answered the wishes

---

[82] Two evangelical harmonies entitled *Monotessaron* were produced in Leuven in the 15th century, one composed by Leuven theologian Johannes Varenacker (*c.* 1413–1475), which is now lost, and another by Leuven professor of philosophy and rhetoric Petrus de Rivo (*c.* 1420–1499), where Gerson's influence is explicitly acknowledged. See Masolini 2020.

[83] Hayden, Greenshields 2005, pp. 81–82: 'The first five dioceses known to have received new Gerson-inspired synodal statutes were Meaux (1493), Paris and Grenoble (1495), Saint Brieuc (1496) and Clermont (1496). The bishops included: Jean l'Huillier, Etienne de Lonwy, Laurent l'Allemand, Jean Simon, Christophe le Penmarch, and Charles de Bourbon'.

[84] Reid 2009, p. 156.

[85] Lemaitre 2018, 2, pp. 13–14.

[86] Letter of 1 April 1400 to Pierre d'Ailly, OC: 2, pp. 23–28: *Item forte expediret sicut olim tempore quarumdam pestilentiarum facultas medicorum composuit tractatulum ad informandum singulos, ita fieret per facultatem uel de mandato eius aliquis tractatulus super punctis principalibus nostrae religionis, et specialiter de praeceptis, ad instructionem simplicium.* '[...I]n these constricted times, so dangerous to souls, [...], just as the schools of medicine once wrote pamphlets to instruct people how to manage in times of plague, so now it would be good if a short work

of these prelates, who were looking for a reasonable foundation to build the future reform of the Church practices in need of change.

Gerson's little manual has a simple organization and a clear structure. It targeted four categories of people in need of basic instruction: simple clergy, all the unlearned, children and youth, and finally, all those, lay or cleric, who care for the sick and dying.[87] Furthermore, prelates were called to provide guidance to all people in need of instruction, including the lower clergy, parents and teachers of children and youth, and administrators of charitable institutions, together with all those who find themselves in care of others. Remarkably, Gerson insisted on the necessity of catechismal education 'pour les josnes escoliers soient filz ou filles qui doiuent estre introduits des leur enfance en poins generaulx de nostre religion. Item les peres et les meres pour leurs enfans',[88] for boys and girls, and fathers and mothers. This rather unusual care to educate both sexes, for which the chancellor never got historical credit, might explain an equally unusual image of the father speaking to his daughter that illustrates the fifteenth century manuscript of Gerson's *Sermons sur la passion*.[89]

Opus tripartitum met with great and quasi-universal success, as it was published under various titles almost without intervals, from 1506 to the 1580s.[90] Paris bishop Etienne Poncher

---

were written [...] dealing with the chief points of our religion, and especially the Ten Commandments, for the sake of the simple folk' (trans. in Bast 2009, p. 2).

[87] Letter accompanying *Opus tripartitum*, OC: 2, p. 75. Gerson also composed a little known *Livret-proverbes pour écoliers*, which represents a rhymed catechism (OC: 7: 1, p. 367).

[88] Letter accompanying *Opus tripartitum*, OC: 2, p. 75: 'Si doiuent quatre manieres de personnes estre diligens que ceste doctrine soit publiee. C'est assauir les prelas de saincte eglise qui ont la prochaine cure des mainres cures et leur sera impute se ilz sont ignorans ou defaillans enners le simple people. Item les peres et les meres pour leurs enfans envers les maistres des escoles. Item les maistres des hospitaus et maisons Dieu. Item generalement tous ceulx et celles qui ont este cause ou sont de paroles ou de faits pechiez dautrui ou qui les doiuent enseignier et ilz nen font ne nont fait riens'.

[89] Delumeau & Roche 1990, p. 63.

[90] Chaunu 1997, p. 169. Here are some of the French editions of *Opus* or works directly derived from it: *Les commendemens de saincte eglise et la confession generale du jour de pasques par les paroisses. Le petit traicte de maistre jehan gerson qui aprent a bien mourir*, Paris, 1516; *Instruction des cures, pour instruire le simple peuple, cest assauir le livre des troys parties des commendements de Dieu, de confession: et de lart de bien mourir*, Poitiers, 1516?; *Instruction des cures pour*

(1446–1524) ordered new editions of the *Opus* and wrote the preface for one of them.[91] His example was followed by François de Luxembourg in the diocese of Mans: 'et nous l'avons [Gerson's *Opus*] pour ceste cause fait correctement imprimer en toutes les deux langues, afin que plus facilement et à vil pris ung chacun le peust avoir promptement et entendre'.[92] Bishop of Meaux Louis Pinelle (d. 1516) ordered *Opus* to be read during Sunday services.[93] Several other bishops recommended its editions, under the titles *Instruction des curez pour instruire le simple people*, *Statuts pour l'Instruction des curéz* or *Manuel des cures*,[94] for use in their dioceses between 1507 and 1517.[95] Bishop of Bayeux Louigi Canessa (1516–1532), a patron of humanists and a close associate of Marguerite de Navarre, who 'measured against the standard of Gerson, Standock, and Seussel',[96] required priests to learn Gerson's *Opus* by heart.[97] The book was also given an official status by being incorporated into the Sunday rituals.[98] In 1556 the cardinal d'Armagnac, following Gerson's instructions, required the use of *Opus* for the instruction of all 'curés and priests for the benefit of their parishioners, all teachers for the benefit of their pupils and those running the hospitals for the benefit of their patients

---

instruire le simple peuple [...] par tout levesche de Saint Malo, Nantes, 1518, 1521; *Instruction des cures et vicaires pour instruire le simple peuple avec la maniere de faire le prosne*, Lyon, 1525; *Instruction des cures, pour instruire le simple peuple, compose par maistre Jehan Gerson ... appelle en latin Opus tripartitum*, Paris, 1531; *Instruction des cures, pour instruire le simple peuple*, Paris, 1533, 1537, 1541; *Jean Gerson, le doctrinal de la foy catholique, auquel est comprins en brief le manipule des curez*, Paris, 1537; *Jean Gerson, Sensuyt le Confessional, aultrement appelle le Directoire des confesseurs: livre tresfructueux et prouffitable et utile contre tous erreurs concernant la foy catholique, a tous fidelles chrestiens pour scavoir et apprendre la maniere de soy confesser et examiner sa conscience*, Paris, 1537, 1547; *Jean Gerson, le Directoire des confesseurs*, 1538, 1539; Johan Quentin, *Heures a l'usage de Rouen, Trois veritez très utiles, et remède ... pour home et femme pour issir de peché ... [selon la doctrine et opinion de Maistre Jehan Gerson, chancelier de Paris, home très expert en sainte moralité*, Paris, vers 1584.

[91] Amalou 2007, p. 191; Chatellier 1995, p. 35; Britnell 1986, p. 192.
[92] Britnell 1986, p. 192.
[93] Reid 2009, p. 161.
[94] Dhotel 1967, p. 30.
[95] Pettegree 2001, p. 90.
[96] Amalou 2007, p. 158.
[97] Amalou 2007, p. 159.
[98] O'Connor 1942, p. 22.

and the poor'.[99] Although 'deriving mainly from Jean Gerson and his successors, the *bonus pastor* tradition initially flourished more in northern than in southern Europe',[100] there is evidence that *Opus'* geography included the diocese of Lyons. The municipal library of this city still has a printed edition of Gerson's *Opus*, both in Latin and in French (under the title of *L'instruction des curez*) that was most likely published in Lyons around 1508 by François de Rohan, archbishop of Lyons and bishop of Angers[101] The Archbishop insisted that all those caring for the needy, whether in hospitals, hostels or other establishments, read *Opus* attentively and often. He also recommended *Opus'* simplified version, together with *De Imitatione Christi*, that was widely attributed to Gerson in France, as well as a small collection of prayers, as a means of fostering popular devotion.[102]

Opus left a substantial mark on the first French movement of catechization, which formed a cornerstone of Catholic religious instruction long before the decrees of the Council of Trent or the Jesuit catechistical catechetical efforts.[103] Several tendencies observable in the Catholic catechization process, 'best to be achieved through the establishment of diocesan and collegiate schools',[104] found their roots in Gerson. The first is the use of the vernacular. Among Lutherans and other Protestants, the use of vernacular expression evolved into an intentional program, a commitment to bring the Scriptures to the people. Among Catholics it became partly a response to the Protestant challenge and partly a continuation of the Gerson-initiated process of 'democratization' of theology. Just as Gerson had done in his vernacular treatise *The Mountain of Contemplation*, and almost in the same expressions, an overwhelming number of Catholic authors openly acknowledged their adoption of the vernacular 'for the sake of the simple folk' and sometimes 'for simple priests'.[105] However, from

---

[99] Lemaitre 2018, 2, p. 13.
[100] Pettegree 2004, p. 292.
[101] Reed 2009, p. 161.
[102] Dhotel 1967, pp. 29–31.
[103] Dhotel 1967, p. 29.
[104] Oakley 2006, p. 190.
[105] Bast 2009, p. 3.

the 1530s the political climate turned against Catholics writing on religion in the vernacular,[106] because this practice was by now firmly associated with Protestantism. Also, even though the Council of Trent did not explicitly forbid the vernacular expression, 'Latin liturgy had become such a symbol of demarcation that in the religiously belligerent sixteenth century change was unthinkable'.[107]

The second Gersonian tendency in French catechization was a strong emphasis on the Ten Commandments, which, just as it happened in the Empire and in England, began to dominate all other moral codes for lay instruction. Many reform-minded Catholic bishops issued diocesan legislation requiring that parish priests teach the Decalogue regularly, some offering special indulgences or other incentives to lay folk who attended such lessons.[108] The aforementioned bishop of Meaux Louis Pinelle, very active in promoting the education for the poor and the peasants, made a decree that those who have difficulties explaining the Ten Commandments to laity should read and study Gerson's *Opus*.[109] Bishop of Troyes, René Benoist (1521–1608), nicknamed 'the Pope of the Halles', was one of the most prolific, although controversial, French Catholic Reformation writers. He translated several of Gerson's treatises in the 1570s and relied on the chancellor's writings in his *Petit fragments catechistic d'une plus ample catechese* (1579).[110] Antoine Dupras (1463–1535), an active anti-Lutheran and Chancellor of France, acting as an Archbishop of Sens, also followed Gerson's pedagogical program with respect to the education of the laity. He required schools for children and instruction during Sunday mass for adults. The third Gersonian characteristic was the tendency of privileging the fourth commandment — to

---

[106] Britnell 2001, pp. 83–109 & pp. 85–86.
[107] O'Malley 2013, p. 269.
[108] Bast 2009, p. 3.
[109] Veissière 1986, pp. 403–04.
[110] The full title is *Petit fragments catechistic d'une plus ample catechese de la magie reprehensible et des magiciens*. While some historians consider Benoit moderate or even irenic, placing him somewhat between Rome and Geneva (see Carter 2005), others see him as a militant Catholic preacher accountable for instigating popular violence against Huguenots in 1570–1571, by declaring that God himself put 'force in the heart and stones in the hands of the rude and imbecile people as executors of his sentence' (Holt 2005, p. 89).

honor your father and mother — with a renewed importance given to the role of the father. This aspect acquired a doubly Gersonian dimension in France and in the rest of Catholic Europe, as it was closely intertwined with Gerson's promotion of the cult of Jesus' early father, St Joseph. The popularity of this saint would reach an unprecedented scale in the sixteenth and especially in the seventeenth centuries. Clearly, more than a century after his passing, Gerson 'continue à garder l'enseignement et la pastorale, notamment dans l'Église de France'.[111]

Opus tripartitum was not the only text of Gerson's appreciated by the French clergy. Well before the Council of Trent, jurist and humanist Claude de Seyssel (d. 1520) found inspiration in Gerson's *Sermo de uisitatione praelatorum*, that articulates five fundamental duties of the *bonus pastor* toward his diocese: obligatory residence, frequent pastoral visitations, spiritual direction of the flock, correction of errors and preaching.[112] Bishop of Saint-Papoul, Pierre Soybert also closely followed the stipulations formulated in *Sermo de uisitatione* in his book *De cultu uinee Domini*.[113] The difficulty of enforcing these requirements is rooted in the sixteenth-century reality that the majority of French bishops did not live in their dioceses or even visit them on a regular basis. Examples as blatant as that of François de Foix, bishop of Aire in Gascony, who never set foot in his diocese in the twenty-four years that he was its bishop, underscore the scale of the issue.[114] Gerson's prestige greatly contributed to the progress in the ecclesiastical discipline, and necessary changes were

---

[111] Venard 2000, p. 206. The increased emphasis on catechization in France does not seem to have been accompanied by a strong vogue for evangelical harmonies. There is no mention of Gerson in François Laplanche's study *La Bible en France entre mythe et critique, 16ᵉ–19ᵉ siècle*. However, few Catholic harmonies that did see the day, such as vernacular 1507 *Les contemplacions histroriez sur la passion nostre seigneur* and 1547 *Tetramonon sive symphonia et concetus quatuor euangeliorum* by the French Benedictine monk Gabriel Dupuyherbault (1490–1566), were fashioned according to Gerson's model.

[112] Reid 2009, p. 156. Herbert Mayow Adams lists following Gerson's editions: *Opera*, 3 editions, 1514, 1518, 1521; *De excommunicationis ualore opuscula*, Paris, 1570; *Dialogus de perfection cordis*, Paris: Jean Petit, 1505; *Meditatio deuota Passionis Dui nostri Jesu Christi*, 1503; *Modus uiuendi omnium christifidelium*, Cologne, 1510; *Sermo de passione domini*, Strasbourg, 1509 (Adams 1967).

[113] Venard 2000, p. 39.

[114] Holt 2005, p. 13.

slowly made. Numerous bishops began considering parochial visits as 'an absolute priority'.[115]

In addition to *Opus* and *Sermo de uisitatione praelatorum*, the persistent attribution to Gerson of *De Imitatione Christi*, usually published together with his *De meditatione cordis*, as in Italy, made the latter treaty 'l'oeuvre la plus massivement diffusée au moins jusqu'en 1582'.[116] Indeed, more than a century-long tradition of publishing these two works in concert extended both the longevity of Gerson's little treaty and the French tradition of attributing *De Imitatione Christi* to him. The chancellor's sermons also retained their audience in France. Thus, Antoine Dupras energetically promoted them as a model for preaching.[117] Gerson's catechetical and spiritual writings were re-edited and translated throughout the sixteenth century, with *Opus* or its parts published as late as 1575, 1583 and 1589. His *Harangue faite par l'université de Paris devant le roy Charles sixième* was published four times between 1560 and 1561 and republished twice in 1588 for political reasons related to the celebration of royal interventionalist policy in church affairs. 'When, in 1584, André Thévet rose up against the Protestants' use of Gerson, he indirectly highlighted the position of the latter on the intellectual horizon of his time'.[118] To sum it up, Gerson remained France's favorite theologian.[119]

The Circle of Meaux: Guillaume Briçonnet, Marguerite de Navarre and Lefèvre d'Etaples

Pierre Chaunu once remarked that the bishops particularly attached to Gerson's pastoral ideal were mostly those with the closest association with humanism.[120] This observation applies to the network of prelates who had Gerson's pastoral ideal at its

---

[115] Venard 1996, p. 203.
[116] Sordet 2011, p. 97.
[117] Pettegree 2004, p. 97.
[118] Denis 2019, p. 43, citing Tallon 1997, p. 444.
[119] Amalou 2007, p. 191.
[120] Chaunu 1997, p. 169.

center: the above-mentioned bishop of Paris Etienne Poncher,[121] son of Antoine Dupras, bishop of Clermont, Guillaume Dupras (1507–1560), bishop of Senlis Louis Guillard,[122] bishop of Carpentras Jacopo Sadoleto (1477–1547), bishop of Avranches Robert Ceneau (1483–1560), bishop of Saint-Malo Denis Briçonnet (1473–1535) and bishop of Troyes Guillaume Petit (1519–1527). This shared vision for the reform of the Church continued at least until 1530.[123] However, while Gerson's pastoral program remained a unifying and stable influence for French reform-minded prelates, they were beginning to diverge on the issue of usefulness of biblical humanism for the advancement of the Church.[124]

These divergences are best illustrated by the example of two brothers, both Gerson enthusiasts, who were born and died within a year of each other, bishops Guillaume (1472–1534) and Denis (1473–1535) Briçonnet. After discovering multiple abuses and irregularities in his diocese of Saint-Malo in 1515, Denis Briçonnet published and then reprinted *Opus tripartitum* under the title *L'instruction des curez pour instruire le simple people*,[125] ordering priests incapable of preaching to read it during early morning services as well as for the high, parochial Mass.[126] As an enticement and reward, he granted forty days' pardon to all those who would read *Opus* aloud in the church, and twenty to those who would listen, thus doubling Gerson's own initial 'remuneration' scale.[127]

---

[121] Veissière 1986, p. 130.

[122] The dates for Louis Gillard seem to be uncertain. I found dates (1525–1553) in Dhotel 1967, p. 30. The date of his death is sometimes given as 1551 and sometimes as 1556.

[123] Venard 1979, p. 117: 'Tel est le sens d'une lettre adressée en 1530 par Sadolet à Erasme, exprimant le point de vue des pasteurs les plus éclairés de l'Église romaine de ce temps, d'autant qu'elle pourrait revendiquer par caution la doctrine toujours respectée de Gerson'.

[124] Reid 2009, p. 156.

[125] Pettegree, Walsby & Wilkinson 2011, p. 675, entry 22721.

[126] Reid 2009, p. 159 & p. 161.

[127] *Le doctrinal aux simples gens*, OC: 10, p. 295: 'Ce present livret en francois qui est de tres grant prouffit et edificacion [...] et afin que lez curés et chappelains soient plus dévots et enclins a lire ou a oir dudit livre au salut de leurs âmes [...] A touz ceulz qui [...] liront ce livret a autrui, vight jours de pardon; et a tous ceulx qui oiront lire et en liront [...] dix jours pour chascune fois a tousjours perpetuelment'.

Fully engaged with Gerson's pedagogical program, Denis Briçonnet offered similar pardons to curates, schoolmasters, parents, and others willing to instruct children and the illiterate using Gerson's manual.[128] His life-long commitment to the chancellor's reforming agenda leaves no doubt, and his brother Guillaume fully shared it. However, Guillaume took his interest in Gerson to a different level, the one where his more traditional brother and many of his confrères were not ready to venture. Besides pastoral theology, Guillaume was attracted to other aspects of the chancellor's legacy: a more personal, internal, subjective and affective spirituality, available to all and adaptable to both monastic and lay audiences. Indeed, Gerson's program of 'democratization [which] transforms what might be called a strictly professional spirituality into more comprehensive terms'[129] struck a resonant chord with Guillaume Briçonnet and the group of his friends, who formed an influential, although short-lived Meaux Cenacle (1521–1525): the sister of King Francis I, Marguerite de Navarre (1492–1549), France's most prominent humanist Lefèvre d'Etaples (1450?–1536), the future bishop of Oloron Gérard Roussel (1500–1550), the Leuven alumnus and Sorbonne theologian Josse Clichtove (1472–1543) and others.[130]

The correspondence between the two most powerful members of the Meaux Cenacle, Marguerite de Navarre and Guillaume Briçonnet, has the theme of spiritual mendicancy as its leitmotif, revealing the correspondents' familiarity with Gerson's vernacular text *La mendicité spirituelle*, that was reedited in 1500 and published in Paris in 1519.[131] This theme is the highest point in

---

[128] Reid 2009, p. 161; Britnell 1986, pp. 192–93.

[129] Burrows 1991 pp. 35–36. For a more detailed analysis on this aspect of Gerson's spirituality see Mazour-Matusevich 2004, chapter 5, part one.

[130] Bedouelle 1976, pp. 91–97. Guillaume Briçonnet was named bishop of Meaux in 1516 but called upon Lefèvre to remain at Meaux permanently. Lefèvre devoted his time at Meaux to translating the New Testament, completing commentaries of the four Gospels and supervising biblical homilies. Lefèvre's friends Pierre Caroli (1480–1546), Gérard Roussel (1500–1550), François Vatable (d. 1547), Michel d'Arande (d. 1528) and Martial Masurier (d. 1550) came with him. Besides them, the Circle of Meaux also comprised, at different moments of its short existence, Guillaume Farel (1489–1565). At the end of September 1521, Marguerite de Navarre and her mother stayed at Meaux.

[131] *La mendicité spirituelle* was published as *Les meditacions de lame: le consolatif de tristesse*. Paris, 1519. See Higman 1996, p. 233.

Gerson's 'theology of seeking'[132] or of spiritual quest, a middle ground between quietism and theology of merits. Although the beggar metaphor is not entirely original to Gerson, and is found in Augustine's homilies ('Profess yourself as beggar of God')[133] and in William of Auvergne's (1180?–1249) *Rhetorica diuina*,[134] Gerson claims to have learned it from a personal encounter with a peasant woman named Agnes, who spiritually 'placed herself like a condemned criminal before her judge, like a poor beggar before a wealthy lord'.[135] The description of this spiritual method, invented by a simple woman, with whom Gerson declared himself to be in complete agreement, served as a promotion of contemplation for laity and particularly for women.

In letters written between 1521 and 1523, Briçonnet and especially Marguerite refer to themselves and to others, as beggars, and adopt 'the profession [mestier] of mendicancy'[136] the safest contemplative method of spiritual advancement. Lefèvre d'Etaples, humanist François Vatable (?–1547) and Gérard Roussel (1500–1550) are presented as 'trois mendiants d'esperit qui sont icy en votre hermitage'.[137] In a letter of November 17, 1521 to Marguerite of Navarre, Briçonnet argues that one can achieve 'divinity' only by 'foieblesse de pauvretté et mendicité d'esprit', 'infirmity of poverty and mendicancy of spirit'.[138] In her answer,

---

[132] Burrows 1991, p. 173.
[133] Augustine of Hippo 2017, p. 318.
[134] See Solère 1994.
[135] *Dialogue Spirituel*, p. 172: 'Je parloye naguerez a une devote femme, nommee Agnes, demourant a Aussoire, a l'occasion de laquelle je fis jadis le livre de mendicité espirituelle, pour ce que on m'avoit recité qu'elle queroit ses aumosnes de grace et faisoit sa procession de saint en saint tres diligement et ardenment pour soy et pour les aultres [...]; et se mettoit devant Dieu comme condempnee devant son juge, comme povre mendiante devant ung riche seigneur [...] qui est, fit elle, le remede ou la deffense plus valable contre toute temtacion? Je respondis que c'estoit humilité [...]. Lors ceste bonne dame dit en sa sage simplesse que s'estoit le signe de la croix. Je lui accorday assez tost et monstray que sa response saccordait a la mienne'.
[136] Marguerite to Briçonnet, before 16 January 1523, Martineau & Veissière, 1975, 2.10.
[137] Herminjard 1866–1897, 1, lettre 59, p. 111. Briçonnet also referred to Lefèvre as a 'spiritual mendicant' (Letter of 16 January 1523, Martineau & Veissière 1975, 2. 12).
[138] Guillaume Briçonnet to Marguerite, 17 November 1521, Martineau & Veissière 1975, 1.54.

written on 22 November, Marguerite prayed to God 'que nous aprenons a mendier', 'so that we learn how to beg'.[139] She continuously referred to herself as a mendicant 'demandant l'aumosne d'oraison' — 'asking for alms of prayer'[140] in other letters, and declared, in January 1523, that the best way to achieve greater spiritual perfection is to 'commencer mestier de mendicité'.[141] Briçonnet answered her with a letter entirely devoted to the same topic:[142]

> Qui par mendicité mendie n'est affamé que de saciété qui le faict mendiant. Plus est assouvy, plus mendie par mendicité pleine. Mendicité est insatiable, mestier plaisant qui l'ame faict vivre en longueur, toutesfois surmontant tout plaisir.[143]

In the same letter Guillaume advised Marguerite to 'dress in the spirit of mendicancy, knowing all of God and nothing of ourselves'.[144] Lefèvre d'Etaples, who might have come across this theme via the published sermons of Geiler von Kaysersberg, whom he knew personally, also uses the term 'mendicant' in his edition of the *Psalms*, in verse 23 of the thirty-fourth Psalm: *Ego autem mendicus sum et pauper*.[145]

This theme of spiritual mendicancy is not the only trace of Gerson's influence in the Meaux Cenacle. Lefèvre d'Etaples cites *De consolatione theologiae* and *De remediis pusillanimitatis* in

---

[139] Marguerite to Briçonnet, 22 November 1521, Martineau & Veissière 1975, 1.70.

[140] Marguerite to Briçonnet, 5 February 1522, Martineau & Veissière 1975, 1.154.

[141] Marguerite to Briçonnet, before 16 January 1523, Martineau & Veissière 1975, 2.10: 'J'ay bien voullu commencer par ceste mon mestier de mendicité'.

[142] Bedouelle has already noticed that 'this word *mendicant* evidently refers to the theme of spiritual mendicancy originated by Gerson' (Bedouelle 1976, p. 124).

[143] Briçonnet to Marguerite, 16 January 1523, Martineau & Veissière 1975, 2. 11. 'Who begs by means of mendicancy hungers for nothing but fulfillment, which makes him a beggar. The more he is satisfied, the more he begs through total mendicancy. Mendicancy is insatiable, a pleasant art that makes the soul live longer, at all times surpassing every pleasure'.

[144] Briçonnet to Marguerite, 16 January 1523, Martineau & Veissière 1975, 2. 12: 'se vestir de l'esperit de mendicité, congnoissant de Dieu tout et de nous rien'.

[145] Bedouelle 1976, p. 124. 'I am a beggar and pauper'.

his *Commentaries on the Psalms* of 1513, as well as in the *Commentary on the Epistle to the Romans* of 1515.[146] The chancellor's theme *Poenitemini et credite euangelio* (Mk. 1:15) is found in Lefèvre d'Etaples' scriptural commentaries,[147] while a close study of his sermons reveals the presence of Gerson's 'reciprocal' theology 'coopérons à la lumière évangélique'.[148] The fact that Lefèvre referred to Gerson as 'a man of piety and great authority, with the spirit of a monk under the garment of a secular priest',[149] shows that it is the malleability of Gerson's spirituality, applicable in both monastic and lay settings, that constitutes one of the attractive elements of his theology in the eyes of Lefèvre and other mystical humanists of the Meaux circle.

Parisian Intellectual Milieu

There is a certain difficulty, due to several factors, in tracing Gerson's distribution in Paris in the post 1517 years of the sixteenth century. The main issue is the significant role that religious persecutions played in the decline of the printing business in the capital. Increased censorship and mounting suspicion discouraged many from entering or maintaining a publishing business: 'tous les quartiers de la rive gauche et l'enceinte étaient sous la juridiction de l'université prédominée par la faculté de théologie qui a le pouvoir de censure et s'érige en tribunal'.[150] From the 1520s onwards many great editors, fearful of harassment by the Catholic

---

[146] Chaunu 1997, p. 385. The direct proof of Lefèvre's familiarity with Gerson is found in his commentaries on Ruysbroeck. For details see Rice 1971.

[147] Bedouelle 1976, p. 195.

[148] *Fête de l'Ascension Marc XVI Epîtres et Evangiles pour les 52 dimanches de l'an*, in Bedouelle & Franco 1976, p. 200. In Protestant tradition Lefèvre has often been presented as a precursor of the Reformation: 'Alors que Renaudet a vu à juste titre Lefèvre d'Etaples comme un des acteurs principaux de l'humanisme parisien, l'historiographie protestante a fait de lui un pré-réformateur [...] C'est la position suivie par la plupart des historiens catholiques' (Bedouelle's replica in Pernot 1995, p. 230). Cenacle de Meaux is part of the Museum of Protestantism in Geneva.

[149] Rice 1971, p. 91.

[150] Pallier 1976, p. 6. Holt 2005, p. 29: 'the dict [of Châteaubriant of June 1551 [...] did proscribe the printing, sale, and even possession of Protestant opinions, as well as outline in much greater detail the powers of censorship of the courts'.

authorities, ran away from Paris. From 1539 to 1572 eighty-one bookstore owners, editors and other book printing professionals, such as well-known publishers Robert Estienne and Jean Le Preux, were persecuted and therefore discontinued their activity, and these are only those whose names are known.[151] Having played a major role in the orientation of the Parisian book printing, the University of Paris eventually transformed the capital into the fief of the Catholic Ligue, that adopted a slogan 'one faith, one law, one king'[152] after the failure of États Généraux in 1576. As the result of this policy printers either fled or complied, and the majority of works published in Paris were royalist. From this point on, the Sorbonne held a monopoly in book printing as well as in book commerce, demanding the strict adherence to its doctrine and regulating all matters concerning printing until at least 1618.[153]

The second difficulty consists in the fact that Gerson's works were more often than not included in compilations with and by other authors or under different titles or were mimicked or directly copied from Gerson, often without mentioning his name.[154] Some authors, such as Jean Columbi, acknowledged that his *Confession generale*, published twice in Lyons, was based on 'Directoire de ceulx qui sont en larticle de la mort: extraict de la bonne doctrine de maistre Johan Gerson'.[155] Others, like Franciscan friar Olivier Maillard, thrice published his *L'exemplaire de confession*, which is none other than Gerson's *Directoire des confesseurs*, as his own.[156] The opposite process also took place, as in the case of the Pseudo-

---

[151] Pallier 1976, pp. 7–8.

[152] Pallier 1976, p. 47.

[153] Pallier 1976, p. 21.

[154] One example of such a compilation is *Miroir de la cour* listed under the authorship of Henry de Harp and Jean Gerson, published in Paris in 1549–1552. Henry de Harp or Henri van Erp was the founder, in 1445, of the Gouda community of the Brethren of the Common Life.

[155] Jean Columbi, *Confession generale, avec certaines reigles au commencement, tresutiles tant a confesseurs que a penitens...*, Lyon, exact year unknown. Columbi, *Confession generale, avec certaines reigles utiles tant a confesseurs que a penitens*, Lyon, 1548, with addition of Gerson's treatise and several poems on the subject of preparation to death (Higman 1996, pp. 161–62).

[156] Olivier Maillard, *L'exemplaire de confession nouvellement imprimeee et corrigee avecques la confession de frere Olivier Maillart, En ce petit livret pourra trouver le confesseur la vraye voye et maniere d'estudier l'enseignement par lequel il pourra*

Gersonian editions in France. For example, translations of Bonaventure were attributed to Gerson in 1529 and 1541.

However, regardless of these difficulties, it is safe to say that Gerson's relevance at French institutions of higher learning was somewhat weaker than among active clergy directly involved in the reform movement. In other words, his influence as a pastor seems to have been stronger in France than his impact as a systematic and mystical theologian. Compared to the dominant mood of the universities in the Empire, such as the universities of Vienna or Heidelberg, devotional and mystical tendencies that made Gerson so popular in German lands were less present at the Sorbonne. Changes in the political climate also affected Gerson's popularity. After the Gallican crisis of 1552,[157] when the relationship with Rome almost reached a breaking point, the Sorbonne's theological faculty were inclined toward very different ecclesiological positions than those that they held under François I. Under the dominance of de Guise's Catholic Ligue, Parisian theologians found themselves in the full-blown situation of *plenutido potestatis*, thus making references to Gerson — 'the symbol of a Gallican Church which recognized the authority of the Pope whilst imposing spiritual and temporal limits to his power'[158] — rather unwelcome. Even among alumni of Gerson's own alma mater, the College de Navarre, only one theologian exhibits some indirect affinity with the chancellor: the forenamed student, friend and longtime associate of Jacques Lefèvre d'Etaples, and academic mentor of Guillaume Briçonnet, Josse Clichtove.[159] Clichtove was the most significant theologian who took part in the 1528 Council of Sens that had the

---

cognoistre la droite voye de confession..., Lyon, 1524 (Higman 1996, p. 300; Renaudet 1916, p. 163).

[157] Amalou 2013, p. 212: 'le théologien Jean Gerson (1363–1429), véritable bannière de 'ceste eschole mesme de Sorbonne florissante en doctrine' avait toujours défendu 'que les royaumes dépendaient de Dieu seul; que comme le pape et les evesques pour le spirituel estoient ses vicaires, les roys l'estoient pour le temporel'.

[158] Denis 2019, p. 44. The crisis might be an explanation for an apparent gap in Gerson's new publications until 1580, with even *Opus* republished in 1560 and 1575, under the title *Traité des dix commandements*, without Gerson's name (Pettegree, Walsby & Wilkinson 2011, pp. 674–76).

[159] Veissière 1986, p. 130.

twofold aim of combating heresy and reforming the church.[160] Foreign to evangelism and one of the earliest refuters of Luther's doctrine, he authored the Council's anti-Protestant decrees, formulating the Catholic position on the relationship between faith and works. A moderate traditionalist, he knew how to disagree without fanaticism and preferred to stay away from open confrontations. Publisher with passion,[161] an academic and professor at Sorbonne after 1506, and 'heir of the *devotio moderna* and of Gerson',[162] Clichtove was also preoccupied with pastoral theology. A passionate reformer of the clergy, he influenced an entire generation of ecclesiastical leaders such as the bishop of Paris Etienne Poncher. In 1538 he published *De doctrina moriendi*, where he argued the possibility for human nature to overcome, at least partly, its sinful condition through the spiritual experiences of penance and repentance.

There was one exception among the Paris institutions of higher learning, where Gerson's authority, although understood in a specific way, was kept very much alive: the aforementioned College of Montaigu, the old fief of Jan Standonck (1450–1504). The chancellor's veneration at this college must have been responsible for the place of honor that he retained in the writings of practically all of its famous graduates: Jacques Almain, John Mair, Jacobus Latomus, Jean Calvin, Ignatius of Loyola, Noël Béda and even the scholastics-hating Erasmus.[163] Conciliarist academics Almain and Mair systematized and developed Gerson's legal ideas, especially his theory of rights. Mair, who was a teacher of John Calvin,

---

[160] O'Malley 2013, p. 65.

[161] Clichtove published works of Hugo of St Victor (Paris 1516), Bernard (Paris 1508, Lyon 1515, Paris 1535) and others.

[162] Cottret 2000, p. 27. Also Lemaitre 2018, 2, p. 14.

[163] For an extensive analysis of Erasmus's attitude toward Gerson, see Bejczy 1998. 'Gerson's exception' possibly extends to Rabelais as well: 'Le fait capital [...] c'est la présence dans ce [de Rabelais] catalogue imaginaire [...] d'un detail sans doute lourd de sens [...] une oeuvre bien reelle: Gerson, *De aufferibilitate papae ab Ecclesia*. Cette exception nous autorise-t-elle à penser que Rabelais se gardait d'assimiler les écrits de Gerson à cette masse de *barbouillamenta surannes*? Ce n'est pas impossible. On sait quelle admiration et quelle affection l'auteur de Gargantua vouait au vieil Erasme [...] Or ce dernier non seulement n'a jamais méprisé l'ieuvre de Gerson, mais pourrait bien avoir été assez profondément marqué par son influence' (Ouy 1983, p. xxix).

François Rabelais and George Buchanan,[164] moved the concept of *dominium* even closer to the notion of private property than Summenhart did: 'Given that *dominium* was simply the *ius* [right] to use something', the most effective use of this right should be private appropriation.[165] His disciple and friend Jacques Almain said the same: *Dominium in tot genere, nihil aliud est: quam ius utendi aliqua re secundum rectam rationem, & ius (ut dicit Gerson) nichil aliud est: quam potestas, uel facultas propinqua competens alicui secundum dictamen rectae rationis [...]*[166] Thanks to the reputation of Parisian scholastics, by the second decade of the sixteenth century Gerson's theory of rights reigned supreme.[167]

Among Montaigu's graduates Noël Béda or Beda (1470–1537), who succeeded Jan Standonck as the principle of this college, holds particular importance in relation to the reception of Gerson in French sixteenth century academia. Formed on the principles of *devotio moderna*, Béda strove to remain faithful to Standonck's strict and narrow understanding of religious life and was dedicated to his mission. He sincerely believed that anything deviating from the traditional beliefs and practices of the past was heresy. Satirized and ridiculed by both Erasmus and Rabelais for his fanatical intransigence, he tried to launch the Inquisition even against the King's sister Marguerite. Gerson was one of Béda's favorite authors, and he claimed to rely on the chancellor's prestige in his polemics against all those, whom he believed, rightly or wrongly, were 'Lutheran'. In his polemical correspondence with Erasmus, whom he accused of undermining the Catholic tradition by applying humanist methods to sacred texts, Béda recommended that the Dutch celebrity read specific texts of Gerson's

---

[164] Mostaccio 2014, p. 31. On Gerson and Mair see Burns 1981. On Gerson and Almain see Burns 1983.

[165] Tuck 1979, p. 28, citing Mair 1509.

[166] '*Dominium* as such is nothing other than the *ius* of using something in accordance with right reason. And *ius* (as Gerson says) is nothing other than a dispositional power or *facultas* which everyone has as a result of the rule of right reason' (Almain 1525, trans. in Tuck 1979, p. 29).

[167] Tuck 1979, p. 29. Secular jurist Fernando Vázquez de Menchaca (1512–1569) defined *dominium* as Gerson did: *Est enim [dominium] naturalis facultas eius, quod facere libet, nisi ui aut iure prohibeatur [...]* '*Dominium* is a natural power, which allows someone to do something unless prohibited by force or law' (Tuck 1979, p. 51, citing de Menchaca 1572).

— *De laude scriptorium*, *De communione laicorum sub utraque specie* and *Collectorium super Magnificat* — providing exact references according to the edition he used.[168] The way Béda spoke of the chancellor in his polemics with Erasmus reveals that, in his eyes, consulting Gerson was sufficient to convince any opponent: 'I wish you had been willing to read what the eminent doctor Gerson said about this [translating Scriptures] in various places of his works'.[169] For Béda and other ultra-conservative theologians like him, Gerson represented the very rock upon which Parisian intellectual tradition was standing, while Erasmus's habit of seeing traditional authorities as 'very great men, but only men after all',[170] appeared as unacceptable arrogance. Like the German anti-Lutheran theologians of the first generation, Schatzgeyer and Cochlaeus, Béda perceived Gerson not only as the latest paternal figure in the long line of unquestionable authorities included, among other compilations of this type, in *Extraits de plusieurs docteurs*,[171] but also as the golden standard against which all new ideas could be safely measured. The attitude toward his favorite theologian was like a litmus paper for orthodoxy or heresy, and Béda, terrified of Luther's rebellion, used this test with his adversaries. One of these adversaries was another one of Montaigu's graduates, the above-mentioned Jacques Lefèvre d'Etaples (1450?–1536). Between 1519 and 1527, Béda repeatedly attacked

---

[168] Erasmus 1994, p. 126, n. 42. Béda uses 'one of the fifteenth-century editions rather than the recent one published by Jean Petit and François Regnault (Paris 1521)' (Dalzell & Nauert 1994, p. 126, n. 42). According to Erika Rumme, Béda also relied on Gerson during his discussion concerning the rights and duties of qualified theologians to pass judgment on matters of Church doctrine, which he considered consequential to their education and status, in other words, *ex officio*. (Rumme 2008, p. 151).

[169] Letter 1579 from Béda to Erasmus, in Dalzell & Nauert 1994, p. 126. Béda quotes from *De laude scriptorium* (OC: 9, p. 432), *De communione laicorum sub utraque specie* (OC: 10, pp. 57–58) and *Super Magnigficat* (OC: 8, p. 350). In letter 1581 Erasmus admits reading 'as a young man [...] a few of Gerson's works' and finding 'in them something to admire' (Dalzell, Nauert 1994, p. 134). In the letter 1596, while stating not having Gerson in his own library, he declares his intention to 'buy a copy or borrow some somewhere' (Dalzell & Nauert 1994, p. 238). 'Yet, even though mediaeval masters were ready enough to disagree with their contemporaries, but it is comparatively rare for anyone to call an ancient author a fool' (Evans 1992, p. 82).

[170] Erasmus 1974, p. 48.

[171] Higman 1996, p. 213.

him, as well as Louis de Berquin (1490–1529) — who was a Josse Clichtove and Erasmus's admirer, humanist and Meaux sympathizer — on several theological grounds, all having to do with the revisions of medieval traditions that humanists considered erroneous and unsupported by scriptural scholarship.[172] While accusing Lefèvre of being complacent with German heresy, Béda blamed him for allegedly despising the authority of his predecessors, and specifically that of Jean Gerson.[173] This accusation is particularly remarkable since Lefèvre knew and venerated Gerson as much as Béda did. Yet, Béda was not entirely mistaken. Lefèvre's respect for the late medieval chancellor had quite a different motivation from his own. For Béda, Gerson embodied the traditional scholastic learning of the University of Paris[174] that had to be preserved at all costs. Lefèvre was interested in the aspects of Gerson's spirituality that he found personally relevant and appealing: interiority, understood as 'a departure from reliance on external standards of conduct',[175] inclusiveness, humility, vernacular expression and Christocentrism. Therefore, even though Béda and Lefèvre emerged from the same milieu, where Gerson's legacy was shared by all parties, they perceived it quite differently. Béda, whose mental state could be qualified as 'piété panique',[176] was inclined to rather restrict Gerson's contemplative innovations, while Lefèvre and other members of the Meaux circle would rather pursue them further. Gerson's legacy, both conservative and innovative, gives ground to both.

Another evidence of Gerson's relevance with the French Catholic polemicists is found in a popular anti-Lutheran book with a playful title *Les Triumphes de la noble et amoureuse dame et l'art d'honnetement aymer*,[177] composed by Jean Bouchet (1476–1558), Rabelais' friend, jurist and poète-rhétoriqueur.[178] Inspired by Gerson's initiative to extend Christian education to ladies, Bouchet

---

[172] See Crane 2010.
[173] Caron 2005, p. 180.
[174] Caron 2005, p. 43.
[175] Depew 2016, p. 31.
[176] Crouzet 1990.
[177] Published in Poitiers in 1530, 1532, 1533, and in Paris in 1535, 1536 (twice), 1537, 1539, 1541 (twice) and in 1545 (Higman 1996, pp. 111–13).
[178] On Bouchet see Hamon 1970; Britnell 1986; Dauvois 2003.

filled his book with moral instructions for 'la noble dame, et l'art de honnestement aymer, tout fondé en amour et dilection charitable, parce que je treuve par la saincte escriture que nostre loy crestienne consiste entièrement en amour'.[179] His choice to follow Gerson in his call to write religious literature for the laity, and especially for women, in the vernacular was rather unusual and brave at this late date for, as it was mentioned earlier, by the 1530s and well into the 1560s, vernacular writings about spiritual matters began to run the risk of falling under the suspicion of being automatically perceived as Protestant.[180] Bouchet appeared to be conscious of this and cited, as the main reasons for his choice, the education of his own children (probably daughters), the desire to produce a piece of pious literature to amend his otherwise purely literary production, and the need to distract women from reading the Bible, which is too dangerous an exercise for their unprepared minds susceptible to Lutheran heresy.[181] In his effort of popularizing knowledge and instruction for the non-Latinate,[182] Bouchet demonstrated broad knowledge of Gerson's texts, which he quoted thirty-four times throughout books two and three, relying on the chancellor's theology of salvation more than on any other source.[183] Bouchet translated, quoted or paraphrased a record number of the chancellor's works: *De consolatione theologiae, Trilogium Astrologiae Theologiae*,[184] *Tractatus de differentia peccatorum mortalium et uenialium, De scientiis mortis, Considerationes pro uolentibus condere testamentum, De mendicitate spirituali, Sermo de oratione factus in Concilio Constantiensi, Tractatus super Magnificat, Expositio super Dimitte nobis debita nostra* and *De oratione et eius ualore*. Also, instead of using Gerson's vernacular works, as could be expected from someone writing in French him-

---

[179] Britnell 1986, p. 223.
[180] Britnell 2003, p. 194: 'Sans que les théologiens de la Sorbonne aient formellement interdit les livres en français [...] il n'en est pas moins vrai qu'une sorte d'ombre de désapprobation pesé sur la littérature théologique à l'intention des laïcs. Cette attitude hostile envers l'enseignement religieux par le livre offre un vif contraste avec le travail accompli par plusieurs évêques dans toutes premières années du seizième siècle'.
[181] Britnell 2003, p. 196.
[182] Britnell 2003, p. 90.
[183] Britnell 1986, p. 230.
[184] Britnell 2003, p. 196.

self, he chose several theologically heavy Latin writings intended for clerical audiences, using the already existing translations or taking pains translating them into French. Such is the case of *De mendicitate spirituali*, originally composed in the vernacular. Bouchet's main source in *Les Triumphes* is *De consolatione theologiae*, and his second most frequent reference is Antoninus of Florence. The fact that 'Gerson and St Antoninus stand out way above all other sources'[185] further augments the weight of Gerson's influence in *Les Triumphes*. Besides being massive, Bouchet's dependence on the late medieval master was also varied. His borrowings included matters of confession, absolution, the nature of sins, the ten commandments, the monastic versus active life, prayer, death preparation, the Eucharist, astrology, etc.[186] In a sense, *Les Triumphes* summarized, in a compressed form, Gerson's theological legacy, as it was received in the first half of the sixteenth century. The combination of two factors considerably extended the longevity of Gerson's literary and theological relevance in France. One factor was that Bouchet answered theological questions 'in the words of Gerson',[187] sometimes borrowing entire sections from his works. The other was that *Les Triumphes* was constantly reprinted, sometimes twice a year, until 1545. This relevance, not limited to the clerical and academic circles, also reached the aristocratic milieu. Duke de Berry himself prepared an edition of *La vie de nostre Benoit Sauveur Ihesuscrist et la Saincte vie de nostre Dame*, that incorporated some of Gerson's writings.[188]

Gerson's significance for Jean Bodin (1529–1596) — member of the Paris Parliament, professor of law in Toulouse and the most important, next to Machiavelli, political writer of the sixteenth century — is controversial. Introduced to the chancellor's authority from his youth, both from growing up under the tutelage of the bishop of Angers, who was 'surely weaned on Gerson's version of the Commandments',[189] and from his studies at the University of Paris, Bodin allegedly absorbed and applied cer-

---

[185] Britnell 1986, p. 231.
[186] Britnell 1986, p. 232.
[187] Britnell 1986, p. 232.
[188] Reinburg 1977.
[189] Bossy 2002, p. 233.

tain elements of the chancellor's intellectual heritage to two fields of his expertise: sovereignty and demonology. The first outcome was the structure of political and moral obligation of civil servants toward the sovereign ruler expounded by Bodin in *Six Lettres de la Republique* published in 1576. In this book, where 'several passages from Gerson's *De ecclesiastica potestate* are quoted', without, however, mentioning his name,[190] Bodin reintroduced the chancellor's conciliarist arguments into the sixteenth-century political discourse in order to create what is now considered the modern definition of sovereignty.[191] According to some Bodin scholars, his experiment bore fruit. In countries where conciliar ideas had taken a stronger hold, such as in France and Germany, there was less resistance to royal absolutism.[192] The connection between conciliarism and absolute monarchy was already formulated by Charles de Guise (1524–1574), the Cardinal de Lorraine and France's representative at the Council of Trent in 1563: 'Je suis François, nourry en l'université de Paris, en laquelle on tient l'autorité du concil par-dessus le pape, et sont censurez comme hérétiques ceux qui tiennent le contraire'.[193] It is probably no coincidence that two early partisans of absolute monarchies, Christopher St Germain and Jean Bodin, relied on Gerson's political thought, favoring different aspects of it according to the needs and circumstances of their respective countries. A comparative study of these two thinkers would be a fascinating endeavor.[194]

---

[190] Howell A. Lloyd states in his Bodin's biography that the names of medieval proponents of conciliarist theory 'are entirely lacking' and 'figure in Bodin's discourse not at all'. Moreover, 'striking as any omissions from the *République* are key arguments over rights (*iura*) which had greatly exercised those same thinkers' (including Gerson)' (Lloyd 2017, p. 125).

[191] Provvidente 2011, p. 114. Bodin's follower in relation to the theory of sovereignty, French jurist and philosopher Pierre Grégoire (*c.* 1540–1597), had also drawn inspiration from Gerson, whom he calls *egregius et pius uir* (Salmon 1987, p. 181).

[192] Fasolt 1997, pp. 385–402. Also see Tierney 1975; Izbicki 1986; van Liere 1997, pp. 597–616.

[193] du Puy 1654, p. 556. Yet, in the eyes of the English King Charles, machinations to arrange marriage between Elizabeth I and the youngest Valois prince, François d'Anjou, 'led yo his being perceived as the 'arch-priest of the papacy' and 'the minister of mischief' (Holt 2005, p. 67).

[194] Zagorin discusses the possibility of such a comparison in passing (Zagorin 2009).

Gerson's role, if any, in Bodin's theory of witchcraft, as described in the *Demonomanie des Sorciers* (22 editions from 1580 to 1616) is unclear. In this 'extremely important and blood curdling book',[195] the same celebrated jurist, historian and political philosopher who was one of the first men to have opposed slavery, and whose tolerance in religious matters has often been celebrated, argues for the suspension of regular legal procedures when dealing with the 'exceptional crime' of witchcraft. In Bodin's view, three witnesses each offering different evidence, would do, while he paid only 'lip service' to the presumption of innocence or Christian mercy.[196] Repentance, even genuine, 'was not enough to avert the death penalty'.[197] Medical arguments that witches were possibly delusional or ill were equally and vehemently rejected.[198] His reasons for the exceptional treatment of witchcraft are mostly, although not exclusively, misogynistic. Women 'are always less credible than men' due to the 'imbecilité & fragilité' of their sex. They are prone to insatiable lust pushing them to copulate with the devil,[199] thus representing 'a danger to social and religious stability'[200] unless tightly controlled. Their crimes all deserve, even if repented, 'la mort esquise',[201] while the potential benefits of punishing witches included: 'to appease the wrath of God and his vengeance on the people as a whole', and 'to earn God's blessing on the entire country'.[202] It has been suggested that Bodin's views, extreme even for his time,[203] were inspired by Gerson. The chancellor's hypothetical influence is specifically associated with identification of witchcraft with idolatry, and validation of the binding character of the Old Testament's command to put witches to death.[204] Although

---

[195] Davidson 2012, p. 102.
[196] Lloyd 2017, pp. 180–81.
[197] Lloyd 2017, p. 180.
[198] Lloyd 2017, p. 180.
[199] Lloyd 2017, p. 181.
[200] Lloyd 2017, p. 187.
[201] Lloyd 2017, p. 180.
[202] Lloyd 2017, p. 180.
[203] These views were critically exposed by the Jesuit controversialist Antonio Possevino or Possevinus (1533–1611) under the direction of the Pope Innocent IX (1591), and consequently put on the *Index of Forbidden Books*.
[204] Bossy 2002, p. 233.

this hypothesis [205] might deserve a due verification, Bodin's blind misogyny, his refusal to consider mental and physical afflictions as possible causes of supposed sorcery, his almost exclusive focus on the Old Testament, accompanied by the relative neglect of the Gospel,[206] as well as heavy reliance not on theological but on legal sources, make Gerson's 'ancestry' in this sphere unlikely.

Part IV. The Catholic Reception in Spain

In comparison with France and the Germanic parts of the Empire, the Spanish Golden Age reception of Gerson was massive, and involved distribution, translation and appropriation of his works and ideas, often mingled with controversy. Indeed, Gerson's theological presence in Spain seems to have been marred by controversy from the very beginning. Thus, the book *De confessione*, in which the professor of theology at the University of Salamanca, Pedro de Osma (or Petrus Martinez de Osma, d. 1480) introduced Gerson in Spain, was later condemned and publicly burned.[207]

---

[205] Neither Sophie Houdard, in her major study of Bodin's demonology (Houdard 1992), nor Lloyd mention Gerson even as a secondary source for Bodin.

[206] In *Demonomanie des Sorciers* the preeminence of the Old Testament is striking. Out of all biblical citations (367 times), the New Testament represents only 4.6%. This is precisely why Possevino accused Bodin to have 'surrendered himself' to rabbinical sources rather than 'to the Gospel of our Lord Jesus Christ' (Lloyd 2017, p. 182). As Andrew Fogelman convincingly demonstrated, Gerson, together with Oresme and Heinrich von Langenstein, was altogether disinclined to see supernatural causes in vision-like experiences, suggesting, in *On Distinguishing True from False Revelations*, as well as in other works, that visions often result 'from brain injury or sicknesses' (Fogelman 2009, p. 16). *De distinctione*, OC: 3, p. 44: *Itaque ad parexitium uergunt abstinentia nimia et crapulosa uoracitas; nisi quod irremediabilior est excessus in abstinentia; quia morbos affert incurabiles ex laesione cerebri et rationis perturbatione, quo fit ut permaniam aut fuiiam uel caeteras passiones melancolicas sic profundantur et intime radicantur phantasmata interius reseruata in cerebro. [...] Pleni sunt medicorum libri de portentuosis huiusmodi apparitionibus et iudiciorum corruptionibus ex laesione uirium interiorum nascentibus. De his ait Hieronymus quod magis indigent fomento Hypocratis quam aliorum consilio.* 'Excessive abstinence and drunken overeating both lead to a similar end, except that excessive abstinence is harder to remedy, for it brings incurable illness from brain damage and mental disorder. [...] Medical books are full of such monstrous apparitions and disturbances in the power of judgment resulting from injury to the interior power. Concerning such people, Jerome said that they are more in need of the remedy of Hippocrates than the council of others' (McGuire 1998, pp. 345–46).

[207] Luttikhuizen 2016, pp. 54–64.

The chancellor's legacy found itself at the epicenter of all the most important issues of sixteenth century Spain. Direct references to him are present in the writings of a record number of Spanish historical figures, among whom are all prominent (and mostly Dominican) thinkers of the School of Salamanca[208] — Francesco de Vitoria (1483–1546), Domingo de Soto (1494–1560), Martin de Azpilcueta (1491–1586), Alfonso de Castro (1495–1558) and Bartolomé de Medina (1527–1580); religious leaders Juan de Cazalla, Louis de Grenada (1504–1588), Bartolomé de Las Casas (1474 or 1484–1566), and Bishop of Braga, Bartholomew or Bartolomeu later known as Bartolomeus a Martyribus (1514–1590);[209] mystics Pedro Ruiz de Alcaraz, Francisco de Osuna (1492/1497-c. 1540), John of the Cross (1542–1591) and Teresa of Avila (1515–1582); humanists Juan de Vergara (1492–1557), Juan Ginès de Sepulveda (1494–1573), and Fernando Vázquez de Menchaca (1512–1569); theologians Juan Lopez de Segura (1511–1583),[210] Juan de Valdés (1490?–1541)[211] and Gabriel Vásquez (1549–1604). Considering that most early Jesuits were Iberians as well, Gerson's posthumous presence in this cultural space appears to surpass that of France and the Germanic Empire combined.

School of Salamanca

Gerson's legacy was of central importance for the development of the legal tradition in Spain and particularly at the much-celebrated University of Salamanca, which in the second half of the sixteenth century attained equal rank with the universities

---

[208] Although 'the very concept of the 'School of Salamanca' is under dispute' in related scholarship, this reference will be used here for the sake of convenience' (Decock 2012, p. 51).

[209] Bartholomé's readings included Bernard, Bonaventure and Gerson (Kallendorf 2010, p. 54). The works of medieval authors were grouped into two large anthologies, *Stimulus pastorum* (1565), a very popular book throughout Europe, and *Compendium spiritualis doctrinae* (1582), published under the supervision of Louis de Grenada.

[210] Bataillon 1991, 2, p. 635: 'Both Louis de Grenada and Secular priest Juan Lopez de Segura, who authored, in 1554, *Libro de Instruccion christiana y de Exercicios spirituals y Praparacion para la missa y sancta communion*, declared Gerson among their authorities'.

[211] Luttikhuizen 2016, p. 55: 'Valdés mentions Gerson twice in his *Dialogue on Christian Doctrine* (1529)'.

of Paris, Oxford and Bologna. This legacy mainly concerns four major concepts of moral theology: *certitudo moralis*, *regula magistralis* or safety rule, the relationship between human and divine laws, and the dichotomy *dominium-ius* or right.[212] *Doctor consolatorius* developed his ideas concerning the first notion in *De consolatione theologiae*[213] and in *Regulae morales*. Since it is impossible, except for super-natural certitude,[214] to reach a positive certainty in human matters because of their extreme variety and complexity, one should side with the most morally sound and probable decision and follow it to avoid complete inaction. Such a decision is the best *certitudo moralis* one can achieve here and now, thus allowing for moral decision-making, which involves a certain degree of psychological uncertainty'.[215]

> *Denique certitudo quae moralis dici potest uel ciuilis tangitur ab Aristotele una cum praecedenti certitudine in Ethicorum suorum principio. […] Intelligo praeterea quod in agibilibus humanis, quae tantam habent uarietatem, dicente Aristotele et experientia teste, ut casu magis quam arte constare uideantur, sufficit tertia certitudo qualis non semper scrupulos omnes abjicit, sufficit ut contemnat uel superet sic operando quasi non sint*.[216]

---

[212] The assessment of Gerson's place in the development of Spanish jurisprudence represents in and of itself a separate topic, and it cannot be fully addressed here. His contribution to legal issues regarding the bindingness of civil laws in conscience is addressed in Paolo Prodi's earlier cited book *Una storia della guistizia* (Prodi 2000). Gerson also played a major role in distinguishing between the realm of conscience and the realm of civil laws and thought advocating the theory of 'merely penal laws', meaning that, in his views, not all laws were binding in conscience. This position was deemed very problematic by Spanish scholastics in the sixteenth century. On this subject see Decock 2017, p. 111.

[213] *De consolatione theologiae*, OC: 9, p. 232: *non enim consurgit certitudo moralis ex euidentia demonstrationis, sed ex probabilibus coniecturis, grossis et figuralibus, magis ad unam partem quam ad alteram*. 'For moral certitude does not arise from the evidence of demonstration, but from probable conjectures which are rough and metaphorical, leaning more to one side than to the other' (Miller 1998, p. 229).

[214] *De consolatione theologiae*, OC: 9, p. 231.

[215] Kantola 1994, p. 112. See also Blic 1930, pp. 264–91. 'La certitude morale est donc une forme de certitude, faillible et temporaire, dont même les sceptiques ne peuvent pas se passer 'ils veulent échapper à l'accusation de l'inaction' (Grellard 2018, p. 639).

[216] *De consolatione theologiae*, OC: 9, pp. 231–32. 'The final certitude which can be called moral or political is touched on by Aristotle at the beginning of his

In other words, ethics not being a precise science, one must be content with a degree of certainty in temporal matters that the subject admits, instead of seeking an unattainable absolute. *Et haec uocatur certitudo moralis uel ciuilis, quod homo sufficienter probatus est.*[217]

Gerson's *sufficienter probatus est* engendered a posterity that the medieval chancellor could not possibly imagine. It stimulated the development of 'applied moral theology'[218] that particularly flourished at the School of Salamanca, the alma mater of Francesco de Vitoria (1483–1546),[219] the 'father of international law' and 'a vastly complex thinker',[220] whose 'writings became the standard reference works in ethics and politics for the sixteenth and seventeenth centuries'.[221] Although Vitoria does not refer to the chancellor directly, the latter's 'presence is felt even if he is not named'.[222] It is indeed with Vitoria that the fascinating story of probabilism begins,[223] as he pushes Gerson's *sufficienter proba-*

Ethics in connection with the preceding natural certitude. [...] I understand further that there is such great variety in the actions one should do that they seem to depend more on chance than on art, as Aristotle says and as experience testifies. Here the third kind of certitude suffices to keep one from ever disregarding all scruples and yet to scorn or overcome them by acting as if they did not exist' (Miller 1998, pp. 229–31).

[217] *Regulae morales* OC: 9, p. 123. 'This is called moral or political certainty, which is sufficiently proven by man'. Even though Gerson was not the first to reflect on this topic, with predecessors such as Jean Buridan (*c.* 1300–1361) and Thomas Aquinas, he introduced the idea of moral certainty in moral theology. (Grellard 2018, p. 640). On the subject of probabilism see Otte 1997; Franklin 2001; Schüßler 2003; Schüßler 2006; Schwartz 2014; Tutino 2017.

[218] Schüssler 2021, p. 1007.

[219] 'Vitoria had been a student at Paris in the critical years between 1507 and 1522 and had been exposed both to the last advocates of the Gersonian theory and to the first productions of the juridical humanists' (Tuck 1979, p. 46). On Vitoria's attitude toward Gerson in the light of conciliarist theory, see Varacalli 2016. On Vitoria's reworking of Gerson's and Summenhart's approach to *ius* and *dominium* see Tuck 1979.

[220] Brunstetter 2012, p. 34.

[221] Brett 1997, p. 123.

[222] Prodi 2000, p. 203.

[223] 'Probabilism holds that in a situation of uncertainty one may follow an expert opinion, at least if that opinion is simply 'probable' (*opinio probabilis*), even though a 'more probable' opinion (*opinio probabilior*) exists. Generally speaking, a probable opinion is a standpoint endorsed by an authoritative expert or by sound

tus est further. For Gerson, the necessity for some kind of negotiable moral certainty is linked to and actually originates from his preoccupation with scrupulous conscience in managing confessions, where

> [D]iversity of circumstances surrounding committing a sin should be taken into consideration when assigning a penalty just as the circumstances of a crime must be weighed with circumspection before giving a judgment.[224]

Vitoria picked up Gerson's thread and developed, in pastoral theology, more delineated criteria for confessors presented with difficult cases. If there is an opinion, which appears improbable, the priest clearly cannot give an absolution. If, however, the confessor is torn between two equally probable opinions, he must absolve the penitent even against his own preference of one probable opinion over another.[225] Forging Gerson's proto-probabilistic ideas into a more defined solution forty years before Bartolomé de Medina (1527–1580), Vitoria generated the idea that one can act against the probable opinion if the other opinion is equally probable.[226]

Initially developed by Gerson as an attempt to bring relief to an *anima infermita* of either or both confessant and confessor, and expanded by Vitoria, the new ethical tactic was harvested by Domingo de Soto (1494–1560), Vitoria's student and another brilliant Salamanca faculty. Taking the lead in the probability debate, de Soto metamorphosed Gerson's *sufficienter probatus est* into several interpretations of moral probabilism.

> One's decision must rely on an opinion that is extrinsically probable and that, after a sincere and diligent inquiry, appears to be clearly more probable than its opposite. One is allowed to follow one's individual conscience only when one has based it on reasonable grounds. [...] In other words, in a situation of moral doubt one is allowed to decide to act according to

argument' (Decock 2012, p. 75). It would, however, be inappropriate and unwise 'to open the pandora box on probabilism in this context' (Decock 2012, p. 74).

[224] O'Malley 1993, p. 252.
[225] Blic 1930, p. 283, citing *Relectio de iure belli*, § 23–25.
[226] Blic 1930, p. 283, citing *Relectio de iure belli*, § 18.

one's wishes. One must not assume the risk of performing a materially evil action.[227]

De Soto also applied Gerson's method of moral decision-making to the situation of *dolus incidens* — an incidental or non-intentional fraud that does not affect the essential terms of a commercial agreement. Since the safest way to acquire a relative moral certainty is to combine consideration of the most common similar situations and opinions of relevant authorities with one's own best judgment, the seller's duty to disclose defects in the quality of merchandise to a potential buyer belongs almost exclusively to *forum internum* or *forum conscientiae*. The act of the sale itself should be left to the public sphere, where it is explicitly verifiable by legal professionals.[228] This way, based upon the consultation with both the subjective probabilism of one's own judgment and the extrinsic probabilism of independent qualified authorities or experts,[229] in the case of *dolus incidens* the contract between the seller and buyer remains valid, and there is no obligation to rescind it, unless that would be necessary in order to adjust the price.[230]

Another student of Vitoria, Bartolomé de Medina (1528–1581) — the great Dominican reader of theology and the official father of probabilism, who was the first to defend it publicly — pushed Gerson's reasoning further than both Vitoria and Soto. Concerned with the problem of moral scrupulosity, Medina introduced, in his *Breve istruttione de'confessor*, a special type of 'patients', whom he called *scrupolosi* & *pusillanimi*, whose ills, 'among other infirmities [...] which in the soul, are very difficult to cure, and need great remedies, and a physician of great science and experience.'[231] To find a cure for these ills, that now would prob-

---

[227] Kantola 1994, p. 119, citing Domingo de Soto, *De dubio et opinione*.

[228] Decock & Hallebeek 2010, p. 107.

[229] Kantola 1994, pp. 115–16. According to Kantola, Gerson's 'combination of extrinsic probabilism and subjective probabilism as a solution to the problem of decision-making in uncertainty became more effective in the beginning of the sixteenth century, when Cajetan introduced the distinction between speculation and practical uncertainty'.

[230] Decock & Hallebeek 2010, p. 109.

[231] Medina 1588, p. 220 & p. 222: 'fra le altre infermità [...] che nell'anima sono di cura difficilissima, et hanno bisogno di rimedij grandi, et di medico di grande scienza & esperienza.' *De consolatione theologiae*, OC: 9, p. 202: *Sunt quos*

ably fall within anxiety disorders, Medina introduced 'the third and most radical grade of probability' — the first was that found in Gerson.[232] If for Gerson the term 'moral certainty' meant 'a very high but not complete degree of persuasion',[233] since no one can have complete certainty at any given time, then according to Medina, one is safe to follow a course of action that is probable, even if the opposite might be more probable. The following lengthy quote offers a glimpse into Medina's theory:

> Opinions are of two kinds: those that are probable, confirmed by great arguments and the authority of the wise (such as that one may charge interest for delayed payment), but others are completely improbable, that are supported neither by arguments nor by the authority of many (such as that one may hold a plurality of benefices) [...] an opinion is called probable not because there are apparent reasons adduced in its favor, and it has assertors and defenders (for then all errors would be probable opinions), but that opinion is probable which wise men assert, and very good arguments confirm, to follow which is nothing improbable. This is the definition of Aristotle [...] It could be argued against this that it is indeed in conformity with right reason, but, since the more probable opinion is more in conformity and safer, we are obliged to follow it. Against this is the argument that no-one is obliged to do what is better and more perfect: it is more perfect to be a virgin than a wife, to be a religious than to be rich, but no-one is obliged to adopt the more perfect of those [...][234]

Medina's 'probable' is rather close to modern English 'arguable' (sustainable, defensible), as he thought of 'probability' in terms of the reasons, including reasons endorsed by traditional authorities, that might be listed in favor of an opinion. From this angle, his understanding of what is probable opinion remained within Gerson's line of thinking. In fact, Medina believed that his opin-

---

scrupulorum inquietudi et cordis pusillanimitas ita perturbat ut uix relictus sit in eis spei locus. 'The distress of scruples and weakness of heart so upset some that room for hope is barely left in them' (Miller 1998, p. 103).
[232] Fleming 2006, p. 7.
[233] Franklin 2001, p. 69.
[234] Kantola 1994, pp. 124–30.

ion on the matter did not deviate from Gerson, who had emphasized the need to stop the spread of doubts of conscience that risked being turned into moral defeatism. Having used Gerson's works as a basis for his discussion on probabilism, Medina later used this method to advocate for the Jesuits.[235] Following Medina, *doctrina probabilitatis* spread like wildfire among Catholic and Spanish moral theologians,[236] who found its use expedient.

Gerson developed his revolutionary interpretation of *regula magistralis in dubiis* (master rule in case of doubt) in *De praeparatione ad missam*. This rule is related but not identical to the issue of moral certainty. Following Guillaume d'Auxerre in the general understanding of this concept, Gerson changed the scope of *regula magistralis* by stating that in case of a painful moral doubt one should choose an option that appears to be the safest regarding salvation of the soul. In other less critical cases the application of the 'safety first rule' was not mandatory. Simply put, not all situations of doubt trigger the 'safety first rule', which is binding only when the agent's doubt is critical. If the doubt is only mild and the degree of certainty, based on available information, is relatively high, there was no need for *regula magistralis*. Therefore, from a general prescription for all kinds of probable reasoning or moral uncertainty, the 'safety first rule' was translated into a measure restricted to extreme cases of conscience only. Even though no one could be precluded from choosing a more rigorist interpretation of this rule, Gerson's take on it offered relative freedom to act even in cases when the agent did not possess evident or unwavering certainty. This reasoning was adopted by another Salamanca faculty, an important theologian, the aforementioned Martin de Azpilcueta (1491–1586), commonly known as Doctor Navarrus, in his *Enchiridion confessariorum et poenitentium*.[237] *Regula magistralis* was also taken over by the Jesuits.[238]

---

[235] Astorri 2019, p. 43.

[236] Schüssler 2014, p. 210.

[237] Navarrus did not directly quote Gerson, but the whole section of the text closely followed Antoninus of Florence's discussion, and Gerson was mentioned as a source in other respects. See Decock 2018.

[238] Jesuit Miguel Pérez used the doctrine of moral probabilism to exempt the persons affected by nocturnal pollutions — the subject of obsession for Gerson — from moral responsibility and blame. See Pérez 1995.

The third Gersonian concept of major importance for the School of Salamanca has to do with the difference between binding qualities of human and divine laws, as found in *De consolatione theologiae* and especially in *De uita spirituali animae*. According to Gerson:

> *Lex diuina praeceptoria est signum uerum reuelatum creaturae rationali quod est notificatiuum rectae rationis diuinae uolentis teneri illam creaturam seu ligari ad aliquid agendum uel non agendum pro dignificatione eius ad aeternam uitam consequendam et damnationem euitandam. [...] Lex humana siue positiua praeceptiua pure et appropiate describitur quod est signum uerum humana traditione et auctoritate immediate constitutum, aut quod non infertur necessaria deductione ex lege diuina et naturali, ligans ad aliquid agendum uel non agendum pro consecutione finis alicuius humani.*[239]

What's more, the chancellor does not consider ancient laws and customs, which do not derive from divine laws and do not directly relate to salvation, as imperative and obligatory.[240] The last argument became the point of contention. Among Salamanca faculty Vitoria stands in direct opposition to Gerson, as he believes that 'in order to know how and how much they [human laws] oblige, we have to consider them as if they were divine'.[241] Two academic stars of Salamanca, Doctor Navarrus and the Franciscan theologian and jurist Alfonso de Castro (1495–1558) engaged in a long-lasting controversy concerning these issues in their respective books *Manuale confessariorum* (1549) and *De potestate legis poenalis* (1550). In their arguments, they both relied on Gerson's *De uita spirituali animae*, where the chancellor could be understood arguing against the supreme claim of secular and ecclesiastical legislators that their laws should be treated as divine. Navarrus

---

[239] *De uita spirituali animae*, OC: 3, p. 130 & 135. 'There are divine laws, which derive from the reason and the will of God, as revealed to humans in order to instruct them about the necessary matters pertaining to salvation and avoidance of damnation. [...] Then there are human or positive laws that are appointed and regulated by human traditions and immediate authorities, which are not necessarily inferred by the deduction from divine and natural law, and concern something to be done or not to be done for the attainment of human ends'.

[240] *De uita spirituali animae*, OC: 3, p. 138: *[...] antiquae legis, et quia multae ueritates sunt quae non sunt imperatiuae et ex hinc non obligatiuae.*

[241] Sarmiento 2011, p. 117, n. 101, citing Vitoria, *De potestate ciuili*.

supported the latter interpretation, while de Castro perceived this argument as a starting point for the separation of *culpa iuridica* and *culpa theologica*. He accused Gerson of being a direct precursor and teacher of Luther, who used the chancellor's theory to develop his errors: *Nam ex hac [theoria] occasionem sui erroris sumpsit Lutherus.*[242] The Lutheran threat led the previously mentioned Salamanca theologian Domingo de Soto to join the polemics with his 1556 book *De iustitia et iure libri decem*, also attacking Gerson. The same Soto who embraced the relevance of *forum internum* in the matters of *dolus incidens* in the sphere of commerce, in this case argued that Gerson's position barely differed from the Lutheran heresy, which teaches the preponderance of the individual conscience over any form of institutional authority. Although Jesuit theologian Gabriel Vásquez (1549–1604), who eventually joined this theological melee to defend the reputation of the late medieval theologian, strove to prove Soto's opinion to be a gross exaggeration,[243] the debate shows that what the chancellor thought a century earlier acquired a different political and religious connotation.[244] In these new circumstances the interpretation of what the late medieval chancellor meant in *De uita spirituali animae* became, in the words of Gabriel Vásquez, 'the case Gerson',[245] toward which Catholic theologians had to formulate their position. The majority, including Medina, de Castro, de Soto, and the pope Adrian VI (1459–1523) opposed it, believing that 'a dangerous dualism between divine law and human laws, introduced by Gerson, paved the way for Luther's revolution'.[246] The chancellor's clear-cut division between divine and human laws, as expressed in *De uita spirituali animae*, seemed

---

[242] Vereecke 1957, p. 10, citing Alphonso de Castro, *De potestate legis paenalis*. Daniel suggests that de Castro's negative attitude toward Gerson's theories was conditioned by his opposition to conciliarism, which was at this point assimilated with Lutheranism in Spain (Daniel 1968, p. 23).

[243] Vereecke 1957, p. 29, n. 2, citing Vásquez 1606, Disputatio 154, n. 5: *Si tamen attente considerantur quae hic auctor docet, lectione illa 4 et 2 De uita spirituali, plane constabit uirum religiosum et pium tam absurdam opinionem nunquam docuisse*. 'If we consider carefully what this author teaches in that lection 4 and 2 of *De uita spirituali animae*, it will become clear that a religious and pious man [like him] has never taught such an absurd opinion'.

[244] Prodi 2000, p. 208.

[245] Vereecke 1957, p. 9, n. 1, citing Vásquez 1606, p. 154 & 156.

[246] Prodi 2000, p. 209.

to contain a danger of undermining the authority of the Church and its officials, since:

> *Nam Ioannis Gerson, cancellarius parisiensis, uir quidem pius as doctus, censet solum Deum posse dare leges et praecepta, quorum transgressio sit tam noxia ut hominem constringat ad poenam aeternam. Quia, ut ait, solus Deus est, qui potest homini poenam infligere aeternam.*[247]

'The case Gerson' illustrates another case of his reception as 'response to the response', namely an example of the Catholic reaction to his thought, which was conditioned by the Lutheran reliance on it and fueled by the fear of Protestantism in general. In addition, although de Soto insisted that 'this opinion [of Gerson] differs from the common doctrine not in name only [as some think] but really and to the largest extent',[248] the difficulty of the late medieval theologian's scholastic language clearly complicated the debate, upsetting not only his opponents, but even his admiring defender Vásquez who, however mildly, complained that the chancellor was too verbose.[249]

The fourth concept of right, understood as *ius* or *dominium* became central in the debate about the rights and the very humanity of (anthropo-*status*) of American Indians, which took place soon after Columbus's return from the New World. Both Vitoria, with his lectures known as *De Indis*,[250] and his pupil

---

[247] Vereecke 1957, p. 10, citing Alphonso de Castro, *De potestate legis poenalis*: 'Jean Gerson, chancellor of Paris, otherwise a devout and learned man, considers that God alone can give laws and precepts the transgression of which could be so noxious as to require eternal punishment. For, as he puts it, God alone can inflict eternal punishment on man'.

[248] Vereecke 1957, p. 11, n. 1, citing Domingo de Soto, *De Iustitia et Iure*, Venise, 1573, lib. I: *Quaequidem opinio [Gersoni], non tantum nomine (ut quidam putant) a communi differt, sed re quidem latissime*. On Vitoria and especially Soto's disagreements with Gerson, see Tuck 1979, pp. 45–50. Brett argued that De Soto's harsh criticism of Gerson was the result of a misunderstanding which identified Summenhart's views with those of Gerson. See Brett 1997, pp. 76–87.

[249] On the full complexity of Vásquez's defense of Gerson see Vereecke's monograph. Fernández-Bollo argued that Navarrus's point of view served as a bridge between Gerson and the Post-Tridentine Jesuit development of the Counter-Reformation at the turn of the century (Fernández-Bollo 2013, p. 60).

[250] According to van der Kroef, Vitoria, who opposed the Aristotelian philosophical concept of the natural slave, based his argument that 'before for-

Soto,[251] entered this debate. The Spanish Dominicans strongly objected to Gerson's and Summenhart's assimilation of *ius* and *dominium*, arguing for the understanding of *ius* as an objective legal notion and *dominium* as a power [*facultas*] of possession or lordship over things or beings: *Fit ergo, ut ius non conuertatur cum dominium, sed sit illi superius & latius patens*.[252] The shift from a more subjective understanding of right to a more objective one is illustrated by how Soto changed Gerson's formula that 'right is a power or faculty pertaining to anyone in accordance with the right reason' to 'right is a power or faculty pertaining to anyone in accordance with the law'.[253]

The discussion of the natural and political rights of the native peoples eventually turned into a philosophical watershed that catalyzed the idea of international law and human rights. It culminated in the Valladolid debates,[254] which were organized by the emperor Charles V in 1550. The dispute pitted Dominican friar Bartolomé de Las Casas (1474 or 1484–1566),[255] a missionary in Central America and a powerful figure in the Mexican ecclesiastical conferences of 1535 and 1536, against Juan Ginés de Sepulveda (1494–1573), the Italian trained humanist philosopher, 'a renowned rhetorician, translator of Aristotle and imperial chron-

---

eign nations had heard of Christianity, they did not commit the sin of unbelief on the grounds that they did not happen to believe in Christ' on Gerson (van der Kroef 1949, p. 149) See Vitoria 1992, p. 109, pp. 115–16, pp. 128–30 & pp. 133–35.

[251] 'Soto commence par le définir en reprenant la définition qu'en avaient donnée Gerson et Summenhart, soit comme le pouvoir, le droit ou la faculté d'user d'une chose conformément au droit' (Demelemestre 2018, p. 6). 'Domingo de Soto distinguished legal slavery and natural slavery — the latter being against divine and natural law as well as human liberty' (Orique 2011, p. 200, n. 656).

[252] '*Ius* must therefore not be confused with *dominium*, as it is superior to it and of wider reference' (Tuck 1919, p. 47, citing Soto, *De Iustitia*).

[253] *De uita spirituale animae*, OC: 3, p. 141: *[...] Ius est facultas seu potestas propinqua conueniens alicui secundum dictamen rectae rationis*. Tierney 1997, p. 260, citing Soto, *De Iustitia*: *Ius est potestas uel facultas conueniens alicui secundum leges*. On Thomist versus Nominalist notions of *ius* see Shortall 2009.

[254] A vast literature, spanning generations of scholars, has been written about this famous affair. See, for example, Brunstetter 2012, pp. 27–28.

[255] Las Casas's father knew Christopher Columbus, and Bartolomé de Las Casas was friends with Columbus's son Diego. He also edited Columbus's travel journals. For Las Casas's impressions of Columbus's achievements, see Las Casas 2001.

icler to Charles V'.[256] Sepulveda's extensive knowledge of Aristotle directly impacted his position on the issue, particularly in his application of Aristotle's category of the 'natural slave' to the indigenous peoples.[257] He was not the first to do so, however. In his disputation with Las Casas, he cited another brilliant academic, Sorbonne professor John Mair or Major (1469–1550),[258] whose thesis had great influence on the treatment of the inhabitants in the Indies:

> As the Philosopher [Aristotle] says in the third and fourth chapters of the first book of the *Politics*, it is clear that some men are by nature slaves, others by nature free [...] And this has now been demonstrated by experience, wherefore the first person to conquer [the Indians], justly rules over them because they are by nature slaves.[259]

---

[256] Brunstetter 2012, p. 46.

[257] Aristotle's theory of slavery, albeit notoriously complex, is found in Book I, chapters 3 through 7 in his *Politics*, and in Book VII of his *Nicomachean Ethics*. Aristotle 'posits the existence of persons, and perhaps even peoples, without full possession of the faculty of reason. Such people are often distinguished by bodily difference. [...] He [the slave] is capable of understanding, but not of *phronesis*, or practical reason [...] The slave apprehends, but does not possess reason (Capizzi 2002, p. 34, citing Aristotle 1177a). However, nowhere did Aristotle state how exactly a natural slave is to be identified. For more see Huxley 1980.

[258] Vickery 1996, p. 23. 'It must be added, however, that Sepulvera's views must be placed in their historical context. He based his judgment, in clear and conscious opposition to Luther's doctrine of the bound will, on the presupposition that 'people are given reason and free will, and with it the ability to access the precepts of natural law, to govern themselves civilly, and to turn to God. [...] he later contends the American indigenous were given the same free will and free access to the universally available, natural law, but, his argument continues, they have not turned to God; they neither desire nor accomplish anything good. Therefore, argues Sepulveda, mercy and justice both demand that the indigenous peoples of the Americas be subdued by Spanish arms and in this way are prepared to receive the saving faith of Christianity' (Benjamin 2017, pp. 78–79).

[259] Capizzi 2002, p. 34; Pagden 1982, pp. 38–39. 'Major had recourse to the Philosopher's categories of barbarians, which term initially meant those who were not Greeks, and referred to 1) those who were generally cruel, inhumane, savage, and pitiless, 2) those who knew no Greek, or spoke it poorly, or, more generally, those who spoke another language, and 3) those who were uncultured and uncivilized. Major opined that Indigenous people belonged to Aristotle's third category of barbarians, and accordingly were at best subhuman, although Major did insist that empirical evidence must be garnered to prove that they were indeed bárbaros' (Orique 2011, p. 137).

It was this view that earned Sepulveda the wrath of Las Casas, provoking the Valladolid debates. The two adversaries engaged in a verbal duel, in which both proclaimed to rely on Gerson's authority. Sepulveda sought to use Gerson to argue that in the Spanish conquest, the evils avoided by waging war against the idolatrous Indians were much greater than the evils incurred through violence. Since the chancellor distinguished three kinds of *dominia*, the evangelical, the natural, and the human, Sepulveda specifically relied on his definition of human *dominium* or right as, *potestas propinqua assumendi res alias aut tamquam alias in sui facultatem aut usum secundum regulas politicas et ciuiles iuris humani*[260] to demonstrate that the Indians were pre-social men with no rights or property, including of their own lives. Gerson's own Aristotle-based emphasis on rationality — *[...] Ius est facultas seu potestas propinqua conueniens alicui secundum dictamen rationis*[261] — was also presented as a binding criteria against the Indians, who, as supposedly irrational beings, were 'bestiales e barbaros' and, therefore, devoid of rights.[262] As a result, the Spaniards could freely occupy the territories in America, because de jure these lands could be considered empty of humans.[263] Las Casas responded to him with the following quote:

> The text he [Sepulveda] cites from Gerson goes counter to his argument, and if one looks at it calmly, works much more in favor of what I say against him. Gerson says: 'Only the good of the state excuses from mortal sin, or the avoidance of damage to the common good markedly worse than the danger to individual good stemming from the war'. It is clear what is far worse damage — a bad name for the faith, a horror of Chris-

---

[260] *De uita spirituali animae*, OC: 3, p. 144: '*Dominium* is the adjacent power to take foreign things either into one's own command because they were foreign, or to use them according to political rules or human civil law' (Tellkamp 2013, p. 129). Sepulvera, once again, relied on John Mair's and Jacques Almain's development of Gerson's idea of natural *dominium*.

[261] *De uita spirituali animae*, OC: 3, p. 141. 'Right is the adjacent means or power that is suitable for someone according to the command of reason'.

[262] The first argument of Sepulveda in Las Casas 1988, p. 82: *Ad hoc barbarorum genus pertinent qui uel ira uel odio uel alio affecto uehementi concitati seditiose aliquid defendant, obliti rationis et decoris*. According to Angel Losada, Sepulveda relies here on *De unitate ecclesiae* (OC: 6, pp. 136–42), thus using against the Indians Gerson's arguments against the schismatics (Losada 1970).

[263] Alonzo 2016, p. 227. Also see Tosi 2003.

tian religion. [...] the texts he cites [...] twisting them against a correct and proper meaning, come back, step by step, to their proper sense, and stand in opposition to his mindless ideology.[264]

Las Casas's interaction with Gerson was not limited to the Valladolid debates. His manual for confessors, *Avisos y reglas para confesores de españoles* (*Admonitions and Regulations for the Confessors of Spaniards*), issued in 1545, was based on Gerson's instructions,[265] to which Las Casa added a regulation that priests were to refuse deathbed absolution to anyone who kept slaves or Indian land. To argue this point, Las Casas relied on the same Gerson's teaching concerning divine and human laws in *De uita spirituali animae* that would provoke 'the case Gerson' five years later. Since only precepts of divine law were binding, individual moral decisions were subject neither to royal nor to papal power. Therefore, what was neither commanded nor forbidden by divine law originating from Scripture and extra-scriptural revelations, was adiaphora or the matter of indifference.[266] The chancellor's idea that human beings retained natural rights even in their fallen state also helped Las Casas in his defense of non-baptized Indians as fully capable of reason and voluntary conversion.[267]

Another celebrated defender of the Indians, the Utopian reformist and the first bishop of Michoacán, Vasco de Quiroga (1470/78–1565) drew from Thomas More and Gerson's *De potestate ecclesiastica et origine iuris* in his book *La Utopia en America*. He believed, based on his understanding of Gerson's idea of *dominion*, that 'as Native Americans did not develop a life sanctioned by good laws, they did not have a mechanism to reinforce justice and punish cannibalism and human sacrifices'.[268] Therefore, it was sufficient to provide good government and legal system to remedy this issue. To this end, Vasco, who is still venerated as a saint among people of this region, organized craft-based communities inspired by More's *Utopia*. Gerson's connection to

---

[264] Sullivan 1995, p. 295.
[265] Tentler 1977, p. 367.
[266] Sullivan 1995, pp. 7–8. Also see Laitakari-Pyykkö 2013.
[267] Reynolds & Durham 1996, pp. 40–42.
[268] Alonzo 2016, p. 227. Also see Colon-Emeric 2017.

Latin America in general, and to Mexico in particular, is not limited to Las Casas, Vitoria and Vasco de Quiroga, who followed Gerson's lead in their demands for the proper religious instruction for the Indians.[269] His massive and undetected legacy in this part of the world represents a separate and fascinating subject awaiting investigation.[270]

Spanish Illuminati

The reception of Gerson in the context of the Spanish *illuminati* or *allumbrados* — who extolled seeking of spiritual perfection through inner illumination and rejected many of the ceremonies of the traditional church[271] — takes the tragic character of a trial, as it involves the use of his argumentation in their persecution, however relatively mild. *Allumbrados'* mystical form of Christianity, based on the belief in the possibility of a direct communication with God, came under the scrutiny of the Catholic church in early sixteenth century Spain, and was officially condemned as heretical on April 21, 1529.[272] Gerson's texts were used in deliberations against mostly humble and uneducated peasant women — precisely the type that he wanted to both recognize and emancipate in his writings — convicted of having 'unchecked' illuminations or visions.[273] The Jesuit superior Gil Gonzales Dávila (1559–1658, the namesake of a famous conquistador), taught the fundamentals of Jesuit spirituality to novices, and he is credited with promotion of mutual 'caridad' or spiritual love among the order's members as their *modus operandi*.[274] He turned to Gerson's authority when he became apprehensive about young Jesuits telling him: 'Father, we do not deal with sins anymore, they are of little benefit, all you need is love, love!'[275] More specifically,

---

[269] Pardo 2004, p. 44.
[270] It is telling and not coincidental that Gerson's last name is still used as the first name by people in some parts of Latin America, particularly in Mexico, where his influence may be the strongest.
[271] Donahue 2010, p. 216, n. 44.
[272] Canovas 2008, p. 157.
[273] Canovas 2008, p. 158.
[274] Friedrich 2017, p. 192.
[275] Dávila 1964, p. 391. Trans. in Marín 2014, p. 184.

Dávila was worried by what he perceived as ecstatic or excessive love, which the chancellor so famously distrusted in both men and women. Relying on Gerson's works *De Probatione spirituum*, *De pueris ad Christum trahendis*; *De arte audiendi confessiones*, *De peccato mollitiei* and *Contra Rusbroquio*, Dávila proclaimed to his students that 'we proceed with much modesty in this love; we do not trust our hearts'.[276] In the thorny question of spiritual union with God, Dávila juxtaposes Germanic medieval mystics Tauler and Ruysbroeck to the Parisian theologian, who criticized the latter:

> Thus, Gerson reprehends this in his book against Ruysbroeck: Neither I know what he meant by abyss, annihilation and union without intermediary [...] Gerson is among the most solid teachers of the path of spirit, and he says: do not read those (esos) books.[277]

More importantly, citing Gerson's authority that 'it is necessary to deal with modesty with women',[278] Dávila linked spiritual *melancolía* and Spanish mysticism's tendency for ecstatic raptures to its perilous association with what he called 'little women' (*mulierculas*), leading to sinister and strange relationships with them, 'siniestras relaciones y peregrinas relaciones'.[279]

Another eminent Jesuit, legal scholar, Salamanca alumnus and a long-time Leuven faculty, Martin Antonio del Rio or Delrio (1551–1608), took the matter further. Delrio was known for his habit of citing Gerson so abundantly that even when he claimed that he was quoting other authorities, he actually quoted the chancellor.[280] He succeeded in applying Gerson-derived ideas to the actual persecution of the *illuminati* and witches. He did so by linking the pastoral issue of hearing confessions with the thorny subject of the discernment of spirits. This step, in combination with Delrio's misogyny, culminated in his infamous book *Disquisitionum magicarum libri sex* (1599), whose popularity in Spain

---

[276] Dávila 1964, p. 605.
[277] Marín 2014, p. 186.
[278] Dávila 1964–, p. 742.
[279] Marín 2014, p. 194.
[280] Maxwell-Stuart 2000, p. 151.

superseded even *Malleus Malefecarum*.[281] Emphasizing Gerson's warnings to confessors about the dangers of their dealings even with the most pious of women,[282] Delrio developed criteria for the discernment of witches based on *De probatione spirituum* and *in De distinctione uerarum reuelationum a falsis*. Such an interpretation of these works is not completely unwarranted. In them the chancellor developed an argument that, since it was close to impossible to determine the authenticity of spiritual visions, one must exercise extreme caution and rely on the opinions of trained theologians in this area. It was indeed Gerson who came up with the idea of compulsory veridiction of someone else's hidden thoughts by a professional inquisitor, for, *hanc inquam quisquis propria uirtute, studio uel industria adipisci et seruare crediderit, errat proculdubio*,[283] because 'the one who investigates [...] ought to be a theologian who is trained by education and experience'.[284] Additionally, Gerson's seemingly most accommodating attitudes regarding confession, which Jean Delumeau qualified as 'the benevolent tradition',[285] suffered malevolent transformations in sixteenth century Spain. Put in a different context, his flexible and personalized approach, which suggested taking into consideration circumstances surrounding confessional practices, with a good confessor informing himself, prior to confession, about *aetate, statu, conditione, studio uel officio confessi* ('age, status, con-

---

[281] Wilson 1997, p. 12. See Lea 1955; Lea 1957.

[282] Maxwell-Stuart 2000, p. 150.

[283] OC: 3, p. 50. 'Whoever then believes he is able to make judgements in such matters on the basis of his own mental ability, skill or industriousness, let him know that he is in error' (McGuire 1998, p. 359). Also, OC: 3, p. 42: *[...] de tali noli credere leuiter quod fallatur per daemonum illusiones, quem et credere consilio et in omnibus caeteris moderamen discretionis obseruare perspexeris*. 'Of people [who lack discretion] I say that they will quickly fall for every demoniacal illusion. Therefore, be suspicious of any unusual revelations such people might pronounce' (McGuire 1998, p. 343).

[284] OC: 3, p. 38: *Et quoniam haec similitudo satis idonea est ad id palpabilius ostendendum quod intendimus, prosequamur eam dicentes primum quod examinator huius monetae spiritualis debet esse theologus arte pariter usuque peritus [...]* 'Since the metaphor is quite suitable for showing in a concrete manner what we intend, we will continue to use it, saying first that the one who investigates this spiritual coin ought to be a theologian who is trained by education and experience' (McGuire 1998, p. 337).

[285] Delumeau 1983, p. 111.

dition, education, or the office of the penitent'),[286] turned into an elaborate protocol of Inquisition. According to del Rio's criteria, inquisitors as well as confessors must scrutinize:

- social, psychological and spiritual aspects of a person pretending to have experienced unusual [extraordinaire] manifestations;
- the nature of these manifestations in relation to the conformity and coherence of the teachings of the holy Catholic church;
- the circumstances and all perdurable consequences of these manifestations;
- the emotions that these manifestations provoked in the person being examined;
- the confirmation of a miracle accompanying these manifestations or lack thereof;
- whether the events confirmed or undermined given revelations.[287]

In Delrio's book, Gerson's ideas metamorphosed into their exact opposite. His circumspect position that *quoniam non est humanitas regula generalis uel ars dabilis ad discemendum semper et infallibiliter quae uerae sunt et quae falsae aut illusoriae reuelationes*,[288] transmuted into a one-size-fits-all procedure. Gerson's critical outlook regarding confessors disappeared altogether.

Although the criteria adopted by the Inquisition for the purpose of discerning heretical views of *illuminati* were later applied to witches, it is problematic to speak of a direct connection between the persecution of 'illuminists' and the witch-hunts in Spain.[289] Among European countries, Spain was one of the least affected by witch-hunts, and from 1537 to 1596 the Catholic Church in Spain was rather skeptical of the capacity of witches to undermine

---

[286] *De arte audiendi confessiones*, OC: 8, p. 11: *Coiiecturet confessor post interrogations quasdam praembulas super aetate, statu, conditione, studio uel officio confessi [...]* (*On the Art of Hearing Confessions*, McGuire 1998, p. 368).

[287] Canovas 2008, pp. 422–35.

[288] OC: 3, p. 37. 'There is for human beings no general rule or method that can be given always and infallibly to distinguish between revelations that are true and those that are false' (McGuire 1998, p. 335).

[289] Wilson 1997, p. 41.

the world order. The holy Inquisition produced a series of specific instructions, especially in the Catalano-Aragonian and Basque regions of Spain, in order to make sure that witchcraft affairs did not end up at the stake.[290] It does not mean that the situation in Spain was more benign. What it means is that on the Iberian Peninsula the auto-da-fé were burning mostly with heretics and not with witches.[291] There is a high probability that, according to the macabre moral arithmetic of early modern Europe, it is precisely the Spanish Inquisition's obsession with heretics, in their majority Jewish *conversos* and more rarely other religious dissidents, such as *morescos* or suspected Protestants, which led to the 'substitution' of witches with female heretics.[292] The condemnation of *alumbradas*, although relatively rarely followed by executions, engendered heavy consequences for all Spanish spiritual movements of the sixteenth and seventeenth centuries. Since Jesuit spirituality was itself 'l'aboutissement, très suspect aux inquisiteurs, d'une fermentation spirituelle que l'inquisition qualifiait d'illuminisme',[293] Ignatius Loyola himself was brought before an ecclesiastical commission on a charge of sympathy with the *alumbrados*. He was lucky to have escaped with an admonition.

However, the reception of Gerson in the context of Spanish *illuminati* is not limited to their persecution. The complex and complicated interaction between his legacy and its Spanish adepts is full of paradoxes, twists and turns on both sides of the *illuminati* controversy. On the one hand, illuminism — 'an interiorized Christianity [...] discipline of the soul, that seeks to make itself available for friendship and relationship with God'[294] — is the spiritual heir of the tradition of Christian interiority,[295] which Marcel Bataillon links to Francisco de Osuna and Gerson without, however, connecting the two. On the other hand, most

---

[290] Canovas 2008, p. 42.

[291] Keitt 2013, p. 16: 'But Spaniards wrote comparatively few such books [on witches]'.

[292] See Dedieu 1979. For the guide to what was considered superstition in the first decades of the sixteenth century, see *Tratado de las supersticiones y hechicerías y varios conjuros y abusiones y de la posibilidad y remedio dellas* by Franciscan friar and Spanish inquisitor *Martín de Castariega* (1511–1551).

[293] Bataillon 1991, 2, p. 282.

[294] Bataillon 1991, 1, pp. 180–81.

[295] Bataillon 1991, 1, p. 199.

spiritual writers in *illuminati* or gnesio-*illuminati* circles maintained a special interest in Gerson's admonitions about ascetic raptures.[296] Moreover, the same *De probatione spirituum*, which was used to persecute the *illuminati*, was also studied and appreciated by them. A prominent early leader of *alumbrados*, Pedro Ruiz de Alcaraz — who was already persecuted by the Inquisition in 1523 — was familiar with *De probatione spirituum*,[297] which one of his most devoted followers, Antonio de Baeza, had translated into Spanish. This translation was one of the main 'spiritual guides' for an eminent Spanish Erasmian, Juan de Valdés (*c.* 1490–1541),[298] whose name was mentioned several times in Alcaraz's trial in 1523–1524.[299] Another illustrious humanist and admirer of Erasmus, Juan de Vergara (1492–1557), whom the Inquisition persecuted from 1530 to 1547, referred to Gerson during his trial. Expressing his indignation against what he perceived as an uncouth ignorance of his judges, he appealed to the authority of the Parisian chancellor, who represented, in his eyes, together with Thomas Aquinas and Bonaventure, the golden age of theology.[300]

Both aspects of Gerson's influence — promotion and restriction of experiential interiority — coexisted not only on both sides of the *illuminati* controversy, but sometimes even within one person. The case of Francisco Ortiz (1497-*c.* 1545) — Franciscan friar, Salamanca alumnus and a successful preacher whose writings 'express an unfeigned spiritual quest'[301] — is very instructive in this regard. Initially Alcaraz's opponent, he was himself tried as *allumbrado* from 1529 to 1532. During his trial he exhorted his inquisitors to look to 'Saint Bonaventure and Gerson on the matter that together with science they had experience', so that the

[296] Beltrán 2018, p. 93.
[297] Bataillon 1991, 1, p. 199.
[298] Ortega 2017, p. 357.
[299] Ortega 2017, p. 14. Valdés provided the first Bible commentaries in Spanish and one of the first treatises on the Spanish language, corresponded with Erasmus, and authored *Dialogue on Christian Doctrine* (1529) — 'a comprehensive perspective of true Christianity, covering diverse areas of knowledge, spirituality, and pastoral practice, reaching even to views on church reform', which was officially banned and put on the *Index of Prohibited Books* in 1547 (Ortega 2017, p. 196).
[300] Bataillon 1991, 2, p. 492.
[301] Ortega 2017, p. 95.

inquisitors 'would not confuse the precious with the vile'.[302] Yet, during the same trial, Ortiz's witness Bachiller Olivares, stated that 'particularly after reading Gerson [*De probatione spirituum*], Ortiz restrained some excesses [concerning radical expressions and miraculous claims]'.[303] Among these 'less excessive claims' is, for example, the fact that, unlike the majority of *allumbrados*, Ortiz never denied vocal prayer, which is more in line with Gerson's teaching. In another twist of Gerson's legacy, Bishop of Verissa Juan de Cazalla (1480–1535), the brother of one of the main *allumbradas* accused during the trials of 1532–1534, and 'un vivant trait d'union entre l'Espagne cisnérienne et l'Espagne érasmisante',[304] himself suspected of heresy because of his 1528 book *Lumbre del alma*, quoted Gerson as an authority on demonic temptations.[305] In this manner, Gersonian mysticism, not only initiated 'a late spring of medieval mysticism that will flower in the early modern tropes of the writings of the group we now refer as the Spanish Mystics',[306] but also led to the exposure and persecution of those who followed its promise. Engaged by both persecutors and their victims, the line between the two was not always clear even to themselves, and it was absorbed as an integral part of both accusation and defense discourses. The chancellor's complicated legacy in Spain still awaits its full illumination.

Francisco de Osuna

Gerson's textual presence is the most significant in the writings of the *illuminati*'s contemporary, a Franciscan Observant Friar and a theologian of international reputation, Francisco de Osuna (1492/1497-c. 1540). His major work, *Tercer Abecedario* (1527), written in the aftermath of the first trials of *allumbrados* in 1523–

---

[302] Selke 1968, p. 259. Trans. in Ortega p. 97.
[303] Ortega p. 107.
[304] Bataillon 1991, 1, p. 66.
[305] Bataillon 1991, 1, p. 71. Homza 2006, p. 153: 'Gerson's vernacular and Latin works were of great importance to Spanish writings on witchcraft'. On Martin de Andosilla's pronounced and explicit dependence on Gerson in his treaty *De superstitionibus* see Gaztambide 2010.
[306] Tyler 2017, p. 48.

1525, stayed away from any dangerous expressions of interiority, rather remaining within Gerson's orthodoxy and discretion. Osuna's dependence on the French chancellor, whom he calls the 'el cristianísimo Gersón, no menos santo que letrado' ('most Christian Gerson, a man as holy as he was learned'),[307] extends far beyond hints and occasional citations. *Tercer Abecedario* explicitly referred to Gerson by name fifty-three times, and a detailed analysis of its relation to the French theologian warrants a whole book about it alone. A thoughtful and welcoming recipient of several major features of Gerson's legacy, Osuna absorbed them to the point of making them fully his own. Just like his older and younger compatriots Garcia de Cisneros and Delrio, even when he appears to quote from other mystical writers, such as St Bernard, he actually cited from Gerson's works.[308]

Tercer Abecedario, considered a masterpiece of Franciscan mysticism, combined two major dimensions of Gerson's theological legacy, namely mystical and pastoral. In more theoretical questions concerning mystical theology, Osuna relies on 'Gerson's *De mistica theologia*, which he quoted frequently and with which he was clearly very familiar'.[309] He focused on the interpretation of Pseudo-Dionysius and definitions of speculative and affective branches of Christian theology. Unlike both Vincent von Aggbach, who believed Gerson's adapted version of *theologia mystica* 'to lack both depth and power',[310] and Nicolas of Cusa, who was not interested in accommodating *simplici et rustici*, Osuna valued the chancellor's contribution precisely for his ability to make lofty matters accessible to all the faithful.

> [F]or Gerson, the *theologia speculativa* resides in the *potentia intellectiua* whilst the *theologia mystica* resides in the *potentia affectiua*. The acquisition of the *theologia mystica* does not therefore require great knowledge or extensive study of books. Therefore, the mystical theology may be acquired by any of the faithful, even if she be an insignificant woman or

---

[307] Osuna 2019, p. 388. Trans. in Osuna 1981, p. 211.
[308] Tyler 2017, p. 43.
[309] Tyler 2009, p. 181. In his dissertation Tyler exclusively focused on Osuna's indebtness to Gerson's *De mystica theologia*.
[310] Hopkins 1988, p. 97.

someone who is illiterate. [...] for Gerson, the school of prayer (*scola orandi*) is more praiseworthy, other things being equal, than the school of learning/letters (*scola litteras*). Accordingly, where we see the distinction in Osuna between *theologia speculativa* and *theologia mystica* [...] is a clear reflection of Gerson.[311]

Although Osuna acknowledges that between the two theologies, speculative and mystical (affective), the second is more perfect and better than the first — 'Esta teologia se dice mes perfecta o mejor que la primera, según dice Gerson, porque de la primera como de un principio se server'[312] — his preference for 'the second' is significantly stronger than Gerson's. The equilibrium between *intellectus* and *affectus* that the chancellor strove to maintain, and that was so appreciated by people like Wessel Gansfort and Thomas More, clearly tilts toward the *affectus* in Osuna. His interpretation of affective theology itself also becomes more overtly affective, in the sense of 'a more sensual and libidinized sense of eros'.[313] Indeed, Gerson's concern for harmonizing the two motifs, knowledge and love, is no longer apparent in *Tercer Abecedario*. Careful to avoid the ecstatic language of the *illuminati*, the Spanish mystic appears to be going further than Gerson (and much further than Nicolas of Cusa) in his championing of the *affectus*, indicating the direction of seventeenth century Spanish mysticism.

Pastoral matters, borrowed from Gerson, are numerous. They include, among others, a disapproving position toward excessive austerity (which Marcel Bataillon identified as Osuna's 'ascétisme modéré et humain'),[314] a specific take on confession and

---

[311] Tyler 2017, p. 188.

[312] Osuna 2019, p. 273 (trans. in Tyler 2009, p. 190). Osuna's division in three types of prayer, from the lowest to the highest, into vocal (active and physical), prayer of the heart (active and emotional) and spiritual (passive and mental) likely represents his reworking of Gerson's similar division in music.

[313] Tyler 2009, p. 193.

[314] Bataillon 1991, 1, p. 189. Osuna 2019, p. 466: 'Podríate responder [...] sino el cristianísimo Gersón, que dice: Más empecería, según dicen los médicos y los teólogos, el ayuno indiscreto que no el comer menos templado'. 'I would rather quote the very Christian Gerson who says: 'According to doctors and theologians, imprudent fasting is more injurious than eating less moderately' (Osuna 1981, p. 394).

absolution,[315] as well as directions regarding admissible correction of others:

> [...] dice Gersón, según el cual se requieren seis condiciones para que seamos obligados a corregir nuestro hermano. La primera es cierto conocimiento del pecado, ca por sola sospecha no debe ser corregido. La segunda es mansedumbre en corregir [...]. Ítem, la tercera condición es que en otro no haya tanta conveniencia para corregir al delincuente como en mí; [...] La cuarta es que haya esperanza que siendo de mí amonestado se corregirá; ca si esto no se espera, no lo debo corregir. La quinta condición es que el pecado que él hace sea mortal y no sólo venial. La sexta, que no se crea haber después mayor oportunidad de tiempo o lugar que cuando lo veo pecar o lo quiero corregir.[316]

A cognizant heir to the French theologian, Osuna declared to have chosen the chancellor's approach to contemplation for the laity as the most suitable: 'según el mismo Gersón dice, y según lo he platicado con personas en este negocio muy ejercitadas, que esta vía es segura y tiene menos en que trompicar que otras'.[317]

---

[315] Osuna 2019, p. 660: 'Gersón dice, se da cierta y no dudosa absolución cuando dice hombre la verdad de lo que siente, y no dejes por decir las circunstancias agravantes, y no es menester que digas las que no agravian'. 'For if you admit what you truly feel without omitting any aggravating circumstances, though it is not necessary to speak of those that did not disturb you, then, as Gerson says, you will be granted certain rather than doubtful absolution' (Osuna 1981, p. 545).

[316] 'Gerson said six conditions are necessary before we are obliged to discipline our brothers. The first is certain knowledge of the incident; do not correct on the basis of mere suspicion. The second is meekness in correcting; the third condition is that there be no one else more suitable for correcting besides myself. The fourth is that there must be hope that the counsel will correct him. If there is no such hope, there is no need to correct. The fifth condition is that his sin is mortal, not venial. The sixth is that there does not appear to be a better time or place to discipline than when I see him sin or when I choose to correct him' (based on Osuna 1981, pp. 587–88). Based on Gerson, *De correptione proximi*, OC: 9, p. 171. The same leitmotive of prudence and discretion are present in others of Gerson's works, such as *Contre conscience trop scrupuleuse*, *De distinctione uerarum reuelationum a falsis*, and *De puella Aurelianensi*. On the idea of *discretio* in Gerson see Boland 1959.

[317] Osuna 2019, p. 236. 'According to Gersón himself, and according to what I have discussed with well-trained people in this matter, this route is safe and less deceitful than others'.

Refusing 'to establish a necessarily link between meditation and cloister',[318] the Spanish mystic followed the chancellor's lead in the use of the vernacular to reach out to the laity and extended the invitation to a contemplative life to 'people outside' and to every faithful Christian:

> El cristianísimo Gersón, no menos santo que letrado, por traer a noticia de todos la muy recogida oración, escribió en su romance un libro que se llama Monte de contemplación, y quísolo dirigir a unas hermanas suyas, por que no pensasen que fue su intento de hablar con solas personas religiosas, mas que también quería ver subir al monte de la contemplación personas seglares. [...] Puesto que, según hemos visto, debamos en este negocio hacer maestros a todos y notificar el recogimiento a todo fiel cristiano que lo quiere seguir, porque, según dice Gersón, a ninguno puede dañar y a muchos puede aprovechar, hay, empero, algunos que dicen no ser bien manifestar el hombre el don que ha recibido, ca escrito está (Tob 12:7) ser cosa buena esconder el sacramento del rey.[319]

As to contemplative meditation, that Osuna called *recogimiento* or 'recollection', his emphasis, like Gerson's, was on discretion and humility — 'dice Gersón que este combate tiene la humildad más que otra virtud alguna',[320] with the word *humilidad* being one of the most frequent in his work — and especially perseverance, that the Spanish mystic declares to have learned from 'el gran chanciller de París':[321]

---

[318] Osuna 1981, p. 201.

[319] Osuna 2019, p. 388 & p. 391. 'The most Christian Gerson, a man as holy as he was learned, wrote his book *The Mount of Contemplation* in the vernacular as a way of informing everyone about the prayer of recollection [...] his intention was to speak also to people outside of religious life, for he wished to see the secular as well as the religious to ascend the mount of contemplation. Like Gerson, I do not propose to speak in this treatise only to the cloistered, but to everyone, and especially to those in the world' (Osuna 1981, p. 211). 'Since, as we have seen, we must make everyone teachers in this business and notify every faithful Christian who wants to follow it, because, according to Gersón, it can harm none and it can benefit many, there are, however, some who say It is not good for man to manifest the gift he has received, it is written (Tob 12:7) to hide the sacrament of the king'.

[320] Osuna 2019, p. 1033. 'Gersón says that this combat has got to have humility more than any other virtue'.

[321] Osuna 2019, p. 734: 'Una de las condiciones que hacen la oración digna de ser oída es. que sea perseverante. Y el gran chanciller de París dice sobre aquellas

> No dejes, pues, de te recoger, aunque carezcas de devoción, ni falte por esto en ti la perseverancia, porque no seas como aquel del cual dice Gersón: El que no tiene devoción, y por esto no se quiere dar a contemplar las cosas espirituales, se compara al que padece frío y no se quiere llegar al fuego si primero no siente en sí el calor.[322]

Like Garcia Jimenes de Cisneros in *A Book of Spiritual Exercises*, Osuna relied on *The Mountain of Contemplation* that he must have read either in its French original or in its Latin translation, *De monte contemplationis*, published in Cologne and Basel. Thus, under the rubric 'On the perseverance', he quoted almost the entire conclusion from *The Mountain of Contemplation*, passionately advertising the chancellor's idea of perseverance in spiritual quest: 'es sentencia en Gersón, donde nos ha dicho cuál ha de ser la perseverancia que para este ejercicio se requiere, y lo que él ha puesto que un día se entiende de todos los que viviéremos sobre la tierra'.[323] The concept of active spiritual quest — *buscar a Dios* — is of particular importance, as it is central to Gerson's theology. Indeed, what Marcel Bataillon identified, in Osuna, as 'une méthode par laquelle l'âme cherche Dieu',[324] was none other than Gerson's theology of seeking, that the Spanish mystic internalized and

---

palabras del Señor (Lc 18,1): Conviene siempre orar y nunca desfallecer. Siempre ora el que tiene siempre los ojosa Dios, y el que siempre desea con piadosa y humilde afección'. 'One of the conditions that makes a prayer worth hearing is for it to be persistent. And the great chancellor of Paris says about those words of the Lord (Luc 18.1): It is always advisable to pray and never to lose heart. He who always has his eyes to God, and he who always desires with pious and humble affection always prays'.

[322] Osuna 2019, p. 1238. 'Therefore, do not stop picking yourself up, even if you lack devotion, nor do you lack perseverance for this, so you are not like the one about whom Gersón says: He who has no devotion, and for this reason does not want to contemplate spiritual things, is like the one who suffers from the cold and does not want to approach the fire unless he first feels the heat in himself'.

[323] Osuna 2019, p. 1240. 'it is a sentence where Gerson tells us how we are to persevere as required for this exercise [of contemplation]. May all on earth one day come to understand his advice' (Osuna 1981, p. 602). The emphasis on perseverance is one of the leading themes in *The Mountain of Contemplation*: 'Vrai est que plusieurs empeschemens la ditte personne sentoit, par especial des aultres pensées et fantasies; mais elle se contraignyt par forte perseverance soi tenir en ceste place et ne se partir ou mouvoir iusques a tant qu'elle sentist en soi ce qu'elle queroit et que dou tout fust arestée a ceste priiere et non a aultre cose' (OC: 7: 1, p. 39).

[324] Bataillon 1991, 1, p. 180.

expanded to the point that it became the leitmotif of his work: 'Lo que más somos obligados a hacer es buscar a Dios'.[325] The word 'exercise' in relation to Gerson, common in Osuna's vocabulary, further confirmed the French theologian's contribution to this concept, usually attributed to Ignatius of Loyola.

The active relationality of Gerson's spirituality is the very premise of Osuna's *recogimiento*, that is built on the idea that 'Es Dios nuestro Señor tan deseoso de tener amigos'[326] ('God our Lord is so eager to have friends'). Osuna described God's friendship as warm and caring, and possible already here and now: 'la amistad y comunicación de Dios es posible en esta vida y destierro; no así pequeña, sino más estrecha y segura que jamás fue entre hermanos ni entre madre e hijo'.[327] The last part of this sentence is very indicative, as Osuna, once again, used a very Gersonian way of referring to the bond between God and man as that between mother (rather than father) and her child. Similarly, the Spanish theologian retained Gerson's image of God's love (based on Is. 66. 13) as not only and not as much fatherly as motherly affection, when 'Dios dice [...]: Como la madre consuela a su hijo halagándolo, así os consolaré yo'.[328]

> Dios nuestro Señor a los recibir, abiertos los brazos de su amistad, con mayor alegría y consuelo verdadero que la madre recibe a su hijo chiquito que se viene a ella huyendo de las cosas que le afligen.[329]

This passage is strongly reminiscent of not only *The Mountain of Contemplation* — 'et les attrait Dieu a soi comme la mere son

---

[325] Osuna 2019, p. 589. 'What we are most obliged to do is seek God'.

[326] Osuna 2019, p. 24.

[327] Osuna 2019, p. 22: 'God's friendship and communion with God are possible in this life and exile, and lesser but more intimate than ever existed the bond between brothers or even between mother and child' (based on Osuna 1981, p. 45).

[328] Osuna 2019, p. 26. 'God says: Like a mother who comforts her child by praising him, so will I comfort you'.

[329] 'Lord God [...] welcomes them [people] with open arms of his friendship, with deeper happiness and sweeter consolation than even that of a mother who receives in her arms her little child seeking refuge from whatever afflicts him' (partly based on Osuna 1981, p. 46).

enfant quant il se part d'elle'[330] — but also of other works such as *Contre conscience trop scrupuleuse*: 'O Dieu tout bon, tout doulx, tout misericors, o pere [...] Et se la personne se sent foible [...], elle se doibt [...] demander douceement pardon a Dieu et son ayde, ainsi comme l'enfant qui est cheu tend la main a sa mère'.[331]

It is readily evident that in relation to both theoretical and practical theological questions, Francisco de Osuna consistently selected, absorbed and amplified the most affective and lively traits of Gerson's spirituality, the ones that contemporary readers would likely find the most attractive as well. The Spanish mystic's multifaceted and extensive reception of Gerson represents, along with Thomas More's, another sixteenth century case of a meaningful communion with the spirituality of the late medieval master. With the word 'consolation' being one of the most frequent terms in his *Tercer Abecedario*, Osuna revealed himself as another *doctor consolatorius*.[332]

John of the Cross and Teresa of Avila

Teresa of Avila's reception of Gerson involved two main channels, one was via Francisco de Osuna and the other through the cult of St Joseph. According to her spiritual autobiography, Teresa first read Osuna's *The Third Alphabet* in 1537, while visiting her uncle. It was this book that taught her to practice prayer and gave her the desire and courage to 'start on the way of prayer with it as her guide'.[333] Teresa stated that until reading Osuna's *Third Spiritual*

---

[330] OC: 7: 1, p. 25. 'God brings them to himself as the mother does the child who leaves her' (McGuire 1998, p. 87).

[331] *Contre conscience trop scrupuleuse*, OC: 7: 1, p. 141. 'If a person feels weak [...], if she doubts [...] ask sweetly God for forgiveness and help, like a child who, when he falls, holds his hand to his mother'.

[332] Osuna 2019, p. 390: 'Según dice Gersón, gran señal es del amor de Dios sentir consolación [...] empero, ni una señal ni otra es evidente por que [...] sintamos de Dios en bondad confiando de él solo, y sintamos de nosotros en humildad teniéndonos por siervos inútiles siempre'. 'According to Gerson, it is a great sign of God's love to feel consolation; [...] however, not one sign or another is evident because [...] we know God's goodness by trusting in him alone, and we think about ourselves in humility, always considering ourselves useless servants'.

[333] Osuna 1981, p. 1. 'When I was on my way, that uncle of mine [...] gave me a book. It is called *The Third Spiritual Alphabet* and endeavors to teach the prayer of recollection [...] And so I was very happy with this book and resolved to follow

Alphabet, and irrespective of the Carmelite exhortation to continual prayer, she didn't know how to go about praying or being recollected.[334] Osuna's 'mystical strategy', inherited from Gerson's *De mystica theologia practica*, greatly influenced Teresa, primarily because the Spanish mystic developed 'the notion of *recogimiento*, partly as a reaction to the condemnation of *alumbradismo* in the Edict of Toledo, and partly to defend a type of contemplative prayer that could not be classed as *dejamiento* or abandonment'.[335] Her simple direct style, spiritual relationality and enhanced interiority are also a direct inheritance from Osuna's *Third Spiritual Alphabet*. While the Dionysian corpus presented mystical theology as 'hidden' from the uninitiated, Gerson's more open contemplative tradition, which became the backbone of Osuna's book, finds its way into Teresa's spiritual output. Considering a very high degree of the *Third Spiritual Alphabet*'s dependence on Gerson, the link between the late medieval theologian and Teresa warrants a further investigation. Her mystical theology, neither intellective nor affective, appears, in certain aspects, to be closer to Gerson's than to Osuna's.[336] In her theology she is 'a determined seeker'.[337] For example, using the affective strategies of *theologia mystica*, constructed by her previous 'masters', notably Gerson and Osuna, she asserts the character of the 'fool', as the one who is wise in his spiritual quest,[338] a potentially Gersonian feature. Furthermore, 'Teresa's identification of herself as 'mujercita' or a little woman 'places her firmly in the Gersonian tradition of the poor and unlettered, even women',[339] who can grasp the fundamentals of a contemplative life, as the chancellor preached in his *Mountain of Contemplation*. This feature separates Teresa's 'Gersonian Dionysism'[340] from the Sufi tradition, with which her spirituality

---

that path with all my strength [...] For during the twenty years after this period of which I am speaking, I did not find a master, I mean a confessor, who understood me, even though I looked for one' (Tyler 2017, p. 36).

[334] Avila 1976, 1, p. 20.
[335] Forthomme 2010, p. 201.
[336] Tyler 2017, p. 37.
[337] Ahlgren 2017, p. 108.
[338] Tyler 2009, p. 178, p. 197 & p. 228.
[339] Tyler 2017, p. 40.
[340] Expression of Peter Tyler.

has often been associated, putting her rather within 'a distinctive and known mystical strategy of *theologia mystica*' of Osuna and Gerson 'to which Teresa is knowingly heir'.[341]

As for the cult of St Joseph, Teresa expanded it beyond purely liturgical matters. She dedicated her entire reformist movement to him, founding the first monastic community carrying the saint's name. Inspired by Gerson's highly influential poem *Josephina*,[342] she believed in Joseph's Assumption and greatly expanded his veneration, particularly among the Jesuits and the Carmelites, who elected him their patron saint in 1621. Thanks to her promotions at the beginning of the seventeenth century, St Joseph also became the patron of manual laborers and even, in an interesting twist of Gerson's double influence, the helper of the dying.[343] Additionally, thanks to Teresa's endorsement of the cult of St Joseph, the very idea of marriage, not only spiritual, but of marriage in general, acquired new meaning based on the idea of mutual consent, itself inspired by the model of Jesus' earthly parents.[344] This, in turn, required a modification of the marital law regarding the spousal right on the wife's body and a radical refiguration of the qualities and demands on the husband and the father. In a sense, the application of Gerson's ideas of marriage emerged in Spain not in a purely judicial sphere of marital law, as in fifteenth century Northern France and Burgundy, but via Teresa's spiritual ratification. As a result, St Joseph became not only 'the model of the emotional type of theologian that Gerson devoted so much energy to promote',[345] but also an archetype of the new husband and father, which the chancellor endorsed no less vigorously.

Teresa's disciple and Carmelite reformer, John of the Cross, who studied at Salamanca before being ordained, was attracted not to the legal dimension of Gerson's thought but to his mysti-

---

[341] Tyler 2009, p. 196. Teresa's mystical theology, 'has more affinity to the 'affective Dionysianism' of the West than the severe and rather pure apophasis (or fanā) of the Sufi tradition' (Tyler 2009, p. 202).

[342] See Iribarren 2011.

[343] Venard 1996, p. 1000. Also see Dompnier 2008.

[344] *Pour la fete de la desponsation Notre Dame*, OC: 7: 1, p. 14: 'Et ce n'est mie petite grace que l'omme et la femme vivent en mariage par bon accort, sans suspicion ou descort ou séparation; et que la femme ensuive l'omme, et l'omme aussi ne face chose pour quoy la femme le doye laissier, ne l'omme ta femme'.

[345] Iribarren 2016, p. 223.

cal theology.[346] His major works, the *Ascent of Mount Carmel* and *The Dark Night of the Soul*, stand as the culmination of the Western tradition of affective mysticism[347] which John of the Cross 'inherited from Osuna, Gerson and the Parisian schools'.[348] Moreover, John's spirituality represents another comeback of affective theology that Gerson sought to revive and to which John of the Cross returned.[349] Several Gersonian features are found in St John's writings. The search of contemplation as a place of 'quietude, repose or rest', developed by Gerson and adopted by Osuna, 'will be used most memorably by John of the Cross in the final stanza of the *Cantico Espiritual*'.[350] The same is true for the accent on the silent prayer of the heart as the most pleasing to God, which is also part of the *Cantico*'s lyricism. The theology of spiritual quest is one of the core elements in *Ascent of the Mount Carmel* and in other works, where John taught his disciples to 'seek and strive after the Glory of God':[351] 'O Lord, my God, who will seek you with simple and pure love, and not find that you are all one can desire, for you show yourself first and go out to meet those who seek you?'[352] This quest, expressed in terms highly reminiscent of Gerson's or Osuna's, is met by an equally intense quest on the part of God 'who is searching the reins and hearts' of men and 'seeks, being Himself God by nature, to make us gods through participation, just as fire converts all things into fire'.[353] The last affirmation would probably have put the reserved chancellor of Paris rather ill at ease. Compared to Teresa's spirituality, still somewhat balanced between intellective and affective

---

[346] Mondello 2018, p. 4.

[347] Mondello 2018, p. 4.

[348] Tyler 2010, p. 128. Tyler argues for a strong Gersonian connection on (Tyler 2010, pp. 61–65 & p. 128). On Gerson's spiritual lineage see Mazour-Matusevich 2004.

[349] Mondello 2018, p. 40.

[350] Tyler 2009, p. 195.

[351] 'By means of this drawing [of the Spiritual Mount]', testified one of his disciples, 'he used to teach us that, in order to attain to perfection, we must not desire the good things of earth, nor those of Heaven; but that we must desire naught save to seek and strive after the glory and honour of God our Lord in all things' (St John of the Cross, *Ascent of Mt. Carmel*, online).

[352] St John of the Cross, *Spiritual Canticle*, online.

[353] St John of the Cross, *Spiritual Canticle*, online.

tendencies inherited from Gerson, John of the Cross' ardent mysticism is fully bent toward powerful affectivity, able to transform his theology into poetry. In him the lineage of affective mysticism from Bernard, Victorines, Gerson and 'intermediaries such as the sixteenth century Franciscan writer Francisco de Osuna',[354] finds its apogee.

Part V. The Early Jesuits

> 'Les jésuites sont un sujet inépuisable,
> et que nous ne scruterons jamais trop'.[355]

The Question of *De Imitatione Christi*

The topic 'Gerson and the Early Jesuits' alone is worth a book, and much more research is needed to elucidate it. Here it will be limited to tracing the main lines of interaction between the chancellor's theological heritage and the inexhaustible subject of the history of the Jesuits, as Marcel Bataillon put in the quote opening this section. One of the major challenges of investigating the early Jesuit reception of Gerson is his alleged authorship of *De Imitatione Christi*, because the Jesuits definitely believed him to be its author. Their belief was part of a general European tendency, in which Thomas à Kempis's name was associated with its authorship more frequently in the Germanic parts of Europe, while Gerson's name was largely preferred in the Romance-language lands.[356] Early Jesuits, nearly all Iberians,[357] were so certain of Ger-

---

[354] Tyler 2010, p. 64. It remains to be seen whether the metaphor of the 'Mount', with various degrees of spiritual perfection as its planes, which John very frequently used for all kinds of religious instruction, has anything to do with Gerson's metaphor of the Mountain of Contemplation.

[355] Bataillon 1991, 1, p. 283.

[356] Habsburg 2002, p. 258. According to Francesco Cancellieri, Johannes Trithemius was the first to attribute *De Imitatione Christi* to Thomas à Kempis (Cancellieri 1809, p. 207).

[357] The second largest group of the Society of Jesus was represented by Italians. French and Germans were represented to a much lesser degree (Maryks 2008, p. 43). In later centuries, Polish Jesuits formed an important percentage of the Jesuit cohort.

son's authorship of *De Imitatione Christi* that they affectionately renamed the book *Gersonzito* or even simply 'Gerson'. Ignatius of Loyola initiated this trend: 'The same can be said of Gerson [*De Imitatione Christi*] — living with Father [Ignatius] seems to be nothing else than reading Gerson translated into action'.[358] Ignatius's companion Jeronimo Nadal (1507–1580) stated, while describing his novitiate experience at the Society: 'Ignatius said to me that [...] each day I was to read a chapter of Gerson [*De Imitatione Christi*] and meditate on it.'[359] Considering the tremendous role that this work played during the formative years of the Society of Jesus, how do we separate the reception of Gerson proper from that of *De Imitatione Christi* credited to him?

There appear to be ways of dealing with this problem. First, it seems logical to elucidate the reasons behind the association of Gerson's name with *De Imitatione Christi* on the one hand, and his link to the Company of Jesus during its early, formative years, on the other hand. Second, it is important to look beyond *De Imitatione Christi* for other possible ties between the late medieval theologian and the early Jesuits. Beginning with the first task, the theological assessment of Gerson's relevance in the Jesuit context suggests that his nexus with both the Company and its book of choice is far from random. Quite to the contrary, 'it is of profound importance that *De Imitatione Christi* was attributed by the early Jesuits to Jean Gerson'.[360] There are several features in Gerson's theology that correspond to the program of the early Jesuits and especially to Ignatius's spiritual aspirations, making him a suitable candidate for *De Imitatione Christi* author. Among them are Gerson's focus on the Passion of Christ in *Monotessaron*,[361] his general Christocentric tendency, his interiority, relationality and affectivity, his practical advice concerning a suitable time and manner for meditations and a strong accent on humility. In addition, the explicit presence of the theme *imita-*

---

[358] Palmer 1996, p. 29.
[359] Endean 1980, p. 73. On Nadal see O'Malley 1984.
[360] Habsburg 2002, p. 233.
[361] O'Malley suggests that besides Ludolph of Saxony's *Vita Jesu Christi*, which 'had an excessive impact on the structure of the *Exercises*, Gerson's *Monotessaron* influenced Loyola's meditation in Episode 5, *Kingdom of Christ Kingdom of the Heart*' (O'Malley 1993, p. 46).

tio Christi, developed in *De consolatione theologiae* — *Nos itaque Iesum debemus imitari*[362] — might be another factor favoring his association with this book. However, even a superficial reading of *De Imitatione Christi* makes it hard to disregard the obvious fact that Kempis, unlike the French master, clearly addressed his work to those 'to whom affairs of the world are of no concern'.[363] This condition would clearly exclude the Jesuits explicitly thrown into the midst of an active life in the *seculum*. Yet, the early Jesuits chose to overlook this prerequisite. They were able to adopt *De Imitatione Christi* thanks to two unintentionally applied tactics engendered by the very nature of their mission. The first consisted in dissociating *De Imitatione* from its monastic roots because '[W]hatever order St Ignatius founded, it was not a monastic one'.[364] Indeed, despite its obvious monastic disposition, early Jesuits did not consider *De Imitatione* to be a monastic text *per se*.[365] The second tactic entailed associating *De Imitatione* with the name of a mystical writer and scholar of international reputation who was not a monk. Gerson's candidacy matched the description. If in the fifteenth century Gerson's legacy was at the center of a conflict between monastic and secular humanistic circles (exemplified by the quarrel between Abbot Johannes Trithemius and printer Jacob Wimpheling) that both claimed it as their own, in new historical circumstances the chancellor's status as a secular clergyman gave him a clear advantage in the eyes of the Society of Jesus, which was not an order of monks but of priests.

The early Jesuits' exposure to Gerson's legacy is beyond doubt. In Paris they studied at the college of Montaigu and at Sorbonne, two places where the chancellor had a celebrity status, and took classes taught by his intellectual heirs such as Jacques Almain and John Mair. Loyola and his first companions certainly were made aware of Gerson's reputation and the major facts of his biography, in which almost everything (with the notable exception of his conciliarist views) was bound to please future members of the Society of Jesus. His association with late medieval scho-

---

[362] OC: 9, p. 208.
[363] Janz 2008, p. 10.
[364] O'Malley 1984, p. 9.
[365] Habsburg 2002, p. 233.

lasticism hindered his popularity with Erasmians, but it made him only more attractive in the judgment of Loyola's companions who were inclined to 'praise both positive theology and that of the Scholastics [...] because Scholastic doctors belong to more recent times, [and] have the advantage of correct understanding of Holy Scripture.'[366] His engagement in worldly affairs could not but delight the nascent Jesuit movement, whose credo was summarized by Ignatius's doctrine of 'contemplation in action'.[367] His story of an exiled wanderer, initially promulgated by his German biographers and generally accepted by all, including his Gallican editors, offered an image that corresponded perfectly to the Jesuits' newly-formulated credo of a professed itinerant life 'in journeys and missions to whatever place either the supreme pontiff or their general might send them for the sake of ministry'.[368] To maintain spiritual focus even in situations 'synonymous with distractions and dissipation of spirit',[369] and to be 'constantly on the move'[370] was to be, in words of the author of the *Constitutions of the Society of Jesus* Jeronimo Nadal, 'the distinctive mark of our vocation'.[371] Finally, Gerson's definition of mystical theology, written a century and half earlier, was the one adopted by the Society of Jesus:

> *Sicut apud Ciceronem orator describitur, quod est uir bonus dicendi peritus, ita theologum nominamus bonum uirum in sacris litteris eruditum; non quidem eruditione solius intellectus, sed multo magis affectus; ut ea quae per theologiam intelligit, traducat per jugem ruminationem in affectum cordis et executionem operis.*[372]

---

[366] Janz 2008, pp. 428–29.
[367] O'Malley 1984, p. 5.
[368] O'Malley 1984, p. 8.
[369] O'Malley 1984, p. 10.
[370] O'Malley 1984, p. 8.
[371] O'Malley 1984, p. 7.
[372] *De consolatione theologiae*, OC: 9, p. 237. 'If Cicero describes the orator as 'a good man skilled in speaking', we describe the theologian as a 'good man with learning in sacred letters' — not with the learning of the intellect alone but even more of the affections, so that what he understands through theology he through constant reflection transfers into the feelings of his heart and into Christian practice' (O'Malley 1993, p. 252).

All these factors speak in favor of the premise that the Jesuits' firm association of Gerson's name with *De Imitatione Christi* represents not only a spiritual, but also an anthropological choice. The young order consciously or unconsciously chose texts and characters that best suited its mission and dispensed with the rest, be it *De Imitatione*'s monastic rationale or Gerson's conciliarism. His authority and reputation, in combination with his secular status, made the chancellor an ideal candidate for the *Imitatione*'s authorship, while *De Imitatione Christi*, in combination with selective elements of Gerson's theology and biography, provided early Jesuits with what every young religious or political movement always longs for: legitimacy.

Besides and Beyond *De Imitatione Christi*

Among the links between Gerson's legacy and the early Jesuits, independent of *De Imitatione Christi*, is the connection via Garcia Jimenes de Cisneros (1455–1510), who was long considered one of Ignatius's spiritual ancestors.[373] Although the two Spaniards' methods and styles reveal a disparity too deep to ignore, and their comparison fails to substantiate a straight correlation between them, a careful reading suggests a more nuanced link between their respective approaches. This link passed through Gerson and Mombaer, on whose ideas Cisneros depended in *Ejercitatorio de la vida spiritual*.[374] Thus, Loyola's concern with adapting exercises to different individuals, according to their occupations, circumstances, vocations, temperaments and degrees of preparation, strongly reverberated with the specifically Gerson-

---

[373] O'Malley 1993, p. 46: 'The Exercises, including their very title, were probably influenced by Abbot Cisneros's *Ejercitatorio de la vida spiritual*, which Ignatius might have seen in compendium form during his stay at Montserrat or Manresa. The suggestion that the title of Cisneros's *Ejercitatorio de la vida spiritual* might have inspired Loyola's *Ejercicios Espirituales* is not new. 'As long ago as 1641 Constantino Cajetan [...] affirmed that the *Spiritual Exercises* of the founder of the Jesuits were 'in large measure borrowed from the *Exercitatorium* of the Venerable Garcia de Cisneros' (Guibert 1964, p. 152). Guibert considers the borrowing of Cisneros's title a possibility but hesitates 'to affirm this as a proven fact when we recall how frequently this expression was used at that time' (Guibert 1964, p. 159).

[374] See chapter I.

ian insights spelled out in *The Mountain of Contemplation*, which Cisneros cited so profusely. Indeed, one of the first rules given by Ignatius to the Jesuit directors of conscience was that they should 'adapt the *Exercises* to the age, capacity, strength of the person about to perform them'.[375] This is almost verbatim Gerson's advice to introduce people to a contemplative life 'according to person, place, time, the grace of God, and the learning or knowledge that one possesses'.[376] Considering that Cisneros was one of the authors to have retained Gerson's unique psychological insights, similarity of Loyola's psychological and pedagogical approaches with Gerson's makes more sense. *The Mountain of Contemplation* is also the work where the chancellor advocates a contemplative way of life for the laity that corresponds to one of the main goals of the Society of Jesus. It is also in this text that he advances his innovative argument concerning compatibility and complementarity of contemplative and active lives, as well as the revolutionary idea that 'la vie mixte est supérieure aux deux autres prises séparemment'[377] — the position that will become the Jesuit modus operandi. Truly, the following quote from *The Mountain of Contemplation* could serve as a slogan for the Society of Jesus: 'Et tel estat doient avoir les prelas, qu'ilz soient de vie contemplative si parfaicte et enracinee qu'ilz descendent a l'active sans du tout laissier la contemplative comme les angels qui nous gardent sa jus sans delaissier la vision a de Dieu la sus'.[378]

---

[375] Saint Ignatius, *Exercises, Retreats with notes of addresses*, London, 1893, p. xxv. For a more recent translation, see Loyola 1991. Francis Rapp brings up the interesting fact that Gerson's influence is also responsible for the differentiation of the days of the week thanks to his spiritual exercise, which regroups seven mediation themes for seven days of the week (Rapp 1994, p. 261).

[376] *The Mountain of Contemplation*, McGuire 1998, p. 113, already cited. This theme is recurrent in Gerson. Letter to his brother Nicolas, around 1408: *Sunt enim complexiones diuersae hominum; sunt uocationes Dei similiter uariae [...]* (OC: 8, p. 89). 'Complexions of men are diverse, similarly varied are God's vocations [for them]'. *Dialogue Spirituel*: 'Tel remede peut une chascune personne ordonner a soy selond son labeur et son estat' (OC: 7: 1, p. 189).

[377] Vial 2009a, p. 285 & p. 389. Gerson also wrote a treatise specifically titled *De comparatione uitae contemplatiuae ad actiuam* (OC: 3, p. 63).

[378] OC: 7: 1, p. 35. 'They must live in a contemplative life that is so complete and deep-rooted that they can descend to the active life without wholly leaving the contemplative one' (McGuire 1998, p. 99).

Ignatius also expanded upon the very essence of Gerson's spirituality, his theology of seeking, in which the chancellor 'adapted the Scotistic emphasis upon the freedom and priority of God's election to a reconstructed version of the Ockhamist view of the human participation in salvation, while dismissing altogether the language of human merit'.[379] After all, Ignatius spoke of himself as a pilgrim, the one who seeks. However, in Loyola's 'warlike book, which contains all the plan of a campaign of man's struggle against himself',[380] he spoke of obtaining divine love and not just searching for it.[381] His *Spiritual Journal* depicted a 'restless journey and seeking'[382] of intensity and urgency, while Gerson's spiritual quest appears both timid and static.[383] In a similar fashion, contemplation itself transforms from a mountain to climb (with three consoling ladies, Faith, Hope and Charity, waiting for you on its top) into a fortress to be taken. Even though a Jesuit must be heroically patient during his spiritual 'siege', his patience, the unrelenting perseverance of a soldier, is of a quite different kind from Gerson's confident faith in the eventual visit of the Holy Spirit to a penitent heart. Therefore, several aspects of Gerson's spirituality — theology of seeking, a combination of active and contemplative lives, an awareness of the psychological diversity of men, and the willingness to act according to this awareness — are likely to have passed into the Jesuit spirituality via Ignatius of Loyola's familiarity with Cisneros's adaptation of the French master (and, possibly, via other still unknown venues).[384] However, all these features

---

[379] Burrows 1991, p. 173.

[380] Debuchy 1910, p. 227.

[381] O'Malley 1993, p. 2.

[382] Fabre 2007, p. 119. The number of verbs related to movement in Loyola's *Journal* is striking. He speaks of 'doing whatever I could [...] to obtain grace' (Fabre 2007, p. 99); of the grace 'pulling' him and 'the Trinity joining' him (Fabre 2007, p. 105).

[383] Yet, Gerson's description of the spiritual quest can be quite vivid at times: 'Comparez ceulx qui ont la boinne odeur de Dieu et de la bonté et de la gloire des cieulx aux dessusdis quatre chiens, et les aultres mondains qui riens n'en sentent aux aultres chiens' (OC: 7: 1, p. 24). 'Compare with these four dogs the people who have the good scent of God and of the goodness and the glory of the heavens' (McGuire 1998, p. 85).

[384] There are good reasons to believe that Loyola might have had a more direct contact with Gerson's legacy, since the latter's actual works were also read by the early Jesuits following dinners, upon Nadal's recommendation (O'Malley 1993,

underwent both qualitative and quantitative transformation in Jesuit theology. They not only attained extreme expression, definition, and power, but they also were converted into an applied Jesuit methodology. One can safely state that in Loyola all major features of Gerson's theology, even though the same, reached an unprecedented degree of passionate intensity very much at odds with the spirit of moderation that Gerson strove to achieve in his *theologia media*.

Confession and Communion

Another area of Jesuit reception of Gerson involves his contributions to new approaches to confession and communion. The new movement transformed the general confession from a rare and almost unknown spiritual ritual into 'one practiced by students, noblemen, women'[385] and introduced changes that were both quantitative and qualitative. The first were related to the desired frequency of confession and communion; the second to the narrow association of confession with communion, better training of the confessors, more structured and systematic confessions, the view of confession as a consolatory experience and the confessors' role as that of consolers. All these features had already been spelled out and promoted by Gerson in a series of some thirty Latin and vernacular works dedicated to this subject, which were copied and recopied throughout Europe after his death.[386] The early Jesuits, who believed Gerson to be the author of *De Imitatione Christi*, 'found double confirmation when they quoted his authentic works on the question of frequent [once a month] communion',[387]

---

p. 358). O'Malley also mentions a possible influence of *Monotessaron* on the 'Kingdom of Christ' meditations in *Spiritual Exercises*, (O'Malley 1993, p. 46) Some scholars also believe that 'Jean Gerson [...] exerted an enormous influence on Ignatius and on later Jesuits, especially regarding women and sexuality. Yet Gerson's mostly negative views concerning spiritual friendships between men and women, and between religious males, remains largely unexplored in the early modern Hispanic context' (Marín 2014, p. 95).

[385] O'Malley 1993, p. 186.

[386] McDonnell 1993, p. 414. Among them the most significant are *De elucidatione scholastica mysticae theologiae, De arte audiendi confessiones, De remediis contra recidiuum, De potestate absoluendi* and *Doctrinal aux simples gens*.

[387] O'Malley 1993, p. 152.

which he recommended for men and women, 'le masle en aage de quatorze ans et la femelle de douze ans'.[388] Besides urging to 'se souvent confesser et communier dignement',[389] Gerson was also among the few authors who accepted the practice of daily confession and communion.[390] The latter modification was retained and promulgated by Loyola's early companion Nicolas Bobadilla (1511–1590).[391] Ignatius Loyola himself declared more modest goals of 'the yearly reception of the most blessed sacrament, and praised more highly monthly reception, and still more weekly Communion.'[392]

Jesuit innovations concerning quality, purpose, circumstances and benefits of confession also derive from Gerson's pastoral legacy. The chancellor declared confession to be 'comme un second baptisme et comme une fontaine ou sont lavés et pardonnez tous les pechiez quels qu'ilz soient',[393] gave a detailed description of what a full confession should be,[394] and praised its benefits: 'car nul ne pourroit dire le prouffit, la grace et la vertu que on y acquiert, et le guerredon que on aura de se souvent confesser et communier dignement'.[395] His recommendations regarding confessions delineate the conduct of the confessor as well. Gerson developed detailed psychological insights, which would become a trademark of Jesuit casuistry, in *Quelques conseils aux confesseurs*:

---

[388] *Le doctrinal aux simples gens*, OC: 10, p. 310: *De communier voulentiers et souvent*: '[...] le masle en aage de quatorze ans et la femelle de douze ans [...]'.

[389] *Le doctrinal aux simples gens*, OC: 10, p. 310: 'St Augustin loe et conseille aux devotes personnes communier tous les dimanches; et les sains canons que au moins se facent communier aux festes solennelles'.

[390] O'Malley 1993, p. 155; Tentler 1977, pp. 72–76; Popelyastyy 2018, p. 203.

[391] The Fourth Lateran Council determined an absolute minimum of confession for all faithful who have reached the age of discernment as 'at least once a year' (Popelyastyy 2018, p. 202, citing Tanner & Alberigo 1990, 1, p. 245).

[392] Janz 2008, p. 423.

[393] *Le doctrinal aux simples gens*, OC: 10, p. 310.

[394] *Le doctrinal aux simples gens*, OC: 10, pp. 314–15: 'Pour bien confesser. Si tu te veux bien confesser, tu dois premièrement bien penser à ta conscience comme cellui qui veut render compte a Dieu, et dois dire tous les péchés dont il se souvient que tu as faiz ou que tu eusses voulentiers faiz se tu eusses osé, ou peu, ou eu temps et lieu de faire'.

[395] *Le doctrinal aux simples gens*, OC: 10, p. 310. 'because no one could tell the profit, the grace and the virtue acquired through it [confession], and the healing that one receives through frequent confession and worthy communion'.

> *Non enim omnia possunt explicari secundum particulares circumstancias: tanta siquidem uariatas est hominum, tum in natura quoad complexionem corporum, et consequenter quoad animas que in multis secuntur ipsa corpora, tum in modo conuersacionis et educacionis, ut uix tradi possit aliqua doctrina que conueniat equaliter omnibus et qua non possit abuti.*[396]

Indeed, a confessor should carefully proceed case by case. Other qualities required of a confessor are tactfulness and gentleness so that

> *[...] ne formident quod propter peccata dicenda confessor sit eos postmodum osurus aut contempturus, aut accusaturus; immo tenerius eos diliget sicut filios carissimos et qui suae fidei se totos commiserunt.*[397]

One finds similar admonitions in Loyola, who taught that the annual confession should be 'in secret or in another manner which may be more pleasing or spiritually consoling'; guided 'with great humility, integrity and charity', and performed 'without concealing anything which is offensive to the Lord'.[398] The Jesuits' perception of confession as a 'consoling experience [...] when the penitent reviewed sinful patterns and sought counseling in order to eradicate bad habits and behaviors',[399] equally comes from *doctor consolatorius*, who viewed confession as an act of both penance and consolation. Although the origin of the general confession

---

[396] Ouy 1990, p. 296. 'It is not enough that he [confessor] seeks to understand the particular circumstances of the acts; he must also and first be aware of the diversity of humans, who naturally differ in complections of their bodies, and therefore in their temperaments and consequently in their souls which, in many respects, depend on physical body; and they are just as different in the environment in which they live, in the education they have received. There is therefore no single doctrine that is equally suitable for all, and which could not be potentially abused'.

[397] OC: 8, p. 12. 'the penitents do not fear that if they tell their sins, the confessor will afterward be hateful or contemptuous or accusatory toward them. Rather, he should love them more tenderly as cherished offspring who have committed themselves totally to his trust' (*On the Art of Hearing Confessions*, McGuire 1998, p. 368). The theme is found in vernacular Gerson's works as well: 'Que les curés et gens d'Eglise qui a ce sont ordonnez, mettent diligence a traiter doulcement tous ceux qui se confessent' (*Note sur la confession*, OC: 7: 1, p. 412).

[398] Loyola 1970, p. 93.

[399] Maher 2000, pp. 184–85.

is commonly attributed to Garcia de Cisneros,[400] he gathered it from Gerson, and its description is found in Cisneros's *Book of Spiritual Exercises*.[401] Loyola experienced the benefits of general and consolatory confession during his stay at Cisneros's Benedictine abbey of Montserrat in 1522. Later he incorporated this type of confession into his *Spiritual Exercises*, requiring 'it of all novices entering the Society of Jesus'.[402] The Spanish abbot served, once again, as a bridge between the founder of the Society of Jesus and the 'greatest voice in the cure of souls',[403] in whose theology 'consolation was a governing idea'.[404] Subsequently, the Jesuits conceived confession as a delivery, and confessors as doctors of conscience. The first companions, like Jeronimo Nadal, saw themselves as mainly 'consolers' whose primary intention and goal was spiritual consolation.[405] *Formula of the Institute* that Ignatius composed in 1539, presented to Pope Paul III, and reworked, together with his companions, for the approval of Pope Julius II in 1550, specified as one of the purposes of the new Jesuit order 'the spiritual consolation of Christ's faithful through hearing confessions'.[406]

The Jesuits' continuous reliance on Gerson in confessionary matters is plainly evident from *Directory for Confessors* by Juan Alphonso de Polanco (1517–1576), a figure of great significance, who was Ignatius's early companion and personal secretary. Loyola's assistant since 1541, he became the official secretary of the Society of Jesus, taught at the Jesuit College in Lyons, and authored the *History of the Society of Jesus*. His *Directory for Confessors* was the most popular among similar texts and dominated

---

[400] Bireley 2018, 1, p. 34: 'At the same time the use of the general confession came into use; it too seems to have originated from Garcia de Cisneros'. Maher claims that 'exact beginnings of this type of confession are unknown' (Maher 2000, p. 185). This is a rather odd statement, considering that Maher links this type of confession to Garcia de Cisneros, who himself borrowed it from Gerson.

[401] See Chapter 1.

[402] Bireley 2018, 1, pp. 29–48, p. 34.

[403] Tentler 1977, p. 46.

[404] O'Malley 1993, p. 83.

[405] Maryks 2008, p. 19.

[406] Maryks 2008, p. 184.

the printing market from 1554 until 1590.[407] It reflects the concerns and organization of Gerson's *Opus tripartitum*, although in a much more detailed and extended format, while closely following his *De remediis contra recidiuum* as the best treatise for dealing with those who are prone to commit the same sins again and again. Keeping with Gerson's practical and moderate approach, Polanco proposed the following advice for chronic offenders: fasting the day after the sinner lapses, psalm-reciting, giving something the sinner loves dearly or money to someone who might need it, according to the person's needs and means, making sure to confess the recurring sin within three days of occurrence and finally, even if he/she is unable to resist the temptation, say some prayers so that God can have mercy on his soul. All these measures were taken directly and without the slightest modification from Gerson's *De remediis contra recidiuum*.[408] Polanco directly quoted that 'the same doctor [Gerson] in grave maladies [meaning mainly relapse in sin] adds a bearable penance: in the memory of received grace something light like Pater or Ave, or something similar, that the afflicted person should say every day so that every day he could repair what he committed earlier'.[409]

Gerson's liberal stance toward reserved cases of conscience provoked mixed reactions. Martin de Frias, Salamanca professor of Sacred Scripture, vicar general, and a man so learned that whenever he competed for a professorship all other competitors simply fled,[410] seconded the chancellor's opinion. In 1528 he quoted Gerson's assertion that 'the bishops by these reservations

---

[407] Maryks 2008, p. 1. The real title is *La Vraye guide des curez, vicaires, et confesseurs: diuisee en trois parties: la premiere contient la pratique d'administrer les Saincts Sacraments du Baptesme, Penitence, ... la seconde, est la vraye methode d'assister & consoler les malades ... la troisiéme contient le directoire des confessions*.

[408] Polanco 1608, pp. 31–32. OC: 8, pp. 67–68: *Primo, quod in casu illo teneretur uno die sequenti, in pane et aqua ieiunare, infra tres dies; secondo, diceret certum psalmorum numerum; tertio, si foret sui iuris, daret in ecclesiam certum iocale aut aliud bene carum sibi aut summam pecuniae etc.*

[409] Polanco 1608, p. 32. Polanco also authored a version of *ars moriendi*, *Methodus ad eaos adiuvandos qui moriuntur*, which appeared separately in 1578 and in 1582, bearing no reference to Gerson. A probable explanation for such an omission might be the fact that by the end of the sixteenth century, Gerson's major contribution to *ars moriendi* literature became an integral and indistinguishable part of the genre itself.

[410] Brodrick 1956, p. 194.

plunged innumerable souls into hell', and added that reserved cases did not work because most people simply refused to go 'for a second confession or flee'.[411] Yet, generally speaking, the chancellor's 'benevolent'[412] position did not prevail. Beginning from the 1530s 'the impression made by Gerson passed away', and the lists of reserved cases became 'enormously overgrown', embracing 'almost all offenses'.[413] The situation became so bad that emperor Charles V himself found it necessary to intervene. His *Formula of Reformation* of 1548 was designed to simplify the confessional for both the confessor and the penitent by abolishing, as Gerson would have it, all reserved cases. However, this position did not find support at the Council of Trent, which sided with the bishops[414] and created a lasting conflict with all those who opposed the practice of reserved cases, beginning with the Jesuits.

The best example of such a conflict was that between the 'rigoroso e austere cardinale'[415] Carlo Borromeo (1538–1584) in the diocese of Milan and the Jesuit preacher Giulio Mazzarino. The disagreement ended in Borromeo's full-blown confrontation with the Jesuits in general. Motivated by the struggle to preserve

---

[411] Lea 1896, p. 318. OC: 2, p. 90: *Quod si remittantur ad praelatum uel poenitentiarium de longinquo uel in publico, refugiunt et horrent; expertumque est millesies quod non uadunt'*.: 'But if such matters are left to the bishop or to confessors who come from far away and whose presence is publicly known, such penitents will take flight in terror. [...] We have seen thousands of people fail to come' (McGuire 1998, p. 241). As usual, Gerson was most concerned about women's safety: *Expertum est itaque quod hic terror reseruationis nullos aut paucissimos cohibet peccare; innumeros autem sic retrahit confiteri propter dictas causas et etiam alias, quoniam mulieres praedpue tali modo retrahuntur: primo, timentes notari a maritis, cum tales confessores adirent; qui cum zelotypi sint, statim sinistram contra uxores suas sumerent occasionem, unde surgerent iurgia, lites, discordiae et amoris interruptio, et cetera quae peiora procurarent mala, utinam non saepius mortem* (OC: 2, p. 90). 'In our experience, this terror of reserved sin keeps no one or very few from sinning, but it holds untold persons back from confessors. Women especially in this manner are kept away. First of all, they are afraid of being noticed by their husbands when such confessors come. When the husbands become jealous, they immediately turn the situation against their wives, and so there are arguments, fights, discord, with the result that love is broken. Other things happen that create even worse evils: would that dissension did not often end in death!'

[412] Delumeau 1983, p. 111.
[413] Lea 1896, p. 317.
[414] Lea 1896, p. 318.
[415] Rurale 1992, p. 256.

'the power of ecclesiastical judges to act against lay people'[416] and the archbishop's power in general, which was confirmed by the Council of Trent,[417] Borromeo insisted on reserving the absolution of grave sins to the higher office of bishops. His 'overstrained and contested disciplinary machine provoked a major crisis'[418] in the diocese, as the local population, priests and the civil government found the reserved cases too many and the penances too severe and disproportionate to the sins committed. Mazzarino was among those who opposed Borromeo's policies of 'zero tolerance'. He claimed that this course of action threw 'penitents into desperation, confessors into confusion, and the city into scandal'.[419] Criticizing the excessive power of Borromeo and ridiculing his religious radicalism in 1579, Mazzarino spoke of 'the very serious damage to souls from an unscrupulous use of reserved cases', with confessors unable to confess for the reason of so many reserved cases that had been published there [in Milan]'.[420] Echoing Mazzarino, Milan's ambassadors to Rome also complained, basing their opinions on 'holy doctors', and arguing when 'discipline is not accompanied by mercy, or rigor by clemency'[421] the best intended moral policies simply do not work.

Besides confession and communion, the chancellor's influence is apparent in at least two other areas of Jesuit pastoral theology: catechization and care for the sick and dying. Both matters found fulfillment in 'the second apostle of Germany', Dutch Jesuit Peter Canisius (1521–1597), 'indisputably a giant among the many giants of the early Society of Jesus',[422] whom Protestants feared and called, among other insults, *papstesel* and 'dog of a monk'.[423] Canisius, a passionate pastor, who made education-related activities his priority, founded several Jesuit colleges and 'managed to create a true and proper network of Jesuit communities work-

---

[416] Terricabras 2018, 2, p. 235.
[417] Terricabras 2018, 2, p. 247.
[418] de Boer 2000, p. 129.
[419] Rurale 1992, p. 270, n. 97.
[420] Rurale 1992, p. 234.
[421] de Boer 2000, p. 131.
[422] Blake, Foreword to Pabel 2013, p. vi.
[423] Walsham 2017, p. 100.

ing for the Catholic Reconquista'.[424] Inspired by the pedagogical works of the French chancellor [425] who aimed to create catechisms for audiences of all states and ages,[426] Canisius produced a series of catechisms: the *Large (major) Catechism*, also called *Summary of Christian Doctrine*, in 1555, the *Tiny (minimus) Catechism*, in 1556, and *An Abridged (minor) Catechism*, planned for students in the middle grades, published in 1558. All three are sometimes combined and referred to as the *Triple Catechism*. In direct response to Martin Luther's tremendously popular catechisms, Canisius's books knew 347 editions in every corner of Europe, as well as in India, Ethiopia, China and Japan.[427] The 1561 edition of his *Catechism*, published in Augsbourg, closely follows the organization of Gerson's *Le doctrinal aux simples gens*, with sections and sub-sections being virtually the same. There are, however, some significant differences. Despite the fact that Canisius's *Catechismus* is considerably longer than either the Latin *Opus tripartitum* or the vernacular *Le doctrinal auz simples gens*, some sections, such as the one on the sacrament of marriage, are drastically reduced (to a couple of lines) compared to Gerson's in-depth treatment of this topic, while others, such as the section concerning the nature of sins, are greatly expanded. Although Canisius shared, like all Jesuits, Gerson's optimistic view of the possibility of cooperation between divine grace and human will — *Si Iesu Christi gratiae cooperemur*[428] — the emphasis on human sinfulness is stronger in the *Catechismus*. Compared to Gerson's rather easy approach to the satisfaction of sins,[429] Canisius sounds more demanding. In the section on penitence Gerson spoke of 'troys choses requises: c'est contrition, confession et satisfaction'.[430] Retaining the same threefold format Canisius, in contrast, makes

---

[424] Mostaccio 2014, p. 50.
[425] Blake, Foreword to Pabel 2013, p. vi.
[426] Pabel 2013, p. 17.
[427] Walsham 2017, p. 100.
[428] Canisisius 1561, no pagination.
[429] *Le doctrinal aux simples gens*, OC: 10, p. 317: 'Se tu es malade et en peril de mort et vray repentant, chascum prestre te doit et peut absoldre de tous tes péchés quelz qu'ils soient [...] Item, se tu n'avoies prestre pour le confesser et tu es vray repentant de tous tes péchez, et te confesseroies voulentiers se tu avoies prestre [...] il souffist a Dieu'.
[430] OC: 10, p. 314.

significant additions to the first and the third requirements: *contritio uel dolor animi peccata* (contrition and pain of the sinful soul) 3. *satisfactio seu uindicta punitioque* (satisfaction and vengeance and punishment)'.[431] In 1556 Canisius became the superior of the Upper German Province. In 1568 he inserted Gerson's *Ars moriendi* in a German edition of his *Small Catechism*, titled *Betbuch und Catechismus: Nach rechter Catholischer Form und Weyß*. The section on the art of dying, *Gebett, Underweisung und Fragstuck für sehr krancke und sterbende Menschen*, closely follows *Opus'* structure and objectives, including questions, exhortations and Gerson's method of addressing the needs of not only the gravely ill, but also of those who accompany them.[432] Just as for Gerson, Canisius's ministry to the dying was not just a clerical professional obligation, but a duty of friendship, shared by all.[433] Besides his contributions to education, Canisius distinguished himself as a Catholic historian. Asked by Pope Pius V to refute Mathias Flacius's *Magdeburg Centuries*, which took Catholics by surprise, Canisius attempted a Catholic historiography in his astonishingly erudite *Commentarii de uerbi Dei corruptelis*. Besides its focus on early Christianity, the book exhibits a strong 'German flavor' and includes hagiographical accounts of predominantly German and German Swiss saints. Among the few non-German exceptions, the chancellor Gerson once again came in for praise, just as it was the case in Johannes Trithemius' fifteenth century *Catalogus illustrium uirorum Germaniae*.[434]

Gerson's contribution to jurisprudence, deepened by Summenhart and forged with Medina's probabilistic approach, was further adopted, extended, and refined by the Jesuits Luis de Molina (1535–1600) and Francisco Suarez (1548–1617).[435] Molina, a Salamanca alumnus and Thomist professor of moral theology at the University of Madrid, was a famous author of philo-

---

[431] Canisisus 1561.
[432] Pabel 2013, p. 6.
[433] Pabel 2013, pp. 6–7.
[434] Janssen 1909, p. 368.
[435] 'The Spanish Dominicans of this period raised issues that were to be further discussed and elaborated by their Jesuit successors, Luis de Molina and Suarez, and, in the Italy of the Counter-Reformation, by Bellarmine' (Burns 1991, p. 155).

sophical-theological doctrine of the 'middle knowledge', a middle ground between God's prescience and human free will. He turned to Gerson's ideas on the nature of rights in his books *Concordia* (1588) and *De Iustitia et Iure* (1592).[436] Like Gerson, he considered *ius* in terms of dispositional power of its possessor, as *facultas* of 'the person who has it to the thing to which the person has such power'.[437] Although Molina's views could be considered as 'a revival of Gersonian rights theory',[438] and the definition of human *dominium* and *ius*, as they are presented in *De uita spirituali animae*, was one of the points of departure for Molina,[439] the Jesuit theologian was also critical of the chancellor's take on the subject. Molina rejected Gerson's account of *dominium* as unduly broadened to non-humans, such as, for example, the horse's right over the grass it eats or the sun's right to shine.[440] For Molina *dominium* is a human institution only, bound to the ability to argue and give reasons. The concept of *dominium*, which gradually gained in importance relative to the term *ius*,[441] expresses claims within the limits of natural or positive laws, if those claims do not contradict them. As a human institution, *dominia* may have various forms such as property (*dominium proprietatis*) and political power (*dominium iurisdictionis*).[442]

Another Salamanca alumnus, a highly influential philosopher and theologian, Francisco Suarez, 'firmly allied himself with those like Gerson and Molina, who analyzed a right as a facultas'.[443] He referred to Gerson's *De uita spirituali animae* in his *Treatise on Laws and God the Lawgiver*, known as *De legibus*, 'listing specific chapters where Gerson discussed the meaning of *ius*.[444] Although Suarez called Gerson's definition of natural law 'more comprehen-

---

[436] See Eisenberg 1998.

[437] *[...] faculatas [...] quam habitudinem, seu relationem personae, a quo habent, ad id quod est talis facultas* (Tuck 1979, p. 53).

[438] Tuck 1979, p. 54.

[439] Tellkamp 2013, pp. 128–29.

[440] Tellkamp 2013, p. 149.

[441] Schüssler 2014, p. 257.

[442] Tellkamp 2013, pp. 141–42, citing Luis de Molina, *De iustitia et iure*, 1, II, 3, col. 31D.

[443] Tuck 1979, p. 55.

[444] Tierney 1997, p. 54. On Suarez and the School of Salamanca see Skinner 1978, 2, pp. 135–73.

sive than necessary',[445] he endorsed the latter's idea of a natural right or *dominium* as 'a moral power that anyone had concerning his own property'.[446] He also endorsed the understanding of *ius* as the human ability to act according to reason, including exercising a choice in performing some actions or refraining from others 'in the attainment of their natural end'.[447] Suárez also appears to be the first notable sixteenth century theologian to have imagined the return to a more rigorist interpretation of 'safety first rule' compared to Gerson's. However, he did not seek to apply his reading in practice.[448] Leonardus Lessius (1554–1623), a professor of moral theology at the Jesuit College of Leuven, entered the Society of Jesus in 1572 and is best known for his fundamental work *On Justice and Right*, where 'the casuistry of the legal and moral tradition is ordered within a systematic whole'.[449] For the exercises in practical ethics and casuistry, which he considered to be the hallmark of the Jesuit order, Lessius made use of *Enchiridion confessariorum et poenitentium* (*Handbook of confessors and penitents*) by the aforementioned Martin de Azpilcueta (1491–1586), commonly known as Doctor Navarrus.[450] Azpilcueta's book was partly based on Gerson's ideas transmitted through Antoninus of Florence.[451] Although Lessius was intimately familiar with Gerson's writings, he strongly disagreed with the chancellor's take on contractual law.[452]

Gerson remained a solid authority figure for the Society of Jesus with his name among the most respected.[453] Several elements of his theology, although greatly modified both quantitatively and qualitatively — the fusion of active and contemplative lives,

---

[445] Brown 1964, p. 191.
[446] Mäkinen 2006, p. 71.
[447] Brown 1964, p. 191.
[448] Schüssler 2019.
[449] Decock 2012, p. 63.
[450] Decock 2012, p. 62. Navarrus did not directly quote Gerson, but the whole section of the text closely followed Antoninus of Florence's discussion, and Gerson is mentioned as a source in other respects.
[451] See chapter 1.
[452] See Decock 2007; Decock, 2012.
[453] O'Malley 1993, p. 358: 'Among the titles recommended to be read at meals were, besides Fathers of the Church and *Imitatatio*, St Bernard, St Bonaventure and Gerson'.

relationality, educational program, catechization, more frequent and more conscientious confessions, psychological nuancing and judicial influence — remained distinctive features of Jesuit spirituality.[454] In 1616, the Jesuit list of books recommended for spiritual reading included the works of Chancellor Gerson.[455] The only occasions when Gerson's name was 'not invoked with reverence'[456] by the Jesuits were all related to the issue of conciliarism, to which the Society of Jesus, dedicated to Rome, naturally had an aversion.

Part VI. The Council of Trent

Gerson's name was not explicitly quoted during the Council of Trent (1545–1563).[457] Yet, just as justifiably as Marcel Bataillon could use the term 'Erasmism' in relation to Erasmus's presence in Spain's evangelical and humanist movement of *illuminati*, one could talk about 'Gersonism' in relation to the Gerson-inspired reform agenda adopted at Trent. In fact, regarding the reception of Gerson at the Council, it makes sense to view Trent as the culmination of previous reform efforts not only in France but in Europe in general. In relation to France, one can distinguish between two closely related reform movements: one that took place before the Council of Trent and was native to Gerson's homeland, and the other, which was established by the Council of Trent and elaborated by Carlo Borromeo.[458] The second, centralized, formalized and imported, profited from and was prepared by the 'native' and 'Gerson-inspired fluid response',[459] with its 'hopes for renewal' 'reposed less in the efforts of pope and curia

---

[454] 'Although Aquinas enjoyed a position of hegemony in the Jesuits' studies, they were also prepared to consider (under the wishes of their founder) the adoption of a guide 'more appropriate to our time'; this intellectual openness, combined with with their determination to clarify the difference between Protestant and Catholic, led them naturally to consider the possibilities represented by Louvain and therefore ultimately by Gerson' (Tuck 1979, p. 52).

[455] Guibert 1964, p. 217, n. 86.

[456] O'Malley 1993, p. 292.

[457] Based on Jedin's and O'Malley's accounts of the Council of Trent.

[458] Hayden & Greenshields 2005, p. 180.

[459] Hayden & Greenshields 2005, p. 180.

than in those of bishops and local pastors'.[460] Thus, the French Council of Sens, which gathered in 1528 'with the twofold aim of combating heresy and reforming the church',[461] suggested that priests prepare their instructions for the laity based on *Opus tripartitum* or, when they are incapable of it, at least read directly from this text to their parish audience.[462]

However, even though it is largely true that in the later sixteenth century Gerson's *bonus pastor* ideal was more widely implemented in France because of the exceptional institutional support there,[463] it was 'an astonishingly stable concept' in the whole Empire of Charles Quint, and it was taken over by German humanists 'without any substantial alternations'.[464] Thus, *Vita Bennonis*, by the aforementioned Saxon anti-Lutheran theologian Hieronymus Emser, 'was inspired by Upper Rhenish humanists drawing on Jean Gerson's ideas of an ideal bishop'.[465] In Spain, bishop Francisco Jimenes de Cisneros (1436–1517) applied Gerson's ideas concerning duties of prelates in the early sixteenth century.

The Gersonian connection was also manifest at the Council of Trent itself, even before the arrival of the French delegation there. His image of *de officio pastoris* became the foundation on which the Council of Trent constructed its picture of the episcopal office, with its most important elements of residence in the diocese, personal involvement in pastoral care, preaching and the holding of diocesan synods, theological instruction and visitation as forms of supervision and guidance of the parish clergy.[466] Articulating the role of a bishop as *cura animarum*, the chancellor drew up a list of a bishop's concrete duties, according to which a bishop should also test candidates for pastoral benefits personally, hold

---

[460] Oakley 2006, p. 189.
[461] O'Malley 2013, p. 65.
[462] Jean-Claude Dhotel cites the resolution of Concile de Sens: 'Avec ce manuel, les évêques entendaient faciliter la tâche des curés: soit pouvoir préparer leurs prônes à partir des éléments du premier traité, soit 's'ils n'en sont pas capables, de lire un chapitre de l'*Opus tripartitum* au moment du prone' (Dhotel 1967, p. 29).
[463] Oakley 2006, p. 90 & p. 98.
[464] Volkmar 2018, p. 219.
[465] Volkmar 2018, p. 446.
[466] Volkmar 2018, p. 219.

frequent synods, make sure that the people knew the basic articles of faith and provide priests with texts enabling them to perform their duties effectively. These recommendations, borrowed from *Nova epistola pro instructione episcoporum et prelatorum*, were presented during the last period of the Council as part of thirty-four articles of the French program of reform, and became subjects of intense debate at Trent.[467] After much controversy, these proposals made their way in the Council's final decrees, thrusting the Gerson-inspired reform program into one of the major impetuses for Trent. The chancellor's efforts paved the way for Trent's success in reforming the office of the bishop, bringing him back to his essential duties of preaching and living amongst his flock'.[468]

Other major Trent decisions signaled both continuity and discontinuity with Gerson's pastoral legacy. On the one hand, the emphasis on the secrecy of confession in the *Catechismus Romanus*, and the invention of the confessional, introduced by Carlo Borromeo and widely adopted after the council of Trent, correspond to the chancellor's priorities, as he repeatedly expressed his wish for a higher degree of privacy in confessional matters. On the other hand, 'despite numerous appeals to the therapeutic function of the confessor's role and recourses to medical terminology and images in the documents of the Council of Trent itself',[469] the balance between the two functions was definitely lost. 'The emphasis was placed [...] on the judicial function of the priest at the expense of the therapeutic one',[470] which clearly goes against Gerson's vision of *bonus pastor*. In some regards Trent resolutions even went back in time, as the Council rejected the formulation of the Lateran Council that decreed that the confessor 'shall be discerning and prudent [...] carefully inquire about the circumstances of both the sinner and the sin [...] not to betray the sinner

---

[467] Forrestal 2004, p. 24.

[468] François & Soen 2018, p. 10.

[469] Popelyastyy 2018, p. 215: 'Nevertheless, it is obvious that in both the Tridentine and post-Tridentine period the emphasis on the judicial function of the confessor has remained dominant in the Latin Church, in spite of numerous appeals to the therapeutic function of the confessor's role and recourses to medical terminology and images in the documents of the Council of Trent itself, as well as the endeavors of the *Catechismus Romanus* and the *Rituele Romanum*, to restore the lost balance'.

[470] François & Soen 2018, p. 10.

at all by word or sign or in any other way',[471] 'because of a lack of well-educated priests with high spiritual and moral standards'.[472]

Even though not all of Gerson's pastoral innovations found continuity in Trent's final outcome, they were not lost. The great Council itself provided a forum for them, making his voice reverberate throughout Catholic Europe. It was heard. The aforementioned *Directory for Confessors* reflects what its author, Alfonso Polanco, who was present at the Council, learned there. Thus, concerning pastoral duties, he wrote that 'a bishop cannot leave his flock if he knows that the salvation of his subjects requires the presence of the Pastor'.[473] Republished in 1619 and widely distributed on the Iberian Peninsula, Polanco's manual contributed to 'Gersonian pattern of influence',[474] which eventually led not only to the net increase in pastoral visits but to the 'interest in teaching and social services in the years immediately following the Council'.[475] Also, Jesuit confessional practice fully 'inherited a benevolent medieval tradition that described the confessor as a physician, and the sacrament as a font of encouragement, consolation and healing'.[476]

Gerson's theological views also met a mixed reception at the Council. The core of his spirituality, the theological middle way, clearly prevailed, as the Council of Trent 'steered a middle course between Pelagianism on the one hand and on a determinist form of predestination on the other, affirming the absolute initiative of God as well as the role of man's free will'.[477] According to the official policy spelled out in Trent's decrees, salvation is found à mi-chemin between God's grace bestowed by the Holy Spirit and human's move toward God:

> Although God touches a person's heart through the light of the Holy Spirit, neither does that person do absolutely

---

[471] Popelyastyy 2018, p. 212.
[472] Popelyastyy 2018, pp. 212–13.
[473] Polanco 1608, p. 57.
[474] Hayden & Greenshields 2005, p. 89.
[475] Hayden & Greenshields 2005, p. 89.
[476] Fleming 2006, p. 3.
[477] Bireley 2018, 1, p. 44.

nothing in receiving that movement of grace, for he can also reject it, nor is he able by his free will and without God's grace to move toward justice in God's sight. Hence, when Scripture says, 'Return to me and I will return to you', we are being reminded of our freedom, when we answer 'Restore us to yourself, O, Lord, that we may be restored', we are admitting that we are forestalled by the grace of God.[478]

Although 'the representation of a virile Joseph able to support and defend his family'[479] is currently associated with Pope Gregory XV's promulgation of Joseph's feast in 1621, the prior incorporation of Joseph's feast into the Roman calendar by Sixtus IV's and the relevant proceedings of the Council of Trent were made possible by Gerson's assiduous promotion of his cult more than a century earlier. In this respect Trent also presented another pattern of continuity with the chancellor's legacy. His promotion of Mary's immaculate conception was not retained by the Council that left this matter unresolved. An extended inquiry into Trent's decrees is likely to identify other traces of Gerson's influence.

Some rather exotic elements of Gerson's influence surfaced soon after the Council. They concern its aesthetic reform and ecclesiastical supervision of the arts. Trent's initially rather vague recommendations concerning artistic expressions 'furnishing occasion of dangerous error to the uneducated',[480] soon led to increasing preoccupation with the issue of propriety among Catholic authorities. The same Carlo Borromeo was at pains removing all traces of nudity in his diocese,[481] while the prior mentioned Antonio Possevinus, in his book *De Poesi et Pictura*, professed that art should be 'not merely chaste, but decent and dignified'.[482] Flemish theologian Johannes Molanus (1533–1585) labored in a similar vein, providing concrete artistic

---

[478] Tanner 1990, 2, p. 672.

[479] Boffa 2016.

[480] 'If any abuses have crept in amongst these holy and salutary observances, the holy Synod ardently desires that they be utterly abolished; in such wise that no images, (suggestive) of false doctrine, and furnishing occasion of dangerous error to the uneducated, be set up' (Waterworth 1848).

[481] Taveneaux 1980, p. 449.

[482] Janelle 2007, p. 165.

recommendations in his *Historia Sanctorum Imaginum et Pecturarum*, where he urged artists to maintain the general simplicity of clothes and surroundings in their paintings and forbade all depiction of nudity, including babies, with drapes completely covering the genitals. Molanus did not limit himself to the directive stating that all *Nouitas omnis diligenter est examinanda in picturis antequam approbetur*.[483] He also took upon himself the task of censoring the inappropriate images of old, that 'have elicited disapproval of learned men because they have no origin in the scripture and because our holy fathers did not know them'.[484] Under the 'learned men' he meant none other than Jean Gerson, whose opinion Molanus highly valued and whom he explicitly cited as his trusted authority. Stressing the far higher impact of an image on the imagination as compared to the word, Molanus, in his *De Picturis et Imaginibus Sacris*, defined an inappropriate image by quoting the chancellor nearly verbatim: 'In my opinion such an object has neither beauty nor pious sentiment and can be a cause of error and lack of devotion'.[485] Under inappropriate images Gerson and Molanus meant the type of representation of the Virgin Mary commonly known as 'vierge ouvrante', in whose wooden 'belly' were 'placed' not only baby Jesus but sometimes 'both adult and child images of Christ, as well as God the Father, the Holy Spirit often represented as a dove, and sometimes even the entire hell as vanquished by the Son of the Virgin'.[486] Following the Council of Trent's and, in this particular case, Gerson's wishes, Molanus 'had special reprehension reserved for the Trinity misrepresented as a tricephalic monster and as the Godhead enfleshed within the Virgin's body'.[487] He preferred images with 'la bienheureuse Vierge Marie peinte à genoux mains jointes devant son fils rayonnant déjà de lumière', and the baby Jesus represented 'avec décence et honnêteté'.[488] Molanus's injunctions against improper 'vierges ouvrantes' were

---

[483] Freedberg 1971, p. 235. 'novelty should be carefully examined in all the pictures before being approved'. For more details see Fabre 2013.
[484] Gertsman 2015, p. 2.
[485] Gertsman 2015, p. 3.
[486] Gertsman 2015, p. 2.
[487] Gertsman 2015.
[488] Fabre 2013, p. xv.

widely and strictly enforced in Catholic countries, leading to the 1745 official censure and banning of the Trinitarian version of the statues by Pope Benedict XIV in his *Sanctissimi Domini Nostri Benedicti Papae XIV Bullarium*.[489]

Conclusion

Gerson had a significant and profound, albeit geographically and thematically uneven, impact on early modern Catholicism. A rather fragmented panorama of his reception in the German-speaking world mirrors the general disorientation of the first 'after-shock' reaction characteristic of German Catholic theologians of Luther's generation. The world they knew crumbled around them under blows from within, struck by their own kind — their colleagues, mentors, pupils and friends — with whom only yesterday they constituted one guild. Gerson was not only part of this guild. He was also its recognized master. As such, he was an anchor of stability amidst the chaos that ensued following Luther's conflict with Rome, and a familiar father figure to whom his spiritual children could turn in their distress. For the first responders to Luther's crisis in the Empire, the chancellor's legacy represented secure ground on which they could build their defenses, and be certain that their Protestant opponents, raised within the same tradition, would recognize his authority. In the world of rapidly changing references, the late medieval theologian became the reference par excellence.

As the initial shock began to die down, however, these theologians began to think about strategies that could be used to confront the reality of the conflict. This realization led to a more calculated and specific interest in Gerson, as, for example, in the case of Cochlaeus's intentional effort to recover and re-appropriate the French theologian's authority from Lutheran rivals. Adam Walasser took this re-appropriation to a different level by recycling the Lutheran reworking of Gerson for Catholic use. By doing so, he possibly launched the tendency of mutual borrowing and manipulation between Protestants and Catholics, which would become commonplace in the later sixteenth and seven-

---

[489] Gertsman 2015, p. 4.

teenth centuries. Finally, theologians such as Johann Staupitz and Jacobus Latomus came into a deep contact with Gerson's thought in an effort to produce a systematic theological response aimed at repudiating major points of Lutheran doctrine. From this point one can surely speak of the Counter-Reformation, since efforts of all the above-mentioned theologians were directed against the spread of what they perceived as a new and deadly heresy. Thus, the new oath for all prospective priests in the diocese of Constance, composed by Johann Fabri in 1523, leaves no doubt that Catholic orthodoxy was to be understood as a belief system specifically built against Protestant doctrines, which a good Catholic priest ought to 'wish malice and intend to resist them [...] in no way shield those who hold to, dispute, protect, preach or take up either secretly or publicly [...] their teachings, that are erroneous and devoid of love'.[490]

In relation to France, however, it is more appropriate to speak of a Catholic Reformation, which began with implementing the Gerson-inspired reform program as early as the late fifteenth century, and continued until it blended with the post-Tridentine reform efforts. The reliance of high clergy on Gerson's pastoral legacy was more systematic and consequential in France, resulting in concrete and effective measures, which greatly facilitated the implementation of Trent's resolutions there. While Gerson's pastoral theology was generally the most important component of his *postérité* in France, his mystical humanism and novel approaches to contemplation found a good reception at the Meaux Cenacle, whose members were interested in the introspective side of his spirituality. When, suspected of Lutheran sympathies, Meaux scholars found themselves in conflict with the Sorbonne, the differences between the opposing parties partly revolved around their interpretation of Gerson's legacy. The situation is best illustrated by a small fragment of the polemical poem *The Farce des Theologastres* by Louis de Berquin, who was executed for heresy. In the poem the character of Faith disputes Gerson's name with the character of Theologian (likely a caricature of Noël Béda) who disavows Gerson for his conciliarist sympathies.

---

[490] Oberman 1981, p. 243.

FAITH
Point ne veux de leurs ergotis
Bien me bailleroit guerison
Le textuaire Jehan Gerson
Car il me fault c'est ma nature
Le texte de saincte escriture

THEOLOGASTES
Maistre Jehan Gerson nares ia
Car cest ung malvais papaliste
Sa doctrine plus ne consiste
Sur les apostres de Sorbonne.[491]

Gerson's thought, simultaneously conservative and innovative, was just as contradictory, complex, and rich as the Parisian theological tradition, to which all the protagonists of this controversy, including the chancellor himself, used to belong. This tradition, even though the concept of tradition might have meant different things for people such as Guillaume and Denis Briçonnet, Clichtove, Lefèvre d'Etaples or Noël Béda, was able, precisely because of its broadness and heterogeneity, to accommodate them all, however loosely. The final and irreversible split brought about by the Reformation would put an end to this tradition for good.[492]

The reception of Gerson in Spain was the most significant, and, like that in England, had a particularly legalistic coloring. As a hypothesis of why this aspect of Gerson's legacy was much stronger in these two locations, one can suppose that the establishment of absolute monarchies in Spain and in England was a factor, as it produced new demands on jurisprudence summoned to justify the interests of early modern power players. In Spain the

---

[491] Berquin 1830, p. 11.
FAITH:
I want nothing of their *ergos*.
The textual scholar John Gerson would cure me better.
For I must — it is my nature —
Have the text of sacred Scripture
Without *ergo*, without *quod*, without *ne*, without *quia*.
THEOLOGIAN:
You will never have Master John Gerson
For he is a bad papalist.
His teaching no longer agrees with the apostles of the Sorbonne (Garside 1974, p. 59).

[492] Smolinsky 2005, p. 80.

conquest of the Indies led to the expansion of Gerson's legacy into colonial matters. Both his take on 'the duality between divine and human laws' and his theory of rights had a fundamental impact on the debate concerning the status of colonized people. In the context of the School of Salamanca his contribution to the new rationalistic approach to ethics, later simply referred to as probabilism, is of particular importance for, 'since probabilism is an ancestor of modern moral philosophy, the problems it creates cannot be easily shrugged off'.[493] His notion of 'probable certainty',[494] which provided a means for a safe conscience on the basis of a relatively satisfactory and not too burdensome process of opinion formation, had an extraordinary posterity in Spain. 'The minimalistic approach to morality, closely related to the notoriously complex debates on decision-making in a context of uncertainty, flourished in early modern scholasticism'.[495] Thinkers such as Vitoria, Soto, Medina and Suarez all argued, although with considerable differences of opinion between them, that meticulous deliberation of conscience should, in all probability, lead one to choose the safest among all reasonably sustainable opinions.[496]

All three of Gerson's main contributions to Jesuit thought — psychological insights, pastoral innovations in pedagogical and confessional matters, and proto-probabilism — had a decisive impact on the formation of casuistry or the detailed consideration of individual 'cases of conscience'.[497] Applied by Jesuits, who

[493] Schüssler 2013, p. 105.
[494] Maryks 2008, p. 67.
[495] Decock 2012, p. 74.
[496] Maryks 2008, p. 115. See also Dhotel 1967, p. 115 & p. 117. Blic 1930, p. 281: 'The majority of authors of following generations continued to rely on his way of thinking'.
[497] Franciscan moralist and canonist Antonio de Córdoba (1485–1578) wrote *Treaty of Conscience Cases* (*Summa de casas de consciencia*), which had at least nineteen editions in Spanish, some quite expanded, and two in Italian, and was published from 1561 to 1592, sometimes twice a year. In his other work, *De indulgentiis tractatus*, published in Ingolstadt by Wolfgang Eder (active 1578–98), Cordoba repeatedly referred to Gerson as a leading authority on this issue. Although Antonio de Cordoba, follower of Vitoria, student of Juan de Medina, opponent of Domingo de Soto, confessor of Emperor Charles V and a professor in Leuven, was a man of great talent and prestige, whose opinions were taken into account well into the eighteenth century, he is all but forgotten, with little to no research devoted to him, let alone to his possible connection to Gerson (del Campo 2005, p. 10) See Barbagallo 2014.

'would become the fiercest advocates of moral probabilism'[498] to all practical needs of Christian Catholic life and worship, casuistry would end up being equally responsible for their immense success as confessors, educators and advisers, and for their sharp downfall as presumably morally lax, corrupt and opportunistic. Probabilistic casuistry became both a solution and a problem, and it posed a challenge to the very spirit of Christianity, as religious rigorists and purists could not eventually fail to realize. As the great mathematician and Jansenist Blaise Pascal famously said during his mostly unfair attack on the Jesuits in the seventeenth century: 'je ne me contente pas du probable, je cherche le seur'.

The reception of Gerson at Trent, although indirect, was substantial in shaping church policies and in implementing them during and after the Council. While the papacy, gravely challenged from all sides, could not afford a display of internal descent, and gave a cold shoulder to the chancellor because of his conciliarist reputation, many Catholic leaders, and especially the Jesuits, continued to rely on his insights in matters ranging from social welfare, such as care for the sick, to human rights, education and even aesthetics. His role in Catholic catechization was the most significant, and it would not be forgotten until at least the end of the sixteenth century. The famous papal envoy, controversialist, encyclopedist and bibliographer, Jesuit Antonio Possevino, intended to establish children's education according to Gerson's model found in *Opus tripartitum*.[499] The selection of books found in 1592 at the home of the Carpentras bishop Giacomo Sacrati (?1572–1593) is certainly representative of the chancellor's popularity at the time, as it contains the Bible, some writings of the Church Fathers, Ludolphe le Chartreux and Gerson.[500] Similarly, his impact would be found not only in the recommendations of the Council of Trent, but also, among others, in François de Sales[501] and in *Rituale Romanum* of 1614.[502]

Concerning Catholic historiography, which began to emerge after the Council of Trent, it is relatively clear that Catholics did

---

[498] Decock 2012, p. 75.
[499] Dhotel 1967, p. 115 & p. 117.
[500] Venard 1996, p. 881.
[501] Delumeau 1983, pp. 86–87, citing de Sales 1928, 23, p. 288.
[502] Delumeau 1983, p. 86.

not put, at least initially, nearly as much emphasis on historiography as their religious opponents did. Thus, despite his fondness for the chancellor and his willingness to reintegrate his legacy into the Catholic discourse, Cochlaeus only briefly mentioned the chancellor in his 1549 *Historiae Hussitarum*.[503] There might be at least three identifiable reasons for this situation. First, under the attacks of their adversaries, Catholic polemicists at first adopted a rather reserved attitude, losing initiative to Protestants immediately after the Lutheran eruption. Second, the Roman Catholic counterattack on Flacius's creations, *Catalogus testium ueritatis* and *Magdeburg Centuries*, was made difficult by the fact that among the 'witnesses' of the Lutheran cause listed in these works were many orthodox Catholic authorities and even some popes. Third, Catholic polemists needed another new and different strategy, but it could only be developed in accordance with the resolutions of the General Council, which took years to emerge, and then dragged on for almost twenty years. Yet, even after the Council a fervent supporter of the papacy in France and professor of theology at the Collège Royal, Gilbert Génébrard (1537–1597), devoted very little space to both Hus and Gerson in his 1581 *Chronography*. Gerson is cited in one sentence in relation to the Council of Constance.[504] Cesare Baronius (1538–1607), who finally came up with an official answer of the Catholic post-tridentine Church to Flacius's historiographical endeavor, does not mention the chancellor in his *Annales ecclesiastici a Christo nato ad annum 1198*, first published between 1588 and 1607, since it covers only a history of the first twelve centuries of the Christian Church. It seems clear that 'Gerson's indifference to the canonical tradition of papal plenitude of power made him a *bête-noire* for later advocates of papal infallibility',[505] and the Vatican hardly could have a vested interest in incorporating or bringing positive attention to the name of a theologian so closely associated, in the minds of many of its subjects, with an anti-papal agenda.

---

[503] Haberkern 2016, p. 240.

[504] Génébrard 1581, p. 1044 & p. 1058, respectively. John Wycliffe, Wycliffe also spelled Wycliff, Wyclif, Wicliffe, or Wiclif.

[505] McGuire 2005, p. 55.

CHAPTER 4

THE RECEPTION OF GERSON IN ENGLAND AND SCOTLAND

Introduction

'The prosecutor had the name of Conscience, for there is nothing she does not know or does not report'.

Jean Gerson[1]

There is no doubt about Gerson's lasting intellectual presence in 16th century England. In fact, his prestige there was so great that Thomas More's scholar Gary E. Haupt spoke of his cult.[2] By 1521 there were five collected editions of Gerson's works available in England,[3] with his name and reputation recognized as an accepted part of the English intellectual pantheon. This situation stands in contrast to his reception during the 15th century, when he does not appear to have made much of an impact. The lack of enthusiasm for Gerson in 15th century England may be explained by his active patriotic stance during the Hundred Years' War (1337–1453), the era's largest conflict, and his proven support for Joan of Arc.[4] He was, after all, a sworn enemy of England, whom Anglo-Burgundians would have executed had they had a chance. By the 16th century the resentment against him must have gradually dissipated because of time and different political and ideological concerns. However, while it is reasonable to note the paucity

---

[1] *Treatise against 'The Romance of the Rose'*, McGuire 1998, p. 378.
[2] Haupt 1976, p. xlv.
[3] Hobbins 2006, pp. 213–16.
[4] See Hobbins 2005, pp. 99–155.

of sources indicating Gerson's early reception in England, it would be inaccurate to presume the complete absence thereof. Thus, while his *Opus tripartitum* was translated into English in 1450,[5] English works written in direct imitation of Gerson's texts appeared much earlier, within years after the Council of Constance.[6] Separate English editions of his *Ars moriendi* circulated in the 1490s,[7] while his other writings continued to appear in collective editions.[8] His name was also kept in circulation as *De Imitatione Christi* continued to be credited to him throughout the 15th and 16th centuries — an erroneous attribution which in itself 'is a measure of his lasting influence'.[9]

Gerson's later return to popularity in England can be linked to two major factors. First, it seems to correspond to the renewed interest in his works in his homeland and the publishing activity of the emerging French presses, which supplied the bulk of the English book market in the late 1520s and early 1530s.[10] Second, England's acute political and later religious crises, following King Henry VIII's conflict with Pope Clement VII over his request to divorce Catherine of Aragon in 1527, rekindled attention to this renowned thinker of the previous century. Another circumstance is political in nature and has to do with the English legation's interest in conciliarist theory as well as in individual conciliarists,[11] among whom Gerson was considered to be the most famous and respected. Thus, a member of the English conciliarist group, political theorist Thomas Starkey (*c.* 1495–1538),[12] who stayed in France between 1528 and 1530 studying law, based his concept of the ecclesiastical constitution on Gerson's ideas.[13] Another member of the same group, the last Roman Catholic Archbishop

---

[5] Comper 1977, p. 7.
[6] Appleford 2015, p. 164.
[7] Rudolf 1957, p. 70. This edition is listed in Duff 1896, p. 38.
[8] Sayle 1900.
[9] Rodgers 2011, p. 243.
[10] Duffy 1992, p. 229.
[11] Mayer 2002, p. 79.
[12] Mayer 1988.
[13] Mayer 2002, p. 79: 'Gerson's view on ecclesiastical constitution was identical to Starkey's'. Considering that it was Starkey who studied Gerson, it must have been the other way around.

of Canterbury and papal legate at the Council of Trent, Reginald Pole (1500–1558), was equally interested in Gerson's conciliarist theory and had the first volume of Gerson's *Opera Omnia* in his library.[14] Cardinal Thomas Wolsey (1473–1530), who failed to negotiate Henry VIII's divorce and was subsequently accused of treason, was also at some point attracted to Gerson's ideas, popularized by a College de Navarre's alumnus and Sorbonne professor, the aforementioned Scottish theologian and logician John Mair (1467–1550). Mair's conciliarism was the reason why Wolsey tried to lure him back to Oxford in 1525.[15] Even John Foxe's Protestant martyrology *The Acts and Monuments* inadvertently brought Gerson's conciliarist theory to attention, leading to the familiarity with his writings by people like the chaplain of King James I, the Anglican theologian Mathew Sutcliffe (1550?–1629),[16] and, as will be shown further on, by King James I himself.

Gerson's overall legacy in England concerns three major areas: theology and pastoral care, legal matters, and the notion of conscience in ethics and literature. All three spheres culminated in Gerson's unparalleled influence on Thomas More, which will be examined separately. Gerson's impact in Scotland also constitutes its own subject. Accordingly, this chapter is organized into five sections. The first part examines Gerson's theological legacy. The second explores Gerson's Scottish connection. Gerson's paramount influence on Thomas More constitutes the third part, and the question of the chancellor's role in the development and implementation of the concept of equity in England is the focus of the fourth. The chapter concludes with a survey of the influence of Gerson's definition of *synderesis* on the notion of conscience in English literary and philosophical traditions.

---

[14] Mayer 2002, p. 79: 'When he died, Pole's library contained the first volume of the Parisian edition of Gerson's *Opera Omnia*, which included all his major conciliarist writing'.

[15] As was explained in the introduction, the conciliarist aspect of Gerson's legacy will not be addressed here.

[16] Francis Oakley remarks that Foxe 'devoted much attention and space to the histories of Constance [...] that '[G]iven the enduring popularity of his *Book of Martyrs* [...] it must have done more to draw attention to conciliarist ideas [...] than anything else since the royal flirtation with conciliarism in the 1530s' (Oakley 2015, p. 273).

Part I. Gerson's Theological Influence

The chancellor's theological input in England involves three main deeply interrelated areas: pastoral care (the art of confession and death preparation), moral and mystical theology, and scriptural literacy. His innovations in the first area fostered what Rudolf Schüssler calls the 'therapy of opinion',[17] and are dominated by two typically Gersonian concerns: certain flexibility toward the sinfulness of actions revealed at confessions, and a search for the solution of the problem of scrupulous conscience. Gerson's *Opus tripartitum*, also known as the book of three 'verities' or *The manner to live well*, published by the Parisian François Regnault, whose production dominated the market,[18] was almost as popular in England as in the rest of Europe. Besides *Opus*, Gerson's manual *On the Art of Hearing Confession* (*De arte audiendi confessiones*) remained the main model for the English clergy throughout the 16th century. It was often copied and imitated without giving him credit, while anonymous Middle English manuals for confessors all share, with only slight variations, basic characteristics of the chancellor's original work.[19] His approach was mimicked so widely that one detects an echo of his confessionary model even in the definition of what constitutes a full confession by Chaucer's character, the Parson:

> First shalt thou understand that Confession is true showing of sins to the priest [...] This is to say 'true', for he must confess himself of all the conditions that belong to his sin, insofar as he can. All must be said, and no thing excused nor hid nor concealed, and do not boast thee of thy good works. And furthermore, it is necessary to understand from whence that sins spring, and how they increase, and what they are.[20]

However, just as it was the case on the Continent, the 16th century attitude toward confessants hardened considerably compared to

---

[17] Schüssler 2011, p. 20.
[18] Duffy 1992, p. 229.
[19] Lochrie 2012, p. 38.
[20] Chaucer online, p. 320. *Le doctrinal aux simples gens*, OC: 10, p. 315: 'Et ne retiens rien a dire a ton escient pour dire a ung prestre car la confession ne vaudroit riens. Et ne te excuse pas, sicomme font aucuns nices gens'.

Gerson's primary intentions. Whereas he was trying to limit confession to the basic Ten Commandments and Seven Deadly Sins, mindful as he was not to cause anxiety in those too scrupulous of mind, subsequent English confessor manuals continuously expanded categories encompassed by a full confession, making it ever more fastidious.[21]

It was *Opus*' last part, known in English translation as *The Craft of Dying*, which was most broadly circulated in manuscript, and with the advent of printing, was given even wider currency, becoming a valued part of the tradition of death preparations.[22] William Caxton's 1490 translation, *The Art and craft to know well to die*, refers to the author of the original text as 'the famous doctor Johan Gerson, chancellor of Parys'.[23] Reprinted in 1540 and 1546 and praised for its didactic and devotional merits,[24] Gerson's *Ars moriendi* became the basis for an influential block-book, which circulated both in England and Continental Europe.[25] Even England's vacillations between Catholicism, the Anglican Church and Calvinist-inspired Protestantism did not affect the high esteem in which Catholics and various Protestants alike held Gerson's *Art of Dying*, a fact which reflects the complexity of evaluating his popularity among different confessions of the period. However, while earlier Catholic renditions of this work tended to accentuate its consolatory value, Protestant versions eventually evolved into a new category of pious literature.[26] Among the English Catholics *Opus* became a favorite companion in times of distress. Besides the already mentioned Archbishop of Canterbury Reginald Pole, another eminent Catholic to have found solace and fortitude in Gerson's treatise on the art of dying was John Fisher (1469–1535), the rebellious Bishop of Rochester and Thomas More's fellow prisoner in the Tower of London. Fisher, who, together with More, refused to recant his views and swear the obligatory Oath of Supremacy, had *Opus* with him during his

---

[21] Lochrie 2012, p. 39.
[22] Duffy 1992, p. 316.
[23] Rudolf 1957, p. 70.
[24] Duffy 1992, pp. 80–81. Also see Houlbrooke 2000; Atkinson 1992; O'Connor 1942; Beaty 1970.
[25] Rudolf 1957, p. 70.
[26] Ariès 1991, p. 303 & p. 304.

imprisonment in the Tower, where he composed his own Gerson-inspired variation of the *ars moridendi* entitled *A Spiritual Consolation ... Spoken in the Person of One That Was Sodainly Preunted by Death*.[27]

William Perkins, Christopher Sutton, Joseph Hall, Richard Baxter

During Elizabeth's rule, when England struggled to maintain a resemblance of peace between the Anglicans, the Roman Catholics and an increasing number of Calvinistic Protestant dissidents, Gerson's theological legacy continued to find favor with religious leaders of different denominations. Protestant or at least Protestant-leaning editions clearly constituted the majority of Gerson's English publications,[28] reflecting the confessional demographic of the contemporary reading public. Thus, among those who owned his works were John Conner, of Magdalen, Oxford (1569), Roger Charnock, of Corpus Christi, Oxford (1577) and Giles Dewhurst, of Christ Church, Oxford (1577), all Protestants.[29] Among Protestant authors with a keen interest in Gerson's pastoral theology was the father of English reformed casuistry William Perkins (1558–1602) — the 'key figure in the rally of Puritan forces that took place in the last decade of Elizabeth's reign, whose writings replaced those of Calvin and Beza at the top of the religious bestseller lists'.[30] A moderate Puritan, known as the 'doctor of conscience' thanks to his willingness and ability to

---

[27] Hatt 2002, p. 351. Catholic polemic writer Thomas Stapleton (1535–1598) mentions Gerson seventeen times in *Replica Ad Honri Flatum*, *Replica Ad Honri Flatum*, *De Principiis Fidei Doctrinalibus*, *Tres Thomae*, *Promptuarium Morale in Euangelia* and *Relectio Principiorum Fidei*. In the majority of cases Stapleton cites Gerson as a supporter of papal authority, which is ironic, considering that the chancellor was held responsible for the opposite position in France and in Italy.

[28] Atkinson 1992, p. xviii.

[29] Yamamoto-Wilson 2013. Protestant reformer at the time of the mid-Tudor dynasty, Thomas Becon or Beccon (1511–1567), who in 1561 authored an *ars moriendi* manual *The Sick Man's Salve*, was likely familiar with Gerson's writings, since his earlier work, *The Flower of Godly Prayers*, published in 1539, contains direct references to him. See Ayre 1844, p. 392 and Howarth & Leaman 2001, p. 31.

[30] Breward 1961, p. 9.

resolve cases of conscience with those who consulted him, Perkins was open to the possibility of learning from his medieval predecessors. He deferentially refers to the chancellor of Paris in his 1596 *Discourse of Conscience*, affirming that Catholics should have learned from 'their owne Doctor Gerson'.[31] Perkins, whose influence on the Puritans was paramount, was also among few pastors to have retained Gerson's emphasis on 'the vital function of the attendants'.[32] In his book *A Salve For A Sicke Man or a Treatise on Godliness in Sickness and Dying* (1595), which was the most influential art of dying manual in the Puritan tradition, Perkins insists upon the importance of the 'fellow members' or 'colleagues' who must 'partly of their counsel be put to help them [the dying], and partly by their prayers to present them to God, and to bring them to the presence of Christ'.[33] Also, unlike the majority of Protestant manuals on the art of dying, and very much like Gerson, Perkins argues that dying 'can become an occasion of great benefit to oneself and to those present'.[34]

Another English devotional writer to have followed Gerson's development of the role of *amicus* in death preparation was a moderate Anglican theologian Christopher Sutton (1565–1629). In his immensely popular *Disce Mori* or *Learn to Die*, constantly reprinted during 17th,[35] 18th and even 19th century, Sutton emphasizes the role of *amicus* in the following passage, strongly reminiscent of Gerson's *La médecine de l'ame*:

Gerson: Si les vrays amys d'ung malade font grant diligence envers luy pour sa vie et santé corporelle et faillable, Dieu et charité requièrent que ilz soient plus soigneux pour son salut et vie espirituelle et pardurable, car a ce dernier besoing voit on qui vray ami est.[36]

Suttun: [...] for if he may be called a friend, that is diligent about a sick person, to administer things necessary for his body, which shall shortly be dissolved, much more he is called a true and

---

[31] In Klinck 2010, p. 119, n. 70.
[32] Curbet 2015, p. 168.
[33] Curbet 2015, p. 168 citing Perkins 1595, pp. 58–59. Also see Vogt 2012.
[34] Keenan 1995 p. 116.
[35] Ollard 1919, p. 99. On Christopher Sutton see Douglass 2011, pp. 209–13.
[36] *La médecine de l'ame* OC: 7: 1, p. 404.

faithful friend [...] to minister things necessary for his soul, which shall never die, but live eternally.[37]

Sutton's affinity with Gerson warrants further investigation, as certain passages from *Disce Mori* are strongly reminiscent of *Opus tripartitum*.

Gerson: Item que on luy mette le moins qu'on porra au devant les amys charnels [...] fors en tant que [...] ne soit point baillé a icelluy tel malade trop grant esperance de revenir en sancte, mais soit dit comme est touché au commencement; car advient que par une telle faulse et vainne consolacion on fait tresbucher en certainne dampnation. On doit dire au malade que par soy mectre en estat envers Dieu et pour son ame, il n'en vauldra que mieulx pour le corps, et en sera plus seur et plus en paix.[38]

Sutton: Care is to be had that those who visit the sick give them hope, but not over great hope of bodily health for vain hopes offen deceive the sick, but let them be comforted in the name of God, but in discreet sort.[39]

Both Perkins and Sutton enhanced, rather than lessened, the role of attendants to the sick, compared to Gerson's original. Although Sutton's *Disce Mori* presents the priest as the main person to whom the care of the dying 'specially appertain',[40] his and Perkins's books are not exclusively addressed to ministers, but rather explicitly entreat lay helpers to sustain their loved ones in their most difficult moments.

Manuals by Perkins and Sutton also attest to a fascinating reappearance of the function of confession at the deathbed, which, from a strictly Protestant viewpoint, is completely at odds with the core of reformed doctrine. Yet, Sutton openly declares: 'Let him make a most sincere and humble confession of all his sins'.[41] Furthermore, while auricular confession had been officially abolished in the practice of the reformed church, its use had been preserved in the 'Order for the Visitation of the Sick' within the

---

[37] Sutton 1841, p. 215.
[38] *La médicine de l'ame*, OC: 7: 1, p. 404.
[39] Sutton 1841, p. 217.
[40] Sutton 1841, p. 214.
[41] Sutton 1841, p. 216.

Anglican *Book of Common Prayer*, which established the patterns that would be followed in the English *ars moriendi*.[42] The confessional function, now practiced without a salvific or any sacred value attributed to the priest, made a return more as a form of psychological and spiritual support for the dying given by a figure of authority or a communal leader. Concerned, like Gerson a century and a half before with the mental well-being of the faithful, Protestant ministers such as Perkins could not fail to recognize the vital necessity for 'the sick party, troubled in mind with the memory and consideration of any of his sins past [...] to receive comfort, and die in peace of conscience'.[43] Eventually confession, although modified on new terms, would become a resource within the framework of the Church of England. Finally, both manuals display the urgent need, which Gerson had rightly felt and tried to fulfill, for a structured protocol for those attending to the dying. This need was definitely recognized and put into practice by both Perkins and Sutton, who adopted Gersonian features such as the order of the preparation of the dying, lists of prayers and 'premeditated [prepared in advance] exhortations'.[44]

An inquiry into the reliance on Gerson of one of the great talents of the Elizabethan era, the philosopher, theologian, polemist and satirist, Anglican bishop Joseph Hall (1574–1656), requires a separate book. The majority of his works, including *Meditations and Vows* (1605), *Arte of Meditation* (1606) *The Peace-Maker* (1624), *Laying Forth the Right Way of Peace in Matters of Religion* (1624) and *The Old Religion* (1628), as well as many of his sermons, contain direct, acknowledged and meaningful references to Gerson as one of their main spiritual sources. Hall possessed a thorough and vast knowledge of the chancellor's writings, including, but far from limited to, *The Mountain of Contemplation, On Distinguishing True from False Revelations, De uita spirituali animae, De schismate et papatu*, as well as an astonishing

---

[42] Curbet 2015 p. 168.

[43] Perkins 1595, pp. 62–63, in Curbet 2015, p. 169. In an interesting twist of history, Curbet detects echoes of the *ars moriendi* tradition in the renewed role of confession in Shakespeare's plays *Measure for Measure* and even *Othello* (Curbet 2015).

[44] Sutton 1841, p. 216: 'A premeditated exhortation, after information taken of the disposition of the sick, is very beautiful'.

variety of sermons. Initially Hall returned to Gerson in his search for piety and mystical contemplation in 'direct conflict with the *Spiritual Exercises* of Ignatius, when fear and hatred of the Jesuits was at its height'.[45] Later, at the opening of the English Civil War (1642), he turned to Gerson with the hope of persuading ministers of God to become 'the counselors and ambassadors of peace'.[46] In the theory and practice of meditation, Hall was foreign to both 'the sectarian exclusiveness of radical Puritanism and the monastic exclusivity of the Roman Catholic tradition',[47] looking for a middle way of moderation:

> There is nothing therefore in the world more wholesome or more necessary for us to learn, than this gracious lesson of moderation [...] this is the centre wherein all both divine and moral philosophy meet; the rule of life; the governess of manners; the silken string that runs through the pearlchain of virtues [...][48]

Using the 1514 edition of Gerson's *Opera* in his most important devotional book *Arte of Meditation*, Hall refers to him by name over twenty times, directly acknowledging him as his source in the preface.[49] Describing circumstances conducive to successful meditation, Hall appears to follow Gerson's *Mountain of Contemplation*, as he advises to 'meet with those circumstances which are necessary for our predisposition to the work, place, time, site of the body'.[50] Considering his close knowledge of Gerson's works and his designation of the chancellor as one of his teachers of meditation[51] and 'a great master of contemplation',[52] Hall's metaphor of the 'the hill of meditation' might allude not

---

[45] Huntley 1981, p. 3.
[46] Hall 1863, p. 661.
[47] Faber 2016, p. 75.
[48] Hall 1863, p. 388.
[49] Hall 1863, p. 54: 'Gerson, whose authority (saving our just quarrel against him for the Council of Constance), I rather use'.
[50] Hall 1863, p. 55.
[51] Hall 1863, p. 57: 'No marvel, therefore, though in this all our teachers of meditation have commended several positions of body, according to their disposition and practice; one, (Gerson), sitting with the face turned up to Heavenward'.
[52] Hall 1863, p. 332.

only to Mount Sinai,[53] but rather or also to *The Mountain of Contemplation*:

> The hill of meditation may not be climbed with a profane foot; [...] only the pure of heart have promise to see God [...] The soul must therefore be purged ere it can profitably meditate.[54]

The English bishop also appreciated the chancellor's psychological insights relating to obsessive thinking and anxiety: 'It is well observed by that learned chancellor of Paris, that some filthy and blasphemous cogitations are better overcome by condemning them than by answering them'.[55] However, Hall's attitude toward Gerson might be characterized as ambivalent and even paradoxical. While he refers to his favorite late medieval authority mostly fondly as 'honest and learned Gerson' or just 'that learned chancellor of Paris', he makes sure to distance himself from the latter's Catholicity by calling him

> a Romish seducer [for being ...] devout client to the saints, and especially to the blessed Virgin Mary, and [the] angels, as Jo. Gerson hath confidently taught us'.[56] Yet, on the same page and in the same paragraph, where he raves about 'the rage of Roman persecution; bloody butcheries of Inquisition; daily bonfires made of the bodies of God's saints; the secret massacres [...]

Hall takes special care to praise the French theologian carefully separating him from the rest: 'so true is that observation of Gerson that there is none so implacable a division as that which goes under pretense of religion'.[57] While much more work is needed to fully elucidate Joseph Hall's complex feelings toward the late medieval chancellor, it appears clear that indifference was not one of them.

One of the most prolific among English Puritan authors, author of the fundamental the *Methodus Theologiae* (1681), Rich-

---

[53] Faber 2016, p. 79.
[54] Hall 1863, p. 51.
[55] Hall 1863, pp. 369–70.
[56] Hall 1863, p. 651.
[57] Hall 1863, p. 661.

ard Baxter (1615–1691) also relied on Gerson in matters pertaining to contemplation, such as, for example, 'the role of the Holy Spirit in meditation'.[58] An example of a skillful amalgamation of Catholic and particularly Jesuit theology with Puritan spirituality, Baxter 'deliberately sets out to recover for the Puritans some of these devotional practices which had fallen away as a result of Calvinist thinking'.[59] Perfectly familiar with Jesuit devotional practices, 'he has wisely limited his overt references to less controversial figures, from whom he could have gained the essentials of his method — especially from Gerson and Hall'.[60] Indeed, his dependence on Catholic sources is exemplified by his reliance on Gerson, to whom he refers in his marginal citations.[61] Even on the account of the thorny question of the nature of the mystical communion with God, Baxter's fondness of Gerson is not as ' surprising'[62] as it may seem. The chancellor had carefully refrained from directly discussing such matters. In *The Mountain of Contemplation*, the work that Baxter knew, Gerson formulated his position on this issue as following: 'La tierce maniere d'avoir grasce est par union, comme eust saint Pol, li excellens contemplatifs. Mais de ceste maniere ne suis je mie digne d'en ouvrir ma bouche; ie la laisse aux plus grans'.[63] Thus formulated, Gerson's attitude toward mystical encounter with God appears to be more in tune with than in opposition to Baxter's. Some of Baxter's metaphors display an interesting fusion of Gersonian and Jesuit contemplative methods. Thus, while the image of spiritual mountain climbing is likely to come from Gerson, Baxter's interpretation of it is rather reminiscent of Ignatius's martial approach: 'there must be vio-

---

[58] Knott 2011, p. 65.
[59] Martz, 1976, p. 168.
[60] Martz 1976, p. 174.
[61] Knott 2011, p. 65; Martz 1976, p. 170. According to Marzt, one of these marginal quotes is from *The Mountain of Contemplation* (Martz 1976, p. 169), but I have been unable to identify it.
[62] Knott 2011, p. 65.
[63] OC: 7: 1, p. 55. 'But concerning this matter [the experience of an outstanding contemplative encounter] I am not worthy to open my mouth. I will leave it to the great' (McGuire 1998, p. 125). As he says in *De Elucidatione scholasticae theologiae*: 'Denique distribuit unicuique Deus mysteria sua prout uult.' (OC: 8, p. 161) 'At the end God distributes his secrets to each as he pleases'.

lence used to get these first fruits [of contemplation], as well as to get the full possession [of them]'.[64]

Gerson's role in the production of evangelical harmonies in England was, on the one hand, particularly long-lasting, with imitations of his harmony *Monotessaron*, often referred to under the title *One from Four*, continuing to appear well into the 17th century, though, on the other, limited to Latin and French language versions. An English gospel harmony was not produced until the late 1620s, when the deacon in the Church of England, Nicholas Ferrar (1592–1637) composed his own *Monotessaron* for his extended family in Little Gidding in Cambridgeshire. Since all previously published evangelical harmonies were either in Latin or in French, Ferrar's main motivation was simply his desire to compose evangelical harmonies in his native tongue. The basic structure of Ferrar's harmonies is still that of Gerson's *Monotessaron*, with which the English deacon must have been familiar, since it was available in the collection of Gerson's works belonging to the Reverend Robert Brooks, whose school Nicholas Ferrar and his brothers attended.[65] Although Ferrar's ambitions were initially limited to his family in Little Gidding, in 1633 his *Monotessaron* attracted the attention of King Charles I (1600–1649). The absolutist king, whose Catholic sympathies ultimately led to civil war and his subsequent execution, requested a copy and made it available to the court. *Monotessaron* also had a formative influence on Thomas More's Tour Works and on the wave of 17th century imitations.

Part II. The Scottish Connection

The amalgamation of Puritan and Catholic methods, accompanied by a reliance on Gerson, is not limited to devotional literature. This trend also finds a curious expression in the political writings of King James I (1566–1625), who 'himself declared that Jesuits are nothing but Puritan-Papists'.[66] The reason for the king's dislike of these religious movements lies in their support,

---

[64] Martz 1976, p. 169. For Ignatius's approach see chapter four.
[65] Ransome 2013, pp. 42–43, n. 20.
[66] McIlwain 1918, p. xxii.

although for different reasons, of the theory of the separation between ecclesiastical and secular jurisdictions. Between the two, the Jesuits appeared more dangerous to James on two grounds: one theological and one political. The first consisted of the fact that, contrary to Puritans (also called Calvinists or, in the case of Scotland, Presbyterians), Jesuits accepted and venerated the papacy as the supreme power on earth, superior to all other authorities and institutions. James was particularly worried about the deposing power of the pope, which was an integral part of the Jesuit theory.[67] Indeed, the Jesuits meant business, and formulated three modes of enforcing papal deposing power. The first was the transfer of power from an old to a new ruler by invasion, the second by rebellion and the third by private elimination of the sovereign through tyrannicide.[68] One of the cases when the Jesuits considered the Pope's deposing power as justified is the situation where a heretical ruler imposes heresy on his subjects. In such cases Jesuits believed that the pope had not just the right but a duty to remove the heretical monarch.

The second reason why King James I viewed Jesuits as a greater threat than Puritans was the reality that they actually possessed material and political means to apply their beliefs with the might of Spain. James went out of his way to prove his religious orthodoxy, so he could not be accused of heresy and therefore become susceptible to the deposing power of the pope. Here is where Gerson's legacy comes into play. James, as King of England, inherited from Elizabeth I the title of Defender of the Faith (which was first obtained, ironically, by Henri VIII from Pope Leo X in 1521) and perceived himself as such in all seriousness. Orthodox in his Catholicity without being papist, James appears to sincerely consider Gerson his ally. For the champion of a national religion to 'which it is entirely proper to apply the term Anglo-Catholicism',[69] the only thing that really mattered was to demonstrate, after speaking 'sufficiently [of Gerson] before [...], that

---

[67] McIlwain 1918, p. xxvi.

[68] McIlwain 1918, p. xxvii: 'It may be truly said that all three are the result of Jesuit influence'.

[69] McIlwain 1918, p. xlvi.

our religion affordeth no rules of rebellion; no any dispensation to suiects for the oath of their allegiance'.[70]

James's little-known dependence on Gerson is found in his *Defense of the King of Kings*, where the English monarch quotes the late medieval chancellor multiple times. The *Defense* was directed against papists in general, and, more specifically, against James's archenemy, the illustrissime French cardinal Jacques Davy Du Perron or Duperron (1556–1618), who was the most successful promoter of absolute papal supremacy in France.[71] In this book, where James declares that there is no supremacy but the king's and no rights for anyone but the king's, since even a wicked king is sent by God,[72] he appeals to Gerson precisely because the latter 'was a deuoute Roman Catholike'.[73] James uses Gerson's authority to his advantage in order to demonstrate several points. First is to show that 'Gerson makes no mention at all of deposing or of any compulsive power over Soueraigne Princes'.[74] Second, to charge Du Perron, not altogether wrongly, with 'his taken out of Gersons famous allegations Oration made before Charles the 6 for the Vniversitie of Paris where he brings in Gerson to affirme, that killing a Tyrant is a sacrifice acceptable to God'.[75] Third, to take advantage of Gerson's perceived Gallicanism by simply placing the argument for the sovereignty of the King of France in an Eng-

---

[70] McIlwain 1918, p. 264.

[71] Both Du Perron and James used Gerson's text according to Edmond Richer's 1606 edition, which, contrary to the declaration of its author to have been 'considerably augmented and improved', was, for the most part, the reprint of Jakob Wimpheling's (Denis 2019, p. 47). For the latest updates on the 17th century reception of Gerson in conciliarist and anti-conciliarist traditions also see Amalou 2018, pp. 11–34. On the cardinal Bellarmine's (1542–1621) opposition to Gerson's conciliarism see Gaille-Nikodimov 2005 and De Franceschi 2007.

[72] McIlwain 1918, p. 67.

[73] McIlwain 1918, pp. 119–20. James continuously refers to Gerson's *De potestate Ecclesia consid.* II (McIlwain 1918, p. 165).

[74] McIlwain 1918, p. 205.

[75] McIlwain 1918, p. 205. Gerson was unwaveringly adamant about the absolute unacceptability of tyrannicide theory, developed in the early 15th century by Parisian theologian Jean Petit at the instigation of the Duke of Burgundy, John the Fearless (1371–1419). He made the condemnation of the tyrannicide theory the main focus of his agenda at the second part of the Council of Constance, and his name is firmly associated with moral resistance to its implementation in a Christian society.

lish context. Fourth, to exploit Gerson's conciliarist reputation and show that one can well be a Catholic without being a papist: 'Gerson was so far from giving the Pope that temporal authority not only over Kings but even over the Church'.[76]

James's knowledge of Gerson's writings, which he quotes correctly, is impressive, and he consciously employs it in order to impress Du Perron, a Frenchman and a trained theologian, whom he accuses of 'omitting' and 'obtruding' the chancellor's thought 'disguised, masked and perverted by his Lordship'.[77] The English king shames the cardinal for not knowing his famous compatriot as thoroughly as the king of England does.[78] James's close knowledge of Gerson, even if purely polemical and utilitarian in purpose, testifies to the chancellor's continuous relevance and prestige in early modern England.

Gerson's Scottish connection far predates the reign of King James, however. It is indeed highly probable that the king's remarkable familiarity with the works of the Parisian master comes from a tradition of study and appreciation of Gerson, which, in turn, is part of a long history of Scottish kinship with France, the main enemy of Scotland's main enemy, and, therefore, its natural ally. Thus, Scottish knight and poet Sir Gilbert Hay, also called Sir Gilbert of the Haye (flourished around 1456), and known for his translations of French popular literature, fought for Joan of Arc during the Hundred Years' War and served as a chamberlain to the King Charles VII of France. Scotland's historical situation logically created 'a fertile terrain for conciliarism'.[79] Both the political and legal philosopher John Mair and the leading Scot-

---

[76] McIlwain 1918, pp. 119–20. According to McIlwain, James's quotes of Gerson are very accurate.

[77] McIlwain 1918, p. 264: 'L. Cardinall should not have omitted that Gerson, in the question of Kings subjection in temporall matters, or of the dependence of their Crownes upon the Popes power, excepteth always the King of France: witnesse that which Gerson a little before alleadged by the Cardinall, hath planely affirmed: Now since Peters time, saith Gerson, all Imperiall Regal, and Secular power is not immediately to draw virtue and strength from the Soueraigne Bishop: as in this maner the most Christian King of France hath no Superior, nor acknowledgeth any such upon the face of the earth'.

[78] McIlwain 1918, p. 264: 'Of Gerson obtruded by the Cardinall we have spoken sufficiently before'.

[79] Denis 2019, p. 46.

tish humanist scholar George Buchanan (1506–1582) considered themselves Gerson's disciples in this regard.[80]

Gerson's impact in Scotland is also found in the writings of a scholar and diplomat John Ireland (c. 1435/1440–1495/1500), whose *Meroure of Wyssdome*, written for James IV of Scotland, 'reveals the most pronounced employment of French political thought, especially Gerson's sermons, to be found in Scottish advice writing at this time'.[81] The book substantially draws, without acknowledgement, on Gerson's works *Adorabunt eum omnes rege terre, Diligite iusticiam, Rex in sempiterne uiue, Veniat pax, Viuat rex* and possibly *Omne regnum in seipsum diuisum desolabitur*, all of which are sermons.[82] *Meroure of Wyssdome* also has an alternative title, *The A.B.C. of Christianity*, a probable hint at the author's indebtedness to Gerson's *A.B.C. pour les simples gens*. This supposition is supported by both Ireland's own occasional references to this work as the *ABC of symple & devote peple Christiane*, Gerson's title verbatim, and by his general aim to offer the vernacular fundamentals of the Christian faith not only to princes, but to all the king's subjects.[83] The influence of Ireland's 'posthumous mentor'[84] is manifest in several aspects of the book besides the title and the aim. The first is its organization. The three prayers offered by Gerson at the beginning of his *A.B.C. pour les simples gens* — Pater Noster, Ave Maria and Credo — are those around which Ireland constructs the first three books of his

---

[80] On John Mair and George Buchanan see Figgis 1962.

[81] Mapstone 1986, p. 10.

[82] See Mapstone 1986, p. 408 & p. 420; McDonald 1991, p. 454. Mapstone explains Ireland's familiarity with Gerson's works by the fact that a Professor of Theology at St Andrews University named Keith (d. c. 1500) had a copy of Gerson's 1489 edition. This edition, however, primarily contained spiritual and theological treatises in Latin. Many of Gerson's compositions, originally written in French, including *Viuat rex* and other political sermons, did not appear in print until the beginning of the 16th century and then only in a Latin translation. Therefore, Ireland must have known Gerson's political works in manuscripts (Mapstone 1986, p. 409).

[83] McDonald 1991, p. 23: 'His professed aim was to instruct the king, specifically, but the Scottish nation, more generally, in the 'ABC's of Christianity', that is, to expound various articles of the Christian faith-the Lord's Prayer, the Creed, the Sacraments, predestination, and the like-with an eye towards strengthening the belief of his king and country'.

[84] McDonald 1991, p. 449.

Meroure, in an order similar to Gerson's. The second is the 'overwhelmingly theological'[85] language of *Meroure of Wyssdome*. The third is its apparent conciliarist tendencies. Finally, in *Meroure*'s Book VII, Gerson's material is borrowed directly in sections discussing the question of the limits of the power of the Pope,[86] the conditions of princely mercy and the virtues of the monarch. In fact, all three Scottish mirrors of princes, Sir Gilbert Hay's *Buik of King Alexander*, an anonymous *The Three Prestis of Peblis*, and Ireland's *Meroure of Wyssdome*, are written in 'a thoroughly Gersonian context'.[87]

Part III. The Very Special Case: Gerson and Thomas More

> 'But the world was not to be won by invincible logic set down systematically in books. The religious future of Christian Europe lay in the hands of young men of passionate temperament who yearned with all their hearts for a direct relation with God, unmediated by hierarchies [...] and in the hands of monarchs who, whatever temperament, looked for greater authority and saw in religious upheaval an irresistible opportunity for worldly advantage'.[88]

Before looking closely at Thomas More's connection to Gerson, I could not imagine the breadth and depth of the late medieval theologian's presence in the writings of the celebrated Englishman. While several More's scholars have mentioned, however briefly, Thomas More's positive reception of Gerson,[89] it appears to be utterly unknown to medievalists and to historians in general. Also, even though the notable role that Gerson played in More's life appears to be a common knowledge among More's scholars, it still has not acquired the attention of a more general public. The chancellor's name is mentioned neither in Richard

---

[85] Burns 1955, p. 90.
[86] Mapstone 1986, p. 369. On Ireland's concilliarist sympathies see McDonald 1991.
[87] Burns 1955 p. 78. See Mapstone 1986; Burns 2018 online.
[88] Marius 1984, p. 331.
[89] See Rodgers 2011; Taylor 2011, pp. 33–52. Marc'hadour mentions Thomas More's life-long dependency on Gerson as his 'vénéré mentor' (Marc'hadour 1995, p. 49). Richard Marius states, in passing, that More 'revered Gerson' (Marius 1984, p. 96).

Marius's influential More's biography nor in Peter Ackroyd's *The Life of Thomas More*, and it is mentioned only once (as a presumed author of *De Imitatione Christi*) in John Guy's book.[90] Yet, already in 1976, Gary E. Haupt had recommended an in-depth comparative study of Gerson in relation to Thomas More,[91] while more recently, in 2002, Ralph Keen also stated the necessity of a comparative analysis of these 'leading minds of the 15th and 16th centuries'.[92] Such a study never took place. Suggesting that the two theologians had much in common, Haupt listed among their shared features their pronounced preference for the warm piety and moral theology over a purely intellectual approach, and their promotion of cautious reforms from within the Church.[93] Their similarities extend far beyond these traits, however. Both men were deeply involved in the affairs of the state, held very high public offices in their respective countries, found themselves at the heart of chief controversies of their times, and had experienced the conflict between their spiritual convictions and worldly obligations. Both were conservative religious leaders and steadfast orthodox Catholics, who loved the Church more than their own lives and were ready to sacrifice themselves as well as others for it. Moreover, both were keenly interested in education, produced pedagogical works, and wrote Latin poetry in their youth. More's extensive knowledge of Gerson is evident from his writings, and his admiration for the late medieval theologian only increased as he aged. In fact, a thread common to all of More's works — 'both those begun before the imprisonment and those begun during it — is his dependence on Jean Gerson as a source of scriptural narrative and moral theology'.[94] Among Gerson's works that most influenced Thomas More are *Monotessaron, De consolatione theologiae, De egressu passionis et resurrectionis Christi, De communione sub utraque specie, Sermo de angelis, De probatione sprituum, De mystica theologia* and *De oratione et eius ualore*. Familiarity with other Gerson's texts, including his sermons and speeches, is

---

[90] Marius 1984 & Guy 2000.
[91] Haupt 1976, p. xlv.
[92] Keen 2002, pp. 284–87.
[93] Haupt 1976, p. xlvi.
[94] Rodgers 2011, p. 243.

also detectable in More's writings. It is important to remember though that More believed Gerson to be the author of *De Imitatione Christi*, which he called *The Following of Christ*.[95]

The Englishman's interest in the late medieval chancellor began in his youth and is related to his humanist pursuits of classical poetry and eloquence. More composed Latin verses over a period of about twenty years, from 1500 to 1520, until other, more pressing and prosaic matters took priority. The major inspiration for More's Latin poetry was *Anthologia Planudea*, which, composed of 2,400 Greek epigrams, was compiled by Byzantine grammarian and theologian Maximus Planudes (1260–1305). More and his friend William Lily (1468–1522), an English classical grammarian and scholar, translated at least 106 poems from this collection.[96] They published their translations as an anthology called *Progymnasmata*, which, because of its great pedagogical value and utility, became an inspiration for subsequent editions of this kind in Germany, France, Italy and other European countries, among Protestants and Catholics alike. More's contribution to *Progymnasmata* consisted of sixteen Greek epigrams followed by their parallel translations in Latin, and one poem based on the French text by Gerson. The fact that Gerson is the only non-classical author that young More included in the anthology indicates the exceptional esteem in which he already held the Parisian master. More's poem, inspired by Gerson's text from *Vivat Rex*, is the following:

> A kingdom in all parts is like a man;
> It is held together by natural affection.
> The king is the head; the people form the other parts.
> Every citizen the king has he considers a part of his own body
> (that is why he grieves at the loss of a single one).
> The people risk themselves to save the king
> and everyone thinks of him as the head of his own body.[97]

---

[95] Monti 1997, p. 65.

[96] Revilo 1984 *CWTM* 3:12. Ackroyd 1999, p. 135: 'Lily belonged to this London circle of English humanists where 'piety was often considered more important than learning'.

[97] *CWTM* 3:164, poem 112:
Totum est unus homo regnum, idque cohaeret amore.
Rex caput est, populus caetera membra facit.

The Englishman's admiration for Gerson only intensified with time, which is remarkable considering that he 'had always been hostile to the French'.[98] This affection cannot be explained by conciliarist solidarity.[99] It has another source: his sympathy toward devotional theology, which, by the time Gerson's voice reached England, was firmly associated with *devotio moderna*.[100] The prestige of the chancellor of Paris as 'the principal oracle of the *devotio moderna*'[101] inspired the Englishman to trust his authority on major theological issues, such as, for example, the thorny subject of distinguishing revelations, which More discussed in his letter to a monk, composed between March and September 1519.[102] In 1522 Gerson's *Sermo tertius de mortuis* about the purgatory serves as the theme for More's unfinished treatise *The Four Last Things*. The main difference in the treatment of this subject lies in the fact

---

Rex quot habet ciues (dolet ergo perdere quenquam)
Tot numerat partes corporis ipse sui.
Exponit populus sese pro rege putatque
Quilibet hunc proprii corporis esse caput
Gerson, *Vivat Rex, Discours pour la réforme du royaume*, OC: 7: 2, p. 1155: 'Selon ce que par l'enseignement de nature tous les membres en ung vray corps se exposent pour le salut du chief, pareillement estre doit un corps mystique des vrayz subgetz a leur seigneur. Mais aussi d'autre part le chief doit adrecier et gouverner les aultres membres. Car aulrement ce seroit destruction: proprement, car chief sans corps ne peust durer'. On the subject of the king's mystical body see Kantorowitz 1957.

[98] Marius 1984, p. 357.

[99] More had 'a great interest in not being explicit about the conciliarist issue at all', as 'conciliarists and papalists alike found themselves swimming for their lives'. (Marius 1980, p. 94). Scholars have been in disagreement as to More's views. Marius states that 'for More the council had much more authority than the pope' (Marius 1984, p. 94); George M. Logan that More was of the opinion that power of the general council 'did not nullify the Pope's primacy' (Logan 2011, p. 243); and Philippe Denis, following Patterson (Patterson 1997, p. 98) that 'Thomas More himself declared from the Tower where he was imprisoned, that he had never considered the pope to be above the Council' (Denis 2019, p. 46).

[100] Along with Gerson's, More favored other works of the anti-speculative nature, such as *The Ladder of Perfection* (*Scala Perfectionis*) by the British mystic Walter Hilton (b. 1340/45–1395/6) (Haupt 1976, p. xciii).

[101] Debongnie 1928, p. 255.

[102] In *A learned epistle from a man of renown, Master Thomas More, in response to a certain monk's ignorant and virulent letter, a senseless invective, belaboring, among other issues, Erasmus's translation 'In the beginning was Speech, etc.'* (*CWTM* 15: 205), More closely follows Gerson's treatises *De probatione sprituum* and *De mystica theologia*.

that Gerson takes the existence of purgatory for granted, while More has to defend this concept against Protestant critics.

For More, Gerson was a highly esteemed theological authority who could weigh in on discussions that mattered. Such a discussion first emerged, when Simon Fish published an anticlerical pamphlet *Supplication for the Beggars*, directly calling upon the laity to seize Church property. Because accusations against the clergy were so broad and violent, More felt compelled, in his 1529 answer entitled *Supplication of Souls*, to not just counteract Fish's pamphlet, but to confront the whole powerful political movement, which was behind it. His goal was to 'restore peace and to defend orthodoxy',[103] which had been threatened by Fish's treatise, especially after it had reached the king himself, most probably through Anne Boleyn, who favored the anti-Catholic fraction. More's defense, based on Gerson's *Sermones de defunctis*, consists in making his readers feel the scandal and shock felt by the potentially abandoned souls of the dead, once they learn 'that eny man shulde need nowe to proue purgatory to crysten men'.[104]

More utilizes Gerson's text, which is more a poem with Verlaine-like rhythm and Verlaine-like overtones than a theological treatise,[105] in order to extol prayer of the living for the dead and of the deceased for the living, as the means of maintaining solidarity between *vivi et mortui* — the essence of the pre-modern community of the faithful, as More knew and valued it:

---

[103] Marc'Hadour 1981, *CWTM* 7: lxvi.

[104] The second book of *Supplication of Souls, A Cruel Attack on the Souls in Purgatory CWTM* 7: 170.

[105] *Complainte des ames au purgatoire*, OC: 7: 1, pp. 363–67: 'Pour esmouvoir les vifz a prier pour les mors qui sont en purgatoire est composée ceste complainte en la personne des mors. Priés pour nous, o vous qui estes vivans sur terre; priés pour nous, pourez et dolentes ames qui sommes en l'apre et dure prison de purgatoire et ne nous pouons aider. Priés pour nous et nous regardez en pitié et en compassion. Aydes nous a délivrer et estre hors des peines et griefs tourmens que nous soustenons en ceste chartre de purgatoire par la iuste sentence des nostre souverain juge. Priez pour nous qui sommes hors de l'estat auquel nous nous puissions aidier par nostre propre priere ou euvre méritoire'. This highly poetic treatise ends with a poem:
Les mors a ung chascun vivant:
Arreste et nous regarde et pleure
Tus eras tel quoy qu'il demeure.
Prie Dieu pour nous qu'il nous sequeure.
Fiche en ton cuer tousdis ceste heure.

And therfore yf god accept the prayour after hys own fauour born toward hym [...] our prayer ys for you so feruent / that ye can no where fynde eny such affeccyon vppon erth. And therfore syth we ly so sore in paynys & haue in our great necessyte so gret need of your help & y ye may so well do yt/ wherby shall rebownd yppon your self an inestimable profyte: let neuer eny slouthfull oblyuyon race vs of your remembrance.[106]

More appeals to Gerson's authority even more frequently as he grows older. He summons the French master's opinion in his polemical works, such as *Apology* and *Debellation of Salem and Bizance*, prompted by the escalating political unrest in England, as well as in his devotional writings such as *Instructions and Prayers*. His virulent polemic with an anti-Catholic legal writer and lawyer, 'one of the intellectual fathers of the new order in England',[107] Christopher of St Germain or St German (1460–1540),[108] who was 'less witty than Machiavelli but much more practical and profound',[109] makes More turn to Gerson again and again. St Germain, himself an avid reader of Gerson, gained fame as the author of the controversial *Dialogues between a Doctor of Divinity and a Student of the Laws of England*, his *magnum opus* on questions of English law, which was initially published in Latin in 1528 and translated into English by the author in 1530. The popularity and impact of this treatise are evident from the fact that it was reprinted twenty-eight times between 1528 and 1630, remaining one of the major legal references for over a hundred years. In *Doctor and Student*, St Germain argues that [unless] 'all men within the realm, both spiritual and temporal, be ordered and ruled by one law in all things temporal', a layman cannot judge what is heresy.[110] Consequently, the clergy should stay away from secular matters. 'Showing an intimate familiarity with the works of Pierre d'Ailly and Gerson',[111] St Germain extensively and exactly cites the

[106] *The Supplication of Souls*, CWTM 7: 227–28.
[107] Haigh 1993, p. 117.
[108] There are multiple spellings of this name: St Germain/St German, St-Germain/St-German and St German/St Germain. Here I chose the spelling St Germain as it is the one used by Francis Oakley.
[109] Marius 1984, p. 380.
[110] St Germain 2006, p. 107.
[111] Denis 2019, p. 45.

latter in his arguments, referring to the chancellor by name nine times. 'Galling' Thomas More 'by drawing heavily on Gerson',[112] the Englishman quotes from *De uita spirituali animae*, *Tractatus de contractibus* and *Regulae morales*, the last work being the standard 'background of general notions' for 'the law student of the later Middle Ages',[113] in support of his criticism of the traditional church, and in paving the way the new order:

> Whereupon John Gerson, in the treatise of the spiritual life of the soul, the second lesson, and the third corollary, says thus All the canons of bishops nor their decrees be not the law of God: for many of them be made only for the political conservation of the people. And if any man will say, Be not all the goods of the church spiritual, for they belong unto the spiritualty, and leading to the spiritualty? We answer, that in the whole political conservation of the people, there be some specially deputed and dedicated to the service of God, the which most specially (as by an excellency) are called spiritual men, as religious men are. And other, though they walk in the way of God, yet nevertheless, because their office is most specially to be occupied about such things as pertain to the commonwealth, and to the good order of the people, they be therefore called secular men or lay men. Nevertheless, the goods of the first may no more be called spiritual than the goods of the other, for they be things more temporal, and keeping the body, as they do in the other. [...] These be the words of John Gerson, in the place alleged before.[114]

St Germain is never shy to use the French medieval chancellor as his favorite backup to prove a point. Using to his advantage Gerson's sharp distinction between divine and human laws, as is described in *De uita spirituali animae*, St Germain proclaims, surely to Henry VIII sheer delight:

> And though that law binds not now Christian people, yet a like law thereto might be made by Christian princes, which then by that new institution ought to be observed and kept, as

---

[112] Marc'Hadour 1981, *CWTM*, 6: 533, note 2.

[113] Jacob 1953, p. 110. Marc'hadour remarks that 'Christopher St Germain galled More by drawing heavily on Gerson's *Regulae morales*' (Marc'Hadour 1981, *CWTM*, 6: 533, n. 2).

[114] St Germain 2006, p. 6.

diverse of the said judicials have been in many countries. Thus far be the words of John Gerson.[115]

His attacks become increasingly radical in his subsequent book, the *Treatise concernynge the diuision betwene the spiritualtie and the temporaltie*, published in 1532, where he focuses his attention on the breadth of jurisdiction of the ecclesiastical courts.[116] He also condemns many traditional Catholic practices, including the use of images in churches, using Gerson's name as a backup:

> [...] but here it is to be nooted/ that Iohan Gerson fyndeth not defaulte in settynge vp of ymages/ for he commendeth it in many places of his werkes, but he fyndeth defaulte at the varietie of them in theyr peyntyng and garnysshyng with golde/ syuer, precious stones, and suche oher/ with so great ryshes about them/ that some simple persons might lightly be enduced to beleue some special working to be in the ymages/ that is not in them undead. And so he fyndeth defaute at the abuse of ymages: and not at the settying vppe of ymages.[117]

Considering that the king was 'siding inexorably with St Germain's new imagination of English law',[118] and that on 15 May 1532 the English bishops submitted to the power of the king by surrendering their ancient liberties, it is not surprising that Thomas More perceived St Germain's allegations as a personal affront and a dangerous political provocation. He responded immediately by publishing, in 1533, *The Apologye of Syr Thomas More, Hnyght*, known as *Apology*. By this time, in 1532, he had already resigned from his office of the chancellor. Although this work is crucial for the understanding of the evolution of Thomas More's thought, special expertise is needed in order to unravel the immensely complex labyrinth of arguments, counter-arguments and counter-counter-arguments entangled in it. Here only few particularly relevant and important points will be addressed. The first concerns his changing attitude toward exegesis. While his

---

[115] St Germain 2006, 167.
[116] Trapp 1979 *CWTM*, 9: lv.
[117] St Germain, *Treatise concerning the division between the spirituality and temporality*, *CWTM* 9: 183.
[118] Cummings 2011, p. 45.

Dialogue Concerning Heresies, written in 1529, advocated Erasmus's position concerning spiritual benefits of lay people reading the Bible in vernacular languages, his *Apology*, written only four years later, reveals quite a different point of view. Retreating from the Erasmian view, and embracing that of Gerson, More was now convinced that the Church was the sole legitimate authority on the interpretation of the Bible, providing laymen with enough information to assure their salvation.

The second point concerns More's stance on heresy, which, like almost everybody else's positions, had evolved during this period in the direction of rigidity. Not surprisingly, his opinion of Jan Hus stands in direct opposition to that of Martin Luther and John Foxe, who included the Czech preacher into his *Book of Martyrs*. According to More:

> [...] the country of Boheme fallying into many heresyes, began [...] receiuying it [the communion] under bothe the forms but also tooke upon them farther, to reproue & reproch for dampnable, the common longe continued custome of the whole corps of Christendom, upon this demeanure of theirs, the general counsyle of Constance, condemned in theyr so doying their ouer arrogant error.[119]

For More, who 'refers to heretics in the way that today passionate journalists and comedians refer to drug-dealers, child-molesters and suicide-bombers',[120] 'heresye of al crimes is the wurste',[121] as it undermines the social order by arrogantly opposing one's personal opinion to the whole Christian community. Since religion was 'the foundation of human society', More rightly 'realized that a new doctrine meant a new order',[122] and did all he could to prevent this from happening. Dealing with Protestant heresy 'was the single most time-consuming issue in his chancellorship' and possibly even 'his chief motive in accepting this office'.[123] During his chancellorship six people were burned at the stake for heresy and, as he declared, those convicted of heresy

---

[119] *The Treatise Upon the Passion*, CWTM 13:149–50.
[120] Rex 2011, p. 103.
[121] *CWTM* 9:45.
[122] Rex 2011, p. 111.
[123] Rex 2011, pp. 106–07.

were 'well and worthily burned'.[124] Yet, Foxe's charges that the chancellor had often personally used violence or torture in his interrogations of heretics cannot be substantiated.[125] In *Apology* More writes that he ordered corporal punishment on only two occasions: a child was caned in front of his family for heresy regarding the Eucharist, and a 'feeble-minded' man was whipped for molesting a woman at a church and disrupting public prayers. However scandalous such practices may appear to modern readers, in the context of the gruesome reality of the 16th century, they are far from excessive punishments. Although Sir Thomas More was neither a sadist nor a 'deepest-dyed villain',[126] he was not a man of all seasons either. He, like the rest of us, was a man of only one season, his own.

Responding to St Germain's use of Gerson, More accused him of having deliberately distorted and manipulated the meaning and purpose of the chancellor's original criticism of clerical abuses. Based on the chancellor's distinction of what the laity should and should not know, More argued that the French theologian never meant to reprimand the prelates before common people the way St Germain (whom he calls 'this pacyfyer') did, thus undermining their authority:

> If he saye that he ment as Gerson dyd, that he maketh mencyon of them bycause he wolde haue the clergy mende them/ surely who so for suche good wyll telleth a man hys fawtes, vseth to tell hit hym secretely/ and so dyd Iohan Gerson hym selfe when he wrote them in latyne, & not in the vulgare tunge. But this pacyfyer contrary wyse bycause he wolde haue the lay peple both men & women loke on them, doth translate them into englysh/where as Iohan Gerson wolde not that a man sholde reproche & rebuke y prelates before the people.[127]

In *Apology* More clearly sides with the Catholic understanding of Christianity as being continuously revealed through the Holy Spirit and carried by the Church *in libris scriptis et sine scripto tra-*

---

[124] *CWTM* 9:113.
[125] See Rex 2011.
[126] Rex 2011, p. 93.
[127] *Apology*, *CWTM* 9: 60.

ditionibus.[128] There was no reason to believe that God, after the completion of the New Testament, would choose to remain silent forever, which was, generally speaking, the position advocated by the Reformers in their *sola scriptura*-doctrine.[129]

St Germain made an immediate reply to More's *Apology* in the same year, 1533, with the crude and, in More's eyes, politically dangerous *Dialogue betwixte two Englishmen, whereof one was called Salem and the other Bizance*,[130] also published anonymously. In the 'Conclusion of this answere to Sir Thomas More's *Apology*', which is part of *Salem and Bizance*, and his final published work, St Germain claimed to do nothing but 'recite the words of maister Gerson',[131] in his discussion of issues including the necessity of fasting and the clergy's supposed idleness. His use of Gerson is particularly paradoxical, as the latter was the most dedicated servant and partisan of the Catholic Church, whose power St Germain sought to contest. Now this power stood in the way of the king of England himself, resisting his royal supremacy over religious matters. The Act of Supremacy was passed in November 1534; hence the main target of St Germain's attack was clerical immunity from secular jurisdiction. Interpreting the 'Word' in a whole new sense as the laws and customs of England, St Germain, presaging the future, believed that power should be exercised exclusively through secular law and institutions.

St Germain's invective was met with More's *The Debellacyon of Salem and Bizance* published the same year. Pretending not to know the authorship of *Salem and the other Bizance*,

---

[128] Wassilowsky 2018, p. 80.

[129] On the relation between Scripture and unwritten tradition(s) see: Congar 1960; Ruppert 1962; Rahner 1986; Ratzinger 1966; Barth 2010, pp. 29–125.

[130] Curtright 2012, p. 142 & p. 160.

[131] *Salem and Bizance*, chapter 21, Appendix, *CWTM* 10: 382. The evaluation of St Germain's actual dependence on Gerson in *Salem and Byzance* is hindered by the fact that the majority of times his quotes come from the works that are not his. Thus, when St Germain discusses his grievances against the clergy, his citations come from *Declaratio compendiosa defectuum uirorum ecclesiasticorum*, a work by the already-mentioned professor of the University of Vienna, Heinrich von Langenstein. On the subject of the confusion of Gerson's works and biography with Langenstein's see chapter 1.

and continuing to ironically call his opponent 'the Pacifier',[132] More, once again, threw himself into battle against what he now perceived to be a political provocation. But the wind had definitely changed in the England of 1534, where More would soon find himself almost alone, together with the elderly bishop John Fisher, still standing against it. While More's *Apology* had already met with Henry VIII's disapproval, his *The Debellacyon of Salem and Bizance* exasperated the king. More's opponent's views on the nature of kingship, which would end up openly justifying the monarch's absolute supremacy, were, on the contrary, bound to please Henry, leading to St Germain's victory in this battle of ideas, and to Thomas More's demise. On 17 April 1534 Thomas More was arrested.

Arrest and imprisonment greatly reinforced More's bond with the French theologian. In fact, it is in prison where Gerson's sway over More became the most powerful and direct. There is a strange resemblance between the two men's personalities, struggles and circumstances. All his life, until his imprisonment, More, like Gerson but more acutely, was a divided man, torn between his worldly obligations and his spiritual longing for the contemplative life of a cloister. This division is heightened in More for, unlike Gerson, who still belonged 'corps et âme' to the mother Catholic Church, the Englishman's obligations were often indistinguishable from his aspirations and even ambitions, with the divide between the outer and inner lives, powerfully embodied by his hidden hair shirt, being literally more tangible. Still, the similarities between the two men's respective situations are too great not to outweigh the differences. Besides, More's awareness of the intensity of his own Catholicity increased under the pressure of circumstances, making him feel even closer to the orthodox Catholic theologian of the previous century. Indeed, considering the state of affairs in which the former Lord Chancellor found himself in, Gerson's Frenchness and More's previously proudly valued Englishness mattered very little now, as the two men's denominational and spiritual accord and their Catholic identity

---

[132] Curtright 2012, p. 143: 'The conventional view is that More knew St German was the author of the *Division and Salem*, though both texts were published anonymously'.

canceled all other factors. Gerson's inner struggle between his engagement in politics — which earned him nothing but disgrace, death threat and exile and his desire to retire from the world and become a monk, is certainly something with which More could easily identify. This identification must have become irresistible from the moment of More's own imprisonment, when he, like Gerson in his exile, finally embraced the monk-like existence that he craved. This psychological similarity reveals itself in what is commonly referred to as Tower works: *Dialogue of Comfort Against Tribulation, Treatise Upon the Passion*, and *De Tristitia Christi*,[133] where Gerson's presence is felt the strongest.[134]

Everything indicates that More kept copies of Gerson's writings with him in the Tower, turning to his favorite author in moments of extreme difficulty, anxiety and doubt. In the *Dialogue of Comfort*, written first, two fictional Hungarians, Uncle Antony and Nephew Vincent, discuss various problems concerning human suffering. The goal of the dialogue is to gradually withdraw the mind from the world, easing it into meditation on the future of a Christian soul: the pains of hell, the joys of heaven, and especially the Passion of Christ. Louis L. Martz and Frank Manley, editors of the *Dialogue of Comfort* in the *Complete Works of Thomas More*, mention Boethius, with whom More's career is so remarkably similar, and his *De consolatione philosophiae*, as likely inspirations for More's dialogue.[135] Bringing attention to a number of similarities between the two works, Martz and Manley state that the 'essentially rational and philosophical' approach in Boethius contrasts sharply with the 'fundamentally religious, drawing upon the Christian scheme of salvation' one found in More.[136] This contrast no longer exists once one thinks of Gerson's *De consolatione theologiae*, itself patterned on Boethius's *De consolatione philosophiae*, as More's literary model. Written in the summer and autumn of 1418, when the chancellor found himself in disgrace and exile after having been one of the most powerful

---

[133] The sequence of Tower works, which is the subject of debate, is given here in accordance with the chronology supported by Martz & Manley 1976 *CWTM* 12: lvii.
[134] Taylor 2011, p. 223.
[135] Martz & Manley 1976 *CWTM* 12: cvii.
[136] Martz & Manley 1976 *CWTM* 12: cvii.

political actors in Europe, *De consolatione theologiae* is a far more suitable archetypal candidate for several reasons. Just like Gerson in *De consolatione*, More makes it clear that his *Dialogue of Comfort* is a theological and not a philosophical work, offering not the consolation of philosophy but the comfort of the Christian faith. The goal of both books is consolation, which is threatened by fear: 'withdraweth the mynd of a man fro the spirituall consolacion of the good hope that he shuld haue in godes helpe'.[137] Just like in *De consolatione*, *Dialogue of Comfort* has two main fictional characters engaged in a dialogue. Both books are composed as humanist soliloquies. The three books of the *Dialogue* correspond to faith, hope and charity, the trinity with which Gerson's *De consolatione theologiae* concludes. Both in Gerson's and in More's works, charity fully emerges in the last part of their respective books. As in *De consolatione*, the understanding of charity in Book III of the *Dialogue* arises from a rational process, and not from a pure affectivity. Indeed, even in his treatises on mystical theology Gerson has always held onto reason, without which no balanced judgment is possible, and we go insane like 'those madmen who take images of their imagination for reality and who upon awakening discover that they were taken advantage of'.[138] Even love — and Gerson means the charitable Christian love — needs the safeguard of reason for 'alone [it] remains too much, too wanton: love impels.'[139] However, for Gerson reason alone cannot guarantee sound judgment and protection against anxiety. Without God's will, as it is expressed in Scriptures, reason is deprived of moral and spiritual guidance and therefore, 'at the highest level the will properly called rational is joined to higher reason, which deals with the eternal laws'.[140] Hence his painstaking quest for a balance between Christian virtues and reason, which is central to *De consolatione theologiae*. Since human intelligence needs constant verification by Christian virtues of love, hope and faith, 'philosophy has no power to confer [...] the formal operations by

---

[137] *Dialogue of Comfort*, CWTM 12: 2:170.
[138] Miller 1984, Introduction, *CWTM* 14: 173. As Marc Vial attempts to demonstrate in his book *Gerson: théoicien de la théologie mystique*, this position might have shifted during the chancellor's sojourn in Lyons at the end of his life.
[139] Miller 1998, p. 169.
[140] Miller 1998, p. 127.

which this state [of truth] is objectively reached in the intuitive knowledge of God'.[141] These words must have been of particular appeal to the English prisoner of faith whose treatment of hope, which he interprets as God's assistance, is in line with Gerson's. Indeed, even though the virtue of hope is seen as emerging from the foundation of faith in *Dialogue of Comfort*, it is a faithful hope, just as it is in *De consolatione theologiae*. The salvation of any particular individual is not an article of faith but a matter of hope: 'Not faith alone as they [Lutherans] do, but accompanied wyth hope, and wyth her chyefe syster well workynge charytie'.[142] One noteworthy difference in More's treatment of faith, hope and charity is that at the end of his *Dialogue* the attainment of these virtues metamorphoses not into a peace of mind, as in Gerson's *De consolatione*,[143] but into their quasi-military victory, the transformation probably reflecting the violent reality of uncompromising religious strife and looming Muslim invasions in the 16th century:

> And let us fence us with faith, & comfort us with hope, & and smyte the devill in the face with a firebrand of charitie [...] that fire of charitie throwne in his face, stryketh the devil sodaynly so blynd, that he can not see where to fasten a stroke on us.[144]

The style of the *Dialogue* also differs sharply from that of Gerson, as it is less scholastic and cumbersome, exhibiting the conversational ease, graceful language and highly constructed logical argumentation characteristic of More's literary brilliance. Another major difference is More's Menippean humor, 'rising discordantly from the grim circumstances of fear, suffering, and death',[145] and expressed in anecdotes, stories, jokes and tales. Witty and sharp-minded, More could not resist being himself even in the face of death.

Dialogue of Comfort refers to Gerson's authority as it pertains to several major theological issues. The first time the fictional char-

---

[141] Miller 1998, p. 59.

[142] *The Confutation of Tyndale's Answer*, CWTM 11: 223.

[143] Miller 1998, p. 265: 'For this reason there are up in the biblical figure three cities of refuge, faith, hope and charity. They contain the cleansing of penance and the refuge of immunity, insofar as the peace disturbed by what a man fears he has done may be reestablished'.

[144] *Dialogue of Comfort*, CWTM 12: 318.

[145] Martz & Manley 1976 CWTM 12: xcvii.

acter Antony brings up Gerson directly is during the argument on the utility of bodily penance and its contribution to the salvation of the soul, especially where a man has a hardened heart, and 'can not wepe nor in his hart be sory for his synnes':[146]

> And therefor wold I ferther advise one in that case, the counsaile which master Gerson giveth every man/ that sith the body & the sowle together make the hole man/ the less affliccion that he feeleth in his sowle/ the more payne in recompense let hym put uppon his body/& purge the spirite by the affliccion of the flesh/ And he who so doth, I dare lay my life/ shall haue his hard hart after relent into tears/ & his sowle in a holesome hevynes & hevenly gladnes too/ specially yf he ioine faythfull prayour therewith/[147]

The second time is when Antony recommends, concerning the issue of true and false revelations, to read 'whole together diuers goodly tratice of that good godly doctor master Iohn Gerson, intitlid *De probatione spirituum*'.[148] Although the issue of spiritual pride acquires more importance in the *Dialogue* than it does in *De probatione spirituum*, where it is mentioned only in passing, this theme is present in other Gerson's writings. In *Mountain of Contemplation* the author warns about the dangers of spiritual pride for all those who might falsely believe themselves safe from it in their quest for a contemplative life: 'car toute fois que la personne se plaist et s'esioist en soi et de soi, soit certaine qu'elle n'a mie vraie humilité'.[149] There is a striking similarity between this passage and More's statement that 'proude/which will somewhat apere, by his delite in his own prayse/or yf of wiliness/ or of a nother pride for to be praysid of humilite/'.[150] A comparison between the *Dialogue of Comfort* and *Mountain of Contemplation* reveals other parallels, as in the following fragments:

---

[146] *Dialogue of Comfort*, CWTM 12: 97.
[147] *Dialogue of Comfort*, CWTM 12: 98.
[148] *Dialogue of Comfort*, CWTM 12: 133.
[149] *La Montagne de contemplation*, OC: 7: 1, p. 55. 'For whenever a person is pleased with herself and takes joy in herself and for herself, she can be certain that she does not have true humility' (McGuire 1998, pp. 124–25).
[150] *Dialogue of Comfort*, CWTM, 12: 133.

More: He is fynally sad of that of which he may be glad. For sith he taketh such thoughtes displesauntly & striveth & fighteth against them/ he hath therby a good token that he is in godes favour/ and that god assisteth hym and helpeth hym/[151]

Gerson: [...] la personne se desplaist et est vile et abhominable a soi meismes, et nient mains a plaisance très grand, mais c'est en la grasce et misericorde et bonté divine.[152]

More: And ouer that [tribulation]/ this beside that, this conflict that he hath agaynst his temptacion shall [...] be an occasion of his merite, & of a right greate reward in hevin/ and the payne that he taketh therein/ shall for so much (as master Gerson well sheweth) stand him in stede of his purgatory/[153]

Gerson: Et combien qu'on désire que la tribulation passe et cesse, pour la doleur [...] toutes fois elle engendre et apporte fruit très paisible [...] ne se puet partir sans tribulation en voie, par dehors ou prise par penitance volentaire et par mortification de sa charnalité.[154]

In *Dialogue of Comfort* More also concurs with Gerson on the issue of special revelations.[155] Considering such revelations to be extremely rare and requiring a careful approach, More believed that: 'For no man except reuelacyon, can be sure whyther he be partener of the pardon or not/'[156]

A special and lengthy attention is given, to the distinctly Gersonian issue of a scrupulous conscience. More, with his 'notoriously fastidious tendency to scrupulosity',[157] dedicates chapter fourteen[158] to troubles of a '[scrupulous person who] confessith

---

[151] *Dialogue of Comfort*, CWTM, 12: 153.

[152] OC: 7: 1, p. 55. 'A person becomes displeasing and is vile and repulsive to herself, even though she will derive much joy from the grace, mercy and goodness of God' (McGuire 1998, p. 125).

[153] *Dialogue of Comfort*, CWTM 12: 153.

[154] OC: 7: 1, p. 26. 'And although one desires that tribulation should cease, the pain [...] nevertheless brings an undeniable good. One cannot get rid of one's carnality without tribulation' (McGuire 1998, p. 87).

[155] Oberman 1963, p. 231.

[156] *The Confutation of Tyndale's Answer*, CWTM 8: 1: 290.

[157] Cummings 2009, p. 480.

[158] Edmund Colledge and Noel Chadwick point at the total absence of exact parallels between *De Remediis contra Temptaciones* (1359) by an English mystic William Flete and More's works (Colledge & Chadwick, 1968, vol. 5).

& confessith agayne, & confessith hym selfe [...] yet he is not satisfied, but yf he say it agayne & yet after that agayne [...] as litell is he satisfied at the last as with the first/'.[159] One substantial difference between Gerson's and More's treatment of this topic is the importance given to the role of the devil. Gerson does not mention him, while More makes him an active protagonist in the drama of too scrupulous a conscience:

> With this nights feare the devil sore trouleth the mynd of many a right good man [...] and will kepe hym without consolation [...] More ouer maketh hym [man] to take for synne, some hyng that is none/& for dedly, some such as are but veniall/to the entent that he shall fall into them, he shall be reson of his scriple synne wherels he shuld not [...] Yee & further the devil longeth to make all his good workes & spirituall exercise so paynfull & so tedious unto hym, that with some other suggestion or false ease wily doctrine of a false spirituall libertie, he shuld for the false ease & pleasure that he shuld soddenly fynd therin, be easely conveyd from that evill faute into a much worse.[160]

Indeed, in *Dialogue of Comfort* the devil evolves into the main character appearing practically on every page. For example, when Gerson advises, in order to avoid being frightened to the point of complete despair, to have a firm hope in [God's] goodness,[161] More, on the same matter, reassures that:

> [...] no devil is so diligent to destroy hym/as god is to preserve hym/ nor no devil so nere hym to do hym harme/as god is to do hym good/ nor all the devils in hell so strong to invade & assawte hym/ as god to defend hym/yf he distrust hym not but faithfully put his trust in hym.[162]

Why the devil makes such frequent appearances in More's text is a fascinating question for historians and cultural anthropologists,

---

[159] *Dialogue of Comfort CWTM* 12: 113.
[160] *Dialogue of Comfort CWTM* 12: 113–14.
[161] *La Montagne de contemplation*, OC: 7: 1, p. 53: 'Ou second estaige ou tabernacle ou maison, demeure esperance qui baille fiance a la personne devote affin que par trop grant paour elle ne se desespoire et se perde. Et yci doibt considérer tout ce qui fait a avoir bonne esperance de la bonté de Dieu'.
[162] *Dialogue of Comfort CWTM* 12: 153.

but this pattern surely brings to mind Luther's well known obsession with the evil spirit, whom he believed to be involved in every aspect of our daily life, since whatever is not of God must necessarily be of the devil.[163] Compared to More's, Gerson's handling of the issue of a tremulous conscience reads as a milder, more confident and more practical take on the subject:

> Premierement soit oublié le temps passé [...] pour mieulx aler au pardeuant en vostre service et demander pardon a Dieu par generale constriction, comme en disant jusques a cy, sire, l'ay perdu mon temps par malhaise vie et dissolue etc. [...][164]

The closing pages of the *Dialogue of Comfort* speak of the Passion of Christ, leading toward the Tower writings, where Gerson's impact reaches its maximum: the English *Treatise upon the Passion* and the Latin work on the same subject, *De Tristitia Christi* (*About the Sorrow, Weariness, Fear, and Prayer of Christ Before he Was Seized*). These works pick up where *Dialogue of Comfort* left off: the agony of Christ. More's focus on the Passion comes from a long medieval tradition, resurfacing each time, when the world appears to be in turmoil and the last days to be at hand. Both works use the method developed by Gerson in *Monotessaron*, which is explicitly acknowledged as the major source for them both.[165] More speaks about his personal copy of *Monotessaron*, which he had with him in prison:

> Here I will gyue the reader warnynge, that I wyll rehearse the words of the evangelistes in this process of the passion, in latyne, word by word after my copy, as I fynde it in the worke of that worshipful father maister Iohn Gerson, which worke he entitled Monotessaron [...][166]

The number of places in which *Treatise upon the Passion* agrees with *Monotessaron* rather than with the Vulgate suggests that it was indeed the main source of More's work. The reliance on the

---

[163] Luther believed in the existence of an entire church of Satan and preached that 'the Devil is beside you'. See Gordon 2000, p. 89 & p. 101, citing Luther's *Sermo de angelis*.

[164] *Contre conscience trop scrupuleuse*, OC: 7: 1, p. 140.

[165] See Hallett & Bassett, 1941, pp. 45–74.

[166] *The Treatise Upon the Passion*, CWTM 13: 50.

Parisian master is so significant that 'More seems to ascribe to Gerson an authority nearly as great as that of Scripture itself'.[167] He keeps his exposition:

> in suche wyse as the right famous clerk Maister Iohn Gerson rehearseth in his woorke called *Monatessaron*, gathered of the woordes of al the three evangelists, saint Mathewe, saint Marke, and sainte Luke, and in a conuenient order, linked and chained ensewinglye together [...][168]

Favoring Gerson's sequencing of events in Jesus's life,[169] and quoting very large sections of *Monotessaron*, More, sometimes translating, sometimes closely paraphrasing Gerson's text, retains its literal sense and its system of abbreviations. Following his strong desire 'to come closer to the language of Gerson himself',[170] More declares in the *Warning to the Reader* in *Treatise Upon the Passion*, his determination to stick to the chancellor's text verbatim 'in englyshe, nothing wil I put of myne own [...]'.[171] The only real deviation from *Monotessaron* is the insertion of the name 'Iohn' in place of the usual abbreviation for the Gospel of John ('I').[172] Adopting a format that provides the reader first with an English translation of the relevant passage from Gerson's Latin harmony, and then with the Gospel verse, the Englishman lets '[the Word] speak in the form of his terse and simple translations from Gerson's harmony of the four Gospels'.[173]

Yet, in spite of repeated declarations that 'I wil not in any worde wyllinglye, mangle or mutilate that honourable mans worke',[174] More does not translate the whole *Monotessaron*, nor does he quote its entire text in Latin. A careful stylist and humanist, he cannot help editing Gerson's original, trying to avoid that 'som

---

[167] Logan 2011, p. 244.
[168] *The Treatise Upon the Passion*, CWTM 13: 118.
[169] Rodgers 2011, pp. 244–45.
[170] Miller, 1984, Commentary I to *The Treatise Upon the Passion*, CWTM 14: 2: 909.
[171] *Treatise Upon the Passion*, CWTM 13: 50–51.
[172] *Treatise Upon the Passion*, CWTM 13:50.
[173] Martz 1900, p. 43.
[174] *Treatise Upon the Passion*, CWTM 13: 50–51.

one sentence wyth so little chaunge so often repeted'.[175] Besides, *Monotessaron* is not the only Gerson's text that More relies upon in *Treatise Upon the Passion*. His concept of three attributes of *oratio* — actual, virtual, and habitual — is taken from *De oratione et eius ualore*. His translation of a passage from this text displays, once again, his tendency to explicitly warn against 'an evil spirit [...] that may creep into our imaginations',[176] whilst Gerson speaks of *phantasia* or mental wandering during a prayer as one of many physical and psychological obstacles to proper concentration.[177] There are also parallels between More's *Treatise Upon the Passion* and two other Gerson's texts: *De communione sub utraque specie* and *Sermo de angelis*.[178] It is also likely, considering More's great familiarity with Gerson's works, that he had some knowledge of other works centered on the Passion, such as the *Sermo alius in cena Domini* or *Expositio in passionem Domini*.

The great esteem in which More held Gerson in the *Treatise Upon the Passion* reaches crescendo in his Latin and last Tower Work *De tristitia* or *De Tristitia Christi*,[179] which represents an extended evangelical harmony also built upon *Monotessaron*. More's view on the idea of evangelical harmony differs sharply from Protestant users of the same period, since he believed that one needs guidance to understand the Scriptures, and this guidance must come from an established spiritual authority of the Church, and not from a private person's arbitrary understanding.[180] Consequently, no passage should appear without an extended and learned theological commentary. In *De Tristitia* the commentary is that of Gerson. Apart from combining it with

---

[175] *Treatise Upon the Passion, CWTM* 13: 50.

[176] *De Tristitia Christi CWTM* 14: 1: 139.

[177] *De oratione et eius ualore*, OC: 2, p. 186: *[...] alioquin nunquam potest cor suum quietare, quia nititur ad impossibile sibi per naturam uel complexionem uel consuetudinem uel phantasiae turbationem quae nunquam potest, sicut tradunt medici.* 'otherwise one can never quiet his heart, because one strives by himself for the impossible, which can never be due to nature or complexion or habit or agitation of imagination, as physicians teach'.

[178] See Curran 1956.

[179] There seems to be no consensus concerning the correct writing of the title of this work. Most sources, including *The Cambridge Companion to Thomas More* and the journal *Moreana*, use *De Tristitia Christi*, with the capitalized 'T', while the editor of the volume 14 of *CWTM*, C. H. Miller, spells it *De tristitia Christi*.

[180] *De Tristitia, CWTM* 14: 1: 21.

illustrations, there are three basic problems with harmonizing the text of the Scriptures. One is chronology, which consists of establishing a unified time sequence for the new narrative of Christ's life compiled out of four different stories, each with its own sequence of events. Another is reconciling variations in accounts of the same episode in the four gospel sources. The third is needing to retain every word of Holy Writ, while avoiding redundancies that would hinder the narrative flow. In More's opinion *Monotessaron* was successful in addressing all three challenges, implicitly or explicitly, and in providing a readily available composite text that blended variations and offered a widely-accepted chronology.[181] The last part of *Monotessaron*, *De egressu passionis et resurrectionis Christi*, serves as the foundation for More's *De Tristitia*,[182] which follows the Gersonian pattern even closer than *Treatise upon the Passion*. Thus, *De Tristitia*'s structure coincides almost exactly with that of *Monotessaron*, which is a single narrative divided into one hundred fifty chapters and three parts: *De origine Christi et ingressu eius* (On the lineage and birth of Christ), *De praedicatione Ionannis et de progressu praedicationis Christi* (On the preaching of John and the diffusion of Christ's preaching), and *De egressu passionis et resurrectionis Christi* (On the Passion and Resurrection of Christ). This system is entirely preserved by Thomas More. More appropriates Gerson's expressions, metaphors and sometimes extended passages. One example is the word *distractio* in the context of inattention during prayer, with which More struggled personally. Clinging to 'the reassuring advice'[183] of 'this remarkable man Gerson',[184] the Englishman is comforted by the reflection that 'involuntary distractions in no way distract from the merit of the original intention to pray, any more than the mental wanderings of a pilgrim on his way to a shrine could nullify decision to make the pilgrimage'.[185] Another case is the Gersonian metaphor of prayer being like a rock that continues to move long after the thrower tossed it.[186] Even though More differs

---

[181] Monti 1997, p. 366.
[182] Rodgers 2011, p. 244.
[183] Monti 1997, p. 395.
[184] *De Tristitia CWTM* 14: 621.
[185] *De tristitia CWTM* 14: 313–14.
[186] Miller 1984, Commentary 1 *CWTM* 14: 910.

from Gerson in some instances, such as the timing of Jesus's arrest in the Garden of Gethsemane, when he argues, against Gerson, that the capture took place as soon as Judas kissed the Lord, these minor deviations only underline his respect for the French theologian, which borders on adoration:

> Exactly when they first laid hands on Jesus is a point on which the experts disagree [...] For Matthew and Mark relate the events in such an order as to allow the conjuncture that they laid hands on Jesus immediately after Judas' kiss. And this is the opinion adopted not only by many celebrated doctors of the church but also approved by that remarkable man John Gerson [...] in his work *Monotessaron* (the work which I have generally followed in enumerating the events of the passion in this discussion.[187]

Even when disagreeing with his kindred spirit, More frames his difference 'less as a criticism than as an appreciation and acknowledgment of Gerson's *Monotessaron* as a source'[188] of his Tower works. At this stage of his imprisonment, he sees the act of composing a Gospel harmony as an occasion for a deep meditation on the text of the Gospels, just as Gerson wanted such an exercise to be. It is indeed a spiritual exercise, a scripted meditation.

In addition to *Monotessaron* More relies on the insights that *eruditissimus idemque optimus Iohannes Gerson in eo tradit opusculo quod de oratione et eius ualore composuit*.[189] In fact, his quotes from *De oratione et eius ualore* are so exact as to suggest that he had this text with him in the Tower.[190] The choice to arrange *De Tristitia* into three parts — biblical text, commentary and prayer — corresponds to the structure of Gerson's *Expositio in passionem Domini*, which begins at the same moment of the Lord's Passion as More's *De Tristitia*: in the Garden of Gethsemane.

In *De Tristitia* More returns, once more, to the subject of scrupulous conscience. Sensing that behind Gerson's formal-

---

[187] *De Tristitia CWTM* 14: 1: 623.
[188] Rodgers 2011, p. 243.
[189] *De Tristitia CWTM* 14: 1: 326–27. *De ualore orationis et de attentione*, OC: 2, pp. 175–91.
[190] Miller 1984, Commentary 2, Historical and Explanatory Notes, *CWTM* 14: 1034.

istic language lies personal experience of anxiety, More advises all those 'who are troubled and saddened because their attention slips away',[191] 'whom this distraction of mind made so terribly anxious that they repeated the individual words of their prayers [...] and still got nowhere and [...] through sheer weariness, lost all sense of consolation from their prayers and [...] were ready to give up'[192] to look for comfort in the writings of the unique spiritual doctor:

> Nevertheless, since I bore down on this point as vigorously as I could by attacking that sort of prayer in which the mind is not attentive but wandering and distracted [...] it would be well at this point to propose an emollient from Gerson to alleviate this sore point, lest I seem to be like a harsh surgeon touching this common sore too roughly, bringing to many tender-souled mortals not a healing medicine but rather pain [...] In order to cure these troublesome inflammations of the soul, Gerson uses certain palliatives which are analogous to those medications which doctors use to relieve bodily pain and which are called 'anodynes' ('*medici uocant anodyne*')[193]

One such remedy is the idea of mental pilgrimage,[194] which found an enthusiastic imitator in Geiler von Kaysersberg.[195] It is only natural that the idea of a mental or virtual (as we would say now) journey would appeal to a man deprived of freedom of movement:

> For such a person sometimes goes forward on his journey and at the same time mediates on the holy saint and the purpose of the pilgrimage. And so this man throughout this whole time continues his pilgrimage by a double act, namely (and I shall use Gerson's own words) by a 'natural continuity' and a 'moral continuity', thus bringing double benefit.[196]

---

[191] Miller 1984, Introduction, *CWTM* 14: 1: 327.
[192] *De Tristitia CWTM* 14: 1: 315–17.
[193] *De Tristitia CWTM* 14: 1: 314–15.
[194] *De Tristitia CWTM* 14: 1: 315–17.
[195] One short English manual by Thomas Winchelsae (d. 1437), *Instructorium Provide Peregrini*, 'was influenced by the spiritual works of Jean Gerson, notably by the latter's *Testamentum Peregrini*'. (Roest 2004, p. 442).
[196] *De Tristitia Christi*, 14: 1: 319.

The main dissimilarity between Gerson's and More's harmonies is, once again, stylistic. The Englishman's humanist elegance contrasts sharply with Gerson's scholastic expression. While quoting Augustine's classical Latin verbatim,[197] the humanist in More could not help embellishing and clarifying Gerson's 15th century idiom. Humanist stylizing did not result in shortening of the text though. For example, in rendering one of Gerson's passages concerning an analogy between prayer and pilgrimage, More, covering 'almost exactly the same ground', used 444 words where Gerson used only 291.[198] It should be taken into account that Gerson's audience was almost exclusively clerical, while More's readers belonged to quite a different social milieu of Renaissance humanists and cultured laity, who greatly valued stylistic sophistication and verbal virtuosity. The latter never fail in *De Tristitia*, a highly personal, intense and, at times, heartbreaking work, beautifully written during the most extreme moments of dread and abandonment experienced by its author awaiting his execution:

> If a man saves his life by offending God, he will find the life he has saved in this way to be hateful. For if you save your life in this way, on the very next day you yourself will find your life hateful and you will be very sorry indeed that you did not suffer death the day before. How foolish is it to avoid a temporary death by incurring an eternal one! And not even to avoid the temporary one, but merely to put it off for a little while! Finally you are doubtless aware that when the fatal disease arrives and your anguish begins to grow worse in the throes of death, you will wish you had died long before [...] Therefore you should not be so desperately afraid of what might happen, since you know that a little later you will wish that that very thing had happened.[199]

'Desperately afraid' and 'in the throes of death', More, 'the most medieval'[200] of the 16th century intellectual giants, is clearly out of line with the modern concept of freedom of conscience

---

[197] *CWTM* 14: 2: 7 65.
[198] *CWTM* 14: 2: 765.
[199] *De Tristitia Christi*, *CWTM* 14: 2: 639, 643, 645.
[200] Suzanne 1981, p. 241.

'that he is often quoted as an example of'.[201] Indeed, More's conscience conforms to the position of the Catholic Church: 'Carefully orthodox and conservative' conscience for More is not 'an arbitrary act of will',[202] but the law of God, as formulated by the holy Catholic Church. His determination not to cave in to Henry VIII's pressure to recognize the king as the head of the Church of England was based on the same foundation as Gerson's resolve to resist John's the Fearless attempts to legitimize political murder by the theory of tyrannicide. This foundation comprises of Christian faith and morality as upheld by the Roman Catholic Church. Nothing could be more absurd in the view of both Gerson and More 'than to go willingly to death on account of a personal opinion'.[203] More's Tower writings, just like Gerson's spiritual testimony *De consolatione theologiae*, reveal a deeply introspective work of a Christian focused on his main purpose: personal salvation, which cannot, according to both authors, be sacrificed, to no matter for how great a cause. Just as a good end cannot justify immoral means, collective good cannot justify the loss of an individual soul, be it through a violent crime or a slow corruption. This final consideration is of principal importance. For Gerson and More personal salvation is an absolute, non-negotiable boundary at which all other considerations must stop. This, by itself, leads to an increased personal awareness. In other words, even if the motive for Gerson's and More's affirmation of individual conscience is exactly opposite of what we understand as freedom of conscience today, since it affirms not the right to be different but the right to remain the same (in More's case the right to remain loyal to the Catholic Church), in new historical circumstances the affirmation of this right *de facto* becomes an act of individual defiance.

---

[201] Cummings 2007, p. 4.
[202] Cummings 2007, p. 4.
[203] Rex 2011, p. 97.

Part IV. Gerson's Influence on the Growth of Common Law in England

> Law is central to the story of early modern ideas in ways now hard to appreciate.'[204]

Although the importance of Gerson's intellectual contribution to the emergence of the early modern judicial order has recently attracted an unprecedented notice of legal scholars,[205] his influence on English jurisprudence still awaits a full evaluation. This chapter will focus on just one aspect of his impact in this area: the development of the concept of equity or *epikeia* (ἐπιείκεια in Greek), 'a sphere where Gerson's historical importance has yet to be gauged'.[206] The idea of *epikeia* or judgment delivered according to fairness intending to correct the law, where the latter might err because of its too universal and standardized nature, is derived from Aristotle's book five of *Nicomachean Ethics* and book one, chapters thirteen and fifteen, of the *Rhetoric*. This concept, already difficult to assess already in Aristotle, who provides no unified concept of it,[207] has a long history in Western thought. It begins in Greco-Roman antiquity, continues in the High Middle Ages with the rediscovery of Aristotle by Thomas Aquinas,[208] and remerges in the late medieval period with Gerson, who based his reworking of *epikeia* on Aristotle and Thomas's *Summa Theologica*.[209] In the English tradition *epikeia* is associated with the English Court of Chancery,[210] commonly understood as the gentle inter-

---

[204] Franklin 2016, p. 5.

[205] Bauer 2004; Thierny 2005; Varkemaa 2005; Mäkinen 2006; Varkemaa 2009; Decock & Hallebeek 2010; Decock 2012; Bader 2014; Majeske 2014; Schüssler 2014; Astorri 2019.

[206] Hobbins 2006, p. 66.

[207] Shanske 2005, p. 1: 'Because there is neither a unified concept nor a direct evolutionary history nor a simple account, i.e. Aristotle's, which would allow one to bypass the confused reality of the tradition, appealing to equity is more fraught than is commonly recognized'.

[208] According to Norbert Horn, Thomas Aquinas retains virtually all of the aspects that are first found in Aristotle himself (Horn 1968, *supra* note). Thomas's innovation consists in connecting equity with a fixed natural law given by God. See Goerner 1983.

[209] Also known as *Summa theologiae* or simply *Summa*.

[210] The American institution of a Supreme Court closely resembles the Chancery. Bernadette Meyler argues that the founding fathers opted for a double dose

pretation of a law',[211] or a 'particularized justice'.[212] This concept has remained relevant in Anglo-American jurisprudence and in the countries of the British Commonwealth, being continuously appealed to in arbitration, federal procedures,[213] environmental law, international law,[214] and in sentencing.[215]

A particular interest in *epikeia* in the English-speaking world has its own history. According to Donald R. Kelley, who saw in the introduction of *epikeia* an example of English legal nationalism,[216] it was reinstated on the island independent of continental developments and, therefore, untainted by medieval deviations, due to the 'direct' reception of Aristotle in the 16th century England.[217] This opinion is no longer supported by legal researchers who agree that the rising importance of the concept of *epikeia* in the 16th century England is related to the English reception of Gerson's interpretation of this notion.[218] It is during the battle of books, which animated English intellectual life for the five years between the first publication of St Germain's *Doctor and Student* in 1528, and 1533, the publication year of Thomas More's *Apology*, that Gerson's reading of *epikeia*, which he 'aligned with the Roman legal appeal to *aequitas* or fairness',[219] found itself at the center of public attention. Both famous lawyers, Thomas More and St Germain, quoted Gerson, and claimed him as their main authority.

The antagonism between the legal subject and the objective, public legal order, which increased during the King of England's consolidation of absolute authority and power, must have made Gerson's take on *epikeia* particularly pertinent. Although not completely original, his interpretation of this concept is unique

---

of equity through mandating jury trials in many cases, which were also justified by appeal to their equitable discretion (Meyler 2006, pp. 38–39).

[211] Hobbins 2006, p. 66.
[212] Shanske 2005, p. 7.
[213] See Main 2003, p. 429.
[214] See DeVine 1989.
[215] See Nussbaum 1993, p. 83, & the discussion in Shanske 2005, pp. 1–2.
[216] Shanske 2005, pp. 13–14.
[217] Kelley 1974, p. 28 & p. 30.
[218] See Rueger 1982; Zahnd 1996; Behrens 1999; Curtright 2012; Hutson 2002.
[219] Oakley 2006, p. 192.

and highly influential for several reasons. The first is Gerson's 'dramatic new emphasis on cases' as an 'intellectual tool to deal with complexity in all its forms because every moral issue should be judged according to circumstances and [...] no general rule can be applied to every problem'.[220] This process of 'thinking in terms of specific cases as opposed to what he called "general rules"'[221] is exemplified in *De consolatione theologiae*, where its author affirms that *non satis est intelligere quid uerum est et quod rectum, sicut cadit sub arte trader, sed particulares circumstantias, quae uariabiles sunt, neque sub arte neque doctrina ueniunt.*[222] This idea is central to Gerson's thought process, and is found in many of his writings, both in major works such as *De uita spirituali animae, De non esu carnium apud carthusienses, De religionis perfectione et moderatione*, and *Regulae morales*, and in a variety of shorter texts, from sermons to letters.

The second reason that makes Gerson's take on *epikeia* notable is that he considers its application in Christian society to be a desired norm rather than an exception. Suggesting it should be inbuilt in every law and followed in every case,[223] and be the basis of political and judicial decisions, he claimed that *aequitas quam nominat Philosophus epikeiam, praeponderat iuris rigori.*[224] The Parisian chancellor hoped to apply the principle of *epikeia* widely, affirming that reforms of ecclesiastical law are to be 'undertaken in the spirit of Aristotle's doctrine of justice of the *Ethics*'.[225] He extended the famous definition of the canon lawyer Hostiensis or Henry of Segusio (1200–1271) — *aequitas est iustitia dulcore mise-*

---

[220] Hobbins 2006, pp. 66–67.

[221] Hobbins 2006, p. 66.

[222] *De consolatione theologiae*, OC: 9, 239. 'It is not enough to understand what is true and right, as it falls under art to teach this. But one must understand particular circumstances which are changeable and which come under neither art nor doctrine' (Miller 1998, p. 263).

[223] Rueger 1982, p. 15.

[224] *Regulae morales*, OC: 9, pp. 95–96. 'equity, which the Philosopher named *epieikeia*, supersedes rigorous justice'.

[225] Rueger 1982, p. 6. Behrens's argument that for Gerson *epikeia* was exclusively 'a principle the practical significance of which lay in its ability to explain why the Church could in an emergency call a general council without papal approval', does not seem to hold true for the integrity of Gerson's oeuvre. Even if our inquiry were to be restricted to the presence of the words *epikeia* or equity in Gerson's writings, Behrens's evaluation would appear too narrow (Behrens 1999, p. 26).

ricordiae temperate[226] — to the formula [...] *est autem aequitas iustitia pensatis omnibus circumstantiis particularibus, dulcore misericordiae temperate.*[227] Moreover, Gerson's application of *epikeia* is not restricted to canon law and ecclesiastical government, but extends to worldly justice and royal politics. Thus, his legal treatise *Diligite iustitiam*, containing a plea to restrict death penalties to a minimum, exemplifies *justice se doit faire par amer bien.*[228] The definition of equity in his treatise *De quatuor uirtutibus cardinalibus* is clearly applicable to civil life:

> *Epikeia seu epiekya uel aequitas uel iustitia interpretatiua, est iustitia qua quis inclinatur obedire legibus, respiciendo ad intellectum quem habebat uel uerisimiliter habuisset legislator in particulari hoc casu, circumstantiis omnibus hinc inde ponderatis.*[229]

In this regard, Gerson continued the line of his famous mentor and friend Pierre d'Ailly (1351–1420) who 'regularly appealed to secular analogies and thought the concept of mixed government applied to any "rightly ordained policy"'.[230] Notwithstanding the crucial difference between the secular and political nature of Aristotle's *epikeia* and the Christian notion of *misericordia*, Gerson promoted equity not as a charitable concession but simply as fairness due to each Christian subject.[231]

---

[226] Lefebvre 1963, p. 123, citing Hostiensis, *Summa Aurea*, Book V, *De dispensationibus*: 'Equity is justice tempered by the sweetness of mercy'.

[227] *Regulae morales*, OC: 9, pp. 95–96. 'Equity is justice which, after taking into consideration all given circumstances, is tempered with the sweetness of mercy'. Glorieux put the date of the *Regulae morales* among the large number of works written in 1400–1415.

[228] *Diligite iustitiam*, OC: 7: 1, pp. 611–12. See also *Requête pour les condamnés à mort* (opus 323), OC: 7: 1, p. 341: 'Dieu ne veult pas que tous maulx soient punis en ce monde car aultrement il n'auroit que juger en l'aultre'. The *Requête* is mainly a plea for granting confession to the condemned before their execution.

[229] *De quatuor uirtutibus*, OC: 9, p. 152. '*Epikeia* or *epiekya* or equity or interpretative justice is the kind of justice by which a person inclines to obey the law in some particular case, taking into account his own understanding or the probable understanding of the legislator, after carefully weighing off all circumstances'.

[230] Mayer 2002, p. 82.

[231] Andrew Majeske credits Gerson with a noble but unsuccessful attempt to combine Christian mercy with Aristotelian thought. Majeske 2014, p. 22.

> [...] *epikeia meditante, quam latine possumus aequitatem nominare, cuius est iura scripta non ad uerborum corticem sed ad intentionis medullam inspicere [...] Medulla uero intentionis qualis altera est quam pax, quam caritas, nam finis legis caritas secundum Apostolum.*[232]

Denouncing as 'vicious extremes of bad judgment' both — 'severity, austerity or judicial rigour' and 'foolish mercy or too outspoken softness'[233] — he thought of *epikeia*, a political virtue compatible with, and modified by, Christian morality, as an equilibrium between the two.

Gerson's promotion of Christian *epikeia* was not bound to theory. In 1391, while still a young man of twenty-eight, he urged King Charles VI, in his text *Adorabunt eum*, to apply balanced and compassionate judgments in response to the shortcomings of his subjects and to avoid harsh measures that sow discord.[234] In the early 15th century he proceeded to advertise the same idea to Charles's sons via two epistolary treatises addressed to their preceptors. The first, *Claro eruditori*, was written between 1408 and 1410 on the request of Jean d'Arsonval († 1416), tutor of Prince Louis (1397–1415), the oldest son of King Charles VI. The second, *Erunt omnes docibiles*, probably composed in 1417, was intended for the newly appointed preceptor — perhaps the physician Jean Cadart († 1449) — of Louis's younger brother Charles (1403–1461), who would ascend the throne in 1422 as Charles VII.[235] The virtues to be upheld by the dauphin are *humanitas*, *clementia* and *humilitas*, which are qualities that preclude, in Gerson's opin-

---

[232] *Fax uobis*, OC: 5, p. 442. 'Reflecting on *epikeia*, which we can call in Latin equity, which is the law written to look not into the surface of words but into the core [marrow] of intentions [...] The core of intentions is truly other than peace, other than charity, for charity is the end of law according to the Apostle'.

[233] *De quatuor uirtutibus*, OC: 9, p. 152: *Seueritas uel austeritas uel rigor iudicii, spectat ad hoc uitium per excessum. Stulta misericordia uel nimius dulcor, spectat ad hoc uitium per remissum*. The same view is found in Gerson's vernacular *Diligite iustitiam*, OC: 7: 1, p. 603: 'En sa justice fera justice sans exceder en trop grande rigidite, ou decouler en trop grande langueur; sera fourme, sans fourvoier ca et la, a dextre ou a senestre'.

[234] *Adorabunt eum*, OC: 7: 2, pp. 519–38.

[235] The letters are edited as opera 42 and 86 in OC: 2, p. 335 & p. 38, respectively. For more on their dates and addressees see Picascia 1987, pp. 235–36.

ion, harsh, abusive or arbitrary forms of government.[236] The chancellor's emphasis on justice tempered by love (as in *Adorabunt eum*) or *iustitia moderata* (as in *Claro eruditori*) corresponds to *epikeia* in the domain of secular government, with moderate justice upheld as the prime political virtue of French monarchs and an essential quality for royal government in Christian countries in general. This is one of the most significant aspects of Gerson's reworking of the concept of *epikeia*,[237] and the one that would later be of special interest in 16th century England.

The third reason that renders Gerson's contribution to the development of the concept of *epikeia* extraordinary[238] is his attentiveness to individual differences, without which the proper understanding of human positive law is impaired:

> [...] pro intelligentia iuris humani positiui utilis est conuersio deorsum ad conditionis humanae multiplicis statum uarium ubi relucet aliquod remotum ualde et imperfectum Dei uestigium, et hoc ut epikeia uel aequitas conseruetur.[239]

This alertness to human variety, which Pierre Pascal once called 'psychology',[240] is not an isolated trait, but runs throughout Gerson's works, where he 'tried to appreciate human weakness, diversity, and perplexity, and offered mercy to strict and suffering consciences'.[241] Whether in the guidance of contemplative practices, the art of hearing confessions or the administration of judicial proceedings, the extreme diversity of human types, circumstances and even moods must be taken into consideration:

---

[236] Gerson's views were deeply rooted in legal Western tradition and particularly in canon law. 'The [equity] theory adopted by the canonists included certain civil law elements which canonical tradition had handed down to them. Like Justinian's equity, the equity celebrated in certain canonical texts is the supreme ideal toward which the law, properly subordinated, must tend. It is thus to be contrasted with the positive law, and is marked by special characteristics of humanity, benevolence, and mercy' (Lefebvre 1963, p. 130).

[237] Rueger 1982, p. 15.

[238] Rueger 1982, p. 9.

[239] Gerson, *Conversi estis*, OC: 5, p. 175. 'In order to understand human positive laws it is necessary to direct one's attention to the diverse and manifold nature of the human condition, where the trace of God is imperfect and very remote, so that *epikeia* or equity may be preserved'.

[240] Pascal 1944, p. 33: 'au départ de son système il y a une psychologie'.

[241] Tentler 1977, p. 159.

> Et ie respons que on ne tient mie une maniere de penser tousiours, mais tres diverse selonc les personnes, le lieu et le tamps, et la gracse de Dieu, et la doctrine ou science que on a. L'un y va ainsi, li autre autrement; voire un meismes ira ung par une maniere, demain par l'autre.[242]

The chancellor's idea of equity comes as much from the Aristotelian tradition as from his pastoral experience.

All three aspects of Gerson's contribution to the concept of *epikeia (sometimes spelled epieikeia)* resurfaced almost a century after his passing in English political and legal discourse. It was Thomas More who, during his two and a one-half years of service (October 1529-May 1532) as Lord Chancellor, 'planted a seed that was to flower much later into a "new" perspective on common law methodology in the common law courts themselves, specifically construing equity to be inherent to the common law'.[243] Using his role as the Chancellor 'to arbitrate in exceptional cases, to prevent an injustice that might occur through the strict application of the law, and to insist that obligations were carried out',[244] More began to apply Gerson's idea of *epikeia* in the legal practice of common law more widely 'than in the practical business of Chancery'.[245] Although the Court of Chancery had emerged already in the 15th century, More, unlike the majority of his predecessors, who had been clerics, was a lawyer,[246] and he used his experience and training to expand the tradition of secular chancellors applying equity. While the law demanded a strict construction of statutory and precedential text, equity, which permitted a looser interpretation,[247] needed to be introduced where the common law was too rigid. Seeking to limit inappropriate judgments by blocking the verdicts of the common-law judges, whenever necessary, More established the practice that, when the

---

[242] OC: 7: 1, p. 46. 'One does not always stick to one manner of thought but will react differently according to person, place, time, the grace of God, and the learning or knowledge that one possesses' (McGuire 1998, p. 113).

[243] Bader 2014, p. 434.

[244] Cummings 2009, p. 479.

[245] Cummings 2009, p. 479.

[246] Marius 1984, p. 360: 'Laymen had been chancellors before, but not in the living memory of anyone in the realm'.

[247] Bader 2014, p. 437.

common law courts failed to provide an adequate remedy, plaintiffs could petition the Court of the Chancellor directly, thus providing an additional opportunity for a fair hearing of a complicated case. Eventually the Court of Chancery would be identified as a court of equity.[248] The significance of this step has only recently been acknowledged:

> Despite the fact that his view of equity at common law was not immediately accepted, Thomas More was a legal prophet. He realized that the common law method allowed, indeed mandated, an equitable calculus. A 'loose construction', if you will, was necessary at times to discern the common law's just and reasonable intent in a particular case.[249]

Thomas More's role 'as the first judge to actively encourage the broad use of equity principles in deciding common law cases has been eclipsed'[250] by his more successful rival, St Germain, who defeated him in their political duel. Besides, what More attempted to achieve in everyday practice, St Germain instituted theoretically:

> at the same time as Christopher St Germain was setting out for the English reader the new learning about equity to be found in Aristotle and Gerson, Thomas More was trying to persuade judges of the common law courts to mitigate the rigour of their procedure by following the example of Chancery.[251]

Indeed, with regard to the subject of *epikeia*, the More — St Germain conflict presents a double paradox. On the one hand, 'by a curious irony, More's practice as a lawyer conformed more and more to the ideals set out in St Germain's *Doctor and Student*,[252] while, on the other hand, in *Doctor and Student* 'the concept

---

[248] John A. Guy questions More's achievements in jurisprudence, maintaining that his policies were no different from Wolsey's 'policy of equitable relief', while 'More's main contribution to the refinement of Wolsey's system came in the field of the better enforcement of equitable decrees' (Guy 2000, pp. 133, 135 & 137).
[249] Bader 2014, p. 436.
[250] Bader 2014, p. 434.
[251] Hutson 2002, pp. 145–46.
[252] Cummings 2009, p. 479.

of *epikeia* was pressed into service in a theory aimed at explaining, and providing an apology for, the peculiar jurisdiction of conscience claimed by the English Chancellor'.[253]

Christopher St Germain

The majority of scholars [254] believe Gerson's influence on St Germain's political and legal views to be very significant: 'if the English lawyers learned from Christopher St Germain, he learned directly from Gerson'.[255] A keen politician, St Germain perceived the potential that Gerson's take on *epikeia* represented and seized it, arguing that now was the moment when *epikeia* needed to be introduced:

> [...] makers of law take heed to such things as may often come, and not to every particular case, for they could not though they would. And therefore, to follow the words of the law were in some case both against justice and the commonwealth. Wherefore in some cases it is necessary to love the words of the law, and to follow that reason and justice requires, and to that intent equity is ordained; that is to say, to temper and mitigate the rigor of the law. And it is called also by some men epieikeia; the which is no other thing but an exception of the law of God, or the law of reason, from the general rules of the law of men, when they by reason of their generality, would in any particular case judge against the law of God or the law of reason: the which exception is secretly understood in every general rule of every positive law.[256]

Thus formulated, *epikeia* becomes a general legal principle, an acceptable adjustment to the written law: 'when human law conflicts with the law of God or the law of reason, human law suffers an exception'.[257] St Germain not only 'transplanted Gerson's theory of *epikeia* from a context of reflection about the institu-

---

[253] Behrens 1999, p. 26.
[254] Among these researchers are Behrens, Curtright, Klinck, Oakley, Rueger and Janda (Janda 1997).
[255] Rueger 1964, p. 478.
[256] St Germain 2006, p. 24.
[257] Behrens 1999, p. 25.

tional structure of the Roman Church to the context of reflection about that of the English judicial system',[258] but he also retained key features of the Gersonian understanding of this concept: its potential universality and its joined application with Christian mercy. The first is expressed by the following: 'Such an equity must always be observed in every law of man, and in every general rule thereof [...] Laws covet to be ruled by equity'.[259] The second is taken from Gerson's *Regulae morales* verbatim: 'Equity is a right wiseness that considers all the particular circumstances of the deed, the which also is tempered with the sweetness of mercy'.[260] Based on Gerson, whose 'concept of equity may not be as cohesive as it is sometimes portrayed',[261] St Germain's idea of equity is also a mixed and ambiguous notion: it looks at all the particular circumstances in which the law is to be applied; it is tempered with mercy; it is an exception to the general rules of positive law and to the letter of law, and it is also a principle of interpretation.[262] Gerson's interpretation of Aristotle's doctrine of equity, as explained in the *De non esu carnium apud carthusienses* and further defined in *Regulae morales*, provided the substance of St Germain's chapter *What is Equytie*, which was highly influential in the 16th and 17th centuries England. Even though St Germain might not have been personally or politically concerned with the fairness of trials or the establishment of the degree of guilt by means of *epikeia*, his absorption of Gerson's legal thought served as a channel for the distribution of the Frenchman's ideas, ensuring that 'the strictly medieval conception of equity had a longer life in England than in any other country in Europe'.[263] It must be added that St Ger-

[258] Behrens 1999, p. 26.
[259] Behrens 1999, pp. 25–26.
[260] St Germain 2006, p. 24. *Regulae morales*, OC: 9, pp. 95–96: *Aequitas quam nominat Philosophus epikeiam, praeponderat iuris rigori. Est autem aequitas iustitia pensatis omnibus circumstantiis particularibus, dulcore misericirdiae temporata.*
[261] Klinck 2010, p. 52.
[262] Klinck 2010, p. 48.
[263] Holdsworth 1903–72, IV, p. 279. Although researchers agree on St Germain's indebtedness to Gerson in this matter, opinions vary in relation to the degree of manipulation that the notion of *epikeia* underwent in the Englishman's interpretation. Some argue that this degree is rather low, since St Germain extensively quotes *Regulae morales* and *De non esu carnium apud carthusienses* (Rueger

main's promotion of the concept of equity was not purely theoretical. In 1531, he involved himself in drafting parliamentary legislation that would implement the ideas of *Doctor and Student* and *New Additions* into judicial practice.[264]

Edmund Plowden

In the third quarter of the sixteenth century Gerson's concept of *epikeia*, reworked and popularized by St Germain, found reception and another application in a conservative lawyer Edmund (Edmunde) Plowden (1518–1585) for whom equity became 'a principle that guides the interpretation of statutory law'.[265] Plowden's name achieved notoriety thanks to his collection of legal cases, which he attended from 1550 to 1579, known as *Les Comentaries* and published at his own expense in 1571. For Plowden, just as for St Germain, equity corrects the letter of the human law by looking to the law of God and the law of reason:

> [...] Both St Germain and Plowden seek to correct positive law by recurring to higher justice [...] The difference is that Plowden, but not St Germain, identifies the sense of the law with the intention of the legislator.[266]

This last remark deserves special attention. What Plowden understands under 'the intent and meaning of the makers of the law [is] an exercise of imagination by the judge',[267] when, in order to form a right judgment of what is the equity in any given cases 'it is a good way to suppose [...] what the legislator would have said',[268] were he present to evaluate particular circumstances. This reference to a plausible understanding of *epikeia* by a legislator as one of the defining factors of what equity is irresistibly brings to mind

---

1982, p. 17). Others argue that St Germain's formulation of equity is not really Gerson's position (Guy 1986, p. 184).
[264] Monti 1997, p. 314.
[265] Behrens 1999, p. 25.
[266] Behrens 1999, p. 35.
[267] Behrens 1999, p. 32.
[268] Behrens 1999, p. 32.

Gerson's already quoted definition of *epikeia* in his treatise *De quatuor uirtutibus cardinalibus*:

> *Epikeia seu epikya uel aequitas uel iustitia interpretatiua, est iustitia qua quis inclinatur obedire legibus, respiciendo ad intellectum quem habebat uel uerisimiliter habuisset legislator in particulari hoc casu, circumstantiis omnibus hinc inde ponderatis.*[269]

Whether Plowden's exercise in legislative imagination originates from Gerson's 'probable understanding by the legislator' remains to be seen. Plowden's note in *Les Comentaries* , suggesting that 'the imaginative test for legislator intent is guided by normative rather than by factual constrains [and that] the proper construction of the term 'right' is the construction, which any 'reasonable man' would adopt',[270] sounds quite like Gerson's 'right is an immediate faculty or power pertaining to anyone according to right reason'.[271] Although the relation, if any, between the French theologian's legal thought and Edmund Plowden's ideas needs to be investigated further, the above-mentioned parallels show that, thanks to St Germain, Gerson's judicial legacy remained current in England. Even in the 17th century bishop of Bristol, Gilbert Ironside the elder (1588–1671), who 'went so far as to argue that 'that which cannot be deduced out of the principles of naturall reason [...] without revelation' could be neither moral law nor perpetually obliging', felt it necessary to appeal to Gerson's authority against St Paul's in order to argue that perhaps it is not 'alwaies a sinne [...] to goe against the feares and scruples of our minds'.[272]

---

[269] *De quatuor uirtutibus*, OC: 9, p. 152. '*Epikeia* or *epiekya* or equity or interpretative justice is the kind of justice by which a person inclines to obey the law in some particular case, taking into account his own understanding or the probable understanding of [it] by the legislator, after carefully weighing off all circumstances'.

[270] Behrens 1999, p. 35.

[271] *De uita spirituali animae*, OC: 3, p. 146, cited earlier.

[272] Sampson 1988, p. 104. On Gerson's legalistic influence, through Suarez, on another English Puritan thinker, Nathaniel Culverwell (1619–1651), see Culverwell 2001.

Part V. Synderesis and the Notion of Conscience in English Literary and Philosophical Traditions

Gerson's contribution to the development of the concept of conscience provided a strong ground for both 'expansiveness of humanism and expansiveness of the Reformation.'[273] The main conduit of this contribution was the same Christopher St Germain, whose dependence on Gerson in this area might be even more extensive than direct quotations from the chancellor reveal. Thus, in his chapter *Of Conscience*, St Germain is indebted to the sequence and the line of argument from Gerson's *De natura conscientiae*, without, however, acknowledging his source. In his attempt to define private conscience, St Germain also relies on Gerson's reflections concerning the nature of *synderesis* in *De uita spirituali animae*, which he quotes and paraphrases quite liberally.

Even though the concepts of *synderesis* and conscience do not denote the same reality, since 'conscience, unlike *synderesis*, is not the disposition but an action and actualization',[274] historically the emergence of the former in the early modern times is linked to the medieval belief in the latter. While Thomas More, 'like Luther, begins the slow historical process of abandoning the distinction between *synderesis* and *conscientia*',[275] this process is far from being complete in St Germain's works, where it is still centered on the former.[276] Indeed, Gerson's definition of *synderesis* is a 'red thread' running throughout the 16th century.[277]

Gerson was quite taken with the *synderesis*, as it is the foundation of his theology of spiritual quest, the very power that enables the human soul to answer the Holy Spirit, to receive grace and to cooperate with God for her salvation. He defines *synderesis* as

---

[273] Suzanne 1981, p. 235. Prodi grants Gerson a pioneering role concerning the emergence of conscience (Prodi 2000, p. 182).

[274] Klinck 2010, p. 33.

[275] Cummings 2009, p. 482.

[276] Klinck 2010, p. 55. It appears that even for Gerson's contemporaries the exact difference between *synderesis* and conscience was not always clear. Thus, in his letter to Gerson, his friend Nicolas de Clamanges seems to use both terms interchangeably: [...] *aut enim per pugnam istam in unoquoque homine gestam remurmurante synderesi, remordente conscientia* (OC: 2, p. 145) 'in each individual this battle is won either by the murmuring *synderesis*, or by the biting conscience'.

[277] Suzanne 1981, p. 234.

uis animae appetitiua suscipiens immediate a Deo naturalem quamdam inclinationem ad bonum per quam trahitur insequi motionem boni ex apprehension simplicis intelligentiae praesentati.[278] The chancellor develops this concept not only in his Latin learned treatises, such as *De theologia mystica*, but also in vernacular works addressed to popular audiences, such as this sermon *Pour le 4ᵐᵉ mercredi de Carême*:

> [la syndérèse] ne te laisseroit dormir ou reposer et aguillonner par ces paroles; car nez maismement dit elle vérité aux dyables et aux dampnez: quantum est synderesim. C'est elle qui fait tant de maulz a tous pechéurs que elle ne puet estre en paix ne laissier son pere et sa mere, entendement et raison, en paix se justice et discipline ne se prent des forfaiz contre Dieu. Cest office et condicion lui a baillee le grant maistre de nostre escole. Si saichiez certainement que elle ne faura point a tesmoingnier la vérité, et tant luy soit dure ou contraire [...] Prenons que ta conscience fust enfondree en l'ordure jusque dessus la teste, se dira elle tousiours que tu as fait offense et te accusera et fera rens, etc.[279]

Among the several definitions of *synderesis* one finds in his works, it is the following description that made it known by a variety of other names such as *superior pars rationis, uertex animae, scintilla intelligentiae* and *instinctus indelebilis*.

> *Synderesim autem aliis nominibus appellamus: uel habitum practicum principioum, uel scintillam intellegentiae ratione cuiusdam suae euolutionis uel ardoris ad bonum, uel portionem uirginalem animae, uel stimulum naturalem ad bonum, uel apicem mentis, uel instinctum indelebilem, aut aliquot tali nomine ut quod est coelom primum in affectiuis potentiis.*[280]

---

[278] Gerson's *De theologia mystica*, OC: 3, p. 260. 'An appetitive power of the soul which receives a certain natural inclination to good immediately from God, through which it is led to follow a good motion presented to it from the apprehension of pure intelligence' (trans. in Greene 1991, p. 195). McGuire translates the same definition as the following: '*Synderesis* is an appetitive power of the soul that comes immediately from God. It takes on a certain natural inclination to the good. Through this proclivity it is drawn to follow the movement of the good on the basis of the understanding presented to it in the simple intelligence' (*On Mystical Theology*, Second treaty, McGuire 1998, p. 279).

[279] *Pour le 4ᵉ mercredi de Carême*, OC: 7: 2, p. 1089.

[280] *De theologia mystica*, OC: 3, p. 261. '*Synderesis* is a practical habit of principles, or the spark of intelligence [...] or a virginal part of the soul, or a natural

Although 'Gerson was not the only Scholastic to define *synderesis* as an instinct,[281] it is the French theologian's explicit and recurring characterization of *synderesis* as *instinctus indelebilis* or *naturalis instinctus ad bonum* that became particularly important for the future development of the notion of conscience. Furthermore, Gerson's inclusion of the term *instinctus naturae* in his brief handbook for students of moral theology, *Definitiones terminorum theologiae moralis*, gave it the status of a term of art in ethics and later in anthropology, where it acquired a whole different meaning.[282] His definition of *instinctus naturae* as 'a divine gift guiding all creatures to their appointed ends even if it is open, in the case of man, to distortion by the sensuality arising from original sin',[283] will have long lasting implications, both in England and on the continent.

Whereas on the Continent Gerson's definition of synderesis as *instinctus indelebilis* was greatly popularized by its inclusion, as *instinctus naturalis in boni*, into Johannes Altensteig's influential dictionary *Vocabularius theologie*, published in 1576, 1579, 1580, 1583 and 1619,[284] in England it was through St Germain's *Doctor and Studen* that became the last serious and sustained subscription to the theory of *synderesis* (using that term) in English, that it reached a wider audience.[285] Dedicating an entire chapter 13 to 'What sinderesis is', St Germain defines *synderesis* 'a natural power of the soul, set in the highest part thereof, moving and stirring it to good and abhorring evil'.[286] St Germain's endorsement of the

---

stimulus to good, or the apex of the mind, or an imperishable instinct, or such other names as the first heaven among the affective powers' (trans. in Greene 1991, p. 200, n. 10). See also Greene 1997, pp. 173–98.

[281] Ojakangas speaks of 'the instinctual nature of *synderesis*' in Bonaventure (Ojakangas 2013, p. 52 & p. 54).

[282] Greene 1997, pp. 188–89. In fact, what Anja-Leena Laitakari-Pyykkö claims to be Melanchthon's influence on the formation of English law, regarding both the definition of instinct in animals ('They preserve their kind; they nourish their offspring by natural instinct'), and in men ('The lawe of nature [...] is called the law of reason, which natural reason has established among all men so that there is a natural instinct present in all men to preserve it') is in fact Gerson's legacy in both Melanchthon and St Germain. See Laitakari-Pyykkö 2013.

[283] Greene 1997, pp. 188–89.
[284] Greene 1997, p. 189.
[285] Greene 1991, p. 208.
[286] St Germain 2006, p. 21.

French theologian's metaphorico-mystical understanding of *synderesis* as the virginal part of the soul led to an English epithet for *synderesis* as the unadulterated and incorruptible component of conscience. Thus, English diplomat and scholar Sir Thomas Elyot (*c.* 1490–1546) laconically described *synderesis* as 'the pure part of conscience' in his Latin-English Dictionary of 1538. This definition continued to be frequently repeated in dictionaries during the late 16th and early 17th centuries, superseding some 'locally developed' and slightly different versions of *synderesis*, as found, for example, in the 1447 *Mappula Angliae*, written by an Augustinian friar Osbern Bokenham (1393–1463), where he defines it as 'naturalle reson & kyndly gratitude', moving man to establish positive laws for the ceremonial honor and worship of God.[287] English physician and lexicographer John Bullokar (1574–1627), who in 1616 published the first English dictionary, still identified 'synteresie' as 'the inward conscience, or a natural quality engrafted in the soul, which inwardly informeth a man whether he do well or ill'.[288]

Although it is generally true that Latin lexicons were much more likely to include the word *synderesis* than their English counterparts, and that works written in Latin were naturally more likely to preserve outdated scholastic terminology,[289] Gerson's definition of *synderesis* endured in English literary works during both the Elizabethan and Jacobean periods thanks to the exceptional popularity of St Germain's *Doctor and Student*. In fact, it was revived in the Elizabethan era with dramatists and poets using the term in the sense given to it by the late medieval theologian.[290] Thus, John Marston (1576–1634), who read *Doctor and Student* in the 1590s in its twentieth edition, included the following invocation (for which he was later satirized)[291] in his notorious 1598

---

[287] Horstmann 1887, p. 14: 'Very naturalle reson & kyndly gratitude determynythe at at every secte & dyversite of namys & mannys lyf schulde alle-wey dyfferryn & reverencyce god-heed & honorwryne & worschipyne hit wt sum righte or synguler cerymonye. Throughe e whiche ynstynnct mevid & steryd, Molmucius, the XXIII kynge of the Brytouns [...] made a statute'.
[288] Bullokar 1616.
[289] Greene 1991, p. 207.
[290] Greene 1991, p. 208.
[291] Greene 1991, pp. 208–09.

parody, *The Scourge of Villanie*: 'Returne, returne, sacred Synderesis/ Inspire our trunckes, let not such mud as this/ Pollute us still'.[292] In 1621 this medieval term was given a new prominence when poet Robert Burton (1577–1640) used it at in his *Anatomy of Melancholy*:

> The agent is that which is called the wit of man, acumen or subtlety, sharpness of invention, when he doth invent of himself without a teacher, or learns anew [...] That which the imagination hath taken from the sense, this agent judgeth of, whether it be true or false; and being so judged he commits it to the passible to be kept. The agent is a doctor or teacher, the passive a scholar; and his office is to keep and further judge of such things as are committed to his charge; as a bare and rased table at first, capable of all forms and notions. Some reckon up eight kinds of them, sense, experience, intelligence, faith, suspicion, error, opinion, science; to which are added art, prudency, wisdom: as also synteresis, *dictamen rationis*, conscience [...][293]

Even Francis Bacon (1561–1626) did not remain unaffected by the English fascination with *synderesis*. In fact, his understanding of it, presented in his 1605 *Advancement of Learning, Divine and Human*, is particularly reminiscent of Gerson's:

> So it must be confessed, that a great part of the law moral is of that perfection, whereunto the light of nature cannot aspire: how then is it that man is said to have, by the light and law of nature, some notions and conceits of virtue and vice, justice and wrong, good and evil? Thus, because the light of nature is used in two several senses; the one, that which springeth from reason, sense, induction, argument, according to the laws of heaven and earth; the other, that which is imprinted upon the spirit of man by an inward instinct, according to the law of conscience, which is a sparkle of the purity of his first estate; in which latter sense only he is participant of some light and discerning touching the perfection of the moral law.[294]

---

[292] Marston 1966.
[293] Burton 2004, pp. 1012–13.
[294] Bacon 1969, p. 254.

In 1625 English linguist John Minsheu (1560–1627) added the description of 'synteresis' to the second edition of his *Ductor in Linguas* and defined it, echoing Gerson, as both 'the remorse or prick of conscience, that parte of the soule which opposeth it selfe against sin', and, in a separate entry, as 'the pure part of conscience'.[295] In his controversial book *De Veritate*, published in 1624, poet and religious philosopher Edward Herbert (1583–1648), known as the father of English theism, revived Gerson's term *instinctus naturae*, giving it something of the recognized status that *synderesis* used to enjoy in the Middle Ages. Herbert devoted two pages to the inextinguishable nature and infallibility of *instinctus naturae* in mankind even after death, a topic regularly treated in medieval *synderesis* debates.[296] Since *De Veritate* was read and commented upon by René Descartes (1596–1650), Hugo Grotius (1583–1645) and Pierre Gassendi (1592–1655), Herbert's revival of *instinctus indelebilis*, as the faculty enabling the human mind to know truth,[297] received further notice in the rest of Europe.[298]

The idea of *synderesis* continued in England for an exceptionally long time, until at least the very end of the 17th century. In 1695, English philosopher and physician John Locke (1632–1704) used this word, being 'well aware of its implications, in his *The Reasonableness of Christianity*'.[299] He spoke of the divine 'spark' of the mind, which is:

> [...] the same spark of the Divine Nature and Knowledge in Man which making him a Man, [...] shewed him the Law he was under as a Man, and asserted that he that made use of this Candle of the Lord [...] could not miss to find [...] the Way of Reconciliation and Forgiveness.[300]

In fact, Gerson's association of *instinctus naturae* with *synderesis* still colors the very meaning of the English word 'instinct', and influences the modern definition of instinct as 'an innate propen-

---

[295] Greene 1991, p. 206.
[296] Greene 1997, p. 122.
[297] Herbert 1937, p. 83. See Bedford 1979, pp. 123–25.
[298] Greene 1997, p. 191.
[299] Greene 1991, p. 210.
[300] Marciniak 2006, p. 246.

sity in organized beings [...] varying with the species, and manifesting itself in acts which appear to be rational, but are performed without conscious design'.[301] The second part of this definition, which focuses 'on human as distinct from animal knowledge, brings the meaning closer to *synderesis*'[302] as it was understood by Gerson. Hence, even though the word *synderesis* eventually fell out of use in the vernacular, its meaning remained deeply engraved in the English language. It shines through the everyday use of expressions such as 'spark', 'sparkle' or 'natural instinct' understood as natural, 'God-given' ability to be exceptional at something or to do something exceptionally well. The medieval meaning of the biblical phrase 'the spirit of man is the candle of the Lord',[303] understood as eternal, divine and incorruptible light within, has also been revived. When we casually say that he or she has a 'divine sparkle', meaning a special natural gift, we inadvertently make reference to the medieval concept of *synderesis* as the best part of a human being that is able to redeem the whole person, a concept cherished by Gerson and all those who, knowingly or unknowingly, followed in his steps.

Conclusion

A full evaluation of Jean Gerson's legacy in England might never be possible, precisely because it is so wide, deep, varied, and long-lasting, encompassing many spheres of English culture and society. Shaped by historical circumstances and the personal preferences of powerful members of society, Gerson's legacy encompassed three main areas: theology, literature, and law, with the last sphere overshadowing all the others. And how could it not be so in a society and culture, which have been rightly called obsessed with law and legal relationships?[304] The conversation regarding just one aspect of Gerson's judicial impact in England — his vision and development of the concept of *epikeia*, which both More and St Germain sought to address — is far from over even now. The

---

[301] Greene 1997, p. 190. Frederickson 2014, p. 1.
[302] Greene 1997, p. 190.
[303] Proverbs 20:27. Greene 1991, p. 209.
[304] Ackroyd 1999, p. 54.

French chancellor turned the medieval tradition of equity 'in a sharp new direction by emphasizing the need to relieve the pressure of prescriptive law on the conscience'.[305] He achieved this by expanding the concept of *epikeia* simultaneously in two ways. One is his advocacy for the cultivation of *epikeia* in the context of moral theology in order to 'mediate, interpret, and even silence the threatening language in canon law'.[306] The other is his promotion of *epikeia*, merged with Christian mercy to create one concept of temperate fairness, as a normative form of judgment in ecclesiastical and civil matters. Both developments, augmented by his emphasis on individual differences and circumstances, made his take on *epikeia* particularly appealing for the changing realities of 16th century England. In the later evolution of the application of equity these two aspects mostly followed separate trajectories, however. The pastoral function of equity soon blended into what has become to be known as theological probabilism (also recently credited to Gerson).[307] The debate about the role of equity in legal practice, for the most part oblivious of equity's medieval and early modern roots, lost its theological underpinnings, but greatly gained intensity with the passage of time. American 21st century lawyers argue for the defense and promotion of *epikeia* in Anglo-American law,[308] and point out to the United States' movement of zero tolerance in criminal justice as a modern illustration of the neglect or even rejection of equity, especially when compared to a more equitable construction of law advocated by both Gerson and Thomas More.[309]

Gerson's contribution to the emergence of the early modern judicial order has attracted the notice of an impressive number of legal scholars, not only in relation to the development of the concept of equity, but also in other areas, such as the theory of indi-

---

[305] Hobbins 2006, p. 66. For the debate on the understanding of conscience in early modern England see Cummings 2007, 2009, 2011.
[306] Hobbins 2006, p. 69.
[307] See Schüssler 2011.
[308] Zahnd 1996, p. 264.
[309] Bader 2014, p. 437. Neither for Gerson nor for Thomas More was equity an abstract moral principle. It was fully embedded in their Catholic faith, which for them represented the truth. This explains the intransigence of both authors toward heretics, who transgress this in truth and, therefore, are exceptions to the application of the principles of equity.

vidual, subjective, and natural rights.[310] His role in the emergence of these concepts is an object of a particularly sharp controversy, with no clear consensus among law historians and jurists. Some argue that by defining right as 'is an immediate faculty or power pertaining to anyone according to right reason', the chancellor took 'an important step toward the naturalization of right at the same time that he asserted the priority of the individual',[311] and thus 'created room for an idea of individual right (*ius*)'.[312] Others object to the use of the term 'subjective right' in relation to thinkers like Gerson as premature, anachronistic and 'surely inappropriate', since he and other medieval and early modern conciliarists referred to the theory of subjective rights in relation to 'rulers or those of communities' and not in relation to individuals.[313] Yet, even though his thought is only 'potentially individualistic'[314] in its implications, the late medieval chancellor has also been credited with the idea of a natural right of self-defense against a tyrannical pope or secular authority and with the concept of a natural right as a liberty through which a Christian could seek his own salvation. The crucial distinction between *ius* and *lex*, or between a subjective right and an objective law, 'typically seen as a 17th century discovery [...] that does not occur until Hobbes',[315] has also been traced to the Parisian chancellor. In sum, while the 'conscious continuity in Gerson's thinking on rights throughout his literary career'[316] still awaits a full professional evaluation, 'there is

---

[310] Among scholars who consider Gerson one of the first to develop the idea of the individual rights are already-mentioned Tierney, Mäkinen, Varkemaa, Brett as well as Gary B. Herbert (Herbert 2003), Oliver O'Donovan and Joan Lockwood (O'Donovan & Lockwood 2004). However, it was Richard Tuck who, already in 1979, explicitly argued that 'it was Jean Gerson, who really created the theory. He did so in a work entitled *De uita spirituali animae*, dedicated to d'Ailly and written partially with his help during the early months of 1402'.

[311] Herbert 2003, p. 73.

[312] Herbert 2003, p. 73.

[313] Oakley 2015, p. 251.

[314] Oakley 2015, p. 251.

[315] Mäkinen 2006, p. 71. James E. G. de Montmorency in *Great Jurists of the World* has attempted to show that much of Hobbes's thought about the common law was derived from Edmund Plowden's *Reports and Quaeries* but 'there is no knowing whether Hobbes did in fact use and rely upon Plowden' (Campbell 1958, pp. 25–26).

[316] Varkemaa 2006, p. 130.

little doubt among historians of subjective right that Jean Gerson is a major figure in their story'.[317]

Besides law, the formative impact of Gerson's thought in England extends to pastoral care, biblical exegesis, moral theology and literary expression. His contribution to religious practices remained significant among Catholics, Anglicans and Puritans of the 16th and 17th centuries.[318] The impact of his biblical harmony *Monotessaron* lasted longer in England than on the Continent, and the creative development of his pastoral impulse in English *Scientia mortis* literature continued well into the 17th century. The chancellor retained significant prestige and textual presence in the mystical works of Puritan theologian Richard Baxter and Anglican bishop Joseph Hall, as well as in the polemical writings of King James I, whose close knowledge of and extended reliance on the Parisian master marks the highpoint of Gerson's Scottish connection, which began in the early 15th century. The weight of his authority is reflected in the fact that in Scotland, as in Sweden, his name became associated with the inauguration of a national literature, as John Ireland's *Meroure of Wyssdome*, dependent on Gerson's writings, is the earliest extant example of Scottish prose.[319]

Synderesis' definition as *instinctus indelebitis ad bonum* was given extraordinary currency in England through St Germain's *Doctor and Student*. The popularity of this work assured Gerson's interpretation of *synderesis* a long life not only in religious context, but also in philosophical and literary circles. His optimistic opinion that every human, no matter how seemingly depraved, still possesses 'a certain natural inclination to the good' through which a person 'is drawn to follow the movement of the good on the basis of the understanding presented to it in the simple intelligence',[320] lived on, perceptible in strangely similar beliefs

---

[317] Brett 1997, p. 77.

[318] Gerson's reputation, together with that of other 'divines of Paris', was enhanced after Edmond Richter's 1606 publication of his complete works. This edition was used, for example, by the Calvinist writer and jurist Melchior Goldast (1576 or 1578–1635), who published several of Gerson and Almain's conciliar tracts in his *Monarchia S. Romana Imperii*.

[319] Burns 1991, p. 139.

[320] McGuire 1998, p. 279. *De theologia mystica*, OC: 3, p. 260, quoted earlier.

expressed by Diderot and Rousseau, among others. It is just as tenaciously persistent now. It is just as tenaciously persistent now.

Gerson's decisive importance for Thomas More corresponds to all three main areas of his legacy in England, due to the fact that the Englishman was a lawyer by profession, a religious leader 'par la force des circonstances' and a brilliant writer by his natural talent. More's intimate dialogue with Gerson embraces the entire oeuvre of the latter and permeates the entire active life of the former. Indeed, Gerson's textual presence in More's works suggests that the English saint had absorbed the French theologian's legacy in concert, as an integral whole. The degree of More's mental intimacy with Gerson renders his reception possibly unique, and might be compared to Petrarch's life-long literary, intellectual, and spiritual conversation with Augustine. For More, the late medieval chancellor was not only an authoritative spiritual guide from the past and the main human source of support, understood as both validation and assistance, but he was also a kindred spirit. The Englishman might be the last English, and possibly European, thinker to have ever felt so.

GENERAL CONCLUSION

> 'Ne se laissant pas facilement réduire en thèses rigides, la pensée de Gerson autorisait les interprétations les plus divergentes'.[1]

The theme of Jean Gerson as Father, as specified in the title of this book, has unfolded in three dimensions: father as a founder of a movement or development, father as a parental figure or mentor for a particular historical character, and father as a member of an established group of elders who were guardians of the common tradition. These three interconnected and sometimes inextricably blended connotations were differently received chronologically and geographically. Tracking the reception of Gerson revealed no straight line. There was neither consecutive growth nor a continuous decline of influence but rather a tortuous road created by an incessant traffic of political agendas, religious tensions, and above all strong personalities for whom the late medieval Parisian theologian had remained or had become a spiritual father. Their degree of intimacy with Gerson varied greatly. Though perceived in different ways, that intimacy reached the highest levels in the cases of Thomas More, Francisco de Osuna, Johannes Staupitz and Martin Luther. Also, while some authors focused on a small selection of Gerson's works, others were 'Gerson's gluttons' such as Jean Bouchet, Thomas More, and Johannes Staupitz (Table 1).

It was in the Holy Roman Empire of the German Nation that the Parisian chancellor was initially elevated to the status of the fifteenth century addition to the fathers of the Church: venerated among members of *devotio moderna*, and copiously quoted, translated and edited by Johannes Geiler de Kaysersberg and Jacob Wimpfeling in Strasbourg, and Gabriel Biel in Tübingen.

---

[1] Vereecke 1957, p. 10.

In these cities, his pious humanism was welcomed by secular and cloistered scholars, who also forged his personal legend as father of 'Teutonic' learning and the agent of *translatio studii* from Paris to Germany. His absorption and adoption by the network of German humanists — via Trithemius's *Catalog of the Most Illustrious Men of Germany* and Geiler von Kaysersberg's and Wimpheling's editions of Gerson's works — allowed for his continuous and favorable presence in a large number of 16th century catalogs, chronicles and indexes, starting with *Catalogus testium ueritatis* by the father of Lutheran historiography Matthias Flacius Illyricus. In this literature Gerson was designated not only as literally *generator* (father) of German learning, but also as a precursor to true (Lutheran and other Protestant) Christianity. An example of such a catalog is the 1580 *Index chronologicus* by Abraham Buchholzer (1529–1584) — Melanchthon's close friend and Protestant theologian, pedagogue, and historian — wherein Gerson figures as one of the precursors of Lutheranism.[2] Another example, *Genealogia imperatorum*, by an antiquarian, historian, physician, and professor of history and poetry at Jena University, Elia or Elias Reusner (1555–1612),[3] includes the story of the French chancellor in the catalogue which is otherwise exclusively dedicated to the genealogy of German emperors, princes, and other aristocrats.[4] The unwillingness of Lutherans and even Calvinists to exclude Gerson from their historiographies, or even to spell out the truth about his role in the fate of their martyr Jan Hus, clearly demonstrates that the need to include the illustrious chancellor among their 'spiritual ancestors' had prevailed over denominational loyalty, resulting in Gerson achieving a position of honor simultaneously as a victim, as a precursor, and finally as a hero.

The century-long integration of the French thinker into the German intellectual landscape carried on into the new era of religious dissention. The story of Martin Luther's relations with Gerson can be seen, throughout his life,[5] as that of a son torn between,

---

[2] Buchholzer 1599, reprint 1876, p. 481.

[3] Reusner's only translated work is *Religion and the Virtues of the Christian Prince Against Machiavelli* (Moore 1949).

[4] Reusner 1592.

[5] See chapter 2.

on the one side, the desire for independence and, on the other, the filial attachment to *noster pater Iohannes Gerson*. Luther's difficulty in disengaging from the French theologian, frustrating for some Protestant scholars, was not unique in the Lutheran camp. The abundance of Protestant documents containing references to Gerson indicates that Protestantism, both Lutheran and other Reformed, brought a new dimension to Gerson's legacy, but did not diminish its importance. Thus, Luther's right-hand man, Philipp Melanchthon, whose filial connection with the French theologian is less personal, less intense, but more constant and more consciously aware, never seemed to want to break the umbilical cord with the chancellor, while the radical Andreas von Karlstadt struggled to rid himself of Gerson's authority — the last bulwark left standing between Karlstadt's personal vision of Christian faith and the Bible. Whether it was Luther's paradoxical attachment, Melanchthon's discreet loyalty, Martin Bucer's painful wavering, or Karlstadt's resolute disavowal, Lutheran theologians clearly experienced difficulties withdrawing from the consoling doctor, and, thereby along with him, from the spiritual and intellectual traditions in which they were all formed.

However, the reception of Gerson within the Protestant camp also had its clear-cut limitations, and *die Grenze* passed through Scriptures. For Lutherans, the fact that 'Gerson fait passer en premier lieu les vérités contenues dans la Bible, les vérités déterminées par l'Eglise ne venant qu'ensuite',[6] signaled the rupture with medieval tradition and the opening of a new era. Yet for the chancellor the primacy of Scriptures did not mean studying them in isolation from tradition. On the contrary, the very opposition between 'written books and unwritten traditions',[7] 'orality and scripturality',[8] was inconceivable for him. For him Scripture was a non-apophatic text in the sense that it lives in and through the Church, and, as a living organism, grows and yields up the fullness of its senses under the inspiration of the Holy Spirit.[9] Even

[6] Delaruelle, Labande & Ourliac 1964, p. 522.
[7] O'Malley 2018, p. 59, citing Tanner & Alberigo 1990, 2, p. 663.
[8] See François 2020.
[9] Flanagan 2006, p. 147: 'For Gerson, the solution [...] will ultimately be found not within the biblical text itself, but through the guidance of the Holy Spirit over both the Scripture and the Church'.

in the case of the Bible, which Gerson took to be wholly reliable, the fallibility of both the human mind and human language mitigate against certainty, which can only be assured through the fundamentally polyphonic reading of the Church, even if it ends up in 'a nightmare of multiple interpretations, all with equal claims to authority'.[10] Such a 'choral solution' was equally unacceptable to Luther, Karlstadt, Osiander or Calvin, for whom, regardless of their differences, Scripture was an ultimate, exclusive, eternal, universal, and only authority. Not to see it this way was at best a sign of confusion and at worst a symptom of disobedience to God. The polyphonic world of the Middle Ages was being forever replaced by a screaming match of autonomous voices of endlessly competing interpretations. However, with the majority of Protestant denominations eventually moving away from their uncompromising biblical fundamentalism, while binding themselves to sources of historical legitimacy, the late medieval chancellor would find a renewed favor in the second-generation Lutherans such as Martin Chemnitz.

Although Gerson's 'fatherhood' initially was more readily acknowledged among the Protestants than among the Catholics, it was German Catholic theologians of Luther's generation who perceived the Parisian master as a father figure on whom they could call in the midst of the chaos that followed the clash between Rome and Martin Luther. In this sense, at the early stage of the religious conflict German Catholic theologians' motivations to appeal to Gerson did not necessarily differ from those of their opponents, be it Melanchthon, Johannes Brenz, or Martin Luther himself: Gerson was Father to them all. However, even outside of the German-speaking world, and despite ambivalence about his status due to his reputation as the founder of conciliarism, the chancellor enjoyed fatherly prestige among practically all principal actors of the century. In France, the dean of the Sorbonne Faculty of Theology Noël Béda saw the chancellor as one of the fathers of Parisian university tradition, while Béda's opponent, Jacques Lefèvre d'Étaples, considered Gerson's theology as an opening to 'an insurrection of conduct internal to Christianity'.[11] When, in

---

[10] Hobbins 2006, p. 69.
[11] Depew 2016, p. 32.

1605, the Société des libraires de Paris that was 'initially founded for the publication of the Church fathers' asked Edmond Richer to 'revise' Gerson's works and to 'oversee their publication', the chancellor of Paris had acquired sufficient notoriety in the circles of theologians and jurists for the project to be seen as viable'.[12]

Gerson's importance as one of the founding fathers of modern jurisprudence is multifaceted. *De uita spiituali animae*, in all probability his most cited work after *Opus tripartitum* (Table 1), and definitely his most influential intellectual contribution, has developed ideas and conceptions that would evolve, via Summenhart, Parisian academia and Spanish scholastics, into modern natural rights theory. His promotion of Christian *epikeia* or equity, based on Aristotle but enriched with Christian mercy, played an important role not only in the development of Luther's and Melanchthon's similar concepts, but also in the formation of the English law and the genesis of rights in general.[13] Finally, one cannot understand modern principles of contract law without appreciating the role of Gerson's *De contractibus*, which had a seminal impact on legal theory and practice. His omnipresence as an *auctoritas* on legal matters is epitomized by reliance on his treatise *De non esu carnium* (*On not eating meat*) across the Catholic and Protestant spectrum, as Francisco de Vitoria, Leonardus Lessius and Martin Luther all consulted it.[14] The case of Gerson's influence in jurisprudence exemplifies the general truth that:

> Law is indebted to theologians. The transformations which the Roman law of antiquity underwent during medieval and early modern times need not be regarded as repugnant forms of degeneration. Roman law lived one of its most intense, prolonged and productive stages by participating in the rich life of the Church. [...] moral theologians [...] who transformed the civilian tradition belonged to an institution, the Roman Catholic Church, which, for centuries, vied for normative power with the secular authorities. The state, winner from this intense power struggle with the Church in the process absorbed a lot of the normative structures which had been

---

[12] Denis 2019, p. 46.
[13] See Shortall 2009, p. 388.
[14] *De non esu carnium* (*On not eating meat*), OC: 3, pp. 77–95. For the detailed analysis of Vitoria's dependence on Gerson in this area, see Fleming 2008, p. 101.

developed by the moral theologians.[15] Therefore, even though we might not know it, Gerson is part of our own universe, our society, and, as such, capable of offering us a surer grasp of principles amid the complexities of the modern world.[16]

As the father of moral theology[17] the chancellor deserves a very special place in the story of this transformation, which has traditionally been associated with the School of Salamanca. The indebtedness to him concerns two inextricably related concepts: the idea of moral certainty and 'the safety-first rule' (*regula magistralis*). Gerson's formulation of relative or minimal moral certainty, aimed at easing painful moral doubts, had a substantial impact on pastoral practice, intellectual history, and law. This concept combined two distinct foundations: 'Aristotle's dictum that in ethics we should expect less certainty than in mathematics', and 'an approach in moral theology that declared Jesus's yoke to be soft (*iugum suave*)'.[18] This 'minimalistic approach to morality', closely related to the notoriously complex debates on decision-making in a context of uncertainty, 'flourished in early modern scholasticism',[19] allowing greater flexibility in many areas, including new business practices, which a more rigorous Christian ethics previously prohibited. Although Gerson adopted and adapted the *regula magistralis* from Guillaume d'Auxerre, his subtle interpretation of it, which dominated Catholic moral theology for at least two hundred years after his death,[20] deserves special credit. Even though not always having generated original ideas himself, the French chancellor often played a major role as their mediator. Blessed with the unique gift of making explicit what needed to be explicitly stated, Gerson was often the one who clarified earlier interpretations for the 15th, 16th and even 17th centuries, contributing to the emergence of moral theology as an

---

[15] Decock 2012, pp. 12–13.
[16] Figgis 2011, p. 4.
[17] Schüssler 2011, p. 453: 'It is not excessive to claim that he was the most important single instigator of the changing shape of scholastic moral theology in the early modern era'. Gerson actually wrote a treatise explicitly titled *Definitiones terminorum theologiae moralis* (OC: 9, p. 133).
[18] Schüssler 2011, p. 452.
[19] Schüssler 2011, p. 452.
[20] See Schüssler 2019.

independent theological discipline. The interpretations of moral theology would differ on the Catholic and Protestant sides of the religious divide, however. 'Generally speaking, to the Protestant reformers, *ius commune* and canon law' would no longer be 'valid sources for the solution of moral problems',[21] while for Catholics, more than ever, 'as Lessius noted, the knowledge (*scientia*) that a good confessor must possess pertains not only to theology but also to canon law'.[22]

If in relation to German humanism Gerson acted as *translatio studii* in the geographical dimension, with respect to mystical theology he represented a crucial link of *translatio traditionis* between the earlier medieval tradition, represented by Victorines and Bernard, and affective theologies of the 16th century. 'Doing theology for everyone',[23] and 'believing in the virtue of the individual effort',[24] he succeeded in transferring spiritual methods reserved for members of the monastic community to a public forum. His risky proclamation that 'simples crestiens qui ont ferme foy de la bonté de Dieu et l'aiment ardanment, ont plus vraie sapience et mieulx doivent estre appelés saiges que quelxconques clers'[25] had a galvanizing effect on those who engaged themselves in personal pursuits of spiritual enlightenment. Lutherans, starting with Luther himself, Spanish orthodox and unorthodox mystics, *devotio moderna*, moderates from the fast-shrinking middle zone, English Anglican, Puritan and Catholic thinkers, as well as early Jesuits, all found inspiration and consolation in his spirituality. Gerson's promotion of private meditation, his rather unprecedented openness to spiritual creativity, his circumstantial flexibility in matters of devotional practices, his soul-searching personal interiority,[26] the use of the vernacular in spiritual matters, and especially his generous invitation, extended to the laity,

---

[21] Decock 2012, p. 48.
[22] Decock 2012, p. 69.
[23] McGuire 2005, p. 33.
[24] McGuire 2005, p. 54.
[25] OC: 7: 1, p. 20. '[...] simple Christians who have firm faith in the goodness of God and love him ardently have more true wisdom and greater claim to be called wise than any scholars' (McGuire 1998, p. 80).
[26] On the subject of Gerson's approach to contemplation Mazour-Matusevich forthcoming.

to seek a contemplative life, electrified his broad-based audience. The words that Karl Rahner (1904–1984) once used to credit Ignatius of Loyola as a pioneer who first treated contemplative life not as the 'special privilege of a person chosen for an elite',[27] but rather as a grace that is available for all and as a normative feature of devotional life potentially accessible to the laity and even to unlearned women, almost verbatim correspond to the program formulated by Gerson in his *Mountain of Contemplation*, which almost all of the historical characters mentioned in this study knew. Almost one hundred fifty years before Loyola, and two centuries before François de Sales, Gerson made 'a major breakthrough' with respect to lay devotion.[28]

Gerson's affectivity, which was aimed at balancing the academic over-intellectualization prevalent in his time, would become the leading spiritual approach for practically all religious movements, factions, and figures in the 16th century. Both Evangelical and Catholic mystics promoted the path of mystical theology, as it is understood in Gerson's *De mystica theologia practica* — at the expense and even rejection of the speculative one. Moreover, Gerson's initiative to offer the benefits of contemplative life to the largest possible number of the faithful,[29] and especially to women, resulted in a spiritual creativity for which existing society was woefully unprepared. '[D]evotion was a messy business, and easily classified as potentially troublesome'.[30] Gerson himself was perfectly aware of it:

> *Si ueniat aliquis igitur qui se reuelationem habuisse contendat quemadmodum Zacharias et alii Prophetarum cognoscuntur ex historia sacra recepisse, quid agemus, quo pacto nos exhibebimus?*[31]

---

[27] Rahner 1986, pp. 175–76.
[28] Hobbins 2006, p. 52.
[29] Combes 1963, 1, p. 138.
[30] Hobbins 2006, p. 50.
[31] *De distinctione uerarum reuelationum a falsis*, OC: 3, p. 38. 'If someone comes who claims to have had a revelation of the type that Zachariah and prophets in sacred history are known to have received, what are we to do, and how are we to act?' (McGuire 1998, p. 337).

In one of the paradoxes of Gerson's legacy, faced with what was perceived as exaggerated 'over-affectivity', theologians in charge of maintaining religious orthodoxy likewise turned to him for guidance. His book *De probatione spirituum* was used both for taming excessive *caridad* among Jesuit novices and for the theorization of witchcraft.[32]

It was in Spain where both the persecutors and the persecuted credited Gerson with a reputation (deplorable by today's standards) as the father of discernment in the area of mystical revelations. His opinions were used in the oppression of Spanish illuminati and are sometimes believed to have contributed to Europe-wide acts of violent misogyny and frenzied witch-hunts. Whether he can be deemed guilty of these later developments has become another 'case Gerson'.[33] With opinions of his posthumous judges greatly depending on his or her selection of sources, and the dangers of parsing through Gerson's thoughts in order to weigh their merits on the scale of contemporary values being evident, it seems safe to say that to limit his 'impressive although somewhat enigmatic legacy' to 'two historical developments — the promotion of rational and just government, and the development of the European concept of the witch'[34] — is a gross oversimplification. Upon closer examination, the very same features of his spirituality for which Gerson has been commended — affectivity, relationality, and democratization of theology — are at least partly responsible both for the emotional excesses of those who followed Gerson's new interpretation of contemplative life and for the backlash against them. By way of illustration, the term 'mujercita' or 'the little woman',[35] which Teresa of Avila used toward herself to emphasize her humility, and which Jesuit priest Gil Gonzales Dávila used derogatively toward women in general, in both cases, comes from Gerson.

---

[32] Haliczer 1990, p. 146.

[33] See, to name just few, Peters 1978; McLoughlin 2016. Juan Miguel Marín holds Gerson responsible for the misogyny of the Jesuit order in general: 'Does this problem [of misogyny] reappear among later Jesuits, those who followed Ignatius in taking not St Francis but Gerson as primary exemplar?' (Marín 2014, p. 16).

[34] McLoughlin 2015, p. 1.

[35] Tyler 2017, p. 40; Marín 2014, p. 194.

In another twist in the reception of Gerson's legacy, he is simultaneously considered as the father of the 'feminization of religious life in France',[36] and the source of Jesuit misogyny in Spain.[37] Moreover, his encouragement of female spirituality would be denigrated in both Catholic and Protestant 16th century Reformations. On the Lutheran side, women's reality did not correspond to Johannes Cochlaeus's scornful description of it:

> The Lutheran women, with all womanly shame set aside, proceeded to such a point of audacity that they even usurped for themselves the right and office of teaching publicly in the Church [...] Luther himself [...] taught that women too were true Christian priests.[38]

In fact Lutheranism reinforced women's obligation to marry, which became the only choice. The internal life of an ideal female was to be confined within the family. On the Catholic side, 'a decree of enclosure for all religious women has passed, although it was not universally enforced',[39] and female spirituality mostly retreated back into the monastery, as illustrated by a formidable example of Teresa of Avila. In the later 16th century the Jesuit ministry suffered a drastic diminution in the feminine sector,[40] and even Teresa of Avila's spirituality and Gerson's inspired silent prayer were seen as suspicious by Jesuit superiors.[41] As for the chancellor's promotion of a third way for female devotional life — neither cloistered nor married[42] — it had no immediate continuity in the 16th century. Except for a very few remaining

---

[36] Bireley 2018, p. 42.

[37] 'Jean Gerson, the most important theologian of the previous century, exerted an enormous influence on Ignatius and on later Jesuits, especially with regard to women and sexuality. Yet Gerson's mostly negative views [...] remain largely unexplored in the early modern Hispanic context' (Marin 2014, p. 95).

[38] Eriksson, Gunner & Blader 2012, p. 211.

[39] Russell 2018, 1, p. 267.

[40] Iparraguirre 1946, p. 225.

[41] See Marin 2014.

[42] Gerson's 'third way' is not entirely original. Informal female communities, where women lived, from the canon law point of view, in the middle ground between religious rule and secular society (and therefore referred to as semi-religious or quasi-religious women) existed already in the 13th century. As in many other regards, it is Gerson's vigorous promotion and popularization of an already existing phenomenon that distinguishes his contribution.

béguinages in the Low Countries, female devotion ended up, once again, literally walled in on both sides of the religious divide.

While Gerson might not have left a cohesive theology, he did leave a coherent reform program. There is little doubt that in the 16th century 'Gerson appears above all as a pastor',[43] and as such can be considered as one of the fathers of the Council of Trent. Surely, some measures tending in the direction of the education of priests — obligatory residence of and visitations by bishops, catechization and normalization of confession — were already taken before him. Yet it was the systematic nature of his pastoral efforts and of his works written to this end that distinguished the chancellor's legacy. If 17th century Catholic emphasis on confession 'reflected the legacy of the Council of Trent',[44] the latter was largely based on Gerson's contributions to this matter. His quasi-therapeutic psychological approach — insistence on privacy, discretion, and respect of the penitent's confession — shaped Jesuit and non-Jesuit confessional practices for centuries to come.[45] From Trent onward 'for Protestants, the individual's conscience was now judge; for Catholics it was the confessor'.[46] Unlike conscience, however, the confessor was supposed not only to judge but also to console. Aware that 'if at any time and in all spheres of life man is called upon to live in accordance with the highest norms, then life becomes unbearable',[47] Gerson insisted on confession as a form of spiritual consolation and healing. This quality would have 'a very special place in Jesuit spirituality and ministries',[48] with the word 'consolation' being so common in early Jesuit documents that it would become a 'conventional greeting', meaning 'not much more than 'blessings''.[49]

Several tendencies observable in early modern catechization also find their roots in Gerson. The first is the use of the vernacu-

---

[43] Delaruelle, Labande & Ourliac 1964, p. 867: 'Gerson apparaît avant tout comme un Pasteur'.

[44] Fleming 2006, p. 2.

[45] Spanish Jesuit, Saint Alphonso Rodríguez (1532–1617), in *Ejercicio de perfección y Virtudes Cristianas*, published in 1609, also abundantly quotes Gerson.

[46] Decock 2012, p. 47.

[47] Decock 2012, pp. 73–74.

[48] Maryks 2008, p. 17.

[49] O'Malley 1993, pp. 82–83.

lar. Among Lutherans and other Protestants, the use of vernacular expression evolved into an intentional program, a commitment to bring the Scriptures to the people. Among Catholics it became partly a response to the Protestant challenge and partly a continuation of Gerson-initiated process of 'democratization' of theology. Just as he had done in *Le doctrinal aux simples gens*, and using almost the exact same expressions,[50] an overwhelming number of his Catholic readers, such as Francisco de Osuna, Teresa of Avila, and Peter Canisius, openly acknowledged their adoption of the vernacular 'for the sake of the simple folk' and 'simple priests'.[51] The second tendency was a strong emphasis on preaching the Ten Commandments, which began to dominate all other moral codes for lay instruction on both sides on the confessional divide. The third is an educational 'program minimum' offered to both priestly and lay audiences:

> *Item forte expediret sicut olim tempore quarumdam pestilentiarum facultas medicorum composuit tractatulum ad informandum singulos, ita fieret per facultatem uel de mandato eius aliquis tractatulus super punctis principalibus nostrae religionis, et specialiter de praeceptis, ad instructionem simplicium.*[52]

Based on the biblical 'prevent not the little children from coming to me',[53] this educational program was carried out uninterrupted on both sides of denominational rift, while being received and implemented with equal enthusiasm by Catholic reform-minded clergymen, Jesuits, Lutherans, and other emerging Protestants. Even though 'there was never a catechetical vacuum in the Middle Ages',[54] Gerson's plan of daily education not only of boys but also

---

[50] *Le doctrinal aux simples gens*, OC: 10, p. 296: 'Ce qui est en ce petit livret doivent enseigner les prestres a leurs parochiens; et pour les simples prestres qui n'entendent mie les escriturez et pour les simples gens, est il fait en francois, plainement, par grand conseil; et pour ce qu'il a esté fait briefment'.

[51] Bast 2009, p. 3.

[52] Letter of 1 April 1400 to Pierre d'Ailley, OC: 2, pp. 23–28. 'Just as the schools of medicine once wrote pamphlets to instruct people how to manage in times of plague, so now it would be good if a short work were written [...] dealing with the chief points of our religion, and especially the Ten Commandments, for the sake of the simple folk' (Bast 2009, p. 2).

[53] Gerson 2019, p. 1.

[54] Walsham 2017, p. 100.

girls and even their mothers, qualifies him as the father of early modern catechization movement, and by extension the creator of a pan-European system of mass elementary education.

Modern psychologists also might find themselves amazed at Gerson's practical advice for the treatment of depression and anxiety, which was much appreciated and transmitted by Martin Luther among others. Gerson's psychological insights that naturally introverted persons need to 'develop the active side of their personality and the naturally extraverted need to develop their contemplative side'[55] anticipate 'Carl Jung's division of 'personality types' into 'extravert' and 'introvert' by 500 years'.[56] The following words from his *Tractatus de paruulis ad Cristum trahendis* have as much merit now as they did when Gerson wrote them more than a half-millennium ago:

> Et pour cause que aucuns ont les esperilz si ligiers et mouvans, si enclins aux oeuvres du monde, que ce leur serait uns petis enfers estre sans compaignie ou ficheement en un lieu par bien petit tamps. Sont ceulx a peu ou néant proufitables a la vie contemplative; et mieus leur vault la laissier et se donner a la vie active, se n'estoit que par force d'acoustumance il vainquissent leurs conditions. Li aulcuns sont qui[...] voient par bonne experience que trop mieus est estre en compagnie et en labeur par dehors, car ne pensent mie a telles coses [...] la vie contemplative[...] leur est trop dure et très perilleuse. Les àoltres sont qui ou par nature ou par grasce ou par tous deux ensemble aiinent solitude.[57]

As for championing child psychology, Gerson most definitely deserves admiration. This aspect of his creativity warrants a whole book to it alone. Contrary to Philippe Ariès's still commonly

---

[55] Tyler 2017, p. 48.
[56] Tyler 2017, p. 48.
[57] *La Montagne de contemplation*, OC: 7: 1, p. 36. 'Some people have a spirit [...] so inclined to the deeds of the world, that it would be a minor form of hell for them to be without company or to be in a fixed place for even a short while. Such people [...] better leave it [contemplative life] and to give themselves over to the active life, unless by force of habit they can overcome their situation. [Others] learn through experience that it is much better for them to be in company and to do physical work, for then they will not be brood. [...] contemplative life [...] is for them too hard and very dangerous. There are yet others who by nature or by grace, or through both together, love solitude' (McGuire 1998, pp. 98–99).

accepted opinion that children were not perceived as children until the 17th century, the chancellor's experience-based pedagogy (which Ariès ignored) clearly demonstrates his awareness that children are not adults, and that they cannot be expected to act or learn as grown-ups:

> *Contemperemus denique sermonem pro paruulis, non magnopere pensantes rudia et uulgate uerba, si opus est, balbutire more nutricum et matrum, bleso ore sermonem cum paruulis dimidiantium, dummode sic intelligatur id quod dicere uolumus satis est, cum ad animandum docemdumque paruulos uenire ad Christum, cum ad tollendum uiarum scandal, magis quam ad quempiam satirica dicacitate acriter coarguendum.*[58]

His reputation as the father of evangelical harmonies originates once again in the Holy Roman Empire, from whence the fashion for them would spread throughout the continent and beyond, continuing on into the 18th century. His *Monotessaron* attracted an enormous following on both sides of the religious split, and it became the gold standard for future harmonizers, to the point that it is said that 'after all attempts of this kind have been tried, by the most eminent theologians, the result must be either *Monotessaron* or the object has not been attained'.[59] Now that the missionary and polemical intents were directed not against outsiders but against adversaries within Christianity itself, *Monotessaron* and its direct descendants enjoyed an exceptional popularity not only as exegetical tools or objects of meditation but also as instruments of catechization. Gerson's creation, although equally unacknowledged by authors who used it, and by researchers who studied

---

[58] *De paruulis ad Christum trahendis*, CO: 9, p. 669. 'In fine, when pleading on their behalf, let us regulate our language in accordance with nature and dispositions of children themselves, not being anxious to use the language of contention and disputation or even an ordinary style of human speech but being ready, if need be, to lisp and babble in our words as mothers and nurses are wont to do when they speak with little ones. If only we make ourselves understood in what we say we shall be quite content. The object we have in view is not to argue, not to convict others of error, much less to cast ridicule upon them but merely to bring forward certain reasons why children should come to Christ, and to remove, as far as may be, those obstacles which, unhappily, but too often prevent them from coming to Him. We shall, therefore, in the following little work be as simple, clear and orderly as we can' (Gerson 2019, pp. 2–3).

[59] Thompson 1828, p. iv.

these authors, is still discernible in Jean Le Clerc's (1657–1736) *Harmonia Euangelica* published in 1699, Bernard Lamy's 1699 *Commentarius* in *Concordiam Euangelicum*, and even Johann Jacob Griesbach's (1745–1812) *Synopsis Euangeliorum* of 1776.[60]

In summation, Jean Gerson is properly acclaimed as the father of biblical harmonization, mass catechization, conciliarism, the internal reform that led to the Council of Trent, proto-probabilism, and several major developments in modern jurisprudence. Having given a remarkable boost to the cult of St Joseph, who became Spain's official protector and Mexico's patron saint beginning in 1679,[61] Gerson prepared the way for Josephism and, since this concept emphasizes the Holy Family as the model for all Christian households, qualifies as a father of the post-Tridentine accent on marriage. As one of the founders of the genus *ars moriendi*, the chancellor can also be considered a father of what would eventually become palliative or hospice care, to which he gave 'den character freundschaftlichen Dienstes'.[62] Whether this feature of Gerson's *ars moriendi* had continuity onward into early modern times remains to be seen, but it might be worth exploring that Saint Louise de Marillac (1591–1660), the co-founder of the Daughters of Charity — which was one of the first services to provide care to the sick, elderly, and poor in their homes, as well as in orphanages, institutions, prisons, etc. — was an avid reader of Gerson.[63] Finally, Melanchthon relied on Gerson's authority as a common point of reference and a unifying factor in the *Augsburg Confession*, the document whose aim was to restore peace and religious unity within the Holy Roman Empire. Gerson would be seen from this angle again after the utter devastation of the Thirty Years' War, when a new generation of theologians turned to the pre-national and pre-divisional authority of the *doctor consolatorius* as the father of peace.

---

[60] See Watson 2013. Even though neither Gerson nor his *Monotessaron* are mentioned in this book, descriptions of subsequent evangelical harmonies, found therein, leave no doubt that they were based on his work. In case of Le Clerc in particular, his familiarity with Gerson's writings is beyond doubt.

[61] McCulloch 2004, pp. 614–15.

[62] Neher 1989, p. 48.

[63] Ryan & Rybolt 1995, p. 42.

The 16th century acted like a gigantic magnifying glass, detailing and expanding specific elements found in Gerson's theology to their extreme limits. What was, in his legacy, a potential, would be transformed into a program and ultimately put into action. His rather mild mysticism would metamorphose into ecstasies of the *illuminati*, his psychological adjustments into a full-blown casuistry, his circumstance-based recommendations for meditative and confessional practices into devices of the Inquisition, and his *sufficienter probatus est* into probabilistic sophistry. His teachings on the certainty of hope and on the cooperation between the soul and its Creator, as well as his theology of 'a covenant of seeking',[64] were expanded and intensified in Jesuit theology, and integrated into mainstream Catholic doctrine through the Council of Trent. For Catholics, the attractiveness of Gerson's theology consisted in his conviction that with the help of sacramental grace and upon the invitation of the Holy Spirit, man can, by using all intellectual and spiritual resources, succeed in his search for God. Although Gerson kept a distance between God and man, it was not 'a categorical break' like in Luther's theology. He saw the relationship between God and man as reciprocal. 'The arbitrary freedom of God's will was necessarily matched by a similar freedom of man's will — there could be no opposition between them'.[65] In Protestant theologies it was Gerson's *regula fidei*,[66] his emphasis on the role of laity as bearers of church life, and his lifelong interest in mystical theology in its relation to Scripture that took a whole different dimension.

The strong reception of Gerson within different religious groups, movements, and peoples, often in substantial disagreement and even in open conflict with one another, has as much to do with the recipients of his legacy as with the paradoxical evolutions and conflicting inconsistencies of the chancellor himself.

---

[64] Burrows 1991.

[65] Tuck 1979, p. 30.

[66] *De necessaria communione laicorum sub utraque specie*, OC: 10, p. 55, already cited: *Scriptura Sacra est fidei regula, contra quam bene intellectum non est admittenda auctoritas uel ratio hominis cuiuscumque; nec aliquanda consuetudo, nec constitutio, nec obseruatio ualet si contra Sacram Scripturam militare conuincatur. Haec regula fundamentum est commune nobis et haereticis quos impugnare conamur.*

His internal dynamism, which seemed at times to surprise and overwhelm even himself, his restless energy, feverish productivity and quasi-megalomaniac need to be everything simultaneously — preacher, administrator, poet, theologian, playwright, inquisitor, philosopher, politician, musician, mystic and educator, resulting in the eclecticism of his writings and a personal mark left in several fields of knowledge — testify to him being not only an early French humanist, but a Renaissance man, although of a very special kind. The fact that people as different as Savonarola, Wessel Gansfort, Luther, Bucer, Latomus, Brenz or Thomas More turned to the chancellor's authority in moments of indecision or acute personal crisis speaks for the evidence that he was an *auctoritas* of exceptional magnitude. He represented a sum of the qualities in a man that command respect for his person, opinions, achievements, talents and integrity. The case of Thomas More, for whom the chancellor became during his imprisonment a true spiritual father and the main source of moral support besides Scriptures, represents a striking testimony to his monumental stature. Despite polemical abuse [67] and religious wars, 'Gerson et sa production subissent en quelque sorte une canonisation',[68] becoming a classical reference in both Protestant and Catholic 16th century sources.[69]

---

[67] An example of such abuse is the English translation of *Augsburg Confession*. In order to project a negative image of monks and monasteries in accordance with the interests of Henry VIII, Melanchthon's Latin reference to Gerson's description of *uita monastica* was rendered as 'monkish life', while the expression 'contemplative life' was translated as a 'holiday'. *Et ante hæc tempora reprehendit Gerson errorem monachorum de perfectione et testatur, suo tempore nouam hanc uocem fuisse quod uita monastica sit status perfectionis* (Melanchthon pp. 118–19) 'And before this tyme also Gersen rebuketh the errour of religious persons/ as touchynge perfection/ and witnesseth that to say the monkisshe or religious lyfe/ to be a state of perfection/ was but a newe founde halydaye and a straunge sayeng euen in this time' (English translation of Augsburg Confession, 1536, in Laitakari-Pyykkö 2013, p. 249).

[68] Vendrix 1997, p. 4.

[69] Gerson and his ideas were universally referenced in the early modern era, yet most people are unaware of his influence. Though he is perhaps the most significant figure to receive this treatment, he is not alone. He is in a good company of other theologians put on the tacit index by modernity due to the impact of the ideology of laïcité that eclipsed contribution by the theologians almost completely (Decock 2012, p. 12).

Gerson's Future

This necessarily synoptic study was not undertaken to explore all the aspects of the early modern reception of Gerson. This is clearly an impossible task. However, if Gerson emerges from this endeavor as a figure worthy of insertion into the lineage of Europe's great minds and as a character meriting further investigation, this book has achieved its goal. I hope that the aspects, characters and sources selected for this inquiry shed enough light on this fascinating figure to stimulate future research projects that will explore his impact in both synchronic and diachronic directions. Concerning the latter, we are barely aware of the ways in which Jean Gerson was still relevant in the 17th century. Among obvious continuities there are Lutheran and other Reformed historiographies, such as the Calvinist *Historiae Christianae secula* written by the German scholar Friedrich Spanheim (1600–1649), wherein the late medieval chancellor retained a place of primal importance. The Society of Jesus's bond with the chancellor also carried on into the next century, as he continued to be cited as an authoritative source in Japanese and Portuguese Jesuit texts such as the *Instructions on the Sacraments and Various Other Matters* published in Nagasaki in 1605. His role in the history of probabilism and the formation of 17th century moral theology involves, among others, his presence in late scholasticism and especially in Jansenists versus Jesuits conflict. The subject of Gerson's potentially huge influence in Mexico, and in Latin America in general, is a virgin territory awaiting its first pioneer. His influence in the spirituality of François de Sales (1567–1622) on the one hand, and in the writings of Lutheran theologians during the period of Orthodoxy, such as Johann Gerhard (1582–1637), on the other, might yield a considerable harvest of new insights. Similarly, his connection to Jacques-Bénigne Bossuet (1627–1704) and his importance to the 17th century German Pietism of theologians like Gottfried Arnold (1666–1714) represent other possible directions for future investigations. What can be assumed with confidence, is that the 17th century found the *doctor consolatorius* equally relevant.

Table 1[70]

De uita spirituali animae (21)	Johannes Nider, Nicolas Kempf, Conrad Summenhart, Martin Luther, Philipp Melanchthon, Martin Chemnitz, John Calvin, Simon Goulart, Kaspar Schatzgeyer, Johann Staupitz, Francesco de Vitoria, Bartolomè de Medina, Domingo de Soto, Alfonso de Castro, Gabriel Vazquez, Bartolomé de Las Casas, Francisco Suarez, Juan Ginès de Sepulvera, Luis de Molina, Christopher St Germain, Joseph Hall
Monotessaron (17)	J. Geiler von Kaysersberg, G. Biel, J. Mombaer, G. J. de Cisneros, Ph. Melanchthon, Ottimar Luscinius, Johannes Bugenhagen, Andreas Osiander, Petrus de Rivo, G. Rosemondt, Jansenius Cornelius of Ghent, Martin Chemnitz, Jean Calvin, Leo Jud, Thomas More, Nicholas Ferrar, Ignatius of Loyola?
La Montagne de Contemplation (10)	Johannes Geiler von Kaysersberg, Johannes Wessel Gansfort, Caritas Pirckheimer, Garcia Jiménez de Cisneros, Pietro Ritta da Lucca, Richard Baxter, T. More, M. Luther, Francisco de Osuna, J. Hall
De theologia mystica lectiones sex (*Theologia speculatiua*) (9)	Vincent von Aggbach, Nicolas of Cusa, B. von Waging, Gabriel Biel, P. Ritta da Lucca, Marsile Ficino, F. de Osuna, J. Staupitz, T. More
De mystica theologia practica (8)	B. von Waging, N. of Cusa, G. J. de Cisneros, Johannes Mombaer, F. de Osuna, J. Staupitz, Ph. Melanchthon, T. More
De consolatione theologiae (9)	J. Nider, N. Kempf, B. von Waging, M. Luther, Chemnitz, J. Staupitz, Hieronymus Dungersheim, Jacques Lefèvre d'Etaples, T. More
De probatione spirituum (8)	T. More, Antonio de Baeza, Martin Antonio del Rio, Perdo Ruiz de Alcaraz, Juan de Valdés, Bachiller Olivares, Francisco Ortiz, Gil Gonzales Dávila
Collectorium Super Magnificat (8)	J. Nider, J. Wessel Gansfort, G. Biel, J. Staupitz, J. Bouchet, Noel Béda, Nicolas Bobadilla
Contre conscience trop scrupuleuse (7)	J. Geiler von Kaysersberg, Antoninus of Florence, J. Nider, M. Luther, Bartolomè de Medina, F. de Osuna, T. More
Tractatus de contractibus (7)	J. Nider, St Antoninus of Florence, C. Summenhart, Martin Chemnitz, Johannes Staupitz, Leonardus Lessius, Ch. St Germain

[70] The table does not represent a positive, comprehensive statistics of Gerson's readership in the late 15th and the whole of 16th centuries, but includes his texts, except *Opus tripartitum*, mentioned in this study in relation to particular authors who read them.

De remediis contra pusillanimitatem (6)	B. von Waging, Antoninus of Florence, *P. Ritta* da Lucca, J. Lefèvre d'Etaples, M. Luther, B. de Medina?
De potestate ecclesiastica (5)	J. Wessel Gansfort, C. Summenhart, Matthews Flacius Illyricus, J. Staupitz, Vasco de Quiroga, James I
De non esu carnium (5)	Thomas Müntzer, M. Luther, F. de Vitoria, Ch. St Germain, L. Lessius
La mendicité spirituelle (5)	J. Geiler von Kaysersberg, Marguerite de Navarre, Guillaume Briçonnet, J. Lefèvre d'Etaples, J. Bouchet
De arte audiendi confessiones (4)	G. Rosemondt, Juan Alphonso de Polanco, M. A. del Rio, G. G. Dávila
Regulae morales (4)	J. Bouchet, J. Staupitz, Ch. St Germain, T. More
De modo uiuendi omnium fidelium (3)	M. Luther, Georg Spalatin, Adam Walasser
Bonus pastor (3)	G. J. de Cisneros, H. Dungersheim, Hieronymus Emser
De preparatione ad missam (3)	Sylvestro Mazzolini, Martin de Azpilcueta, Antoninus of Florence
De laude scriptorium (3)	Johannes Trithemius, N. Béda, Johannes Reuchlin
De necessaria communione laicorum sub utraque specie (3)	Martin Bucer, N. Béda, T. More
De distinctione uerarum reuelationum a falsis (3)	J. Staupitz, M. A. del Rio, J. Hall
De simplicatione cordis (3)	Johannes Mickel, Biel, Staupitz
De potestate absoluendi (3)	S. Mazzolini, G. Rosemondt, J. Staupitz
De remediis contra pusillanimitatem (3)	Waging, da Lucca, Lefèvre d'Etaples
De indulgentiis (3)	Gansfort, Luther, Staupitz
De examinatione doctrinarum (3)	Andreas Bodenstein von Karlstadt, Martin Chemnitz, K. Schatzgeyer
De consiliis euangelicis (3)	Gansfort, Martin Chemnitz, Staupitz
Spiritus domini repleuit orbem terrarium (2–3)	Ficino, Staupitz, Cusa?
Viuat rex (2)	John Ireland, T. More
De miseria humana	Dietrich Ulsenius, Thomas Wolff
Remède contre les tentations de blaspheme (2)	Geiler von Kaysersberg, Luther
Tractatus de canticis (2)	M. Luther, J. Staupitz
Contra sectam flagellantium (2)	Gansfort, Staupitz
De oratione et eius ualore (2)	J. Bouchet, T. More
De natura conscientiae (2)	Geiler von Kaysersberg, Ch. St Germain, T. More

Contra Matthaeum de Fussa (2)	Gansfort, Staupitz
De sensu litterali Sacrae Scripturae (2)	Christopher Columbus, Jacobus Latomus
A Deo exiuit (2)	Ficino, Staupitz
Sermo de uisitatione praelatorum (multiple)	Claude de Seyssel, Pierre Soybert, Council of Trent
De pueris ad Christum trahendis (2)	Wimpheling, Gonzales Dávila
Traité Enhortant a prendre l'estat de virginité plus que de marriage (2)	Geiler von Kaysersberg, J. Mombaer
De schismate et papatu (2)	Martin Chemnitz, J. Hall
Monochordum Iesu Christi (1)	Mombaer
Trilogium astrologiae theologiae (1)	Bouchet
Sermo de oratione factus in Concilio Constantiensi (1)	Bouchet
Tractatus de differentia peccatorum mortalium et uenialium (1)	Bouchet
Expositio super Dimitte nobis (1)	Bouchet
Figura scacordi musicalis simul et militaris (1)	Mombaer
De meditatione cordis (1)	Pietro da Lucca
De exercitio deuotorum simplicium (1)	Geiler von Kaysersberg
De quatuor virtutibus (1)	St Germain
De uiagio regis Romanorum (1)	Hieronymus Dungersheim
Considerationes pro uolentibus condere testamentum (1)	Bouchet
Sermo de angelis (1)	T. More
De egressu passionis et resurrectionis Christi (1)	T. More
Veniat pax	J. Ireland
Adorabunt eum omnes rege terre (1)	J. Ireland
Diligite iusticiam (1)	J. Ireland
Rex in sempiterne uiue (1)	J. Ireland
De peccato mollitiei (1)	G. Gonzales Dávila
Contra Rusbroquio (1)	G. Gonzales Dávila
Centilogium de impulsibus (1)	J. Staupitz
Iosephina (1)	Staupitz
Regulae mandatorum (1)	Staupitz
De primis motibus et consensus (1)	Staupitz

De nuptiis Christi et ecclesiae (1)	Staupitz
De impulsibus (1)	Staupitz
De directione cordis (1)	Staupitz
Contra curiositatem studentium (1)	Staupitz
Super uictu pompa praelatorum (1)	Staupitz
Exsultabunt (1)	Staupitz
Fulcite me (1)	Staupitz
De quatuor domibus (1)	Staupitz
Considerate lilia (1)	Staupitz
Sermo St Bernardo (1)	Staupitz
De passionibus animae (1)	Staupitz
Regula mandatorum (1)	Staupitz
Considernati mihi (1)	Staupitz
A Dei uadit (1)	Staupitz
Nova epistola pro instructione episcoporum et prelatorum (1)	Council of Trent
Requête pour les condamnés à mort (1)	Geiler von Kaysersberg?
De perfectione cordis (1)	Chemnitz
De unitate ecclesiæ (1)	Chemnitz
De quatuor domibus (1)	Chemnitz

# BIBLIOGRAPHY

Primary Sources

Pierre d'Ailly, *Ymago mundi de Pierre d'Ailly*, 3 vols, éd. E. Buron, Paris: Maisonneuve, 1930.

Jacques Almain, *Aurea opuscula omnibus theologis perquam utilia*, Paris: N. de Pratis, 1525.

Aristotle, *Nicomachean Ethics*, trans. W. D. Ross, http://classics.mit.edu/Aristotle/nicomachaen.html (access 20/02/2020).

Augustine of Hippo, *Confessions*, trans. R. S. Pine-Coffin, NY: Penguin classics, 1961.

Augustine of Hippo, *Sermon on the Mount; Harmony of the Gospels; Homilies on the Gospels*, ed. A. Uyl, Woodstock, Ontario: Devoted Publishing, 2017.

St Augustine, *De Consensu evangeslistarum*, ed. J.-M. Roessli; academia.edu/7998644/Augustine_De_Consensu_evangeslistarum (accessed 28/01/2021).

Teresa of Avila, *The Collected Works of Saint Teresa of Avila*, trans. K. Kavanauch, first edition, Washington DC: ICS Publications, Institute of Carmelite Studies, 1976.

Francis Bacon, *Advancement of Learning*, ed. Henry Morley, Oxford: Clarendon Press, 1969.

Bernard de Clairvaux, *Sur le Cantique des Cantiques, Oeuvres mystiques*, préface et trad. A. Béguin, Paris: Seuil, 1953.

Louis de Berquin, *La Farce des théologastres à six personnages*, éd. P. A. Gratet-Duplessis, Lyons: G. de Rossary, 1830.

Sebastian Brant Maternus Berler & Bischof Wilhelm von Hoenstein, *Chronik, code historique et diplomatique de la ville de Strasbourg*, Strasbourg: Silbermann, 1843.

Johannes Brenz, *Frühschriften*, ed. M. Brecht, G. Schäfer & F. Wolf, vol. 2, Tübingen: Mohr, 1974.

Guillaume Briçonnet and Marguerite d'Angoulême, *Correspondance (1521–1524)*, éd. Martineau & Veissière, Geneva: Droz, 1975.

Martin Bucer, *Deutsche Schriften: Schriften zu Taufertum und Spiritualismus 1531–1546*, ed. S. E. Buckwalter, Gütersloh: Mohn, 1960.

Martin Bucer, *Opera Latina*, ed. W. I. P. Hazlett, Leiden/New York: Brill, 2000 (Studies in Medieval and Reformation Traditions).

Martin Bucer, *Schriften zur Kölner Reformation*, ed. S. E. Buckwalter, H. Schulz & T. Wilhelmi, Gütersloh: Mohn, 2003.

Abraham Buchholzer, *Abrahami Bucholzeri Index chronologicus*, Görlitz: Rhamba, 1599.

John Bullokar, *An English Expositour*, London, 1616.

Jean Calvin, *Institutes of the Christian Religion*, ed. J. T. McNeill, trans. F. L. Battles, Philadelphia: Westminster John Knox, 1960.

Peter Canisisius, *Catechismus*, Augsbourg, 1561.

Wolfgang Capito, *Monumentum instaurati patrum memoria per Heluetiam regni Chrsiti et renascentis Evangelii, id est Epistolarum d. Johannis Oecolampadii et Hulduchi Zwinglii ...*, Basel: Sebastian Henricretri, 1592.

Martin Chemnitz, *Loci theologici Dn. Martini Chemnitii*, Frankfurt & Wittenberg: D. Tobiae Mevii & Elerdi Schumacheri, 1653.

Martin Chemnitz, *Examinis Concilii Tridentini. D.h. Prüfung des Concils von Trient*, St Louis, MO: Verlag von L. Volkening, 1875.

Martin Chemnitz, *Examination of the Council of Trent*, trans. Fred Kramer, St Louis, MO: Concordia Publishing House, 1971.

Martin Chemnitz, J. Gerhard & P. Leyser, *Harmonia Quatuor Euangelistarum, a Theologis Celeberrimis, D. Martino Chemnitio Primum Inchoata: D. Polycarpo Lysero Post Continuata*, Geneva: P. Chouet, 1645.

Martin Chemnitz, *Loci Theologici*, trans. J. A. O. Preus, St Louis: Concordia, 1959.

Garcia Jimenes de Cisneros, *Ejercitatorio de la vida spiritual*, Barcelona: Librería Religiosa, 1857.

Garcia Jimenes de Cisneros, *A Book of Spiritual Exercises, and a Directory for the Canonical Hours*, trans. by a monk of St Augustine's monastery, Ramsgate, Oxford: Burns and Oates, 1876.

Johannes Cochlaeus, *Historiae Hussitarum per Ioannem Cochlaeum, atrium ac sacrae theologiae magistrum*, s.l. Rome: Francisci Behem, 1549.

Johannes Cochlaeus, *Des Johannes Cochlaeus Streitschrift de Libero arbitrio hominis (1525)*, ed. H. Jedin, Breslau: Müller & Seiffert, 1927.

Johannes Cochlaeus, *Responsio ad Iohannem Bugenhagium Pomeranum*, ed. R. Keen, Nieuwkoop: De Graaf, 1988.

Jean Crespin, *Histoire des vrays témoins de la vérité de l'Évangile depuis Jean Hus jusqu'à present. Comprinse en VIII livres contenans actes memorables du Seigneur en l'infirmité des siens: non seulement contre les forces & efforts du monde, mais aussi à l'encontre de diverses sortes d'assauts & heresies monstrueuses; les prefaces montrent une conformité de l'estat ecclesisastique en ce dernier siecle, à celuy de la primitive Eglise de Jesus Christ*, Geneva: Crespin, 1570.

Jean Crespin (2011), *Recueil de plusieurs personnes qui ont constamment enduré la mort pour le nom de N. S. J. C. depuis Jean Hus jusqu'à cette année présente 1554 (1555)*, in *Zwingliana*, 38, pp. 35–52.

St John of the Cross, *Ascent of Mt. Carmel*, ed. & trans. E. A. Peers, https://jesus-passion.com/ASCENT_OF_MT._CARMEL.htm (access 20/02/2022).

John of the Cross, *Spiritual Canticle* and *Sayings of Light and Love*, https://www.jesus-passion.com/Minor_Works_StJohn.htm (access 20/02/2022).

Nathaniel Culverwell, *An Elegant and Learned Discourse of the Light of Nature*, ed. R. A. Greene & H. MacCallum, Indianapolis, IN: Liberty Fund, 2001.

Martin A. Delrio, *Investigations into Magic*, trans. P. G. Maxwell-Stuart, Manchester: Manchester University Press, 2000.

Denis the Carthusian, *Dionysii cartusiensis opera selecta*, ed. K. Emory, Turnhout: Brepols, 1991.

Desiderius Erasmus, *The Correspondence of Erasmus – Letters 446 to 593, 1516–1517*, trans. R. A. B. Mynors & D. F. S. Thomson, Toronto: University of Toronto Press, 1974.

Desiderius Erasmus, *The Correspondence of Erasmus – Letters 1535–1657 (1525)*, trans. A. Dalzell & A. Ch. G. Nauert, Toronto: University of Toronto Press, 1994.

Pierre Dupuy, *Dupuy (Du Puy), Instructions et lettres des rois tres-chrestiens et de leurs ambassadeurs et autres actes concernant le Concile de Trente pris sur les originaux*, Paris: Sébastien & Gabriel Cramoisy, 1654.

Marsilio Ficino, *Theologia Platonica*, 3 vols, trans. M. J. B. Allen, Cambridge, MA: Harvard University Press, 2001.

Matthias Flacius Illiricus, *Catalogus testium ueritatis, qui ante nostrum aetatem reclamarunt Papae*, Basel: Perna, 1556.

Matthias Flacius Illiricus, *De translatione imperii Romani ad Germanes*, Frankfurt a. M.: Kopffius, 1612.

Robert Gaguin, *Epistolae et orations*, Paris: Bocard, 1498, 1903, reprint 1977.

Johannes Wessel Gansfort, *Farrago rerum theologicarum*, Basel: Adamus Petri, 1522.

Johannes Wessel Gansfort, *Wessel Gansfort: Life and Writings. Principal Works*, trans. J. W. Scudder, ed. E. W. Miller, New York/London: Knickerbocker, 1917.

Johannes Geiler von Kaysersberg, *Peregrinus. Der bilger mit seinen eygenschaften (Der Pilger)*, Strasbourg, 1494.

Johannes Geiler von Kayserberg, *Doctor keyserspergs Trostspiegel So dir Vatter, muter, kynd, od freünd gestorben synt*, Strabourg, 1503.

Johannes Geiler von Kaysersberg, *Passion des herrn Jesu [...] geteilt in stückes weiß eins süßen Lebkuchen ußgeben*, Strasbourg: Johanes Grüninger, 1514.

Johannes Geiler von Kaysersberg, *Der Passion oder das lyden Jesu Christi vnsers herren/noch dem text der fyer Euangelisten*, Strasbourg: Schott, 1522.

Johannes Geiler von Kaysersberg, *Die Augsburger Predigten*, ed. K. Freiehagen-Baumgardt & W. Williams-Krapp, Berlin: De Gruyter (Deutsche Texte des Mittelalters), 2015.

Gilbert Génébrard, *Genebrardi Gilberti ..., Chronographiae libri quattuor*, Paris: Johann Gymnich, 1581.

Jean Gerson, *Ioannis Gersonii doctoris et cancellarii parisiensis opera*, ed. Edmond Richer, Paris, 1606.

Jean Gerson, *Ioannis Carlerii de Gerson de Mystica Theologia*, éd. A. Combes, Lugano: Thesaurus Mundi, 1958.

Jean Gerson, *Œuvres complètes*, éd. P. Glorieux, 10 vols, Paris: Desclée & Cie, 1960–1971.

Jean Gerson, *Jean Gerson: Early Works*, trans. B. P. McGuire, New York: Paulist Press, 1998.

Jean Gerson, *The Consolation of Theology / De consolatione theologiae*, trans. C. L. Miller, Indianapolis: Abaris Books, 1998.

Jean Gerson, *Josephina*, éd. G. M. Roccati, Paris: LAMOP, CD-ROM, 2001.

Jean Gerson, *Sylvula precationum pathetikon ex Johannis Gersonis scriptis collecta*, Nürnberg: J. Jugler, 1603.

Gil Gonzalez, *Pláticas Sobre las Reglas de la Compañía de Jesús*, Barcelona: Juan Flors, 1964.

Simon Goulart, *Catalogus testium ueritatis*, Genève: J. Chouet, 1608.

Joseph Hall, *The Arte of Divine Meditation. The Works of the Right Reverend Joseph Hall*, Oxford: Oxford University Press, 1863.

Isidoro Isolano, *Summa de donis sanctis Joseph*, Rome: P. Berthier, 1887.

King James, *The Political Works of James I, King of England*, ed. C. H. McIlwain, Cambridge, MA: Cambridge University Press, 1918 (Harvard Political Classics).

Thomas A Kempis, *The Imitation of Christ*, trans. L. Sherley-Price, Baltimore: Penguin, 1972.

Wolf Krüger, *Onomasticon uel historicum, darinnen berhumter Keyser, König ... Geburt, Lebens und Sterbenszeit ... verzeichnet und begriffen*, Nürnberg, 1603.

Wolf Krüger, *Catalogus et historologia mille uirorum et monte, arte et morte, genio atque ingenio illustrium*, Erfurt: Jacob Singe, 1616.

Bartolomé de Las Casas, *In Defense of the Indians*, trans. & ed. S. Poole, Decalb, Illinois: Northern Illinois University Press, 1992.

Bartolomé de Las Casas, *A Short Account of the Destruction of the Indies*, trans. Nigel Griffin, New York: Penguin Classics, 1999.

Bartolomé de Las Casas, *Obras completes*, ed. R. Hernándes, Madrid: Alianza, 1988.

Bartolomé de Las Casas, *Las Casas on Columbus: The Third Voyage*, ed. G. Symcox & J. Carrillo, trans. M. Hammer & B. Sullivan, Turnhout: Brepols (*Repertorium Columbianum*, 11), 2001.

Jacobus Latomus, *De trium linguarum ratione, in Gesschriften uit den tijd der hervorming in de Neberlandes*, Leiden: F. Pijpe, 1905.

Ignatius of Loyola, *Exercises, Retreats with Notes of Addresses*, trans. J. Morris, London, 1893.

Ignatius of Loyola, *Letters of St Ignatius of Loyola*, trans W. J. Young, Chicago: Loyola University Press, 1959.

Ignace de Loyola, *Journal des motions intérieures*, trad. & éd. P.-A. Fabre, Paris: Lessius, 2007.

Pietro Ritta da *Lucca, Regule de la uita spirituale et secreta theologia*, Venezia: Comino de Luere, 1526.

Othmar Luscinius, *Musurgia seu praxis musicae*, Strasbourg: Johannes Schott, 1536.

Martin Luther, *Luthers Werke, Kritische Gesamtausgabe*, gen. ed. Ultich Köpf, 73 vols, Weimar: Herman Böhlaus Nachfolger, 1883–1929.

Martin Luther, *Luther's Works*, ed. J. Pelikan et al., 55 vols, Philadelphia/St Louis: Concordia, 1957–1986.

John Mair (Major), *Quartus Sententiarum*, Paris: Jean Granjon, 1509.

Sylvestro Mazzolini de Prierio, *Summa Summarum quae Silvestrina nuncupatur*, Lyons: Jacques Huguetan, 1539.

Bartolomé de Medina, *Breve istruttione de confessori, come si debba amministrare il Sacramento della Penitentia*, Salamanca, por los herederos de Mathias Gast, 1579.

Bartolomé de Medina, *Breve istruttione de' confessori, come si debba amministrare il Sacramento della Penitentia*, Roma, 1588.

Philipp Melanchthon, *Didymi Faventini versus Thomam Placentinum pro M. Luthero oratio*, Basel: Adam Petri, 1521.

Philipp Melanchthon, *Loci communes theologici*, Wittenberg: Joseph Klug, 1535.

Philipp Melanchthon, *De obitu Lutheri historia de uita et actis reuerendis*, Heidelberg, 1548.

Philipp Melanchthon, *Corpus Reformatorum: Philippi Melanchthonis Opera quae supersunt Omnia*, 28 vols, ed. C. Bretscheider & E. H. Birdseil, Halle: Schwetschke & Son, 1834–1860.

Philipp Melanchthon, *The Confession of Faith: Which Was Submitted to His Imperial Majesty Charles V At the Diet of Augsburg in the Year 1530*, trans. F. Bente & W. H. T. Dau, Project Wittenberg, 1921; intratext.com/ixt/eng0204/ (accessed 22/01/2021).

Philipp Melanchthon, *Melanchthons Werke in Auswahl*, ed. R. Stupperich, 7 vols, Gütersloh: Bertelsman, 1951–1952.

Philipp Melanchthon, *Loci Communes 1543*, trans. Ch. Preus, St Louis, MI: Concordia, 1992.

Philipp Melanchthon, *Loci Communes 1521*, trans. H. G. Pöhlmann, Gütersloh: Gerd Mohn, 1993.

Philipp Melanchthon, *Common Places: Loci Communes 1521*, trans. Ch. Preus, St Louis, MI: Concordia, 2014.

Thomas More, *The Complete Works of St Thomas More*, gen. ed. G. L. Carroll & J. B. Murray, 15 vols, New Heaven, CT: Yale University Press, 1963–1997.

Johannes Nider, *Consolatorium timoratae conscientiae*, Paris: Gering, 1478.

Andreas Osiander, *Gesamtausgabe, Schriften und Briefe*, ed. G. Seebass, Gütersloh: Mohn, 1985.

Andreas Osiander, *Harmoniae euangelicae libri quatuor Graecae et Latine*, Basel: Matthias Crom, 1537.

Francisco de Osuna, *Tercer abecedario spiritual*, 1527, e-book, 2019; www.vidasacerdotal.org/index.php/descargas/libros-de-vida-espiritual/file/93-tercer-abecedario-espiritual.html (accessed 23/02/2021).

Francisco de Osuna, *The Third Spiritual Alphabet*, trans. M. E. Giles, New York/Toronto: Paulist Press (Classics of Western Spirituality), 1981.

William Perkins, *A Salve For A Sicke Man or a Treatise on Godliness in Sickness and Dying*, London: Cambridge, 1595.

Francesco Petrarca, *Opera*, Seniles IX, Basel, 1581.

Francesco Petrarca, *Opere*, Firenze: Sansoni, 1975.

Conrad (Konrad) Peutinger, *Sermones conviviales de finibus Germaniæ contra Gallos*, Strasbourg, 1530.

Juan-Alfonso de Polanco, *Le Directoire des confesseurs tres brief, par lequel tant le confesseur que le penitent pourront se regler à bien parfaire & accomplir ce qui est de leur devoir au Sacrement de Penitence*, Toulouse: J. Colomiez & R. Colomiez, 1608.

Petri Poiret, *Oeconomiae divinae, Dei erga hominess proposita, agenda rationes, atque opera demonstrator*, libri sex, Frankfurt a. M, 1705.

Juan-Alfonso de Polanco, *Vita Ignatii Loiolae et rerum Societatis Iesu historica*, Madrid: Avrial, 1894–1898.

Edmond Richer, *Apologia pro Ioanne Gersonio pro suprema Ecclesiae & concilii generalis auctoritate ... aduersus scholae Parisiensis, & eiusdem doctoris christianissimi obtrecatores*, Leiden: Paul Moriaen, 1676.

Godschalck Rosemondt, *Confessionale*, Antwerp, 1553.

François de Sales, *Avertissements aux confesseurs*, Oeuvres complètes, vol. 23, Paris: Annecy, 1928.

Girolamo Savonarola, *Selected Writings: Religion and Politics, 1490–1498*, trans. A. Borelli & P. M. Pastore, New Haven, CT & London: Yale University Press (Italian Literature and Thought), 2006.

Kaspar Schatzgeyer, *Scrutinium diuinae scripturae pro conciliatione dissidentium dogmatum* (1522), ed. U. Schmidt, Münster: Aschendorff, 1922.

Nikolaus Selnecker, *Operum latinorum: pars prima, continens formam explicationis examinis ordinandorum olim scripti a Philippo Melanthone*, Leipzig: Steinman, 1584.

Christopher St German, *Doctor and Student*, (1518), based on 1874 edition, Lonang Institute, 2006; lonang.com/wp-content/download/DoctorAndStudent.pdf (accessed 28/01/2021).

Johannes Staupitz, *Tubingen Prediger, Quellen und Forschungen zur Reformationsgeschichte*, ed. G. Buchwald & E. Wold, 8 vols, Leipzig:

Heinsius Quellen und Forschungen zur Reformationsgeschichte, 8), 1927.

Johannes Staupitz, *Johann von Staupitzes Sämmtliche Werke*, ed. J. K. F. Knaake, vol. 1, Potsdam: Deutsche Schriften, 1867.

Caspar Herrmann Sandhagen, *Kurtze Einleitung in die Geschichte unsers Herrn Jesu Christi, der Apostel, wie auch den Faden des Neuen Testaments nach der Zeitordnung aus den vier Evangelisten, der Apostelgeschichte und Briefen, wie auch Offenbarung Johannis zu betrachten*, Lüneburg: Johann Stern, 1684.

Francisco Suarez, *Selections from Three Works*, trans. G. L. Williams et. al., Indianapolis: Liberty Fund, 2015.

Christopher Sutton, *Disce mori: learn to die*, New York: Appleton & Co, 1841.

Johannes Trithemius, *Catalogus scriptorium ecclesiasticorum*, Cologne: Petrus Quentell, 1531.

Johannes Trithemius, *Opera historica*, Frankfurt a. M.: Marquard Freher, 1604.

Fernando Vázquez de Menchaca, *Controuersiarum Illustrium ... libri tre* Frankfurt a. M: Johann Theobald Schönwetter, 1572.

Vasquez, G. *Commentariorum ac Disputationum in Primam Secundae St Thomae Tomus secundus*, Ingolstadt: A. Angermarius, 1606.

Francisco de Vitoria, *Doctrina sobre los Indios*, trans. R. H. Martín, second edition, Salamanca: Editorial San Esteban, 1992.

Adam Walasser, *Kunst wol zusterben: ein gar nutzliches hochnothwendiges Büchlein*, 1585, 1572, 1579, reprinted in 1607 and 1612.

Adam Walasser, *Der Seelen Artzney: Ein Geistreichs Büchlin, darin[n] begriffen, die siben Buß Psalmen, inn verstendtlichen Teutschen Versen, neben andern andechtigen Gebetlin vnd haylsamen Ermanungen, samt etlichen schönen geistlichen Tractätlin, wie im Register zu end dises Büchlins zusehen ist*, S. Meyer, 1571.

Jacobus Wimpheling (Wimfeling), *Adolescentia*, Strasbourg: Martin Flach, 1500.

Jacobus Wimpheling, *De uita et miraculis Iohannis Gerson*, Strasbourg: Iohannes Prüss, 1506.

Jacobus Wimpheling, *Prima Pars Operum Ioannes Gerson*, Strasbourg: M. Schürer, 1502, 1514.

Johannes Wolf(f), *Lectionum memorabilium et reconditarum centenarii XVI, s.l.*, Lauingen: Rheinmichel, 1600.

Johannes Wolf(f), *Rerum Germanicarum ueteres iam primum publicati Scriptores VI, s.l.*, Frankfurt a. M: Marnius & Aubrius, 1607.

Secondary Sources

Ackroyd, P. (1999), *The Life of Thomas More*, New York: Anchor.

Adams, H. M. (1967), *Catalogue of Books Printed on the Continent of Europe, 1501–1600 in Cambridge Libraries*, London: Cambridge University Press.

Adams, M. M. (1977), 'Ockham's Nominalism and Unreal Entities', *The Philosophical Review*, 86 (2), pp. 144–76.

Ahlgren, G. T. W. (2017), 'Wise Action in a World of Suffering and Injustice', in P. Tyler & E. Howells (ed.), *Teresa of Avila: Mystical Theology and Spirituality in the Carmelite Tradition*, London & New York: Routledge, pp. 107–20.

Aichele, A. & M. Kaufmann (2013), *A Companion to Luis de Molina*, Leiden: Brill (Brill's Companions to Christian Tradition, 50).

Akkerma, F., G. C. Huisman & A. Vanderjagt (ed., 1997), *Wessel Gansfort (1419–1489) and Northern Humanism*, Leiden: Brill (Brill's Studies in Intellectual History, 40).

Alcantara, M. P. de (1978), 'Dos sermones inéditos sobre S. José del Beato Bernardino de Feltre', in *Archivum Franciscanum Historicum*, 71 (1–2), pp. 65–111.

Alderson, P. M., 'Melanchthon's Authorizing of Luther: An Examination of the Narrative Origins of Sixteenth-Century Historical Life-Writing' (unpublished doctoral thesis, Durham University, 2014).

Alonzo, M. M., *The Thomist Philosopher and the Cannibals: Alonso de la Veracruz's Theses on Cannibalism and Crimes against Nature* (2016); file:///Users/yelenamatusevich/Downloads/1157-1766-1-PB.pdf (accessed 28/01/2021).

Amalou, T. (2007), *Une concorde urbaine: Senlis au temps des réformes, vers 1520-vers 1580*, Limoges: Presses Universitaires.

Amalou, T. (2013), 'Les disputes académiques et l'espace public parisien au XVIᵉ siècle', dans T. Amalou & B. Noguès (éd.), *Les universités dans la ville*, Rennes: Presses universitaires, pp. 179–215.

Anderson, C. C. (2007), *Great Catholic Reformers, From Gregory the Great to Dorothy Day*, Mahwah, NJ: Paulist Press.

Anderson, M. P., 'Melanchthon's Authorizing of Luther: An Examination of the Narrative Origins of Sixteenth-Century Historical Life-Writing' (unpublished doctoral thesis, Durham University, 2014).

Andersen, R. (2016), *Concordia Ecclesiae: An Inquiry into Tension and Coherence in Philipp Melanchthon's Theology and Efforts for*

Ecclesiastical Unity, Especially in 1527–1530, Münster: LIT Verlag (Arbeiten zur historischen und systematischen Theologie 21).

Angerer, J. (1974), *Die Liturgisch-musikalische Erneuerung der Melker Reform*, Wien: Der Österreichischen Akademie der Wissenschaften (Studien zur Erforschung der Musikpraxis in den Benediktiner-Klöstern des 15. Jahrhunderts).

Ankwitz-Kleenoven, H. (1959), *Der Wiener Humanist Johannes Cuspinian. Gelehrter und Diplomat zur Zeit Kaiser Maximilians I*, Vienna: Bohlau.

Anttila, M. E. (2013), *Luthers Theology of Music: Spiritual Beauty and Pleasure*, Berlin: De Gruyter (Theologische Bibliothek Töpelmann, 161).

Anzelewsky, F. (1979), 'Ein Humanistischer Altar Dürers', in E. Grassi (ed.), *L'humanisme allemand (1480–1540): XVIIIe Colloque International de Tours*, Paris: Vrin, pp. 525–36.

Appel, H. (1938), *Anfechtung und Trost in Spatmittelalter und bei Luther*, Leipzig: Heinsius.

Appleford, A. (2015), *Learning to Die in London, 1380–1540*, Philadelphia, PA: University of Pennsylvania Press (The Middle Ages Series).

Aquillon, P. (1979), 'La réception de l'humanisme allemand à Paris', dans E. Grassi (éd.), *L'humanisme allemand (1480–1540): XVIIIe Colloque International de Tours*, Paris: Vrin, pp. 45–81.

Ariès, Ph. (1991), *An Hour of Our Death: The Classic History of Western Attitudes Toward Death over the Last One Thousand Years*, Oxford: Oxford University.

Arnold, M. (2017), *Martin Luther*, Paris: Fayard.

Arnaud, M. (2006), *Annoncer l'Évangile (XVe-XVIIe siècles). Permanences et mutations de la predication*, Paris: Le Cerf.

Astorri, P. (2019), *Lutheran Theology and Contract Law in Early Modern Germany*, Paderborn: Brill/Schoningh (Law and Religion in the Early Modern Period/Recht und Religion in der Frühen Neuzeit, 1).

Atkinson, D. W. (1992), *The English ars moriendi*, New York: Peter Lang (Renaissance and Baroque/Studies and Texts).

Auke, J. (1998), *Frontiers of the Reformation: Dissidence and Orthodoxy in Sixteenth-century Europe*, Farnham, UK: Ashgate (St Andrews Studies in Reformation History).

Avis, P. (2008), *Beyond the Reformation?: Authority, Primacy and Unity in the Conciliar Tradition*, New York: T & T Clark.

Ayre, J. (ed., 1844), *Prayers and Other Pieces of Thomas Becon*, Cambridge, UK: University Press.

Backus, I. (2004), 'Bullinger als Neutestamentler: Sein Kommentar zu den Paulusbriefen und den Evangelien', in *Zwingliana*, 31, pp. 105–32.

Backus, I. (2008), *Life Writing in Reformation Europe*, Farnham, UK: Ashgate (St Andrews Studies in Reformation History).

Backus, I. (2013), 'Quels temoins de quelle vérité? Le *catalogus testium veritatis* de Mathias Flacius Illyricus revu par Goulart', dans O. Pot (éd.), *Simon Goulart un pasteur aux intérêts vastes comme le monde*, Geneva: Droz (Travaux d'humanisme et Renaissance), pp. 125–39.

Bader, W. D. (2014), 'Saint Thomas More: Equity and the Common Law Method', in *Duquesne Law Review*, 52 (2), pp. 433–38.

Bailey, M. D. (2003), *Battling Demons: Witchcraft, Heresy, and Reform in the Late Middle Ages*, University Park, PA: Penn State University Press (Magic in History).

Bainton, R. (1995), *Here I Stand: A Life of Martin Luther*, New York: Plume.

Balbach, E. (1999), 'Using Case Studies to Do Program Evaluation', California Department of Health Services, Online.

Barbagallo, A. (2014), 'Los Casos de consciencia de Fray Antonio de Cordoba', in G. Carrascón et al. (ed.) Estudios Aldo Ruffinatto *en el IV centenario de las Novelas Ejemplares*, Alessandria: Edizioni dell'Orso, pp. 295–302.

Barbier, F. (2006), *L'Europe de Gutenberg. Le livre et l'invention de la modernité occidentale (XIIIᵉ-XVIᵉ siècle)*, Paris: Belin (Histoire et société).

Barbier, F. (2011), 'Quelques observations sur les origines d'un succès européen', dans M. Delaveau & Y. Sordet (éd.), *L'Imitatio Christi*, Paris: Bibliothèque Nationale de France, pp. 35–51.

Barge, H. (1905), *Andreas Bodenstein von Karlstadt*, Leipzig: Brandstetter.

Barth, H.-L. (2010), 'Die katholische Lehre von den zwei Quellen der Offenbarung: Philologische und theologische Überlegungen zu einem umstrittenen Text des Konzils von Trient, seiner Vorgeschichte und seiner Rezeption', in *Una Voce Korrespondenz*, 40, pp. 29–125.

Bast, R. J. (1997), *Honor Your Fathers: Catechisms and the Emergence of Patriarchal Ideology in Germany (1400–1600)*, Leiden: Brill (Studies in Medieval and Reformation Thought, 63).

Bast, R. J., 'The Political Dimension of Religious Catechisms in Fifteenth and Sixteenth Century Europe', dans *La Révolution française*; Les catéchismes républicains, le 16 novembre 2009; journals.openedition.org/lrf/123journals.openedition.org/lrf/123, pdf (accessed 28/01/2021).

Bast, R. J. & A. C. Gows (ed., 2000), *Continuity and Change: The Harvest of Late-Medieval and Reformation History, Essays Presented to Heiko A. Oberman*, Leiden/Boston/Cologne: Brill.

Bataillon, M. (1991), *Erasme et l'Espagne: Recherches sur l'histoire spirituelle du XVIe siècle*, 3 vols, Geneva: Droz.

Bataillon, M. (2009), *Les jésuites dans l'Espagne du XVIe siècle*, Pierre-Antoine Fabre (éd.), Paris: Belles Lettres.

Bauch, G. (1903), *Die Reception des Humanismus in Wien. Eine litterarische Studie zur deutschen Universitätsgeschichte*, Breslau: M. & H. Marcus.

Bauer, D. (2004), 'The Importance of Medieval Canon Law and the Scholastic Tradition for the Emergence of the Early Modern International Legal Order', in R. Lesaffer (ed.), *Peace Treaties and International Law in European History: from the Late Middle Ages to World War One*, Cambridge, UK: Cambridge University Press, pp. 198–221.

Baümer, R. (1980), *Johannes Cochlaeus (1479–1552), Leben und Werk im Dienst der Katholischen Reform*, Münster: Aschendorff (Katholisches Leben und Kirchenreform im Zeitalter der Glaubensspaltung).

Baylor, M. G. (1977), *Action and Person: Conscience in Late Scholasticism and the Young Luther*, Leiden: Brill (Studies in Medieval & Reformation Thought, 20).

Beaty, N. L. (1970), *The Craft of Dying: A Study in the Literary Tradition of the Ars moriendi in England*, New Haven, CT & London: Yale University Press (Yale Studies in English).

Bedford, R. D. (1979), *The Defence of Truth: Herbert of Cherbury and the Seventeenth Century*, Manchester: Manchester University Press.

Bedouelle, G. (1976), *Lefèvre d'Etaples et l'Intelligence des Écritures*, Genève: Droz.

Bedouelle, G. & F. Giacone (ed., 1976), *Jacques Lefèvre d'Étaples et ses disciples. Epistres et Evangiles pour Les Cinquante et Deux Dimanches de L'an. Texte de l'édition Pierre de Vingle. Édition Critique avec Introduction et Notes*, Leiden: Brill.

Behrendt, W., 'Übersetzung eines Gerson-Textes von Georg Spalatin' in *Lehr-Wehr- und Nährstand. Haustafelliteratur und Dreistände-*

lehre im 16. Jahrhundert, Berlin, 2009; refubium.fu-berlin.de/handle/fub188/10734 (accessed 28/01/2021).

Behrens, G. (1999), 'Equity in the Commentaries of Edmund Plowden', in *The Journal of Legal History*, 3, pp. 25–50.

Bejczy, I. (1998), 'Erasme explore le moyen âge: sa lecture de Bernard de Clairvaux et de Jean Gerson', dans *Revue d'Histoire Ecclésiastique*, 93, pp. 461–76.

Belinda, E. A. (2001), *Oswaldi de corda opus pacis*, Turnhout: Brepols (Corpus Christianorum Continuatio Mediaevalis, 179).

Benjamin, K. M., 'A Semi-Pelagian in King Charles's Court: Juan Gines de Sepulveda on Nature, Grace, and the Conquest of the Americas' (unpublished dissertation, Duke University, 2017).

Bellitto, C. (2008), *The Church, the Councils, and Reform*, Washington DC: The Catholic University of America Press.

Beltrán, M. (2018), 'Mística del abandono en los primeros alumbrados', in *Cahiers d'études des cultures ibériques et latino-américaines*, 4, pp. 87–105.

Bender, G. (1975), *Die Irenik Martin Bucers in ihren Anfängen (1523–1528)*, Hildesheim: Gerstenberg (Studia Irenica 5).

Berman, H. J. & H. J. Witte Jr., 'The Transformation of Western Legal Philosophy in Lutheran Germany', in *Southern California Law Review*, 62 (6), 1989.

Berry, Ph. (1999), *Shakespeare's Feminine Endings: Disfiguring Death in the Tragedies*, New York: Psychology Press (Feminist Readings of Shakespeare).

Bess, B., 'Johannes Gerson und die Kirchenpolitischen Parteien Frankreichs vor der Konzil zu Piza' (unpublished doctoral dissertation, Marburg University, 1890).

Bibliotheque Numerique de Lyon, numelyo.bm-lyon.fr/f_view/BML: BML_00GOO01001THM0001ars_moriendi_3.

Bieber, A. (1993), *Johannes Bugenhagen zwischen Reform und Reformation - Die Entwicklung seiner frühen Theologie anhand des Matthäuskommentars und der Passions- und Auferstehungsharmonie*, Göttingen: Vandenhoeck & Ruprecht (Forschungen zur Kirchen und Dogmengeschichte, 51).

Billanovich, V. G. & G. Ouy (1964), 'La première correspondance échangée entre Jean de Montreuil et Coluccio Salutati', dans *Italia medievale e umanistica*, 7, pp. 337–74.

Binski, P. (1996), *Medieval Death: Ritual and Representation*, New York: Cornell University Press.

Bireley, R. (2018), 'The Religious Movements of the Sixteenth Century as Responses to a Changing World', in W. François & V. Soen (ed.), *The Council of Trent: Reform and Controversy in Europe and Beyond (1545-1700). Volume 1: Between Trent, Rome and Wittenberg*, Göttingen: Vandenhoeck & Ruprecht, pp. 29–48.

Blake, R. A. (2013), 'Fear and Consolation: Peter Canisius and the Spirituality of Dying and Death', in *Studies in the Spirituality of Jesuits*, 45 (1), pp. i–vii.

Blankenburg, W. (1991), *Johann Walter: Leben und Werk*, Hohengehren: Schneider.

Blick, J. de (1930), 'Barthélémy de Medina et les origines du probabilisme', in *Ephemerides Theologicae Lovanienses*, 7, pp. 46–83/pp. 264–91.

Blot, M. L. (2016), *La Mort. Un choix pour la vie: Du Mourir en France aujourd'hui?*, Books on Demand.

Blythel, J. M. (2005), *Le gouvernement idéal et la constitution mixte au Moyen Âge*, Fribourg: Cerf (Vestigia).

Boer, J.-H. de (2017), *Die Gelehrtenwelt ordnen: Zur Genese des hegemonialen Humanismus um 1500*, Tübingen: Mohr (Studies in the Late Middle Ages, Humanism and the Reformation).

Boer, W. de (2000), 'The Politics of the Soul: Confession in Counter-Reformation Milan', in K. L. Parker & A. T. Thayer (ed.), *Penitence in the Age of Reformations*, Aldershot: Ashgate (St Andrews Studies in Reformation History), pp. 116–33.

Boffa, S., 'Joseph of Nazareth as Man and Father in Jerónimo Gernónimo Gracián's Summar s Summary of the Excellencies of St Joseph (1597)' (unpublished doctoral dissertation, University of Notre Dame, Australia, 2016).

Boland, P. (1959), *The Concept of Discretio Spirituum in Jean Gerson's De Probatione Spirituum and De Distinctione Verarum Visionem a Falsis*, second edition, Washington DC: The Catholic University of America Press.

Bollbuck, H. (2010), 'Testimony of True Faith and the Ruler's Mission', in *Archiv für Reformationsgeschichte*, 101 (1), pp. 238–62.

Bond, L. (2005), *Nicolas of Cusa, Selected Spiritual Writings*, Mahwah, NJ: Paulist Press (Classics of Western Spirituality).

Bonnechose, F. P. E. de (1846), *Les réformateurs avant la Réforme: Jean Hus, Gerson, et le Concile de Constance*, Paris: J. Cherbuliez.

Borries, E. (1926), *Wimpheling und Murner im Kampf um die ältere Geschichte des Elsasses*, Heidelberg: Winter.

Bossy, J. (2002), 'Moral Arithmetic: Seven Sins into Ten Commandments', in E. Leites (ed.), *Conscience and Casuistry in Early Modern Europe*, Cambridge, UK: Cambridge University Press, pp. 214–34.

Bott, G. (1983), *Martin Luther und die Reformation in Deutschland*, Leipzig: Insel Verlag.

Boudet, J.-P. (2007), *La Dame à la licorne*, Paris: Le Peregrinateur.

Bourdin, B. (2010), *The Theological-Political Origins of the Modern State: The Controversy Between James I of England and Cardinal Bellarmine*, trans. S. Pickford, Washington DC: The Catholic University of America Press.

Braakhuis H. A. G. (1993), 'Wessel Gensfort, between Albertism anf Nominalism', in F. Akkerma, G. C. Huisman & A. Vanderjagt (ed.), *Wessel Gabsfort (1419–1489) and Northern Humanism*, Leiden: Brill (Brill's Studies in Intellectual History, 40), pp. 30–43.

Brady, T. A. (1992), 'Some Pecularities of German Histories in the Early Modern Era', in A. C. Fix & S. C. Karaut-Nunn (ed.), *Germania Illustrata, Essays on Early Modern Germany*, vol. 18, Ann Arbor, MI: Edwards Brothers (Sixteenth Century Essays & Studies Volume XVIII), pp. 197–216.

Brady T. A. (2009), *German Histories in the Age of Reformations*, 1400–1650, Cambridge: Cambridge, University Press (Sixteenth Century Essays & Studies).

Brann, N. (1981), *The Abbot Trithemius (1462–1516), The Renaissance of Monastic Humanism*, Leiden: Brill (Studies in the History of Christian Traditions, 24).

Brann, N. (2002), *The Debate Over the Origin of Genius During the Italian Renaissance*, Leiden: Brill (Brill's Studies in Intellectual History, 107).

Branya, J., 'Synderesis According to Leonardo Polo Barrena' (doctoral dissertation, Strathmore University, Nairobi, Kenya, 2016); Su-plus.strathmore.edu/bitstream/handle/11071/4808/Synderesis%20according%20to%20Leonardo%20Polo%20Barrena.pdf?sequence=5&isAllowed=y (accessed 28/01/2021).

Brauer, S. & J. Helmar. (1989), *Der Theologe Thomas Müntzer. Untersuchung zu seiner Entwicklung und Lehre*, Berlin: Evangelische Verlagsanstadt.

Braun, K.-H. (2006) *Johann Falri und Michael Heldung, zwei katholische Theologen aus Obenschwaben im Umfeld Karls V und Ferdinands I, Heimatkundliche Blätter für der Kreis Biberach*, Freiburg: Sonderdrucke aus der Albert-Ludwigs-Universität Freiburg.

Brecht, M. (1966), *Die frühe Theologie des Johannes Brenz*, Tübingen: Mohr.

Brecht, M. (ed., 1993), *Der Pietismus vom sibzehnten bis zum frühen achzehnten Jahrhundert*, Göttingen: Vandenhoeck & Ruprecht (Geschichte des Pietismus).

Brett, A. (1997), *Liberty, Right and Nature: Individual Rights in Later Scholastic Thought*, Cambridge, UK: Cambridge University Press (Ideas in Context, 44).

Breward, I. (1961), 'William Perkins and the Origins of Reformed Casuistry', in *Church Dogmatics*, 3, 4, 1961, pp. 3–20.

Britnell, J. (1986), *Jean Bouchet*, Durham: Univerity of Durham (University of Durham Series, I).

Britnell, J. (2001), 'Religious Instruction in the Work of Jean Bouchet', in A. Pettegree & P. Nelles (ed.), *The Sixteenth Century French Religious Book*, London, UK: Routledge (St Andrews Studies in Reformation History), pp. 83–109.

Britnell, J. (2003), 'Fictions au service de la foi: les Triumphes de la noble et amoureuse dame (1530)', in J. Britnell & N. Dauvois (ed.), *Jean Bouchet, traverseur des voies périlleuses. Acts of Poitiers Colloquium*. Paris: Champion, pp. 193–208.

Brodrick, J. (1956), *Saint Ignatius Loyola: The Pilgrim Years 1491–1538*, San Francisco: Ignatius Press.

Brogl, T. (2013), 'Yeglichs nach Sin vermugen: Johannes Niders Idea of Consience', in S. Müller & C. Schweiger (ed.), *Between Creativity and Norm-Making: Tensions in the Early Modern Era*, Leiden: Brill (Studies in Medieval and Reformation Traditions, 165), pp. 61–76.

Brooks, Ch. W. (2009), *Law, Politics and Society in Early Modern England*, Cambridge, UK: Cambridge University Press.

Broutin, P. (1953), *L'évêque dans la tradition pastorale du XVIe siècle*, Paris: Desclée de Brouwer.

Brown, D. C. (1987), *Pastor and Laity in the Theology of Jean Gerson*, New York: Cambridge University Press.

Bruening, M. W. (2006), *Calvinism's First Battleground: Conflict and Reform in the Pays de Vaud, 1528–1559*, Dordrecht: Springer Science & Business Media (Studies in Early Modern Religious Tradition, Culture and Society, 4).

Brunstetter, D. R. (2012), *Tensions of Modernity Las Casas and His Legacy in the French Enlightenment*, New York: Routledge (Routledge Innovations in Political Theory).

Bubenheimer, U. (1977), *Consonantia Theologiae et Iurisprudentiae: Karlstadt als Theologe und Jurist*, Tübingen: Mohr (Jus Ecclesiasticum).

Büchner, F., 'Thomas Murner, Sein Kampf und die Kontuität der kirchlichen Lehre in den Jahren 1511–1522' (unpublished doctoral dissertation, Berlin, Kirchliche Hochschule, 1974).

Buck, A. (1993), *Rom-Idee und nationale Identität in der italienischen Renaissance*, in T. Klaniczay, N. S. K. Nemeth & P. G. Schmidt (ed.), *Antike Rezeption und nationale Identität insbesondere in Deutschland und in Ungarn*, Budapest: Balassi Klado, pp. 19–31.

Brunstetter, D. R. (2012), *Tensions of Modernity: Las Casas and His Legacy in the French Enlightenment*, New York: Routledge (Routledge Innovations in Political Theory).

Burke, P. (2007), *Cultural Translation in Early Modern Europe*, Cambridge, UK: Cambridge University Press.

Burns, J. H. (1955), 'John Ireland and The Mercoure of Wyssdome', in *The Innes Review*, 6 (2), pp. 77–98.

Burns, J. H. (1981), '*Politica regalis et optima*: The political Ideas of John Mair', in *History of Political Thought*, 2 (1), pp. 31–61.

Burns, J. H. (1983), 'Jus Gladii and Jurisdictio: Jacques Almain and John Locke', in *The Historical Journal*, 26 (2), pp. 369–74.

Burns, J. H., 'Wisdom and Kingship: John Ireland, John Mair and George Buchanon', in St Andrew Intellectual History Archive, Institute of Intellectual History; arts.st-andrews.ac.uk/intellectualhistory/welcome (date unknown) (accessed 22/03/2018).

Burns, J. H. (1991), 'Scholasticism: Survival and Revival', in J. H. Burns (ed.), *The Cambridge History of Political Thought, 1450–1700*, New York: Cambridge University Press.

Burns, J. H. & M. Goldie (ed., 1991), *The Cambridge History of Political Thought 1450–1700*, Cambridge, UK: Cambridge University.

Burns, J. H. & T. M. Izbicki (ed., 1998), *Conciliarism and Papalism*, Cambridge, UK: Cambridge University Press (Cambridge Texts in the History of Political Thought).

Burrows, M. S. (1991), *Jean Gerson and De consolatione theologiae (1418): the Consolation of a Biblical and Reforming Theology for a Disordered Age*, Tübingen: Mohr (Beitrage Zur Historischen Theologie).

Burton, R., *The Anatomy of Melancholy*, Project Gutenberg; https://www.gutenberg.org/files/10800/10800-h/10800-h.htm (accessed 28/01/2021).

Bussi, R. (1987), *Libri, idee e sentimenti religiosi nel Cinquecento italiano: 3–5 aprile 1986*, Modena: Panini (Istituto di studi rinascimentali).

Büttgen, Ph. (2011), *Luther et la philosophie*, Paris: Vrin (Contextes).

Cahill, T. (2014), *Heretics and Heroes, How Renaissance Artists and Reformation Priests Created Our World*, Norwell, MA: Anchor (The Hinges of History).

Calvot, D. & G. Ouy (1990), *L'œuvre de Gerson à Saint-Victor de Paris*, Paris: Catalogue des manuscrits.

Campbell, E. (1958), 'Thomas Hobbes and the Common Law', in *Tasmanian Law Journal*, 1, pp. 20–46.

Cameron, E. (1993), 'Medieval Heretics as Protestant Martyrs', in D. Wood (ed.), *Martyrs and Martyrologies*, Oxford: Oxford University (Studies in Church History), pp. 185–207.

Campi, E. (ed., 2004), *Heinrich Bullinger, und seine Zeit: Eine Vorlesungsreihe*, Zürich: Theologischer Verlag (Zwingliana. Beiträge zur Geschichte Zwinglis, der Reformation und des Protestantismus in der Schweiz).

Campo, del U. A (2005), *Vida y obra de fray Luis de Granada*, Salamanca: Editorial San Esteban.

Camus, A. (1992), *The Rebel: An Essay on Man in Revolt*, reissue edition, New York: Vintage.

Cancellieri, F. (1809), *Dissertazioni epistolari bibliografiche di Francesco Cancellieri sopra Cristoforo Colombo: di Cuccaro nel Monferrato, discopritore dell'America, e Giovanni Gersen di Cavaglia' abate di S. Stafano in Vercelli, avtore del libro De imitatione Christi, al ch. sig. Cavaliere*, Roma: Gianfrancesco Galeani Napione di Cocconato Passerano.

Canovas, A. 'La sorcière, la sainte et l'illuminée, les pouvoirs féminins en Espagne à travers les procès (1529–1655)' (unpublished doctoral dissertation, Toulouse 2, 2008).

Capizzi, J. E. (2002), 'The Children of God: Natural Slavery in the Thought of Aquinas and Vitoria', in *Theological Studies*, 63, pp. 31–53.

Carnahan, D. H. (1916), 'Some sources of Olivier Maillard's Sermon on the Passion', in *Romanic Review*, 7, pp. 144–70.

Caron, P. & A. Laimé (2005), *Noël Béda*, Paris: Les Belles Lettres.

Carter, A. (2005), 'René Benoit: Scripture for the Catholic Masses', in L. Racaut & A. Ryrie (ed.), *Moderate Voices in the European Reformation*, Farham UK: Ashgate (St Andrews Studies in Reformation History), pp. 162–77.

Caspers, C. M. A. (1999), 'Magister Consensus Wessel Gansfort (1419–1489) und die Geistliche Kommunion', in F. Akkerma, A. Vanderjagt & A. Laan (ed.), *Northern Humanism in European Context, 1469–1625: From the 'Adwert Academy' to Ubbo Emmius*, Leiden: Brill (Brill's Studies in Intellectual History, 94), pp. 82–98.

Cave, T. C. (1967), 'The Protestant Devotional Tradition: Simon Goulart's Trente Tableaux de la Mort: Parallels Between Catholic and Protestant Devotion', in *French Studies*, 21 (1), pp. 1–15.

Cechetti, D. (1966), 'L'elogio delle arti liberali nel primo umanesimo francese', in *Studi Francesi*, 28, pp. 1–14.

Cechetti, D. (1982), *Petrarca, Pietramal e Clamanges: storia di una 'querelle' inventata*, Paris: CEMI.

Cechetti, D. (1992), 'Sic me Cicero laudare docuerat. La retorica nel primo umanesimo francese', dans C. Bozzolo & E. Ornato (éd.), *Préludes à la Renaissance. Aspects de la vie intellectuelle en France au XVe siècle*, Paris: CEMI, pp. 47–106.

Chaconac, P. (1963), *Grandeur et adversité de Jean Trithème, Bénédictin abbé de Spanheim et de Wurtzbourg, 1462–1516: la vie, la légende, l'oeuvre*, Paris: Éditions Traditionnelles.

Chafe, E. T. (2000), *Analyzing Bach Cantatas*, Oxford: Oxford University Press.

Charrier, S. (1996), *Recherches sur l'œuvre latine en prose de Robert Gaguin (1433–1501)*, Paris: Champion (Renaissance Library, 35).

Chartier, R. (1976), 'Les arts de mourir, 1450–1600', dans *Annales. Histoire, Sciences Sociales*, 31, pp. 51–75.

Chartier, R. (1989), 'Le monde comme représentation', dans *Annales. Histoire, Sciences Sociales*, 6, pp. 1505–1520.

Chatellier, L. (1995), *Le catholicisme en France, limites actuelles*, Paris: Sedes.

Chaucer, G., s. d. *The Parson's Tale*; sites.fas.harvard.edu/~chaucer/teachslf/parst-tran.htm (accessed 28/01/2021).

Chaunu, P. (1971), *Examination of the Council of Trent*, Fred Kramer (trans.), St Louis, MO: Concordia.

Chaunu, P. (1981), *Eglise, culture et société: Essais sur Réforme et Contre-Réforme (1517–1620)*, Paris: Société Edition Enseignement Supérieur.

Chaunu, P. (1997), *Le temps des Réformes: Histoire religieuse et système de civilisation. La crise de la chrétienté. L'éclatement (1250–1550)*, Paris: Fayard.

Christ-von Wedel, C. (2011), 'Der Bibelübersetzer Leo Jud und sein biblisches Erbauungsbuch *Vom lyden Christi* (1534)', in *Zwingliana*, 38, pp. 35-52.

ChulHong Kang, P. (2006), *Justification: The Imputation of Christ's Righteousness from Reformation Theology to the American Great Awakening and the Korean Revivals*, Berlin: Peter Lang.

Classen, A. (2007), Introduction, *Old Age in the Middle Ages and the Renaissance: Interdisciplinary Approaches to a Neglected Topic*, Berlin: De Gruyer (Fundamentals of Medieval and Early Modern Culture, 2).

Cole, D. E. (2003), 'Judicial Discretion and the 'Sunk Cost:' Strategy of Government Agencies', in *British Columbia Environmental Affairs Law Review*, 3, pp. 710–14.

Collard, F. (1996), *Un historien au travail à la fin du XVe siècle: Robert Gaguin*, Geneva: Droz (Travaux d'humanisme et Renaissance).

Collins, E. F., 'The Treatment of Scrupulosity in the *Summa Moralis* of St Antoninus: A Historical-Theological Study' (unpublished doctoral dissertation, Rome, Pontificia Universitas Gregoriana, 1961).

Colón-Emeric, E. (2017), 'Human Sacrifice: Religious Act or Vicious Desire? Testing the Limits of Tolerance with Vitoria and Las Casas', in *Journal of Early Modern Christianity*, 4 (2), pp. 227–61.

Combes, A. (1963–1965), *La théologie mystique de Gerson: profil de son evolution*, 2 vols, Rome etc.: Desclée et Libraria Editrix Pontificiae Universitatis Lateranensis.

Comper, F. M. M. (1977), *The Book of the Craft of Dying and Other Early English Tracts Concerning Death*, New York: Arno Press.

Congar, Y. M. (1960), *La Tradition et les traditions*, Paris: Fayard (Collection Le Signe).

Connolly, D. K. (2009), *The Maps of Matthew Paris, Medieval Journeys through Space, Time and Liturgy*, Woodbridge, UK: Boydell.

Connolly, J. (1928), *John Gerson: Reformer and Mystic*, Leuven: Librairie Universitaire.

Connolly, T. (1994), *Mourning into Joy: Music, Raphael, and Saint Cecilia*, New Heaven: Yale University Press.

Conti, F. (2011), *Preachers and Confessors against 'Superstitions'. The Rosarium Sermonum by Bernardino Busti and its Melanese Context (Late Fifteenth Century)*, Central European University, Budapest, 2011.

Cottret, B. (2000), *Calvin: A Biography*, Grand Rapids, MI: Wm. B. Eerdmans.

Coumet, E. (1970), 'La théorie du hasard est-elle née par hasard?' dans *Annales. Histoire, Sciences Sociales*, 25, pp. 574–98.

Coville, A. (1974), *Jean Petit. La question du tyrannicide*, Genève: Slatkine.

Crane, M. (2010), 'A Scholastic Response to Biblical Humanism: Noël Béda Against Lefèvre d'Etaples and Erasmus (1526)', in *Humanistica Lovaniensia*, pp. 71–97.

Creo, R. A. (2004), 'Mediation 2004: The Art and The Artist', in *Pennsylvania State Law Review*, 108, pp. 1017–1037.

Crouzet, D. (1990), *Les Guerriers de Dieu. La violence au temps des troubles de Religion (vers 1525-vers 1610)*, Seyssel: Champ Vallon (Époques).

Cubillos, R. H. (2009), 'Consolation as Theme in Luther's Sermons and Correspondence: Insights into his Theological Ethics', in *Asbury Journal*, 64/2, 36–67.

Cummings, B. (2007), 'The Conscience of Thomas More', in A. Höfele, S. Laqué & E. Ruge (ed.), *Representing Religious Pluralization in Early Modern Europe*, Berlin/Münster: Hopf, pp. 1–14.

Cummings, B. (2009), 'Conscience and Law in Thomas More', in *Renaissance Studies*, 23 (4), pp. 463–85.

Cummings, B. (2011), 'Conscience and Law in Thomas More', in H. E. Braun & E. Vallance (ed.) *The Renaissance Conscience*, Malden, MA: Wiley-Blackwell, pp. 29–51.

Curbet, J. (2015), Rewriting the '*ars moriendi*': Society and the Dying Self in William Shakespeare's 'Measure for Measure' and 'Othello', in *Medievalia*, 18 (1), pp. 165–74.

Curran, M., 'St Thomas More's Treatise Upon the Passion' (unpublished doctoral dissertation, Dublin University College, 1956).

Curtright, T. (2013), *The One Thomas More*, Washington DC: The Catholic University of America Press.

Dacheux, L. (1876), *Jean Geiler de Kaysersberg prédicateur à la cathédrale de Strasbourg, 1478–1510: étude sur sa vie et son temps*, Paris: C. Delagrave.

Dacheux, L. (2010), *Les plus anciens écrits de Geiler de Kaysersberg: Todtenbüchlein, Beichtspiegel, Seelenheil, Sendtbrieff, Bilger*, LaVergne, TN: Nabu Press.

Dagens, J. (1952), *Bibliographie chronologique de la littérature de spiritualité et de ses sources, 1501–1610*, Paris: Desclée/De Brouwer.

Daniel, W. (1968), *The Purely Penal Law Theory in the Spanish Theologians from Vitoria to Suarez*, Rome: Gregorian Biblical BookShop (Analecta Gregoriana).

Daumas, M. (2007), *Au Bonheur des mâles: adultère et cocuage à la Renaissance, 1400–1650*, Paris: Armand Colin.

Davenport, A., 'Is there a Sixth Sense in the Lady and the Unicorn Tapestries?' in *The New Arcadia Review*, 4 (2011); bc.edu/publications/newarcadia/archives/4/is_there_a_sixth_sense/H (28/01/2021).

Davidson J. P. (2012), *Early Modern Supernatural: The Dark Side of European Culture, 1400–1700*, Santa Barbara, CA: ABC-CLIO (Praeger Series on the Early Modern World).

Denis, Ph. (2014), *Edmond Richer et le renouveau du conciliarisme au XVIIe siècle*, Paris: Cerf (Sagesses chrétiennes).

Denis, Ph. (2019), *Edmond Richer and the Renewal of Conciliarism in the 17th Century*, bilingual edition, English trans. by C. Beckett, Göttingen: Vandenhoeck & Ruprecht (Refo500 Academic Studies, 62).

Denis, Ph. (2019a), 'Edmond Richer, la Sorbonne et les métamorphoses du conciliarisme', dans *Dix-septième siècle*, 285, pp. 109-24.

Derrida, J. & B. Stiegler (1996), *Échographies de la télévision. Entretiens filmés*, Paris: Galilée.

Debongnie, P. (1927), 'Une œuvre oubliée de Mauburnus: *Le Rosarum Hortulus*', dans *Revue d'Ascétique et de Mystique*, 8, pp. 392–402.

Debongnie P. (1928), *Jean Mombaer de Bruxelles: ses écrits et ses réformes*, Louvain-Toulouse: Librairie universitaire.

Debongnie, P. (1980), *Dictionnaire de spiritualité ascétique et mystique*, Paris: Beauchesne.

Debuchy, P. (1910), *Exercices spirituels de Saint Ignace de Loyola*, Paris: Lethielleux.

Decock, W. (2007), 'Leonardus Lessius on Buying and Selling (1605). Translation and Introduction', in *Journal of Markets & Morality*, 10 (2), pp. 433–516.

Decock, W. (2012), *Theologians and Contract Law: The Moral Transformation of the Ius Commune (ca. 1500–1650)*, Leiden: Martinus Nijhoff (Legal History Library, 9/4).

Decock, W. & J. Hallebeek (2010), 'Pre-contractual duties to inform in Early Modern Scholasticism', in *The Legal History Review*, 78 (1–2), pp. 89–133.

Decock, W. (2017), 'Collaborative Legal Pluralism. Confessors as Law Enforcers in Mercado's Advice on Economic Governance (1517)', in *Rechtsgeschichte — Legal History*, 25, pp. 103–14.

Decock, W. (2018), 'Martín de Azpilcueta', in R. Domingo & J. Martínez-Torrón (ed.), *Great Christian Jurists in Spanish History*,

Cambridge, UK: Cambridge University Press (Law and Christianity), pp. 116–33.

Dedieu, J.-P. (1979), *L'Inquisition Espagnole XVe–XIXe siècles*, Paris: Hachette.

Delaruelle, E., E.-R. Labande & P. Ourliac (1962 & 1964), *L'Église au temps du Grand Schisme et de la crise conciliaire (1377–1449)*, Paris: Bloue et Gay.

Delsaux, O. & T. Van Hemelryck (2014), *Les manuscrits autographes en français au Moyen Âge: Guide de recherches. Avec trois articles de Gilbert Ouy*, Turnhout: Brepols.

Delumeau J. (1983), *Le cas Luther*, Paris: Desclée.

Delumeau, J. (1983), *Le péché et la peur, La culpabilisation en Occident (XIIIe-XVIIIe siècle)*, Paris: Fayard (Nouvelles Etudes Historiques).

Delumeau, J. (1990), *L'aveu et le pardon: les difficultés de la confession, XIIIe-XVIIIe siècle*, Paris: Fayard (Nouvelles Etudes Historiques).

Delumeau, J. & D. Roche (1990), *Histoire des pères et de la paternité*, Paris: Larousse.

Deman T. (1936), 'Probabilisme' dans J. M. A. Vacant, E. Mangenot & E. Amann (éd.), *Dictionnaire de Théologie Catholique*, vol. XIII, part 1, cols 417–619, Paris: Letouzey et Ané.

Demelemestre, G. (2018), 'Philosophie et droit chez les humanistes', Conférence 'La Renaissance, parlons-en', Paris: Sorbonne, April 2018.

Denifle, H. (1917), *Luther and Lutherdom, from Original Sources*, Somerset, OH: The Torch Press.

Depew, J. F. (2016), 'Foucault Among the Stoics: Oikeiosis and Counter-Conduct', in *Foucault Studies*, 21, pp. 22–51.

DeVine, S. W. (1989), 'Polyconnotational Equity and the Role of *Epieikeia* in International Law', in *Texas International Law Journal*, 24, pp. 149–259.

Dhotel, J.-C. (1967), *Les origines du catéchisme moderne d'après les premiers manuels imprimés en France*, Paris: Aubier-Montaigne.

Doebler, B. A. (1994), *Rooted Sorrow: Dying in Early Modern England*, Vancouver BC: Fairleigh Dickinson University Press.

Dompnier, B. (2008), 'La dévotion à saint Joseph au miroir des confréries', dans B. Dompnier & P. Vismara (éd.), *Confréries et dévotions dans la catholicité moderne (mi XVe - début XIXe siècle)*, Rome: École française de Rome, pp. 285–309.

Dompnier, B. (2010), 'Thérèse d'Avila et la dévotion française à saint Joseph au XVIIe', dans *Mémoires et documents*, 117, pp. 291–308.

Donahue, C. (2007), *Law, Marriage, and Society in the Later Middle Ages: Arguments about Marriage in Five Courts*, New York: Cambridge University Press.

Donahue, D. (2010), 'The Mysticism of Saint Ignatius Loyola', in H. Kallendorf (ed.), *A New Companion to Hispanic Mysticism*, Leiden: Brill (Brill's Companions to Christian Tradition, 19), pp. 201–29.

Dotted, C. (1904), 'The Tercentenary Exhibition of the Musicians' Company', in *The Musical Times*, 45 (737), pp. 429–35.

Douglass, J. D. (1966), *Justification in Late Medieval Preaching: A Study of John Geiler of Keisersberg*, Leiden: Brill (Studies in Medieval and Reformation, 1).

Dragseth, J. H. (2011), *The Devil's Whore: Reason and Philosophy in the Lutheran Tradition*, Minneapolis, MN: Fortress Press (Studies in Lutheran History and Theology).

Dress, W. (1931), *Die Theologie Gersons*, Gutersloh: E. Bertelsmann.

Duby, G. (1996), *Love and Mariage in the Middle Ages*, Chicago: University of Chicago Press.

Duff, E. G. (1896), *Early English Printing*, London: Kegan, Paul Trench, Trübner and Company, Limited.

Duffy, E. G. (1992), *Stripping of the Altars: Traditional Religion in England, 1400–1580*, New Heaven: Yale University Press.

Dykema, P. A. (2000), 'Handbooks for Pastors: Late Medieval Manuals for Parish Priests and Conrad Porta's *Pastorale lutheri* (1582)', in R. J. Bast & A. C. Gow (ed.), *Continuity and Change: The Harvest of Late Medieval and Reformation History: Essays Presented to Heiko A. Oberman on His 70th Birthday*, Leiden: Brill, pp. 143–62.

Ebeling, G. (1977), *Lutherstudien: Disputatio de homine, Band 2: Teil 1: Text und Traditionshintergrund*, Tübingen: Mohr.

Ehmer, H. (2009), 'Brenz und Paul', in W. Holder (ed.), *A Companion to Paul in the Reformation*, Leiden: Brill (Brill's Companion to the Christian Tradition, 15), pp. 165–86.

Eisenberg, J. 'Theology, Political Theory, and Justification' (unpublished doctoral dissertation, New York, CUNY, 1998).

Elias, N. (1969) *The Court Society*, Dublin: UCD Press (Collected Works of Norbert Elias).

Ellington, D. S. (2001), *From Sacred Body to Angelic Soul. Understanding Mary in Late Medieval and Early Modern Europe*, St Louis, MO: The Catholic University of America Press.

Endean, Ph. (1980), 'Origins of Apostolic Formation: Jerome Nadal and Novitiate Experiments', in *The Way*, Supplement 39, pp. 57–82.

Enenkel, K. & W. Melion (ed., 2010), *Meditatio — Refashioning the Self: Theory and Practice in Late Medieval and Early Modern Intellectual Culture*, Leiden: Brill.

Engen, J. van (2008), 'Multiple Options: The World of the Fifteenth-Century Church', in *Church History*, 77 (2), pp. 257-284.

Erb, P. (1989), *Pietists, Protestants and Mysticism: the Use of Late Medieval Spiritual Texts in the Work of Gottfried Arnold (1666–1714)*, Lanham, ML: Scarecrow.

Eriksson, A.-L., G. Gunner & N. Blader (2012), *Exploring a Heritage: Evangelical Lutheran Churches in the North*, Eugene, OR: Wipf and Stock (Church of Sweden Research Series, 5).

Ernst, T. (1996), *Schwarzweiße Magie. Der Schlüssel zum dritten Buch der Steganographia des Trithemius*, in *Daphnis* 25 (1), Amsterdam: Rodopi.

Esquivel, J. (1979), 'Assassination and Tyrannicide', in *Crítica: Revista Hispanoamericana de Filosofía*, 33 (11), pp. 3–17.

Estes, J. (2007), *Christian Magistrate and Territorial Church: Johannes Brenz and the Gerson Reformation*, Toronto: Centre for Reformation and Renaissance Studies (Essays and Studies, 12).

Evans, G. R. (1992), *Problems of Authority in the Reformation Debates*, Cambridge: Cambridge University Press.

Ewig, E. 'Die Anschauungen des Kartäusers Dionysius von Roermond über den christlichen Ordo in Staat und Kirche' (Inaugural dissertation, Bonn, 1936).

Ex-classics Project, 2009, exclassics.com.

Faber, B. (2016), 'The Art of Divine Meditation in George Herbert's *The Temple*', in *Christianity & Literature*, 66 (1), pp. 73–89.

Fabre, I. (éd., 2005), *La doctrine du chant du coeur de Jean Gerson*, Genève: Droz (Publications romanes et françaises, 235).

Fabre, P. A. (2013), *Décréter l'image? La XXVe session du concile de Trente*, Paris: Les Belles Lettres.

Faesen, R., 'The Turn to Interiority in the Early Modern Period', in T. Merrigan et al. (ed.), *The Crisis of Religion and the Problem of Roman Catholic Self-Definition*, Leiden: Brill, forthcoming in 2022.

Faini, M. (2019), 'Vernacular Books and Domestic Devotion in Cinquecento Italy', in *Journal of Early Modern Christianity*, 6 (2019), pp. 299-318.

Falk, F. (1907), *Drei Beichbüchlein nach den Geboten aus der Frühzeit der Buchdruckerkunst*, Münster: Aschendorff.

Farge, J. K. (1985), *Orthodoxy and Reform in Early Reformation France: The Faculty of Theology of Paris, 1500–1543*, Leiden: Brill (Studies in Medieval and Reformation Traditions, 32).

Fasolt, C. (1997), 'William Durant the Younger and Conciliar Theory', in *Journal of the History of Ideas*, 58 (3), pp. 385–402.

Fernández-Bollo, E. (2013), 'Conciencia y valor en Martín de Azpilcueta: ¿un agustinismo práctico en la España del siglo xvi?' in *Criticón*, 118, pp. 57–69.

Fernández-Santamaria, José A. (1975), 'Juan Ginés de Sepúlveda on the Nature of the American Indians', in *The Americas*, 31 (4), 1975, pp. 434–51.

Fétis, F.-J. (1841), *Biographie universelle des musiciens*, 8 vols, Bruxelles: Meline, Cans & Compagnie.

Fèvre, L. (1957), *Au cœur religieux du XVIe siècle*, Paris: École Pratique des Hautes études.

Figgis, J. N. (1999), *Studies of Political Thought from Gerson to Grotius: 1414–1625*, Kitchener, Canada: Batoche Books.

Fisher, J. (2006), 'Gerson's Mystical Theology: A New Profile of its Evolution', in B. P. McGuire (ed.), *A Companion to Jean Gerson*, New York/Leiden: Brill (Brill's Companions to the Christian Tradition, 3), pp. 205–48.

Flanagan, D. Z. (2006), 'Making Sense of it All: Gerson's Biblical Theology', in B. P. McGuire (ed.), *A Companion to Jean Gerson*, New York/Leiden: Brill (Brill's Companions to the Christian Tradition, 3), pp. 133–78.

Fleming, J. (2006), *Defending Probabilism, The Moral Theology of Juan Caramuel*, Washington DC: Georgetown University Press (Moral Traditions).

Fleming, J. (2008), 'When Meats Are Medicines: Vitoria and Lessius on the Role of Food in the Duty to Preserve Life', in *Theological Studies*, 69, pp. 99–116.

Flete, W. (1968), 'Remedies against Temptations: The Third English Version of William Flete', in E. Colledge & N. Chadwick (ed.), *Archivio Italiano per la Storia della Pieta*, 5, pp. 201–40.

Flint, V. I. J. (1992), *The Imaginative Landscape of Christopher Columbus*, Princeton: Princeton University Press (Princeton Legacy Library).

Fogelman, A. (2009), 'Finding a Middle Way: Late Medieval Naturalism and Visionary Experience', in *Visual Resources: an International Journal on Images and Their Uses*, 1-2, pp. 7-28.

Forrestal, A. (2004), *Fathers, Pasters and Kings, Studies in Early Modern European History*, Mancherster: Mancherster University Press (Studies in Early Modern European History).

Forrestal, A. & E. Nelson (ed., 2009), *Politics and Religion in Early Bourbon France*, London: Palgrave.

Forthomme, B. (2010), Le 'Recogimiento, source franciscaine de la spiritualité carmélitaine au Siècle d'Or', in *Miscellanea Francescana*, 110 (1-2) pp. 184-204.

Franceschi, S. de (2007), 'Gallicanisme, antirichérisme et reconnaissance de la romanité ecclésiale. La dispute entre le cardinal Bellarmin et le théologien parisien André Duval (1614)', dans J.-L. Quantin & J.-C. Waquet (dir.), *Papes, princes et savants dans l'Europe moderne. Mélanges à la mémoire de Bruno Neveu*, Genève: Droz (Hautes Études Médiévales et Modernes, 90).

François, W. (2020), 'Scriptures' and 'Non-Scriptural Traditions': Evolutions at the Beginning of the Reformation Era', in P. De Mey & W. François (ed.), *Ecclesia Semper Reformanda: Renewal and Reform Beyond Polemics*, Leuven: Peeters (Bibliotheca Ephemeridum Theologicarum Lovaniensium), pp. 13-36.

François, W. & V. Soen (ed., 2018), *The Council of Trent: Reform and Controversy in Europe and Beyond (1545-1700)*, 3 vols, Göttingen: Vandenhoeck & Ruprecht.

François, W. & M. Gielis (2017), 'Een herbronning van het ambt van de zielzorgers. De visie van de Leuvense theoloog Jacobus Latomus (1516-1518)', in W. François, L. Kenis & V. Soen (ed.), *Bisdommen, seminaries en de Leuvense theologische Faculteit (16de-20ste eeuw)*, Leuven: Peeters (Annua Nuntia Lovaniensia, 75).

Frank, C. B. M., 'Untersuchungen zum Catalogus testium veritatis des Matthias Flacius Illyricus' (unpublished doctoral dissertation, Tübingen University, 1990).

Franklin, J. (2001), *The Science of Conjecture: Evidence and Probability Before Pascal*, Baltimore: Johns Hopkins University Press.

Franklin, J. (2016), 'Pre-history of probability', in A. Hájek & C. Hitchcock (ed.), *Oxford Handbook of Probability and Philosophy*, Oxford: Oxford University Press (Oxford Handbooks), pp. 33-49.

Frederickson, K. (2014), *The Ploy of Instinct: Victorian Sciences of Nature and Sexuality in Liberal Governance*, New York: Fordham University Press (Forms of Living).

Freedberg, D. (1971), 'Johannes Molanus on Provocative Paintings. *De Historia Sanctarum Imaginum et Picturarum*', in *Journal of the Warburg and Courtauld Institutes*, 34, pp. 229–45.

Frey, W. (2000), 'Die Pilgerreise des Christen und das Christenleben als Pilgerreise in das thor des vatterlandes öwiger säligkait', in D. Klein (ed.), *Vom Mittelalter zur Neuzeit: Festschrift für Horst Brunner*, Wiesbaden: Reichert, pp. 431–45.

Friedrich, M. (2017), 'On Reading Missionary Correspondence: Jesuit Theologians on the Spiritual Benefits of a New Culture', in H. Puff, U. Strasser & C. Wild (ed.), *Cultures of Communication: Theologies of Media in Early Modern Europe and Beyond*, Toronto: University of Toronto Press (UCLA Clark Memorial Library Series), pp. 186–208.

Gaille-Nikodimov, M. (éd., 2005), *Le Gouvernement mixte. De l'idéal politique au monstre constitutionnel en Europe (XIIIe-XVIe siècle)*, Saint-Étienne: Publications de l'université de Saint- Étienne.

Ganzer, K. (1997), *Kirche auf dem Weg durch die Zeit. Institutionelles Werden und theologisches Ringen. Ausgewählte Aufsätze und Vorträge*, H. Smolinsky & J. Meier (ed.), Münster: Aschendorff (Reformationsgeschichtliche Studien und Texte).

Gaquoin, K. & R. Gaguin (1901), *Denkschrift zum 400. Todestage des Robertus Gaguinus*, Heidelberg: Winter.

Garside, C. Jr. (1974), '*La farce des Theologastres*: Humanism, Heresy, and the Sorbonne, 1523–1525', in *Rice University Studies*, 60, pp. 45–82.

Gauvard C. & G. Ouy (2001), 'Gerson et l'infanticide, défense des femmes et critique de la pénitence publique', dans J.-C. Mühlethaler & D. Billotte (éd.), *Riens ne m'est seur que la chose incertaine. études sur l'art d'ecrire au moyen age: Etudes sur l'art d'écrire au Moyen Age offertes à Eric Hicks par ses élèves, collègues et amis*, Genève: Slatkine, pp. 45–66.

Gaztambide, J. G. (2010), 'El tratado 'De Superstitionibus' de Martín de Andosilla', in *Instrucion Príncipe de Viana (PV)* 251, pp. 1011–1069.

Geary, P. (2002), *The Myth of Nations: the Medieval Origins of Europe*, Princeton: Princeton University Press.

Geest, P. van (2008), 'Gabriel Biel: Brother of the Common Life and 'Alter Augustinus?' Aim and Meaning of His *Tractatus de communi vita clericorum*', in *Augustiniana*, 58, pp. 305–57.

Gertsman, E. (2015), *Worlds Within: Opening the Medieval Shrine Madonna*, University Park, PA: Penn State Press.

Gerz-von Büren, V. (1973), *La tradition de l'oeuvre de Jean Gerson chez les Chartreux*, Paris: CNRS.

Gifford, P. M. (2001), *The Hammered Dulcimer. A History*, London: The Scarecrow Press (American Folk Music and Musicians Series, 6).

Gillespie, M. A. (2009), *The Theological Origins of Modernity*, Chicago: University of Chicago Press.

Gilli, P. (1997), *Au miroir de l'humanisme. Les représentations de la France dans la culture savante italienne (c. 1360-c. 1490)*, Rome: École Française de Rome, Palais Farnèse.

Gilmont, J.-F. (1981), *Jean Crespin: Un éditeur réformé du XVIᵉ siècle*, Genève: Droz (Travaux d'Humanisme et Renaissance, 186).

Gilmont, J.-F. (1983), 'Aux origines de l'historiographie vaudoise du XVIᵉ siècle: Jean Crespin, Etienne Noël et Scipione Lentolo', dans *Valdesi e l'Europa* (Collana della Società di Studi valdesi 9), Torre Pellice: Società di Studi Valdesi, pp. 165–202.

Gilmont, J.-F. (1990), *La Réforme et le livre. L'Europe et l'imprimé (1517-v. 1570)*, Paris: Éditions du Cerf (Histoire).

Giraud, C. (2016), *Spiritualité et histoire des textes entre Moyen Âge et époque moderne: genèse et fortune d'un corpus pseudépigraphe de méditations*, Paris: Institut d'Études Augustiniennes (Série Moyen Âge et Temps modernes, 52).

Godet, M. (1912), *La congrégation de Montaigu (1490–1580)*, Paris: Bibliothèque de l'École des Hautes-Études, Sciences historiques et philologiques.

Goerner, E. A. (1983), 'Thomistic Natural Right: The Good Man's View of Thomistic Natural Law', in *Political Theory*, 11 (3), pp. 393–418.

Goetz, W. (1981), 'Luthers Ein Sermon von der Bereitung zum Sterben', in *Luther Jahrbuch*, 48, pp. 97–113.

Golz, R. (1998), *Wolfgang Mayrhofer, Luther and Melanchthon in the Educational Thought of Central and Eastern Europe*, Münster: LIT (Texts on Theory and History of Education, 10).

Gordon, B. (1996), 'The Changing Face of Protestant History and Identity in the Sixteenth Century', in B. Gordon (ed.), *Protestant History and Identity in Sixteenth-Century Europe*, Farnham: Aldershot (St Andrews Studies in Reformation History), pp. 1–22.

Gordon, B. (1996a), 'The Worthy Witness of Christ': Protestant Uses of Savanarola in the 16ᵗʰ Century', in B. Gordon (ed.), *Protestant History and Identity in Sixteenth-Century Europe*, Farnham: Aldershot (St Andrews Studies in Reformation History), pp. 93–107.

Gordon, B. (2000), 'Malevolent Ghosts and Ministering Angels: Apparitions and Pastoral Care in the Swiss Reformation', in B. Gordon & P. Marshal (ed.), *The Place of the Dead: Death and Remembrance in Late Medieval and Early Modern Europe*, Cambridge: Cambridge University, pp. 87–109.

Graf, zu Dohna, L. & R. Wetzel (1987), *Johann von Staupitz, Sämtliche Schriften (Complete Works), Lateinische Schriften, Tübinger Predigten*, Berlin: De Gruyter (Spätmittelalter und Reformation Texte und Untersuchungen 13).

Grant, E. (1974), *A Source Book in Medieval Science*, Cambridge, MA: Harvard University Press.

Greene, R. (1991), 'Synderesis the Spark of Conscience, in the English Renaissance', in *Journal of the History of Ideas*, 52 (2), pp. 195–219.

Greene, R. (1997), 'Instinct of Nature: Natural Law, Synderesis, and the Moral Sense', in *Journal of the History of Ideas*, 58 (2), pp. 173–98.

Gregorovà, M, 'Skrupulózní svědomí v duchovním životě' ('Scrupulous conscience in spiritual life') (unpublished doctoral dissertation, Palacký University, Olomouc, Czech Republic, 2014).

Grellard, Ch. (2018), 'Comment peut-on croire à la transsubstantiation? La certitude morale et ses fondements sociaux chez Jean Mair', dans *Przeglad Tomistyczny*, 24, pp. 627–50.

Greschat, M. (2004), *Martin Bucer: A Reformer and His Times*, Westminster: John Knox.

Grosse, S. (1994), *Heilsungewissheit und Scrupulositas im späten Mittelalter*, Tübingen: Mohr (Beiträge zur historischen Theologie, 85).

Guibert, J. de (1953), *La spiritualité de la Compagnie de Jésus: esquisse historique*, Roma: Institutum Historicum.

Guibert, J. de (1964), *The Jesuits: Their Spiritual Doctrine and Practice — a Historical Study*, Chicago: Loyola University Press.

Guicharrousse, H. (1995), *Les musiques de Luther*, Geneva: Labor & Fides (Histoire et société).

Guillon, E. (1888), *De Johanne Gersonio quatenus in arte politica valuerit*, Paris: Thesim.

Guenée, B. (1992), *Un Meurtre, une société: l'assassinat du Duc d'Orléans, 23 novembre 1407*, Paris: Gallimard.

Guy, J. A. (1986), 'Law, Equity and Conscience in Henrician Juristic Thought', in A. Fox & J. A. Guy (ed.), *Reassessing the Henrician Age: Humanism, Politics, and Reform, 1500–1550*, New York: Blackwell.

Guy, J. A. (2000), *Thomas More*, New York: Oxford University Press. (Reputations Series).

Guzuskyte, E. (2014), *Christopher Columbus' Naming in the 'diarios' of the Four Voyages (1492–1504): A Discourse of Negotiation*, Toronto: University of Toronto Press (Toronto Iberic).

Haas, A. (1998), 'Didaktik des Sterbens in Text und Bild', in *Die Zeitschrift der Universität Zürich*, 2/97 (1997); https://www.kommunikation.uzh.ch/static/unimagazin/archiv/2-97/didaktik.html (accessed 22/02/2022).

Haas, G. H. (1997), *The Concept of Equity in Calvin's Ethics*, Waterloo, OH: Wilfrid Laurier University Press.

Haberkern, Ph. N. (2016), *Patron Saint and Prophet: Jan Hus in the Bohemian and German Reformations*, Oxford: Oxford University Press (Oxford Studies in Historical Theology).

Habsburg, M. von, 'The Devotional Life: Catholic and Protestant Translations of Thomas À Kempis' *Imitatio Christi*, C. 1420-C. 1620' (Unpublished thesis, University of St Andrews, 2002).

Habsburg, M. von (2011), *Catholic and Protestant Translations of the Imitatio Christi 1425–1650: From Late Medieval Classic to Early Modern Bestseller*, Farham, UK: Ashgate Publishing.

Hacking, I. (2006), *The Emergence of Probability: A Philosophical Study of Early Ideas about Probability, Induction and Statistical Inference*, New York: Cambridge University Press.

Haga, J. (2012), *Was there a Lutheran Metaphysics?: The interpretation of communicatio idiomatum in Early Modern Lutheranism*, Göttingen: Vandenhoeck & Ruprecht (REFO500 Academic Studies).

Haigh, C. (1993), *English Reformation: Religion, Politics, and Society Under the Tudors*, Oxford: Clarendon Press.

Haile, H. G. (2014), *Luther: An Experiment in Biography*, Princeton, NJ: Princeton University Press (Princeton Legacy Library).

Haliczer, S. (1990), *Inquisition and Society in the Kingdom of Valencia, 1478–1834*, Berkeley CA: University of California Press.

Haller, W. (1963), *Foxe's Book of Martyres and the Elect Nation*, London: Cape.

Hallett, P. E. (ed.), M. Bassett (trans., 1941), *St Thomas More's History of the Passion*, London: Burns Oates & Washbourne Ltd.

Hamm, B. (1977), 'Frömmigkeit als Gegenstand theologiegeschichtlicher Forschung: Methodisch-historische Überlegungen am Beispiel von Spätmittelalter und Reformation', in *Zeitschrift für Theologie und Kirche*, 74, pp. 464–97.

Hamm, B. (1998), 'Warum wurde für Luther der Glaube zum Zentralbegriff des christlichen Lebens?', in B. Möller & S. E. Buckwalter (ed.), *Die frühe Reformation in Deutschland als Umbruch: Wissenschaftliches Symposion des Vereins für Reformationsgeschichte 1996*, Gütersloh (Schriften des Vereins für Reformationsgeschichte, 199), pp. 103–27.

Hamm, B. (2003), *The Reformation of Faith in the Context of Late Medieval Theology and Piety*, R. J. Bast (ed.), Leiden: Brill (Studies in the History of Christian Traditions, 110).

Hamm, B. (2014), *The Early Luther: Stages in a Reformation Reorientation*, M. J. Lohrmann (trans.), Grand Rapids, MI: Eerdmans (Lutheran Quarterly Books).

Hamon, A. (1970), *Un Grand Rhétoriqueur poitevin, Jean Bouchet, 1476–1558*, Geneva: Slatkine Reprint of 1901 edition.

Hannemann, C., 'Das Bild des Todes in Artes moriendi und Totentänzen des ausgehenden 15. Jahrhunderts' (Magisterarbeit, Hamburg Universität, 2004).

Härdelin, A. (2009), 'Jean Gerson ou la théologie pratique en France et en Suède', dans O. Ferm, P. Förnegård & H. Engel (éd.), *Regards sur la France du Moyen Âge. Mélanges offerts à Gunnel Engwall à l'occasion de son départ à la retraite*, Stockholm: Sällskapet Runica et Mediaevalia and Centre d'études médiévales de Stockholm, pp. 277–97.

Hartmann, M. (2001), *Humanismus und Kirchenkritik: Matthias Flacius Illyricus Als Erforscher des Mittelalters*, Stutgart: Jan Thirbecke (Beiträge zur Geschichte und Quellenkunde des Mittelalters, 19).

Hatt, C. A. (2002), *English Works of John Fischer, Bischop of Rochester (1469–1535): (1469–1535): Sermons and Other Writings, 1520–1535*, Oxford: Oxford University Press.

Hausamann, S. (1970), *Römerbriefauslegung zwischen Humanismus und Reformation. Eine Studie zu Heinrich Bullingers Römerbriefauslesung von 1525*, Zürich/Stuttgart: Zwingli Press.

Hayden, J. M. & M. R. Greenshields (2005), *Six Hundred Years of Reform: Bishops and the French Church, 1190–1789*, Montreal: McGill-Queen's MQUP (McGill-Queen's Studies in the History of Religion, 2).

Headley, J. M., (1963), *Luther's View of Church History*, New Heaven, CT: Yale University Press.

Helmrash, J., U. Muhkack & W. Gerrit (2002), *Diffusion des Humanismus: Studien zur nationalen Geschichtsschreibung europäischer Humanisten*, Göttingen: Wallstein.

Henkel, N. (1988), *Deutsche Übersetzungen lateinischer Schultexte, ihre Verbreitung und Funktion im Mittelalter und in der frühen Neuzeit: mit einem Verzeichnis der Texte*, München: Artemis.

Henze, B. (1995), *Aus Liebe zur Kirche Reform, Die Bemühungen Georg Witzels (1501–1573) und die Kircheneinheit*, Münster: Aschendorff (Reformationsgeschichtliche Studien und Texte, 133).

Herbers, K. (2016), *Jakobsweg: Geschichte und Kultur einer Pilgerfahrt*, Munich: C. H. Beck.

Herbert, E. (1937), *De Veritate, prout distinguitur a revelatione, a verisimili, a possibili, et a falso*, trans. Meyrick H. Carré, Bristol: Arrowsmith.

Herbert, G. B. (2003), *A Philosophical History of Rights*, New Brunswick, N J: Transaction Publishers.

Herding, O. (1970), 'Jakob Wimpfeling — Beatus Rhenanus. Das Leben des Johannes Geiler von Kaysersberg', in *Jacobi Wimpfelingi Opera selecta*, 2/1, München: W. Fink, pp. 53–87.

Herminjard, A. L. (1866–1897), *Correspondance des réformateurs dans les pays de langue française*, Geneva-Paris.

Higman, F. (1996), *Piety and the People: Religious Printing in French, 1511–1551*, Farham UK: Ashgate (St Andrews Studies in Reformation History).

Hirschi, C. (2005), *Wettkampf der Nationen: Konstruktionen einer deutschen Ehrgemeinschaft an der Wende vom Mittelalter zur Neuzeit*, Göttingen: Wallstein.

Hobbins, D. (2005), 'Jean Gerson's Authentic Tract on Joan of Arc: *Super facto puellae et credulitate sibi praestanda* (14th of May 1429)', in *Mediaeval Studies*, 67, pp. 99–155.

Hobbins, D. (2006), 'Gerson on Lay Devotion', in B. P. McGuire (ed.), *A Companion to Jean Gerson*, Leiden: Brill (Brill's Companions to the Christian Tradition, 3), pp. 41–78.

Hobbins, D. (2009), *Authorship and Publicity Before Print Jean Gerson and the Transformation of Late Medieval Learning*, Philadelphia, PA: University of Pennsylvania Press (The Middle Ages Series).

Hoch, A. (1901), *Geilers von Kaysersberg Ars moriendi aus dem Jahre 1497 nebst einem Beichtgedicht von Hans Foltz von Nürnberg*, Freiburg im Breisgau: Herder.

Hoffmann, J., 'Das Bild des Jean Gerson in der europäischen Forschung nach 1945' (Magisterarbeit, Leipzig University, 1995).

Hohenadel, V. (2015), *Das Consolatorium tribulatorum des Bernhard von Waging, Literaturgeschichte Studie und Redaktiongeschichticje Edition*, Münster: Aschendorff.

Holdsworth, W. S. (1902–1972), *A History of English Law*, 17 vols, London: Methuen, vol. IV.

Holmes, U. T. (2002), *A History of Christian Spirituality: An Analytical Introduction*, New York, NY: Church Publishing, Inc. (The Library of Episcopalian Classics).

Holt, M. P. (1995), *The French Wars of Religion, 1562–1629*, Cambridge, UK: Cambridge University Press (New Approaches to European History, 36).

Homza, L. A. (2006), *The Spanish Inquisition, 1478–1614: An Anthology of Sources*, Indianapolis, IN: Hackett Publishing.

Hopkins, J. (1988), *Nicholas of Cusa's Dialectical Mysticism: Text, Translation, and Interpretive Study of De Visione Dei*, Minneapolis, MN: Arthur J Banning.

Horn, N. (1968), *Aequitas in den Lehren des Baldus (1327–1400)*, Köln: Graz.

Horstmann, C. (ed., 1887), '*Mappula Angliae* von Osbern Bokenham', in *Englische Studien*, 10, pp. 6–34.

Horstmann, C. (2003), 'Fictions au service de la foi: les Ttriumphes de la noble et amoureuse dame (1530)', dans J. Britnell & N. Dauvois (éd.), *Acts of Poitiers Colloquium Jean Bouchet, traverseur des voies périlleuses*, Paris: Champion, pp. 193–208.

Horton, M. (2012), *Union with Christ*, Grand Rapids, MI: Zondervan.

Houdard, S. (1992), *La science du diable*, Paris: Cerf (Histoire).

Houlbrooke, R. (2000), *Death, Religion and the Family in England 1480–1750*, Oxford: Oxford University Press (Oxford Studies in Social History).

Howarth, G. & O. Leaman (2001), *Encyclopedia of Death and Dying*, Abingdon, UK: Taylor & Francis.

Hub, B. (2007), 'Material Gazes and Flying Images in Marsilio Ficino and Michelangelo', in C. Göttler & W. Neuber, *Spirits Unseen: The Representation of Subtle Bodies in Early Modern European Culture*, Leiden/New York: Brill (Intersections, 9).

Huntley, F. L. (1981), *Bishop Joseph Hall and Protestant Meditation in Seventeenth-Century England: A Study. with the Texts of The Art of Divine Meditation (1606) and Occasional Meditations (1633)*,

Binghamton, New York: Center for Medieval and Early Renaissance Studies.

Hutson, L. (2002), *The Usurer's Daughter: Male Friendship and Fictions of Women in 16th Century England*, Abingdon-on-Thames: Routledge.

Huxley, G. L. (1980), 'Aristotle, Las Casas and the American Indians', in *Proceedings of the Royal Irish Academy: Archaeology, Culture, History, Literature*, 80, pp. 57–68.

Iparraguirre, I. (1946), *Historia De La Práctica De Los Ejercicios Espirituales De San Ignacio De Loyola...: Desde la muerte de San Ignacio hasta la promulgación del directorio oficial (1556–1599)*, Bilbao: El Mensajero del Corazón de Jesús.

Irribaren, I. (2011), 'Le Théologien: Poète de la Doctrine. Quelques Réflexions Autour de la Josephina de Jean Gerson', dans *Revue des sciences religieuses*, 85 (3), pp. 356–70.

Irribaren, I. 'Joseph en songeur: songe, rapt et prophétie dans la *Josephina* de Jean Gerson', dans *Revue des sciences religieuses*, 90 (2) 2016, pp. 207–23.

Irvin, J. L. (1981), 'The Mystical Music of Jean Gerson', in *Early Music History*, 1, pp. 187–201.

Iserloh, E. (1980), 'From the Middle Ages to the Reformation', in H. Jedin & J. P. Dolan, *History of the Church: From the High Middle Ages to the Eve of the Reformation*, University of Michigan: Burns & Oates.

Iserloh, E. & P. Fabisch (ed., 1984), *Kaspar Schatzgeyer. Schriften zur Verteidigung der Messe*, Münster: Aschendorff (Corpus Catholicorum).

Isnardi, G. C. (2015), *Storia e cultura della Scandinavia: Uomini e mondi del Nord*, Milano: Bompiani.

Izbicki, T. M. (1986), 'Papalist Reaction to the Council of Constance: Juan de Torquemada to the Present', in *Church History*, 55 (1), pp. 7–20.

Izbicki, T. M. & Ch. M. Bellitto (2000), *Reform and Renewal in the Middle Ages and the Renaissance: Studies in Honor of Louis Pascoe*, Leiden/New York: Brill (Studies in the History of Christian Traditions, 96).

Izbicki, T. M. (2012), 'Antoninus of Florence and the Dominican Witch Theorists', in *Memorie Domenicane*, 42, pp. 347–61.

Jackson, R. (2013), *Performance Practice: A Dictionary-Guide for Musicians*, Abingdon-on-Thames, UK: Routledge.

Jacob, E. F. (1953), *Essays in the Conciliar Epoch*, Manchester: Manchester University Press (Historical Series, LXXX).

Jäger, Y. S., *Die Steinätzung von Rosegg. Ein Beitrag zur Ars moriendi des 16. Jahrhunderts* (Magisterarbeit Universität, Wien, 2010).

Janda, R. (1997), 'Legal Architecture, Equity and Christopher St German', dans J. E. C. Brierley (éd.), *Melanges offerts par ses collegues de McGill à Paul-André Crépeau*, Cowansville, Québec, Canada: Yvon Blais, pp. 373–416.

Janelle, P. (2007), *The Catholic Reformation*, New York: Simon & Schuster.

Janssen, J., *History of German People, Canisii Epistulae*, London (1909); archive.org/stream/historyofgermanp14jansuoft/history-ofgermanp14jansuoft_djvu.txt (accessed 28/01/2021).

Janz, D. R. (2008), *A Reformation Reader, Primary Texts with Introductions*, second edition, Minneapolis, MN: Fortress Press.

Jedin, H. (1957), *A. History of the Council of Trent*, 2 vols, trans. E. Graf, NY: Thomas Nelson and Sons (American Council of Learned Societies).

Jepp, A. (1857), *Gerson, Wicefus, Hussus inter se et cum reformatoribus comparati, commentatio in concertatione civium Academiae georgiae Augustae die IV. Jun. a. ... theologorum ordine praemio regio ornata*, Göttingen.

Jeudy, C. (1995), 'La bibliothèque cathédrale de Reims', dans M. Ornato (éd.), *Pratiques de la culture écrite en France au XVe siècle*, Louvain-La-Neuve, pp. 75–91.

Jiménez, P. E. (2017), 'El fInal de la hegemonia hispana en la Compañia de Jesus: los memorialistas italianos (1585–1593)', in *Hispania Sacra*, 69 (140), pp. 619–63.

Johnson, A. M. & J. A. Maxfield (ed. 2012), *The Reformation as Christianization, Essays on Scott Hendrix's Christianization Thesis*, Tübingen: Mohr (Spätmittelalter, Humanismus, Reformation, 66), pp. 321–48.

Jones, C. L. (1886), *Simon Goulart, 1543–1628: étude biographique et bibliographique*, Paris-Geneva: Champion.

Jonge, H. J. de (1990), 'Sixteenth-century Gospel Harmonies: Chemnitz and Mercator', dans I. Backus & F. Higman (éd.), *Théorie et pratique de l'exégèse: actes du troisième Colloque international sur l'histoire de l'exégèse biblique au XVIe siècle, Genève, 31 août-2 septembre, Textes réunis par Irena Backus et Francis Higman*, Genève: Droz (Études de philosophie et d'histoire, 43), pp. 156–60.

Jonsen, A. & S. Toulmin (1988), *The Abuse of Casuistry: A History of Moral Reasoning*, Berkeley: University of California Press.

Jonte-Pace, D. E. & W. B. Parsons (2001), *Religion and Psychology: Mapping the Terrain: Contemporary Dialogues, Future Prospects*, London: Psychology Press.

Jourda, P. (1930), *Marguerite d'Angoulême, duchesse d'Alençon, reine de Navarre (1492–1549)*, Paris: Crépin et Lume.

Kallendorf, H. (2010), *A New Companion to Hispanic Mysticism*, Leiden/New York: Brill (Brill's Companions to the Christian Tradition, 19).

Kaluza, Z. (1988), *Les querelles doctrinales à Paris. Nominalistes et réalistes aux confins du XIVe et du XVe siècles*, Bergamo: Pierluigi *Lubrina* (Quodlibet).

Kantola, I. (1994), *Probability and Moral Uncertainty in Late Medieval and Early Modern Times*, Helsinki: Luther-Agricola Society.

Kantorowitz, E. H. (1957), *The King's Two Bodies: A Study in Mediaeval Political Theology*, Princeton: Princeton Universoty Press (Princeton Classics).

Karant-Nunn, S. (2005), *Reformation of Ritual: An Interpretation of Early Modern Germany*, Oxford: Routledge (Christianity and Society in the Modern World).

Kaup, S. (2013), 'Bernhard von Waging — sein literarisches Werk als Spiegel zentraler Themen der benediktinischen Klosterreform', in F. X. Bischof & M. Thurner (ed.), *Die benediktinische Klosterreform im 15. Jahrhundert*, Berlin: Akademie Verlag (Veröffentlichungen des Grabmann-Institutes zur Erforschung der mittelalterlichen Theologie und Philosophie, 56), pp. 11–53.

Keen, R. (2002), 'Thomas More', in C. Lindberg (ed.) *The Reformation Theologians: An Introduction to Theology in the Early Modern Period*, Oxford: Blackwell (Great Theologians Series), pp. 284–97.

Keenan, J. F. (1995), 'William Perkins (1558–1602) and the Birth of British Casuistry', in J. F. Keenan & T. Shannon (ed.), *The Context of Casuistry*, Washington DC: Georgetown University Press (Moral Traditions), pp. 105–30.

Keitt, A. (2013), 'The devil in the Old World: anti-superstition literature, medical humanism and preternatural philosophy in early modern Spain', in F. Cervantes & A. Redden (ed.), *Angels, Demons and the New World*, Cambridge, UK: Cambridge University Press, p. 15–39.

Kellerman, G., *Jakob Ulvsson och den svenska kyrkan* 1–2 (Stockholm 1935–1940) in *Bälinge församling*, Uppsala län, 14 (1953);

sok.riksarkivet.se/SBL/Presentation.aspx?id=15387 (accessed 28/01/2021).

Kelley, D. R. (1974), 'History, English Law, and the Renaissance', in *Past and Present*, 65 (1), pp. 24–51.

Kelley, D. R. (1983), *The Beginning of Ideology: Consciousness and Society in the French Reformation*, Cambridge, UK: Cambridge University Press (Cambridge Paperback Library).

King, J. N. (2009), *Foxe's Book of Martyrs: Select Narratives*, Oxford: Oxford University Press (Oxford World's Classics).

King, M. & A. Rabil, Introductory essay in *The Other Voice in Early Modern Europe* (1996); othervoiceineme.com/othervoice.html (accessed 28/01/2021).

Kinnell, G. (1982), *The Poems of Francois Villon*, trans. G. Kinnell, new edition, Hanover and London: University of New England Press.

Klinck, D. R. (2010), *Conscience, Equity and the Court of Chancery in Early Modern England*, Forham: Ashgate.

Klomps, H. (1959), *Freiheit und Gesetz bei dem Franziskanertheologen Kaspar Schatzgeyer*, München: Aschendorff.

Knott, J. R. (2011), *The Sword of the Spirit: Puritan Responses to the Bible*, Eugene, OR: Wipf and Stock.

Koch, E. (ed., 1985), *Otto Clemen, Kleine Schriften zur Reformationsgeschichte (1897–1944)*, Leipzig: Zentralantiquariat der DDR.

Köhler, W. (1900), *Luther und die Kirchengeschichte nach seinen Schriften zunächst bis 1521*, Erlangen: Junge.

Kolb, R. (1987), *For All the Saints: Changing Perceptions of Martyrdom and Sainthood in the Lutheran Reformation*, Macon, GA: Mercer.

Köstlin, J. (1897), *The Theology of Luther in Its Historical Development and Inner Harmony*, trans. C. E. Hay, 2 vols, Philadelphia: Lutheran Publication Society.

Kramer, F. (1981), 'Martin Chemnitz, 1522–1586', in J. Raitt (ed.), *Shapes of Religious Traditions in Germany, Switzerland, and Poland, 1560–1600*, New York: Yale University Press.

Kraume, H. (1980), *Die Gerson Übersetzungen Geilers von Kaysersberg: Studien zur deutschsprachigen Gerson-Rezeption*, Zürich: Artemis, (Münchener Texte und Untersuchungen zur deutschen Literatur des Mittelalters).

Kraye, J. & R. Saarinen (2005), *Moral Philosophy on the Threshold of Modernity*, New York: Springer (The New Synthese Historical Library, 57).

Kristanto, B., 'Musical Settings of Psalm 51 in Germany c. 1600-1750 in the Perspectives of Reformational Music Aesthetics' (unpublished doctoral dissertation, Heidelberg University, 2009).

Kristeller, P. O. (1962), 'The European Diffusion of Italian Humanism', in *Italica, American Association of Teachers of Italian*, 39, pp. 1–20.

Kristeller, P. O. (2005), *Il pensiero filosofico di Marsilio Ficino*, Florence: Le Lettere.

Kroef, J. M. van der. (1949), 'Francisco de Vitoria and the Nature of Colonial Policy', in *The Catholic Historical Review*, 35 (2), pp. 129–62.

Krohn, E. (1919), 'The Bibliography of Music', in *The Musical Quarterly*, 5, pp. 231–54.

Kroon, M. de. (2009), *We Believe in God and in Christ, not in the Church: The Influence of Wessel Gansfort on Martin Bucer*, London: John Knox Press (Princeton Theological Seminary Studies in Reformed Theology and History).

Laemers, W. J. J., 'Invincible ignorance and the discovery of the Americas: the history of an idea from Scotus to Suárez' (unpublished doctoral dissertation, University of Iowa, 2011).

Laitakari-Pyykkö, A.-L., 'Philip Melanchthon's Influence on English Theological Thought during the Early English Reformation' (unpublished doctoral dissertation, Helsinki University, 2013).

Lang, M. H. de (1991), 'Jean Gerson's Harmony of the Gospels (1420)', in *Nederlandsch archief voor kerkgeschiedenis*, 71, pp. 35–47.

Langley, Ch. R. (2017) 'Lying Sick to Die: Dying, Informal Care and Authority in Scotland, 1600–1660', in *The Sixteenth Century Journal*, 48 (1), pp. 27–46.

Langston, D. C. (2008), *Conscience and Other Virtues: From Bonaventure to Macintyre*, University Park, PA: Penn State University Press.

Laube, A. (ed., 1992), *Flugschriften vom Bauernfrieg zum Täuferreich (1526–1535)*, Berlin: Akademie.

Laube, A (2000), *Flugschriften gegen die Reformation (1525–1530)*, Berlin: Academie.

Laurent, S. (1989), *Naître au Moyen Age. De la conception à la naissance: la grossesse et l'accouchement (XIIe-XVe siècle)*, Paris: Le Léopard d'Or.

Lea, H. C. (1896), *A History of Auricular Confession and Indulgences*, London: Swan Sonnenschein.

Lea, H. C. (1955), *A History of the Inquisition of the Middle Ages*, New York: The Harbour.

Lea, H. C. (1957), *Materials Toward a History of Witchcraft*, ed. A. C. Howland, New York: Thomas Yoseloff.

Leaver, R. (1985), 'Bach, Hymns and Hymnbooks', in *The Hymn Society of America* 36 (4), pp. 7–13.

Lefebvre, C. (1963), 'Natural Equity and Canonical Equity: Note', in *Natural Law Forum*, 98.

Lefebve-Teillard, A. (1973), *Les officialités à la veille du Concile de Trente*, Paris: R. Pichon et R. Durand-Auzias.

Leget, C. (2007), 'Scientific Contribution: Retrieving the *ars moriendi* Tradition', in *Medicine, Health Care and Philosophy*, 10, pp. 313–19.

Leitch, S. (2010), *Mapping Ethnography in Early Modern Germany: New Worlds in Print Culture*, Basingstoke, UK: Palgrave Macmillan (History of Text Technologies).

Leites, E. (1988), *Conscience and Casuistry in Early Modern Europe*, Cambridge, NY: Cambridge University Press (Ideas in Context Series, 9).

Lemire, J.-J. (1971), 'La pensée théologique de Bernardin de Bustis sur saint Joseph, Saint Joseph durant les quinze premiers siècles de l'Église', dans *Cahiers de Joséphologie*, 19, pp. 481–91.

Leppin, V. (2010), 'Die Wittenberger Reformation und der Prozess der Transformation kultureller zu institutionellen Polaritäten', in *Philologisch-historische Klasse*, 140 (4), Leipzig: Sachsische Akademie der Wissenschaten.

Leaver, R. A. (2007), *Luther's Liturgical Music: Principles and Implications*, Grand Rapids: William B. Eerdmann Publishing (Lutheran Quarterly Books).

Leroux, N. R. (2003) 'In the Christian City of Wittenberg: Karlstadt's Tract on Images and Begging', in *Sixteenth Century Journal*, 34 (1), 73–105.

Leroux, N. R. (2007), *Martin Luther as Comforter: Writings on Death*, Leiden/New York: Brill (Studies in the History of Christian Traditions).

Leroux, N. R. (2009), 'Luther on Music', in T. J. Wengert (ed.), *The Pastoral Luther: Essays on Martin Luther's Practical Theology*, Grand Rapids, MI: Eerdmans (Lutheran Quarterly Books).

Lesnick, D. (1989), *Preaching in Medieval Florence: The Social World of Franciscan and Dominican Spirituality*, Athens, GA: University of Georgia Press.

Lett, D. (2000), *Famille et parenté dans l'Occident médiéval, V^e-XVe siecle*, Paris: Hachette (Carré Histoire).

Lieberman, M. (1963), 'Autour de l'iconographie gersonienne', dans *Romania*, 84, pp. 307–53.

Lieberman, M. (1965), 'Gerson, d'Ailly, Eck et saint Joseph', dans *Cahier de Joséphologie*, 13, pp. 227–72.

Lieberman, M. (1968), 'Jean Gerson, Pierre d'Ailly, Jean Eck et saint Joseph', dans *Cahiers de Joséphologie*, 16, pp. 293–336.

Liere, K. E. van (1997), 'Vitoria, Cajetan and the Conciliarists', in *Journal of the History of Ideas*, 58 (4), pp. 597–616.

Liguori, A. de (1841), *Sermone di S. Giuseppe, Discorsi morali*, Naples.

Lindberg, C. (1996), *The European Reformations*, New York: Wiley-Blackwell.

Lindberg, C. (2001), *The Reformation Theologians: An Introduction to Theology in the Early Modern Period*, New York: Wiley-Blackwell (Great Theologians Series).

Lloyd, H. A. (2017), *Jean Bodin: 'this Pre-eminent Man of France': an Intellectual Biography*, Oxford: Oxford University Press.

Loades, D. (ed., 1984), *The End of Strife: Death, Reconciliation and Expressions of Christian Spirituality. Papers Selected from the Proceedings of the Commission Internationale d'Histoire Ecclésiastique Comparée Held at the University of Durham, 2 to 9 September 1981*, Edinburgh: T. & T. Clark.

Lochrie, K. (2012), *Covert Operations: The Medieval Uses of Secrecy*, Philadelphia, PA: University of Pennsylvania Press (The Middle Ages Series).

Logan, G. M. (2011), *The Cambridge Companion to Thomas More*, Cambridge, UK: Cambridge University Press (Cambridge Companions to Religion).

Losada, A. (1970), *Fray Bartolomé de las Casas a la luz de la moderna crítica histórica*, Madrid: Tecnos.

Luttikhuizen, F. (2016) *Underground Protestantism in Sixteenth Century Spain: A Much Ignored Side of Spanish History*, Göttingen: Vandenhoeck & Ruprecht (Refo500 Academic Studies).

Lyotard, J.-Fr. (1999), *The Hyphen: Between Judaism and Christianity*, New York: Humanities Books (Philosophy and Literary Theory).

Maag, K. (ed., 1997), *The Reformation in Eastern and Central Europe*, Farnham, UK: Ashgate (St Andrews Studies in Reformation History).

Maggi, A. (2006), *In the Company of Demons: Unnatural Beings, Love, and Identity in the Italian Renaissance*, Chicago: University of Chicago Press.

Maher, M. (2000), 'Confession and consolation: the Society of Jesus and its promotion of the general confession', in K. L. Parker & A. T. Thayer (ed.), *Penitence in the Age of Reformations*, Aldershot, UK: Ashgate (St Andrews Studies in Reformation History), pp. 184-200.

Maier, C. (1936), *Girolamo Savonarola: aus grossen Theils handschriftlichen Quellen*, Berlin: Reimer.

Maier, P. L. (1959), *Caspar Schwenckfeld on the Person and Work of Christ*, Assen, Cambridge, UK: Royal van Goreum LTD.

Main, T. O. (2003), 'Traditional Equity and Contemporary Procedure', in *Washington Law Review*, 78, pp. 429-516, p. 429.

Majeske, A. (2014), *Equity in English Renaissance Literature: Thomas More and Edmund Spenser*, Abingdon-on-Thames: Routledge (Literary Criticism and Cultural Theory).

Mäkinen, V. (2006), *Lutheran Reformation and the Law*, Leiden/New York: Brill (Studies in Medieval and Reformation Traditions, 112).

Mäkinen, V. & P. Korkman (ed., 2005), *Transformations in Medieval and Early Modern Rights Discourse*, Berlin: Springer (New Synthese Historical Library, 59).

Mangenot, E. (1856-1922), *Dictionnaire de Théologie Catholique*, Paris: Letouzey et Ané.

Mangrum, B. D. & G. Scavizzi (1998), *A Reformation Debate: Karlstadt, Emser, and Eck on Sacred Images: Three Treatises*, Toronto: Centre for Reformation and Renaissance Studies (Renaissance and Reformation Texts in Translation, 5).

Mansch L. D. & C. H. Peters (2016), *Martin Luther: The Life and Lessons*, Jefferson, NC: McFarland.

Mapstone, S. L., 'The Advice to Princes Tradition in Scottish Literature, 1450-1500' (unpublished doctoral thesis, St Hilda College, Oxford University, 1986).

Marc'Hadour, G. (1995), 'Thomas More et les Concils Oeucuméniques', dans *Moreana*, 121, pp. 33-52.

Marciniak, V. P. (2006), *Towards a History of Consciousness: Space, Time, and Death*, Berlin: Peter Lang (American University Studies).

Marín, J. M., 'A Firestone of Divine Love': Erotic Desire and the Ephemeral Flame of Hispanic Jesuit Mysticism' (unpublished doctoral dissertation, Harvard University, 2014).

Marius, R. (1984), *Thomas More*, Cambridge, MA: Harvard University Press.

Marr, S. C. '*Ars moriendi*: Mittelalterliche Sterbekunst als Vorbild für eine neuzeitliche Sterbekultur' (doctoral dissertation, Medizinische Fakultät Georg-August-Universität Göttingen, 2010).

Marsh, H. (trans., 1823), *Introduction to the New Testament*, London: Rivington.

Marston, J. (1966), *The Scourge of Villainie Three Bookes of Satyres*, London: J. Roberts.

Martin, D. (1992), *Fifteenth-Century Carthusian Reform: The World of Nicolas Kempf*, Leiden/New York: Brill (Studies in the History of Christian Thought, 49).

Martin, H. (1988), *Le métier de prédicateur en France Septentrionale À La Fin du Moyen Age (1350–1520)*, Paris: Cerf.

Martin, H. (2011), 'Les sermons du dominicain Jean Clérée (1450–1507), jalon parmi d'autres, entre les jeux de mystère et la comédie de moeurs', dans Conférence *Predication et performance, Fondation Singer-Polignac*, Paris, 23, 2011; https://www.dailymotion.com/video/xjkp6q (accessed 2022).

Martinez, P. de Alcantara (1978), 'Dos sermones indéditos sobre S. José del Beato Bernardino de Feltre', in *Archivum Franciscanum Historicum*, 71 (1-2), pp. 65-111.

Martz, L. L. (1976), *The Poetry of Meditation: A Study in English Religious Literature of the Seventeenth Century*, New Heaven, CT: Yale University Press (Yale Studies, English).

Martz, L. L. (1990), *Thomas More: The Search for the Inner Man*, New Heaven, CT: Yale University Press.

Maryks, R. A. (2008), *Saint Cicero and the Jesuits: The Influence of the Liberal Arts on the Adoption of Moral Probabilism*, Abingdon-on-Thames, UK: Routledge (Catholic Christendom, 1300–1700).

Maryks, R. A. (2014), *A Companion to Ignatius of Loyola: Life, Writings, Spirituality, Influence*, Leiden: Brill (Brill's Companions to the Christian Tradition, 52).

Masolini, S. (2020), 'How to Order Four into One. Harmonizing the Gospels at the Dawn of Biblical Humanism', in A. Dupont, W. François et al. (ed.), *1516: Towards Erasmus and More*, Turnhout: Brepols (LECTIO, Studies in the Transmission of Texts and Ideas, 10).

Massaut J.-P. (1968), *Josse Clichtove. L'humanisme et la réforme du clergé*, Paris: Les Belles Lettres (Bibl. de la Faculté de Philosophie et Lettres de l'Université de Liège).

Matnetsch, S. (2012), *Calvin's Company of Pastors, Pastoral Care and the Emerging Reformed Church, 1536–1609*, Oxford: Oxford Studies in Historical Theology (Oxford Studies in Historical Theology).

Matthews, S. (2013), *Theology and Science in the Thought of Francis Bacon*, Farham, UK: Ashgate Publishing, Ltd (Church History and Religious Culture).

Mauro, D. di, 'Jan Hus' Chalice: Symbol of Christian Freedom' (unpublished MA thesis, Reformed Theological Seminary, Jackson, MS, 2006).

Mayer, T. (1988), 'Thomas Starkey, an Unknown Conciliarist at the Court of Henry VIII', in *Journal of the History of Ideas*, 49, pp. 207–27.

Mayer, T. (2002), *Thomas Starkey and the Commonwealth: Humanist Politics and Religion in the Reign of Henry VIII*, Cambridge, UK: Cambridge University Press (Cambridge Studies in Early Modern British History).

Mazour-Matusevich, Y. (2002), 'Jean Gerson (1363–1429), Nicholas of Cusa (1401–1464), Jacques Lefèvre d'Etaples (1450–1537): The continuity of Ideas', in T. M. Izbicki & Ch. Bellitto (ed.), *Nicholas of Cusa and His Age: Intellect and Spirituality. Essays Dedicated to the Memory of F. Edward Cranz, Thomas P. McTighe and Charles Trinkaus*, Leiden/New York: Brill (Studies in the History of Christian Thought, 105), pp. 237–63.

Mazour-Matusevich, Y. (2003), 'Gerson et Pétrarque: humanisme et l'idée nationale', dans *Renaissance et la Réforme*, 25 (1), pp. 45–80.

Mazour-Matusevich, Y. (2004), *Le siècle d'or de la mystique française: un autre regard. Étude de la littérature spirituelle de Jean Gerson (1363–1429) à Jacques Lefèvre d'Étaples (1450?-1537)*, Paris-Milan: Archè (Fides nostra, 2).

Mazour-Matusevich, Y. (2006), 'Jean Gerson (1363–1429) and the Formation of German National Identity', in *Révue de l'Histoire Ecclésiastique*, 101 (3–4), pp. 963–87.

Mazour-Matusevich, Y. (2006a), 'Gerson's After Life', in B. P. McGuire (ed.), *A Companion to Jean Gerson*, Leiden/New York: Brill (Brill's Companions to the Christian Tradition, 3), pp. 357–400.

Mazour-Matusevich, Y. (2010), 'Jean Gerson and the Creation of German Protestant Identity', in *Revue d'Histoire Ecclesiastique*, 105 (3–4), pp. 632–51.

Mazour-Matusevich, Y. (2010a), 'Jean Gerson's Legacy in Tübingen and Strasburg', in *Medieval History Journal*, 13 (2), pp. 259–86.

Mazour-Matusevich, Y. (2013), 'Jean Gerson's (1363–1429) Assessment of the Issue of Religious Zeal in the Context of the Tyrannicide', in *Medieval History Journal*, 16 (1), pp. 121–37.

Mazour-Matusevich, Y. (2016), 'Humor as a Teaching Tool in Jean Gerson's (1363–1429) Morality Plays', in *European Medieval Drama*, 20, pp. 1–20.

Mazour-Matusevich, Y. (2017), 'The Calvinist Stance Toward Chaotic Modality: The Case of Visual Arts', in *Protestant Traditions and the Soul of Europe*, Leipzig: Evangelische Verlag (Beihefte zur Ökumenischen Rundschau, 110), pp. 217–30.

Mazour-Matusevich, Y. (2018), 'Contextualizing Bakhtin's Intuitive Discoveries: The End of Grotesque Realism and the Reformation', in S. Grachev & H. Mancing (ed.), *Bakhtin's Heritage in Literature, Arts, and Psychology*, Lanham, MD: Rowman & Littlefield, pp. 137–56.

Mazour-Matusevich, Y. (forthcoming), 'Interiority in Jean Gerson (1363–1429): An Invitation to a Further Inquiry', in T. Merrigan et al. (ed.), *The Crisis of Religion and the Problem of Roman Catholic Self-Definition*, Leiden: Brill, forthcoming in 2022.

McCulloch, D. (2004), *The Reformation: A History*, New York: Penguin.

McDonald, C. (1991), 'Mirror, Filter, or Magnifying Glass? John Ireland's *Meroure of Wyssdome*', in *Studies in Scottish Literature*, 26 (1) pp. 448–55.

McDonnell, K. (1993), 'The *Summae Confessorum* on the Integrity of Confession as Prolegomena for Luther and Trent', in *Theological Studies*, 54, pp. 405–25.

McDougall, S. (2014), 'The Transformation of Adultery in France at the End of the Middle Ages', in *Law and History Review*, 32 (3), pp. 491–525.

McDougall, S. (2014a), 'The Opposite of the Double Standard: Gender, Marriage, and Adultery Prosecution in Late Medieval France', in *Journal of the History of Sexuality*, 23 (2), pp. 206–25.

McGinn, B. (2002), 'In Search of Bernard's Legacy: Jean Gerson and a lifetime devotion', in E. Rozanne (ed.), *Praise no less than Charity, Studies in Honor of M. Chrusogonus Waddell Monk of Gethsemani Abbey*: contributions from colleagues, confrères, and friends on the occasion of the fiftieth anniversary of his monastic profession, Kalamazoo, MI: Cistercian Publications (Cistercian Europe: architecture of contemplation, 193), pp. 285–328.

McGinn, B. (2005), *The Harvest of Mysticism in Medieval Germany*, New York: Crossroad Publishing Company (The Presence of God, 4).

McGinn, B. (2017), *Mysticism in the Golden Age of Spain (1500–1650)*, New York: The Crossroad Publishing Company (The Presence of God, 6).

McGuire, B. P. (1997), 'Late Medieval Care and Control of Women: Jean Gerson and his Sisters', in *Revue d'histoire ecclésiastique*, 92, pp. 5–37.

McGuire, B. P. (2005), *Jean Gerson and the Last Medieval Reformation*, University Park, PA: Penn State Press.

McKim, D. (ed., 1998), *Historical Handbook of Major Biblical Interpreters*, Westmont, IL: InterVarsity Press.

McLoughlin N. (2015), *Jean Gerson and Gender: Rhetoric and Politics in Fifteenth-Century France*, London, UK: Palgrave Macmillan (Genders and Sexualities in History).

Meier, Fr. C. (1836), *Girolamo Savonarola: aus grossen Theils handschriftlichen Quellen*, Berlin: Reimer.

Meijering, P. H. (1983), *Melanchthon and Patristic Thought: the Doctrines of Christ and Grace, the Trinity, and the Creation*, Leiden/New York: Brill (Studies in the History of Christian Traditions, 32).

Meiss, M. & E. H. Beatson (éd. 1977), *La vie de nostre Benoit Sauveur Ihesuscrist et la Saincte vie de nostre Dame translatee a la requeste de tres hault et puissant prince Iehan, duc de Berry*, NY: New York University Press (Monographs on archaeology and the fine arts, 32).

Melchior, A. (1620), *Vitae Germanorum theologorum, qui superiori seculo ecclesiam Christi uoce scriptisque propagarunt et propugnarunt*, Heidelberg: Iona Rose.

Melion, W. S. & W. L. Palmer (2010), *Early Modern Eyes*, Leiden/New York: Brill (Intersections).

Mennecke-Haustein, U. (2003), *Conversio ad Ecclesiam: Der Weg der Friedrich Staphylus zurück zur katholischen Kirche*, Göttingen: Hubert & CO (Quellen und Forschungen zur Reformationsgeschichte, 74).

Mennecke-Haustein, U. (ed., 1989), *Luthers Trostbriefe*, Gütersloh: Mohn (Quellen und Forschungen zur Reformationsgeschichte, 56).

Mentzer, R. A. & Spicer A. (2007), *Society and Culture in the Huguenot World, 1559–1685*, Cambridge, UK: Cambridge University Press.

Metzler, R. (2008), *Stephan Roth, 1492–1546, Stadtschreiber in Zwichau und Bildungsbürger der Reformationzeit; Biographie;*

Edition der Briefe seiner Freunde Franz Pehem, Torgau/Leipzig: Sächsische Akademie (Quellen und Forschungen zur sächsischen Geschichte; 32).

Meyer-Baer, K. (2015), *Music of the Spheres and the Dance of Death: Studies in Musical Iconology*, Princeton, NJ: Princeton University Press (Princeton Legacy Library, 1307).

Meyler, B. A., 'Substitute Chancellors: The Role of the Jury in the Contest between Common Law and Equity', in *Cornell Law Faculty Publications* 39 (2006); scholarship.law.cornell.edu/lsrp_papers/ (accessed 28/01/2021).

Middleton, E. (1816), *Biographia evangelica*, Oxford: Oxford University Press.

Milway, M. (2000), 'Forgotten Best-Sellers from the Dawn of the Reformation', in R. J. Bast & A. C. Gows (ed.), *Continuity and Change: The Harvest of Late-Medieval and Rformation History, Essays presented to Heiko A. Oberman*, Leiden: Brill, pp. 119–43.

Mixson, J. & B. Roest (2015), *A Companion to Observant Reform in the Late Middle Ages and Beyond*, Leiden/New York: Brill (Brill's Companions to the Christian Tradition, 39).

Monahan, A. P. (1994), *From Personal Duties Towards Personal Rights: Late Medieval and Early Modern Political Thought, 1300–1600*, Montreal: McGill-Queen's Press – MQUP (McGill-Queen's Studies in the History of Ideas, 17).

Mondello, G. K. (2018), *The Metaphysics of Mysticism, St John of the Cross: Reason, Revelation, and the inexorable Logic of the Ascent of the Soul to God*, Independently published.

Monfalcon, J.-B. (1866), *Histoire monumentale de la Ville de Lyon*, 2 vols, Lyon: Firmin Didot.

Montagu, J. (2002), *Timpani and Percussion*, New Heaven, CT & London: Yale University Press.

Monti, J. (1997), *The King's Good Servant but God's First: the Life and Writings of Saint Thomas More*, San Francisco: Ignatius Press.

Montover, N. (2011), *Luther's Revolution: The Political Dimensions of Martin Luther's Universal Priesthood*, Eugene, OR: Wipf and Stock (Princeton Theological Monograph Series Book, 161).

Moore, G. A. (trans. & ed., 1949), *Practical Politics by Giovanni Botero; Religion and the Virtues of the Christian Prince against Machiavelli by Pedro Ribadeneyra*, Chevy Chase, Maryland: The Country Dollar Press.

Mornet, E. (1995), 'Gerson en Scandinavie', dans M. Ornato et N. Pons, *Pratiques de la culture écrite en France au XVe siècle. Actes* *du Colloque international du CNRS, Paris, 16–18 mai 1992, organisé en l'honneur de Gilbert Ouy par l'unité de recherche 'Culture écrite du Moyen âge tardif*, Louvain-la-Neuve: Fédération internationale des instituts d'études médiévales, 1995, pp. 93–108.

Morrall, J. B. (1960), *Gerson and the Great Schism*, Manchester: Manchester University Press.

Mossakowski, S. (2004), 'Trent'anni dopo: ricerche sul significato della *Santa Cecilia* di Raffaello', in P. D. Ferrara (ed.), *Per la storia dell'arte in Italia e in Europa: studi in onore di Luisa Mortari*, Rome: De Luca Editori d'Arte, pp. 269–76.

Mostaccio, S. (2014), *Early Modern Jesuits Between Obedience and Conscience During the Generalate of Claudio Acquaviva (1581–1615)*, Farham, UK: Ashgate.

Mozley, J. F. (1940), *John Fox and his Book*, London: Society for Promoting Christian Knowledge.

Müller, G. M. (ed., 2010), *Humanismus und Renaissance in Augsburg: Kulturgeschichte einer Stadt zwischen Spätmittelalter und Dreißigjährigem Krieg*, Berlin: De Gruyter (Frühe Neuzeit).

Müller, H. (2006), *Habit und Habitus: Mönche und Humanisten im Dialog*, Heidelberg: Mohr (Studies in the Late Middle Ages, Humanism, and the Reformation, 32).

Müller, R. (2017), *Die Ordnung der Affekte: Frömmigkeit als Erziehungsideal bei Erasmus von Rotterdam und Philipp Melanchthon*, Bad Heilbrunn: Julius Klinkhardt (Historische Bildungsforschung).

Muller, R. (2003), *After Calvin: Studies in the Development of a Theological Tradition*, Oxford: Oxford University Press (Oxford Studies in Historical Theology).

Mullett, M. A. (1999), *The Catholic Reformation*, Bloomberg: Psychology Press.

Nederman, C. J. (1990), 'Conciliarism and constitutionalism: Jean Gerson and medieval political thought', in *History of European Ideas*, 12 (2), pp. 189–209.

Neddermeyer, U. (1998), *Von der Handschrift zum gedruckten Buch: Schriftlichkeit und Leseinteresse im Mittelalter und in der frühen Neuzeit; quantitative und qualitative Aspekte*, Wiesbaden: Otto Harrassowitz (Buchwissenschaftliche Beitrage, 61).

Neher, P. (1989), *Ars moriendi — Sterbebeistand durch Laien: eine historisch-pastoraltheologische Analyse*, St Ottilien: Verlag St Ottilien.

Nelson, B. (1981), *On the Road to Modernity: Conscience, Science and Civilizations. Selected Writings by Benjamin Nelson*, T. Huff (ed.), Lanham, MD: Rowman & Littlefield.

Needham, N. (2017), 'Seeds of Reformation', in *Metropolitan Tabernacle*, 2017; https://files.metropolitantabernacle.org/School-of-Theology/2017-Our-Glorious-Reformation-Legacy/Seeds-of-the-Reformation (assessed 20/2/2022).

Newman, B. (2013), *Medieval Crossover, Reading the Secular against the Sacred*, Notre Dame, ID: Notre Dame University Press (Conway Lectures in Medieval Studies).

Noye I. (1961), 'Examen de Conscience', dans *Dictionnaire ascétique et mystique*, Paris: Beauchesne, t. 4, *c.* 1820–1829.

Nussbaum, M. C. (1993), 'Equity and Mercy', in *Philosophy and Public Affairs*, 22, pp. 85–88.

Oakley, F. (1999), *Politics and Eternity: Studies in the History of Medieval and Early Modern Political Thought*, Leiden/New York: Brill (Studies in the History of Christian Traditions, 32).

Oakley, F. (1999), 'Bronze-Age Conciliarism: Edmond Richer's Encounter with Cajetan and Bellarmine', in *History of Political Thought*, 20, pp. 65–86.

Oakley, F. (2000), 'Conciliarism in England: St Germain, Starkey and the Marsiglian Myth', in T. M. Izbicki & Ch. Bellitto (ed.), *Reform and Renewal in the Middle Ages and Renaissance: Studies in Honor of Louis Pascoe S.J.*, Leiden: Brill (Studies in the History of Christian Traditions, 96), pp. 224–39.

Oakley, F. (2003), *The Conciliarist Tradition: Constitutionalism in the Catholic Church, 1300–1870*, Oxford: Oxford University Press (*ACLS Centennial Series*).

Oakley, F. (2006), 'Gerson as Conciliarist', in B. P. McGuire, *A Companion to Jean Gerson*, New York/Leiden: Brill (Brill's Companions to the Christian Tradition, 3), 2006, pp. 179–204.

Oakley, F. (2015), *The Watershed of Modern Politics: Law, Virtue, Kingship and Consent (1300–1650)*, New Heaven, CT: Yale University Press (The Emergence of Western Political Thought in the Latin Middle Ages).

Oberman, H. A. (1963), *Harvest of Medieval Theology, Gabriel Biel and Late Medieval Nominalism*, Cambridge MA: Harvard University Press.

Oberman, H. A. (1965), *Spätscholastik und Reformation. Der Herbst der The Concept of Discretio Spirituum in Jean Gerson's De Probatione Spirituum and De Distinctione Verarum Visionem a Falsis mittelalterlichen Theologie*, Zürich: Mohr.

Oberman, H. A. (1981), *Masters of the Reformation: the Emergence of a New Intellectual Climate in Europe*, trans. Denis Martin, Cambridge: Cambridge University Press.

Oberman, H. A. (1981a), *Forerunners of the Reformation*, trans. Paul L Nyhus, 1st edition, Minneapolis, MN: Fortress Press (Library of Ecclesiastical History).

Oberman, H. A. (1986), *The Dawn of the Reformation: Essays in Late Medieval and Early Reformation Thought*, New York: T. & T. Clark.

Oberman, H. A. (1991), *Initia Calvini: The Matrix of Calvin's Reformation*, Amsterdam: Koninklijke Nederlandse Akademie van Wetenschappen.

Oberman, H. A. (1993), 'Wessel Gansfort: Magister contradictionis', in F. Akkerma, G. C. Huisman & A. Vanderjagt (ed.), *Wessel Gabsfort (1419–1489) and Northern Humanism*, Leiden/New York: Brill (Brill's Studies in Intellectual History, 40), pp. 97–121.

Oberman, H. A. (1999), 'Varieties of Protest', in *New Republic*, 16 August, pp. 40–45.

Oberman, H. A. & C. Caspers (1999), Magister Consensus Wessel Gansfort (1419–1489) und die Geistliche Kommunion', in F. Akkerma, G. C. Huisman & A. Vanderjagt (ed.), *Wessel Gansfort (1419–1489) and Northern Humanism*', Leiden/New York: Brill (Brill's Studies in Intellectual History, 30), pp. 82–98.

Oberman, H. A. (2008), *The Two Reformations: The Journey from the Last Days to the New World*, ed. Donald Weinstein, New Heaven, CT: Yale University.

O'Connor, M. C. (1942), *The Art of Dying Well: The Development of the Ars moriendi*, New York: Columbia University Press.

O'Donovan, O. & J. Lockwood (2004), *Bonds of Imperfection: Christian Politics, Past and Present*, Cambridge, MA: Eerdmans.

Oglaro, M. (2012), 'L'auteur de l'*Imitation de Jésus-Christ*: une longue controverse', dans M. Delaveau & Y. Sorbet (éd.), *L'Imitatio Christi*, Paris: Bibliothèque Nationale de France.

Ojakangas, M. (2013), *The Voice of Conscience: a Political Genealogy of Western Ethical Experience*, London/Oxford/New York: Bloomsbury Academic (Political Theory and Contemporary Philosophy).

Ollard, S. L. (1919), *A Dictionary of English Church History*, New York: Morehouse Publishing Company.

Olson, O. K. (2002), *Matthias Flacius and the Survival of Luther's Reform*, ed. Paul Strawn & S. Krieger, Wiesbaden: Harrassowitz.

O'Malley, J. (1984), 'To Travel to Any Part of the World: Jeronimo Nadal and the Jesuit Vocation', in *Studies in the Spirituality of Jesuits*, 16 (2), pp. 1–17.

O'Malley, J. (1993), *The First Jesuits*, Cambridge, MA: Harward University Press.

O'Malley, J. (2013), *Trent: What Happened at the Council*, Cambridge, MA: Harvard University.

Oosterhoff, R. J. (2018), *Making Mathematical Culture: University and Print in the Circle of Lefèvre d'Etaples*, Oxford: Oxford University Press (Oxford-Warburg Studies).

O'Reilly, T. (1995), *Loyola to John of the Cross: Spirituality and Literature in Sixteenth-century Spain*, Brookfield, VT: Variorum Studies.

Orique, D. T. *The Unheard Voice of Law in Bartolomé de Las Casas's Brevisima Relacion de la Destruction de las Indias* (unpublished dissertation, University of Oregon, 2011).

Ortega, M. M. (2017), *Juan de Valdés (c. 1490–1541) in Light of his Religious Background*, Amsterdam: Vrije Universiteit Amsterdam.

Osslund, R., 'Melanchthon's Understanding of the Will in the *Loci Communes*', (Unpublished Master thesis, St Louis, MI, 1984).

Østrem, E., J. Fleischer & N. H. Petersen (2003), *The Arts and the Cultural Heritage of Martin Luther*, Special Issue of *Transfiguration: Nordic Journal for Christianity and the Arts*, Copenhagen : Museum Tusculanum Press.

Otte, R. (1987), 'Subjective Probability, Objective Probablity, and Coherence', *Southern Journal of Philosophy*, 25 (3), pp. 373-80.

Ouy, G. (1961), 'Enquête sur les manuscrits autographes du chancelier Gerson et sur les copies exécutées par son frère le célestin Jean Gerson', dans *Scriptorum, Revue internationale des études relatives aux manuscrits*, 16, pp. 275–311.

Ouy, G. (1970), 'Le Collège de Navarre, berceau de l'humanisme français', dans *Actes du 95ᵉ Congrès National des sociétés savants*, Reims, pp. 276–99.

Ouy, G. (1985), 'Quelques conseils de Gerson aux confesseurs (Ms. Paris, B.N. lat. 14920, ff. 101-103v)', dans *Codex in context: Studies over codicologie, kartuizergeschiedenis en laatmiddeleeuws geestesleven aangeboden aan Prof. Dr. A. Gruijs*, Nijmegen: Alfa, pp. 289-312.

Ouy, G. (1993), 'Les recherches sur l'humanisme français des XIVᵉ et XVᵉ siècles', dans E. Follieri, G. Orlandi & M. Regoliosi (éd.), *La Filologia Medievale e Umanistica Greca e Latina nel Secolo XX. Atti del Congresso Internazionale, Roma, Consiglio Nazionale delle Ricerche Università La Sapienza 11–15 dicembre 1989*, Roma: Scuola Tipografica S. Pio X, pp. 276–326.

Ouy, G. (1998), *Gerson bilingue*, Paris: Honoré Champion.

Ouy, G. (2003), 'Le célestin Jean Gerson. Copiste et éditeur de son frère', dans Spilling Harald (éd.), *La collaboration dans la production de l'écrit médiéval*, Paris: École des Chartes, pp. 281–308.

Ozment, S. E. (1969), *Homo Spiritualis. A Comparative Study of the Anthropology of Johannes Tuler, Jean Gerson and Martin Luther (1509–1516) in the Context of their Theological Thought*, Leiden/New York: Brill (Studies in Medieval and Reformation Thought, IV).

Pabel, H. M. (2013), 'Fear and Consolation: Peter Canisius and the Spirituality of Dying and Death', in *Studies in the Spirituality of Jesuits*, 45 (1), pp. 1–31.

Pagden, A. (1982), *The Fall of Natural Man: The American Indian and the Origins of Comparative Ethnology*, New York: Cambridge University Press (Cambridge Iberian and Latin American Studies).

Page, Ch. (1978), 'Early 15th Century Instruments in Jean Gerson's *Tractatus de Canticis*', in *Early Music*, 6, pp. 339–50.

Pallier, D. (1976), *Recherches sur l'imprimerie à Paris pendant la Ligue (1585–1594)*, Geneva: Droz.

Palmer, M. (trans., 1996), *On Giving: the Spiritual Exercises. The Early Jesuit Manuscript Directories and the Official Directory of 1599*, St Louis: Institute of Jesuit Sources.

Pannen, F., '*Luther über Johannes Gerson*: Eine Untersuchung der Aussagen Luthers über den Doktor des Trostes' (2000); friedemann-pannen.de/resources/Luther+zu+Gerson.pdf (accessed 28/01/2021).

Pardo, O. F. (2004), *The Origins of Mexican Catholicism: Nahua rituals and Christian sacraments in Sixteenth-century Mexico*, Ann Arbor: University of Michigan Press (History, Languages, and Cultures of the Spanish and Portuguese Worlds).

Parker, T. H. L. (1993), *Calvin's New Testament Commentaries*, Westminster: John Knox.

Pascal, P. (éd., 1944), *Gerson, Jean. Initiation à la vie mystique*, Paris: Gallimard (Les Arcades, 1).

Pascoe, L. B. (2005), *Church and Reform: Bishops, Theologians, and Canon Lawyers in the Thought of Pierre d'Ailly, 1351–1420*, Leiden/New York: Brill (Studies in Medieval and Reformation Traditions, 105).

Patterson, W. B. (1997), *King James VI and I and the Reunion of Christendom*, New York: Cambridge University Press (Cambridge Studies in Early Modern British History).

Pauck, W. (1969), *Melanchthon and Bucer*, Westminster: John Knox (Library of Christian Classics).

Payan, P. (2006), *Joseph, Une image de la paternité dans l'Occident médiéval*, Paris: Aubier (Collection historique).

Payan, P. (2008), 'Famille du Christ et pastorale familiale dans la *Vita Christi* de Francesc Eiximenis', dans *Famille et parenté dans la vie religieuse du Midi (XIIe-XVe siècle), Cahiers de Fanjeaux*, 43, pp. 189–207.

Payan, P. (2012), 'La sanctification *in utero* de Joseph: une proposition gersonienne', dans *Revue electronique du Centre des Recherches Historiques* 10; acrh.revues.org/4246?gathStatIcon=true#ftn (accessed 28/01/2021).

Peignot, G. (1835), *Histoire de la Passion de Jesus-Christ, par Olivier Maillard*, Paris: Crapelet.

Pelikan, J. (1948), 'Luther's Attitude toward John Hus', in *Concordia Theological Monthly*, 19, pp. 747–63.

Pennington, K. (2008), 'Lex Naturalis and Jus Naturale', in *Jurist: Studies in Church Law and Ministry*, 68, pp. 569–91.

Pérennès, F. M. & D. Humphry (1838), *Dictionnaire de bibliographie catholique, présentant l'indication et les titres complets de tous les ouvrages qui ont été publiés dans les trois langues grecque, latine et française, depuis la naissance du christianisme, en tous pays ...*, Paris: J. P. Migne.

Pérez, M. (1995), 'Sex, morals and medicine in Counter Reformation Spain. An unpublished report on pollution by the Jesuit (1550–1605)', in *Dynamis*, 15, pp. 443–57.

Pernot, J.-F. (éd., 1995), *Jacques Lefevre d'Etaples (1450?-1536). Actes du colloque d'Etaples, les 7 et 8 novembre 1992*, Paris: Honoré Champion.

Peters, E. (1978), *The Magician, the Witch, and the Law*, College Town, PA: University of Pennsylvania Press (The Middle Ages Series).

Peterson, C. W., 'The Humanistic, Fideistic Philosophy of Philip Melanchthon (1497–1560)', (unpublished doctoral dissertation, Marquette University, Milwaukee, Wisconsin, 2012, epublications. marquette.edu/dissertations_mu/237, accessed 23/02/2021).

Petersen, W. L. (1994), *Tatian's Diatessaron: Its Creation, Dissemination, Significance, and History*, Leiden/New York: Brill (Vigiliae Christianae, Supplements, 25).

Petersen, W. L., J. Krans & J. Verheyden (ed., 2011), *Patristic and Text-Critical Studies: The Collected Essays of William L. Petersen*,

Leiden/New York: Brill (New Testament Tools, Studies and Documents, 40).

Pettegree, A. (ed., 2004), *The Reformation, Critical Concepts in Historical Studies*, London: Routledge.

Pettegree A., M. Walsby & A. Wilkinson (ed., 2011), *French Books III & IV: Books published in France before 1601 in Latin and Languages other than French*, Leiden/New York: Brill (Preliminary Material, I).

Petzold, K. (1969), *Die Grundlagen der Erziehungslehre im Spätmittelalter und bei Luther*, Heidelberg: Quelle und Meyer (Pädagogische Forschungen, 42).

Picascia, M. L. (1987), 'Messaggi al precettore del Delfino: *Tractatus* e *Instructiones* di Jean Gerson', in *Mélanges de l'Ecole française de Rome: Moyen âge–Temps modernes*, 99, pp. 235–60.

Pieper, F. (1953), *Christian Dogmatics*, 4 vol., St Louis: Concordia Publishing House.

Pietsch, S. (2016), *Of Good Comfort: Martin Luther's Letters to the Depressed, and their Significance for Pastoral Care Today*, Hindmarsh, SA: ATF.

Piton, M. (1966), 'L'idéal Episcopal selon les prédicateurs français de la fin du XVe et du début du XVIe siècle', dans *Revue d'Histoire Ecclésiastique*, 61 (1–2), pp. 77–118/392–423.

Plard, H. (1979). 'L'Utopie communiste agraire d'Eberlin de Günzburg: les pays de Wolfaria', dans E. Grassi (éd.), *L'humanisme allemand (1480-1540): XVIIIe Colloque International de Tours*, Paris: Vrin, pp. 387–403.

Platt, P. (2009), *Shakespeare and the Culture of Paradox*, Farham, UK: Ashgate (Studies in Performance and Early Modern Drama).

Pohlig, M. (2010), 'Themenschwerpunkt / Focal Point: The Protestant Reformation and the Middle Ages', hg. v. M. Greengrass & M. Pohlig, in *Archiv für Reformationsgeschichte*, 101, pp. 233–304.

Polman, P. (1932), *L'Elément historique dans la controverse religieuse du XVIe siècle*, Paris: J. Duculot.

Poncet, Ch. (2010), 'L'image du char dans le commentaire de Marsile Ficin au Phèdre de Platon: Le véhicule de l'âme comme instrument du retour à dieu', dans *Revue des sciences philosophiques et théologiques*, 94 (2), pp. 249–85.

Popelyastyy, V. (2018), 'The Post-Tridentine Theology of the Sacrament of Penance on the Basis of the *Rituale Romanum* (1614)', in W. François & V. Soen (ed.), *The Council of Trent: Reform and*

Controversy in Europe and Beyond (1545–1700), 3 vols, Göttingen: Vandenhoeck & Ruprecht, pp. 191–220.

Posset, F. (2003), *The Front-Runner of the Catholic Reformation: The Life and Works of Johann von Staupitz*, Aldershot, U.K: Ashgate (St Andrews Studies in Reformation History).

Posset, F. (2005), *Renaissance Monks: Monastic Humanism in Six Biographical Sketches*, Leiden/New York: Brill (Studies in Medieval and Reformation Traditions, 108).

Posset, F. (2015), *Johann Reuchlin (1455–1522): A Theological Biography*, Berlin: De Gruyter (Arbeiten zur Kirchengeschichte Book, 129).

Pot, O. (éd., 2013), *Simon Goulart, Un Pasteur aux intérêts vastes comme le monde*, Genève: Droz (Travaux d'Humanisme et Renaissance, 514).

Prodi, P. (2000), *Una storia della guistizia. Dal pluralismo dei fori al moderno dualismo tra coscienza e diritto*, Bologna: Milano.

Prosperi, A. (2016), *Infanticide, Secular Justice, and Religious Debate in Early Europe, trans. H. Siddons*, Turnhout: Brepols (Europa Sacra).

Provvidente, S. (2011), 'Inquisitorial Process and *plenitudo potestatis* at the Council of Constance (1414–1418)', in *Filosoficky Casopis*, 59 (3), pp. 98–114.

Prügl, T., 'Dissidence and Renewal: Developments in Late Medieval Ecclesiology', in *Les nouveaux horizons de l'ecclésiologie: du discours clérical à la science du social. Ecclesiologie, hérésiologie et dissidence*, Bulletin du centre d'études médiévales d'Auxerre, BUCEMA, 2013: file:///Users/generalusenopw/Downloads/cem-12782.pdf (accessed 28/01/2021).

Puyol, P. E. (1898), *Descriptions des manuscrits et des princivales editions du livre de Imitatione Christi*, Paris: V. Retaux.

Racaut, L. (2003), 'Religious Polemic and Huguenot Self-Perception and Identity, 1554–1619', in R. A. Mentzer & A. Spicer (ed.), *Society and Culture in the Huguenot World, 1559–1685*, Cambridge: Cambridge University Press, pp. 29–43.

Rahner, K. (1986), 'The Immediate Experience of God in the Spiritual Exercises of Saint Ignatius of Loyola', in P. Imhof & H. Biallowons (ed.), D. E. Harvey (trans.), *Karl Rahner in Dialogue: Conversations and Interviews 1965–1982*, New York: Crossroad.

Rahner, K. & J. Ratzinger (1966), *Revelation and Tradition*, trans. W. J. O'Hara, New York: Herder and Herder (Quaestiones Disputatae, 17).

Rainer, R. (1957), *Ars moriendi' von der Kunst des heilsamen Lebens und Sterbens*, Köln: Böhlau.

Raley, J. M. (2012), 'Traversing Borders – Defining Boundaries: Cosmopolitan Harmonies and Confessional Theology in Georg Rhau's Liturgical Publications', in *The Sixteenth Century Journal*, 43 (4), pp. 1079–1105.

Ransome, J., *Monotessaron: The Harmonies of Little Gidding*, 2013; file:///Users/yelena/Downloads/Courtesy_at_Little_Gidding.pdf (accessed 28/01/2021).

Ranum, O., *D'Encre et de sang: Simon Goulart et la Saint-Barthélemy*, 2007; muse.jhu.edu/journals/ren/summary/v061/61.4.ranum.html (accessed 28/01/2021).

Rapp, F. (1976), 'Die elsässischen Humanisten und die geistliche Gesellschaft', in O. Herding & R. Stupperich (ed.), *Die Humanisten in ihrer politischen und sozialen Umwelt*, Bonn: Boldt (Kommission für Humanismusforschung, 3), pp. 87–108.

Rapp, F. (1982), *Le diocese de Strasbourg*, Paris: Beauchesne.

Rapp, F. (1994), 'Les caractères communs de la vie religieuse', in J.-M. Mayeur et al., *Histoire du christianisme*, vol. 7, Paris: Desclée, pp. 215–308.

Rasmussen T. & J. Flaeten Øygarden (2015), *Preparing for Death, Remembering the Dead*, Göttingen: Vandenhoeck & Ruprecht (Refo500 Academic Studies 022).

Rathey, M. (2016), *Johann Sebastian Bach's Christmas Oratorio: Music, Theology, Culture*, New York: Oxford University Press.

Reid, J. A., (2009), *King's Sister — Queen of Dissent: Marguerite of Navarre (1492–1549) and her Evangelical Network*, Leiden/New York: Brill (Studies in Medieval and Reformation Traditions, 139).

Reinburg, V. (2012), *French Books of Hours: Making an Archive of Prayer: 1400–1600*, Cambridge: Cambridge University Press.

Reinis, A. (2007), *Reforming in the Art of Dying: The Ars Moriendi in the German Reformation (1519–1528)*, Farham, UK: Ashgate (St Andrews Studies in Reformation History).

Renaudet, A. (1916), *Préréforme et humanisme à Paris pendant les premières guerres d'Italie (1494–1517)*, Paris: Champion.

Resch, C. (2006), *Trost im Angesicht des Todes: Frühe reformatorische Anleitungen zur Seelsorge an Kranken und Sterbenden*, Tübingen und Basel: Francke (Pietas Liturgica Studia).

Reynolds, N. B. & W. C. Durham Jr. (1996), *Religious Liberty in Western Thought*, Grand Rapids, MI: Eerdmans (Emory University Studies in Law and Religion).

Révolution française, Les catéchismes républicains, mis en ligne le 16 novembre 2009; lrf.revues.org/123 (accessed 28/01/2021).

Rex, R. (2011), 'Thomas More and the Heretics: Statesman or Fanatic?' in G. M. Logan (ed.), *The Cambridge Companion to Thomas More*, Cambridge: Cambridge University Press (Cambridge Companions to Religion), pp. 93–115.

Rice, E. (1971), 'Jacques Lefèvre d'Etaples and the Medieval Christian mystics', in J. G. Rowe & W. H. Stockdale (ed.), *Florilegium Historiale, Essays presented to Wallace K. Ferguson*, Toronto: University of Toronto Press (Heritage), pp. 89–124.

Richardson, C. M. (2011), 'St Joseph, St Peter, Jean Gerson and the Guelphs', in *Renaissance Studies*, 26 (2), pp. 243–68.

Riemann, H. D. 'Der Briefwechsel Bernhards von Waging und Johannes von Eych (1461–1463): *Speculum pastorum et animarum rectorum Epistula impugnatoria Defensorium speculi pastorum et animarum rectorum: zur Kontroverse über Rang und Verdienst des Aktiven und des kontemplativen Lebens*' (unpublished doctoral dissertation, University of Cologne, 1985).

Ritchey, S. (2013), 'Wessel Gansfort, John Mombaer, and Medieval Technologies of the Self: Affective Meditation in a Fifteenth-Century Emotional Community', in B. Gusick (ed.), *Fifteenth-Century Studies*, 38, Rochester, New York: Boydell & Brewer. pp. 153–74.

Ritter, F. (1955), *Histoire de l'imprimerie alsacienne aux XVe et XVIe siècles*, Strasbourg-Paris: F.-X. Leroux.

Ritter, G. (1971), 'Romantic and Revolutionary Element in German Theology on the Eve of the Reformation', in S. E. Ozment (ed.), *The Reformation in Medieval Perspective*, Chicago: Quadrangle Books (Modern scholarship on European history).

Rittgers, R. (2012), *The Reformation of Suffering, Pastoral Theology and Lay Piety in Late Medieval and Early Modern Germany*, Oxford: Oxford University Press (Oxford Studies in Historical Theology).

Rittgers, R. (2012a), 'Christianization Through Consolation: Urbanus Rhegius's Soul-Medicine for the Healthy and the Sick in These Dangerous Times (1529)', in A. M. Johnson & J. A. Maxfield (ed.), *The Reformation as Christianization, Essays on Scott Hendrix's Christianization Thesis*, Tübingen: Mohr (Spätmittelalter, Humanismus, Reformation, 66), pp. 321–48.

Roccatti, G. M. (1995), *La formation des humanistes dans le dernier quart du XIVe siècle*, dans M. Ornato & N. Pons (éd.), *Pratiques de la culture écrite en France au XVe siècle*, Louvain-la-Neuve: Fédération Internationale des *Instituts* d'Études Médiévales, pp. 55–73.

Roccatti, G. M. (1992), 'Humanisme et préoccupations religieuses au début du XVe siècle: le prologue de la *Josephina* de Jean Gerson', dans C. Bozzolo & E. Ornato (éd.), *Préludes à la Renaissance*, Paris: CNRS, pp. 113–61.

Rodgers, K. G. (2011), 'The lessons of Gethsemane: *De Tristitia Christi*', in Logan G. M. (ed.), *The Cambridge Companion to Thomas More*, Cambridge: Cambridge University Press (Cambridge Companions to Religion), pp. 239–64.

Rodriguez-Grahit, I. (1957), *La Devotio moderna en Espagne et l'influence française*, Geneva: Droz.

Roest, B. (2004), *Franciscan Literature of Religious Instruction before the Council of Trent*, Leiden/Boston: Brill (Studies the History of Christian Traditions, 117).

Rollo-Koster, J. & T. M. Izbicki (2009), *A Companion to the Great Western Schism (1378–1417)*, Leiden/New York: Brill (Brill's Companions to the Christian Tradition, 17).

Rueger, Z. (1964), 'Gerson, the Conciliar Movement and the Right of Resistance', in *Journal of the History of Ideas*, 25 (4). pp. 467–86.

Rueger, Z. (1982), 'Gerson's Concept of Equity and Christopher St German', in *History of Political Thought*, 3 (1), pp. 1–30.

Rumme, E. (2008), *Biblical Humanism and Scholasticism in the Age of Erasmus*, Leiden: Brill (Brill's Companions to the Christian Tradition, 9).

Rupp, G. (1972), 'Protestant Spirituality in the First Age of the Reformation', in *Studies in Church History*, 8, pp. 155–70.

Ruppert, G. J. (1962), *Die Heilige Schrift und die Tradition. Zu den neueren Kontroversen über das Verhältnis der Heiliger Schrift zu den nichtgeschriebenen Traditionen (Quaestiones disputatae)*, Freiburg: Herder.

Rupprich, H. (1934), *Der Briefwechsel des Konrad Celtis*, München: Beck.

Rurale, F. (1992), *I gesuiti a Milano, Religione e politica nel secondo Cinquecento*, Rome: Bulzoni (Biblioteca del Cinquecento/Europa delle Corti, Centro studi sulle società di antico regime).

Russell, J. S. (1980), 'More's Dialogue and the Dynamics of Comfort', in *Moreana*, 65–66, pp. 41–56.

Ruys, J. F. (2014), 'Dying 101: emotion, experience, and learning how to die in the late medieval artes moriendi', in *Parergon*, 31 (2), pp. 55–79.

Ryan, F. & J. Rybolt (ed., 1995), *Vincent de Paul and Louise de Marillac: Rules, Conferences, and Writings*, New York: Paulist Press (Classics of Western Spirituality).

Ryan, J. (1998), *Apostolic Conciliarism of Jean Gerson*, Oxford: Oxford University Press (An American Academy of Religion Book, 4).

Saak, L. (2017), *Luther and the Reformation of the Middle Ages*, Cambridge, UK: Cambridge University Press.

Sackville, T. (1938), *The Mirror for Magistrates* (1563), ed. L. B. Campbell, Cambridge, UK: Cambridge University Press.

Salmon McMillan, J. H. (1987), *Renaissance and Revolt: Essays in the intellectual and social history of early modern France*, New York: Cambridge University Press (Cambridge Studies in Early Modern History).

Sampson, M. (1988), 'Laxity and Liberty in Seventeenth-Century English Political Thought', in E. Leites (ed.), *Conscience and Casuistry in Early Modern Europe*, Cambridge, UK: Cambridge University Press (Ideas in Context Series, 9).

Sarmiento, A. (2011), 'The Obligation to fulfill Civil Laws According to Francisco de Vitoria', in K. Bunge, A. Spindler & A. Wagner (ed.), *Die Normativitat Des Rechts Bei Francisco de Vitoria. The Normativity of Law According to Francisco de Vitoria*, Stuttgart: Frommann-Holzboog (Politische Philosophie und Rechtstheorie des Mittelalters und der Neuzeit), pp. 98–122.

Sayle, C. E. (1900), *Early English Printed Books in the University Library, Cambridge, 1475 to 1640*, Cambridge, UK: Cambridge University Press.

Schädle, K., 'Sigmund Gossenbrot: ein Augsburger, Kaufmann, Patrizer und Frühhumanist' (unpublished doctoral dissertation, München, 1938).

Schaff, Ph. (1997), *History of the Christian Church, vol. VII. Modern Christianity. The German Reformation, § 64. Melanchthon's Theology*, Oak Harbor, WA: Logos Research Systems, Inc.

Shaffern, R. W. (1988), 'Indulgences and Saintly Devotionalisms in the Middle Ages', in *The Catholic Historical Review*, 84 (4), pp. 643–61.

Scheible, H. (1996), 'Der *Catalogus testium veritatis*. Flacius als Schüler Melanchthons', in *Ebernburg-Hefte*, 30, pp. 91–105.

Schepers, K. (2008), 'Het *Opus tripartitum* van Jean Gerson in het Middelnederlands', in *Ons Geestelijk Erf*, 79 (2), pp. 146–88.

Schmidt, Ch. (1989), *Essai sur Jean Gerson, chancelier de l'Université et de l'église de Paris*, Strasbourg: Schmidt & Grucker.

Schmitt, Ch. (2001), *Biographisch-bibliographisches Kirchenlexikon*, 19.

Schneider, J. (1953). 'Die Verpflichtung des menschlichen Gesetzes nach Johannes Gerson', in *Zeitschrift für katholische Theologie*, 75, pp. 1–54.

Schnerd, B. (2005), *Jean Sans-Peur — le prince meurtrier*, Paris: Payot (Biographie Payot).

Schoepff, F. G. P. (1857), *Aurora, siue bibliotheca selecta ex scriptis eorum, qui ante Lutherum ecclesiae studuerunt restituendae*, Dresden: Adler et Dietze.

Scholz, W. G. (2002), *Paracelsian Moments: Science, Medecine and Astrology in Early Modern Europe*, Kirksville, MO: Williams Truman State University Press (Sixteenth Century Essays and Studies Series, 64).

Schüssler, R. (2006), *Moral im Zweifel. Die Herausforderung des Probabilismus*, Paderborn: Mentis (Perspektiven der Analytischen Philosophie).

Schüssler, R. (2011), 'Jean Gerson, Moral Certainty and the Renaissance of Ancient Scepticism', in H. E. Braun & E. Vallance (ed.), in *The Renaissance Conscience*, London: Wiley-Blackwell, pp. 445–62.

Schüssler, R. (2013), 'On the Anatomy of Probabilism', in J. Kraye & R. Saarinen (ed.), *Moral Philosophy on the Threshold of Modernity*, New York: Springer (The New Synthese Historical Library, 57), pp. 91–113.

Schüssler, R. (2014), 'Scholastic Probability as Rational Assertability: The Rise of Theories of Reasonable Disagreement', in *Archiv für Geschichte der Philosophie*, 96, pp. 202–21.

Schüssler, R. (2014), 'The Economic Thought of Luis de Molina', in A. Aichele & M. Kaufmann, *A Companion to Luis de Molina*, Leiden/New York: Brill (Brill's Companions to the Christian Tradition, 50), pp. 257–88.

Schüssler, R. (2019), *The Debate on Probable Opinions in the Scholastic Tradition*, Leiden/New York: Brill (Brill Studies in Intellectual History, 302).

Schüssler, R. (2021), 'Kant, Casuistry and Casuistical Questions', in *Journal of Philosophy of Education*, 55, pp. 1003–16.

Schütze, H. (1879), *Auslese aus den Werken berümter Lehrer und Pädagogen den Mittelalters: Alcuin, Rabanus Maurus, Joh. Gerson*, Gütersloh: Mohn.

Schwab, J. B. (1858), *Johannes Gerson, Professor der Theologie und Kanzler der Universität Paris*, Würzburg: Stahel, 1858.

Schwartz, D. (2014), 'Probabilism Reconsidered: Deference to Experts, Types of Uncertainty, and Medicines', *Journal of the History of Ideas*, 75 (3), pp. 373-93.

Seebass, G. (1997), *Die Reformation und ihre Aussenseiter: Gesammelte Aufsätze und Vorträge. Zum 60. Geburtstag des Autors. Festschrift Seebaß*, Göttingen: Vandenhoeck und Ruprecht.

Seidel, K. J. (1970), *Frankreich und die deutschen Protestanten Die Bemühungen um eine religiöse Konkordie und die französische Bündnispolitik in den Jahren 1534/35*, Münster: Aschendorffsche Verlagsbuchhandlung (Reformationsgeschichtliche Studien und Texte, 102).

Selke, A. (1968), *El Santo Oficio de la Inquisición: proceso de Fr. Francisco Ortíz: 1529–1582*, Madrid: Guadarrama.

Sère, B. (2007), *Penser l'amitié au Moyen Âge. Étude historique des commentaires sur les livres VIII et IX de l'Éthique à Nicomaque' (XIIIe-XVe siècle)*, Turnhout: Brepols (Bibliothèque d'histoire culturelle du Moyen Âge, 4).

Sère B. (2018), *Les Régimes de polémicité au Moyen Âge*, Rennes: PUR.

Sère, B. (2016), Les débats d'opinion à l'heure du Grande Schisme *Ecclésiologie et politique*, Turnhout: Brepols (Ecclesia militans, Histoire des hommes et des institutions de l'Église au Moyen Âge, 6).

Shanske, D. (2005), 'Four Theses. Preliminary to an Appeal to Equity', in *Stanford Law Review*, 57 (6), pp. 2053–2085.

Shortall, M. (2009), *Human Rights and Moral Reasoning: A Comparative Investigation by Way of Three Theorists and Their Respective Traditions of Enquiry: John Finnis, Ronald Dworkin and Jürgen Habermas*, Rome: Gregorian Biblical BookShop.

Sider, R. J. (1974), *Andreas Bodenstein von Karlstadt: The Development of His Thought, 1517–1525*, Leiden/New York: Brill (Studies in Medieval and Reformation Thought, 11).

Simpson, J. (2004), *Reform and Cultural Revolution*, Oxford: Oxford University Press (The Oxford English Literary History, 2).

Simut, C. C. (2003), 'The Development of the Doctrine of Justification in the Theology of Philip Melanchthon: A Brief Historical Survey', in *Perichoresis*, 1 (2) pp. 119–27.

Skinner, Q. (1978), *The Foundations of Modern Political Thought: The Age of Reformation*, 2 vols, Cambridge, New York: Cambridge University Press.

Slemon, P. J. 'Adam von Fulda on Musica Plana and Compositio. De Musica, Book II: A Translation and Commentary' (dissertation, University of British Columbia, 1975).

Sluhovsky, M. (2017), *Becoming a New Self: Practices of Belief in Early Modern Catholicism*, Chicago: University of Chicago Press.

Smolinsky, H. (1976), *Domenico de Domenichi und seine Schrift De potestate pape et termino eius*, Münster: Aschendorff (Vorreformations-geschichtliche Forschungen).

Smolinsky, H. (1993), *Kirchengeschichte der Neuzeit*, Düsseldorf: Patmos Verlag.

Smolinsky, H. (2005), *Im Zeichen von Kirchenreform und Reformation: gesammelte Studien zur Kirchengeschichte in Spätmittelalter und Früher Neuzeit*, in K.-H. Braun, B. Henze & B. Schneider (ed.), Münster: Aschendorff (Reformationsgeschichtliche Studien und Texte).

Smolinsky, H. (2013), 'The Better Human Being: The Dispute on Morality in Humanism and Reformation', in S. Mueller (ed.), *Between Creativity and Norm-Making: Tensions in the Early Modern Era*, Leiden/New York: Brill (Studies in Medieval and Reformation Traditions, 165), pp. 189–202.

Smolinsky, H. (2014), 'Lutheran Roman Catholic Critics', in R. Kolb, I. Dingel & L. Batka (ed.), *The Oxford Handbook of Martin Luther's Theology*, Oxford: Oxford University Press (Oxford Handbooks), pp. 502–10.

Smoller, A. L. (2017), *History, Prophecy, and the Stars: The Christian Astrology of Pierre d'Ailly, 1350–1420*, Princeton: Princeton University Press (Princeton Legacy Library).

Smyth, E. (1996) Memorial Lecture, unfinished text, presented 23 March 1996 in London at Saint Edmund the King church, Lombard Street, the City of London, pdf (accessed 25 July 2018).

Solère, J.-L. (1994), 'De l'orateur à l'orant. La 'rhétorique divine dans la culture chrétienne occidentale', dans *Revue de l'histoire des religions*, 211 (2), pp. 187–224.

Sommerville, J. (2014) *Royalists and Patriots: Politics and Ideology in England, 1603–1640*, Abington, UK: Routledge.

Sönke, L. et al. (2002), *Bücher, Bibliotheken und Schriftkultur der Kartäuser: Festgabe zum 65. Geburtstag von Edward Potkowski*, Berlin: Steiner (Contubernium, 59).

Spinrad, P. S. (1987), *The Summons of Death on the Early Modern Stage*, Columbus, OH: Ohio State University Press.

Spitz, L. W. (1957), *Conrad Celtis: The German Arch-Humanist*, Cambridge, MA: Harvard University Press.

Spitz, L. W. (1963), *The Religious Renaissance of the German Humanists*, Cambridge, MA: Harvard University Press.

Spitz, L. W. (1996), *Luther and German Humanism*, Abingdon-on-Thames, Oxfordshire, England, UK: Routledge (Variorum Collected Studies).

Srolz, P. (2004), 'Bullingers Bild des Mittelalters', in E. Campi (ed.), *Bullinger, Heinrich und seine Zeit*, Zürich: Theologische Verlag (*Zwingliana*. Beiträge zur Geschichte Zwinglis, der Reformation und des Protestantismus in der Schweiz), pp. 37–60.

Staubach, N. (1997), '*Memores priscae perfectionis*. The Importance of the Church Fathers for Devotio moderna', in I. Backus (ed.), *The Reception of the Church Fathers in the West (From the Carolingians to the Maurists)*, Leiden/New York: Brill), vol. 1, pp. 411–15.

Stefaniak, R. (2008), *Mysterium Magnum: Michelangelo's Tondo Doni*, Leiden/New York: Brill (Brill's Studies in Intellectual History, 164/1).

Steinmetz, D. C. (1968), *Misericordia Dei: The Theology of Johannes von Staupitz in Its Late Medieval Setting*, Leiden: Brill (Studies in Medieval and Reformation Thought, IV).

Stelzenberger, J. (1928), *Die Mystic des Johannes Gerson*, Breslau: Müller & Seiffert.

Stepien, K. (2014), '*Sinderesis* and the Natural Law', in *Studia Gilsoniana*, 3, pp. 377–98.

Stieber, J. W. (1978), *Pope Eugenius IV the Council of Basel and the secular and ecclesiastical authorities in the Empire*, Leiden/New York: Brill (Studies in the History of Christian Traditions, 13).

Sordet, Y. (2011), 'Usages, appropriations, transmission de l'*Imitatio Christi*: l'enseignement des exemplaires', dans M. Delaveau & Y. Sordet (dir.), *Édition et diffusion de l'Imitation de Jésus-Christ (1470–1800). Étude et catalogue collectif des fonds conservés à la bibliothèque Sainte-Geneviève, à la Bibliothèque Nationale de France, à la bibliothèque Mazarine et à la bibliothèque de la Sorbonne*, Paris: BNP, pp. 93–107.

St Clare, L. D. 'As the Crone Flies: the Imagery of Women as Flying Witches in Early Modern Europe' (unpublished doctoral dissertation, Norman, Oklahoma, 2016).

Stolz, P. (2004), 'Bullingers Bild des Mittelalters', in *Zwingliana*, 31, pp. 37–60.

Strauss, G. (1993), *Enacting the Reformation in Germany*, Farham, UK: Ashgate (Variorum Collected Studies).

Strickland, M., 'Evangelicals and the Synoptic Problem' (unpublished doctoral dissertation, University of Birmingham Research Archive, E-theses Repository, 2011).

Stumpf, Ch. (2006), *The Grotian Theology of International Law: Hugo Grotius and the Moral Foundations of International Relations*, Berlin: De Gruyter (Religion and Society, 44).

Stupperich, R. (ed., 1962), *Martin Bucers Deutsche Schriften*, vols 2, 6, 9 & 11, Paris: Presses Universitaires de France.

Sullivan, F. P. (ed. & trans., 1995), *Indian Freedom, The Cause of Bartolomé de Las Casas*, Milwaukee, WI: Sheed & Ward.

Suzanne, H. (1981), 'Conscience in the Early Renaissance: the Case of Erasmus, Luther and Thomas More', in *Moreana*, 51, pp. 231–44.

Tallon, A. (1997), *La France et le Concile de Trente, 1518-1563*, Rome: École française de Rome.

Tallon, A. (2000), *Le concile de Trente*, Paris: Le Cerf.

Tanner, N. & G. Albergo (1990), *The Decrees of the Ecumenical Councils: Trent to Vatican II*, 2 vols, Washington DC: George Town University Press.

Taveneaux, R. (1980), *Le catholicisme dans la France classique 1610–1715*, Paris: SEDES.

Tavuzzi, M. (1997), *Prierias: The Life and Works of Silvestro Mazzolini Da Prierio (1456–1527)*, Durham, NC: Duke University Press (Duke Monographs in Medieval and Renaissance Studies).

Taylor, A. (2011). 'In stede of harme inestimable good': A Dialogue of Comfort against Tribulation', in G. Logan (ed.), *The Cambridge Companion to Thomas More*, Cambridge, UK: Cambridge University Press (Cambridge Companions to Religion), pp. 216–38.

Taylor, S. (2007), 'L'aage plus fort ennaye': *Scientia mortis, Ars moriendi* and Jean Gerson's Advice to an Old Man', in A. Classem (ed.), *Old Age in the Middle Ages and the Renaissance: Interdisciplinary Approaches to a Neglected Topic*, Berlin-New York: De Gruyter (Fundamentals of Medieval and Early Modern Culture, 2), pp. 407–20.

Tellkamp, J. A. (2013), 'Rights and *Dominium*', in A. Aichele (ed.) & M. Kaufmann (trans.), *A Companion to Luis de Molina*, Leiden: Brill (Brill's Companions to the Christian Tradition, 50), pp. 125–54.

Tenenti, A. (1989), *Il senso della morte e l'amore della vita nel Rinascimento (Francia e Italia)*, Torino: Giulio Einaudi.

Tentler, T. (1977), *Sin and Confession on the Eve of the Reformation*, Princeton NJ: Princeton University Press (Princeton Legacy Library).

Terricabras, I. F. (2018), 'The Catholic Reformation and the Power of the King', in W. François & V. Soen (ed.), *The Council of Trent*, 3 vols, Göttingen: Vandenhoeck & Ruprecht, vol. 2, pp. 221–53.

Thompson, J. S. (1828), *A Monotessaron; Or the Gospel of Jesus Christ, According to the Four Evangelists: Harmonized and Chronologically Arranged. In a New Translation from the Greek Text of Griesbach*, New York: J. Robinson.

Thompson, N. (2005), *Eucharistic Sacrifice and Patristic Tradition in the Theology of Martin Bucer: 1534–1546*, Leiden/New York: Brill (Studies in the History of Christian Traditions Series, 119).

Tierney, B. (1975), 'Divided Sovereignty at Constance: a Problem of Medieval and Early Modern Political Theory', in *Annuarium Historiae Conciliorum*, 7, pp. 236–56.

Tierney, B. (1997), *The Idea of Natural Rights: Studies on Natural Rights, Natural Law, and Church Law 1150–1625*, Atlanda: Scholars Press (Emory University Studies in Law and Religion).

Tierney, B. (1988), 'Aristotle and the American Indians — Again', in *Cristianesimo nella Storia*, 9, pp. 81–111.

Tierney, B. (1996), 'Religious Rights: an Historical Perspective', in J. Witte & J. D. van der Vyver (ed.), *Religious Rights in Global Perspective: Legal Perspectives*, The Hague: Martinus Nijhoff, vol. 1, pp. 17–47.

Tierney, B., 'The Idea of Natural Rights-Origins and Persistence', in *Northwestern University Journal of International Human Rights*, 2 (2) (2004); law.northwestern.edu/journals/jihr/v2/2/ (accessed 21/01/2021).

Tierney, B. (2005), 'Dominion of Self and Natural Rights Before Locke and After', in V. Mäkinen & P. Korkman (ed.), *Transformations in Medieval and Early Modern Rights Discourse*, Berlin: Springer (The New Synthese Historical Library, 59), pp. 173–207.

Tilly, A. 'Pädagogik, Mystic und Pietismus bei Pierre Poiret' (unpublished doctoral dissertation, Bonn University, 1930).

Tilly, M. (1990), *Biographisch-bibliographisches Kirchenlexikon*, Nordhausen: Verlag Traugott Bautz GmbH, vol. 2, col. 810–12.

Toussaint, S. (2011), 'Zoroaster and the Flying Egg', in P. J. Forshaw & R. Valery (ed.), *Laus Platonici Philosophi: Marsilio Ficino and His Influence*, Leiden/New York: Brill (Brill's Studies in Intellectual History, 198).

Treusch, U. (2011), *Bernhard von Waging (g. 1472), ein Theologe der Melker Reformbewegung*, Tübingen: Mohr (Beiträge zur historischen Theologie, 158).

Todd, M. (2002), *Culture of Protestantism in Early Modern Scotland*, New Heaven, CT: Yale University.

Tosi, G. (2003), 'A doutrina subjetiva dos direitos naturais e a questão indígena na Escuela de Salamanca e em Bartolome de Las Casas', in *Cunadernos Salmantinas de Filosofia*, 30, pp. 577–87.

Trotsky, L. (1965), *The History of the Russian Revolution*, London: Sphere Books.

Tsui, J. & B. Lucas, 'Methodologies for measuring influence', in *Governance and Social Development Resource Centre* (2013); http://www.gsdrc.org/docs/open/hdq905.pdf (accessed 28/01/2021).

Tuck, R. (1979), *Natural Rights Theories: Their Origin and Development*, Cambridge: Cambridge University Press.

Tucker, J. (2017), *The Construction of Reformed Identity in Jean Crespin's Livre des Martyrs*, London & New York: Routledge (Routledge Research in Early Modern History).

Turchetti, M. (2001), *Tyrannie et tyrannicide. De l'antiquité à nos jours*, Paris: Presses Universitaires de France (Renaissance Library, 11).

Tutino, S. (2018), *Uncertainty in Post-Reformation Catholicism: A History of Probabilism*, Oxford: Oxford University Press.

Tyler, P. M. 'Mystical strategies and performative discourse in the theologia mystica of Teresa of Avila: A Wittgensteinian analysis' (unpublished doctoral dissertation, Durham University, 2009).

Tyler, P. M. (2018), 'Oración Mental, Mindfulness, and Mental Prayer: The Training of the Heart in the Iberian School of Abbot Garcíade Cisneros of Montserrat and St Teresa of Avila', in *Buddhist-Christian Studies*, 38, pp. 253–66.

Tyler, P. M. (2017), 'Mystical Affinities: St Teresa and Jean Gerson', in P. M. Tyler & E. Howells (ed.), *Teresa of Avila: Mystical Theology and Spirituality in the Carmelite Tradition*, London: Routledge, pp. 36–50.

Tyler, M. P. (2010), *St John of the Cross*, London, UK: Bloomsbury.

Ullmann, C. (1863–1877), *Reformers Before the Reformation: Principally in Germany and the Netherlands*, Edinburgh: T. & T. Clark.

Undorf, W. (2014), *From Gutenberg to Luther: Transnational Print Cultures in Scandinavia 1450–1525*, Leiden/New York: Brill (Library of the Written Word, Handpress World Series, 28).

Vanderpoel, M. (2018), 'The Rhetoric of Sacred Scripture in Jean Gerson', paper presented at 'Jean Gerson écrivain', Colloquim, Montpellier, April 2018, forthcoming in *Jean Gerson écrivain*, Geneva: Droz.

Vandiver, E. & R. Keen (2003), *Luther's Lives: Two contemporary Accounts of Martin Luther*, trans. T. Frazel Manchester: Manchester University.

Vansteenberghe, E. (1920), *Le cardinal Nicolas de Cues, l'action et la pensée*, Paris: Champion.

Vansteenberghe, E. (1939), 'Un programme d'action épiscopale au début du XIVe siècle', dans *Révue des sciences religieuses*, 19 (1), pp. 39–47.

Varacalli, T. F. X., 'The Thomism of Bartolomé de Las Casas and the Indians of the New World' (unpublished doctoral dissertation, Louisiana State University, 2016).

Varkemaa, J. (2012), *Conrad Summenhart's Theory of Individual Rights*, Leiden: Brill (Studies in Medieval and Reformation Traditions, 159).

Varkemaa, J., 'Conrad Summenhart's Theory of Individual Rights and its Medieval Background' (unpublished doctoral dissertation, University of Helsinki, 2009).

Varkemaa, J. (2006), 'Summenhart's Theory of Rights: A Culmination of the Late Medieval Discourse of Individual Rights', in V. Mäkinen & P. Korkman (ed.), *Transformations in Medieval and Early Modern Rights Discourse*, Berlin: Springer (The New Synthese Historical Library Book, 59), pp. 119–49.

Varkemaa, J. (2005), 'Justification through Being: Conrad Summenhart on Natural Rights', in J. Kraye & R. Saarinen, *Moral Philosophy on the Threshold of Modernity*, New York: Springer (The New Synthese Historical Library, 57), pp. 181–93.

Vaughan, R. (2002), *John the Fearless*, Woodbridge: Boydell.

Veissière, M. (1967), 'Un précurseur de Guillaume Briçonnet: Louis Pinelle, évêque de Meaux de 1511–1516', dans *Bulletin de la Société d'histoire et d'art du Diocèse de Meaux*, 18, pp. 7–61.

Veissière, M. (1986), *L'evêque Guillaume Briçonnet: contribution à la connaissance de la Réforme catholique à la veille du Concile de Trente*, Provins: Société d'histoire et d'archéologie.

Veit, P. (1986), *Das Kirchenlied in der Reformation Martin Luthers, eine thematische und semantische Untersuchung*, Stuttgart: Steiner (Abteilung für Abendländische Religionsgeschichte).

Venard, M. (1979), 'Dans l'affrontement des reformes du XVIe siècle: regards et jugements portés sur la religion populaire', dans G. Duboscq, B. Plongeron & D. Robert (éd.), *La Religion populaire. Actes du colloque international, Paris, 17–19 octobre 1977*, Paris: CNRS, pp. 115–27.

Venard, M. (1996), *De la réforme à la réformation (1450–1530)*, dans *Histoire du christianisme des origines à nos jours*, 14 vols, v. VII, Paris: Desclée.

Venard, M. (2000), *Le catholicisme à l'épreuve dans la France du XVIe siècle*, Paris: Cerf.

Venard, M. (1995), 'Volksfrömmigkeit und Konfessionalisierung', in W. Reinhard & H. Schilling (ed.), *Die katholische Konfessionalisierung*, Münster: Aschendorff (Reformationsgeschichtliche Studien und Texte, 135), pp. 258–70.

Vendrix, Ph. (1997), 'La difusion de textes théoriques français à la Renaissance', in A. Beer, K. Pfarr & W. Ruf (ed.), *Festschrift Christoph-Hellmut Mahling zum 65. Geburtstag*, Tutzing: Hans Schneider (Mainzer Studien zur Musikwissenschaft), pp. 1453–1462.

Vereecke, L. (1957), *Conscience morale et loi humaine*, Paris: Declée & Cie (Bibliothèque de théologie 2, Théologie morale).

Verger, J. (1995), *Les universités françaises au Moyen Âge*, Leiden/New York: Brill (Education and Society in the Middle Ages and Renaissance, 7).

Verkamp, B. (1975), 'The Limits Upon Adiaphoristic Freeedom: Luther and Melanchton', in *Theological Studies*, 36, pp. 52–76.

Vial, M. (2006), *Jean Gerson: théoricien de la théologie mystique*, Paris: J. Vrin.

Vial, M. (2004), 'Zum Funktion des Monotessaron des Johannes Gerson', in Ch. Burger, A. den Hollander & U. Schmid (ed.), *Evangelienharmonien des Mittelalters*, Assen: Royal van Gorcum (Studies in Theology and Religion, 9), pp. 40–72.

Vickery, P., 'The Prophetic Call and Message of Bartolomé de Las Casas (1484–1566)' (unpublished dissertation, Oklahoma State University, 1996).

Virdung, S. (1993), *Musica Getutscht: A Treatise on Musical Instruments (1511)*, ed. & trans. B. Bullard, Cambridge, New York: Cambridge University Press.

Vogelsang, E. (1932), *Der Angefochtene Christus bei Luther*, Berlin: De Gruyter (Arbeiten Zur Kirchengeschichte).

Vogt, Ch. P. (2012), 'Dying Well in Historical Perspective: The *ars moriendi* Tradition of the Sixteenth and Seventeenth Centuries', in M. T. Lysaught et al. (ed.), *On Moral Medicine: Theological Perspectives on Medical Ethics*, Grand Rapids, MI: Wm. B. Eerdmans, pp. 1065–1070.

Volkmar, Ch. (2019), *Catholic Reform at the Age of Luther: Duke George of Saxony and the Church 1488–1525*, Leiden/New York: Brill (Studies in Medieval and Reformation Traditions, 209).

Walsham, A. (2017), 'Wholesome Milk and Strong Meat: Peter Canisius's Catechisms and the Conversion of Protestant Britain', in A. Flüchter (ed.), *Translating Catechisms, Translating Cultures: The Expansion of Catholicism in the Early Modern World*, Leiden: Brill (Studies in Christian Mission, 52), pp. 92–126.

Warme, L. G. (1996), *A History of Swedish Literature*, Omaha: U of Nebraska (Histories of Scandinavian Literature Series).

Wartenberg, G. (ed., 1999), *Werk und Rezeption Philipp Melanchtons in Universität und Schule*, Leipzig: Evangelische Verlagsanstalt (Herbergen der Christenheit).

Wasserman, D. (1994), 'Wissenschaft und Bildung in der Erfurter Kartause im 15 Jahrhundert', in J. Helrath & H. Müller (ed.), *Studien zum 15 Jahrhundert: Festschrift für Erich Meuthen*, München: Oldenbourg Verlag, pp. 483–503.

Wassilowsky, G. (2017), 'The Myths of the Council of Trent and the Construction of Catholic Confessional Culture', in W. François & V. Soen (ed.), *The Council of Trent: Reform and Controversy in Europe and Beyond (1545–1700)*, Göttingen: Vandenhoeck & Ruprecht (Refo500 Academic Series, 35, 1–3), pp. 69–98.

Watanabe, M. (1993), 'Nicolas of Cusa and the Reform of the Roman Curia' in J. W. O'Malley, T. M. Izbicki & G. Christianson (ed.), *Humanity and Divinity in Renaissance and Reformation: Essays in Honor of Charles Trinkaus*, Leiden/New York: Brill (Studies in the History of Christian Thought, 51), pp. 185–204.

Waterworth, J. (trans., 1848), *The Council of Trent Canons and Decrees*, the Twenty-Fifth Session, London: Dolman, pp. 232–89.

Watrigant, H. (1897), *La Genèse des exercices de Saint Ignace de Loyola*, Amiens: Imprimerie Yvert & Tellier.

Watson, L. J., 'The Influence of the Reformation and Counter Reformation upon Key Texts in the Literature of Witchcraft' (unpublished doctoral dissertation, University of New Castle, 1997).

Watson, F. (2013), *Gospel Writing: A Canonical Perspective*, Grand Rapids, MI: Eerdmans.

Wedel, Ch. von (2011), 'Der Bibelübersetzer Leo Jud und sein biblisches Erbauungsbuch *Vom lyden Christi (1534)*', in *Zwingliana*, 38, pp. 35–52.

Weiler, A. G. (1999), 'The Dutch Brethren of the Common Life, Critical Theology', in F. Akkerma, A. Vanderjagt & A. Laan (ed.), *Northern Humanism in European Context, 1469–1625: From the 'Adwert Academy' to Ubbo Emmius*, Leiden/New York: Brill (Brill's Studies in Intellectual History, 94), pp. 307–32.

Weiss, J. M. (1992), 'The Harvest of German Humanism: Melchior Adam's Collective Biographies as Cultural History', in M. P. Fleischer (ed.), *The Harvest of Humanism in Central Europe: Essays in Honor of Lewis W. Spitz*, St Louis, MO: Concordia, pp. 341–50.

Wengert, T. (1998), *Human Freedom, Christian Righteousness: Philip Melanchthon's Exegetical Dispute with Erasmus of Rotterdam*, Oxford: Oxford University Press (Oxford Studies in Historical Theology).

Wengert, T. (2012), *Defending Faith: Lutheran Responses to Andreas Osiander's Doctrine of Justification, 1551–1559*, Tübingen: Mohr.

Werner, E. (1991), *Jan Hus, Welt und Umwelt eines Prager Frühreformators*, Weimar: Böhlaus (Forschungen zur mittelalterlichen Geschichte, 34).

Wheatley, L. A. (1891), *The Story of the Imitatio Christi*, London: Elliot Stock.

Wicks, J. (1992), *Luther's Reform: Studies on Conversion and the Church*, Mainz: Philipp von Zabern.

Willshire, W. H. (1874), *An Introduction to the Study & Collection of Ancient Prints*, Oxford: Oxford University Press.

Willy, A. (1948), *Deutschland vor der Reformation*, Stuttgart: Deutsche Verlags-Anstallt.

Wilson, G. (1897), *Philip Melanchton*, London: The Religious Tract Society.

Witte, J. & J. D. van der Vyver (ed., 1996), *Religious Rights in Global Perspective: Legal Perspectives*, Leiden: Martinus Nijhoff.

Witte, J. & J. D. van der Vyvar (ed., 1996), *Religious Rights in Global Perspective: Religious Perspectives*, Leiden: Martinus Nijhoff.

Witte, J. Jr. & J. J. Latterell (2015), 'Christianity and Human Rights: Past Contributions and Future Challenges', in *Journal of Law and Religion*, 30, pp. 353–85.

Wolf, E. (1927), *Staupitz und Luther: ein Beitrag zur Theologie des Johannes von Staupitz und deren bedeutung für Luthers theologischen Werdegang*, Leipzig: M. Heinsius Nachfolge.

Wollersheim, H.-W. (1999), 'Philipp Melanchtons Einfluß auf das sächsische Schulwesen', in G. Wartenberg (ed.), *Werk und Rezeption Philipp Melanchthons in Universität und Schule bis ins 18. Jahrhundert*: Tagung anlässlich seines 500. Geburtstages an der Universität Leipzig, Leipzig: Universität Verlag, pp. 83–97.

Woods, M. (2016), 'Trailblazers for Martin Luther: 5 Great Reformers', in *Christian Today*, 31 October 2016; https://www.christiantoday.com/article/trailblazers-for-martin-luther-5-great-reformers/99005.htm (assessed 20/02/2022).

Worstbrock, F. J. (1972), 'Über das geschichtliche Selbstverständnis des deutschen Humanismus', in W. Müller-Seidel, H. Fromm & K. Richter (ed.), *Historizität in Sprach-und Literaturwissenschaft; Vorträge und Berichte der Stuttgarter Germanistentagung*, München: Fink, pp. 499–519.

Worstbrock, F. J. (1981), 'Gossembrot (Gossen-, Cosmiprot), Sigismund', in W. Stammler, K. Langosch & K. Ruh (ed.), *Die deutsche Literatur des Mittelalters*, Verfasserlexik, vol. 3, Berlin/New York: De Gruyter, pp. 105–08.

Worstbrock, F. J. (1994), 'Hartmann Schedel's, *Index Librorum* Wissenschaftssystem und Humanismus um 1500', in J. Helmrath & H. Müller (ed.), *Studien zum 15 Jahrhundert: Festschrift für Erich Meuthen*, Berlin: De Gruyer, pp. 697–715.

Wriedt, M. (1996), 'Luther's Concept of History and the Formation of anEvangelical identity', in B. Gordon (ed.), *Protestant History and Identity in Sixteenth-Century Europe*, Farnham, UK: Aldershot (St Andrews Studies in Reformation History), pp. 31–45.

Wrightson, K. (1982), 'Infanticide in European History', in *Criminal Justice History*, 3, pp. 1-20.

Wünsch, D. (1983), *Evangelienharmonien im Reformationszeitalter*, Berlin: De Gruyter (Arbeiten zur Kirchengeschichte, 52).

Yamamoto-Wilson, J. R. (2013), 'Robert Persons's *Resolution* and the Issue of Textual Piracy in Protestant Editions of Catholic Devotional Literature', in *Reformation and Renaissance Review*, 15 (2), pp. 177–98.

Young, W. J. (ed. & trans., 1959), *Letters of St. Ignatius of Loyola*, Chicago: Loyola University Press.

Zagorin, P. (2009), *Hobbes and the Law of Nature*, Princeton, NJ: Princeton University Press.

Zahnd, E. G. (1996), 'The Application of Universal Laws to Particular Cases: A Defense of Equity in Aristotelianism and Anglo-American Law', in *Law and Contemporary Problems*, 59, pp. 263–96.

Zeeveld, W. G. (1974), *The Temper of Shakespeare's Thought*, New Haven, CT: Yale University Press.

Zumkeller, A. & A. Krümmel (ed., 1994), *Traditio Augustiniana: Studien über Augustinus und seine Rezeption. Festgabe für Willigis Eckermann OSA zum 60. Geburtstag*, Würzburg: Augustinus-Verlag.

NAME INDEX

Ackroyd, Peter   365-366, 408
Adam, Melchior   235
Adams, Herbert Mayow   267
Adams, Marilyn McCord   18
Adams, Phyllis   13
Adrelini, Faustus   193
Adrian VI, Pope   293
Aggbach von, Vincent   43-44, 46, 306, 431
Agnes of Mansfeld, Countess   253
Agricola, Johannes   56, 215
Ahlgren, Gillian T. W.   313
Ailly, Pierre d'   133-134, 185, 369, 393, 410
Aindorffer, Gaspard   43-44
Alberigo, Norman P.   324, 415
Albert the Great   28, 41
Albrecht III of Austria   36
Albrecht V of Austria   34
Alcaraz, Pedro Ruiz de   285
Alexander VI   130
Almain, Jacques   83-84, 276-277, 297, 318, 411
Alonzo, Manuel Méndez   297-298
Altenstaig (Altensteig), Johannes   63, 404
Amalou, Thierry   13, 102, 264, 268, 275, 361
Ambrose, Saint   41, 160
Amerbach, Johann   48
Anderson, C. Colt   18
Andersson, Thorer   135
Anselm, Saint   41, 89, 204

Antoninus of Florence   121-123, 281, 283, 291, 333, 431-432
Anttila, Miikka E.   42, 125, 164, 168
Antoninus of Florence   121-122, 281, 292, 333, 431-432
Appleford, Amy   105, 348
Aquillon, Pierre   99
Aquinas, Thomas   29, 39, 41, 64-65, 96, 160, 169, 204, 287, 304, 334, 390
Arc, Joan of   347, 362
Archimedes   111
Arias, Santa   23
Ariès, Philippe   93, 351, 425-426
Aristotle   39, 129, 243, 286-287, 295-297, 390-393, 396-397, 399, 414, 417-418
Arnaud, Matthieu   49, 54, 152, 171
Arnold, Gottfried   430
Arsonval, Jean de   394
Astorri, Paulo   21, 121, 176, 203-206, 291, 390
Atkinson, David William   351-352
August of Saxony, Elector   191
Augustijn, Cornelius   73
Augustine of Hippo, Saint   29, 35, 111, 144, 160, 196, 226
Auke, Jelsma   174
Auxerre, Guillaume de   291, 418
Avila, Teresa of   26, 169, 248, 285, 312-315, 421-422, 424
Ayre, John   352

Azpilcueta, Martin de 285, 291, 333, 432

Bach, Johannes Sebastian 169, 195
Backus, Irene 50, 216, 219, 236
Bacon, Francis 406
Baeza, Antonio 109, 304, 431
Bader, William D. 21, 390, 396-397, 409
Bainton, Roland 153
Balbach, Edith 26
Barbagallo, Antonio 343
Barbier, Frédéric 99, 133-134
Barge, Hermann 186
Baronius, Cesare 345
Barth, Heinz-Lothar 374
Bassett, Mary 282
Bast, Robert James 19, 97, 118, 174, 218, 255, 263, 265-266, 424
Bataillon, Marcel 245-246, 285, 303-305, 307, 310, 316, 334
Bauch, Gustav 56, 119-120
Bauer, Dominique 21, 390
Bäumer, Remigius 254
Baxter, Richard 352, 358, 411, 431
Beatus Rhenanus 48
Beaty, Nancy Lee 251
Becon or Beccon, Thomas 352
Béda, Noël 29, 83-84, 276-279, 341-342, 416, 431-432
Bede the Venerable, Bede or Beda 41
Bedford, Ronald David 407
Bedouelle, Guy 270, 272-273
Beebe, Kathryne 54
Behrendt, Walter 150
Behrens, Georg 391-392, 398-401
Bellarmine, Robert 331, 361
Bellitto, Christopher 18, 32
Beltrán, Miquel 304
Bender, Gottfried 189
Benedict XIV, Pope 340
Benedictis, Giovanni Antonio de 123
Benjamin, Katie Marie 296
Benoist, René 266
Bernard de Clairvaux 41, 101, 111, 156, 158, 160-161, 204, 209, 219, 233, 252-253, 276, 285, 306, 316, 333, 419, 434
Berquin, Louis de 279, 341-342
Beza, Théodore 230-231, 235, 252
Bieber, Anneliese 177
Biel, Gabriel 27, 65-67, 72, 76, 83-84, 137-138, 150, 175, 252, 255, 413, 431
Billanovich, V. Giuseppe 118
Binski, Paul 93
Bireley, Robert 114, 326, 337, 422
Blader, Niclas 422
Blankenburg, Walter 164
Bledsoe, Craig 13
Blic, Jacques de 286, 288, 343
Blythe, James M. 18
Bobadilla, Nicolas 324, 421
Boccacio, Giovanni 29, 63
Bodin, Jean 281-284
Boer, Jan-Hendryk de 129, 259, 329
Boer, Wietse de 129
Boethius, Anicius Manlius Severinus 41, 376
Boffa, Sophia 338
Bokenham, Osbern 405
Boland, Paschal 308
Boleyn, Anne 368
Bollbuck, H. 209-211, 216, 218-219
Bonaventure, Saint 41, 96, 101, 111, 158, 204, 219, 275, 285, 304, 333, 404
Boquet, Damien 92
Borries, Emil 58
Borromeo, Charles 169, 328-329, 334, 336, 338
Bosch, Hieronymus 132
Bostius, Arnold 56, 142
Bossuet, Jacques-Bénigne 430
Bossy, John 23, 87, 102, 151, 174, 196, 247, 281, 283
Bott, Gerhard 144
Bouchet, Jean 279-281, 413, 431-433
Boudet, Jean-Patrice 109
Bourbon, Charles de 262
Bouyer, Jean 101

NAME INDEX

Brann, Noel 58, 61-63, 99, 123, 131-132, 142-143
Brant, Sebastian 48, 193
Branteghem, Wilhelm van 198
Brett, Annabel 67, 70, 287, 294, 410-411
Bracciolini, Poggio 215
Brady, Thomas A. 217
Brecht, Martin 238
Brenz, Johannes 237-238, 241-242, 416, 429
Brett, Annabel 67, 70, 287, 294, 410-411
Breward, Ian 352
Briçonnet, Denis 269-270, 342
Briçonnet, Guillaume 55, 268, 270-272, 275, 342, 432
Brindisi, Saint Lawrence of 128
Britnell, Jennifer 264, 266, 270, 279-281
Brodrick, James 327
Brogl, Thomas 37, 171
Brooks, Christopher W. 222
Brooks, Robert 359
Brown, Catherine 17-18, 66, 103, 138, 224, 242, 261, 333
Bruening, Michael W. 190
Bruni, Leonardo 119
Brunstetter, Daniel R. 287, 295-296
Bubenheimer, Ulrich 150, 184-187
Bucer, Martin 148, 188-192, 207, 211, 226, 237, 240, 242, 415, 429, 432
Buchanan, George 277, 363
Bucholzer, Abraham 32, 414
Buchwald, Georg 253
Buck, August 118
Buck, Thomas Martin 215-216
Bugenhagen, Johannes 148, 192, 194-195, 219, 224, 250, 431
Bullard, Beth 193
Bullinger, Heinrich 224, 226, 229, 236, 240
Bullokar, John 405
Bureau, Laurent 56, 98-99
Büren, Gerz von 18, 41-42
Buridan, Jean 287

Burns, James Henderson 66-67, 71, 84, 277, 331, 364, 411
Burrows, Mark Steven 17-18, 270-271, 322, 428
Burton, Robert 406
Bury, Pierre 56
Bushnell, Katelyn 13
Bussi, Rolando 123
Busti, Bernardino di 125-128, 137-138, 218
Büttgen, Philippe 22, 150, 243

Cadart, Jean 394
Cahill, Thomas 18, 248
Cajetan, Thomas 84, 170, 247, 289, 320
Calvin, Jean 84, 220-227, 241, 276, 352, 416, 431
Cameron, Euan 216
Campi, Emidio 161, 199, 203, 226
Campo, Urbano Alonso del 343
Camus, Albert 15
Cancellieri, Francesco 135, 316
Canessa, Louigi, Bishop of Bayeux 264
Canisius, Peter 246, 329-331, 424
Canovas, Anny 299, 302-303
Capito, Wolfgang 236
Capizzi, Joseph E. 296
Carion, Johann 211, 213, 216-218
Carnahan, David Hobart 103
Caron, Pierre 279
Caspers, Charles M. A. 73-74, 259
Castiglione, Sabba da 125
Castro, Alfonso de 285, 293-294, 431
Cave, Terence C. 131, 220
Cazalla, Juan de 285, 305
Cecchetti, Dario 119
Celtis, Conrad 56, 62, 119, 140, 142
Ceneau, Robert 269
Chacornac, Paul 56
Chadwick, Noel 380
Chafe, Eric Thomas 195
Cicero, Marcus Tullius 29, 64, 142, 319
Charles I of England 282, 359

509

Charles V, Emperor   178-179, 328, 335, 343
Charles VI of England   361
Charles VI of France   394
Charles VII of France   362, 394
Charles VIII of France   98, 100
Charles de Guise   282
Charnock, Roger   452
Charrier, Sylvie   58
Chartier, Roger   88
Chatellier, Louis   264
Chaucer, Geoffrey   350
Chaunu, Pierre   47, 263, 268, 273
Chemnitz, Martin   20, 183, 199-207, 210, 240, 242, 416, 431
Chrysostome, Saint John   191-192, 219
Cisneros, Francisco Jimenes   335
Cisneros, Garcia Jimenes   109-117, 137-139, 306, 310, 320-322, 326, 431-432
Clamanges, Nicolas   101, 210, 229, 402
Classen, Albrecht   93, 96
Clement VII, Pope   348
Clérée, Jean   103
Clichtove, Jesse   98, 270, 275-276, 278, 342
Cochlaeus, Johannes   249-250, 253-255, 257-258, 278, 340, 345, 422
Collard, Franc   58, 99-100
Colledge, Edmond   380
Collins, Eduardo F.   122
Colon-Emeric, Edgardo   298
Columbi, Jean   274
Columbus, Christopher   20, 130, 133-134, 294-295
Combes, André   71, 83-84, 174, 420
Congar, Yves M.   374
Conner, John   352
Connolly, Thomas   123-124
Conti, Fabrizio   126
Corda, Oswald de   35
Córdoba, Antonio de   343
Cottret, Bernard   276
Coville, Alfred   32
Crane, Mark   279

Crantz, Martin   99-100
Crespin, Jean   148, 225, 227-230, 232-233
Christ-von Wedel, Christine   224
Comper, Frances M. M.   348
Crouzet, Denis   279
Cubillos, Denis   152
Culverwell, Nathaniel   201
Cummings, Brian   151, 155, 371, 380, 389, 396-397, 402, 409
Curbet, Jean   353, 355
Curran, Michael   384
Curtright, Travis   374-375, 391, 398
Cusa, Nicolas of   43-47, 66-67, 82, 97, 138, 161, 201, 236, 306-307, 431-432

Dacheux, Léon   49-50, 55
Dagens, Jean   98
Dalberg, Johannes von   56
Dalzell, Alexander   278
Daniel, William   293
Daumas, Maurice   107
Dauvois, Nathalie   279
Davenport, Anne   109
Davidson, Jane P.   283
Dávila, Gil Gonzales   299, 421, 431, 433
Debongnie, Pierre   31, 56, 71, 83, 85-86, 367
Debuchy, Paul   322
Decock, Wim   19, 21, 121, 285-286, 288-289, 291, 333, 343-344, 390, 418-419, 429
Dedieu, Jean-Pierre   303
Delaruelle, Etienne   19-20, 242, 415, 423
Delsaux, Olivier   98
Delumeau, Jean   16, 107, 127, 156-157, 263, 301, 328, 344
Demelemestre, Gaëlle   295
Demine, Vlad   13
Denifle, Heinrich   149, 171
Denis, Philippe   18, 60, 368, 275, 282, 361-362, 367, 369, 417
Denys van Leeuwen (Denys the Carthusian)   41

510

Depew, James F.   70, 74, 279, 416
Derrida, Jacques   15
Descartes, René   407
Dewhurst, Giles   452
Dhotel, Jean-Claude   264-265, 269, 335, 343-344
Diderot, Denis   412
Digulleville, Guillaume de   54
Dinkelsbühl, Nikolaus von   35, 88
Dionysius the Areopagite   41, 44, 46, 132, 306, 313
Dobeneck, Johannes   254
Dompnier, Bernard   314
Donahue, Charles   107, 299
Douglass, Jane Dempsey   49, 54, 61, 255, 353
Dragseth, Jennifer H.   182, 243
Driedo, John   260
Duff, Edward Gordon   348
Duffy, Eamon   248, 348, 350-351
Duglioli, Beata Elena   123
Dumoulin, Charles   225
Dungersheim, Hieronymus   255-256, 431-433
Dupras, Antoine   266, 268-269
Dupras, Guillaume   269
Dupuyherbault, Gabriel   267
Dürer, Albrecht   139
Durham, W. Cole   29
Dykema, Peter   87, 101, 236, 241

Eck, Johannes   20, 152-153, 184, 208, 247, 249, 254-255, 257-258
Eder, Wolfgang   343
Eisenberg, Jose Monroe   332
Egan, Belinda A.   35
Elias, Norbert   26
Ellington, Donna Spivey   127-128
Elizabeth I, Queen of England   282
Emery, Kent   41
Emser, Hieronymus   257
Endean, Philippe   317
Engen, John van   29
Erb, Peter   238
Enenkel, Karl A. E.   18
Erasmus, Desiderius   29, 56, 83-84, 142, 172, 181-182, 247, 259, 276-279, 304, 334, 367

Eriksson, Anne-Louise   422
Erlinger, Georg   193-194
Ernst, Thomas   56
Estaing, Francois de   262
Estaing, Antoine de   262
Estes, James   238
Esquivel, Javier   32
Eusebius of Caesarea   72
Evans, Gillian Rosemary   278
Ewig, Eugen   41

Faber, Johann   356-357
Fabisch, Peter   250-252
Fabre, Isabelle   42, 322
Fabre, Pierre-Antoine   13, 322, 339
Fabri, Johann   246, 249, 255, 257, 341
Faesen, Rob   50
Fairclough, George   13
Faini, Marco   123-124
Falk, Franz   97
Farel, Guillaume   270
Fasolt, Constantin   282
Fernández-Bollo, Eduardo   294
Ferrar, Nicholas   359, 431
Fétis, François-Joseph   169
Fèvre, Lucien   48
Fichet, Guillaume   100
Ficino, Marsilio   56, 130-133, 431-432
Figgis, John Neville   16, 32, 282, 363, 418
Finck, Thomas   34
Fish, Simon   368
Fisher, Jeffrey   67
Fisher, John, Bishop of Rochester   351, 375
Flacius, Matthias Illyricus   20, 63, 72, 148, 158, 195, 207, 210-219, 225, 228, 230-233, 235, 238-239, 242, 331, 345, 414, 432
Flanagan, David Zachary   186-187, 197, 415
Fleischer, Manfred P.   164
Fleming, Julia   38, 83, 290, 337, 417, 423
Flete, William   380
Flint, Valerie I. J.   133

Fogelman, Andrew 284
Foix, François de 267
Forrestal, Alison 336
Forthomme, Bernard 313
Foxe, John 216, 227, 349, 372-373
Frias, Martin de 327
Franceschi, Sylvio Hermann de 361
Francis of Assisi 175, 422
Francis I, King of France 182, 270
François, Wim 13, 30, 245, 259-260, 336, 415
Frank, Christina Beatrice Melanie 211-212, 217
Frank, Sebastien 217, 225
Franklin, James 130, 287, 290, 390
Freedberg, David 339
Freiehagen-Baumgardt, Kristina 50-53
Freinsheim, Johannes Wischler von 33
Freudenberger, Theobald von 256
Frey, Winfried 54
Friburger, Michael 99
Friedrich, Markus 299
Fulda, Adam von 162-164, 168
Fyner of Esslingen, Conrad 42

Gaguin, Robert 58, 99, 118
Gaquoin, Karl 58
Gaille-Nikodimov, Marie 361
Gansfort, Johannes Wessel 24, 71-85, 130, 137, 139, 172, 209, 259, 307, 429, 431
Gassendi, Pierre 407
Gauvard, Claude 105, 108
Geiler, Johannes von Kaysersberg 24, 27, 47-55, 57-58, 60-61, 63, 66-67, 78, 82, 87-88, 94-95, 137, 139, 143, 175, 189, 235, 240, 272, 387, 413-414, 431
Geiselmann, Josef Ruppert 374
Genebrard, Gilbert 345
George, Duke of Saxony 153, 249, 256-258
Gerhard, Johann 198, 200-201, 430
Gering, Ulrich 99-100
Gertsman, Elina 339-340

Gifford, Paul M. 125
Gilbert, Lisa 13
Gillespie, Michael Allen 18
Gilli, Patrick 118
Giraud, Cédric 16, 83, 85, 138
Glorieux, Palémon 106, 192, 238, 393
Glowa, Josef 13
Godet, Marcel 83
Goerner, Edward Alfred 390
Goetz, Werner 152
Goldast, Melchior 411
Golz, Reinhard 174
Gordon, Bruce 168, 208-209, 212, 218-219, 255, 382
Goulart, Simon 148, 225, 230-235, 237, 431
Graf zu Dohna, Lothar 252-253
Grant, Edward 133
Grégoire, Pierre 282
Gregorová, Miroslava 121-122
Gregory the Great 41, 111-112, 144, 219
Greene, Robert 155-156, 220-221, 403-405, 407-408
Greenshields, Malcolm R. 262, 334, 337
Grellard, Christophe 286-287
Grenada, Louis de 285
Greschat, Martin 189
Griesbach, Jacob 427
Grosse, Sven 37, 39, 50, 121
Grüninger, Johanes 53
Grünrade, Otto von 231
Guénée, Bernard 32
Guibert, Joseph de 110, 320, 334
Guicharrousse, Hubert 162
Guillaume of Paris 41
Guillard, Louis 269
Gunner, Goran 422
Guy, John 365, 397, 400
Guzuskyte, Evelina 134

Haga, Joar 150, 238
Haas, Alois 152, 222
Haberkern, Phillip N. 254, 345
Habsburg, Maximilian von 71, 85, 134, 169, 316-318

Haigh, Christopher 369
Hallebeek, Jan 289, 390
Haliczer, Stephen 421
Hall, Joseph 352, 355-358, 411, 431-433
Haller, William 216
Hallett, Philip E. 382
Hamm, Berndt 30-31, 49, 52, 88, 120, 130, 149, 152, 252-253, 257
Hamon, Auguste 279
Hannemann, Cornelia 89
Härdelin, Alf 135
Harp, Henry de 274
Hartmann, Martina 215, 217, 219
Hatt, Cecilia A. 452
Haupt, Gary E. 176, 347, 365, 367
Hausamann, Susi 224, 226
Hay, Gilbert 362, 364
Hayden J. Michael 262, 334, 337
Hazards, Hugues des 262
Haselbach, Thomas Ebendorfer von 97
Hazlett, William Ian P. 189-190
Heftinger, Maureen 13
Hekel, Johann Friedrich 32
Henkel, Nicholas 64, 163
Henneberg, Berthold von 97
Henry VIII, King of England 182, 348-349, 370, 375, 389, 429
Henze, Barbara 257
Herbert, Edward 407
Herbert, Gary B. 410
Herding, Otto 49
Herminjard, Aimé Louis 271
Heynlin (Lapide), Johannes 48, 67, 99-101
Higman, Francis 270, 274-275, 278-279
Hilarius, Saint 226
Hilton, Walter 367
Hirschi, Caspar 62, 119, 141-142
Hobbins, Daniel 15-18, 30, 34, 37, 41-43, 68, 71, 87, 97, 118, 125, 144, 347, 390-392, 409-410, 416, 420
Hoch, Alexander 53, 60, 88, 95
Hoeck, Jacob 74, 77, 80-81
Hoffman, Jana 20

Hoffman, Steffen 13
Hohenadel, Victoria 34, 46, 140, 144
Holdsworth, William S. 399
Holt, Mack P. 48, 220, 266-267, 273, 282
Hopkins, Jasper 43-44, 306
Horn, Norbert 390
Horstmann, Carl 405
Hotman, François 226
Houdard, Sophie 284
Houlbrooke, Ralph 351
Howarth Glennys 352
Hugues of St. Victor 41
Huiklene, Johannes 40
Huntley, Frank Livingstone 356
Hus, Jan 31, 153-154, 157-158, 190-191, 207, 214-216, 219, 227-228, 232, 234-235, 237, 260, 345, 372, 414
Hutson, Lorna 391, 397
Huxley, George Leonard 296

Innocent IX, Pope 283
Iogna-Prat, Dominique 13
Iparraguirre, Ignacio 422
Iribarren, Isabel 314
Ironside, Gilbert 401
Irvin, Joyce L. 124-125
Iserloh, Erwin 250-252
Isolano or Isolani, Isidore 127-128
Isnardi, Gianna Chiesa 137
Izbicki, Thomas 18, 32, 84, 121, 282

Jackallen, Jalil 13
Jacob, Ernest Fraser 45, 73, 82, 370
Jäger, Yvonne Silke 88-89, 92, 241
James I, King of Scotland and England 20, 349, 359-363, 411
Janda, Richard 398
Janelle, Pierre 338
Jansenius, Cornelius of Ghent 261, 431
Janssen, Johannes 331
Janz, Denis R. 318-319, 324
Jedin, Hubert 255, 334

Jerome of Prague   31, 151-154, 215, 219, 228, 232, 234-235
Jerome, Saint   35, 41, 155, 160
Jeudy, Colette   98
John XXIII, Pope   215
John of the Cross   169, 248, 285, 312, 314-316
John the Fearless   32, 361, 389
Jones, Leonard Chester   232
Jonge, Henk Jan de   201
Jud, Leo   224
Julius II, Pope   326
Jung, Carl   425
Juvenal (Juvenalis), Decimus Junius   253

Kallendorf, Hilaire   285
Kaluza, Zenon   16, 241, 286, 289-290
Kang, Paul ChulHong   195
Kantola, Ilkka   286, 289-290
Kantorowitz E. H.   367
Karlstadt, Andreas Bodenstein von   146, 183-188, 192, 210, 237, 240-242, 255, 415-416, 432
Kaup, Susanne   46
Keen, Ralph   365
Keenan, James F.   353
Keitt, Andrew   303
Kellerman, Gösta   136
Kelley, D. R.   147, 188, 208, 226, 232, 391
Kempf, Nicolas   40, 63, 82, 138, 431
Kempis, Thomas à   62, 65, 84-85, 134, 169, 316, 318
Kim, Sylvia   13
King, John N.   227
Klinck, Dennis R.   238, 253, 398-399, 402
Klomps, Heinrich   251-252
Knaake, Joachim Karl Friedrich   253
Knott, John R.   358
Koch, Ernst   255
Köhler, Walther   149, 154, 171
Kolb, Robert   215-216, 219
Kraume, Herbert   17-18, 30, 34, 49, 57-58, 62, 66

Kristanto, Billy   164, 168-169
Kristeller, Paul Oscar   132, 143
Kroef, Justus van der   294-295
Kroon, Marijn de   73-74, 77
Krüger, Wolfgang   32

Labande, Edmond-René   19-20, 45, 423
Laitakari-Pyykkö, Anja-Leena   298, 404, 429
l'Allemand, Laurent   262
Lamy, Bernard   427
Landkron, Stephan von   94
Langenstein, Heinrich von   35-37, 233, 284, 374
Las Casas, Bartholomé de   20, 133, 285, 295-299
Latomus, Jacobus   84, 259-261, 276, 341, 429, 433
Laube, Adolf   256
Laurent, Sylvie   108
Lea, Henry Charles   328
Leaver, Robin   162-166, 168, 195
Le Clerc, Jean   427
L'Écuy, Jean Baptiste   32
Lefebvre, Charles   393, 395
Lefebvre-Teillard, Anne   107
Lefèvre d'Étaples, Jacques   55, 98, 268, 270-273, 275, 278-279, 342, 416, 431-432
Le Gall, Jean-Marie   13
Leib, Kilian or Chilian   255-256
Lemaitre, Nicole   101, 262, 265, 276
Leites, Edmund   96-97
Lemire, Jean-Jacques   126
Leo X, Pope   360
Le Penmarch, Christophe   262
Leppin, Volker   27-28
Leroux, Neil   89, 152, 187
Le Roy, Guillaume   101
Lesnick, Daniel   135
Lessius, Leonardus   333, 417, 419, 431-432
Lett, Didier   105, 108
Levet, Pierre   101
Leyser, Polycarp   198
l'Huillier, Jean   262

Lieberman, Max   50, 55, 60, 63
Liere, Katherine Elliot van   282
Lily, William   366
Lindberg, Carl   22-23, 245
Lloyd, Howell A.   282-284
Lochrie, Karma   128, 350-351
Locke, John   407
Lockwood, Joan   410
Loewe, Andreas   163, 165, 168
Logan, George M.   367, 383
Lonwy, Etienne de   262
Louis XI of France   100
Louis XII of France   98
Loyola, Ignatius of   20, 49, 84, 245, 276, 303, 311, 317, 324, 326, 356, 358-359, 420-421
Lovere, Simone da   124
Lucas, Brian   26
Lucca, Pietro Ritta da   123-124, 138-139, 431-433
Ludolphe le Chartreux   344
Ludolph of Saxony   317
Luscinius, Ottimar   192-193, 431
Luther, Martin   20, 24, 65, 67, 72-73, 77, 83-84, 89, 97, 117, 140, 143, 148, 150-168, 170-171, 173-174, 180-185, 188, 190, 194-195, 206-210, 212, 215, 217, 219-220, 226, 237-238, 240-243, 247-250, 252, 254-256, 258-259, 276, 278, 293, 296, 330, 340, 372, 382, 402, 413-417, 419, 422, 425, 428-429
Luttikhuizen, Frances   109, 284-285
Lynch, C. Arthur   192
Lyotard, Jean-François   245

Maas-Kisha, Heather   138
Mac Culloch, Dearmaid   427
Maher, Michael   325-326
Maillard, Olivier   103, 274
Mair, John   83-84, 276-277, 296-297, 318, 349, 362-363
Majeske, Andrew   390, 393
Mäkinen, Virpi   68, 333, 390, 410
Mangrum, Bryan D.   255
Manley, Frank   376, 378

Mansch, Larry D.   73
Mapstone, Sally Louise   363-364
Marc'hadour, Germain   364, 368, 370
Marchant, Guy   101
Marciniak, Vwadek P.   407
Marguerite de Navarre   55, 264, 268, 270-272, 277, 432
Marillac, Louise de   427
Marín, Juan Miguel   299-300, 323, 421-422
Marius, Richard   254, 364-365, 367, 369, 396
Marlorat, Augustin   224
Marquard, Freher   61
Marr, Stefanie Christiane   94
Marsh, Herbert   198
Marston, John   405-406
Martin V   101
Martin, Dennis   35, 40-41
Martineau, Christine   101, 271-272
Martin, Hervé   103
Martinez, Pedro de Alcantara   126
Martyribus, Bartolomeus a   285
Martz, Louis L.   358-359, 376, 378, 383
Maryks, Robert A.   38, 110, 316, 326-327, 343, 423
Masolini, Serena   192, 261-262
Massaut, Jean-Pierre   40, 42, 65
Matnetsch, Scott M.   234
Mattesilani, Mattheo de   186
Mauro, Dennis di   189
Mayer, Sebald   249
Mayer, Thomas   348-349, 293
Maximilian I   64
Maxwell-Stuart, Peter G.   300-301
Mazour-Matusevich, Yelena   30, 32, 35, 43-44, 71, 76, 101, 108, 154, 223, 241, 270, 315, 419
Mazzarino, Giulio   328-329
Mazzolini, Sylvestro   128-130, 139, 432
McDonald, Craig   363-364
McDonnell, Kilian   128-129, 323
McGinn, Bernard   22, 43-44, 50, 110

McGuire, Brian Patrick   13, 17, 20, 32-34, 44, 47-48, 51-52, 93, 106, 112-113, 116, 129, 133, 138, 140-141, 144, 147, 243, 284, 301-302, 312, 321-322, 325, 328, 345, 347, 358, 379-380, 396, 403, 411, 419-420, 425
McIlwain, Charles Howard   359-362
McKim, Donald   242
McLoughlin, Nancy   17, 421
Medina, Bartolomé de   285, 288-291, 293, 331, 343, 431-432
Meier, Fr. Carolus   131
Meijering, Piet Hein   182
Melanchthon, Philipp   20, 24, 26-27, 48, 58, 67, 72, 148, 158, 171-183, 188, 193-195, 199, 203-206, 209-211, 213, 215-216, 219, 225-226, 230, 232, 236-238, 240-242, 247, 254-255, 404, 414-417, 429, 431
Melion, Walter Simon   18
Menchaca, Fernando Vázquez de   277, 285
Mennecke-Haustein, Ute   161, 236
Menot, Michel   103
Mentzer, Raymond A.   231
Metzler, Regina   64-65, 163
Meyer-Baer, Kathi   42
Meyler, Bernadette   390-391
Mézières, Philippe de   92
Mickel, Johannes   64-65
Middleton, Richard of   41
Middleton, Erasmus   236
Milway, Mike   29
Minsheu, John   307
Mirandola, Giovanni Pico della   63
Mirandola, Gianfrancesco Pico della   130-131
Mladonovice, Peter of   215, 228
Molanus, Johannes   338
Molina, Luis de   331-332, 431
Mombaer, Johannes   71, 83-86, 110, 138, 259, 320, 431-433
Monahan, Arthur P.   18
Mondello, Geoffrey K.   315
Monfalcon, Jean-Baptiste   99

Monti, James   366, 385, 400
Monte Rocherii (Monterochen or Monterocher), Guido de   87
Montmorency, James E. G. de   410
Moore, George Albert   414
More, Thomas   20, 24, 26-27, 180, 247, 254, 259, 298, 307, 312, 347, 349, 351, 359, 364-365, 367, 370-371, 373-376, 384-385, 391, 396-397, 402, 409, 412-413, 429
Mornet, Elisabeth   135
Morrall, John B.   18
Mossakowski, Stanisław   124
Mostaccio, Sylvia   270, 330
Müller, Gernot Michael   64
Müller, Ralf   174
Muller, Richard   230, 235
Müller, Sigrid   121
Moses   202, 255
Müntzer, Thomas   242, 432
Murner, Thomas   48, 58, 100

Nadal, Jeronimo   317, 319, 322, 326
Napoléon (Bonaparte)   19
Nauclerus, Johann   217
Nauert, Charles G.   278
Neddermeyer, Uwe   121
Nederman, Cary J.   18
Needham, Nick   73
Neher, Peter   93-94, 427
Newman, Barbara   17, 25, 197
Nicolai, Ericus   100, 136-137
Nider, John   24, 35, 37-40, 46, 97, 121, 138, 159

Oakley, Francis   18, 45, 82, 185, 265, 335, 349, 360, 391, 399, 410
Oberman, Heiko A.   17-18, 48, 59, 66-67, 71-74, 81, 89, 127, 144, 147, 152, 162, 170, 175, 180, 209, 220, 246, 249, 341, 380
O'Connor, Mary Catharine   87, 90, 95, 264, 351
O'Donovan, Oliver   410
Oglaro, Mario   120, 134

Oecolampadius, Johannes   226, 236, 238
Olivares, Bachiller   305
Ollard, Sidney Leslie   353
Olson, Oliver K.   154, 210-212, 215-218, 230
O'Malley, John   23, 117, 190, 266, 276, 288, 317-320, 322-324, 326, 333-335, 415, 423
Oosterhof, Richard J.   74
O'Reilly, Terence   110
Oresme, Nicolas   284
Orique, David T.   295-296
Ortega, Martinez M.   304-305, 431
Ortiz, Francisco   304-305, 431
Osiander, Andreas   24, 148, 192, 194-198, 200, 225, 236-237, 255, 415, 434
Osma, Pedro de   284
Osslund R.   182
Østrem, Eyolf   164
Osuna, Francisco de   24, 248, 285, 303, 305-316, 413, 424, 431
Otter, Jacob   240
Ourliac, Paul   19-20, 242, 415, 423
Ouy, Gilbert   35, 49, 98, 101, 104-105, 108, 118, 276, 325

Pabel, Hilmar M.   329-331
Pagden, Anthony   296
Pallier, Denis   273-274
Palmer, Martin   317
Pantaleon, Heinrich   234
Pardo, Osvaldo F.   299
Parker, Thomas Henry Louis   223-224, 228
Pascal, Blaise   156, 344
Pascal, Pierre   395
Pascoe, Louis   32, 34, 117
Paul III, Pope   326
Payan, Paul   30, 105-106, 126-127
Peignot, Gabriel   103
Pelikan, Jaroslav   149, 153, 155, 159, 162
Pérez, Miguel   291
Perkins, William   452-455
Pernot, Jean-François   273

Perron, Jacques Davy Du   361-362
Peters, Curtis H.   73
Peters, Edward   421
Petersen, Nils Holger   164
Petersen, William Lawrence   192, 196
Peterson, Charles William   180
Pinelle, Louis   102, 262, 264, 266
Piroska, Nagy   92
Page, Christopher   167
Pannen, Friedemann   150, 158-159, 170
Pappus, Johannes   209, 216
Pappus, Peter   76
Patterson, William Brown   367
Pauli, Johannes   55
Peignot, Gabriel   103
Pepin, Guillaume   101
Petit, Guillaume   269
Petit, Jean   278
Petrarch, Francesco   29, 64, 118-119, 212, 412
Petri, Adam   177
Pettegree, Andrew   102-103, 264-265, 268-269, 275
Peutinger, Konrad   64
Peuntner, Thomas   35, 88-89
Pfeffinger, Johannes   225
Picascia, Maria Luisa   394
Pieper, Francis   183
Pigouchet, Philippe   101
Pirckheimer, Caritas   139
Pirckheimer, Euphemia   139
Pirckheimer, Willibald   139
Piton, Michel   102
Pius IV, Pope   169
Pius V, Pope   331
Planudes, Maximus   366
Plowden, Edmund (Edmunde)   400-401, 410
Plumetot, Simon de   98
Polanco, Juan Alphonso   24, 316-327, 337, 432
Pole, Reginald   349, 351
Pohlig, Matthias   211, 230-232
Pöhlmann, Horst G.   174, 176
Polanco, Juan-Alphonso   24, 326-327, 337, 432

517

Polman, Pontien 153, 210-212, 214-215, 225-226, 232, 247
Poncet, Christophe 132
Poncher, Etienne 262-263, 269, 276
Popelyastyy, Vasyl 324, 336-337
Posset, Franz 36, 49, 57, 62, 252-253
Possevino (Possevinus), Antonio 283-284, 338, 344
Pot, Olivier 234
Preus, Christian 171-172, 177, 183
Preussen, Heinrich von 33
Prodi, Paulo 21, 237, 286-287, 293, 402
Prosperi, Adriano 104, 108
Provvidente, Sebastián 282
Prügl, Thomas 31
Puy, Pierre du 282

Quentin, Johan 264
Quiroga, Vasco de 298-299, 432

Rabus, Ludwig 212
Racaut, Luc 230
Rabelais, François 247, 276-277, 279
Rahner, Karl 374, 420
Raley, J. Michael 169
Ransome, Joyce 359
Raphael (Raffaello), Sanzio da Urbino 124-125
Rapp, Francis 55, 83, 321, 377
Rathey, Markus 169
Ratzinger, Josef 374
Raulin, Jean 102
Regnault, François 278, 350
Reichenthal, Ulrich von 215
Reid, Jonathan A. 262, 264, 267, 269-270
Reinburg, Virginia 281
Reinis, Austra 240-242
Renaudet, Augustin 56, 273, 275
Reuchlin, Johannes 48, 56-57, 172, 175, 217, 434
Reusner, Elia or Elias 414
Reusner, Nicolaus von 234
Revilo, Oliver 366

Reynolds, Noel B. 298
Rex, Richard 372-373, 389
Rhegius, Urbanus 240
Rice, Eugène 273
Richardson, Carol 105-106, 126
Richer, Edmond 60, 361, 417
Rieman, Heide Dorothea 46-47
Ringmann, Matthias 177
Rio (Delrio), Martin Antonio del 300-302, 306
Ritchey, Sara 85, 87
Ritter, François 49, 60
Rittgers, Ronald 150-151, 240
Rivo, Peter de 261-262, 431
Roccati, Giovanni Matteo 35, 119
Roche, Daniel 16, 127, 263
Rodgers, Katherine Gardiner 348, 364-365, 383, 385-386
Rodríguez, Alphonso 423
Rodriguez-Grahit, Ignacio 110
Roest, Bert 97, 387
Rohan, François de 265
Rollo-Koster, Joëlle 18
Rosemondt, Godescale 259, 261, 431
Rosenheim, Peter von 36-37
Roth, Johannes 143
Roth, Stephan 65
Rousseau, Jean-Jacques 57, 412
Roussel, Gérard 270-271
Rudolf, Rainer 33, 88-89, 348, 351
Rueger, Zofia 390-391, 395, 398-399
Rumme, Erika 278
Rupp, Gordon 73
Rupprich, Hans 140
Rurale, Flavio 328-329
Russell, J. Stephen 422
Ruys, Juanita 89-90, 93
Ruysbroeck, John van 45, 273
Ryan, Frances 18, 427
Rybolt, John 427

Saak, Leland 30
Saarinen, Risto 149
Sacrati, Giacomo 344
Sadoleto, Jacopo 169
Sales, François de 344, 420, 430

Sandhagen, Kaspar Hermann   198
Salmon, John Hearsey M.   282
Salutati, Coluccio   119
Sampson, Margaret   401
Santen, Henrik von   97
Sarmiento, Augusto   292
Savonarola, Girolamo   20, 130-131, 137, 233, 429
Scavizzi, Giuseppe   255
Schädle, Karl   64
Shaffern, Robert W.   75
Shakespeare, William   109, 355
Schatzgeyer, Kaspar   249-252, 255, 258, 278, 431-432
Schaumberg, Peter von   63
Schedel, Hartmann   64
Schepers, Kees   259
Schmidt, Charles   103
Schmitt, Christoph   61
Schmutz, Jacob   13
Schott, Peter (Pierre)   48, 55, 57, 63
Schüssler, Rudolf   13, 38, 70, 114, 121-122, 287, 291, 332-333, 343, 349-350, 390, 409, 418
Schwartz, Daniel   287
Schwab, Johann Baptist   17
Schweiger, Cornelia   121
Schalk, Carl F.   162
Shanske, Darien   390-391
Schedel, Hartmann   64
Shindler, Solomon   13
Shortall, Michael   295, 417
Segusio (Hostiensis), Henry of   392-393
Segura, Juan Lopez de   285
Selke, Angela   305
Selnecker, Nicolaus   204
Sepulveda, Juan Ginès de   285, 295-297
Sère, Bénédicte   13, 18
Seyssel, Claude de   267
Sider, Ronald J.   184, 186-187
Sieben, Hermann Josef   18
Simon, Jean   262
Simpson, James   198
Sixtus IV, Pope   126, 152, 338
Skinner, Quentin   18, 332

Sleidan, Johannes   226
Smoller, Ackerman Laura   133
Smolinsky, Heribert   48, 58, 64, 143, 172-173, 250, 342
Soen, Violet   30, 245, 336
Solère, Jean-Luc   271
Sordet, Yann   268
Sönke, Lorenz   42, 65
Soto, Domingo de   285, 288-289, 293-295, 343, 431
Soybert Pierre   267
Spalatin, Georg   151, 241, 258, 432
Spanheim, Friedrich   430
Spicer, Andrew   231
Spitz, Lewis W.   56, 119
Standonck, Jan   71, 83-84, 86, 100, 109, 259, 276-277
Staphylus, Friedrich   236
Stapleton, Thomas   352
Starkey, Thomas   348
Staubach, Nikolaus   31, 71
Staupitz, Johannes   24, 27, 67, 153, 175, 249, 252-253, 255-256, 258, 260, 341, 413, 431
Stefaniak, Regina   126-127
Steinmetz, David Curtis   252
Stieber, Joachim W.   41
Strigel, Victorinus   225
Stoeckel, Wolffgang   240
Stolz, Peter   224, 226
St. Germain, Christopher   24, 36, 222, 282, 369-371, 373-375, 391, 397-402, 404-405, 408, 411, 431
Strauss, Gerald   58, 217
Suarez, Francisco   331-333, 343, 401, 431
Sullivan, Francis Patrick   298
Summenhart, Konrad   65, 67-71, 277, 287, 294-295, 331, 417, 431-432
Sumpf, Johannes   214
Sutcliffe, Matthew   349
Sutton, Christopher   352-355
Suzanne, Hélène   38, 388, 402

Tallon, Alain   268
Tanner, Norman   324, 338, 415

Tardif, Guillaume   100
Tauler, Johannes   143, 300
Taveneaux, René   338
Tavuzzi, Michael   128
Taylor, Andrew W.   364, 376
Taylor, Scott   91, 93, 96
Thévet, André   268
Tellkamp, Jörg Alejandro   69, 297, 332
Tentler, Thomas   37, 121, 235, 298, 324, 326, 395
Terence (Publius Terentius Afer)   253
Terricabras, Ignasi Fernández   329
Teuler, Johannes   184
Thompson, John Samuel   426
Tilly, Michael   48
Tilsworth, Debbie   13
Timm, Kat   13
Tosi, Giuseppe   297
Toussaint, Stéphane   120, 131-132
Trapp, Joseph Burney   233, 371
Tierney, Brian   67, 130, 282, 295, 332, 410
Treusch, Ulricke   46
Trithemius, Johannes   47-48, 56, 60-63, 99, 120, 133, 137, 141-143, 217, 233, 235, 316, 318, 331, 414, 432
Trotsky, Leo   143
Tsui, Josephine   26
Tuck, Richard   67-71, 122, 130, 260, 277, 287, 294-295, 332, 334, 410, 428
Tucker, Jameson   215, 227-231, 254
Turchetti, Mario   32
Tutino, Stefania   130, 287
Tuysselet, Guillaume   98
Tyler, Peter   110, 305-307, 313-316, 421, 425

Ulfsson, Jacob   136-137
Ullmann, Carl   73
Ulsenius, Dietrich   64
Undorf, Wolfgang   257
Utenheim, Christoph von   48

Valdés, Juan de   285, 304, 431

Vanderpoel, Mathew   197
Vansteenberghe, Edmond   17, 43, 91, 117
Verger, Jacques   16, 254
Varacalli, Thomas Francis Xavier   287
Varenacker, Johannes   262
Varkemaa, Jussi   21, 67-70, 390, 410
Vásquez, Gabriel   285, 293-294
Vatable, François   270-271
Vattlin (Fattlin), Melchior   255-256, 260
Vaughan, Richard   32
Veissière, Michel   266, 269, 271-273, 275
Venard, Marc   22, 117, 267-269, 314, 344
Venatorius, Thomas V.   241
Vendrix, Philippe   42, 429
Vereecke, Louis   293-294, 413
Vergar, Juan de   285, 304
Verger, Jacques   16, 254
Verlaine, Paul   368
Vial, Marc   17, 43, 137-138, 155, 192, 220, 321, 377
Villon, François   109
Virdung, Sebastian   193
Virgil (Publius Vergilius Maro)   142, 253
Vitelli, Vitellozzo   169
Vitoria, Francisco de   260, 285, 287-289, 292, 294-295, 299, 343, 417, 431-432
Vog, Christopher   253
Volkmar, Christoph   24, 140, 153, 248-249, 256-258, 335

Wabrigant, Henri   110
Waging, Bernhard or Bernard von   24, 43, 45-47, 63, 66, 89, 117, 138-139, 431
Walasser, Adam   255, 258, 340, 432
Walcher, Wolfgang   34
Walsby, Malcolm   102-103, 269, 275
Waldburg, Otto Truchseß von   249

NAME INDEX

Walsham, Alexandra   329-330, 424
Wandel, Lee Palmer   87
Warf, Barney   23
Warme, Lars G.   135, 257
Wassermann, Dirk   43
Wassilowsky, Günther   239, 274
Watanabe, Morimichi   45
Waterworth, James   338
Watson, Francis   226-231
Weiler, Antonius Gerardus   75
Weiss, James Michael   235, 239
Weissenhorn, Alexander   254
Weller, Jerome   161
Wengert, Timothy J.   195, 254
Westphalia, John of   133
Wetzel, Richard   252-253
Wheatley, Leonard Abercromb   62
William of Auvergne   271
Wilkinson   102-103, 269, 275
Williams-Krapp, Werner   50-53
Willshire, William Hughes   36
Wilson, George   172, 301-302
Willy, Andreas   119
Wimpheling, Jacob   36, 47-49, 55-65, 99-100, 120, 137, 141, 144, 172-173, 175, 177, 193, 217, 240, 318, 361, 413-414, 433

Winchelsea, Thomas   387
Witzel, Georg (Georgius Wicelius)   255-258
Wolf, Ernst   252
Wolf (Wolff), Johannes   97, 218
Wolff, Thomas   64, 432
Wollersheim, Heinz-Werner   175
Wolsey, Thomas   349, 397
Woods, Mark   73
Worstbrock, Franz Josef   64, 120
Wriedt, Markus   208
Wrightson, Keith   108
Wünsch, Dietrich   193-194, 198, 225, 261
Wycliff, John   207, 260, 345

Yamamoto-Wilson, John R.   352
Young, William John   246

Zagorin, Perez   282
Zahnd, Eric G.   391, 409
Zediltz, Georg von   154
Zediltz, Sigismund von   154
Ziska, Jan   235
Zumkeller, Adolar OSA   252
Zwingli, Huldrych   164, 185, 224, 226, 242, 250